End-to-End Arguments in the Internet

End-to-End Arguments in the Internet: Principles, Practices, and Theory

Matthias Bärwolff

Berlin 2010

Book version of a PhD thesis submitted to the Department of Electrical Engineering and Computer Science at Technische Universität Berlin

Advised by Prof. em. Dr. iur. Bernd Lutterbeck, Technische Universität Berlin, and Dr. David D. Clark, Massachusetts Institute of Technology

---

www.bärwolff.de matthias@baerwolff.de

Self-published via CreateSpace
(DBA of On-Demand Publishing LLC,
part of the Amazon group of companies)

ISBN-10: 1456331353
EAN-13: 9781456331351

The body of this work is a verbatim copy of the thesis version available from http://www.bärwolff.de — scaled by 85 percent and slightly offset to the outer margin so as to fit the 5.5 x 8.5 inches digest size instead of the original A4 paper size.

Cover illustration by the author, using a painting by: Caravaggio, Michelangelo (1571-1610). Basket of Fruit (oil on canvas, c. 1599). Biblioteca Ambrosiana, Milan, Italy.

Free PDF versions and accompanying materials can be found at
http://www.bärwolff.de/publications/2010-10-PhD-thesis.html

PRINCIPLES are often more effective guides for action when they appear as no more than an unreasoned prejudice, a general feeling that certain things simply "are not done"; while as soon as they are explicitly stated speculation begins about their correctness and their validity. [. . .] Once the instinctive certainty is lost, perhaps as a result of unsuccessful attempts to put into words principles that had been observed "intuitively", there is no way of regaining such guidance other than to search for a correct statement of what before was known implicitly.

— Friedrich August von Hayek (1973, p. 60)

Abstract

The end-to-end arguments — a founding principle of the Internet — have inspired a world of opinionated interpretations, re-articulations, and comments about their lower-level technical and higher-level normative merit. However, their precise meaning and scope of applicability have remained diffuse — arguably as diffuse as the constituency of stakeholders in the very Internet itself. Our thesis elaborates the end-to-end arguments by putting them into a meaningful context of other principles as well as the current realities of the Internet. Also, it elaborates their normative content in view of a defendable set of purposes. To these ends we have conducted a most thorough study of primary literature going back to the intellectual predecessors of the Internet in the early 1960s, and developed the several notions of this thesis in a largely desk-based research effort.

Following a comprehensive discussion of the various different versions of the end-to-end arguments both prior to and subsequent to the seminal Saltzer et al. (1981*a*) formulation we trace the actual manifestations of the end-to-end arguments walking from the Arpanet as developed in the late 1960s to the eventual Internet architecture emerging from the mid-1970s. We find that the descriptive content of the end-to-end arguments is, in fact, broader than their self-contained formulation as a logical argument about application completeness implies. Second, we find that they are best conceived as one principle within a framework of other, no less relevant principles. And, third, we argue for a revised normative take on the end-to-end arguments that emphasizes the importance of edge redundancy as a crucial means of extending their scope beyond the classic considerations of data integrity alone. In all, we add much needed focus and clarity to a notion that has been carried so far away from its original content as to cloud its true relevance in both today's Internet and tomorrow's.

Zusammenfassung

Seit ihrer ursprünglichen Fassung von Saltzer u. a. (1981*a*) wurden die „End-to-End Arguments" – der Kern eines der grundlegenden Prinzipien des Internets – im Hinblick auf ihre technische und normative Bedeutung stetig neu interpretiert und bewertet. Indes, der eigentliche Gehalt und die Grenzen ihrer Gültigkeit sind dabei weitgehend diffus geblieben – ebenso diffus wohl wie das Internet und die Menge derer, die es prägen und nutzen. Diese Arbeit entwickelt die „End-to-End Arguments" weiter, indem sie sie in einen sinnvollen Kontext aus anderen Prinzipien führt und dabei nicht nur den Realitäten des heutigen Internets gerecht wird, sondern zudem eine sorgfältige Zweckbestimmung für deren normativen Gehalt vornimmt.

Basierend auf einer ausführlichen Erörterung der verschiedenen Versionen der „End-to-End Arguments" betrachten wir die technischen Artefakte, in denen sich jene von der Entwicklung des Arpanets in den späten 1960er Jahren bis hin zum Internet in den 1970er Jahren spiegeln. Es zeigt sich, dass die „End-to-End Arguments" auf deskriptiver Ebene deutlich breitere Anwendbarkeit finden, als sich dies aus dem logischen Kern der ursprünglichen Formulierung ergibt. Weiterhin zeigt sich, dass der Gehalt der „End-to-End Arguments" sich in einem systematischen Kontext aus weiteren für die Platzierung von Funktionen relevanten Prinzipien am besten fassen lässt. Nicht zuletzt entwickelt die Arbeit eine sinnvolle normative Fassung der „End-to-End Arguments", die die Wichtigkeit von Redundanz an den Rändern des Internets, dort wo die Enden Zugang nehmen, betont. Dadurch verbreitert sich deren Geltungsbereich weit über den klassischen Betrachtungsgegenstand von Datenintegrität hinaus. Insgesamt gewinnen die „End-to-End Arguments" durch unsere Arbeit an Fokus und Klarheit im Hinblick auf deren, auch künftige, Bedeutung.

Preface

Who Should Read this Thesis

This thesis has been written first and foremost in pursuit of an academic degree, but we hope that it will also be read by more than six people.[1] Broadly speaking, this thesis aims at (1) scholars, students, and reflective practitioners at the intersection of computer science and economics, (2) those interested in the broader history of the Internet, but also (3) regulators and all those with a stake in technology policy ranging from political parties to technology industry representatives and strategists.

We neither strictly assume the reader to be familiar with basic textbook descriptions of the Internet (e. g., Peterson and Davie 2007; Kurose and Ross 2005; Stallings 2007) nor with historical accounts of networking (e. g., Norberg et al. 1996; Hafner and Lyon 1998); however, having some general intuition about the basic notions of computer networking will substantially ease the reading of this thesis. Also, we highly recommend to have read the original paper on "end-to-end arguments in system design" by Saltzer et al. (1981*a*).

Technical Aspects of This Thesis

This thesis is written in (American) English language.[2] Largely this is because the bulk of the underlying literature and controversy is in English. Also, in all modesty, we hope that this work will be read beyond the confines of the German speaking world.

As for the content, while it does get technical in some places, we have tried to keep the text concise and accessible. Also, we have chosen to move the notes — which are often very copious, sometimes bordering the pedantic—into the back matter, (1) to make the body of the text readable and coherent in its own right, and (2) to allow for the flexibility of adding comprehensive asides where they are suitable (if only for completeness' sake).

As for the broad structure of this thesis, while it obviously follows some linear sequence, most sections are self-contained, and the reader may choose to jump over sections and generally read them in the order they prefer (see the contents).

A note on style, particularly regarding the endnotes: at times, we have here included copious digressions which are not central, sometimes not even strictly relevant, to the arguments in the main text. However, often we felt that such asides would add to the broader discussion—be it by providing additional perspectives, or by recounting obscure but instructive literature threads (see the index of interesting asides).

Last, we should like to mention the most important layout choices and LaTeX packages we have used:

- The notes have been moved away from the main body of the text by using the endnotes package with a slight customization for obtaining hyperlinks from the notes back to the places in the main text that spawned them.
- The headers and footers have been customized using the fancyhdr package, plus tweaks for which credit goes to Philipp Lehmann.
- The bibliography has been managed with the biblatex package, again by Philipp Lehmann, with some minor customizations.
- Also, we have made rather extensive use of the hyperref package.

Acknowledgments

Many thanks to Prof. Dr. Bernd Lutterbeck — first, for letting me work on a subject as ambitious and difficult as this research turned out to be; second, for guiding my efforts such that the whole work became manageable; and, third, for being patient with me, and letting me get away with taking a fair bit longer than we had planned.

Speaking of getting away with things, I also want to thank the School of Electrical Engineering and Computer Science at Technische Universität Berlin for accepting my thesis, even though I do not hold an proper university degree in computer science. Horst Bamberg, Lutz Haase, and Gabriela Ernst handled my 'case' with a most professional and flexible attitude. Thanks also to Prof. Dr. Adam Wolisz for handling my exam.

The third paragraph of this list of acknowledgments firmly goes to Dr. David D. Clark of the Massachusetts Institute of Technology. He took me on as a visiting student for the academic year 2008/2009 despite a lack of any meaningful references other than a thesis proposal. He also has taken ample time out of his schedule to answer my (certainly sometimes boring and redundant) questions, and put me in touch with a host of interesting people to interview. He was in all respects instrumental to the various stages of my work.

Most sincere thanks to the many more people that have answered my questions in person or via email. David Walden clarified many Arpanet and BBN related points for me with great patience and immense care. BBN librarian Jennie Connolly had me as a guest for three full days. Their help was truly immeasurable. There have been many more people who have taken substantial time and efforts to answer the many questions I put to them — I cannot hope to compile a full list of all those with a stake in this work, so I had better not try.

Last but not least, I want to thank Frank Pallas and Kei Ishii of Technische Universität Berlin who have provided me with thoughtful feedback and helped keeping the scope of my thesis under control. Thank you very much.

Finally, thanks to Prof. Dr. Manfred Bräuer for kindly sponsoring a quiet office during the later stages of my writing up this thesis. And, before I let you go: thanks to Nicole and Cosima; you have been awesome, and will forever be.

Contents

Chapter 1

Introduction

There is no such thing as a logical method of having new ideas or a logical reconstruction of this process.

— Karl Popper

All the lessons about networking that have accrued over the last 40 years and all the criticism that may rightfully be leveled against the Internet do not change its core principles. At the heart of the Internet architecture stands the premise of an irreducibly minimum common protocol that does little more than establish an address space to move data packets within — a premise which, in turn, allows for almost arbitrary complexity and specificity to be erected upon it. True, we could have larger address fields; but once we turn to issues such as routing, congestion management, QoS schemes, security, and accounting, it is much less certain that a new version of the Internet (if we could just turn back time) would look much different from the one we have. In spite of all historical accident, eventual ossification, and strategic capture, the basic architecture of the Internet is one of great clarity and elegance, and one that, in retrospect, seems very natural a result of the early efforts to build wide-area general purpose data communication networks.

And yet even though the core architectural principles of the Internet in abstract seem very sound and definitive, upon closer inspection it turns out that there is great ambiguity in their actual implications — they are only principles, after all. In particular, there has been a continuous paradox about the right amount of minimality at the heart of the Internet: Turing completeness in the abstract rarely makes a usable or useful system,[3] and with the Internet having become the commandingly dominant universal public data communication system, it would only be fair for it to evolve from a lowest common denominator system to one that reflects its being deployed for ever more critical applications, and have 'surrounding entities' conform to a minimum standard specification above best effort as in no effort at all. The principles once considered inviolable—above all the unqualified minimality in the core protocols and services—have thus become strained in recent years, and subject to heated public debates about the future of the Internet.[4]

What can be done to shed clarity on the principles of the Internet? One approach would be to 'go back to the basic problem' and try to elaborate principles anew, not by drawing them from real-world practices and successes, but by deriving them in scientific manner from truly invariable axioms rather than the whims of history.[5] Another approach would be to declare the written principles from the very early days of the Internet to be inviolable rules, rather than mere rules of thumb subject to a broader context of other such rules. Accordingly, any deviation from those principles would be considered a violation of normative rules and a case for government regulation to reobtain the 'foundational' architecture of the Internet.[6] It is easy to see the shortcomings of either of these approaches: the one breaks with all received notions, and the other forecloses any dynamic developments that adapt the overall system to changing contexts and needs—neither position being a meaningful premise if we acknowledge the political dimension of any such efforts and the need to appreciate the legitimate concerns of the multitude of stakeholders involved.

The third approach, and the one we subscribe to, is to take the existing principles about the Internet as loose rules that (1) are informed by customs and practices, (2) properly need constant re-articulation so as to maintain their relevance in a dynamically moving system, and (3) must never be taken as absolutes in either descriptive or normative sense.[7] This is in line with well-established notions from other fields inherently shaped by principles rather than strict rules—chiefly law and economics,[8] as well as architecture[9]—and promises to be more fruitful than the former two approaches.[10] Of course, this is not to say that our approach has no weaknesses,[11] or that the above two approaches have no merit whatsoever;[12] but we feel that ours—while offering less potential for bold conclusions—is much better suited to add to a reasoned debate about how best to develop the existing principles without falling into what Hayek (1973) termed the problem of "constructivist rationalism".[13]

1.1 Research Subject, Problems, and Questions

It is not possible in a 'lone-scholar, no-budget mode' to conclusively tackle the whole subject area of Internet principles. Hence the *subject* of this thesis is more modest — we confine ourselves to the end-to-end arguments in the Internet, a line of resonings first articulated explicitly by Saltzer et al. (1981*a*), and which in recent years have seen a heightened interest from legal scholars,[14] regulators,[15] politicians,[16] and computer scientists.[17] Yet despite this flurry of interest it has proven difficult to maintain the precision and elegance of the early formulation,[18] and derive reasonable and useful normative implications from the originally descriptive notion.

The *research problem* we address in our thesis is thus twofold: (1) the inconclusive state of the articulation of the end-to-end principle and its surrounding concepts, and (2) the lack of comprehensive historical and empirical foundation to those notions and thus the arguments based thereupon. These are very basic and profound problems indeed, to which the existing literature offers a rather confusing picture.[19] For example, on the one hand, policy makers are being told that specific versions of the end-to-end principles, also referred to as network neutrality, are essential grounds for innovation, social welfare, and democratic values (e. g., Schewick 2009); on the other hand, some argue that there is more harm than benefit from imposing preemptive ex ante regulation in the face of what may well be a very limited problem in the first place (e. g., Farber 2009).

While our thesis offers no explicit 'policy implications', our work shall provide a firm basis for future debates on the merit and normative scope of the end-to-end arguments. More specifically, the *research goal* of this thesis is to interpret and articulate the end-to-end design arguments such that they (1) appreciate rather than romanticize the history of the Internet and (2) make sense given today's realities in the Internet. Such an effort will reveal a host of subtleties in the end-to-end arguments, and, in particular, develop them beyond the perfunctory examples and self-contained logic typically associated with them.

To this end we pursue a number of *research questions*, among them:

- What is the causality between end-to-end principles and practices along those lines?
- What is the causality between end-to-end principles and practices on the one hand, and specific higher level purposes such as innovation, social welfare, and democracy on the other hand?
- What is the relationship between principles as flowing from established practice, and principles that are normative in their nature and have to be enforced by a regulator?
- Is there a hierarchy between various, possibly conflicting, design principles of the Internet?
- What are reasonable higher level values that a global and virtually non-discriminatorily accessible Internet can be built to pursue?

Note that neither is this list complete, nor are all of the questions here listed dealt with in full exhaustion. But, this is the type of questions that our thesis deals with.

1.2 Synopsis

Our thesis features three distinct but related parts — all three have merit as original research efforts in their own right, and yet they combine to a logical sequence of elaborating the end-to-end arguments, helping to address our research problem: the proper appreciation of the nature and due scope of the end-to-end arguments.

In *Part I* we venture a detailed review and discussion of the existing literature leading up to and building on Saltzer et al. (1981*a*), the original paper on end-to-end arguments. The objective here is to elaborate the host of re-articulations, interpretations, and applications of the end-to-end arguments, and discuss their respective merits and shortcomings. We find that the notion of end-to-end arguments can be traced to the early 1960s, and by 1981 there was a good theoretical understanding of the various trade-offs regarding the position of different functions in the continuum between end points and network intermediary nodes. From 1981 onwards several elaborations of the original, basic end-to-end arguments evolved — diffusing the notion well beyond their original scope and meaning. In fact, we also add to the elaboration here by developing several novel ideas, particularly our 2009 distinction between vertical and horizontal end-to-end arguments.

Part II is a collection of case studies about the history of the Internet, arranged in an analytical fashion so as to obtain a reasonably self-contained part which adds not only to our thesis, but also to the broader 'research grade' secondary literature about the Internet, its architecture, and its history. Our focus here is with the end-to-end arguments as an empirical matter, and how they developed along with the evolution of the Internet (and its earlier predecessors). We find that the basic architectural separation of functions as articulated by Saltzer et al. (1981*a*) was arrived at very early in the history of wide-area packet switching data networks — seminally exemplified by the Arpanet. Also, almost right away, it was discovered that different applications would require markedly different lower level services (the canonical case being that of interactive speech versus file transfer) leading to the appreciation of the merit of exposing a plain unreliable datagram interface to end hosts. In fact, such an interface can be found as early as 1974 in the Arpanet, well before the UDP/TCP distinction in the Internet took shape. Finally, we find that with the advent of the TCP/IP Internet some interesting factual observations can be made about the dynamics of positioning functions such as fragmentation and congestion control which are not spoken to by the original arguments.

Part III elaborates on the previous two, discussing (1) the broader merit of the original end-to-end arguments, (2) their descriptive scope beyond the perfunctory application level examples typically associated with the end-to-end arguments, and (3) the elusiveness of their more recent normative incarnations, and approaches toward framing meaningful higher-level normative end-to-end arguments. It would be impractical to list all our results in due detail, but it is worth noting several original insights that emerge from this part:

- In elaboration to the descriptive content of the end-to-end arguments, we argue that the end-to-end arguments can be seen as part of a broader principle of 'interface simplicity and implicitness'. Some of the empirical cases considered in Part II support the notion that it is often prohibitively expensive and thus infeasible to distribute logical functions across trust boundaries and maintain explicit control interfaces between the modules that are part of such a distributed function. As a result, discrete functions end up either with the network intermediary nodes *or* (as in XOR) the end hosts, hardly ever with both. Due to the fact that very few functions can be fully implemented in the network without control input by the hosts, the bulk of functions goes with the end hosts rather than the network intermediary nodes.

- We develop a systematic context for the end-to-end arguments by placing them within a framework of other design principles which also speak to the shape and position of functions in the Internet. Our framework features the principles of modularity, minimal coupling, layering, best effort, least privilege, cascadability, symmetry, 'running code', complexity avoidance, and rough consensus — all of which contribute to the shape and placement of functions in the Internet. While the end-to-end arguments are inherently logically prior to the other principles (all the functions of a network ultimately serve the applications on user behalf), we argue that the other principles add substantial elaboration to the overall trade-offs of where to place functions of networking.

- We argue that any higher-level versions of the end-to-end arguments based on notions of end user empowerment and autonomy must be clearly separated from the lower-level original version of 'application completeness'. Yet we find merit in the articulation of a normative end-to-end argument (or rather, the rediscovery of a specific version of the end-to-end arguments we have elaborated in Part I) that calls for an increased appreciation of the availability of redundant Internet attachment points for end users — a notion not at all well catered for in the existing Internet architecture, but which would (1) help improve end user empowerment and autonomy without violating the tussle separation principle by having regulators resort to ex ante constraint of ISP behavior, (2) improve the ability of end points to perfect parameters other than data integrity, most notably throughput and delay to the standard they require.

Part I

End-to-End Arguments in the Academic Debate

[T]here are philosophical ideas, values and insights that remain relevant beyond the disparate events of history. There is no conflict in finding relevant insights in principles that contribute to our civilisation and the recognition of their limited impact on the course of history.

— *Ernst-Joachim Mestmäcker (2007, p. 61)*

Chapter 2

Prior Arguments about End-to-End Arguments

The notion that we can dismiss the views of all previous thinkers surely leaves no basis for the hope that our work will prove of any value to others.

— *M. R. Cohen (1931, p. x)*

The end-to-end arguments have become one of those items of computer science (and beyond) that are typically taken as a given rather than a tentative and falsifiable set of statements. While such may be the fate of all statements which capture in arguably unambiguous clarity a complex notion and reduce it to a simple formula with predictive value; with the history behind those statements slowly vanishing from sight, it is most instructive to revisit their predecessors.[20] In particular, we feel that current debates about issues such as tussles and network neutrality rules cannot be understood and meaningfully developed without looking at the large body of existing accounts leading up to and based upon the 1981 paper by Saltzer et al. — specifying and diversifying its initial scope and meaning.

It is only fair to consider the end-to-end arguments as a principle (or set of principles) that requires interpretation — just like a 'law' formulated by a legislator does; our chief interest is not in what a 'legislator' has *thought* when articulating a notion, but in what they reasonably *should have* thought and what a certain principle *means* in a given context.[21] Especially in so far as the end-to-end arguments are to be a principle of universal scope (that is, a principle of spontaneous order discovered rather than normatively imposed), it is useful to also consider accounts dealing with it prior to the seminal formulation of Saltzer et al. (1981*a*). We thus develop the history of the end-to-end notion along the lines of Lakatos (1978*a*): as the emergence and contestation of a research programme, complete with a hard core of irrefutable statements, a protective belt of auxiliary statements, and a positive heuristic, as well as contentions between different such programmes along similar lines of subject and purpose.[22] While we submit that such an exercise runs the risk of becoming more solemn than is necessary or useful (it is 'only' a principle, after all), we think that not only is doing so a vital requisite to any further reinterpretation, but also is it a valuable research effort in its own right—merging textual interpretation of the seminal articulations with teleological and historical approaches.[23]

As for the structure of this chapter plus the following one: we will proceed largely in a sequential fashion, walking through the literature on end-to-end arguments and relevant asides from the early 1960s to more recent accounts, covering specifically (1) the contestation over end-to-end error control in a distributed system; (2) the question of supporting application diversity beyond virtual circuits, and arriving at a minimum common ground for interconnecting different networks; and (3) the intricacies of the interplay between applications and end hosts, on the one hand, and the network at large, on the other. A focused discussion of the actual artifacts that those arguments have effectively been about is largely deferred to Part II.[24]

2.1 Networking, Redundancy, and Checksums

The notion that there is a trade-off between placing functions at the end points of a communication path and in between, as well as the issue of the proper level of redundancy of functions has been recognized and discussed well before the 1981 Saltzer et al. paper. In fact, accounts of general long distance communication problems featuring basic control procedures (or 'protocols') can be traced back hundreds if not thousands of years into human history (Holzmann and Pehrson 1994).[25] And yet, while the history of human messengers, communication via torches and other optical means, and, eventually, electronic telegraphy are no doubt instructive and entertaining, we are here more interested in the past-telegraphy takes on the trade-offs between end-to-end and node-to-node functions. For it was only by the early 1960s that a profound change in the whole notion of networking was ignited in earnest, bestowing upon the end-to-end arguments the relevance they have commanded to this very day.

Arguably, the first relevant discussion of end-to-end problems in computerized data communication is due to Paul Baran and his series of papers and research memoranda in the early 1960s.[26] At that time, computer networking was in its very infancy, there were no large scale computer networks apart from a handful of airline reservation and banking systems, and those had very little in common with today's Internet by any measure.[27] Baran introduced some ideas that — while conceivable as incremental improvements to modern telegraphy[28] — manifested no less than a revolutionary departure from previous practices. The notion that interactive traffic such as voice could be carried by a network more closely related to telegraphy than telephony was unheard of at the time.[29] Baran's network — featuring (1) digital rather than analog communication, (2) individual message blocks rather than a continuous flow of data, and (3) the automatic and uncorrelated routing of those individual blocks of data rather than the setup of permanent circuits for the duration of a connection — proved seminal for the later advent of packet switched data networks.[30]

In elaborating his ideas, Baran came to touch on some of the aspects of the balance of functions between the network and its end hosts that would later become more pronounced. He only brushed over the narrower notion of end-to-end error control and correction, noting that "[p]owerful error removal methods exist" (Baran 1964*d*, p. 5), alluding to existing checksum, acknowledgment and retransmission schemes widely used in existing telegraphy networks.[31] However, and interestingly for our purposes, he did give prominent consideration to the level of redundancy necessary to obtain a reliable network from unreliable components; a question very much addressing the pragmatic engineering side of the issue of end-to-end reliability.[32] Baran seminally concluded that even moderate redundancy (combined with digital blocks of data adaptively switched through computer relays) could obtain almost perfect reliability.[33] And, along the lines later detailed by Saltzer et al. (1981*a*) he concluded that there is a pragmatic limit to the redundancy that should be built into a network:

> [E]xtremely survivable networks can be built using a moderately low redundancy of connectivity level. Redundancy levels on the order of only three permit the withstanding of extremely heavy level attacks with negligible additional loss to communications. [. . .] [T]he optimum degree of redundancy can be chosen as a function of the expected level of attack [or unreliability of nodes or links for that matter]. *Further redundancy gains little.* (Baran 1964*d*, p. 3, emphasis added)

A second point that Baran made is that the payoff to redundancy of node connections is larger at the edges compared to the core of the network:

> [In the case of "attack", or just: random node or link failure] most of the non-connected stations are found on the periphery of the matrix. This result is caused by the number of probable connections being lower for those stations on the outside fringe. [. . .] *[A] higher degree of redundancy is desirable at the outside edge of distributed networks than needed in the interior.* (1960, p. 23, emphasis added)

This is an argument very much amenable to 'end-to-end' considerations, for it offers a specific advice on the balance of redundancy as reliability functions between the end points and the network.[34] And, as we shall see toward the end of this thesis, there is more merit to the redundancy notion put forward by Baran than is generally acknowledged in the protocols and mechanisms of today's Internet.

At the time of their articulation, however, the arguments put forward and elaborated by Baran were to remain only abstract discussions of the problems of data networking. While there is little uncertainty about the seminal role that Baran played in rewriting the fundamental premises of networking,[35] his ideas were not yet to see an actual implementation—largely due to a lack of commitment and funding by the relevant government agencies.[36] Getting a data network along the lines of Baran off the ground and working out the more tedious details was to remain the work of ARPA, BBN, and the host sites that would connect to the network conceived and implemented by the former two: the Arpanet.

2.2 Dealing with Errors, All the Way

The emergence of the Arpanet beginning in 1969 gave rise to a highly instructive exchange of arguments about the proper place of various functions to be part of distributed and packet oriented data networking—above all, the question of error control. It is useful to begin by noting that much of the Arpanet architecture (and thus the way functions would be arranged along the continuum between application end points and network intermediary nodes) resulted from the Request for Quotations (RFQ) issued by ARPA in 1968 (Scheblik et al. 1968). The stated objective of the Arpanet RFQ was to build a network in which that which was to sit in between the actual end hosts (who would ultimately make use of the network) would assume as many as possible of the functions of the overall network, and appear to the hosts as a most trivial and perfectly reliable I/O facility, much like a printer or a keyboard.[37] Conceptually, the notion of having the hosts connected to one another by means of interfacing with the Interface Message Processors (IMPs) was not too far removed from the then conventional notion of telephones interfacing with the telephone network (Figure 2.1).[38] And, as in the telephone network, the hosts were not to implement *any* network specific functions whatsoever. The only thing they would do is pass chunks of data (of up to 8 times 1008 bits) to their IMP ("at the convenience of the IMP"), and have it sent to the destination IMP who would then pass it on to the destination host and thus consider the task done.[39]

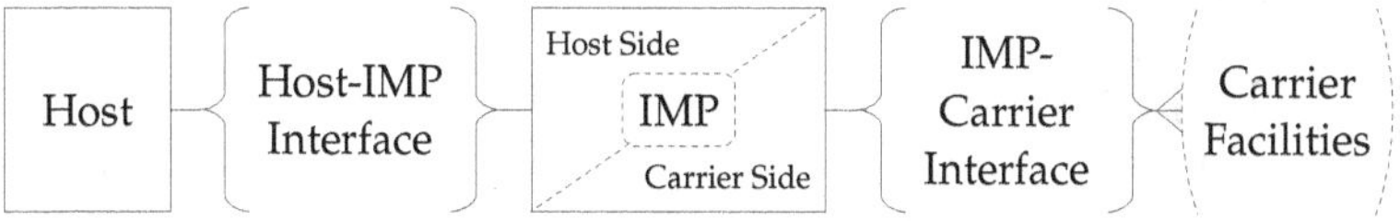

Figure 2.1: Connection between Host, IMP and common carrier; Source: Scheblik et al. (1968, p. 26)

In fact, the hosts were seen as very much secondary in the whole design of the Arpanet (Figure 2.2)—whenever in doubt, a liability rather than an asset, if not a downright nuisance that the network would have to protect itself against. This point is elaborated in Heart et al. (1970), the first published paper on the design of the IMP subnetwork of the Arpanet;[40] a short version of which is offered by BBN's William Crowther as quoted in Postel and Crocker 1970*a*:

> We assume all kinds of users, and protect ourselves accordingly. (p. 3)

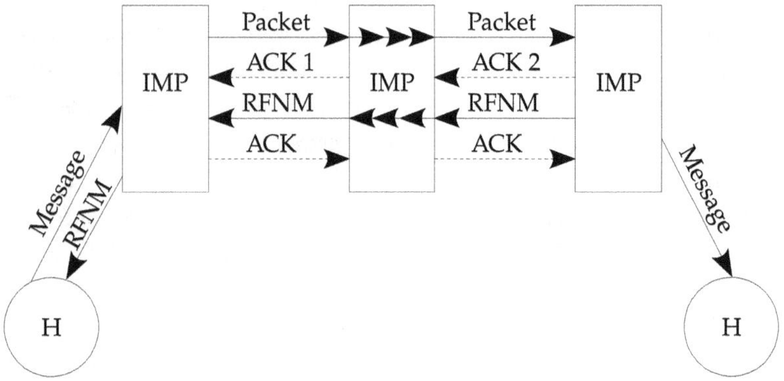

Figure 2.2: RFNMs and acknowledgments; Source: Heart et al. (1970, p. 554)

The host sites, naturally, had a very different take on who was and who was not to be trusted in the relationship between hosts and IMP network. When the prospective host sites convened in early 1969 they were not at all convinced of the infallibility of the network they would come to attach to. The first ever RFC published in April 1969 put it adamantly:

> The point is made by Jeff Rulifson at SRI that error checking at major software interfaces is always a good thing. He points to some experience at SRI where it has saved much dispute and wasted effort. On these grounds, we would like to see some Host to Host checking. Besides checking the software interface, it would also check the Host-IMP transmission hardware. (BB & N claims the Host-IMP hardware will be as reliable as the internal registers of the Host. We believe them, but we still want the error checking.) (S. D. Crocker 1969, pp. 4 f.)

S. D. Crocker (1969) thus proposes that messages at the host level would carry "a message number, bit count, and a checksum", all transparent to the IMPs (p. 6) — by no means an adventurous position; after all, the IMPs would be making extensive use of checksums themselves to guard against both link and IMP failures.[41]

Moreover, as alluded to in S. D. Crocker (1969), the position of the host sites on checksums and end-to-end reliability checks in general had a firm footing in the experiences from software engineering at the time. The notion that software and hardware may fail and one better designs systems with the anticipation of such failures in mind has certainly been around ever since the very first computers, and it was little more than plain reasonable for those with a computer science background to apply these insights to computer networks, too (Rulifson 2009).[42] Thus the host sites kept insisting on doing error control themselves, and various follow-up RFCs elaborate the point made in RFC 1.[43] In chapter 4 we will see why they would still content themselves with dispensing with even a most basic checksumming procedure; even though they proved essentially correct: only a complete host level procedure could fully deal with host level issues — host-host, or, as it was later put, end-to-end. But there was another issue to resolve, and a surprisingly subtle one at that. What was one to do when an error was discovered at the host level, possibly resulting from errors in the host-host protocol procedures?

Actually arriving at a comprehensive notion of how to treat the whole conceivable range of errors at the host level turned out to be no trivial endeavor at all. Early host-host protocol proposals remained distinctly vague on how to deal with errors at all. Crocker et al. (1970*a*), in RFC 33 on the "new host-host protocol", made no mention of error control procedures. Comments on the specifications of the protocol proposed some notion of error handling,[44] but remained cumbersome, and ultimately unconvincing, as Postel and Crocker (1970*b*) conclude:

> With respect to true errors [that is, errors other than resource errors from errant flow control procedures], we are not certain what the value of the <ERR> command is to the recipient. Presumably his NCP is broken, and it may only aggravate the problem to bombard it with error commands. (p. 7)

The next 'official' version of the host-host protocol and the Network Control Program (NCP) (Crocker et al. 1970*b*; Newkirk et al. 1970) included an error command message, but this would be used only for diagnostics rather than any corrective measures:

> Errors are queued for later attention by system programmers, and are considered to be a system error in the host that originated the exchange. (Not associated with any state). (Newkirk et al. 1970, p. 21)

Crocker et al. (1970*b*) elaborate:

> [A]n ERR command is included for notifying a foreign host it has (apparently) made an error. At present, no specific list of errors is defined, and no action is defined for the receipt of ERR commands. (p. 5)

But, ultimately, they had to admit that they had no good idea what to do about errors at the host level:

> As we gain some experience with the network, we will develop a better understanding of what errors can occur and, perhaps more importantly, what to do about these errors. We expect the protocol to change as we understand error control. (p. 8)

Somewhat ironically, it took a comment from BBN's Walden in response to S. D. Crocker's "Host-Host Protocol Document No. 1" to resolve the quandary of error control at the host level. The solution recommended by Walden was to do away with all host-host protocol error messages, and correct for errors by retransmitting any message for which no positive acknowledgment has been returned after a certain time-out:[45]

> If I implemented an NCP, all ERRs would be treated like NOP [that is, be discarded]. As an error control mechanism ERR is complicated and insufficient. Who wants to debug a complicated mechanism which only catches bugs due to the primary mechanism being undebugged. The one error control mechanism I would provide is a receive process to send process acknowledgment on every message. If this is not received for too long, the send process can send the message again if it has been saving it. This acknowledgment catches errors causing message loss at the process/NCP, NCP/NCP, Host/IMP, IMP/IMP, etc. levels. (1970, p. 2)

The answer to the question of what to do about errors—all the way from low level bit errors to high level protocol violations—thus turned out to be: "Do nothing". Instead, acknowledge every action that has completed *without* error, thus making the tacit assumption of errors the default, rather than the exception to be caught. It is completely immaterial "what errors can occur"; as long as the correct termination of actions that are part of the mutually agreed upon protocol can be determined and acknowledged, or, absent acknowledgment simply be repeated until such acknowledgment results, in principle to all eternity.[46] Everything else would be bells and whistles, possibly (not necessarily) improving the performance of the protocol and recovery from errors,[47] but not fundamentally changing the bottom line which holds that positive acknowledgments are the *only* way to obtain certainty about the achievement of intended actions.[48]

When we later close in on the end-to-end arguments as articulated by Saltzer et al. we shall discuss how such improvements may be objectionable on theoretical and empirical grounds. But before we get there, we will turn to the changing premises about the service a network would have to deliver in the first place, making for a second fundamental shift in the whole notion of networking—just a few years after the Arpanet had gotten off the ground.

2.3 Evaporating the Network

We have noted above that the Arpanet had been designed very much as a network delivering a complete and reliable service to the attached hosts, and very much with the assumption of untrustworthy hosts in mind.[49] Even more importantly, when the Arpanet project started, host sites were less than happy about the prospect of having (1) to share their resources with third parties, and thus (2) to help build the network in the first place. The benefits from being part of a network whose explicit objective it was to share computer resources were simply too vague to be appealing to those already in possession of computers, and even with a subnetwork doing virtually all the networking, there were still plenty of unresolved issues to be tackled for the host machines.[50]

Thus there was almost by necessity a very high level and strict line between the IMP subnetwork and the host machines. *High level* to ease the burden for hosts to attach to the network, and *strict* to separate clearly between the functions and responsibilities of subnetwork and attached hosts. The set of functions to be resolved in a cooperative fashion between the network and the hosts was thus kept to a bare minimum.[51]

However, the host sites' initial reservations toward networking quickly gave way to outright enthusiasm among many computer scientists. The Arpanet had exceeded expectations, and quickly proved a useful foundation for many applications which in turn drew ever more people to join the network. By 1972 the Arpanet was reliable and *useful* enough to be demonstrated to a broader audience at the first International Conference on Computer Communication (ICCC) in Washington, DC, and establishing much beyond doubt that packet switched data networking was both feasible and sensible.[52] Packet switched computer networking became an accepted notion and was starting to be pursued by other groups outside the Arpanet project, too.

But, while some of the general principles of computer networking such as layering and information hiding became universally accepted, that of the right balance between networking functions in the hosts and those in the 'inner' network became hotly contested. Arguably, once the people concerned with host level issues realized (or came to believe) that a network could never be made such that it would provide a 'simple' telephone like interface to the hosts, they became hungry for more: if the end hosts already had to do flow control and error correction, then why not take over even more functions?

The first to explore and actively advocate for an approach along those lines was Louis Pouzin in a French project called Cyclades starting in 1972.[53] Having had been to the U.S. and seen the work on Arpanet, he consulted BBN in the run-up to and throughout the Cyclades project taking much of his inspiration from the experiences in the early Arpanet, but also developing notions that departed markedly from the BBN work.[54] The most decisive difference in Pouzin's approach was to void the 'inner' network (that is, everything outside the actual end host computers) from all the functions that could also sensibly be performed by the end hosts themselves. The functions that in the Arpanet were performed by the IMPs would in the Cyclades network be performed by the end hosts — the network would literally extend into the hosts rather than offering them an interface to a complete and self-contained network. Only the irreducible functions to be performed in between the end hosts would be assumed by a packet switching network called Cigale (Pouzin 1974*b*).[55] The packet switching subnetwork underneath Cyclades would still do node-to-node error checking (Pouzin 1974*b*),[56] but altogether offer no guarantees for reliable or otherwise sane transmission of data. The experience from Arpanet showed that it was possible, by and large, to offer a reliable service, but it also showed that many crucial functions would have to be implemented at or very close to the ultimate end points to the networks — a notion that Pouzin (1976*b*) named "focal points" (Figure 2.3).[57] The only service thus

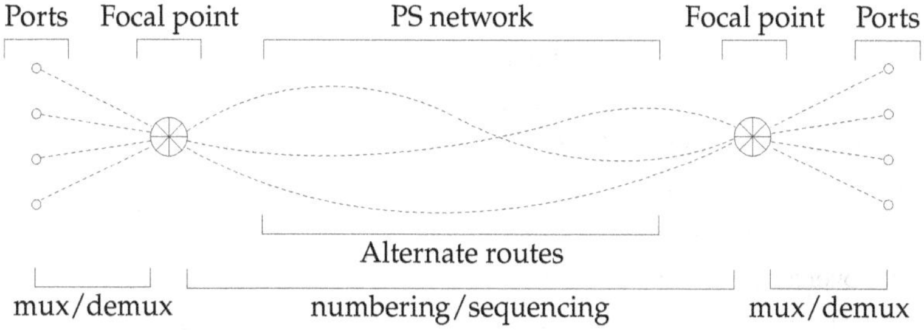

Figure 2.3: Focal points; Source: Adapted from Pouzin (1976*b*, p. 486)

offered by Cigale was a most simple 'datagram' facility, moving packets of data from one host to another, with packets possibly getting lost, duplicated, or arriving in an order other than that in which they were sent off.

Why would Pouzin do this? To a certain extent, this departure from the Arpanet approach owed to the political situation at the time, namely the fear of the French that they would lose out to the then burgeoning U.S. computer industry.[58] However, the printed literature adds other, more technical reasons, too. According to Pouzin (1973*b*) there were two primary motivations behind the design of Cyclades/Cigale: (1) building an evolvable network, with heterogeneous sites all having it "their way" (p. 80); and (2) building a network that could "inter-network" with other networks. A network thus, which would "leave room for expansion not only upwards as usual, but also sideways" (p. 83).[59] Advocating the simplicity of a datagram network for inter-networking to a broader community, Pouzin (1974*a*) notes:[60]

> Most of the apparent difficulties [in network interconnection] stem from peculiar functions which are not mandatory features of a packet switching service. They smack more of accidental design, rather than intrinsic requirement. In this category fall virtual circuits, end-to-end acknowledgements, buffer allocation, and the like. [...] [P]acket switching would not be the least impaired, should these functions be left out. On the other hand, any end-to-end function, which users might desire, can be implemented over one or several networks at the user interface. (p. 2)

Another reason for Pouzin's adamancy about keeping the core of the network as basic as possible, and not as convenient as possible for the hosts has been emphasized in another line of reasonings: the objective to contain the power of state monopolies that would offer public data networks, very much along the lines of the then existing PTTs. The experience of government controlled state monopolies on telecommunication services in Europe had gone along with (1) prices substantially higher than in the U.S., (2) a very limited prospect of competition in data networking, and (3) a dismal state of public data networking services.[61] Most importantly, there was a material danger that PTTs would try to add more and more functions to a public data network, leaving no flexible network to end users—while private competition would be outlawed by the government regulation aimed at protecting their monopolies:

> Wherever possible, private nets will be outlawed or deterred with exorbitant line tariffs. State monopolies can do that.
>
> Terminal manufacturers will have to queue up for months or years to get their products supported by public networks. Even if they conform to PTT specifications, a stamp of approval will likely be necessary. Innovation will be decided by PTTs. [...]
>
> [T]he packet clan will have to walk a thin line, and tends to operate by political coups rather than by open policy. (Pouzin 1976*b*, p. 492)

Given those political realities on the one hand, and the feasibility of having the hosts implement the bulk of network functions on the other,

Pouzin (1976*b*) sees little point in settling on anything other than a balance of functions between carriers and end hosts which allows the latter to implement end-to-end protocols at their liking, and the former to be confined to most simple datagram services:

> CVC's [Carrier Virtual Circuits] may have a minor advantage over DG's [Datagrams], when the customer *agrees to trust* the carrier, because a CVC protocol is perhaps a little more compact than an E-E [End-End User Protocol] plus a DG protocol. But this cannot be held true until it has been validated from experience for *a number of protocols*.
>
> On the other hand, *if the customer wants to insure his own E-E control, a DG interface would unquestionably take less overhead than CVC's*. (p. 490, emphasis added)

A simple packet switching service, the 'datagram facility' would thus serve as the sole common ground between end hosts and carriers, on top of which end hosts could implement whichever end-to-end transport protocols and applications they saw fit—at the discretion of the end hosts' users, not the carriers in between.

On the other side of the Atlantic Ocean, over in the U. S., it took much longer to arrive at the notions championed by Pouzin. While work at TCP, commencing in 1973, took aim at interconnecting networks via gateways that would be tasked with the necessary conversions between the networks it connected,[62] it was only by 1977 that a clear conceptual delineation of host level and (inter)network level issues was arrived at.[63] Postel (1977*b*) submits:

> We are screwing up in our design of internet protocols by violating the principle of layering. Specifically we are trying to use TCP to do two things: serve as a host level end to end protocol, and to serve as an internet packaging and routing protocol. These two things should be provided in a layered and modular way. I suggest that a new distinct internetwork protocol is needed, and that TCP be used strictly as a host level end to end protocol. (p. 1)

And, thus it happened. While the PTTs in Europe built networks based on the then settled upon X.25 standard which left VCs in the province of network operators,[64] in the U. S. the principles of datagrams and inter-network end-to-end VCs together with the hands-on experience of the Arpanet laid the foundation of what was to become today's Internet. In an odd twist of history, TCP and IP adopted the central notions developed by the Cyclades team in light of the presence of omnipotent state monopolies in Europe (PTTs)—just before the Cyclades project ceased in 1978 precisely due to the power of those PTTs—, [65] and developed them into the Internet protocols that are essentially still with us to this very day.

2.4 End-to-End Arguments Taking Shape

We have now walked through the basic intellectual developments that led to much of the modern notion of networking with a particular focus on end-to-end arguments. Before we continue with the main thrust of this chapter, we may thus briefly pause and recapitulate the high level rationales considered thus far for moving functions into the end hosts rather than leaving them to the network:

Diminishing marginal utility of redundancy No level of redundancy of functions 'in' the network can ever minimize the probability of failure down to zero. Depending on the expected level of node and link failure, there is a level of redundancy (in node interconnection) adding to which any further redundancy gains so little as not to warrant the costs thus incurred (section 2.1).

End-to-end correctness Only end-to-end error control based on positive acknowledgment can cover the whole communication path between two processes at host level and thus provide perfect reliability, if so desired be the end hosts (section 2.2).

Flexibility of the host functions The more general a network is in its basic functionality, the more flexible the hosts are in their uses of the network. With "as few features as possible at levels buried in the sensitive parts of the network" "heterogeneous sites can have their way, and still communicate with others in a consistent manner" (Pouzin 1973*b*, p. 80). It would thus be up to the hosts to decide which networking functions were essential to them in the first place, rather than having the network offer a uniform service to all hosts regardless of their specific requirements (section 2.3, pages 19 f.).

Interconnection of heterogeneous networks The fewer functions there are at the common ground of a network, the more other networks it can interconnect to. If we assume different networks to be different in their services, then only an "intersection of properties" (Pouzin 1973*b*, p. 83) can provide the basis for global interconnection (section 2.3, pages 19 f.).

Competition and empowering end users The fewer functions there are under the control of monopoly network operators, the lower the risk of them controlling what applications end users may employ in the first place, and the more of the social surplus ends up with customers rather than operators (section 2.3, pages 20 f.).

It is fair to conclude that by the mid-1970s there was a good general understanding of the engineering trade-offs in the placement of functions in packet switching networks to be shared stochastically by multiple users and applications. In the following chapter we will turn to the elaboration of the end-to-end arguments that started with the 1981 Saltzer et al. paper on "end-to-end arguments in system design." However, before moving our discussion to these increasingly abstract arguments we shall in the final section of this chapter (section 2.5) discuss the growing concerns at the time about hosts assuming vital networking functions and thus removing the operation of the network from central control and management. For just as it was understood that there is merit in moving functions toward the end points, it was also understood that there might be considerable costs to doing so.

2.5 First Responses: Of Power and Responsibility

There are no good 'arguments' without reasonable and plausible points on both sides, and so it is with the slowly emerging 'end-to-end arguments'. While research into broadening the scope of data network beyond the confines of the Arpanet, other smaller networks, and the emerging Local Area Networks (LANs) kept progressing very much along the lines sketched by

Pouzin, some were not quite buying into the arguments of the 'datagram' (as opposed to virtual circuit) proponents.

We have already mentioned that moving functions of the networks from a physically separated subnetwork into the host machines themselves runs very much counter to the premises the Arpanet was based on,[66] but that with the growing confidence in the basic notion of packet switching many came to believe that the benefits from moving network functions into the immediate sphere of the host computers would outweigh the costs thus incurred (see page 18).

BBN (1974*d*)[67] take up the emerging discussion which they summarize as this:

> An important part of the ARPA Network design which has become controversial is the ARPA Network system of messages and packets within the subnetwork, ordering of messages, guaranteed message delivery, and so on. In particular, the idea has been put forth that many of these functions should be moved from subnetwork to Host level. [. . .] Differing views on specific design choices in this area have been proposed by the designers of the Cyclades network [Pouzin 1973*b*], writers on the subject of inter-network communication [Cerf and Kahn 1974], and ARPA Network researchers commenting on their experience [Cerf 1974]. [. . .]
>
> [T]he principles usually given for eliminating message processing from the communications subnetwork [are]: (a.) For complete reliability, Hosts must do the same jobs and therefore, the IMPs should not. (b.) Host/Host performance may be degraded by the IMPs doing these jobs. (c.) Network interconnection may be impeded by the IMPs doing message processing. (d.) Lockups can happen in subnetwork message processing. [and] (e.) The IMP would become simpler and have more buffering capacity if it did not have to do message processing. (pp. 3 ff.)

After elaborating each of the points (pp. 4 ff.), only the latter of which they acknowledge in principle, they offer a summary response to the objections put forward by Pouzin, Cerf and Kahn, and Cerf,[68] which, put very briefly, boils down to three essential points:

- Hosts are to deal with host level issues (flow control, end-to-end error control, host level resources), but none of their efforts can render superfluous the subnetwork having to deal with issues logically at the subnetwork level (congestion, resource management, offering reasonable performance to the hosts).[69]
- Any feasible trade-off between reliability, throughput and delay that might be desired by the hosts (e. g., delay sensitive but loss insensitive applications such as voice, rather than the initially more important loss sensitive but delay insensitive applications such as file transfer and remote login) can be added as a service of the subnetwork with little cost to other hosts, and in fact more conveniently than by having to coordinate all the end hosts. None of the functions that the IMP subnetwork offers prejudices hosts who might want to add further functions, or impedes the possibility of inter-networking with other networks by using a simpler service than that typically offered by the Arpanet.[70]
- Debugging and improving on the network is much eased by central control over network functions. Even fundamental design changes in the subnetwork can thus be obtained with very little coordination overhead.[71]

It is only fair to note that these arguments pertain to a setting that is much more tractable than today's Internet, and have some obvious problems when generalized to a more complex interconnection of networks, as BBN readily acknowledge in closing:

> With the growth of the ARPA Network, and the introduction of new technology in IMPs and circuits, including satellites, all the parameters above must be reexamined. (p. 15)

The Internet has shown that a truly global network may comprise arbitrarily idiosyncratic networks,[72] but a 'local' network may never grow as large as the Internet has.

And yet, while the Internet of today — owing to its much reduced set of global functions mandatorily to be performed by the networks involved —

is much larger than the Arpanet could ever hope to become, it is also plagued by precisely the problems touched on by BBN: congestion control is a problem that is conceptually unresolved in the Internet (Briscoe 2008; Briscoe 2009), the lack of Quality of Service (QoS) on the global Internet arguably precludes some applications,[73] and updating functions of the networks or even changing its design is practically impossible today (Handley 2006).[74] Moreover, placing control over the network with a decentralized and largely anonymous set of hosts may jeopardize the very operations of the overall network and the hosts attached to it, for it robs the network of efficient means of governing the sharing of its resources. Roberts (1978) comments with regard to the Cyclades network which, as we have discussed above, very much embodies the design philosophy of the then emerging Internet:[75]

> Since a major part of the organization and control of the network is imbedded in the Cyclades [host] computers, the subnetwork, Cigale, is not sufficient by itself. [. . .] The Cyclades structure provides a good testbed for trying out various protocols, as was its intent; but it requires a more cooperative and coordinated set of hosts than is likely to exist in a public environment. (p. 1309)

With hindsight it has, of course, turned out that the benefits from leaving the bulk of functions, power, and responsibilities with the end hosts rather than network intermediary nodes has far outweighed the risks and costs of doing so. In the following chapter we shall thus elaborate the further history of the end-to-end arguments — from the seminal articulation in Saltzer et al. (1981*a*) (section 3.1) to the variations and extensions built thereupon (sections 3.2 through 3.4).

Chapter 3

Classic End-to-End Arguments and Beyond

Sometimes a few stable statements are borrowed over and over again by many papers; but even in these rare cases, the statement is slowly eroded, losing its original shape, encapsulated into more and more foreign statements, becoming so familiar and routinised that it becomes part of tacit practice and disappears from view!

— *Bruno Latour (1987, p. 43)*

The end-to-end arguments may have been contested before Saltzer et al. wrote them up in 1981; however, the wealth of reformulation and contestation was to build up subsequent to their original formulation. On the one hand, this continuous reshaping of content, objectives, and normative scope is unfortunate, for no account of the end-to-end arguments can thus ever hope to be conclusive; on the other hand, it is precisely this malleability that helps keep the end-to-end arguments a relevant principle for the Internet. The challenge is to make informed judgments about which versions of the end-to-end arguments make sense and which do not.

The previous chapter featured some subjectivity on our part in choosing which threads to amplify and which to neglect.[76] That subjectivity features prominently in this chapter, too; particularly since it entails continuous critical assessments of the various articulations at hand. Despite this bias, we feel that it offers a good overview of the relevant threads that have been ensuing from the original end-to-end arguments. Note well, though, that we do not include here sizable treatments of the network neutrality discussion, a subject we defer to footnotes as well as some incidental discussion in Part III.[77] As for the detailed structure of the remainder of this chapter, it continues the outline given at the beginning of the previous chapter, reflecting on the Internet and its emerging conceptual problems — all at the level of theoretical elaboration rather than the detailed reflection of real-world artifacts.

3.1 The Original End-to-End Arguments

Having elaborated the end-to-end arguments about the emerging data communication systems from the 1960s to the 1970s, and thus prior to the Saltzer et al. paper, we are now turning to the 'original' source that articulated the notion of end-to-end arguments in system design (Saltzer et al. 1981*a*).

It is apt to start out by noting an oddity about the notions of *arguments* and *principles* as they occur in the paper. While the Abstract therein is bold in claiming that their reasonings give rise to a design principle, the rest of the paper is very much silent on the notion of an end-to-end *principle*. The word principle only appears, much in passing, in the second as well as in the penultimate sentence of the body of the paper.[78] Indeed, the paper is more of a loose set of *arguments* (as in: debates) about the proper place of functions in a distributed communication system than it is about stating a categorical principle (or, argument, as in: logically derived statement).[79] This may be a fine point, but it is an important one, for Saltzer et al. have often been charged with having invented, or at least seminally articulated, a categorical end-to-end *principle* with categorical implications about the *only* proper place of functions in a communication system — when all they have done, instead, is to consider a number of arguments about the proper place of functions in a distributed network such as the Internet.[80]

At its very core, the end-to-end arguments as framed in the 1981 paper are a set of rationales for putting functions of a communication system (mostly those concerned with reliability of data transfer) with the end hosts rather than with the communication 'subsystem' — a notion very much in line with what we have considered in the preceding sections, and something the authors readily acknowledge:

> The individual examples of end-to-end arguments cited in this paper [. . .] have accumulated over the years. (Saltzer et al. 1984, p. 285)

In fact, at first glance, the paper adds little more than an appealing metaphor — "end-to-end arguments" — to the existing state of knowledge at the time.[81] The notion that end hosts would have to implement error control themselves rather than trust it to the network in between the ends had been well established by the late 1970s. Pouzin and Zimmermann (1978) offer no less than nine casual references in support of this point (p. 1362), visualized in Figure 3.1. Moreover, the chief principle as well as the atten-

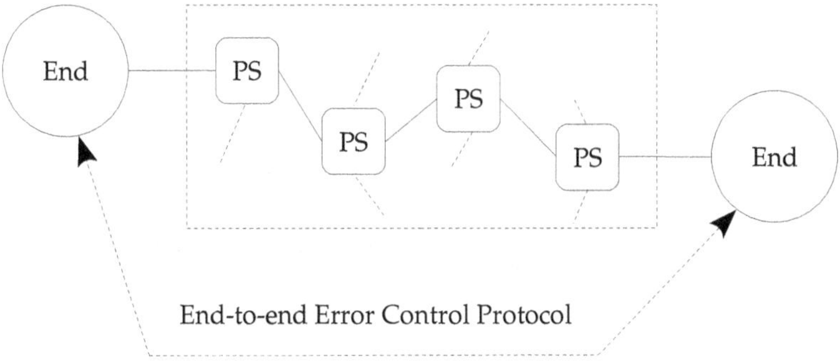

Figure 3.1: End-to-end error control; Source: Adapted from Pouzin and Zimmermann (1978, p. 1362)

dant performance trade-offs connotated by the 1981 end-to-end arguments had already been voiced with considerable clarity during the mid-1970s debates about the proper design of gateways in an inter-network.[82]

In a sense, thus, Saltzer et al. (1981*a*) is largely about taking stock of the previous years of discussions on the questions raised by Heart et al. in 1970: "What tasks shall be performed by each [the hosts and the subnetwork]? What constraints shall each place on the other?",[83] their answer being:

> *The function in question can completely and correctly be implemented only with the knowledge and help of the application standing at the*

> *endpoints of the communication system. Therefore, providing that questioned function as a feature of the communication system itself is not possible. (Sometimes an incomplete version of the function provided by the communication system may be useful as a performance enhancement.)* (Saltzer et al. 1984, p. 278, emphasis in original)

It is worth paying attention to the immediate context of this quote, which points to the applicable scope of this "line of reasoning against low-level function [called] the end-to-end argument". They note:

> The argument appeals to application requirements. [. . .] [It is] the requirements of the application [that] provide the basis for the [argument]. (pp. 277 f.)

Thus the end-to-end argument is about functions as they are required by applications, presumably at the end hosts, that use the subnetwork in order to communicate based on a set of requirements that ultimately they, and not the subnetwork, can articulate, and thus implement and monitor. And, of course, the whole purpose of the subnetwork is to further those of the end hosts and their users; the subnetwork serves no purpose in and of itself.

So, what functions does the end-to-end argument pertain to? The authors largely confine the scope of their paper to "encryption, duplicate message detection, message sequencing, guaranteed message delivery, detecting host crashes, and delivery receipts" (p. 278), all of which are functions directly related to the problem of host level (end-to-end) data transfer in a packet switching network. Considering just that problem as a case study, the authors conclude, somewhat predictably:

> In order to achieve careful [meaning perfectly reliable] file transfer, the application program that performs the transfer must supply a file-transfer-specific, end-to-end reliability guarantee — in this case, a checksum to detect failures and a retry-commit plan. For the data communication system to go out of its way to be extraordinarily reliable does not reduce the burden on the application program to ensure reliability. (p. 280)

As we have indicated above, this reasoning put forward by Saltzer et al. is very much in line with the earlier articulations of the argument that functions pertaining to end-to-end reliability should sit with the end hosts, ultimately with the very processes that originate and terminate the data communication.[84] Lower level attempts aimed at obtaining perfect reliability are useful only to a certain degree, from which on they become cost-ineffective.[85]

The more interesting and original part of the paper comes with the considerations about applications that do *not* need perfectly reliable data transfer, and which rather have the subnetwork be unreliable, fast, and cheap, instead of reliable, slow, and expensive. Common functions in a subsystem that go beyond what some applications require as a minimum service may thus not only be redundant, they may in fact be wholly unnecessary and thus futile if not downright harmful:

> [P]erforming the function at the lower level may cost more—for two reasons. First, since the lower level subsystem is common to many applications, those applications that do *not* need the function will pay for it anyway. Second, the low-level subsystem may not have as much information as the higher levels, so it cannot do the job as efficiently. (p. 281, emphasis added)

The prime example along those lines of reasoning is, of course, real-time interactive voice traffic which is inherently delay-sensitive but can easily cope with less than perfect reliability:

> For those connections that carry voice packets, an unusually strong version of the end-to-end argument applies: If low levels of the communication system try to accomplish bit-perfect communication, they will probably introduce uncontrolled delays in packet delivery, for example, by requesting retransmission of damaged packets and holding up delivery of later packets until earlier ones have been correctly retransmitted. Such delays are disruptive to the voice application, which needs to feed data at a constant rate to the listener. (pp. 284 f.)

While this argument is not entirely new, either;[86] it neatly wraps up the overall case against providing functions in the common subnetwork which are redundant at best, and harmful at worst.

There are thus two main arguments to the end-to-end argument: First, many functions of a network are specific to the applications sitting at its end points in such a way that they cannot be implemented "completely and correctly" by the network subsystem without the applications' "knowledge and help". Thus a lower level implementation may be helpful, but ultimately futile in and of itself. The canonical example here is *reliable data transfer*. Second, functions that *inhibit* certain applications (rather than merely adding redundancy) should not be implemented in the subnetwork lest they narrow the scope of applications (including unforeseeable ones) of the network. Here, the canonical example is *interactive voice*.

In sum, the end-to-end argument may be generalized as an economic trade-off about the functions in question, and be stated as follows:

Argument 1 *A common subnetwork should provide functions only to the extent that (1) applications at the end hosts that require certain functions (that go beyond an irreducible reasonably minimum of service by a distributed network) are not capable of making up for the lack of those functions at the subnetwork at reasonable cost, and (2) there are (potential) applications which are harmed rather than helped by those very functions if part of the subnetwork. The line between functions to be provided at the subnetwork and functions to be implemented at the application level depends on the benefit of providing common subnetwork functions to the applications that may thus be helped, versus the cost of doing so to those applications that do not need those functions at all. While the functions in question may be provided optionally and thus be of no prejudice against applications not needing them,*[87] *as far as the costs of those functions have to be born by all applications the trade-off remains pertinent.*

To venture a preliminary judgment of Saltzer et al. (1981*a*), their principal achievement was to give explicit articulation to an argument in favor of placing functions with the end hosts rather than with the network, and coin a metaphor (metaphors) that would—despite its vagueness, or maybe just because of it—serve as an umbrella for all coming discussions about the balance of functions in a distributed system.[88] Still, the vagueness of the paper is somewhat unfortunate, because it leaves the designer at loss as to how precisely to resolve the broad trade-off between flexibility and performance. On the one hand, "lower levels need not provide 'perfect' reliability" (p. 281), on the other, "some effort at the lower levels to improve network reliability can have a significant effect on application performance" (p. 281). In a sense, thus, the end-to-end argument advances a default rule, an "Occam's razor" as the authors submit, to be applied whenever "the communication subsystem is [. . .] specified before applications that use the subsystem are known" (p. 287). However, any communication subsystem will have to do *something* in order to be useful in the first place, and the end-to-end argument is nowhere near conclusive about what features a communication subsystem will have to provide, and which ones it will better leave to the end hosts attached.

An even more serious objection to the reasoning behind the end-to-end argument is that it gives *no* consideration whatsoever to issues of congestion, fairness, and overall stability and order in general. It assumes that a network can simply be provided, very much as an exogenous given rather than an artifact at interplay with the end hosts it is serving and the applications it is being put to. While this is fair enough for a policy statement and a model that necessarily has to abstract away from reality (and also makes explicit its assumptions and scope), it is nevertheless an omission worth noting and being aware of — the more so since the authors had no doubt been well aware of the issues raised by extremely thin "subnetworks" such as those of Alohanet — air —, and Ethernet — copper cable —, which required elaborate access control schemes to which all of the hosts would have to adhere to very strictly, with a misbehaving host effectively being able to collapse the entire network.[89]

We have pointed above to the premise of Saltzer et al. (1981*a*) that "the requirements of the application provide the basis for the [end-to-end arguments]" (pp. 277 f.). However, in reality not only will the subnetwork have requirements of its own (e. g., not to be overwhelmed by traffic from the hosts) that will potentially give rise to other equally legitimate "arguments"; those requirements will in turn very much reflect back on the requirements of the applications and what service they can effectively obtain from the network, the end-to-end arguments notwithstanding. All other things being equal, the end-to-end arguments make for a useful principle; but in reality, the all-other-things-being-equal assumption rarely holds. The additional arguments that may be raised from different premises may not just complement the end-to-end arguments, but may as well run counter to them — a notion we shall further explore in section 7.2. Note that this is not so much a critique of the Saltzer et al. paper,[90] as it is a caveat against progressing carelessly from end-to-end *arguments* to end-to-end *argument* to end-to-end *principle*. While much of the discussion based on the end-to-end arguments has been mindful of the conceptual limitations of the end-to-end argument; as we shall see in the remainder of this chapter, some writers have also taken it very much out of context, leaving little more than a caricature of the original formulation and its subtleties.

With the original paper on end-to-end arguments leaving considerable scope for elaboration, it is not surprising to find various refinements, restatements, and comments on the issues raised therein. The points made subsequent to Saltzer et al. (1981*a*) may be grouped roughly along the categorization put forward in their paper: (1) reliability and fitness for application requirements generally requires the functions in those respects to be implemented by the applications at the end hosts, and (2) functions beyond an irreducible and reasonable level of service in the subnetwork may impose unacceptable or even prohibitive costs on applications not requiring those functions.[91] The reasonings detailed in section 3.2 and section 3.3 largely pertain to the former argument, and those in section 3.4 to the latter.

3.2 Fate Sharing and Orthogonality

An early elaboration of the end-to-end argument is offered by Clark (1988), a widely acknowledged paper detailing the design goals and decisions of the Internet. According to Clark the top priority goal of the Internet architecture was "survivability in the face of failure", and the chief means by which this goal was achieved was what he calls the "fate-sharing approach to survivability" (pp. 107 f.).

Effectively, the fate-sharing argument assumes that the subnetwork (especially in an inter-networking scenario) is inherently unreliable, and thus no state information about ongoing connections between end hosts should be maintained in the subnetwork (only). "It is acceptable to lose state information associated with an entity if, at the same time, the entity itself is lost" (p. 108), but it is not acceptable for such state to get lost because of subnetwork failures, precisely because such failures are assumed the norm rather than the exception. In fact, the argument follows straight from the overall architectural premise of the Internet:

> The most important goal [. . .] is that the Internet should continue to supply communications service, even though networks and gateways are failing. In particular, this goal was interpreted to mean that if two entities are communicating over the Internet, and some failure causes the Internet to be temporarily disrupted and reconfigured to reconstitute the service, then the entities communicating should be able to continue without having to reestablish or reset the high level state of their conversation. [. . .] [A]t the top of transport, there is only one failure, and it is total partition. The architecture was to mask completely any transient failure. (pp. 107 f.)

Thus, according to the fate-sharing argument, a host should not delegate state into the network lest it loses control over the state of its network operations, because the network cannot (and should not) be relied on to maintain the state associated with end points to ongoing connections in a sane and predictable manner. The only state that end points may delegate inside the network is "soft state", that is, state that "can be lost and reconstructed" (Clark 1989, p. 15).[92] The fate-sharing argument is thus very much an elaboration of the first of the 1981 end-to-end arguments concerned with reliability.[93]

At a practical level, the consequence of this reasoning, according to Clark (1988) and IAB (1996), is that the network should not provide virtual circuits on behalf of the end hosts. Instead, end hosts themselves are the better places to maintain the state necessary for virtual circuits; they would have to replicate any state maintained in the network, anyway, should they wish to guard against network failures. Thus a network that is assumed to suffer from transient failures better be a simple datagram network facility only, leaving any further elaboration of the network services to the — presumably more reliable — end hosts.[94]

It is useful to note that the fate-sharing argument is *not* (no more than the original end-to-end arguments) an argument against *any* state in the subnetwork. IAB (1996) acknowledges this point,[95] and so do Bush and Meyer (2002):

> [T]he End-to-End Argument does not imply that the core of the Internet will not contain and maintain state. In fact, a

> huge amount coarse grained state is maintained in the Internet's core (e. g., routing state). However, the important point here is that this (coarse grained) state is almost orthogonal to the state maintained by the end-points (e. g., hosts). (p. 3)

In fact, this note about orthogonality between state associated with application requirements and state associated with the core operations of the internal network is little more than a reminder that the original end-to-end argument is effectively a host level or application layer argument, not an argument about the design of the network at large.[96] And, it gets us not much closer yet to those interrelations between host state and internal state of the network that cannot be resolved by arranging them orthogonally. We will return to this issue in later segments of this thesis; suffice it here to note that expanding the end-to-end argument from its application layer focus to a broader principle about all networking functions involves a number of subtleties that go well beyond the original scope of the end-to-end arguments.

3.3 Trust and Delegation

The basic premise of the original end-to-end arguments had been that the end hosts are inherently more trustworthy to perform networking functions to the standard of the application at hand than a subnetwork which was inherently beyond the control of the end hosts. Those operating the end host computers were assumed to be both willing and capable to take on the burden of implementing all those functions that in the Arpanet were provided by the IMPs rather than the hosts. Also, the end-to-end arguments were very much about making an abstract and general point, not too much about weighing the performance and cost trade-offs in detail. Thus the notion of delegating vital application layer functions at the discretion of the end hosts away from them and into the network was not covered by Saltzer et al. (1984).

And yet, from the very beginning of host-host communication considerations has there been the firm notion of a dedicated transport program at the hosts that would multiplex and perform the communication requests of various application processes at the host computer. A process wanting to communicate with a process at a remote host would simply invoke some 'network program' and hand it the payload data to be transmitted plus control parameters such as remote address and desired priority of the communication.[97] In the Arpanet this was the task of the Network Control Program (NCP) (S. D. Crocker 1970*a*), in the Internet it became the task of the Transmission Control Program (TCP) (Postel 1981*f*).[98] Thus a process would not itself have to implement all the functions needed for networking; instead, it could use a common network program, very much like a subroutine. Not only did such approach save the various applications at a host from having to implement the complexities of networking themselves; also, a central entity controlling access to a network link would be much better suited to manage the fine-grained multiplexing of several applications onto the underlying communication link(s).[99]

Moors (2002) argues that this notion is effectively a violation of the end-to-end arguments, for according to them it is the "applications, not transport layers, [that] should check integrity" (p. 1215). He then argues that delegating functions to the transport layer (as implemented at the system in question) is justified because the benefit from doing so vastly exceeds the cost thus incurred. More generally, functions are referred to the transport program because it is trusted to be effectively as reliable (if not more so) than the application, and both sit at the same computer system, anyway:

> [T]he decision to implement reliable transfer in the transport layer is not justified on the basis of end-to-end arguments, but rather on the basis of trust. (p. 1215, emphasis omitted)

This is indeed a useful point to generalize: functions may be delegated away from the ultimate application processes on the basis of trust.[100] In a 2007 paper Clark and Blumenthal take up this notion[101] and develop it into a whole new version of the original end-to-end argument — sharpening its application level focus (as opposed to conceiving it as being applicable to *all* functions of a network), and exploring the *horizontal* issues raised by the overall problem of distributed networking (as opposed to the *vertical* issues addressed by the original end-to-end argument).[102] Acknowledging the limitations of the original argument,[103] they argue that from the user perspective the problem addressed by the end-to-end argument essentially boils down to one of human end users acting as principals invoking a set of 'trustworthy' agents to perform the functions on their behalf. From the individual user perspective there is nothing that 'in principle' prevents such functions to reach beyond the confines of the host computers they physically attend. In fact, there may not even be an all too close relation between the location of a user and that of the end points to the relevant transactions.[104] Thus Clark and Blumenthal arrive at a restatement of the end-to-end notion in terms of trust—trust by the end user to have entities, wherever they are located, to perform the desired functions to their standard.[105]

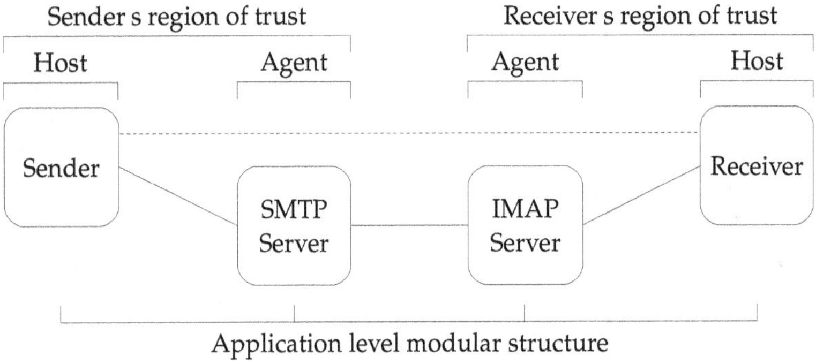

Figure 3.2: Regions of trust in email; Source: Clark and Blumenthal (2007, pp. 11 f. and Figure 1 at p. 12)

The argument firmly derives from the original reasoning, but it only becomes apparent in the face of the realities of today's Internet which break many of the assumptions that were true back in the early 1980s, particularly that for an end user the *end node* and the *trusted node* converge into one.[106] The crucial point is that from the functions migrating away from the ultimate application end points and into the network it does not follow that applications become less reliable; much rather they may become *more* reliable,[107] with the principals (hopefully) making informed decisions as to where to delegate which functions and to which ultimate purposes.[108] It is important to note here that the narrow conception of reliability in the original end-to-end arguments, meaning little more than correct transmission of application level data, preferably in a fully transparent fashion, has in the Clark and Blumenthal version given way to a broader application level conception that comprises all sorts of functions related to application level use of a networking facility—basically anything that a third party may offer as a service to an application sitting at a end host; e. g., identity management, payment services, or proxy services.[109] And, not only is there a 'bilateral' social surplus to be obtained by such transactions if guided by the discretion of both network owners and end users; it is crucial to note that there are also very few if not fully negligible side-effects to moving functions inside the network along horizontal lines at the application layer, for doing so will only rarely impose specific functions on third parties the way it would when moving functions to a a shared common layer in a vertical protocol stack.[110] There is thus next to no point in limiting the movement of functions from end hosts into the network as long as that takes place at the application layer and at the discretion of the end users in their capacity as principals in what may be conceived essentially as a classic principal-agent setting.

Thus framed, the result of the (to adopt an economics term here) 'make-or-buy decision' for the hosts as well as the more global policy implications are completely different from those entailed by the original end-to-end arguments. Clark and Blumenthal put it succinctly:

> The analog to the original end-to-end argument might be that it is better for the end-nodes to solve what problems they can by themselves, because involving a third party can only add to the complexity, and perhaps to the lack of certainty about trust. But the outcome of the analysis, in this case as in the original paper, is not a dogmatic stricture but a preference, to be validated by the facts of the situation. And this construction by analogy may be nonsense. There is no reason to believe that the original reasoning about an unreliable communications subsystem makes any sense at the application level. So perhaps at this level there should not be a preference for end-to-end patterns of communication, but a preference for the use of third-party services and multi-way patterns of communication. (p. 15, footnotes omitted)

Thus, seen from the perspective offered by Clark and Blumenthal, the original end-to-end arguments are essentially about the division of functions along vertical lines — the network protocol stack —, and especially about the question which functions shall be provided as common ground to all end hosts and applications partaking in the Internet thus formed. They do not address the (horizontal) structure of the network at the application layer, for back in the early 1980s applications were very much assumed to sit with their ultimate end points. The coincidence of applications and many of their functions being logically above the common internetwork layer *and* at the same time at the horizontal edges of the overall network rendered a more elaborate version of the end-to-end arguments largely unnecessary.

In all, the trust-to-trust variation of the original end-to-end arguments holds that all those functions that are *not* conceptually part of the inter-network layer, especially those functions that are orthogonal to those that are provided as common ground, are not covered by the original end-to-end arguments and will thus have to be considered using a different principle, namely the trust-to-trust argument. To quote from Clark and Blumenthal again:

> "The function in question can completely and correctly be implemented only with the knowledge and help of the application standing at a point where it can be trusted to do its job in a reliable and trustworthy fashion." Trust, in this context, is determined by the ultimate end points — the principals that use the application to fulfill their purposes. Because the locus of trust is naturally at the ends, where the various principals are found, "trust-to-trust" is preferable to "end-to-end" from the point of view of the principals, because it more directly invites the important question of "trusted by whom?" (p. 10)

That is, above the common ground of the Internet (whose functions are firmly spoken to by the end-to-end principle) it is not that everything is fair game, or (worse still) has to be structured by way of a horizontal analogy to the originally vertical end-to-end arguments,[111] but that a different class of arguments is needed to speak to the structure of applications and control at the application layer. The trust-to-trust argument firmly falls into the category of horizontal arguments, and has thus paved the way for a further elaboration of such principles.

One such elaboration has been proposed by the author of this thesis in a 2009 paper. Following the broad notion of horizontal arguments, we may arrive at a conceptual argument that is broader than trust and hence more general — without losing any of its relevance and generality. Instead of considering trust to be the ultimate criterion for the degree of delegation of functions away from the ends and into the network we may have the ends deciding on the basis of a more general cost-benefit analysis. While this notion has been alluded to in Clark and Blumenthal (2007)[112] and also in Blumenthal and Clark (2001),[113] our broader argument holds that trust is but one of the parameters in a multivariate cost-benefit analysis, determining the optimum place for any given function.[114] Other such parameters may be the value of a given function, the costs and risks of implementing them oneself versus outsourcing them, the positive externalities gained by performing them at a central place, etc.:

> [A]s long as the intermediaries perform their functions to the standard of the ultimate ends, with the expected net benefit from doing so exceeding that of internalising the functions by those ends, [. . .] [the application structure serves the end users and thus conforms to a horizontal end-to-end argument]. The functions that are logically between the two ends can be regarded as having been delegated by those ends. Thus we can reduce the relevant trade-offs [of where to place functions in a network] to a simple utility function of the ends that use the application. (Bärwolff 2009c, p. 3)

Hence some functions may better rest with the end hosts, others with nodes in the network; some may better be under full control of the ultimate principal (the user, or, in fact, his employer or some other principal for that matter), others under the control of third parties, and still others be controlled by multiple parties at once — all largely without prejudice to the flexibility of the Internet and the freedom of its users at large.[115]

Another important point bears noting here. In the vertical end-to-end arguments, if an end goes down, it takes the application state down with it — which is the very rationale for the fate sharing argument (see our section 3.2). However, if the end 'dies' involuntarily (e. g., due to a DDoS attack or a failure in the end host), then the shared application state is also lost involuntarily. The problem cannot be solved satisfactorily at the level of the classic vertical end-to-end arguments, for they have no notion of end point redundancy; the end here is exogenously given and beyond reproach. The horizontal end-to-end arguments, on the other hand, allow for such application state to be distributed beyond the end points that take the ultimate interest in that state—if many 'ends' cooperate in maintaining the application level state, then this state may only be lost if all the redundancy thus obtained gets lost.[116]

Before closing this section, we note an important caveat about the horizontal end-to-end argument: unlike the vertical variant, it evades simple and tractable implications. Where the latter has a well articulated focal point[117] there is no such plain focal point that makes tangible the core content of the horizontal arguments. Arguing that functions are at *some* place along a continuum is much vaguer a statement than arguing that functions are best put in a very *specific* place. On the other hand, there has been some elusiveness in the focal points of the vertical end-to-end arguments, too. For, arguably, none of the functions to be balanced along vertical lines can escape the fact that any subnetwork of non-trivial size necessarily has to assume *some* functions, many of which are likely to be intertwined with functions to be performed at host level. In all, we may summarize the vertical and horizontal end-to-end arguments in a way that usefully expands on the original end-to-end arguments (see page 32), and which explicitly addresses the horizontal dimension to the problem in its own right vis à vis the original vertical version:

Argument 2 *Whereas the original vertical end-to-end argument implies a firm default for having functions at the host rather than the network layer because of the (potential) negative externalities otherwise incurred, the horizontal balance of functions may be determined chiefly by weighing the costs and benefits of the various possible arrangements from the point of view of the ultimate end users. One such result could be that entities outside the end hosts and inside the network are not trusted to maintain the state of an application in case of transient network failures. Thus a replication of state inside the network serves no useful purpose while making the overall application more complex and thus costly. However, users may as well shift substantial portions of application level functions to inside the network, and thus become substantially better off compared to having to implement functions at the end points only. This is particularly true for cases* *in which the end hosts are less capable or trustworthy than third party services inside the network. The crucial difference between the classic vertical arguments, and the horizontal arguments considered here is that other end users and (potential) applications are only marginally affected by having functions sit inside the network—horizontally at the application layer.*

3.4 A Common Minimum Ground

We are in this section taking up two main threads from earlier sections, one that we left in section 3.1—"functions beyond an irreducible and reasonable level of service in the subnetwork may impose unacceptable or even prohibitive costs on applications not requiring those functions" (page 34)—, and one that we touched on in section 2.3, and which states that it is more efficient to "leave room for expansion not only upwards as usual, but also sideways" rather than "piling layer upon layer of functions, with the associated overhead and duplication" (Pouzin 1973*b*, p. 83).

Many of the questions about how the balance of functions should best be distributed between hosts and network parts in between have already been addressed in the sections just mentioned. We will here trace some additional relevant history of the basic notion that the network should only provide the most minimal common ground of functions to the hosts attached, for reasons of simplicity, scalability, and flexibility. This section is thus something of a flip side to the preceding sections (sections 3.2 and 3.3); and while it is useful to devote some space to this purpose for reasons of structural coherence alone, we also raise some points that go well beyond the dichotomy implied in the original Saltzer et al. paper and discussed in section 3.1.

Our task here is not a trivial one, however; for the question that we have dealt with in the preceding sections—as to which degree functions should rest with the end hosts to a network—is vastly easier to tackle than the one we are concerned with here—the question of which functions should *not* be part of the underlying network. Both questions are loosely related; but the former is much more tractable, and also lends itself much better to the articulation of general design principles. The latter is much more about arguably vague concepts of performance, flexibility, and—to draw from more recent debates—generativity (Zittrain

2008) and innovation (Schewick 2007).[118] Also, the central trade-off to the end-to-end arguments—about the value of adding what may essentially be considered redundancy to the network, and the importance of leaving as many as possibly functions out of the network—is much more pronounced here. Taken to the extreme, every function beyond the physical transmission of signals on a medium may be dispensed with in favor of the hosts assuming them instead.[119] Accordingly, hosts may blame the network whenever they deem a function at the network level to be redundant or harmful; the network, on the other hand, has no such standing vis à vis the hosts, its raison d'être is solely to match what hosts need at minimum, not blame them for duplication. At the same time, while it *should* not go much above the minimum host requirements, it also *must* not fall below such line either.

The issue of design principles about this elusive minimum has been dealt with—if somewhat tacitly—very early on in the debate about networking, chiefly inter-networking which is inherently less tractable than a local setting under accountable control. Already, the core lesson from early networking experiments, particularly from the Arpanet, was that a network simply cannot guarantee flawless service within tight performance specifications.[120] The notion of "connected nets subject to stochastic flow" (Kleinrock 1964, p. 8) made this problem no easier; and no later than upon moving to a setting involving multiple interconnected networks did it become clear that a sensible global service definition of the network would have to encompass any service potentially down to *zero*. There simply is no positive specification of the minimum performance that a host can be guaranteed to obtain from the network at large—it effectively boils down to no service at all, and has remained just that to this day.[121] When reasoning about reliability over the whole range of likely scenarios, then the worst case is what defines which means will be needed to obtain perfect reliability. Thus any application requiring guarantees pertaining to reliability will have to implement *all* the necessary functions by itself—which is precisely what the high level reasoning behind TCP (as a function of the end hosts) in the 1970s was.[122]

The beauty of this solution is that neither the network nor its applications can ever fail, conceptually. The problem with this notion, on the other hand, is that it does not say anything positive about just *what* the network will have to do at all — why expend any material effort when the requirements state that none will do just fine, and anything done in excess may just be redundant, anyway? The answer to those questions is twofold. First, while a 'no effort' network may be rendered reliable by higher level mechanisms, its performance may be so bad as to be completely useless. Some effort beyond zero will be necessary in order for the network to be of any use whatsoever to host applications (most of which will also expect some interactivity).[123] It is thus that instead of basing the higher level design of a global network on the somewhat tautological worst case scenario of zero absolute service (the categorical case), it is useful to refer to statistical assurances (the empirical case), too. If, on average, the network drops no more than 1 percent of the packets, then an application willing to accept this level of unreliability need not implement any higher level reliability enhancements, or just implement them with that very assumption of 1 percent failure, no more. In fact, it is entirely reasonable to assume a given failure rate (say 1 percent) and then add lower level reliability enhancement only to those links which do not meet this nominal target (and which are too costly to bypass with alternative links) — so as to maximize the performance of the overall system.[124]

The second reason why a 'no effort' network is infeasible is that the overall performance and robustness trade-off speaks very much for placing a good amount of effort if not intelligence at lower levels. Much like the fate-sharing argument (see section 3.2) is but an extreme take in the continuum of possible results obtained by trading off function placements along horizontal lines of reasoning (see section 3.3), so is the minimality argument in its 'emptiness version': both performance and robustness trade-offs speak for a departure from the extreme position of having no more than an absolute minimum of functions in the network. Clark (1988) pointed to this trade-off regarding robustness:

> [T]he goal of robustness, which led to the method of fate-sharing, which led to host-resident algorithms, contributes to a loss of robustness if the host misbehaves. (p. 110)

There is probably no perfect way to resolve this conceptual paradox, but the central implication here is that a sensible second-best alternative of how to balance functions between the network and the hosts attached very likely beats an extreme version of the arguments of both fate-sharing and network minimality.

The above reasoning helps understand why, despite an inherent service definition of zero, the network will have to go above this for important conceptual reasons. But, we are not quite finished yet, for it does not say anything about the value there is from leaving functions out of the network in the first place. A discussion of the various lines of thought here may again be structured along vertical and horizontal lines of reasoning (see section 3.3), the former pertaining to the issue of raising the value on top of a common layer, and the latter primarily pertaining to the issue of extending the horizontal reach of the interconnected system of networks. Whereas our previous discussions, chiefly in sections 3.2 and 3.3, dealt with the stylized question of how an optimum network would have to look like from the perspective of an *existing* application, we are here dealing with the question of how a network should look like in order to cater for *new* applications and users in the first place.

A high level common sense case along *vertical lines* has been made about keeping the 'core of the network' generally as minimal as possible, arguing that minimality in the actual functions implemented at the common internetwork layer will promote flexibility and growth—both of the network itself, and the uses it can be put to. The point had been alluded to in the original paper by Saltzer et al., as we have discussed in section 3.1 (specifically page 31); and Reed et al. (1998) reiterate it explicitly in discussing the merit of programmable network resources at the inter-network layer:

> Part of the context of an end-to-end argument is the idea that a lower layer of a system should support the widest possible variety of services and functions, to permit *applications that cannot be anticipated.* That is, minimize the lower-layer function, get out of the way, and let the higher layer do its thing. (p. 70, emphasis added)

Specifically, they argue that complexity is to be avoided unless weighty performance or other concerns speak for the opposite.[125] Driven to the extreme, and viewed in very general terms, the argument against functions in the lower common levels of the network would result in what

Isenberg (1997) calls "stupid network", a network that does nothing else but deliver digital data from one end to another.[126] While such notions do make sense as general guidelines of intuition, they lack the stringency and concreteness that result when viewing the problem from the perspective of existing application needs (such as reliable file transfer or real-time interactive voice). A minimality principle like this one will always have a speculative touch which requires a certain amount of ex ante belief rather than strict logical derivation from empirical fact.

Less elusive is the thread of reasoning along *horizontal lines* that developed in the 1970s in the transition from Arpanet to Internet, and which dealt with the question of just how minimal a global network of interconnected networks would have to be, mostly as a positive engineering concern derived from the rationale of interconnecting different networks. In section 2.3 we have already begun considering the ease of inter-networking as one of the principal reasonings for keeping as many functions of networking as possible out of the common network parts. The notion that any inter-network would *by necessity* have to be as simple as possible was quickly accepted by the researchers concerned with the goal of interconnecting different networks beyond the then most prominent Arpanet. Cerf (1972*a*) reports on the first discussions within INWG:

> [I]nterworking between packet switching networks should not add complications to the hosts, considering that networks will probably be different and thus gateways between networks will be required. These gateways should be as uncomplicated as possible, whilst allowing as much freedom as possible for the design of individual networks. (p. 1)

Thus very early on there was a firm notion that the mechanisms concerned with network interconnection would have to be most simple and minimal so as to allow as many as possible networks to participate in the resulting federation of networks.[127]

Also, there was some recognition that the function of interconnecting networks would best be left entirely unrelated to those of host level concerns, in order to leave the function of inter-networking free from any host level idiosyncrasies that would make harder the task of connecting different networks with as wide a variance of performance characteristics as possible.[128] Any host level issues would have to be dealt with by host level protocols—not because of completeness and correctness concerns, but because it would limit the set of tasks to be dealt with by the inter-networking protocol, and thus help further its objective to connect as many as possible individual networks.[129] Recall from section 2.3 the conceptual line between an inter-network protocol and a host level transport protocol logically separating the part of networking that was to be performed by the network at large, on the one hand; and that to be performed by the host (and the hosts *only*), on the other. Any degree of elaboration could be added to the host level procedures without affecting the common inter-network protocol which was solely to be concerned with a most simple and irreducibly low level datagram service. This in turn allowed gateways to implement the protocol in between and atop of almost arbitrary individual networks—the common protocol was logically outside both the hosts and the underlying networks thus connected, allowing virtually arbitrary concatenation of different network by means of gateways on the one hand,[130] and uninhibited development of host level protocols and applications on the other.[131] The notion advanced by Pouzin (1973*b*) (as discussed in our pages 19 f.) took prominent shape, eventually.

In summary to this section we note that arriving at sound principles about the concrete shape of minimality of the network below and in between hosts as called for by the broader notion of end-to-end arguments is no trivial matter indeed. There is an intuitive case for keeping a network minimal so as to allow unanticipated applications to emerge, but one may object that as long as the sophistication of a network does not prejudice the availability of an interface to a simpler network service there is no reason per se not to offer more elaborate network services (see our discussion in section 2.5). A strong case, however, can be made for minimality of an inter-network protocol in an interconnection of arbitrarily different networks, for it is there that only an intersection of properties of the constituent networks allows their interconnection in the first place. The case for interconnection of different networks and minimality, in turn, makes for a strong case for minimality along vertical lines too, for keeping an elaborate lower level service consistent across a multitude of networks not only limits the potential scope of that service but would also introduce undesirable complexity to the gateways connecting the different networks.

Conclusion of Part I

It is probably hard to find another principle in networking that is at once so evidently simple and true, yet so rich in interpretative scope. The end-to-end arguments have long left the realm of the authority of the original authors, and have become a subject of sometimes heated debate, extending to all sorts of different stakeholders, each adding another facet to their meaning.[132] We have in this part of the thesis offered an exhaustive review on the history of the end-to-end arguments, going back in time to before the original Saltzer et al. paper, and considering various themes through to today.[133] We have thus uncovered the huge breadth of arguments surrounding the original articulation; in fact, to our knowledge we are the first to have ventured such an in-depth systematic review.[134]

In sum, we have arrived at the following major insights about the end-to-end arguments:

Rich pre end-to-end arguments history to the notion The general notion behind end-to-end arguments has been building up from the early 1960s through to the mid-1970s. As we have summarized in section 2.4, by the time the original end-to-end arguments were articulated by Saltzer et al. (1984) the general case for as well as the subtleties of placing functions with the end hosts rather than lower level elements inside the network had been well understood.

Application level view versus lower level view There are two principal perspectives to the end-to-end arguments as framed by Saltzer et al. (1984) (section 3.1) and the developments to the notion thereafter. From the perspective of an application there is often a case for assuming functions (or controlling the delegation to trusted agents), because the network in between the application instances typically lacks the precise knowledge of the application needs, and often cannot even implement them "completely and correctly" in the first place. On the other hand, and notwithstanding the needs of individual applications and the performance trade-offs in their respect, there is a strong case for offering an irreducibly low level of service at a shared common inter-network layer in order to allow flexible "expansion not only upwards [. . .] but also sideways" (Pouzin 1973*b*, p. 83).

Vertical versus horizontal end-to-end arguments There is merit in distinguishing between end-to-end arguments along vertical lines, and end-to-end arguments along horizontal ones (section 3.3). The former is concerned with the balance of functions between the vertically stacked layers in a network, but does not speak to the horizontal structure of the application layer across the network. Horizontal end-to-end arguments are concerned with just that structure, and have implications that are vastly different from the conventional vertical arguments. Largely, this is because there is no case for negative externalities here as there is with the vertical arguments. It is thus important to separate the two notions, and not carry over the reasoning from the former to the latter, for such "construction by analogy may be nonsense" (Clark and Blumenthal 2007, p. 15).

While those results are interesting in and of themselves, already; we think that they can serve as valuable inputs for any discussion about the merit of the end-to-end arguments, their logical structure, and possible reformulations. As for the remainder of this thesis, we have thus set the scene for further theorizing, but also to an informed consideration of how the end-to-end arguments played out in actual fact. We leave the theorizing to Part III of this thesis and will in the following part turn to the question of how the development of the Internet historically accords to or conflicts with the notions here elaborated.

Part II

End-to-End Arguments in Motion: From Arpanet to Internet

It is the factual observance of the rules which is the condition for the formation of an order of actions; whether they need to be enforced or how they are enforced is of secondary interest. Factual observance of some rules no doubt preceded any deliberate enforcement. The reasons why the rules arose must therefore not be confused with the reasons which made it necessary to enforce them. Those who decided to do so may never have fully comprehended what function the rules served.

— *Friedrich August von Hayek (1973, p. 96)*

Chapter 4

Basic Structures

It is a capital mistake to theorize before you have all the evidence. It biases the judgment.

— *Sherlock Holmes*

It is one thing to develop a principle by continuous cycles of articulation, promulgation, and debate; it is quite another thing to describe the very patterns that such principle intends to capture and inform. For no matter how intriguing or seemingly 'right' a normative facet of an argument; if there is no equivalent practice to support it, then there is very little ground indeed for the principle to legitimately reflect back to the realm of real-world practices. Recall that the end-to-end arguments were not written as a mere logical exercise, but precisely as such a distillate from actual practices at the time. In fact, for any practical purposes, it is far more instructive to consider how the problem at the heart of the end-to-end arguments — the question of how to arrange the functions of networking so that they best serve and live up to the requirements of the applications standing at its end points — played out in the realm of pragmatic reality rather than elegant theory.

By studying the history of the Internet we aim in this part of the thesis to (1) recount how the end-to-end arguments developed as factual rules, long before the original articulation by Saltzer et al. (1981*a*), and (2) elaborate some of the aspects that go beyond the perfunctory examples typically associated with the end-to-end arguments. To this end we develop in a descriptive approach along analytic lines the meta case study of the Internet ranging from the early Arpanet to its eventual structure as of today.[135] Of course, we cannot hope to map each and every event in the history of the Internet to the causalities underlying their sequence, and how those bear on the end-to-end arguments — but it is by such analytical narration that we hope best to inform the discourse about their proper shape and merit, thus helping to further develop them beyond vague intuitions and into a notion that offers sound guidance to actual engineering practices.

In this chapter we recount how the basic structures of large-scale distributed networking emerged in the Arpanet,[136] while we leave in-depth consideration of the emergence of the Internet and some of its core conceptual problems to the following chapter. More specifically, the logical sections presented in this chapter plus the following one cover the various analytical aspects connotated by the end-to-end arguments as detailed in Part I, and are arranged roughly along a sequential timeline — from (1) the late 1960s and 1970s, reflecting on the Arpanet, to (2) the 1980s, reflecting on the emerging Internet, to (3) more recent accounts, reflecting on the various conceptual problems of the Internet. While this part may be seen as complementary to the previous one, note that the dichotomy between the two is not perfectly clear cut: in the preceding part we pointed to real world events, and in this part we will point to theoretical notions, in turn.

4.1 The Arpanet Line Between Subnetwork and Hosts

The Arpanet ventured an experiment that had never been tried before, earlier theoretical advances and small-scale experiments notwithstanding.[137] Connecting computers as peers, supporting general purpose uses not specified in advance, was a notion totally remote at the time — computers had been built according to a master-slave paradigm, not a peer-to-peer communication one.[138] The overall challenge of building a network of computers was thus twofold, neither one aspect being trivial. First, for a multitude of computers to be connected, a network was to be built which would allow multiplexing of traffic from various computers on links and intermediary nodes thus shared between the end hosts.[139] The theory of multiplexing and routing, however, was only emerging, and practical experience was virtually non-existent.

Second, the computers to be connected would have to be made to appreciate the existence of peer computers with whom to communicate, and protocols would have to be devised to allow the network to be used for applications beyond the emulation of terminals or other peripheral devices — and beyond use for predetermined tasks such as those found in existing airline reservation and banking networks.[140] And, of course, new applications beyond existing paradigms would have to be invented in the first place.[141] With hindsight, the former problem may be considered as the lower level problem, and the latter as the higher level one. At the time, however, this distinction was only beginning to become clear.

Adding to those hurdles, there was a strong initial skepticism by many host sites at the time about the usefulness of connecting to a network which would allow others to remotely access resources previously at the sole discretion of those in physical possession of the computers in question.[142] Moreover, the host computers at large were seen with great suspicion from the perspective of the lower level network, as we have noted in section 2.2.[143] This lack of common purpose was largely remedied by the power of ARPA to specify the characteristics of the network to be built, plus its discretion over the funding of computer procurement of prospective host sites.[144] However, this integration by 'command and control' did not render unnecessary the drawing of an engineering line between the various concerns of different stakeholders.

It was thus that ARPA decided to separate the issue of (1) building a general purpose data network from that of (2) devising useful applications to such a network. The line between those two was drawn by specifying the design of the network such that a 'subnetwork' would essentially offer a reliable VC service to the actual host computers who could then communicate transparently with other host computers by simply handing the subnetwork the data to be communicated and without having to worry about any of the intricacies of getting the data to their peer hosts in the first place.[145] Thus the host sites could concentrate on addressing host level issues, and ARPA would have a sensible definition of what service the subnetwork was to offer to the host sites and to which it could hold its contractors accountable.[146] Keeping the host computers out of the definition of the network made the initial steps toward a general purpose network far more tractable.[147]

Thus, from a high level architectural perspective, the Arpanet became a virtual circuit network: the host computers would invoke a reliable virtual circuit service subject only to a protocol (or rather, an interface) that specified the communication between a host computers and its appropriate counterpart computer *inside* the IMP subnetwork.[148] In particular, there was no need for hosts to perform end-to-end error checks, acknowledge received data, or for source hosts to buffer sent data once it was sent to the IMP (Figure 4.1).[149] In section 2.2 we have considered the theoreti-

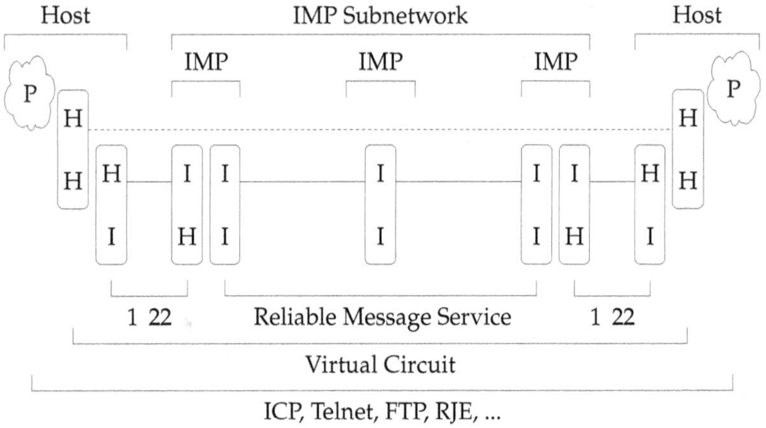

Figure 4.1: Arpanet layered architecture with IMP subnetwork as a black box

cal futility of such an approach, and established that this assessment was very much common ground amongst host sites before the first IMP was even delivered.[150] It was pursued nevertheless: BBN, who were building the subnetwork as a chief contractor to ARPA, persuaded the host sites not to include end-to-end error control mechanisms in the common host-host protocol, arguing that doing so would for one be redundant, and also reduce the overall performance of the Arpanet. Thus end-to-end error control did not become part of the host-host protocol, but remained the province of the IMP subnetwork.[151]

And yet, the Arpanet worked.[152] Well enough, in fact, that ARPA kept continuing the initial contract with BBN such that the network grew at a steady rate of roughly one new IMP per month for the first couple of years,[153] making the Arpanet the world's largest wide-area packet switching network at the time, featuring a huge variety of experimentation at both the network and the host level, and eventually spawning the Internet as we know it.[154] Not only did the Arpanet subnetwork see a host of qualitative improvements over its lifetime which remedied its initial problems to considerable extent;[155] most notably with respect to the end-to-end arguments, even when the fallibility of the subnetwork was plainly acknowledged by BBN and ARPA (McQuillan 1973),[156] did the host-host protocol in its basic design remain unchanged from its 1972 version which assumed a perfectly reliable IMP subnetwork. While there was a lively discussion in the NWG community on how to add proper reliability by error control and correction to the host-host protocol,[157] none of those suggestions were to be implemented in the official network-wide host-host protocol—arguably because the Arpanet with the host-host protocol as it was worked relatively fine for the purposes then at hand.[158]

Regarding the end-to-end arguments, this episode reminds us that any principle, no matter how self-evidently true, should always be seen as one variable in a complex setting of other principles and plain practical constraints that will often entail conflicting implications. That does not invalidate a principle as such, but it emphasizes the need for considering the broader picture rather than relying on categorical implications. Plus, it reiterates the point that even principles bordering truisms are often better regarded as *arguments* whose implications depend on the actual circumstances of a given situation, not just their theoretical abstract validity. Complete host level end-to-end error control based on the principles expounded in Part I was simply not the most pressing issue at a time when the Arpanet was an experimental network, a chief objective of which it was to gather insights into the feasibility of packet switching, computer communications, and the applications of such a system. As for the second explicit objective, that of resource sharing, the problems of getting host computers to work in a paradigm of peer-to-peer rather than master-slave communication, building interoperable application software on different host computers, and arriving at the various standards of host level communication that we take very much for granted today, all proved vastly more formidable challenges than restarting an application in the face of occasional message losses inside the subnetwork.[159] Plus, the pervasiveness of errors and plain uncertainties at the very level of the hosts themselves did not speak too much for end-to-end checks.[160] In particular, adding complexity to an already complex distributed system of host level processes was considered much less sensible than building a reliable subnetwork that could be maintained, monitored, and debugged by one central agency, rather than in a distributed fashion involving various host sites.[161]

The story does not end here, of course. For the overall trade-off did change once the Arpanet grew in size and use beyond the initial handful of host sites exchanging largely experimental traffic in pursuit of getting the host level protocols and applications right in the first place. It took until early 1972 to arrive at a host sites wide agreement on the specification of the basic host-host protocol;[162] however, once the basic host level protocols were in place, the assumption of a reliable subnetwork became ever more of a burden given that in a growing Arpanet this assumption could not be maintained to hold true. Heart et al. (1978) submit:

> [R]esolving various possible lockups has required the subnetwork to discard a message occasionally, and the topology of the network has evolved into long series of machines and lines that increase the probability of involuntary message loss. (p. III-52)

In a sense, it was the very success of the Arpanet that spelled the need for considerable relaxation of the initially adamant reliability requirements from the network.[163] By the time BBN submitted the Arpanet Completion Report in 1978,[164] it had become common ground among the relevant stakeholders that hosts would have to play a far more active role in the basic operations of distributed computer networking—because both the overall objectives and the context had changed considerably.

Before we turn to the development of the later Internet protocols and architecture, however, we will in the following sections keep elaborating how the communications functions came to be placed inside the Arpanet's IMP subnetwork, how they took shape at its edges, and the question of which services to place at a common level to be shared by all participants in the first place. Returning to the issue of end-to-end arguments, suffice it for now to conclude by noting that the approach of drawing a firm line between the subnetwork and the hosts that would leave the subnetwork with virtually all of the networking work and the hosts with only host level application issues was no less valid than the coming TCP approach (see section 5.2). Each had its time, and neither is inherently more 'correct' than the other.

4.2 The Inner Architecture of the Arpanet

To the hosts in the Arpanet, the IMP subnetwork was a black box delivering a virtual circuit service. There was, however, more to the internals of the subnetwork than meets the casual eye. Not only was the Arpanet a packet switching network, in a number of important respects it anticipated the later Internet with its premise of best effort packet rather than perfectly reliable virtual circuit service.[165] Most notably, one can clearly distinguish between two very different levels inside the Arpanet: the IMP-to-IMP level (hop-by-hop) on the one hand, and the source-IMP-to-destination-IMP level ('end-to-end') on the other (Figure 4.2).[166]

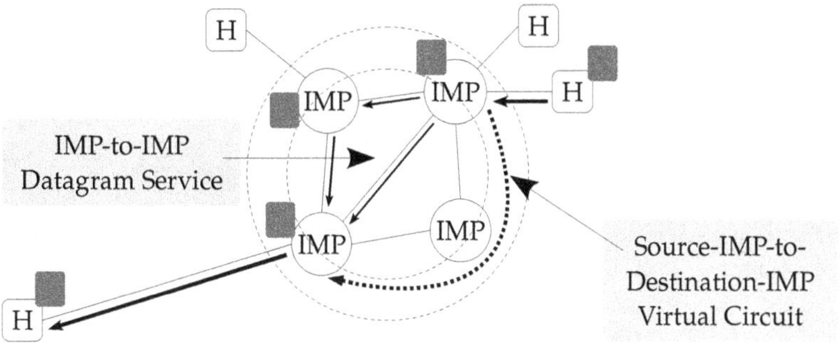

Figure 4.2: Basic Arpanet IMP level architecture

The procedures governing the two levels are different in that it is the latter that provides the virtual message switching circuit on behalf of the hosts, while the former provides a low level packet transport service only. The lower level thus resembles very much the IP service of today's Internet, whereas the source-IMP-to-destination-IMP procedures perform very much the functions that TCP would later come to assume: reordering, duplicate detection, and defragmentation, as well as some aspects of error and flow control. All of these functions were managed by protocols between the source IMP and the destination IMP, rather than hop-by-hop or in a true switched circuit manner.[167] The one mechanism that was implemented hop-by-hop in addition to packet forwarding based on a distributed adaptive routing scheme was error control and retransmission—every packet received had to be acknowledged IMP-to-IMP, and would be retransmitted absent such acknowledgment (Figure 4.3).[168]

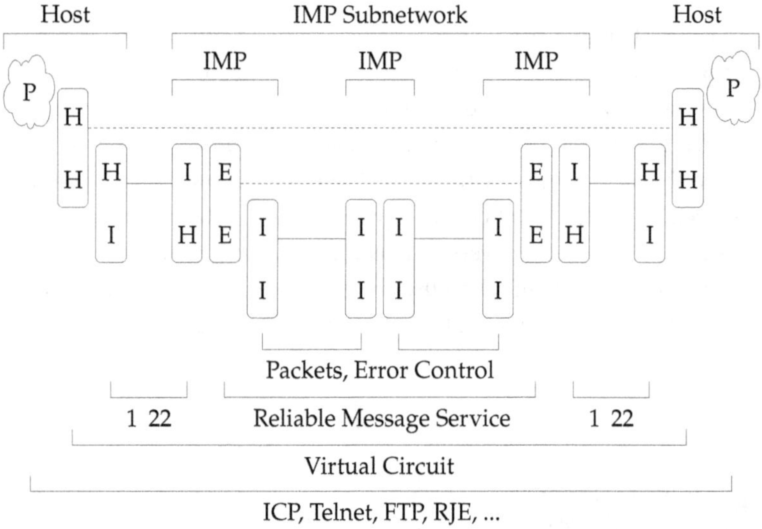

Figure 4.3: Arpanet layered architecture with IMP subnetwork level elaboration

Thus, while the hosts delegated the bulk of networking tasks to 'their' IMPs,[169] and the subnetwork provided a virtual circuit service to the hosts, the inside of the Arpanet IMP subnetwork clearly demonstrated the principal balance of functions in a packet switched network—the conceptual distinction between the elementary IMP-to-IMP operations and the end-to-end operations implemented by the source and destination IMPs. Inevitably, there would be lost packets and duplicates,[170] and packets would potentially arrive out of order.[171] To remedy those artifacts, the Arpanet designers chose the balance of functions just detailed.

In all, the design of the overall subnetwork from source-IMP-to-destination-IMP was very much complete, and able to deal with most of the errors that could occur at the IMP level. As long as the IMPs tasked with the transfer of messages on behalf of two hosts actually passed on the packets that they acknowledged 'upstream',[172] and the interface between the source and destination IMPs and their respective hosts was fine, the data transmission would be very much reliable—almost as in "completely and correctly".[173]

However, this arguably elegant state of affairs was not to remain satisfactorily for a long time. We will in the following sections discuss how the premise of hosts being intimately linked to an agent providing perfectly reliable data transmission service became futile once the the interfaces between IMPs and hosts grew significantly more challenging, and applications came to require markedly different services of the network. The approach set out in the 1968 Arpanet RFQ may have been a feasible start to get the Arpanet, and computer networking in general, off the ground; however, in view of the many host level considerations that were to arise, it was by no means to remain the most efficient point of equilibrium to arrive at.

As for the end-to-end arguments, the important conclusion to this section is that delegating material networking tasks away from the ultimate ends of a communication network does not render the end-to-end arguments futile or less valid. The relevant end points often coincide with conceptual boundaries between higher level transport services and lower level packet switching; and while such boundaries may be hidden inside a 'subnetwork black box', they are still a crucial piece of the overall architecture. We have seen in section 2.3 that the packet switching paradigm inherently results in an architecture where certain higher level functions are *necessarily* implemented at or at least very close to the ultimate end hosts. Even when end hosts delegate those functions to intermediaries inside the network, the core principle of packet switching—breaking large user level messages into smaller packets to be transmitted independently and self-sufficiently across the network—dictates that the relevant conversion functions have to be implemented at logical end points of the packet switching network.[174] In a very basic sense, the end-to-end arguments are a logical implication of packet switching. Or, as Clark (2007*a*) puts it succinctly:

> The discovery of packets is not a consequence of the end-to-end argument. It is the success of packets that make the end-to-end argument relevant. (slide 31)

4.3 The Fringe Architecture of the Arpanet

Once the core architecture of the Arpanet — the IMP subnetwork — was in place, it turned out that the strict conceptual line between IMPs and hosts, bridged by a simple serial bit interface, was an insufficient premise to maintain if the network was to be put to reasonably efficient uses. The notion that the Arpanet would consist solely of host computers with an IMP very close by (which, at that, was exclusively dedicated to this one very host) might have been a useful starting point for specifying the system that potential contractors would bid on, but it was a substantial limitation if a larger number of host computers were to be connected to the Arpanet. After all, the Arpanet project was chiefly about the sharing of host resources; and the larger and more diverse the number of host computers, the more resources there would be to share in the first place. Also, dedicating an IMP to every computer participating in the network would not only have been prohibitively costly, but also mostly redundant given the possibility of multiplexing traffic from multiple hosts or simple terminals on a single IMP with little performance cost to each of the sources thus connected.[175] Real-time traffic such as remote login sessions would generate mostly stochastic low volume traffic patterns (a prime candidate for multiplexing), and file transfer applications requiring greater traffic volume would not need a highly responsive service, anyway. Thus a substantial elaboration of the whole notion of interfacing IMPs with actual end hosts and even simple terminal boxes found at the time followed, very much diffusing the once firm line separating IMPs and hosts, and bringing into focus the nature of vertical layering so commonly referred to in networking today.

There were three main logical steps in elaborating the fringe architecture of the Arpanet: (1) allowing more than one host to be attached to an IMP, (2) allowing hosts to be farther than a mere couple of feet away from an IMP, and (3) having IMPs serve less potent terminal boxes directly through dial-up connections rather than through a dedicated host computer connected to the IMP. The fringe architecture of the Arpanet was thus to become vastly more complex, not only by (1) serving a growing number of hosts by way of multiplexing, but also by (2) implementing communication protocols for serving hosts at greater distance from IMPs, and (3) serving terminals at the 'application layer'. We shall in this section discuss all three notions in turn.

Serving more than one host per IMP was a requirement added very early in the process of designing the IMPs and specifying their operations.[176] BBN thus made use of the IMPs' hardware (and specified the relevant data formats) so as to allow four distinct hosts per IMP.[177] The software routines were designed such that each host would be served in a "fair round robin (random) order" (BBN 1974*b*, pp. 11 f.), thus equally sharing the available IMP resources between the attached hosts. There were some issues — mostly theoretical — with slow hosts at a destination IMP holding up faster hosts by "tying up buffer space [at the IMP] for abnormally long periods of time thus depriving the other hosts of the IMP of the use of this space" (p. 12). But, by and large, serving more than one host per IMP remained a relatively trivial enhancement to the initial Arpanet design, not substantially changing the philosophy of how to distribute the functions of networking between IMPs on the one hand and hosts on the other.

The more challenging requirement that emerged following the first IMP installations was to increase the distance between an IMP and its hosts beyond the initial 30 feet limit. The founding assumption for the host-IMP connection had been that they would be very close by, possibly separated by a wall (so as to help fend off "inquisitive graduate students"), but not much more than that. Thus connecting an IMP and a 'local' host computer initially required little more sophistication than a serial interface between them: data to be sent between the two was transfered bit-wise, using a simple "Ready-For-Next-Bit, There's-Your-Bit handshaking procedure" (BBN and Kahn 1976, p. 4-2).[178] However, the premise of hosts and IMPs standing literally beside each other had to be dropped almost instantly, right after the first few IMPs had been deployed. Heart et al. (1978) recall:

> No sooner were these [first four] IMPs in the field than it became clear that some provision was needed to connect hosts relatively distant from an IMP [. . .]. Thus in early 1970 a "distant" IMP/host interface was developed. Augmented simply by heftier line drivers, these distant interfaces made clear, for the first time, the fallacy in the assumption that had been

> made that no error control was needed on the host/IMP interface because there would be no errors on such a local connection. (p. III-55)

By adding some elaboration regarding delay and noise, thus, the maximum distance between a host and its IMP was increased to 2000 feet, while leaving the logical operation of the interface unchanged and upholding the initial premise of a serial, reliable, and error-free interface (BBN 1970*a*, p. 6; BBN and Kahn 1976, p. 4-8, pp. 4-22 ff.) (Figure 4.4).

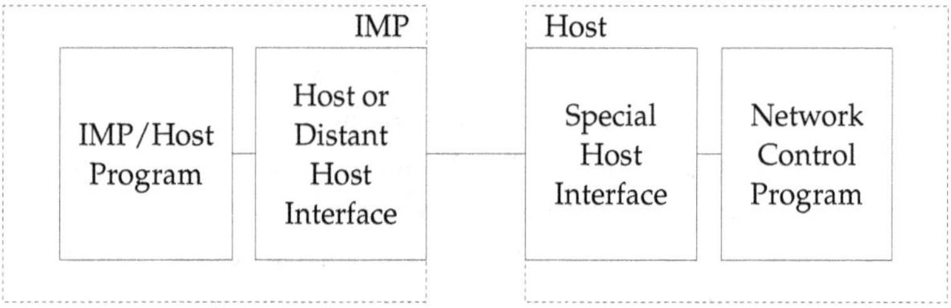

Figure 4.4: Classic IMP-Host interface for local and distant hosts (without error control); Source: BBN and Kahn (1976, p. F-2), BBN (1972*a*, p. 9)

However, by 1971 the 2000 feet limit came under increasing strain, and the conceptual premise of an inherently error free IMP-host interface became finally untenable—there was no good theoretical reason (other than that of keeping with the initial specification of the Arpanet) why hosts could not be at arbitrary distance to their IMP, and be connected using arbitrary links.[179] Far away hosts and error-prone lines to an IMP, however, required a full-blown transmission protocol rather than a simple serial bit-copy interface. By early 1972 the design of the Very Distant Host (VDH) interface was largely complete and included various functions from (1) error control, acknowledgment and retransmission; to (2) the detection of duplicates; to (3) control functions such as pinging the opposite side to see if it is still alive (BBN 1972*a*, pp. 9 ff.).[180]

Effectively, the VDH interface implemented what amounts to a reliable virtual circuit based on the exchange of packets which could be lost, scrambled, duplicated, or arrive out of order—a notion not much different from the core processes inside the IMP subnetwork of the Arpanet (see section 4.2).[181] In fact, the similarities with the IMP-to-IMP transmission protocols were so great that it is fair to consider the VDH interface a set of protocols that logically extended the Arpanet from the IMPs to the hosts. No more were the hosts mere trivial sources and sinks of data outside the actual network—data were exchanged in packets rather than bits,[182] and acknowledgments were piggybacked just like in normal IMP-to-IMP packet acknowledgments.[183]

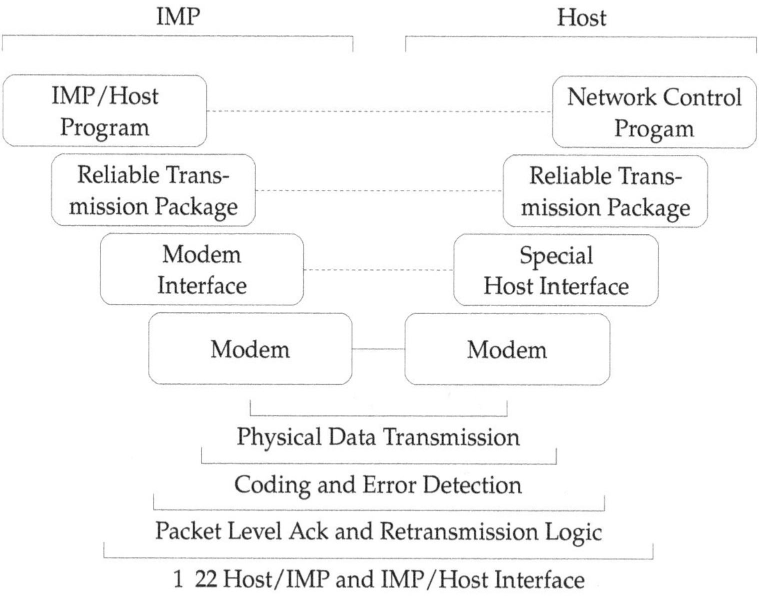

Figure 4.5: Layered IMP-Host connection for very distant hosts (VDHs) (with error control); Source: Adapted from BBN and Kahn (1976, p. F-4), BBN (1972*a*, p. 10)

The resulting structure was very much a layered one, featuring on either side (1) the high-level processes concerned with the data transfer, (2) a reliable transmission package (RTP) responsible for packing and unpacking the payload data, and issuing acknowledgments and retransmissions, and (3) a line interface tasked with error detection (Figure 4.5).[184] It is by no means far-fetched to speak of the IMP-host link as a 'local network'[185] in its own right—the RTP being the local network protocol to achieve a reliable communication service, and the Arpanet message facility being the 'inter-network' protocol connecting the IMP-host network to the Arpanet IMP subnetwork (another 'local' network) (Figure 4.6).[186]

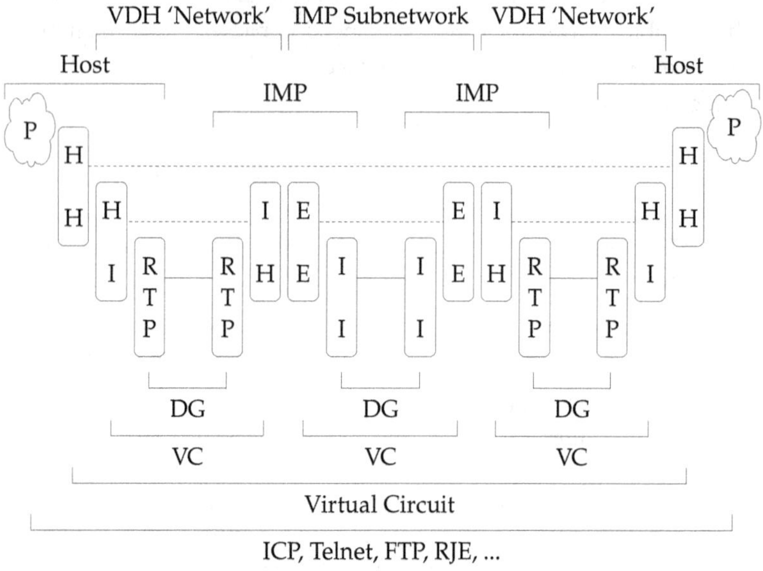

Figure 4.6: Arpanet layered architecture with IMP subnetwork level elaboration and extended VDH fringes

Having discussed the developments from the initial trivial IMP-host interface to one that (1) allowed a multitude of hosts to share one IMP (page 63), and (2) allowed those hosts to be located at virtually arbitrary distance, connecting to the IMP via telephone circuits and modems (pages 63 ff.), we shall now turn to the final consideration of this section: the development of Terminal IMPs, or TIPs, that would allow a range of different terminals to be connected to an IMP directly via a local line or dial-up without first having to connect to a proper host, first.[187] The introduction of the VDH interface may be regarded as having spread lower level protocols to 'outside' of the Arpanet's IMP subnetwork and into the hosts; the innovation of TIPs, on the other hand, moved host level functions to inside the IMP subnetwork—another development that appreciably changed the initial Arpanet architecture with its strict horizontal separation between IMPs and hosts, and bears directly on our question of how the end-to-end arguments developed prior to the advent of the early Internet.

The notion that IMPs were more than mere low-level packet switches had been around for some time before TIPs were introduced. An IMP was designed such that any process part of the IMP software requiring networking services itself — routing updates, gathering and reporting of statistics, local teletype handling, distribution and loading of the IMP core program, etc. — would be implemented as a 'fake host' or 'back host', essentially using the existing program structures dealing with normal hosts, too. Such processes used the same mechanisms talking to the lower level packet switching processes that any normal local host would have to use; in particular did they generally have to abide by the flow control provided by Ready for Next Messages (RFNMs), and make sense of all the other control messages that an IMP would issue to a host in the course of its operation.[188] However, those processes were typically low-profile;[189] and, more importantly, they were in no substantial ('hard state') way linked to the processes sitting in the ultimate application end points. Hosts appreciated when the IMP subnetwork ran smoothly, but the states in either of them were largely unrelated — when an IMP (other than the source or destination IMP) failed, hosts would typically remain unaffected (unless the failure resulted in sustained partitioning of the network); and when a host failed, only the hosts in peer relation to it would be affected, the IMPs were designed to depend in no way on the sanity of their hosts.

This all changed with the introduction of Terminal IMPs, or TIPs, work on which started in 1970, and the first of which were operational in 1971.[190] Heart et al. (1978) recount:

> At the outset all terminal access to the network was via terminal connections to the hosts themselves. After a time it became clear that there was a population of users for which terminal access to the network was very desirable, but who were not conveniently able to access the network via a host computer. Thus, a new nodal switching unit, a Terminal Interface Message Processor, or TIP, was defined to serve the purpose of an IMP plus an additional function of direct terminal access. This shift resulted in the design of a TIP which really was *a tiny host embedded in a switching node itself* and permitted the

> direct connection of up to 63 asynchronous character-oriented terminals to the switching node. The TIP became the nodal switching unit of choice, often even where there was a local host computer; this allowed connection of both hosts and terminals at that location directly to the network. (pp. II-21 f., emphasis added)

With TIPs it was thus no longer that hosts in effect delegated packet switching tasks to an IMP;[191] the concept of TIPs turned the IMPs into very hosts—of rather, host level intermediaries—themselves,[192] assuming a substantial subset of host level functions not ordinarily found in IMPs, plus an additional set of functions pertaining to the handling of a growing variety of terminals (Figure 4.7).[193] More specifically, TIPs would

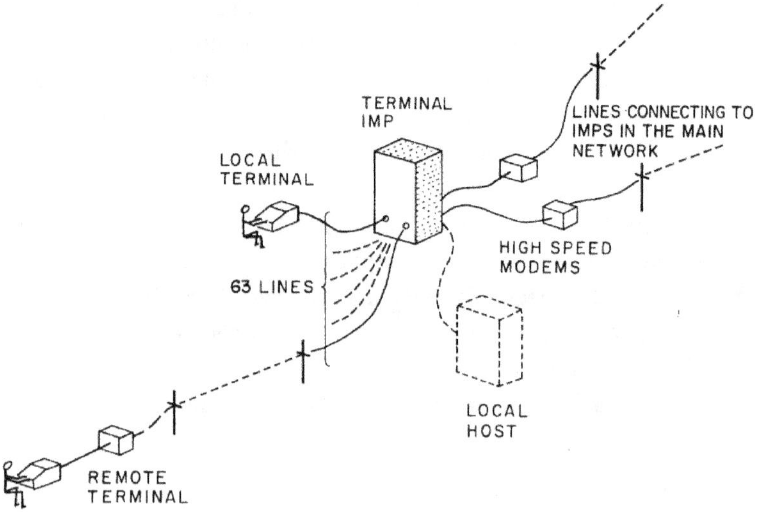

Figure 4.7: BBN's Arpanet Terminal IMP (TIP); Source: Rettberg (1972, p. 2), Ornstein et al. (1971, p. 246)

provide 63 physical access ports for connecting arbitrary terminals to it,[194] and allow these terminals to communicate via Telnet with arbitrary hosts on the Arpanet. To this end a TIP would have to perform three major functions: (1) communicating with the terminals attached so as to allow them to set TIP parameters, initiate connections to hosts, etc.; (2) communicating with other IMPs and hosts, using the whole hierarchy of protocols from the IMP level up to the host level, including the host-host protocol (NCP), ICP, and Telnet (neither of which originally much of a province of BBN); and (3) character conversion back and forth from the local terminal character format to a common Network Virtual Terminal (NVT) code.[195] Put differently, the lower level part of the TIP (the IMP portion) was in the subnetwork, and the higher level part (the terminal handling portion) in the host 'layer'—administratively they were in the network, but architecturally they extended up to the host level (Figure 4.8).

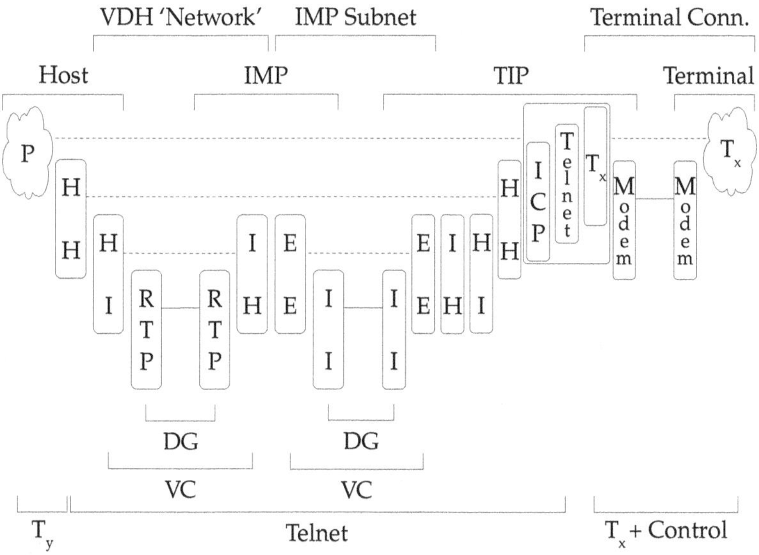

Figure 4.8: Arpanet layered architecture with TIPs and terminals

The introduction of TIPs thus brought into focus a firm notion of vertical layering that not only goes well beyond the initial abstractions carried over from the telephone paradigm of communication networks,[196] but also stretches firmly beyond a simple mapping from a horizontal conception of function separation. No longer were 'higher layers' confined to end devices at user premises (the fake and back hosts inside the IMPs notwithstanding); inside the network, too, could there be functionality directly related to the applications executed at the ultimate end points of communication—an early instance of horizontal end-to-end arguments as considered in section 3.3. It is fair to conclude that the TIPs—as high level focal points—have moved host level functions to those very position in the horizontal scope of the network where they generated the greatest benefit, meaning both technical sensibility and economic efficiency. Whilst at first only 'normal' hosts assumed 'host level' functions, the reality of terminal devices lacking the processing capabilities to act as proper hosts (that is, implement all the protocols necessary to communicate with remote hosts across the Arpanet) meant that it was most sensible to place at least a useful subset of host level functions right with the IMPs, so as to allow terminals to connect to remote hosts by linking directly to an IMP, and without having to go through a local hosts (or even requiring one in the first place).

Not only did TIPs bundle the entire vertical scope of protocol layers found in the Arpanet. In view of the end-to-end arguments it is important to note that the terminals moved significant (or 'hard') application state to the TIPs, a constellation very much contra the fate sharing argument discussed in section 3.2. The TIPs are thus a prime example of the trade-off to be had when weighing the costs and benefits of implementing all necessary functions at the very ends of a communication versus implementing them at intermediate points.

The broader conclusions to be drawn from this section are that the place of functions in a horizontal continuum between ultimate end hosts and the inner network is often highly malleable. Our discussion of increasingly elaborate host access, or IMP-host interfaces (pages 63 ff.), revealed that lower level functions may usefully be extended to the ultimate end hosts so as to guard against transmission errors in the access networks. On the other hand, the TIP discussion just above (pages 66 ff.) points to the sensibility of multiplexing simple and reasonably well defined host level functions with entities 'inside' the network.[197] In fact, it is only because TIPs assumed vital conversions and other intermediary functions, that less potent terminal devices could gain access to the network on their limited terms rather than having to conform to a wealth of network-wide higher layer conventions, or having to go through a local host.

To generalize with the due preliminary caution: if the functions at all layers are moving rather freely between the core and the ultimate edges of a network, subject to the various trade-offs to be found, then the line between the network and its ultimate applications is equally blurry. Logical, physical, and administrative separation lines may thus diverge quite substantially. What does this mean for end-to-end principles? Already, Saltzer et al. (1981*a*) have argued that the end points to any end-to-end argument must be identified with great care, for they may reside at intermediate points rather than the ultimate end points of a communication network. We would add that the delegation of hard state 'into the network' may not be as disturbing as it sometimes appears,[198] for the divergence of logical and administrative separation lines between the network and its applications may make the overall economic setup more complex and impede seamless horizontal expansion, but in itself is not a per se irremediable or unfeasible situation. Thus, rather than watering down existing design principles, it is probably more useful to complement them by principles dealing explicitly with the divergence of those lines. We have in section 3.3 already pointed to such possible extensions, and will in later segments of the thesis further elaborate on the set of such principles.[199]

In the following sections, however, we will first turn from the question of horizontal placement and migration of functions (this section) in a somewhat exogenously given protocol architecture (sections 4.1 and 4.2) to the question of how those functions have initially come to be distributed across the vertical scope of the network protocol stack — for one, discussing the problem of arriving at reasonably 'complete and correct' designs of application layer protocols such as Telnet and FTP (section 4.4); and, for another, discussing the Arpanet history of applications with no need for either completeness or correctness (most notably: voice) (section 5.1). Thereafter, we will draw in on the developments toward the Internet as we know it today (sections 5.2 ff.).

4.4 Completeness and Robustness at the Host Level

Any useful reasoning about the Arpanet and its design principles inevitably entails a closer look at its higher level host layer(s) — for the network is ultimately no more than the agent of its applications. Much like its lower-level counterpart, the host level design of the Arpanet became very much a layered one; the core difference, however, being that there had never been an equivalent to the Arpanet RFQ for the subnetwork that could guide the development efforts at the host layer. Nor was there a designated contractor to implement the higher layer applications and protocols. The design process thus followed the inherent distributiveness of higher level resources across a multitude of sites, and, literally, common sense. Even though ARPA and BBN exerted some influence (the former with its funding and coercive power, the latter by virtue of its intimate knowledge of the subtleties of wide-area packet switching), much of the work was ultimately done by a loose federation of people at various host sites — the Network Working Group, or NWG.[200] Notwithstanding all experimentation and proposals about host level application design,[201] a basic structure quickly set in, and we shall in this section look at the basics of this structure, and how it bears on the end-to-end arguments. Specifically, we shall consider the various strategies that emerged to obtain the level of end-to-end "correctness and completeness" required by given applications in the face of the limitations of both the host-host protocol and the IMP subnetwork service.

Considering the structure of the host layers in closer detail, it is useful to recall that any host level protocol had to be layered on top of the host-IMP interface provided by the IMP subnetwork. Thus there was a rough two-layer structure to begin with, already. Moreover, if accessing the host-IMP interface was to occur in some orderly fashion, then a sensible means of managing and multiplexing different application level communications would be required. Plus, given the administrative separation between the IMP subnetwork and the host level issues to be addressed, there was a strong case for introducing a lower level host layer to insulate specific application layer protocols from changes to the IMP subnetwork and the interface provided by the IMPs.[202]

Quickly, a rough structure featuring three distinct conceptual layers emerged — with a common host-host protocol at the center, plus 'that which is below' (the actual network) and 'that which is above' (the various applications).[203] By circa 1971, the notion of a general purpose host-host protocol and a certain hierarchy of layers at the host level had taken a firm hold in the host sites community. More specifically, there were three core notions: (1) there was a host-host protocol that took care of multiplexing and managing host level application processes desiring network access onto the host-IMP interface provided by the IMP to which the host was connected; (2) application level connections to peer hosts were generally initiated using an Initial Connection Protocol (ICP);[204] and (3) Telnet and FTP together with suitable common intermediary data representations[205] became sufficiently entrenched so as to allow remote logins and data transfers between virtually arbitrary hosts without having to implement special purpose emulators or adapt to a destination's idiosyncratic data formats, etc. (Figure 4.9).[206] Note that neither of those notions were

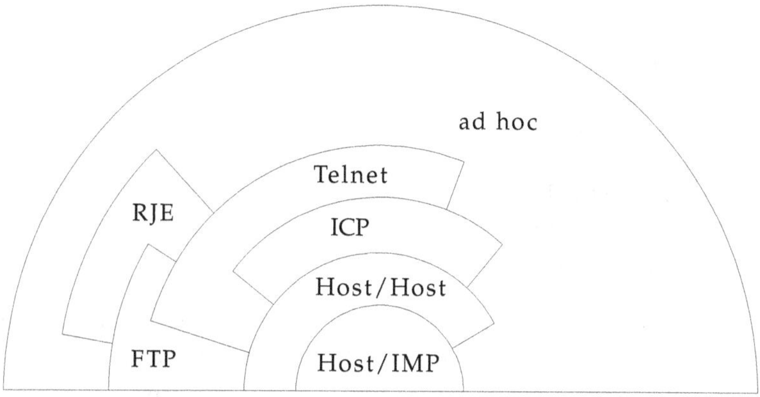

Figure 4.9: Layered relationship of the Arpanet protocols at host level; Source: Walden (1975*b*) (Walden 1978, p. 183)

rigidly enforced by any entity; standards, if any, emerged by what Clark would later call "rough consensus" and "running code" (Clark 1992*a*). Most importantly, there was nothing that kept applications from sidestepping any of the layers depicted in Figure 4.9—note the "ad hoc" space and the variations in layering structure for Telnet, FTP, and RJE.[207]

The one network-wide standard that eventually came to pertain to all of the hosts of the Arpanet was the host-host protocol—constituting the primary spanning layer for host level applications.[208] Everything above and below this spanning layer largely remained subject to much smaller scale local considerations and frequent amendments.[209] We have discussed in section 4.1[210] that the host-host protocol did not contain any provisions for error control or recovery in and of itself—for on the one hand, BBN did not like the notion that its network would effectively be considered as unreliable despite all its effort in pursuit of the reliability requirement as stated in the Arpanet RFQ; on the second hand, the subnetwork turned out to be, in fact, quite reliable (though not completely reliable); and, on the third hand, once the host-host protocol had been in place, it was hard to change it in any material respects.[211] The lack of complete reliability of the subnetwork which went unremedied by the host-host protocol meant that higher-level strategies had to be applied in cases where higher than standard reliability was required. Three principal strategies can be discerned, all of which have been applied in various combinations, depending on the actual problem at hand:

1. Leaving error control to the user (safe the error messages provided by the IMP-host interface, particularly the Incomplete Transmission notifications)

2. Applying policies in the Network Control Program based on the available host-host protocol and IMP/host interface mechanisms so as to increase the reliability of the host-host protocol

3. Devising special purpose application process level mechanisms for error control and recovery (e.g., checkpoints in data transmissions so as to allow automatic resumption of data transfers)

The first option, leaving error control to the user, was the simplest, in a sense most elegant and most 'complete' of all options; but it was, of course, also the least satisfactorily one—workable only in cases where human users were directly in the communication loop and not overwhelmed by having to make up for potentially fallible network services. A user would have to keep a close eye on error messages arriving from the IMP-host interface, close and restart misbehaving connections (e.g., deadlocked "half open" connections), and try to make sense of the results of the inter-process communication obtained by the system, ultimately deciding whether to be content with the service.[212] Depending on human users in the control loop severely limited the generality of data transmission applications.[213]

The second strategy, making the host-host protocol more robust to subnetwork errors by catering for message retransmissions in case of Incomplete Transmission indications from the IMP-host interface, was successfully applied in a number of instances. While not resolving the totality of potential problems from lost messages,[214] such retransmission strategies went a long way to increasing the reliability of host-host connections.[215] A problem with host-host retransmissions was that they required potentially significant resources to be added to the NCP. By 1974 eight messages could be in transit between two hosts at one time,[216] thus in the worst case scenario an NCP would have to buffer roughly eight times 8000 bits—clearly not a negligible burden at the time. However, holding onto messages containing as little as one terminal character until the RFNM arrived from the IMP, or resending them in case of Incomplete Transmission notifications, was a quite reasonable strategy.[217] Indeed, it was just this application setting that such retransmission schemes were quickly added to, thus improving the service for terminal users at relatively little cost.[218]

Third, and finally, applications and their protocols could be designed so as to make up for potential reliability problems at lower layers. Most prominently, the application of file transfer was gradually changed so as to include the option to add checkpoints to the data in transmission, allowing in turn to resume file transfers from such checkpoints in case a connection failed mid-way through a file transfer.[219] The error handling was thus raised from the host-host level to the application level, with recovery procedures applying to application level boundaries in the data to be transmitted rather than to host-host level messages as such. Arguably, for file transfer—where high throughput rather than low delay was required, and one logical data transmission could take many hours rather than split seconds—this was a more sensible strategy than to try and get NCP to make up for transmission errors. Not only did the application level error control keep NCP from having to redundantly buffer large amounts of data, it also addressed both network outages and host level failures including complete host crashes. Once a connection was resumed between a source and destination host to a file transmission, a previously aborted file transfer could simply be resumed at a checkpoint inserted at user discretion.[220]

In conclusion, a large amount of robustness and reliability was added to both interactive terminal sessions and bulk file transfers by augmenting the levels below and above the host-host protocol, respectively.[221] More generally, dealing with errors, and reducing them to a level acceptable for the ultimate use cases manifested by various application scenarios in the

Arpanet, turned out to entail varying efforts distributed among all levels — from (1) the IMP subnetwork, to (2) NCP and the host-host protocol, to (3) the application level protocols as well as the ultimate applications and users. In some instances casual user awareness sufficed, others could be hugely improved by relatively small augmentations to the NCP operations, and still others were best dealt with by introducing application level error control and recovery measures to deal with uncertain network conditions.

What do the episodes recounted in this section tell us about the end-to-end arguments? The specific lesson is that the lack of complete reliability at the host-host protocol layer resulted in a number of target application specific augmentations to variables outside of the common host-host protocol specification. The more general lesson, however, is that in many cases application end points took on certain functions *regardless* of the level of service provided by the subnetwork — see the file transfer checkpoint strategies discussed above. Also, recall from section 4.3 that application end points increasingly dissipated from the immediate vicinity of the Arpanet host-IMP interface, thus firmly removing the concerns of application 'completeness and correctness' from any host-IMP interface level performance expectations. With the requirements of the application in question determining the needed level of reliability, robustness, ease of debugging, and so on, the solutions devised were in a very real sense end-to-end solutions, even if the functions to obtain reliability were not necessarily right with the end applications — see the Telnet/NCP augmentations by the TIPs, discussed at our section 4.3, pages 66 ff..

Given that virtually every application turned out to need some end-to-end reliability augmentation, if only by 'user level reliability protocols', the question may be put as to whether or not IMP subnetwork level efforts toward end-to-end reliability were futile. However, the overhead added by IMP-IMP packet acknowledgment and retransmission facilities were relatively minor, and so was the message level (source to destination IMP) negative acknowledgment and error reporting facility. The benefits from both mechanisms arguably exceeded their costs — the former substantially reduced lost packets due to line errors, and the latter helped hosts in devising strategies to deal with lost messages without having to implement end-to-end acknowledgment schemes.[222] And, neither mechanism significantly prejudiced applications *not* needing the reliability thus obtained. True, there was no service menu other than the implicit choices between single-packet and multi-packet messages, as well as a rudimentary priority mechanism.[223] But, as we shall see in the following chapter, the subnetwork was soon to offer a basic 'raw message' service that dispensed with most of the functions aimed at providing reliable message transmission to the host level, thus providing a service interface for precisely those applications that were better served with less than perfectly reliable message transmissions, and paving the way for the emergence of the Internet as we know it today.

Chapter 5

Letting Go

On any conceivable horizon—I'll say until about 5 billion years from now, when the sun explodes—we're not going to run out of discoveries.

— *Paul Romer (2001)*

In this chapter we turn from the Arpanet to the Internet, from the network that established the feasibility of real-time wide-area networking based on the packet switching paradigm, to the 'supernetwork' that would become the virtual lowest common denominator for potentially any network. While the basic philosophic building blocks of the Internet have been laid in the Arpanet (as we shall see particularly in the first section of this chapter), the Internet brought about a very different overall architecture for it aimed at objectives very different from those of the Arpanet. Consequently, it faced a number of very distinct new problems the resolution of which continued through to the 1980s,[224] and, in fact, to this very day.[225]

It would be surprising if the main principles of networking had stopped evolving with the implementation of the Arpanet specification. So is it with the end-to-end arguments—which we may trace back to the architecture of the Arpanet, but which have seen material elaboration with the episodes to be discussed in this chapter. We shall first look at the history of Arpanet raw messages, an arguably direct predecessor to the notion of IP packets. Then, we recount how the Internet Protocol came about. And, finally, we will elaborate the history of two problems of inter-networking, fragmentation and congestion control, and how these developments bear on the end-to-end arguments.

5.1 Second Thoughts on Subnetwork Services

The most curious, but also one of the most important discoveries in the early days of the Arpanet was that there were applications for which the IMP subnetwork was actually *too* reliable. The network was mostly optimized for reliability rather than delay and throughput,[226] a combination of parameters adequate for most applications, but not for each and every one. While many hosts and applications benefited from the near perfect reliability of the subnetwork, thus being relieved from having to achieve such reliability by host level means, some applications needed no perfect reliability in the first place—in fact, its side effects could be very much counterproductive to their purposes: they would rather have the network deliver their messages with occasional losses but as quickly as possible (and with as low a variation of delay as possible), than having them delivered reliably (and with variable delays of up to 30 seconds)[227]. The two major cases in point were (1) interactive voice traffic,[228] and, to a somewhat lesser extent, (2) network interconnection.[229]

By circa 1974, BBN acknowledged the merit of providing a less than perfectly reliable message service to hosts with tight delay and lax reliability requirements,[230] and in late 1974 introduced an "unordered" or "raw" message facility, available via a Raw Message Interface (RMI). The new interface offered a non-reliable, unordered, and non-flow-controlled service for one-packet messages (meaning host messages no larger than ca. 1000 bits). While raw messages were treated by intermediary IMPs just like any other packets (they were acknowledged hop-by-hop and would be retransmitted absent timely acknowledgment), they were exempted from the normal flow control, buffer reservation, one-packet message retransmission scheme, and other measures intended to deliver a reliable message transmission service to hosts.[231]

However, there was an important restriction to the RMI in that host sites had to obtain explicit permission of the BBN NCC if they wanted to use it. These administrative restrictions were put in place lest the network would become congested with uncontrolled messages, as BBN's Walden explains:

> Because the uncontrolled use of this mechanism will degrade the performance of the network for all users, the set of Hosts

permitted to use this mechanism will be regulated by the Network Control Center. (Walden 1974, p. 2)

It is not entirely clear how access to the RMI was enforced, but we may with reasonable certainty say that without explicit NCC intervention a host could not use raw messages.[232] On the other hand, while the administrative overhead involved in obtaining permission to use it certainly did not help its prominence,[233] we have found next to no indications that applications other than voice were seriously interested in using the facility in the first place, or that reasonable requests for access to the service had been denied by BBN.[234] By 1975 the raw message interface was used by "three or so hosts" (Walden 1975*c*, p. 2),[235] and it is fair to estimate that at no time had there been more than a dozen or so hosts using it.[236]

In practice, the raw message service was predominantly used for packet voice experiments,[237] largely in the course of ARPA initiated and directed research efforts commencing in 1972.[238] By late 1973 the first version of the Network Voice Protocol (NVP) along with the requisite host applications were completed (D. Cohen 1977*b*, p. iv). With the raw message facility in place from 1974, the NVP was augmented so as to make use of uncontrolled messages for its data traffic (D. Cohen 1977*b*, p. 1).[239] Whereas earlier experiments (built on the existing normal message service provided by the IMP-host interface) focused largely on coding and processing strategies,[240] establishing the general feasibility of the whole notion of packet speech;[241] the new interface allowed to experiment with trading off the whole range of relevant parameters for interactive speech transmissions: delay, throughput, and reliability (as in packet loss rate) (see Figure 5.1).[242]

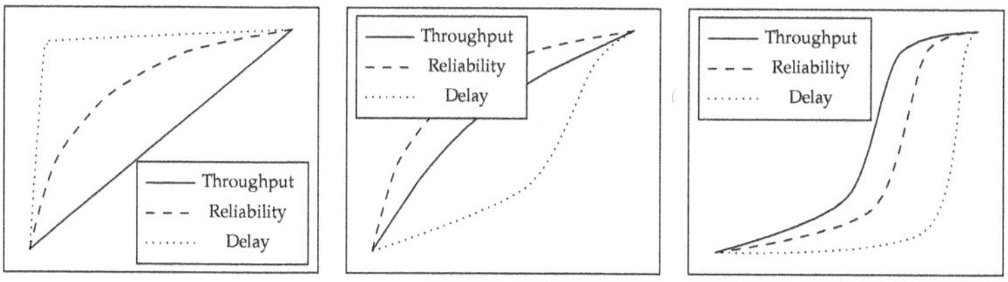

(a) FTP utility (b) Telnet utility (c) Speech utility

Figure 5.1: Utility of canonical application types as a function of throughput, reliability, and delay performance

As one would expect, the delay characteristics of data transmissions generally improved when dropping the prior arsenal of normal IMP subnetwork reliability measures.[243] Weinstein and Forgie (1983) report of one experiment between ISI and LL:

> At a 1 percent lost packet rate, type 3 [uncontrolled message service] is seen to provide about a 0.4 s advantage in overall delay. For higher rates [than 8.6 kbits/s] type 0 [normal controlled message service] became unusable whereas it was possible at the time to support 16 kbit/s CVSD with type 3 packets (but only during hours when network load was light). For lower rates, such as 2.4 kbits/s,the difference between type 3 and type 0 diminished. (p. 971)

Average delays were thus much smaller for uncontrolled messages than for the previous controlled ones.[244] Gold (1977, pp. 1653 f.) arrives at very similar results in their experiments: to successfully transmit 99 percent of packets, each carrying ca. 600 bits of payload data, a delay of ca. 0.5 seconds had to be allowed for; a rate of 95 percent reduces the maximum delay to 0.35 seconds.[245] Reassembly strategies 'jumping over' silent packets allowed to further reduce the fixed delay at the receiver (Gold 1977, p. 1654).[246]

In all, while not comparable to circuit switched speech communication at the time, the experiments showed that packet speech was, in principle, a feasible application to large scale packet switched networks; if only in conditions of light network load.[247] More fundamentally they established that a network service of less than perfect reliability could be beneficial, even vital, for applications—a core reason for the 1978 TCP/IP split.[248] With the 'official' appreciation that perfect reliability might be superfluous, even detrimental to the applications and uses of a network not needing such in the first place, it had now become clear that the range of services to be delivered to applications could well be short of perfectly reliable and ordered data transmission. Why keep considering reliability an essential part of a network's service if, with growing scale, neither rates nor delays can ever be hoped to be specified in advance—especially given that reliability is the *only* parameter of the three that can be arbitrarily perfected by end-to-end measures, anyway?[249]

Furthermore, and with a nod to inter-networking considerations, it was gradually understood there is little point in aiming at any perfection when a neighboring network part of the overall end-to-end path between two hosts is beyond one's administrative control and accountability, and may thus fail to be at par with one's standards of reliability, anyway. Once hosts start to implement reliability functions themselves, then, there is little point in striving for *perfect* reliability (or indeed any performance guarantees) in any one of the subnetworks along the path.[250] In the worst case, these dynamics result in an inefficient race to the bottom; in the desirable case of reasonable interconnectedness and routing flexibility, though, this results in an economically efficient equilibrium of just the right amount of reliability in the network, as opposed to in the hosts.

As for the end-to-end arguments, then, it bears noting that the introduction of raw messages was accompanied by the most crucial appreciation that reliability was neither a broadly necessary, nor even a necessarily helpful characteristic of a subnetwork given that the overall performance trade-off for applications involved a host of parameters other than reliability of the subnetwork. Plus, even with a network trying really hard to maintain a reliable data transmission service, once the fringes of the network turn into networks of sorts, themselves,[251] the administrative coherence of the 'one network' approach is effectively lost. The cost and complexity of maintaining a reliable communication service to the ultimate end devices thus becomes increasingly large, and the case for moving reliability functions to the actual ends becomes accordingly stronger.

Raw messages were a first conceptual step toward the ultimate architecture of the Internet as we know it today, with the bulk of transport logic at the host layer, not delegated to the network. At that, they contained both the promise and the challenges inherent in leaving networking over statistically shared resources to the discretion of ends rather than the management of a central network management entity. Thus they anticipated many of the issues at the heart of the end-to-end arguments, such as:

- How to protect the network from collapsing under the traffic load that hosts are now free to offer to the network?

- How to regulate the now-empowered end hosts without undermining the advantages of end-to-end based approaches to networking?

- And, how to even come to terms with notions such as equality, fairness, and efficiency in such a network?

Answering those questions has remained a central problem in reasoning about networking to this day, but it is instructive to note that the seeds to those questions were sown a long time ago.

Second, a slightly more subtle point emerged from the consideration of packet speech: at the host level, there is no explicit need for a one-size-fits-all general transport protocol offering reliable service to each and every application. Rather, there are to be more than but one transport protocol — in the extreme there may be as many transport protocols as there are applications. Even when there is no diversity in subnetwork services (beyond the standard supposedly reliable service), there is good reason to allow protocols other than the host-host protocol as implemented by NVP to sit conceptually beside NCP.[252] Not surprisingly, thus, NVP was not to remain the only idiosyncratic transport protocol beside NCP. We have already mentioned TCP in passing, and in the following section we shall further detail how the notion of ultimately arbitrary transport services on top of a common (inter)network protocol logically outside of the networks to be interconnected, and implemented in both network gateways and hosts, came to change networking at large.

5.2 Raising the Common Ground Above Arpanet

The Arpanet was by no means the only packet switching network to gain prominence in the early 1970s. Very quickly an impressive body of experience with different approaches to networking emerged, giving rise to (1) a set of robust principles of network design in general, and (2) an increasing need for consolidating the different networks such that resources would be available across network boundaries in a coherent and tractable way. Whereas higher level protocols and applications such as Telnet, FTP, and SMTP,[253] plus a set of common intermediate representations such as NVT[254] had been firmly in place by ca. 1974, using these protocols across network boundaries still necessitated ad hoc solutions involving protocol gateways mediating between incompatible protocols very close to the application protocol layer, thus giving rise not only to the notorious $n \times m$

problem, but also to all sorts of vagaries stemming from different protocol semantics and functions that may not trivially map to one another.[255] Anyone wanting to connect to hosts on the Arpanet had to convert their data to Arpanet messages and abide by Arpanet protocol specifics such as RFNMs, etc. — thus effectively establishing a two-level hierarchy, with the Arpanet as a de facto common standard at the center and several 'satellite' networks connecting to their Arpanet IMP or TIP via a dedicated gateway.

The conceptual limitations of thus extending the Arpanet notwithstanding, using satellite links and special purpose gateways, the Arpanet quickly stretched to Hawaii,[256] Norway,[257] and the UK;[258] and, more decisively, to a burgeoning number of local area networks at Arpanet host sites.[259] The diversity of networks — all logically 'local' ones, but in some way connected to the Arpanet — increased such that by as early as 1973 it was hardly appropriate anymore to consider the Arpanet an inevitable or even useful common ground for inter-networking efforts.[260] In fact, building and maintaining gateways connecting a given network to the Arpanet was typically far from trivial, and often entailed severe limitations to the resulting inter-network service, particularly when connecting to other large-scale or incumbent networks that featured their very own idiosyncrasies.[261]

Consequently, while topologically still very much the 'tier-1' network, the choice for Arpanet protocols as the de facto intermediary standard for connecting different networks was looking increasingly arbitrary — an artifact of the Arpanet's primacy and dominance, rather than a proper solution for inter-networking to be maintained and scaled potentially indefinitely.[262] Most importantly, the Arpanet could not conceptually be extended toward arbitrary networks using gateways without running into scalability problems regarding performance, nor was it anywhere near likely that its specifics would be welcome by each and every host computer, application type, or purpose that the emerging 'network of networks' would be put to. The Arpanet IMP subnetwork protocols, for one, could certainly not be considered an irreducible lowest common denominator for data communication — both regarding a sensible application diversity to be supported, and the interconnection with other, different networks.[263] In short, a coherent and scalable way for interconnecting the proliferating set of different 'local' networks was needed.

Efforts to solve the inter-networking problem in a general manner that would scale with the anticipated and desired rise of both local and large-scale networks started in 1972, before even the famed public Arpanet demonstration[264] took place, and quickly took shape in the work of a group of international networking researchers — the International Packet Network Working Group (INWG).[265] By 1973 a concerted international effort about inter-networking had commenced in earnest, aiming to arrive at a protocol that would be implemented by gateways potentially bridging *all* the different networks found at the time, plus future networks, too.

Cerf (1973) spells out the first ideas toward such a protocol, the initial set of thoughts eventually leading to today's TCP/IP:

> Let us begin with the assumption that we want to interconnect several distinct, resource-sharing computer networks. Each of these networks connects together Host computers whose resources can be shared among the users of the network. If we are to achieve a similar ability between Hosts residing in different networks, we must find a way for a Host in one network to reproduce, without alteration, a stream of messages originating from a Host in another network. This is a primitive but essential necessity, and [. . .] [the requisite] Host level protocol will be implemented through a Host program called the Transmission Control Program (TCP). (p. 4)

Thus the scene was set for the core notion in TCP: hosts were to assume the principal responsibility for achieving the transparent data communication hitherto provided by the Arpanet IMP subnetwork. This design decision was based primarily on the only sensible assumption regarding the dependability of intermediary networks: they could not be assumed to offer any reliable or otherwise predictable services, be it in data transmission, or in control functions. In fact, not even the gateways to mediate between the networks were considered to offer any reliable service. Again, Cerf (1973):

> The ITP [International Transport Protocol] is resistant to failures in intermediate nodes and gateways. This is accomplished by arranging for positive acknowledgement of receipt of message by the receiving Host. Furthermore, sending Hosts are

> expected to time-out and retransmit messages which have not been acknowledged. (p. 6)

The conceptual role of intermediate gateways and networks was thus reduced to the lowest possible common denominator — they would be assumed to offer *some* service on behalf of the ultimate end hosts, but there would be no minimum quantitative specification to this service 'definition'. While gateways would be designed so as to pass messages between networks,[266] they were essentially free to drop packets, otherwise go insane, and generally not be assumed to make up for any insanity of the constituent networks.[267] In short, the inter-network would be a 'best effort' 'datagram' 'virtual' network:

- The service to be obtained from the concatenation of networks in between two hosts would not be subject to a strict service definition. Rather, due to the inherent vagaries of any communication effort, the inter-network would only be expected to offer a "best effort" service (Metcalfe 1973).[268]

- The nature of the inter-network service would be 'datagrams', that is, relatively small discrete pieces of digital data wrapped into 'packets' that would simply be injected into the inter-network, with the gateways expected to interpret the control data found in the packet 'internetwork header' (most importantly, the destination address) so as to forward the packet toward its eventual destination. No state about any one 'connection' or packet need be kept in the gateways.[269]

- The inter-network — built out of different 'local' networks using gateways subject to an inter-network protocol (or at least packet header format) — virtualizes a 'gateway virtual network' (Walden and Rettberg 1975, pp. 119 ff.) from the resources of each of the network it connects.[270] The due inter-network protocol needs to be simple for two reasons: For one, a simple protocol will maximize the generality and flexibility in connecting different networks. For another, only a simple protocol will be 'cascadable', and not reintroduce the $n \times m$ problem.[271]

So far, so simple.[272] However, the specification of TCP did not yet properly separate between 'host level issues' and 'gateway level issues'. There

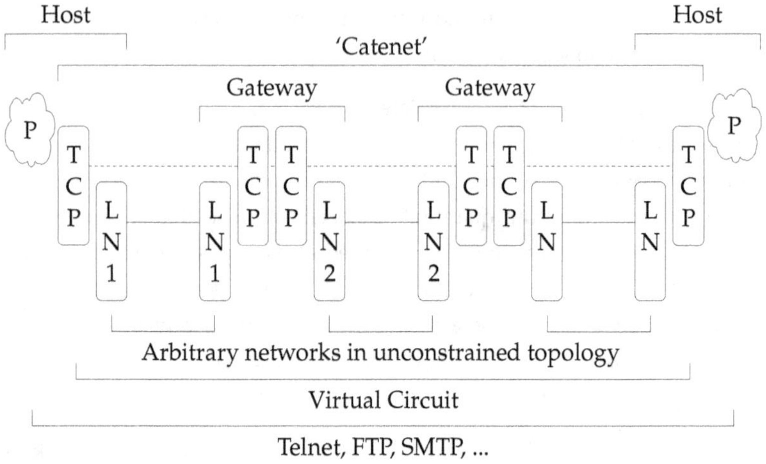

Figure 5.2: Basic TCP gateway inter-network architecture

was some appreciation of the differences between hop-by-hop and end-to-end TCP functions;[273] but, essentially, the gateways were considered to be special purpose *hosts* tasked with the *host level* interconnection of hosts across different networks using a common host level 'inter-network' protocol — without clearly specifying the level to which the inter-network 'host level' protocols inside a gateway would actually reach (Figure 5.2).[274]

Eventually, in 1978 a low level inter-network protocol was split off from the initial, monolithic TCP. The Internet Protocol, or IP, was to be implemented as a host level inter-networking protocol throughout the 'gateway virtual network', that is by all *gateways*. On the other hand, the higher level inter-network protocol — the TCP (which now had turned from a Transmission Control *Program*, Cerf and Postel 1978, to a Transmission Control *Protocol*, Postel 1978c) — was to be implemented by all the *hosts*, much along the lines of the previous NCP host-host protocol (Figure 5.3).[275]

With the 'lower host level' inter-networking protocol properly separated from the more specific host 'transport level' protocol it now became possible to place potentially arbitrary protocols other than TCP on top of IP, thus accounting for diverse requirements by different applications (see section 5.1), or simply the fact that not every host might be powerful enough to implement the entire TCP protocol in the first place. Most no-

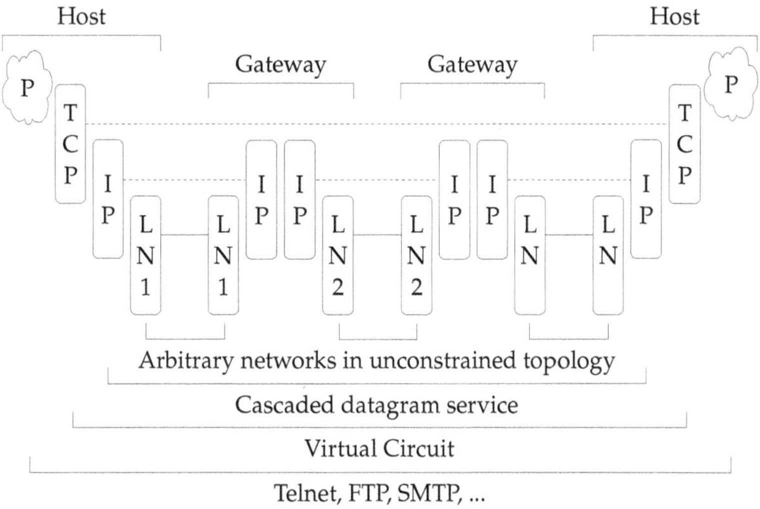

Figure 5.3: TCP/IP inter-network architecture

tably the User Datagram Protocol (Reed and Postel 1979) was defined to allow applications access to the IP protocol with minimum host level protocol overhead ("messages delivery is unordered and unreliable", p. 1).[276] Also, the connection setup overhead of TCP would be dispensed with; only plain messages were sent to a specified port at a destination host.[277] While TCP has remained the commandingly dominant host level protocol, there have been various applications and contexts in which UDP provided the more sensible basis for host level interprocess communication.[278]

In all, despite the novelty of the approach, the TCP/IP architecture was very much equivalent to the Arpanet architecture—with the IP protocol loosely analogous to the IMP-IMP protocol, the TCP analogous to the normal source-IMP-to-destination-IMP protocol, and UDP analogous to the unordered (or 'raw') message service. Curiously, the process of arriving at the appreciation of protocols other than the virtual circuit TCP also repeated very much along the lines of those pursued when arriving at the notion of raw messages. At first, it was thought that everyone would want virtual circuits, anything less than VC was catered for only as an exception to the rule.[279] Only later was it appreciated that the overhead of

VCs would prove inefficient for enough applications to warrant offering a less potent, but possibly faster and lower overhead transport protocol, with only a most basic inter-network protocol having to be shared by *all* participants to the inter-network. Thus the observations regarding the end-to-end arguments made in the previous sections, mostly sections 4.4 and 5.1, largely hold for this episode, too.

The more interesting and novel twists in the history of TCP/IP come from the vagaries of inter-networking as opposed to managing and developing a tractable, centrally managed 'local' network such as the Arpanet. Two aspects stand out, and we shall deal with either of them in turn in the following sections: (1) resolving the contentious issue of fragmentation, and (2) controlling congestion. While the former once more goes back in time before the advent of TCP/IP, the latter only begins once TCP/IP was firmly in place.

5.3 The Rift over Fragmentation

The considerations of host level flexibility and generality discussed in the previous section notwithstanding, the need for a firm separation of host level and gateway level issues owes much of its rationale and elaboration to the heated contentions surrounding the possible fragmentation of packets in inter-networking which we shall elaborate in this section. Two basic philosophical positions marked the controversy over fragmentation: the view that inter-network fragmentation without end-to-end transparency was viable, versus the view that such approach would be ill-advised.

Cerf (1973) argues in favor of the former:

> [M]essages crossing through a gateway may require breaking into more than one message which may not be reassembled before delivery to a Host. (p. 7)

Cerf and Kahn (1973)[280] further develop the notion of gateway level fragmentation, arguing that reassembly of all fragments is best left to the ultimate end point of a TCP transmission and not to be contained to the gateway level operations:[281]

> Gateway reassembly can lead to serious buffering problems, potential deadlocks, the necessity for all fragments of a packet

> to pass through the same Gateway, and increased delay in transmission. Furthermore, it is not sufficient for the Gateways to provide this function since the final Gateway may also have to fragment a packet for transmission. Thus, the destination Host must be prepared to do this task. (p. 7)

The inter-network fragmentation scheme was thus informed to some extent by the concern to keep gateways as simple as possible and not have them implement elaborate virtual circuit notions along with all the latency and statefulness they typically add — precisely the issues that the inter-networking part of TCP was supposed to eliminate. While any local network was, of course, free to transmit TCP messages in whichever way it saw fit,[282] there was great hesitation to burden networks and their TCP gateways with mandatory and possibly unnecessary complexities.

Also, Cerf and Kahn (1974)[283] add that the principal alternative to catering for gateway level fragmentation — legislating a maximum packet size that every network can fit to carry (without incurring the performance penalties of effectively having to establish a virtual circuit for every packet that has to be fragmented) — would "seriously inhibit the long range growth and development of internetwork communication" (p. 639). Once the TCP/IP Internet attained the dominance it later did, this concern proved to be no longer important; but at the time, it was considered vital to allow as broad a range of networks as possible to join the TCP/IP Internet (Clark 2010*a*).

On the other hand, the problem with allowing fragmentation of TCP messages (or the later IP packets) by gateways, but not requiring attendant reassembly, is that it inextricably links the hop-by-hop operations to those taking place end-to-end at the end hosts level. While this was apparently an acceptable situation for the U. S. side to the INWG debates, it proved unacceptable for the Europeans, most notably Pouzin:[284]

> [With the fragmentation scheme proposed by Cerf and Kahn 1974] E-E protocols are definitely tied up with the design of gateways. As a consequence, evolutions in E-E protocols could become completely dependent on PTTs. (Pouzin 1975*b*, p. 2-10)

The same problem was seen to apply vice versa: the gateways, too, depend on the stability of the host-host protocol(s), as Gien et al. (1975) note:

> The Gateway must be party to the Host-Host protocol which in any case might change. Extra complication is involved at the Gateway if more than one Host-Host protocol is in existence. (p. 247)

A third argument is about performance. Note Gien et al. (1975):

> Once fragmented into tiny pieces by one network it is impractical for subsequent networks to reassemble to larger fragments which they might carry with less overhead. (p. 247)

Thus, even without the problems of surrendering control and functions to potentially ill-meaning PTTs, there was a good case for cleanly separating the responsibilities and powers regarding fragmentation given the various additional pertinent trade-offs—either by stipulating a minimum packet size, or by leaving fragmentation, if necessary, to the TCPs in the end hosts only.[285]

In spite of those reservations about inter-network fragmentation, the original fragmentation scheme in TCP stood its ground, until by ca. 1977 the concerns about the disadvantages of inter-network fragmentation were beginning to be echoed in the TCP community, too;[286] along with more general concerns about the appropriateness of mixing gateway level and host level issues in one protocol (see section 5.2). In 1977 discussions inside the ARPA sponsored TCP community finally led to significant amendments in the fragmentation scheme—along with a complete redesign of the whole TCP architecture, the famous TCP/IP split (Cerf 1978*b*).[287] By early 1978 the fragmentation scheme in TCP was finally changed—not only was fragmentation moved into a separate 'internet protocol' layer (Cerf 1978*a*),[288] but it was also elevated from the sole discretion of the intermediate networks to the ultimate discretion of the hosts (Cerf 1978*b*)—setting a "don't fragment" flag would now result in the packet being discarded or subjected to transparent intra-network fragmentation only, rather than be fragmented and passed on in fragments to subsequent networks (Postel 1978*a*, p. 6; Postel 1978*c*, p. 6). Users (as well applications and hosts) were thus empowered to simply outrule any fragmentation of their packets.[289]

In the further development of the TCP/IP Internet, fragmentation was relegated to a relatively minor role, once some consensus about default packet sizes emerged, and a sound appreciation of the disadvantages to fragmentation at the gateway level took hold in the networking community at large (Kent and Mogul 1987).[290] Fragmentation thus turned from a general design problem affecting all parts of an inter-network to the more contained host level issue of choosing the size of IP packets to send out in the first place. The necessary mechanisms came to be almost exclusively confined to the host level proper — without any the need for 'legislatively restricting' a minimum maximum packet size to be accepted by every network. After all, with very little effort, a host could dynamically discover the maximum size packet that a given path through the Internet could bear. It would do this either by observing packet loss rates (which would spike once packets get larger than the MTU) (Mathis and Heffner 2007), or by relying on explicit ICMP feedback from gateways (Mogul and Deering 1990) (effectively as a performance enhancement to the loss observation scheme).[291] Given that routes are typically stable throughout the lifetime of a given connection, and that there are few reasons for a (sane) host or application to send out packets larger than the MTU determined for a given path,[292] fragmentation has very quickly turned from a major source of contention inside INWG to what has effectively reduced to a non-issue.[293] Of the two major functions of the Internet Protocol beyond forwarding — routing and fragmentation (Postel et al. 1981, p. 263) — only the former was to remain a core part.

As for the end-to-end arguments, it is fair to argue that the history of inter-network fragmentation demonstrated a strong case for end-to-end solutions over solutions relying on logically linking hosts and gateways outside the discretion of the hosts. In the beginning of the Internet, inter-network fragmentation provided a crucial benefit: it allowed the interconnection of any network capable of passing on some 61 bytes (the maximum IP header plus 1 byte of payload data) without either the hosts or the gateways having to implement elaborate mechanisms to deal with such networks. And even then, it was agreed that "the gateways must have the least possible knowledge of end-to-end protocols" (Postel 1978c, p. 5). However, the conceptual simplicity and advantages of the scheme notwithstanding, once some common ground consensus about reasonable packet sizes took hold, it was no longer considered useful or even acceptable to logically link the operations of gateways to those of the hosts by way of an inter-network fragmentation scheme without allowing hosts to bypass that scheme at their discretion. Today, it is hard to find any applications that consciously and explicitly choose to have their IP packets fragmented along the way. Rather, the commandingly dominant default is to probe for the path MTU — with minimal to no explicit help from the network routers — and leave any fragmentation, as in choosing the size of packets to be sent across the inter-network, to the end hosts proper.

5.4 Higher Loads and Hidden Hacks

On January 1, 1983, the Arpanet switched from the previous host-host protocol to the TCP/IP protocols, in an ARPA mandated transition that all host sites were to abide by.[294] Use of the new protocols as a common ground enabled Arpanet hosts to connect to arbitrary hosts outside the Arpanet, provided an IP gateway (or a concatenation of such gateways across various networks) could establish a path between the two hosts. And, given that such gateways logically operated at the host layer, they could be implemented in any host facing two different networks, thus providing IP connectivity between potentially *all* the hosts on either of the two networks. A decade after research into inter-networking had commenced, the Internet as we know it came to life — a decentralized virtual 'network of networks', scalable to staggering size, and glued together into a coherent whole by a dispersed set of gateways providing an unreliable but irreducibly simple datagram service.

And yet, despite its seeming simplicity and robustness, there was one chief issue that proved not simple to resolve at all, and has remained a largely open research topic to this day: the problem of controlling congestion and preventing congestion collapses.[295] At a very basic level of abstraction, congestion is a condition in which the traffic admitted to a network exceeds its resources (that is, the number of packets it is capable of holding while still being able to transmit them toward their destination and do otherwise meaningful work).[296] Very broadly, the consequence of this simple logic is a normative "conversation of packets" principle, meaning "[a] new packet isn't put into the network until an old packet leaves" (Jacobson 1988*a*, p. 314). The chief problem in congestion control lies in upholding said principle (1) without introducing excessive complexity and overhead along the lines of circuit switching and reservation schemes in general; (2) doing so in a scalable and robust manner without building on overly unrealistic external assumptions (such as well-behaved hosts and network nodes in an administratively and physically distributed system); and (3) doing so in a manner that allows economically efficient differentiation to obtain without incurring prohibitive transaction costs.

There had been some prior elaboration of 'global' congestion control schemes that would keep the volume of traffic within a given maximum limit,[297] but there was little practical experience in dealing with congestion in a scalable, robust, and efficient manner. The primary predecessor of the Internet, the Arpanet, also had to deal with congestion (then referred to as flow control); but, being a 'local' network, it could resort to two very effective remedies: (1) since there was a clear administrative and physical separation between network and hosts, the network could simply block a host interface so as to stop the flow of traffic into the networks; and (2) given the coherent administration and physical control over network resources, the network could implement and centrally upgrade elaborate internal mechanisms (e. g., resource reservation at the destination IMP) to contain the problem of resource congestion and performance degradation. In general, any local network may feasibly change its internals, control usage, and thus protect itself from badly-behaving or downright malicious hosts.[298]

However, neither of those remedies has been available to the virtual IP gateway network (or just: the 'Internet'). For one, due to the simplicity of the Internet Protocol and the administrative distributiveness of its constituent parts, much of the relative power that used to be with 'the network' was now with the end hosts. Where a normal network deals with traffic from well-known sources, ultimately at the sole discretion of the network; an IP gateway may be subject to traffic originating from potentially anywhere on the entire Internet, with next to no means to verify the source or sender of an IP packet. Plus, the degree of internal sophistication in dealing with congestion problems has been intrinsically limited by the very virtuality and administrative distributiveness of the Internet (as opposed to the tractability of local networks such as the Arpanet). The core functions virtualized from the local networks that make up the Internet have not been the authentication of traffic sources, the monitoring of end-to-end flows, or the routing of money; it has been the best effort passing on of IP packets — to this day the one common ground to all parties of the Internet.[299]

The initial way to control congestion was to try and institute a global, but extremely simple scheme — having gateways signal congestion to the sources of excess traffic which they were unable to forward due to buffer overruns (or impending buffer overruns), and expecting the hosts to back off accordingly, thus maintaining an equilibrium of traffic load bounded by the maximum capacity of the network. In the face of congestion, a gateway would not just drop a packet, but it would also send a "source quench" message to the host whose packets were discarded, thereby requesting the host to slow down, and allow the gateway to recover from congestion (Strazisar 1979).[300] The IP module with the host would then pass this information up to the TCP (or any other host level transport protocols), which in turn would have to slow down so as not to overwhelm the IP module. The source quench mechanism thus obtained a closed-loop system linking the hosts and the routers, in which information about congestion in a router is explicitly fed back to the sources causing the congestion.

While seemingly addressing the congestion problem in a straightforward way, and being easy to implement and uphold, there were a number of conceptual and practical problems with the source quench mechanism. First, a host may choose to ignore such a messages (or simply not have gotten it)[301] and keep sending at prior rates. There is no way of forcing hosts to throttle their rates without building up significant state information inside gateways about logical flows and traffic sources. Also, an outright malign (rather than just badly-behaved) host may forge source addresses (or otherwise confuse any flow identification algorithm in a router) so as to impede such efforts in the routers.[302] Add to this the general cost and potential side effects from making do with any such error message scheme in the first place,[303] and the overall benefit of the source quench facility quickly drops below zero. Second, and somewhat more importantly, the source quench signal itself provided no details about the gateway congestion that would help a host arrive at a reasonable strategy to deal with that signal in the first place. The underlying cause of a source quench message may be anything from severe network disruptions to no more than transient network failures without any appreciable impact on the end-to-end service obtained from the Internet, or simply be due to a faulty implementation of ICMP in a gateway. Notes Clark (1982*a*):[304]

> [A] valuable feature of the Internet [is] that for many internal failures it reconstructs its function without any disruption of the end points. [. . .] In general, error messages give valuable information about what went wrong, but are not to be taken as absolutely reliable. (pp. 11 f.)

And, third, even if the source quench messages were perfectly reliable and offered fine-grained advise on the state of the network, they would still not suffice to inform a reasonable response by the host. In the case of TCP, simply blocking any input from the TCP to the IP module could either make congestion problems *worse* by holding back acknowledgments thus triggering retransmissions, or time out TCP connections by holding back retransmissions (which alleviates the congestion problem but does so in an unacceptably destructive way).[305] With source quench the congestion information has to be propagated from the IP layer up to the TCP, but that means TCP needs some internal sophistication allowing it to reduce its rate — for it is more than just a serial data transmission facility. Lack of such capabilities renders the source quench mechanism futile or even destructive.[306] As for UDP, here the problem of properly choosing what to do about the congestion signal is moving upwards further still, for there are no connections to throttle or windows to adjust at the level of UDP. The source quench mechanism may be sitting at the IP layer, but it can hardly solve the problem of cutting back rates without somehow involving the upper layers on whose behalf, after all, it is operating. Absent such cooperation from the higher layers, the conceptual clarity of the scheme is very much lost.[307]

In all, while the source quench message and the norm of rate reduction is a seemingly simple and effective scheme to alleviate gateway congestion, it is not trivial to align actual implementations with the best interests of the host applications ultimately using IP to communicate with their peers across the Internet, nor is it trivial to do so in a fair and robust manner. For the objective of the source quench message is *not* ultimately about protecting the network from heavy traffic; rather, it is about relaying other end hosts' misgivings about one's sending of packets to the network and thus degrading the service they are able to obtain from the network. Any relevant normative criterion about whose traffic is to absorb how much of the Internet's resources ultimately resides in the end hosts' host layer operations, not the Internet's internal state. ICMP error messages can only ever be a proxy for such considerations, and even their value as an adequate piece of input to the trade-offs to be had at the end hosts is highly questionable. Clark (1981) concludes:

> The existing [congestion control] algorithm, which is based on a source quench message from the gateway to the host, has not been shown to work well. (p. 6)

And, Baker et al. (1995) eventually acknowledge:

> A router *should not* originate ICMP Source Quench messages. [. . .] Source Quench consumes network bandwidth but is an ineffective (and unfair) antidote to congestion. (p. 57, emphasis in original)

Strictly speaking, source quench messages are still part of the Internet standards and "must", in theory, be acted upon in some reasonable way (Braden 1989, pp. 41, 103)—however, they have not lived up to their intended usefulness, and have to all intents and purposes become irrelevant to the operations of the Internet at large.[308]

By the mid-1980s the congestion problem had grown considerably more acute,[309] questioning the feasibility of the whole Internet architecture (vis à vis seemingly better-behaved VC schemes such as X.25/X.75). In early 1986 the matter was becoming a major subject of discussion in the then newly formed IETF (Nagle 1986), and in late 1986 it was so bad that Mockapetris and Dunlap spoke of "gateway crises" and how they severely complicated building applications with even minimal performance expectations (1986, p. 141).[310] The way to solve the congestion problem of the Internet turned out not to lie in the operation of the IP protocol and the interaction of gateways and hosts at that layer; rather, the solution was found in keying the transmission rate of TCP to the frequency of packet losses per RTT inside the Internet, using these as an indication of congestion and thus a signal to back off so as to relieve the packet build-up inside the Internet—the slow-start and congestion avoidance algorithm by Jacobson

(1988*a*).[311] The whole scheme is only very loosely (or: softly) coupled to the Internet routers[312]. Neither does it depend on any explicit state inside the Internet (it does not even care where exactly congestion occurs), nor does it impose inflexible linkages between the hosts and the routers. Provided it is adhered to by the bulk of all hosts, it is an extremely effective means of countering congestion; in fact, it bears the brunt of congestion control to this day, the wealth of alternative proposals put forward ever since notwithstanding.

Apart from relying on hosts to actually implement it in the first place, the principal limitation of Jacobson's scheme in and of itself is that it does not address issues of fairness and economic efficiency in a consistent, defendable way. It treats every TCP connection the same—packet losses trigger rate reductions, no matter how high the relative value of *not* reducing the rate of individual flows in the face of congestion, and no matter how many TCP flows an application uses (in order to crowd out other, better-behaved applications). Worse still, a host may choose to defect from the cooperation assumption tacit in TCP and 'TCP friendly' protocols by actually *increasing* its sending rate and adding forward error correction in response to lost packets. Absent any targeted policing efforts on part of the Internet routers involved, other better-behaved hosts would then scale back, leaving the more aggressive host with an 'unfair' share of the overall capacity.[313]

With the Jacobson mechanism as a given, the most practical way of addressing policy issues of fairness and efficiency is by having gateways drop packets such that badly-behaved and low utility hosts, not the well-behaved and relatively high utility ones, bear the brunt of performance penalties due to congestion. It is, however, not trivial to tell apart a badly behaved host from one that simply gains high utility from heavy network usage—in fact, the only difference is in intention and value creation (and distribution); the *effect* of either is the same.[314] The problem in determining the utility functions of the different end hosts is largely the lack of a feasible mechanism to provide proper incentives for applications and hosts to report the relative value of their IP packets. Absent such incentive everyone will overstate the value of their packets, which is precisely what happened with the Type of Service field in the IP header: it has quickly become completely meaningless.[315] Thus, mirroring the host strategy of ignoring source quench messages from the routers, the more reasonable thing to do for a router wanting to improve service—at least on average, without considering detailed subtleties about the relative value hosts place on their packets—has been to disregard any explicit signals about their service requirements. Rather, it would try and aim at some basic fairness between different logical flows (Nagle 1985); and, beyond that, try and infer any straightforward utility differences from implicit information about the type of application carried in the IP packets, or the traffic pattern they exhibit.

For the router, the central trade-off in either scheme (fairness and utility) is that between excessive statefulness and complexity in the gateways on the one hand, versus the overall value of doing such differentiation on the other hand. Indeed, the costs and side-effects to statefulness in the gateways may easily outweigh the benefits thus obtained, and schemes such as 'fair' queuing may well be too much, already.[316] A more sensible approach—based on utility rather than fairness considerations—has been to observe implicit signals about delay versus throughput requirements from the *individual packets* rather than the *logical flows* they may amount to. Indeed, such schemes have proven a useful means of applying sensible and low overhead discrimination rules in the face of congestion, and have been in place since the early 1970 Arpanet flow control schemes which gave precedence to single-packet messages.[317] Once the congestion problem grew more acute with the increase of Internet traffic—most notably on the NSFNET from 1986 onwards—such precedence schemes gained considerable prominence inside routers so as to maintain a reasonable service to end hosts (Mills 1988).[318] Nowadays, the congestion problem in the large Internet backbone networks is largely contained by the sheer scale of traffic aggregation, very much smoothening out any individual traffic volatility. Neither heavy over-provision, nor intricate precedence schemes are generally needed in those routers.[319]

Moving toward the edges of the Internet, however, and into the stub networks that typically serve residential broadband to end users, there has been more scope for sustained differentiation patterns (1) aimed at controlling congestion, but also (2) in view of legal or business constraints. To begin with, most customers typically have their maximum bandwidth restricted to a certain value—a crude first step to controlling the traffic volume seen by the ISP as a proxy for congestion management. Other, more focused discrimination has often been due to legal constraints and security concerns;[320] much more rarely is it due to poor dimensioning or intrinsically limited capacity.[321] Some cases have also been reported about prioritization schemes along the lines of delay versus throughput precedence considerations much like in the NSFNET Fuzzball scheme.[322] However, very little empirical evidence has yet been found for clandestine traffic discrimination along the lines typically lamented by 'network neutrality' proponents.[323] Thus, while there is some traffic differentiation to be found in the Internet,[324] the IP traffic that is being admitted to the Internet in the first place, and not dropped along the way,[325] is generally transmitted in a reasonably indiscriminate and transparent fashion.

Having discussed the existing mechanisms of dealing with the problem of congestion it is instructive to turn to a brief discussion of further possible remedies to the general problem of congestion management. In the foregoing, we have established that congestion in the Internet is controlled in a very loosely coupled manner[326] by (1) having end hosts adapt their transmission rates according to the packet losses they experience, and (2) having network routers drop IP packets by whichever policy they see fit, possibly (but not necessarily) aiming at some notion of fairness or utility maximization. With a nod to the basic taxonomy of congestion control approaches — "cooperative, authoritarian, and market solutions" (Nagle 1985, p. 5) — we may consider the former a cooperative solution, and the latter an authoritarian one.[327] The one solution that is conspicuously absent from the picture is one involving actual utilities and prices at the user level — 'maximizing the total happiness in the system' (or, 'the sum of the utilities of all the players', see Shakkottai and Srikant 2007). Theoretically, a perfect congestion management scheme would eradicate each and every unpriced externality, maximize the value of all participants to the Internet in the face of any congestion issues, and have congestion at precisely the economically efficient level considering all costs and benefits to building out capacity.[328] The proposal put forward by Briscoe et al. (2005) — "re-inserted explicit congestion notification", a scheme that would allow traffic policers in the access networks to govern the amount of 'congestion volume' a host may cause in downstream networks along the path to a destination host — holds considerable promise in making congestion a

Governance type	Resource allocation approach
Market	Prices for congestion volume as a function of demand and supply interactions
Common property	Global cooperation by voluntary back-off in the face of packet losses or explicit congestion signals
Network authority	Packet forwarding and discarding by authoritarian local rule and arbitrary considerations

Table 5.1: Framework for congestion control approaches

marketable commodity, and thus reduce the inefficiencies from unpriced congestion externalities and proxy solutions such as accounting for bandwidth rather than congestion. However, we are left to speculate whether such a scheme will ever make up for the costs of introducing it in the first place. After all, while incrementally deployable, it requires changes in the IP modules of a critical mass of hosts, as well as policer boxes in the edge networks.[329]

There is now considerable debate as to whether it is prudent to continue the absence of fine grained market mechanisms to address the issue of global congestion (Papadimitriou et al. 2009, pp. 7 ff.). And yet, while the ad hoc solutions, if not hacks, to the problem of congestion we have been left with thus far may only very crudely come anywhere near a perfect market scheme; they have worked reasonably well. In particular, they have worked without requiring any minimum complexity in the Internet, and without requiring any material conceptual linking between the end hosts and the Internet routers. The crucial point to note about congestion control schemes and traffic discrimination inside the Internet — be they based on tail drop packet discard or on any level of conceivable sophistication and statefulness about flows, traffic sources, and traffic destinations — is that they do not create any hard state inside the Internet that bears critical relevance to the end hosts other than with respect to varying performance or precedence considerations.

To conclude this section: the case of congestion control thus a curious example for the broader validity and nature of the end-to-end arguments — end hosts obtain a global congestion management scheme by 'virtual cooperation', for both their information and their resultant actions are, in fact, strictly local. While being subject to continuous criticism for not being the most optimal scheme to deal with congestion in the abstract, the Jacobson congestion avoidance and control scheme in conjunction with some very basic heuristics in packet discarding to achieve some fairness between different end hosts has provided a solid ground for containing congestion collapses even with the assumption of cooperation between end hosts becoming increasingly unrealistic.[330] A tighter control loop between end hosts and Internet routers might make for an improved congestion management; but, it would also increase the cross-dependencies between the two. Much like fragmentation has come to be handled by the hosts; it seems like congestion control is best managed by the hosts, too.

Also, it is important to note that the infeasibility of perfect market mechanisms to be applied to the problem of congestion at its root — the multitude of end hosts sharing scarce intermediate resources — does not imply that the problem cannot be solved at the host layer. Congestion remains a problem conceptually at the host level, not the inter-network level — much like tragedy of the commons type scenarios in general are about talking to the other stakeholders, and devising sustainable usage strategies in concert (rather than individually watching the grass vanish).[331] While the end hosts may be physically linked via mechanisms inside the Internet, the solution to the problem of congestion management lies not primarily (or even necessarily) in linking closer the logical operations of the end hosts to those of the Internet. Rather, it lies in linking closer together the operations of the hosts amongst one another, and have the utility trade-offs and tussles over surplus from Internet traffic play out at that level. Proper market mechanisms may or may not be applied to the congestion problem, eventually. But, as long as no such mechanisms come to be integrated with the Internet architecture at large, the current 'hack' of end based back-off, and Internet based approximation of basic utility concerns are bound to remain the core mechanisms to keep the problem of congestion in check.

Conclusion of Part II

It would be overbold to claim that our history of the Internet is anywhere near conclusive, and that it forms a sufficient basis to reason about the end-to-end arguments as a descriptive matter. And yet it is instructive to reconsider the evolution of the Internet as a set of case studies about the merit of the end-to-end arguments—because the end-to-end arguments are the most appropriate lens through which to reconstruct the events that shaped the Internet; they are the one body of principles that combines essential considerations about the position of functions with issues that go beyond mere technical appropriateness—they have been speaking to issues such as flexibility, open-endedness, end user empowerment in ways that few other principles do. The set of cases detailed in this part thus represent a genuinely useful and valuable research endeavor in their own right, notwithstanding any of the omissions they may have.[332] If we take the end-to-end arguments to be of any significance in the larger societal debates about the architecture of the Internet, then it must be by observing in due detail the history of its core artifacts that we can hope to make solid articulations with descriptive and normative power.

In summary, we may list the following core points as the main results of the two preceding chapters:

Importance of focal points In sections 4.1 and 4.2 we have considered the emergence of the inevitable core division of functionalities and general architecture that the notion of packet switching entails. Low level datagram services, possibly augmented by some error control protocols, can be implemented hop-by-hop; whereas higher level services, particularly end-to-end virtual circuit services can only be implemented in or very close to the end points that originate and terminate those services. Given that such services may be shared by several entities, we arrive at the notion of focal points (first articulated by Pouzin 1976*b*, see Figure 2.3 at page 19 and accompanying text), a prime example being the NCP or TCP module in a host computer. The precise place for such focal points is informed by two converse economies: (1) the economy of sharing network resources by packet switching dictates that the focal points at which higher level virtual services are derived from the low-level service not be too deep in the core of the network; and (2) the economy (and convenience) of sharing such high-level services in turn dictates that the focal points not be too close with the eventual application at the ultimate end points. There may be different such focal points in one system, and the specifics of the situation at hand may result in very different optimal positions for the focal points.

Futility of elaborate services at the network/host boundary We have recounted how it proved virtually impossible to offer a one size fits all lower-level service for all possible applications, fully satisfying each and every application requirement. Even a heroic effort on the part of the network to obtain and offer to hosts complete reliability will rarely suffice for applications requiring perfect reliability (e. g., binary file transfer) (section 4.4). Worse still, such efforts will be excessive for and may even impede those applications not needing perfect reliability in the first place (section 5.1). Hence the early evolution toward a 'raw' packet service leaving any reliability protocols to the ultimate communication ends (Arpanet raw messages and, of course, IP packets).

Cascadability and symmetry for open-endedness Adding to the above points, any elaboration beyond an easily cascadable network service inhibits the open-endedness of a network, in that its edges might potentially extend further outwards beyond the network/host interface (section 4.3). Such cascadability, in turn, speaks very much for symmetric networking modules as can be seen in the history of the IMP/Host interface elaborations in the Arpanet that anticipated much of the later symmetry in the IP protocol module.

End-to-end arguments beyond application completeness We have in sections 5.3 and 5.4 elaborated two cases — fragmentation and congestion control—which carry the core content of the end-to-end arguments to functions that are not intimately related the the actual applications at the network end points. The case for a strong division of functionalities thus extends to the apparent infeasibility (at least in these two cases) of linking the operations across trust and administrative boundaries by explicit interface in the first place.

In all, we have shown with ample historical references the emergence of the core of the end-to-end arguments—the strong case for moving the bulk of networking functions (in the Saltzer et al. 1984 sense of completeness and correctness) to a conceptual layer distinct from the forwarding/routing plane that is the inevitable province of any packet switching network (in the sense Davies 1966 and Baran 1964*d*). That distinct layer may then be used to institute focal points for higher level application use, and which may migrate arbitrarily close to the application end points even with network edges extending outwards away from any *one* network, but also may move 'inwards', away from the ultimate application end points, should the economies of sharing such focal point at the edges force it this way.

However, we have in this part also moved beyond the confines of the original end-to-end arguments articulation by Saltzer et al.—(1) by developing all of the above points in a level of detail that should make for a rather complete empirical account of many of the relevant threads and which may thus serve as a solid basis for future elaborations of individual aspects or the consideration of novel theoretical notions; and (2) by detailing the evolution of two functions not typically considered when elaborating the end-to-end arguments: fragmentation and congestion control. In the following part we will add to the end-to-end arguments by discussing (based on the evidence found here) the notion that there is very little scope for explicitly linking the operations of 'the network' and 'the end hosts', not merely due to concerns of application completeness and open endedness, but also plain technical feasibility. Also, we shall in the remainder of this thesis develop some ideas that should add to our deeper understanding of the ultimate invariants lying behind the vast array of empirical realities to the found in the Internet.

Part III

Toward a Theory of End-to-End Arguments

The only way that a pattern can actually help to make a situation genuinely more alive is by recognizing all the forces which actually exist, and then finding a world in which these forces can slide past each other.

— *Christopher Alexander (1979, p. 304)*

Chapter 6

Revisiting the Classic End-to-End Arguments

And the end of all our exploring will be to arrive where we started and know the place for the first time.

— *T. S. Eliot, Little Gidding*

The Internet—conceived in the mid-1970s, and put into wider-scale practice from the early 1980s—has to this day remained the commandingly dominant infrastructure for public data communication, with the core protocols largely unchanged ever since.[333] Yet this does not imply that the core principles of the Internet must have remained equally unchanged. In fact, it may well be that only by having principles adapt to the ever changing context of the Internet can we hope to say anything meaningful about it and understand which notions are truly invariable, and which ones only have been useful at a certain time, but are not necessarily anymore so.

The end-to-end arguments, "the closest thing that exists to a sacred text for the Internet architecture" (Clark et al. 2004, p. 67), have forever been part presumption, part descriptive principle, and part normative call in view of a set of central values that may be ascribed to the Internet. We have seen in Part I that they have been morphed continuously into ever higher-level statements about the proper position of functions in the Internet, and we have seen in Part II that most every episode from the history of the Internet at large may be usefully interpreted with the end-to-end arguments in mind. In this part we shall return to the quest of a meaningful formulation of the end-to-end arguments so as to maintain their relevance in a time when there have been increasing doubts about the applicability of the classic version to the reality of the Internet at large. While we are building on much of what we have detailed in the previous chapters, here we also take the liberty of advancing ideas that are yet to be fully understood and elaborated (let alone be proven).

This chapter starts out by revisiting the classic end-to-end arguments, a sobering exercise which leaves us with the conclusion that, as a logical argument, they collapse to little more than the recognition that a very limited set of functions — those that can be implemented completely and correctly in the end system without any regard whatsoever to the performance of intermediary communication nodes — best sits with the end hosts. Worse still, as we shall see in the second section of this chapter, the very notion of end points in the first place is almost meaningless in a system where most applications are spread throughout and end users are increasingly delegating major application state to third parties inside the Internet. We are thus left with little more than a vague intuition if not presumption that functions better sit with the end hosts when, in fact, they may as well sit at any other place given the various relevant trade-offs.

6.1 Limits of the Original Argument

In recent years, from ca. 1998 onwards, the end-to-end arguments have seen a steady broadening of scope, gradually turning into an architectural principle at the heart of several second-order objectives in line with certain philosophical premises of the Internet. Before turning to a discussion of the merit of such ever more normative versions based on ever more daring causalities we shall revisit the classic limits of the original descriptive end-to-end arguments, for it is useful to recall that their scope had, in fact, been rather limited in the beginning.

The canonical application of the end-to-end argument has first and foremost been to the simple problem of how to obtain a faithful reproduction of digital data sent from one 'end' of a connection to another 'end', with the two end points connected by a presumably unreliable, untrustworthy, 'thin wire' network. Sophisticated high level reasonings about the end-to-end arguments (such as those considered in Part I) notwithstanding, it bears noting that this is, of course, precisely the problem addressed by the TCP/IP Internet architecture. While it does not follow that TCP is necessarily a supreme protocol only because it neatly accords with a very basic version of the end-to-end arguments,[334] several important observations can be made about this commandingly most successful instantiation of the end-to-end 'principle':

1. TCP only addresses the problem of reliability as in integrity and completeness; it is not concerned about delay and throughput (other than in its strategies about timing out connections and relieving congestion by adapting its sending rate)

2. TCP is interested in no less than virtually perfect reliability; there is no way to specify through the TCP service interface the need for reliability to *some* standard in excess to what the network offers, the only option is *perfect* reliability.

The design of TCP thus addresses a very limited problem, that of obtaining a perfectly reliable virtual circuit from an unreliable datagram service; and it does so in a very general way, with no concern whatsoever about the ultimate applications or the semantics of the data they carry, and with no means for applications to vary the specifics of the service it provides them with.

It is, in fact, surprisingly difficult to relax the above observations about the design of TCP, for its neat generality and congruence with the end-to-end to arguments are very much tied to the case of perfect reliability without non-trivial regard to parameters like throughput and delay. The end-to-end arguments become rapidly more ambiguous (and less useful as a design principle) when considering the whole range of possible application requirements, for reliability is the only parameter that can be arbitrarily perfected by trivial end-to-end measures in the first place.[335] Throughput and delay may be monitored, but can only tangentially if at all be controlled by mechanisms in the end systems rather than in the network at large. True, by leaving the pursuit of perfect reliability to the end systems rather than a concatenation of intermediary packet switches, throughput and delay *may* be improved,[336] but only to the level that can be upheld by the network at large—there is very little an end system can do to improve its throughput on a given path, or the delay that results from the stochastic sharing of resources in the Internet. Blumenthal and Clark (2001) duly note, based on a personal communication with Jerome Saltzer:

> [F]rom the beginning, the end-to-end arguments revolved around requirements that could be implemented correctly at the end-points; if implementation inside the network is the only way to accomplish the requirement, then an end-to-end argument isn't appropriate in the first place. (p. 80)

Consequently, while the argument about applications with less than perfect reliability needs, but stricter delay and throughput needs (mostly, interactive voice applications) features very prominently in the end-to-end arguments literature, it is rarely elaborated in full — because there is nothing to elaborate, it depends on functions necessarily in the network, which the end-to-end arguments are necessarily silent about.[337]

Moreover, once we move beyond the application requirement of 'perfect reliability without regard to delay and throughput costs', and to more complex application specific requirement sets, it becomes comparatively harder to state those requirements in terms of simple parameters communicable through an interface of a shared transport protocol module such as TCP.[338] Both the protocol mechanisms and the broader management functions in support of more complex application level requirements will thus often have to be implemented at the very application level, rather than be delegated to a common host level transport protocol module. This may be deceptively simple for some cases of trivial request/response message communication; but, it may also have to be left for the user to control and implement their performance requirements by user level measures, thus reducing the end-to-end arguments in these cases to an arguably tautological user level version.[339]

In all, the design of TCP seems to indicate that the general principle connotated by the end-to-end argument is easiest applied to clear-cut either-or cases that lend themselves to 'complete and correct' end host implementation — reliable data transfer, extending to "encryption, duplicate message detection, message sequencing, guaranteed message delivery, detecting host crashes, and delivery receipts" (Saltzer et al. 1984, p. 278). The original end-to-end arguments only vaguely speak to the problem of how to design solutions for requirements that are (1) inherently more complex to specify and (2) are bound to non-trivial performance floors of network services.[340]

Adding to the above, there is another fundamental limitations to the end-to-end arguments as a conclusive principle for the position of functions in a network. Even the apparently safe case of perfect reliability acknowledges the importance of network level service performance in view of acceptable application performance.[341] Already, Licklider and Vezza (1978) noted:

> [I]t greatly simplifies most network applications if the network can be counted on to do the error handling. (p. 1340)

While we need not go so far as to require the network to do *all* the error handling, we may carry this reasoning further as a Gedankenexperiment, and postulate a 'network principle' in direct opposition to the 'end-to-end principle', stating that all application related functions should be implemented by the network, absent any efficiency or performance considerations to opposite effect. Given reasonably well-defined trade-offs, such a rule might produce the exact same architecture as does the end-to-end argument—even the 'unpriced' residual connotated with flexibility and option value ascribed to the end-to-end argument may under such rule be left to the end points.[342]

In conclusion, given the limitations of the end-to-end arguments and their ambiguity about leaving functions to the network if sensible reasons speak for doing so, it is fair to ask whether there is any end-to-end argument meriting the appellation of principle at all. Going beyond simple cases of application completeness and correctness (which, at that, are silent on the amount of functions that may be put in the network in support of the application end points) we are left with little more than the intuition that leaving functions to the end systems somehow maximizes the total value of the Internet given to the entire set of possible applications, by not privileging any one type of application over others with different or even conflicting needs. And, even this premise is questionable given that by *not* implementing certain functions the network prejudices against those applications that require features not amenable to implementation in the end systems.[343] A minimal inter-network protocol privileges applications without stringent real-time or rate requirements; to argue that such minimality serves all applications equally is to confuse that which we have with that which might be.[344]

To summarize, the original end-to-end arguments along with the canonical example of careful file transfer correctly argue that any desired level of reliability can only be achieved by having the end hosts implement the necessary functions themselves rather than relying on the underlying network to do so on their behalf. Also, this version very much decouples the end hosts' transport layer from the common inter-network layer, for it involves neither the communication of application requirements to the network, nor the monitoring of network performance. While one may consider this argument a principle of sorts, three caveats are in order. First, it is largely silent on the issues arising when application requirements put greater focus on delay and throughput optimization rather than reliability. While it may be that the lack of mandatory perfect reliability in the network service sufficiently improves the performance with respect to the other two parameters; applications can, in fact, do little more than monitor the performance they receive—adapting their rates and other protocol parameters to a certain degree, or give up in case of underruns. They may also switch between providers, but the exercise of such choices features only tangentially in both the original Internet design and the original end-to-end arguments formulation.[345] Second, it does not lend itself to strict categorical application; in fact, it explicitly allows for functions in the network—so as to resolve the various performance and cost trade-offs in the placement of functions (see the original Arpanet design, sections 4.1 through to 4.3). Third, and arguably, it barely goes beyond existing notions of end user sovereignty and considerations of consumer utility functions in general, and thus reduces to a tautological user level argument with very little technical content.

Having said all that, it is important to note that we are not per se questioning the validity of some of the design choices typically attributed to the end-to-end arguments; yet we question their instrumentality in arriving at certain distributions of functions. It might be that other principles, or reformulations of the end-to-end arguments offer a better framework to explain some of the existing design and anticipate useful future design choices—an exercise we take up in chapter 7. Before turning to this endeavor, however, we will in the following section elaborate on the increasingly unrealistic yet quite typical assumption of fixed and well-defined end points, combining the application end point and its user in one very physical place.[346] We have observed in section 3.3 that the scope of the original end-to-end arguments has gradually collapsed horizontally toward a small core of potent IP modules which at a higher level enlarge the application end point to an ever broader scope ranging from the ultimate users to a distributed set of agents across the network. It is, indeed, striking to see just how elusive the line the line between 'network' and 'applications'—the core premise behind any meaningful end-to-end argument—has become, or may, in fact, have always been.

6.2 The Elusive Notion of End Points

Many considerations about the merit of end-to-end arguments, including most of ours in the previous section, assume an unambiguous dichotomy between 'networking' (moving bits from A to B), on the one hand; and 'applications' (the actual uses of this service), on the other hand. While such a distinction is useful in understanding the general issues involved in networking—the "semantic aspects of communication are irrelevant to the engineering problem" (Shannon 1948, p. 379)—, it is equally useful to relax this very dichotomy in order to appreciate some of the inevitable overlap between the two notions, especially in a rather mature real-world network where application demands shape much of the underlying communication system. For not only is it that application end points migrate ever deeper into the Internet and away from their ultimate end users, it is fair to argue that *any* service that the network renders to its end users is inextricably specific to the ultimate applications: no design decision can ever be entirely value neutral, even the most undisputed augmentations ensue economic and social prejudices that directly bear on the viability and respective attractiveness of different applications and uses.[347]

Adding to those basic philosophical concerns about the nature of lower level common services of a network, there is a very tangible concern about the often sizable economy of shared application level state in the network—many applications have come to depend on some shared state managed by an intermediary third party, and there is often strong economy in sharing application level functions or delegating them to parties better equipped than the ultimate end (Clark and Blumenthal 2007; see also our section 3.3). Conversely, the 'ultimate end' of a communication effort is increasingly becoming an elusive entity, not only because functions move to third parties in the Internet, but also because the congruence between end *user* and end *host* is rapidly vanishing with the advent of increased mobility and a multitude of 'end' devices per user.[348] Ironically, while end users are pushing ever more functions to intermediaries inside the network, the province of networking functions proper becomes ever smaller, for every function beyond the most minimal effort datagram forwarding gets laden with application and user specificity and thus becomes subject to continuous tussles that have little in common with the innocent trade-offs found in the original end-to-end arguments.

When Saltzer et al. put forward the notion of end-to-end arguments they acknowledged that finding the relevant end points to begin with requires great care and diligence. It turns out that finding good end points has become an increasingly hard exercise, for applications have become ever more interwoven with remote third parties in the network and have come to depend on certain (sometimes) tacit network characteristics. Aiming to add to this crucial part of the discussion, we shall in the remainder of this section do three things: (1) look at the continuum of possible definitions for the Internet in the first place, (2) consider the typical sophistications of application level structures, and (3) consider how those structures integrate with a broader notion of the Internet.

At least since the Internet turned from a research exercise in the 1970s to an operational network in the 1980s there has been the question of what actually defines 'the Internet'. At a most basic level, of course, the Internet is no more than a "roughly transitive closure of IP-speaking systems" (as cited in Clark et al. 1991, p. 10) with no performance specifications whatsoever. As long as a non-zero percentage of IP packets makes it from IP module A to IP module B, those two entities are part of the Internet.[349] However, this definition is very much useless if we give even the slightest consideration to actual application needs. Any useful notion of the Internet thus requires a minimum performance criterion—even if it is only probabilistic—that allows *interactive* communication by some reasonable measure, rather than asynchronous communication only (Quarterman and

Carl-Mitchel 1996, pp. 5 ff.).[350] To this end *some* reasonable performance beyond best effort as in 'no effort at all' is clearly required — a "customary packet delivery service" (Clark 2009*b*, p. 10) rather than a no effort Internet service.[351]

Application	Throughput requirement
Transaction processing	<9.6 kbps
Messaging/text applications	<9.6 kbps
Voice	<9.6 kbps
Location services	9.6 kbps
Still image transfer	14.4 to 28 kbps
Internet/VPN access	28 kbps
Database access	28 kbps
Enhanced Web surfing	28 to 64 kbps
Low-quality video	28 to 64 kbps
HiFi audio	28 to 64 kbps
Large file transfer	64 kbps
Moderate video	64 to 144 kbps
Interactive entertainment	144 to 384 kbps
High-quality video	384 kbps

Table 6.1: Throughput requirements for at least adequate performance of various applications; Source: Adapted from Stallings (2007, p. 13, Fig. 1.1)

Adding to this quantitative concern, there has been a longstanding appreciation of (1) the possibility of partial connectedness of IP modules, largely due to local policy considerations, and (2) the application level structure of the Internet and how it bears on the definition of just what the Internet is. Clark et al. (1991) thus include in their definition systems with "partial IP connectivity, restricted by policy filters" as well as systems with "e-mail connectivity to the Internet, whether or not a mail gateway or mail object transformation is required" (p. 10).[352] The crucial point with this broader definition is that transitive IP connectivity is not mandatory to being part of the Internet — in fact, arbitrary connections between Application Level Gateways (ALGs) and end host applications will do.[353]

Another important if not vital aspect of the Internet 'up the stack' has been the name resolution typically required to obtain a routable IP address of a desired service (or *any* address, for that matter) in the first place. Without a standard means to dynamically map from largely invariable and static names to arbitrary and volatile addresses the Internet would still 'work as advertised'—but it would clearly entail a significant burden for host applications to keep track of any pertinent address changes.[354] Thus it could be argued that a broad notion of the Internet would best be conceived not primarily as a set of *applications connectivity* graphs beyond the 'core Internet', but as a *name-based application level scope* that is bound only loosely to any topological addresses, at whichever layer of abstraction (Piscitello and Chapin 1993, pp. 526 ff.). In such a setting, the defining moment of the Internet would be the names of services plus ways to resolve these names into addresses, not the physical addresses of IP modules, or source routes (also referred to as 'bang paths') to email recipients outside the core Internet.[355]

Finally, it is useful to consider two additional functions that typically feature much less prominently, but clearly are of significant concern when thinking about the usefulness of a network from the perspective of applications: (1) routing—the function of obtaining routes from an IP module A to an IP module B subject to a given set of optimization criteria;[356] and (2) caching—the intermediate storage of data some place between A and B, either on their explicit behalf, or as a contingent and transient artifact of the data transmission function.[357]

In sum, it is, in principle, possible to conceive the Internet as a "roughly transitive closure of IP-speaking systems" without any regard to functions 'up the stack' (or beside IP) that are critical for any reasonable application use; yet some functions have proven so vital to the Internet that it would be clearly imprudent to exclude them from a consideration of the invariables that have come to serve the bulk of applications on the Internet. To summarize on the above we may venture a list of canonical functions beyond mere IP packet forwarding which (1) may from an end host perspective reasonably be considered part of the network 'in between' the ultimate end points of an application, and which (2) offer very specific services to the application end points at large, thus helping to extend the application end points to 'inside' the Internet:

Name to address resolution possibly featuring multiple iterations at multiple conceptual levels, with names typically applying to objects such as subscribers, hosts, ports, and services.[358]

Address to route resolution which may be anything from static, to dynamic, to 'just in time' binding; with the locus of control anywhere between the ultimate end users and the network nodes performing the actual data forwarding.

Intermediate storage of data both transient and permanent; at explicit user control or at contingent necessity; and at any level from IP packets to application level payloads.

This simple (if vague) taxonomy[359] offer a very useful means of accommodating the host of real world applications that feature some level of intermediation — from classic email,[360] to the World Wide Web (WWW),[361] to Google's ubiquitous Web search,[362] to Akamai's CDNs and routing overlays,[363] to typical VoIP services,[364] to RIM's 'push' email service[365] — much more meaningful than a simple interpretation in terms of IP and TCP ever could. Note that the level of intermediation complexity in these applications (briefly elaborated in notes 360 through 365) is hardly exceptional; rather, "it is possible that all applications may work in this way in the future, and the need for universal end-to-end transport connectivity will vanish" (Clark 2009*f*, p. 42). In fact, our casual history of Internet applications indicates a common pattern of applications starting out as strictly end-based, with no performance enhancing functions delegated to third parties in between the ultimate end users; later dissolving into a complex application level structure in which substantial intermediary functions along the lines put forward above come to integrate more tightly with the network than would be possible in a mere end-based structure. Even applications with a prominent emphasis on end user autonomy about content management and dissemination typically benefit from some functional network integration — see the current developments toward P2P systems integrating with ISPs so as to optimize the traffic patterns needed to support the P2P application (Aggarwal et al. 2007; Griffiths et al. 2009).

In all, there seems to be a solid case for an extended set of basic functional building blocks beyond the mere Internet Protocol, which in turn indicates the merit of a conceptual augmentation of the current core Internet design so as to explicitly acknowledge for the useful existence of logical intermediaries as "first class citizens" rather than as physical interposition 'hacks' only (Walfish et al. 2004). In fact, the assumption of the irreducible centrality of a universally scoped "transitive closure of IP-speaking systems" may ultimately prove to be a "false" (and thus redundant) "global agreement", rather than a "basic tenet of the stable IP platform" (Clark 2009*a*, p. 10).[366] The seminal case in point here is Internet email — it has always been largely immaterial for the operation of the distributed email application at large, in which way an email client connects to its email server, or in which way email servers pass on emails to other servers. The prime spanning layer for email is not IP, but the application level protocols behind email.[367] Another example is WWW — given suitable gateway integration, it is entirely immaterial for a user whether their web browser uses TCP, UDP or an ad-hoc avian carrier protocol underneath the HTTP protocol, much less whether those are implemented using IP or any other lower level protocol.

The important conclusion regarding the end-to-end arguments is that they better acknowledge the rich application level structure that characterizes today's applications much of which is thoroughly integrated in the Internet infrastructure at large,[368] lest they risk losing their broader relevance. It is neither useful nor innocent to insist that the only valid interpretation and normative use of the end-to-end arguments is that which goes along with the canonical example of file transfer between two end points. For not only are the actual 'user ends' increasingly removed from the 'application end points' as seen from a more classic end-to-end arguments perspective; also, it is fair to argue in outlook that along with this detachment the notion of reasonably fixed application end points is gradually giving way to a more encompassing store and forward application protocol paradigm that renders increasingly futile the notion of distinct end points altogether.[369] There is often substantial merit in 'violating' categorical "broad" versions,[370] and even mixing some semantic aspects of application level communication uses with the engineering of networking functions proper. Put differently, while there is merit in a low level perspective from which every application level function is deemed to be with 'end' hosts, even if they are 'inside' the Internet; the more relevant discussion surely comes from a high level take at which functions exhibit certain patterns of distribution, often across trust boundaries. The original end-to-end argument may not have considered such application level structure, but it would be imprudent to leave such elaborations out of modern (re)formulations. More important still, we come to the conclusion that the end-to-end arguments as such — no matter how they are framed — hardly suffice to explain the distribution of functions found in the Internet. In fact, as we shall see in the following chapter, there is substantial value in elaborating the broader context of other principles that also speak to the problem of where to position functions of networking.

Chapter 7

Toward a Systematic Analysis

Any [. . .] rule will always operate in combination and often in competition with other rules or dispositions and with particular impulses; and whether a rule will prevail in a particular case will depend on the strength of the propensity it describes and of the other dispositions or impulses operating at the same time.

— *Friedrich August von Hayek (1973, pp. 75 f.)*

It is highly unlikely that a rule or principle, even if declared to be an axiom, will suffice to speak conclusively to any non-trivial issues in a large, complex, and distributed real-world system. This is so in law,[371] in architecture,[372] and there is little reason to be believe it not to be so in network architecture. After all, a principle is a principle not because it amounts to an absolute truth, but because it offers a rough rule of thumb about how to go about solving a particular design problem. Such principles are on the one hand informed by existing patterns, and on the other hand they maintain those patterns by giving them name and articulation, thus rendering them fit for discourse, development, and contestation.[373]

We have in the previous chapter established that even if the end-to-end arguments are applied to trivial problems of application completeness, they are subject to a whole host of qualifications and exceptions — while it might be possible to ascertain a meaningful application end point and a way of implementing a given function 'completely and correctly' with that end point, a significant amount of non-orthogonal intelligence and state is bound to remain with the intermediary network, nevertheless. The more so, if we go beyond functions that can be fully implemented on top of an arbitrarily poor service datagram network in the first place. Also, we have in Part II considered many of the developments from the pre-Arpanet notions of networking to today's Internet, establishing a solid empirical foundation to reason about the end-to-end arguments as a function of and informing device for actual practices rather than mere theoretical reasoning.

We are thus in a good position to inquire about the deeper underlying reasons and forces that determine the eventual balance of functions between end points and network intermediary nodes — the principles that valuably accompany the end-to-end arguments. While we have throughout the thesis touched briefly on some of the determinants that combine with the end-to-end arguments to more fully inform the placement of functions, this chapter offers a more focused analysis of the issue. In particular, we add to the systematic interpretation of the end-to-end arguments the following two core notions:

1. We observe, by revisiting some of the problems raised in chapter 5 (Letting Go), that even where there is theoretical scope for (and where one would expect) explicit cooperation between end points and network intermediaries, virtually every discrete and self-sufficient function is conclusively implemented in either the end nodes at the end-to-end layer or the intermediary nodes, very rarely in both (though several functions may combine with complementary effects). We theorize about the reasons for this exclusiveness, advancing a principle which may be called 'interface complexity avoidance' or 'prohibitive costs to explicit interfaces between ends and network nodes in the Internet'.

2. Extending on the above, we put forward a set of principles that add to the end-to-end arguments in speaking to the ultimate position of functions, but also to the actual choice of functions in the first place and the balance of functions, if any. Thus we can further theorize on the proper role and scope of end-to-end arguments in a system of surrounding principles, all of which, depending on the specifics of the context at hand, speak to the choice, placement, and implementation of networking functions.

7.1 Beyond Reliability

It has remained an oddity about the end-to-end arguments that despite all their clarity and elegance in abstract, for the most part they rely on the very trivial if not perfunctory reliability example, plus a set of functions of networking that immediately pertain to the applications using the network in the first place — end-to-end encryption, reordering, acknowledgments, and the like. In fact, from the perspective of the high level abstract argument they make sense only in those cases (Blumenthal and Clark 2001; see also our page 114), and we have noted in section 6.1 that it is hard to uphold even those arguably trivial versions. However, while such limitation of the end-to-end arguments' scope is useful in upholding their integrity as a logical principle, and while TCP offers a reasonable example for a successful application of the end-to-end arguments, not only does such limitation little to clarify how the end-to-end 'argument' informs the balance between end points and network for functions it properly claims to apply to; it also remains silent on the whole gray area of functions that may *not* be perfectly implemented in the end points, and about which there is a subtle choice of how to distribute the overall function across the continuum between end points and network intermediary nodes.

For example, should the end points have exclusive control over routing? Probably they should;[374] alas, despite all efforts to give end users more mechanisms to effect routing policies of their choice,[375] they are typically left with choosing no more than the first outbound router for their IP packets. It is instructive to consider why this is so, an exercise we take up in this section. Also, with reference to sections 5.3 and 5.4, it is instructive to consider in a related exercise why, for that matter, functions such as fragmentation and congestion control have largely become the province of end points rather than intermediary nodes. These functions are bound to the network ends in more subtle ways than the perfunctory examples typically cited along with the end-to-end arguments, for they logically pertain to the operation of the network rather than the completeness and correctness of applications at its end points — accordingly, the end-to-end arguments have traditionally been silent on them. While one may simply remove such examples by definition from the scope of the end-to-end arguments (Blumenthal and Clark 2001),[376] we believe that no such limitation is fundamental to the merit of a descriptive notion of the end-to-end arguments with such cases. After all, as we have discussed in section 6.2, application ends typically rely, at least implicitly, on functions that they cannot implement all by themselves — if all such cases were removed from the scope of a descriptive end-to-end principle, then there would be very little left that the end-to-end arguments would properly speak to, at all.[377]

In this section we shall put forward the notion that many functions shift toward the end points *not* due to their intrinsic need or desire to assume them, but due to the infeasibility of creating a general and stable enough interface between the hosts and the network with respect to functions that cannot be completely implemented inside the network without any control input from or reporting to the end hosts. Conversely, all those discrete functions that cannot be implemented to sufficient degree in the end points will go to the province of intermediary nodes alone, provided they can implement them sufficiently well — the underlying pattern yet again being that an explicit interface for cooperation across trust boundaries is too costly and cumbersome to remain stable. This section may be taken as a complement to section 6.1 in which we argued that the necessary complexity of the interface control communication required to obtain more flexible services from a common end-to-end protocol largely forecloses the feasibility of sophisticated service variation. Here we argue that a comparable problem of interface complexity forecloses sophisticated interfacing between the end hosts and intermediary network nodes so as to perform networking functions by explicit cooperation.

In the remainder of this section we shall look at the empirics of the horizontal distribution of various functions of networking — (1) briefly revisiting the cases of fragmentation and congestion management, (2) considering in some detail the case of routing, and (3) generalizing to application level functions at large. Moreover, we will comment on the implications for the proper interpretation of end-to-end arguments — (1) drawing conclusions about the firm exclusiveness of functions leaning either to the network or the end points, but rarely explicitly bridging both at the same time, and (2) close by noting the need for end-to-end arguments to make statements about functions evidently part of an application end point, but at once placed firmly inside the Internet and controlled by implicit means only.

It is instructive to start out by recalling from section 5.3 (The Rift over Fragmentation) that the core problem with inter-network fragmentation was the logical linkage it would create between hosts and network — thus limiting their conceptual independence and impairing future evolution in either sphere. Also, recall from section 5.4 (Higher Loads and Hidden Hacks) that any elaborate back and forth between the hosts and the network in an effort to control congestion may not only be cumbersome, but also render the whole effort of solving the congestion problem futile.[378] Instead, whenever the network needs to fragment packets for onwards transmission, or discard them in the face of congestion, it has come to do so without involving the hosts — packets are reassembled (or otherwise put back into initial shape) by an egress gateway of the network they were fragmented for (or otherwise adapted), and packet losses are left for the hosts to be discovered by themselves rather than by explicit information from the network. Accordingly, the hosts have come to adopt strategies of finding the maximum packet size that a given path will bear transparently, and adapt their transmission rates so as to minimize packet losses due to congestion. Those two functions demonstrate very clearly the merit of end based solutions to problems not immediately related to the actual applications using the network. They also demonstrate that functions generally tilt towards either that end points or the network, and any cooperation is achieved by implicit control signals, rarely explicit ones.

Another case of a function that is not intimately related to the ultimate applications is that of routing. While routing is generally implemented 'inside' the network, our argument of interface complexity avoidance holds here, too; it just leads to the opposite result to the two cases considered above: the functions have mostly come to sit with the network rather than its end points.[379] The principal difference between fragmentation and congestion control on the one hand, and routing on the other, is that routing in any non-trivial partially connected mesh topology network almost invariably involves part of the overall function to be explicitly performed by the network nodes.[380] The three distinct but closely related subtasks to the problem of routing — (1) exchange of connectivity information, (2) computations thereupon, and (3) choice of next hop and overall path — combine to a set of tasks not readily performable by the end hosts alone. Ultimately, the choice in routing is that about which end-to-end path across multiple hops to use for one's data communication. While it is possible to make such choice in the end systems, in any larger network spanning different administrative domains it is generally necessary to do this on the basis of reasonably current global connectivity information.[381] Such information typically resides in the network nodes; and while one might poll the network nodes from and do the overall connectivity and route computation in the end systems,[382] such approach would scale very poorly, be extremely inefficient (to the point of uselessness), and easily fail to find good routes even in the face of perfectly reasonable connectivity between two end points. The exchange of information about connectivity and other routing related data, and the calculation of connectivity graphs based thereupon, has therefore been mostly the province of network nodes. The end hosts would simply inject their data into the network, possibly along with some routing related performance parameters (priority, throughput, delay, cost, etc.) and leave the detailed routing to the network nodes. Typically, thus, the function of routing gets implemented on a router-to-router basis inside the Internet, with next to no interaction between routers and end hosts (other than the end hosts possibly choosing the very router they directly connect to).

In sum, all three cases considered above support our argument that the continuum of function position between end hosts and network is heavily skewed to either ends, depending on the respective merit and cost of placing a function at one or the other end — functions like fragmentation have moved to the end points, routing has moved to the network, and congestion control is implemented by separate functions in the network and the end hosts. More specifically, it seems fair to argue that even though many of these functions are entirely reasonable augmentations to the best effort (as in, potentially, no effort) Internet service, there is virtually no scope for explicit cooperation between end hosts and network proper via the common IP interface in jointly implementing these functions. Not only has it proven next to impossible to sustain the explicitness of any part of the IP interface that is not strictly necessary for the irreducible core task of the Internet at large — forwarding packets closer to their ultimate destination —, [383] for those cases in which there is something reasonable the network can do about service requests of the hosts (which may not be many), the complexity and attendant costs of any ensuing control communication between network and host may easily thwart the whole effort. The same goes for the delegation of functions from the network toward the end hosts. Thus there have been few if any instances of explicit co-operation between the Internet at large and the hosts at its ends — an issue that has been nicely illustrated by the demise of both IP options and ICMP messages.[384] Absent explicit and trustworthy control signals both sides resort to implicit cues, loosely inferring relevant information from the context at hand rather than by explicit protocol — e. g., as we have discussed in section 5.4, end hosts adapt their sending rates based on packet loss rates rather than explicit congestion feedback, and routers base forwarding decisions on TCP port numbers rather than values set in the IP ToS field.[385]

While this dynamic of function placement is interesting in itself, a further instructive observation that bears directly on the end-to-end arguments can be made about functions 'in' the network as opposed to at its edges: Returning to our example of routing, while most of the constituent tasks take place 'horizontally inside' the network, they do so in a manner that is conceptually ('vertically') detached from the best effort packet forwarding mechanism at the heart of the IP protocol. Thus the entire set of routing functions may as well be assumed on top of plain IP, by a distributed host level mechanism sufficiently omnipresent so as to render superfluous any elaborate routing efforts by routers themselves.[386] Put differently, while routing is a functions of the network in that it is not amenable to do without horizontally going 'inside' the network, it need neither be implemented as part of a common inter-network protocol nor even in dedicated router-to-router protocols — in the extreme, it may be fully assumed by a distributed machinery at the host level proper, reaching horizontally into the network at large.[387] Such machinery may then also address related concerns, those that may be *specified* by the end hosts, but cannot be *implemented* all by themselves — from routing preferences related to cost, security, etc., to specific QoS expectations regarding throughput, delay, availability, etc., to dedicated application level functions such as caching, name resolution, anycast, etc. In all these cases host level structures that achieve a variety of functions not amenable to implementation in the classic end-to-end horizontal form may feasibly be imposed on the plain IP inter-network.

It bears noting, however, that moving 'up the stack' does *not* typically alleviate the concerns about interface complexity between end hosts and network at large — a function residing at a higher layer does not make it easier to contain the complexity of control communication necessary for explicit cooperation between end hosts and network intermediaries. Returning yet again to our case of routing (pages 129 f.), this time at the 'host layer', not the 'inter-network layer', we observe that while explicit communication of control information and the maintenance of complex dynamic state on behalf of the ultimate end hosts is generally more feasible here, the very control communication itself often reduces to one-off out-of-band negotiations of some expected service parameters and contractual obligations between one 'end host' and a third party offering the host level service in question.[388] The actual data communication henceforth is no different than any other IP communication in the Internet at large — any necessary discrimination or control information will be gathered from implicit contexts such as IP addresses or port numbers, no changes to the applications using the service are necessary.[389] In all, due to the attendant complexities there is little scope for explicit cooperation between ends and network, no matter whether at the common IP level or at a distributed host layer.[390] Even at the host layer it seems that only the simplest control structures and choices are generally feasible.[391]

Extending the thread of arguments elaborated in chapter 3 (page 32 and pages 42 f.), we may draw the following argument about functions beyond those typically connotated with end-to-end data transfer reliability:

Argument 3 *While it is possible and often intuitively sensible to involve entities inside the Internet with functions of networking on performance, efficiency, or completeness grounds, it is rarely possible to devise an explicit interface that is stable and flexible enough to warrant wider-spread use for proper end host application based delegation and control. The distribution of functions in networking is thus heavily skewed toward end hosts even where there is ample scope for explicit cooperation. And, any cooperation between end hosts and network entities — no matter at which level or layer — is best based on loose implicit hints, tacit focal points, and host level out-of-band negotiation rather than explicit signals part of a common protocol. Devising such solutions is a non-trivial venture, and leaves ample scope for entrepreneurial activities as well as attendant tussles between end users and potential intermediaries.*

To conclude this section, there seem to be considerable empirical indications that the end-to-end arguments apply to various functions of networking other than reliability to the standard of application end points. In many cases, functions come to sit with the end hosts, even when they are not intimately related with the applications therein. In other cases, it is more viable to leave functions to the network, even when they are very much related to the applications in the end hosts. Either way, there is very little scope for explicit cooperation across trust boundaries, hence all those functions with even minimum relevance for the end points coupled with reasonable economy of implementation with the end points firmly fall to the network edges rather than the network nodes.[392]

Thus, while the end-to-end arguments make for a fitting 'title of a story', it seems fair to argue that in and of themselves they offer very little logical explanation about the actual causes of their validity. We have in this section offered our presumption that the costs of delegation and the ensuing complexity of a proper control interface are crucial factors in determining the eventual outcome of the distribution of the various functions of networking. In the next section, we will carry this reasoning further still, and put forward a broader framework of principles and rules that add to the end-to-end arguments in speaking to the proper position of functions in the Internet.

7.2 Beyond End-to-End Arguments

Complex systems in their entirety can only be understood by abstraction and reasoned about by reference to principles. Rarely, however, does one principle alone offer sufficient scope for useful and non-trivial abstraction from real-world intricacies. More often, it is several, possibly conflicting principles, constraints, and institutions that capture the essence of structure and dynamics of large distributed systems. 'Internet architecture'[393] much like classic architecture in general, is not primarily about the application of singular codified principles; instead it is properly about observing the *systems* of patterns in existing artifacts. Any codified principle — no matter how formally arrived at, and no matter how much empirical reality it commands — is only ever a minor and tentative part in an overall trade-off about the proper application of a whole host of principles which evades conclusive mechanic description (Alexander 1979).[394] Hence in 'Internet architecture' it is as futile to insist on the strict universality of any one principle in isolation, without considering other principles with which it combines to a system of principles that can only be applied with creative judgement to a given purpose.

Arguably, it is fair to consider a number of rules that were evidently critical in the early work on the Internet—as axioms or premises rather than more malleable principles. First, the notion of *packet switching* and flexible multiplexing, in the concrete shape of *datagram networking* may safely be taken as a given.[395] Note Postel et al. (1981):[396]

> The key decision in the design of the ARPA Internet Protocol is the choice of a datagram basis rather than a virtual circuit basis. (p. 269)

Second, there were the very much related notions that almost arbitrary existing as well as future networks could be part of the Internet, regardless of and with no need to change their internal operations (the Internet thus being transparent to them)—which would be achieved by having end hosts and *gateways* implement a *simple* and *unreliable* inter-network protocol in a largely decentralized fashion.[397]

Moving to the realm of principles, however, there is much less clarity about their respective merits, interplay, and hierarchy—even when talking about widely acknowledged ones like layering and complexity avoidance, to name but two. The end-to-end arguments, as we have elaborated in Part I, have over time come to be widely considered the defining if vague normative principle to govern the Internet, often considered vis à vis economic and business trade-offs and legal constraints that are understood to challenge the end-to-end 'nature' of the Internet (IAB 2004) and its original transparency (Carpenter 2000). Yet, as we have already noted,[398] the end-to-end arguments are notoriously prone to overly broad interpretations that border the tautological rather than the empirical, and may thus fail to qualify as proper principles. Instead of formulating ever vaguer principles it shall be more conducive to try and map a system of principles that pertain to the field of end-to-end issues at large—principles that serve useful purposes, are broadly applicable, and go beyond the tautological.[399] In this section we shall thus elaborate the field of principles (as opposed to vague normative concerns) pertaining to the end-to-end arguments, so as to appreciate their systematic role, and inform any broader normative principles that might be drawn from the end-to-end arguments.

It is not trivial to choose from the host of principles (or related such notions that can be found in the literature) a set of principles and concerns that suffice to inform the problem of the proper placement and potential movements of functions in a distributed network such as the Internet.[400] Extending on the considerations about interface complexity avoidance as a critical factor in shaping the balance of function placement in the Internet section 7.1, in this section we propose the following set; we feel that they combine to speak to the placement of functions in far greater depth and detail than the end-to-end arguments alone:[401]

1. original end-to-end arguments and economic efficiency concerns,
2. modularity, minimal coupling, and layering,
3. best effort and least privilege,
4. cascadability and symmetry,
5. running code, complexity avoidance, and rough consensus.

We shall elaborate them in turn.

First, as has been noted by Saltzer et al. (1981*a*), the end points to a data communication are the only places that can specify in arbitrary detail the end-to-end service they require, and are thus the natural place for the complete and correct implementation of functions that do not depend on certain service guarantees by the subnetwork. Non-essential functions added to the common network service may not only prove redundant, but may also add considerable overhead to the network that might have to be borne by all end points, not only those who need the service. Apart from adding costs and inefficiencies, doing so may reduce the generality, flexibility, and scalability of the network at large.[402] While this general rule makes sense for arguably clear-cut cases such as that of perfect reliability (as a function of the network versus in the end hosts), it offers very limited advice on the more granular placement of functions on performance and cost trade-off grounds (see section 6.1, pages 114 f.). It thus relies loosely on what boils down to a marginal cost analysis so as to arrive at proper quantitative values for the level of effort to be placed at the several possible places. However, in general it is very hard to find proper values for the cost and benefit figures to apply to such analysis—they may depend on the application, the opportunity costs of the players involved, and are generally likely to change over time. Thus, at the one extreme, such analysis results in no functions other than random unreliable forwarding of data packets to be in the network; at the other extreme, hosts would be left with no function other than accessing a set of network defined application interfaces at the sole discretion of the network. In all, while the classic end-to-end arguments speak to some concerns of functions placement, they are hardly sufficient to resolve the problem of function placement in a dynamic, large-scale network subject to a multitude of stakeholders with possibly conflicting concerns. However, they are nevertheless central to the overall trade-off of function placement as we shall argue toward the end of this section.

Second, the placement of functions in the Internet has been shaped to significant extent by the notion of layering,[403] as well as the notion of modularity more generally (Parnas 1972; Stevens et al. 1974)[404]—in particular as it goes along with the horizontal stretch across spatial distances and administrative domains.[405] Whereas the abstraction of layering is not a strict necessity for a communications network,[406] it has proven an extraordinarily powerful means of (1) reasoning about common conceptual levels of functionality across a horizontally distributed set of network nodes and application hosts in the first place, and (2) organizing functions and their interfaces so as to obtain a vertical hierarchy of functions that affords a versatile, robust, and scalable general architecture.

At its core, the layered architecture of the Internet reduces to three layers—that which is below the common spanning layer, the spanning layer, and that which is above the spanning layer—of which only the second is by definition a global common standard (the Internet Protocol).[407] Notwithstanding the pertinent trade-offs in the optimal design of the spanning layer, it is difficult to overstate the success of the hourglass structure obtained by having the Internet Protocol as minimal as it turned out to become.[408] In particular, the Internet Protocol—the narrow waist of the hourglass—results in an irreducibly minimal coupling between the functions above and below itself.[409] All an application can ask for via the IP interface is for the Internet to move its data to a given destination, with no guarantees about rate, delay, and loss rates; and, accordingly, all a network can do is forward packets based on the address information in the IP header, indiscriminate of the actual content or application.[410] It has to this day proven futile to extend the basic Internet architecture as defined by the IP protocol and interfaces so as to support anything beyond classic best effort service in a standardized and explicit manner.[411] Thus the IP protocol not only separates the communication peers at either end of the network, it generally maintains a firm separation between the entities above and below it. Arguably, the costs to this structural separation by the de facto complete absence of control data through the IP protocol has been more than offset by the ensuing flexibility and scalability of the system as a whole. At least, this is what may be concluded by the overwhelming success of the Internet over competing systems. In all, the layering principle in its effection of an irreducibly minimal coupling of the distributed entities that form the Internet at large is one of its evidently most vital principles.

Third, the principles of best effort and least privilege seem to be crucial complements to the layering principle in obtaining the degree of robustness that is necessary for scaling a system with a heterogeneous set of stakeholders and accordingly distributed administrative control. While layering and modularity speak to the arrangement of different conceptual levels and the separation of entities along horizontal lines, best effort and least privilege place a firm upper bound on the actual level of interdependency along both vertical lines of interface and horizontal lines of protocol. We have observed as a matter of descriptive fact that the spanning layer of the Internet, the IP protocol, offers next to no means of passing control information or guaranteeing certain levels of services; but it is the principles of best effort and least privilege that explain why that result has been a stable outcome.

Best effort — meaning not only that every party is doing 'its best', but also that every party "expects only as much from the processes upon which it depends" (Metcalfe 1973, p. 6-26) — helps the Internet survive virtually any failure in any of its constituent entities.[412] While there are various more or less tacit assumptions, functional bindings on statistical grounds, and even hard bilateral state; at the bottom, it is failure, not functioning, that is the default expectation for any of the core Internet protocols. Unlike an operating system, there is thus no way that the Internet may fail so as to completely abort any operation, no matter if any of its constituent parts happen to fail. It is fair to argue that the principle of best effort has been a conspicuously central one, not only in the design of the Internet, but in that of the earlier Arpanet, too.[413]

Least privilege, on the other hand, — meaning that no entity must impact others any more than is strictly necessary (Saltzer 1974) —[414] reduces the ways in which the failure or misbehavior of any one part can affect other parts of the system in the first place. As for the Internet, it means that neither is there much scope for end hosts to affect the operation of a router, nor is there much scope for routers to interfere with the operations of the end hosts.[415] Generally, the only control variable that a router accepts as relevant input from the end hosts is the destination address part of the IP packets; and, conversely, the only control information that an end host accepts as input from the routers is the "destination unreachable" message — neither of which offers much potential for horizontal privilege escalation, or adverse effects between IP modules, more generally. In fact, the principle of least privilege would explain why both IP options and ICMP messages have become that limited in their use, and why, for that matter, the notion of active networking has remained that irrelevant.[416] By and large, it is only on the basis of IP modules being within the same trust boundaries that more control passes between them.

Fourth, the notions of cascadability and symmetry feature prominently in the architecture of the Internet at large.[417] While cascadability of functions and protocols affects the scalability of the system, symmetry affects the flexibility of uses to which a protocol may be put. One of the central insights that shaped the design of the Internet was that functions such as virtual circuits, end-to-end acknowledgments, and buffer allocations inhibit the concatenation (or cascading) of networks so as to form 'supernetworks' (Pouzin 1974*a*).[418] Concatenating such functions typically goes along with severe limitations and gross inefficiencies, and may entail inevitable violations of their semantics.[419] Cascadability by virtue of conspicuous lack of elaborate control protocol in the Internet Protocol thus contributes notably to the objective of seamless concatenation of networks in the Internet.[420]

A very much related principle about the design of versatile protocols is that of symmetry — meaning that all communication ends are proper peers with functionally equivalent protocol machines, and neither end being master or slave.[421] Again, abidance by this principle can be found in many of the central Internet protocols, and also in earlier networking efforts, most notably the Arpanet, with both the internal IMP-to-IMP procedures and the NCP host-host protocol being symmetric.[422] While this is not to say that all protocols need to be symmetric,[423] it has turned out that asymmetric protocols generally have a much reduced scope for 'building stuff' upon them. Thus symmetry has been an important principle for all those parts of the Internet which are to flexibly support higher level applications and unspecified uses.

Fifth is the important group of loose concerns about the governance and stability of the very Internet evolution process — the primacy of running code, the strong preference for complexity avoidance, and the notion of rough consensus in strategic advancement. Rough censensus and running code have at least since 1992 been foundational principles to the IETF governed work on the Internet.[424] While the scope of the IETF work is limited,[425] and neither the IETF's nor the IAB's 'rules' have any legal force in and of themselves, the IETF has been *the* central forum in steering the advancement of the Internet at large. Their operational rules thus easily qualify as principles for the Internet.[426]

Closely related is the notion of complexity avoidance, or complexity aversion — a universal and virtually undisputed engineering principle which puts a sizable premium on increased complexity, and is an inevitable complement to all the above concerns, too.[427] It may be paraphrased loosely as: complex systems have complex and unpredictable side effects, and fail in superlinearly complex ways, requiring still more complex solutions; all of which makes them very undesirable for dynamic systems which ought to be reasoned about in terms of and which are subject to substantial division of labor and administrative control.[428] The concern for complexity avoidance has been important, not only on general grounds of tractability and acceptability; also, complexity adds to the cost of making any progress at all, for it typically involves couplings which are difficult to unravel let alone change in a concerted way.[429] While the Internet — even though it is made of simple pieces — has due to its sheer size alone come to exhibit considerable complexity along with the attendant side effects and ossification; there is thus a strong case for avoiding the addition of further complexity which would make the overall system still more complex.

If we accept that the set of principles just taxonomized — from classic end-to-end arguments to complexity aversion — suffices, by and large, to describe the architecture of the Internet and the placement of functions therein, we may consider the ways in which they relate to one another and the overall effects to which they combine by way of the following intermediate conclusions:

- All functions that the Internet performs may ultimately be reduced to be on behalf of the ultimate application ends, with the classic end-to-end arguments putting a *lower bound on the amount of functionality that needs be with the ends*.

- The avoidance of complexity in the constituent parts is a most decisive part of the pertinent economic trade-offs in choosing the proper arrangement of functions. Closely related are the governance principles of rough consensus and running code which speak to the manner in which progress happens in the first place.

- The architecture of the Internet is informed largely by the principles of layering and minimal coupling (speaking to the general structure), best effort and least privilege (speaking to the underlying philosophy), as well as cascadability and symmetry (speaking to the design of protocols, more generally). Those principles also combine to put an *upper bound on the amount of functions that ought to be at the common system level.*

Thus it is the classic end-to-end argument that helps arrive at a strictly necessary minimum of functionality that needs be with the ends, but it is the other principles in our list that inform the actual balance of functions — the principle of complexity avoidance speaking to the placement of functions along the entire continuum, and a number of further principles limiting the maximum of functions that may reasonably sit with the Internet. The combined effect of all these is that the bulk of functions of networking are left with the ends rather than intermediary nodes of the Internet. Consequently, it is apt to interpret the end-to-end arguments more broadly, so as to mean that functions *generally* tend toward the ends — regardless of how intimately important they are for applications standing at the end hosts; but it is equally important to appreciate the underlying set of causes, most of which have little to do with the original classic end-to-end argument as such. The economy of implementation and interface (see section 7.1, particularly page 132) provides a plausible explanation for the empirical observation that discrete functions tend very much completely toward either the network or the ends, based on the due comparative trade-offs. But it is the set of principles considered in this section that more fully explains just why there is so little scope for functions in the network as opposed to the ends.

The important conclusion to this chapter is thus that the end-to-end arguments are — curiously — most important as an abstract design principle, for it is their role to establish whether and which part of a given concern invariably falls to the application ends or their immediate agents. The accompanying set of principles then establishes the amount of functionality beyond this minimum that has to go to the end points, too. The end-to-end arguments may not always be the most decisive principle in this overall trade-off; but given that all networking is ultimately on behalf of the application end points, it is the one that is logically prior to the others.[430]

However, elevating the end-to-end arguments to a more encompassing principle detached from mere integrity and reliability concerns must not lead to confusion about their normative scope. There is little point in advancing arguments about the normative categoricalness of having functions with the end points rather than the network without appreciating why the functions we find at either place have settled the way they did. Appealing to innovation, democratic participation, and the like in pursuit of a stricter and more encompassing formulation of the end-to-end arguments is an altogether different exercise than simply describing reality (see Part II) or mapping a system of principles that work in conjunction with the end-to-end arguments (as we have done in this section). In fact, as we shall see in the following chapter, it is arguably futile to postulate the universal pe se validity of any purposes other than the most basic abstract ones — overall order and individual liberty.

Chapter 8

The Elusive Normativity of End-to-End Arguments

It seems that the specific character usually ascribed to 'norms' which makes them belong to a different realm of discourse from statements of facts, belongs only to articulated rules, and even there only once the question is raised as to whether we ought to obey them or not.

— *Friedrich August von Hayek (1973, p. 79)*

Elevating a descriptive principle to a normative one—that is, one that ought to be observed, but often is not—is no trivial exercise. For one, the raison d'être of any normative principle or rule is to serve a legitimate higher level purpose; and while it is possible to formulate arbitrary such rules and uphold them using a state's monopoly on violence, there is always a very real risk that such rules are unjust in that they "make right the loss of freedom for some by a greater good shared by others" (Rawls 1972, pp. 3 f.). Put differently, there may be good reasons to violate principles which are inherently unjust.[431] For another, any rule, even when scoped so as to further legitimate and broadly agreeable purposes, may come to exhibit unintended side-effects—a problem well known in social sciences (Merton 1936; Hayek 1973), but especially well known in computer science.

Few of those fundamental issues are typically found addressed in the increasingly large and vocal body of advocacy about the "mythical qualities" of the Internet based on the "embrace of engineering principles such as the end-to-end arguments" (Blumenthal 2002, pp. 709, 710). This is unfortunate not only as an academic lapse, but also because it reassigns potentially useless meaning to the original notion of end-to-end arguments, and makes it harder to frame a meaningful discourse on the matters involved without risking to hit territory captured by overbold reinterpretations of the end-to-end arguments.

In this chapter we make a careful attempt to gauge the normative scope of the end-to-end arguments, by (1) discussing the set of defendable purposes that any normative articulation of end-to-end arguments in an Internet subject to tussles among different stakeholders should be geared to, and (2) suggesting a potential shape of such normative articulation, very much outside and unrelated to current popular notions of network neutrality.

8.1 Liberty, Order, and Tussles

In recent years, one of the defining threads in the broader discussion about the end-to-end arguments has been their gradual elevation from a loose descriptive notion toward a decidedly normative one. Some have declared it foundational to the architecture of the Internet, others have given it prime 'constitutional' status—most all of which have turned the end-to-end 'arguments' into an a priori principle that derives straight from a vague set of broadly agreeable ends, from innovation, to economic welfare, to free speech, to democracy at large. However, attempts to develop such arguments in full always run the risk of arriving at a caricature of the original end-to-end arguments, one that is so strict and categorical as to be nonsensical for any practical purposes. The problem here is not so much that the normative core of any such principle (the design guidelines it implies) need necessarily be *wrong*—any principle is a loose rule of thumb, always to be considered within a broader context of other pertinent rules (see section 7.2)—, but that it (1) couches itself in a diffuse batch of 'second-order' purposes that serve to forbid exactly the flexible application that ought to characterize a principle, thus turning it into a non-negotiable rule of sorts, and (2) lacks much of the empirical support that can be found with the original end-to-end arguments (section 7.1).[432] Hence it shall be useful to devote some detailed consideration to the very question of which purposes any broader normative end-to-end argument ought to serve.

One of the first explicitly articulated purposes of the end-to-end arguments beyond reliability guarantees and integrity concerns has been that of application level innovation by end users (IAB 2004). However, given the inherent necessity of intermediaries and integrated chains of value creation in much of the recent Internet application development, it has proven difficult to apply the normative purpose of innovation in a defendable way so as to produce any useful implications about restricting the placement of functions in the Internet at large.[433] In fact, even if a case in favor of functions at the end points not the network could be made, innovation at large is very much exogenous to singular limitations and has thus not been significantly impaired by partial restriction or management of the Internet's application level uses, end user devices, or even complete subnetworks, all of which run counter to an 'innovation centric' end-to-end argument (Gillett et al. 2001*a*; Gillett et al. 2001*b*).[434]

Other purposes that have been put forward range from "economic growth", to "improved democratic discourse", to "a decentralized environment for social and cultural interaction in which anyone can participate" (Schewick 2009, p. 33). However, while these are all laudable goals in the abstract, they offer very little focus by which to judge specific principles in the first place, and offer even less guidance on the proper formulation of normative rules to be enforced, potentially against the will of perfectly legitimate participants to the Internet. Not surprisingly, thus, efforts to align the set of intuitions about non-discriminatory open access with more sober causes along economic lines of reasoning[435] have produced few if any useful results.[436]

We would venture to argue that *any* purposes along the lines of the above are deficient as a means to judge a broader normative end-to-end principle. The only defendable purposes of the Internet that are worth upholding per se are, in fact, the very same as those in any other complex societal settings with a large number of stakeholders: (1) individual liberty and (2) maintenance of the overall order—both of which foreclose the imposition of values by central authority (Hayek 1973).[437] Arguably, the only meaningful normative purpose beyond liberty and robustness of order that may be pursued in an a priori fashion is that of freedom of speech.[438] However, there have been neither empirical indications nor persuasive theoretical arguments in favor of prior restraint rules in support of free speech.[439] Thus, as for non-trivial higher level purposes to narrow the normative scope of the end-to-end arguments we are left with the two classic ones — liberty and overall order. While this may seem very little, it is, in fact, sufficient to elaborate normative articulations of end-to-end arguments that are well suited to broad debate and continuous interpretation by all stakeholders — much better than dogmatic articulations inherently unsuitable for meaningful academic or democratic debate.[440]

To begin with, it is vital to appreciate that the conceptual setting to which any notion of normative principles along the lines of end-to-end arguments sensibly applies is not captured well by the chiefly descriptive notions set forth in the preceding chapter — neither of the principles considered therein helps much in delineating the structure of normative concerns, and even in their combination they do not suffice to do so. Curiously, the false interpretation and development of the classic end-to-end arguments has diluted not only arguments about principles about application completeness and correctness at the technical level, but also those at a higher level firmly aiming at broader 'second order' objectives instead. We have already noted in section 3.3 that false analogies may be nonsensical; they are ill-suited for arriving at any useful framing of a normative debate about the end-to-end arguments in the first place.[441]

The crucial insight about the nature of the problems to be addressed by any normative principles in the first place is due largely to Clark et al. (2002) who have put forward the notion that any conflicts — they call them 'tussles' — between the ever-growing and continuously rearranging set of stakeholders inevitably resulting from the open-ended constituency of the Internet had better be explicitly appreciated in the very design of the Internet architecture.[442] The tussles notion thus develops the 1972 notion of modularity along conceptual boundaries rather than on the basis of hierarchical structures or flowcharts (Parnas 1972), and argues for a modularization along "tussle boundaries" (Clark et al. 2005c, p. 466).[443] The crucial idea about 'designing for tussle' is that tussles are nothing that can be hoped to be designed away by principle or rule,[444] and the only useful thing designers may do about them is reflect them in the design of logical modules such that they do not adversely affect parts that are otherwise unrelated to the actual core of the tussle:

> Functions that are within a tussle space should be logically separated from functions outside of that space, even if there is no compelling technical reason to do so. Doing this allows a tussle to be played out with minimal distortion of other aspects of the system's function. (Clark et al. 2005c, p. 466)

The core principle flowing from this reasoning is that of 'tussle separation' or 'tussle isolation', and while such principle is much less amenable to the illustrative layer and module flowchart structure of the Internet than the end-to-end arguments,[445] it firmly speaks to the way in which to go about distributing functions and shaping the interfaces between abstract modules so as to avoid harmful side effects from tussles playing out in the Internet. One very tangible first conclusion from the tussles arguments is that the notion of 'neutrality' is likely insufficient and ultimately useless with regard to addressing and resolving the various tussles readily identified in the Internet. As for the arguably principal tussle in the Internet—the economic one between end users and network operators over the social surplus—the neutrality position leads to results that are not compatible with those implied by a tussles analysis.[446] While the network neutrality position (by definition) arrives at neutrality on the part of *network* operators vis à vis *end* users as a default remedy for any tussles, the tussle design notion emphasizes mutual choice and liberty as a means to maintain an overall order in the face of unavoidable conflicts in certain parts of the system (Clark et al. 2005c, p. 468)—a result in marked agreement with the value neutral position about eventual purposes as elaborated by Hayek (1973) (see pages 145 f.).[447]

The notion of neutrality as an extreme version of the end-to-end arguments, on the other hand, is in stark contrast not only to tussle design approaches,[448] but is also in violation of the prime objective of overall order. Concerns about potential abuses of monopoly power notwithstanding, it is crucial to appreciate that without some reasonable balance between either sides the very feasibility of the Internet in the first place may be at stake.[449] It is neither useful nor innocent to argue for Internet neutrality and neglect questions about investment and innovation at the level of the underlying facilities.[450] If there is any hope to resolve the various unpleasant issues about the Internet, then it will not be by aligning end users and network operators against one another, but by acknowledging that both sides have legitimate conflicting interests that require adequate tussle spaces so as to play out beneficially.

8.2 Toward a Defendable Normative Articulation

There have been ample versions of the end-to-end arguments which emphasize the desirable lack of functions and control inside the Internet.[451] Yet many of the feared scenarios that have informed such arguments have failed to materialize (see also our note 462), and given that they carry with them substantial risks of undesirable tussle escalations due to the strict boundaries they impose between entities logically inside and those outside the Internet,[452] their merit may be fairly limited.[453] While the original end-to-end arguments provided a useful first stab at the problem of open access and end user empowerment at a time when many were concerned that the Internet would turn into a tightly controlled massive integrated media distribution system for the old giants of mass media entertainment,[454] it is about time to disentangle the normative relevance of the end-to-end arguments in a defendable way from the original articulation. To repeat an apt quote from Clark and Blumenthal (2007):

> There is no reason to believe that the original reasoning about an unreliable communications subsystem makes any sense at the application level. (p. 15)

The first premise in articulating normative arguments about end user empowerment and control would thus be that there is no point in trying to adapt the canonical example of reliable file transfer over an arbitrarily poor performance datagram network. The two arguments cover different realms and there is very little that can be carried over from the one to the other.[455]

However, as we have found in chapter 2, there are versions of the end-to-end arguments other than the 'TCP/IP, UDP/IP versions'. Most important here for our purposes is the one we elaborated in section 2.1 and which states that a higher level of redundancy is required in the "outside edge of distributed networks" to improve survivability in the face of random network outages.[456] If we substitute survivability with choice, then we obtain a very useful notion that aligns end user empowerment and control at the lower level with the pragmatic concerns of having application level functions freely move away from the end users subject to the relevant economic trade-offs. Turned into a broader normative end-to-end principle: end users ought to have a reasonable choice not only of third-party application service providers (by virtue of market competition at large), but also of the very Internet attachment points available to them — thus mitigating concerns about power imbalances and prejudices against certain end points, application types, and contents. Such a principle addresses a broad range of possible concerns, from low-level connectivity to higher-level choices in the view of competing purposes and their respective tussle characteristics.[457] Most importantly, however, its normative pursuit is largely orthogonal to any conceivable 'runtime' tussles, for what it gives to the end users is the option of choosing with whom to tussle in the first place. Thus it does away with the requirement of strict functional separation between end hosts and network nodes that goes along with more conventional normative versions focusing on the power balance between singular end points and networks.

True, such options already exist, for one may multihome with as many providers as one can establish a direct connection to.[458] However, the practical problem when multihoming with several providers is not only that the normal end user will pay for a redundancy that they will, on average, not utilize; but also that existing transport layer end-to-end protocols generally make no use of multiple paths, let alone offer any sophistication in controlling the choice of paths based on application level or user concerns.[459] Arguably, what is lacking from the current broader Internet architecture is a practical (low overhead) way of (1) distributing an application's traffic across several network attachment points, and (2) sharing network attachment points between different users, so as to spread their costs and increase their utilization. Put differently, the sharing paradigm so central for resources 'inside the network' ought to be extended outward to the end points, so that they can enjoy the same redundancy and robustness that can be found in the core networks of the Internet.

We can only speculate as to why this notion has not been pursued in a more pronounced manner; but, given that the broader payoffs to such redundancy were vague to non-existing in the early days of the Internet and the relevant constituency has lacked feasible means of organizing or delegating their concerns to a larger agent on their behalf, it is fair to argue that there have been very little economic incentives as yet to drive the necessary technical developments and standardization efforts.[460] Also, there are several concerns about authentication and accountability that arise when an end user shares their Internet access with other users, and which would have to be addressed in the design of such schemes — complete laissez-faire has not shown to work very well, as the demise of unencrypted WLAN access points has shown.[461]

That being said, we would venture to argue that the payoffs to schemes that improve choice and redundancy at the Internet edges have now become so large that a normative case can be made for their pursuit — even though ISPs may not be interested in them.[462] Ultimately, the prospect of 'mutual discrimination' and tussles in a market like setting, with all parties having access to comparably potent means of discrimination, is far more appealing than that of having to regulate the prices and minimum services of an entire industry: For one, even with end users being in a better bargaining position than before, it is unlikely that profit margins would collapse all the way down to the marginal costs of service provision in inverse linear relation to the surplus now accruing with end users (greater anonymity, better service, lower costs);[463] for another, the scope for viable regulation (along 'network neutrality' lines) is very limited if we continue to care for innovations in all parts of the overall system.[464]

Most notably, however, our principle of edge redundancy is perfectly consistent with the tussle separation principle considered in the previous section. We have noted that both an outright preference for end based solutions and a rule for network neutrality are in marked conflict with the implications of the tussles notion as advanced in Clark et al. (2005*c*) — leaving us at loss about the proper normativity of the end-to-end arguments. On the other hand, the notion put forward in this section, an early version of the end-to-end arguments (see section 2.1), tilts the power balance toward users without having to rely on any strict rules of function placement whatsoever. The only thing it calls for is some redundancy at the edges as well as the due mechanisms for end users to exert a reasonable amount of choice so that they may become true peers with ISPs, armed with the complementary means of discrimination that enable them and the applications on their behalf to counter the means of discrimination available to ISPs.[465]

Moreover, improved edge redundancy of Internet attachment points coupled with the proper means to exploit such diversity would also go a long way toward end based control over service variables other than reliability (as in the perfunctory example of careful file transfer). We have seen in previous sections that the end-to-end arguments originally apply only to functions that can be fully implemented with the end points in the first place — any function not amenable to such control is by definition not subject to the end-to-end arguments.[466] Hence, we have argued, neither delay nor throughput (nor any other parameter, for that matter, that requires entities outside the end points' immediate administrative and trust scope to deliver services above best effort and the maintain application related state beyond zero)[467] would qualify to be subject to the end-to-end arguments. Yet with access to multiple network attachment points at once those parameters become far more susceptible to end user control and perfection: throughput may be improved by spreading a given application's traffic over multiple links; and, as for delay, given a large enough choice of different networks an application may choose the one link with the most suitable delay characteristic, and reserve the option to instantly switch to another link, should the one chosen happen to degrade.

We close this chapter, and thus the main part of the thesis, by offering a final articulation of the end-to-end arguments — a version that acknowledges that high-level arguments about user empowerment, liberty, autonomy, and choice of options cannot be developed meaningfully with reference to the canonical example of reliable file transfer in the original end-to-end arguments.

Argument 4 *The set of functions to be implemented sufficiently 'completely and correctly' to the standard of and with 'the knowledge and help of the application standing at the end points of the Internet' can be substantially increased by enlarging the number of network attachment points an application end point may choose from. Thus we can extend the set of functions to be implemented at the end points beyond (1) functions such as those in the classic file transfer example (that logically collapse into the very application end point and require no service greater than any epsilon greater than zero) to (2) functions such as throughput* *maximization and delay minimization. By enlarging the set of functions at reasonable control of the end user, we explicitly further second-order purposes such as user empowerment and autonomy. The ensuing normative case for 'edge redundancy' by multiplexing between several applications and users on the one hand, and a number of Internet attachment points on the other, is firmly in accordance with the notion of tussle separation, and does away with the need to enforce any rules such as neutrality or minimal service—for given sufficient choice of network attachment points, the disciplining effects of market competition should contain the natural propensity of ISPs to increase their profits without regard to the corresponding and potentially greater loss of surplus on the end user side.*

Conclusion of Part III

The Internet — as any larger non-trivial artifact of computer science — is built on principles that are often imprecise and subject to various qualifications. And, as a dynamic system with a multitude of different stakeholders its principles are bound to be moving targets, and none can credibly claim to persist forever.[468] Thus it is the more important to search continuously for meaningful articulations, reasoned qualifications, and sensible contexts for the principles we have. For it is only by naming, articulating, and developing the patterns that we find and those that we seek, that we can build a shared language about the parts and actions required in the Internet. And it is only by such shared language, not central command, that we can hope to maintain and further the architecture of the Internet.[469]

The end-to-end arguments have developed from their initially mainly technical content to encompass an almost unbounded set of higher-order purposes — its core has in recent years become a common reference not only when reasoning about liberty and autonomy,[470] but also when arguing about economic growth, innovation, and 'social' purposes in general. In this part we have elaborated the end-to-end arguments by

1. discussing their merit as of today, concluding that the original end-to-end arguments speak poorly to many of the application level structures found in the current Internet,

2. developing other principles that support and inform the end-to-end arguments, thus placing them in a systematic context that helps focus their meaning and applicability, and also helps extending their scope beyond example cases such as reliable file transfer, a function that logically collapse into the very application end point and requires no minimum service whatsoever for correctness and completeness.

3. considering the normative content of the end-to-end arguments in accordance with the most vital appreciation of tussles and in view of defendable purposes that can be furthered not primarily by moving functions to the end points, but by improving the means by which end points may multiplex different Internet attachment points on applications and users, and vice versa.

The defining feature, but also the great paradox of the Internet has been that it connects different stakeholders with very different, often conflicting ends. One way to keep such conflicts from spilling across logical tussle boundaries, thus causing greater than necessary harm to the overall system, is by affording all parties with comparable means of mutual discriminations. The central paradigm of the Internet has been that of sharing resources between peers on equal footing; extending this paradigm to include the end points within the end users' locus of control might go a long way toward remedying problems of fragility and power imbalances at the Internet's fringes—upholding both overall order and individual liberty, all without adding to the ossification of the Internet core structures.

Chapter 9

Conclusion

[I]t is not in our power to build a desirable society by simply putting together the particular elements that by themselves appear desirable.

— Friedrich August von Hayek (1973, p. 56)

Any good piece of research should probably raise as many new question as it resolved existing ones. By having addressed some of the empirical and intellectual puzzles about the end-to-end arguments, and having put forward a number of tentative statements for wider debate, we hope to have contributed to the broader theory of end-to-end arguments and Internet principles at large. Yet any such effort can only ever be a small step toward a more refined understanding of all the pertinent issues involved, the relevant trade-offs to be had, and the workable approaches for their resolution. Not because it is impossible to articulate inherently plausible notions here, but because there is no good in claiming unqualified authority in the articulation and interpretation of a principle that has taken on so many meanings for so many different people — for there can be no *one* truth in systems of principles, there can only ever be subjective judgment and opinionated discourse.[471]

9.1 The Value Added

It was our objective in this thesis to shed light on the end-to-end arguments notion by observing the customs and realities that have informed them, and by elaborating their proper construction and systematic context without losing sight of the patterns that they stem from. Beyond offering a comprehensive descriptive account of the very notion of end-to-end arguments (Part I) and their seminal manifestations in the history of the Arpanet and Internet (Part II), a number of useful abstract themes have emerged (particularly from Part III):

1. The end-to-end arguments are more than a self-contained blackboard exercise about the logical correctness and completeness of data transfers. It is especially in conjunction with other principles that the end-to-end arguments extend well beyond cases that obviously collapse into the application end points and require from other entities no level of service greater than any epsilon greater than zero. We have here argued that functions like fragmentation and congestion control have moved to the end points not because of completeness and correctness concerns, but because of the infeasibility of maintaining a meaningful explicit interface for such functions across trust boundaries (section 7.1). Moving from the descriptive to the normative, we have also argued that functions such as throughput maximization and delay minimization can be moved more firmly to the end points if we pursue the normative notion of 'edge redundancy', allowing users and Internet attachment points to multiplex on each other (section 8.2).

2. There is substantial merit in distinguishing between vertical end-to-end arguments and horizontal ones, only the latter of which speaks to the application level structure of today's Internet. The crucial difference between the two is that while the vertical arguments logically entail the notion of irreducibly minimum common ground at the shared inter-network level so as to reduce the adverse effects from negative externalities, the horizontal ones allow functions to float freely between end users and network intermediaries subject to trust and other pertinent trade-offs, for the effects of such sophistication are limited only to the entities part of any such structure. The minimality of the IP protocol is an impressive testament to the power of the vertical arguments. The horizontal arguments, on the other hand, have forever been far more malleable to application specific concerns at the very application (protocol) level. While this notion

is not original to our thesis, we have offered an in-depth discussion and elaboration, particularly in section 3.3.

3. The end-to-end arguments have been notoriously prone to be interpreted pursuant to a vague set of higher-order purposes (innovation, economic growth, and democracy) which together with the widespread confusion between vertical and horizontal arguments has led to a number of nonsensical (policy) implications. With a nod to Hayek (1973), we argue that it is crucial to appreciate that only the purposes overall order and individual liberty can be solidly defended and used as a measure to judge any version of the end-to-end arguments (or, indeed, any other principle or rule). On a very much related note, the appreciation of tussles in the Internet, along with the understanding that they can only be contained but not eliminated, does not go together well with any strict and dogmatic version of the end-to-end arguments. What it does go together well with, however, is the edge redundancy version of the end-to-end principle lending further credence to the notion of tussle separation—a notion we have developed particularly in chapter 8.

9.2 Loose Ends

Where do we go from here? One crucial step in developing the themes expounded here will be to carry them into the broader professional debate about Internet architecture, design principles, and the normative bias we are prepared to introduce.[472] Particularly, the following notions would likely benefit from further elaboration in future studies: (1) the notion of horizontal end-to-end arguments, which has yet to move beyond the level of conference proceedings elaboration and debate;[473] (2) the analysis of end-to-end arguments in a systematic context, as put forward in section 7.2, preferably with some consideration of their dynamics;[474] and (3) the history of the Internet decentralization process with respect to the question of how common principles have been disseminated and upheld given the lack of central authority and control.[475] Finally, an important elaboration of our thesis will be to more fully develop some of the themes by applying them in a practical context—the notion of edge redundancy put forward in section 8.2 would sure benefit from such elaboration, especially since it gives rise to a whole host of problems that need to be addressed or have been addressed in ongoing IETF work.[476]

In all, our thesis is nowhere near a definitive statement on the nature, purposes, and merits of the end-to-end arguments. It is but *one* written manifestation of a necessarily incomplete and subjective set of thoughts,[477] and it is bound to have weaknesses and omissions. And yet we feel that it is a worthwhile piece of research that puts forward a number of insights some of which may not only be interesting, but also prove instructive and useful. More can hardly be achieved in a thesis about the end-to-end arguments — a design principle so broad in scope and rich in implications that all we can do is add our thoughts and insights to a debate that will have to go forward indefinitely.

Notes, Asides, Acronyms, Figures, Tables, Literature

Notes

1 (xi). Latour (1987) put it:

> Readers are devious people, obstinate and unpredictable — even the five or six left to read the paper from beginning to end. (p. 56)

2 (xi). We have generally followed American spelling and writing rules; however, we have put small spaces before and after em-dashes. Also, we have chosen to typeset "e.g." as "e. g." (which is clearly not in accordance with the Chicago Manual of Style). Finally, we have generally normalized the writing of all caps terms from literature sources (such as ALOHANET, HOST, TELNET) to a normal capitalization scheme (Alohanet, Host, Telnet).

Introduction

3 (2). Notes Perlis (1982):

> Beware of the Turing tar-pit in which everything is possible but nothing of interest is easy. (p. 10)

The Internet Protocol may be considered the networking equivalent of such a Turing tarpit — in theory it allows arbitrary elaboration on top and below it, but it offers next to no practical assistance in achieving such elaborations.

DIGRESSION: On a related note, an interesting example from a completely different realm is provided by an episode about German composer Ludwig van Beethoven who was composing 33 variations on a simple waltz theme by Austrian music publisher Anton Diabelli, adding a whole universe of complex originality to the slim material. The point here is that while the base material may have inherently contained the seeds for subsequent sophistication, it took the genius of Beethoven to bridge the gap between something very simple and minimal on the one hand, and something truly original and novel on the other (Boulez 1989; Fastner 2007). More recent examples of variations to existing basic themes come from the rich Jamaican culture of using 'riddims'—typically fairly basic patterns of drum and bass lines—as the basis for more sophisticated song material.

4 (2). See notes 14 through 17 and accompanying text.

5 (2). Day (2008) (elaborating on the notion of protocol nesting put forward by Pouzin 1975*a*) has attempted such feat (for a summary version of the Day book see Day et al. 2008), and tried to formalize efforts based on his book by founding the "Pouzin Society"—"a forum for developing viable solutions to the current Internet architecture crisis."

There are two basic problems with such radical approaches—one philosophical, one practical. As for the former, Alexander (1979) noted valuably:

> Even when a person seems to "go back to the basic problem," he is still always combining patterns that are already in his mind. (p. 205)

And, as a practical matter, moving completely outside the established research and engineering context of the Internet means that few meaningful alliances with incumbent players may be forged.

6 (2). Schewick (2004) offers a comprehensive attempt to link the end-to-end arguments to the notion of network neutrality, and argues that innovation on the Internet has been a result of what she calls the 'broad version' of the end-to-end principle, a particularly strong version that argues against placing any application related functions whatsoever outside the end hosts, even if conventional perfomance or robustness trade-offs would argue in favor of doing so. According to Schewick the 'original Internet' was firmly based on just that principle and is now under thread by "network providers [who] will continue to change the internal structure of the Internet in ways that are good for them but not necessarily for the rest of us."

However, as we shall elaborate in this thesis, the classic end-to-end arguments have never implied strict neutrality or even fairness on the part of the network vis à vis end users and host level applications, nor has the Internet been conceived as a primarily 'neutral' network with the political objectives of Lessig and Schewick in mind—Lovink (2008) has referred to such false beliefs by network neutrality proponent as "foundational myths"; Sandvig (2007) calls them a "fiction", "framed in terms of protecting a non-existent neutral internet" (p. 145). If anything, the Internet was designed to encompass as many as possible networks and users, with users and host computers as active parts of the network, and assuming their generally benign behavior towards both the network resources and other end users. Neither neutrality nor even fairness have featured prominently in comparison with other more central objectives (Clark 1988).

7 (2). Our approach is, of course, not as adventurous as it might seem. Most of the relevant discussion on Internet architecture and design principles moves within those premises. As for the role of practice in informing principles, Denning (2003) notes:

> What we call principles are almost always distilled from recurrent patterns observed in practice. (p. 15)

The need for constant re-articulation and re-evaluation is acknowledged even by those who see current developments surrounding the Internet with great skepticism. Note IAB (2004) about the end-to-end arguments:

> Does the end-to-end principle have a future in the Internet architecture or not? If it does have a future, how should it be applied? Clearly, an unproductive approach to answering this question is to insist upon the end-to-end principle as a fundamentalist principle that allows no compromise. A more productive approach is to return to first principles and re-examine what the end-to-end principle is trying to accomplish, and then update our definition and exposition of the end-to-end principle given the complexities of the Internet today. (p. 8)

And, the case that no principle should be applied too strictly is a logical conclusion of the very notion of principles versus axioms (true by presumption) and normative rules (true by virtue of the state's monopoly on violence).

8 (2). To quote from Hayek (1973):

> [A]rticulation [of rules of what most obeyed in practice] will often become necessary because the 'intuitive' knowledge may not give a clear answer to a particular question. The process of articulation will thus sometimes in effect, though not in intention, produce new rules. But the articulated rules will thereby not wholly replace the unarticulated ones, but will operate, and be intelligible, only within a framework of yet unarticulated rules. (p. 78)

While Hayek's positions have often been dismissed in both economics and law, there is strong merit in the notion that any principles of law ought to arise chiefly from actual cases and the regularities found in a society, rather than from a top-down imposition of those in power or a simple economic cost/benefit trade-off (as has been suggested by Posner; for a fine critical discussion see Wright 2003, for a background see Gilles 2003). Mestmäcker (2007, p. 57) notes that legal rules are as much "path dependent" as they are "past dependent", and develops that point with reference to Hayek (1973) and Epstein (2003) more fully:

> Properly refined and pruned these principles that lie behind the endless array of discrete cases allow us to establish a complete and well-defined set of relationships between private individuals that meet simultaneously the practical concerns of ordinary individuals, the moral concerns of philosophers and the efficiency concerns of economists. (p. 57)

If custom is one, if not the *only* legitimate, source of law, then customary principles and practices from within computer science should qualify as sources of inherent scientific conceptions for computer science, too. Much like in common law, while principles and rules are derived from the past, they are properly being applied to present cases, too (which is, of course, the whole point of articulating such regularities in the first place).

9 (2). It is instructive to note that classic architecture is not primarily about the application of singular codified principles; instead it is properly about observing the systems of patterns in existing artifacts. Not only are principles inherently tentative, and subject to continuous (re)articulation,

promulgation, and debate (Alexander 1979, pp. 268 ff.), but any codified principle — no matter how formally arrived at, and no matter how much empirical reality it commands — is only ever a minor and tentative part in an overall trade-off about the proper application of a whole host of principles which evades conclusive mechanic description (Alexander 1979, p. 223).

10 (2). The elaboration of vague principles is the more instructive exercise compared to formal approached featuring precisely stated hypotheses, axiomatic mathematics, and trivial comparableness — because principles are the most meaningful way to reason about computer science artifacts in social context, and beyond self-sufficient questions of physics and mathematics.

DIGRESSION: Some aside notes about the more general problems with the very notion of computer science vis à vis natural and social sciences proper. Notes Schinzel (2006):

> The missing references to concrete matters remove any bounds and limits from the procedures of computer science. The boundlessness of computer science becomes visible in the exploration and development of ever newer subject areas, and it is impossible to understand the concrete limits of computer science models by formal means alone. The universality should be constrained by considerations of the consequences and a normative reference to usefulness. The proper limits should stem not from what is possible but from what is desirable and sensible. (my translation from German original text)

Fano (1972), in drastic terms:

> The present trend is toward automation of functions in a way that lessens significantly human control over them by removing the pertinent information from easy access on the part of people. This trend is not the result of a conscious choice, but rather because it would be too inconvenient, or too uneconomical, or even impossible to do otherwise in view of the technology that happens to be available at this time. Continuation of this trend is very likely to lead to a society operated by a rigid

> bureaucracy whose power will stem from widespread surveillance and control over information, that is, to a society of the "1984" type. This is most likely to occur unintentionally as a result of the actions of many well-meaning people attempting to solve the problems they face in the best way they know how at the time. (p. 1253)

And, Weizenbaum (1980), who had been notoriously pessimistic about computer science:

> What and whose needs will be satisfied by [. . .] by the ongoing proliferation of computers and computer controlled systems? What will be the indirect effects on a society that increasingly, possibly irreversibly, commits itself to being monitored and controlled by systems that even its own technostructure ill understands? [. . .]
>
> [T]he heralds of its [our euphoric dream] transmutation to disaster are already obvious: the market is inundated with computer games in which the players' main objective is to kill, crush, and destroy. We have spacewar, battleship, tank battles, and so on. (p. 442)

The list of pessimistic takes on the potentially ill effects of technology could be extended almost arbitrarily. However, drawing any useful conclusions from such pessimistic accounts is a different matter altogether (see, e. g., the notoriety of Kaczynski 1995). It is well to ask "hard questions" about the usefulness and purpose of computer science artifacts; but there are few practical implications from such reasoning, as Dertouzos (1980) points out in a reply to Weizenbaum:

> [S]cientific discovery is very often the result of a well-timed accident or the by-product of the pursuit of an altogether different goal. Even the intended use of a scientific discovery does not necessarily forecast the consequences of subsequent uses. Take for example radar, which was developed during World War II. Application of the implicit Weizenbaum doctrine would have characterized that development as societally questionable, since its intended function was to help wage war.

> Yet, the safety of today's worldwide air transportation system rests on that earlier development.
>
> What is it then that we as technologists should do? To begin with, we should not engage in technological research that clearly violates our moral and legal codes, as in the use of human guinea pigs in potentially dangerous experiments. However, the bulk of scientific and technological research is not blessed with such clear and early indicators. Take the internal combustion engine, for example, or nuclear power, or behavior changing drugs. If we ask ourselves today whether these developments have, on balance, helped or hindered the pursuit of worthy societal goals, we are at best in a quandary even though we have lived with these technologies for many years. How, then, in view of such retrospective ignorance can we ever hope to assess the prospective benefits of a contemplated invention let alone look purposefully for a beneficial one that will solve some of our problems?
>
> [. . .] [W]e have no compelling reasons at this time to suppress the development of technologies that will make possible information networks, computers in the home, or, my favorite theme, computer individualization of products and services. (pp. 463 f.)

Last, it is apt to close this excursus with an unmistakably optimistic view by Simon (1971):

> [W]hile technology demonstrably generates some problems, and these problems have to be dealt with (using that same technology!), technology is man's one best and only hope to escape from the curse of Adam. We need more technology, not less. [. . .]
>
> [I]naction is also action, and experimentation on the real world is not as risky as it sounds, at least no more risky than that form of experimentation which consists of doing nothing new or different until all the facts are in. Life requires us to balance risks; it does not permit us to avoid them altogether. Moreover, it is easy to exaggerate how irreversible our experiments

> on nature are. I find it hard to come by genuine examples of important irreversibility. (p. 72)

11 (2). There are two principal problems with our approach: (1) it falls outside the paradigm of 'hard' science, the guiding paradigm for most of computer science (or 'informatics'); and (2) it thus depends on qualitative rather than quantitative methodological approaches, making it less well amenable to the safe statement of falsifiable hypotheses.

DIGRESSION: This is an apt place to briefly discuss our *methodology* which essentially boils down to an exploratory and largely desk based approach involving an extensive literature review and a few case studies. Put more formally, we have employed as concrete research methods (1) review of literature from various fields bordering the subject of Internet and design principles, (2) private interviews with various people involved with the Internet and its design principles, and (3) case studies to illuminate some of the larger points of this thesis.

Some technical elaboration: This is not a 'hard' computer science thesis, but a 'soft' one (see Guba and Lincoln 1994, pp. 105 ff. for the notions of 'hard' and 'soft' sciences), very much in the tradition of hermeneutics as the guiding research paradigm (Ramberg and Gjesdal 2005; Kincheloe and McLaren 2005), grounded theory as a methodological background (Glaser and Strauss 1967), and triangulation as an important methodical device for our practical research efforts (Campbell and Fiske 1959; Jick 1979; Mathison 1988).

Our methodological approach is very much reflective of the fact that science is more than the (random) articulation of falsifiable and non-trivial statements, thus regarded as temporary facts or knowledge (Popper 1935). Instead, it is often the (strategic) proposition of theories that may not even have *any* substantial empirical backing, and yet help further human scientific pursuit, for they have a broader potential explanatory scope, are easier to apply, or just simpler in their articulation. It is not, to paraphrase Braithwaite (1953), that "man proposes and nature disposes" (p. 368), but much rather that "[n]ature may shout *no*, but human ingenuity [. . .] may always be able to shout louder" (Lakatos 1978*a*, p. 111, emphasis in original). Often, while "assumptions that are unrealistic [. . .] do not guarantee a significant theory", it is also true that "the more significant the theory, the more unrealistic the assumptions" (Friedman 1953, p. 14, footnote 12). To quote Lakatos (1978*a*) a little further on this point:

> [T]o give a stern "refutable interpretation" to a fledgling version of a programme is a dangerous methodological cruelty. The first version may even "apply" only to non-existing "ideal" cases; it may take decades of theoretical work to arrive at the first novel facts and still more time to arrive at interestingly testable versions of the research programmes, at the stage when refutations are no longer foreseeable in the light of the programme itself.
>
> The dialectic of research pogrammes is then not necessarily an alternating series of speculative conjectures and empirical refutations. The interaction between the development of the programme and the empirical checks may be very varied—which pattern is actually realized depends only on historical accident. (pp. 65 f., emphasis omitted)

Consider as an apt illustration the research programme of "web science" put forward by Berners-Lee et al. (2006). Shadbolt and Berners-Lee (2008) admit:

> It seems sensible to say that Web science can help us engineer a better Web. Of course, we do not fully know what Web science is, so part of the new discipline should be to find the most powerful concepts that will help the science itself grow. Perhaps insights will come from the work's interdisciplinary nature. (pp. 36 f.)

It is for these types of preliminary considerations that our thesis falls outside the typical 'scientific' realm of computer science which, as Schinzel (2006) notes, prefers "very much in line with its mathematical-technical tradition, 'purely formal' approaches [. . .] [which] ensures provability via formal means, scientificity, and academic recognition." Yet, while computer science may owe its scientific roots to mathematics (e. g., cryptography, convergence of routing tables) and physics (e. g., capacity, noise, reliability), it is also a notoriously 'virtual' science different from 'natural' science. Kay (1977) notes that computers "made new universes available that could be shaped by theories to produce simulated phenomena" (p. 236). These new universes may also just be "splendid nonsense" (p. 244). Rheingold (1985) adds:

> According to the rules of scientific induction, first set down by Francis Bacon three hundred years ago, scientific knowledge and the power granted by that knowledge are created by first observing nature, noting patterns and relationships that emerge from those direct observations, then creating a theory to explain the observations. With the creation of a machine that "obeyed laws you wanted to be held true," it became possible to specify the laws governing a world that doesn't exist, then observe the representation created by the computer on the basis of those laws. (p. 245)

Crowcroft (1997) concludes:

> Computer science is not a "Natural Science". We construct systems, which we then examine by some means, so it is a "Virtual Science". The number of possible worlds we can build in computing makes this feasible. This also makes PhDs somewhat odd compared with natural science or engineering.

Few if any computer science problems can thus be solved by formal 'mathematical-technical' means alone. Instead, core computer science issues such as software development, IT security, and Internet design are constrained and actively shaped by three major "regulatory nests" (Tsiavos and Hosein 2003): (1) the mathematical features of information, ontologies of languages, etc., (2) the capabilities and characteristics of computer and network technology, and, most important, (3) the psychology of humans that interact with computer science artifacts, plus the sociology of human society regarding computer science artifacts. Arguably, the former two aspect are becoming increasingly usurped by their antecessors mathematics and electrical engineering, leaving the latter, admittedly more elusive aspect in the actual center of the computer science discipline. It is primarily this set of three forces that drive and address the core computer science problems and their dynamics (Figure N.1).

Returning to the discussion of our methodology we note that there are some practical caveats about our approach. First, history, no matter

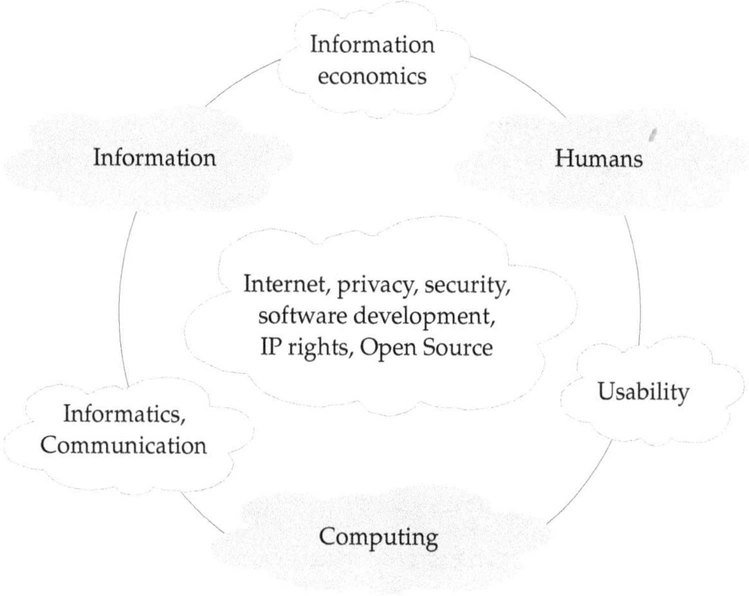

Figure N.1: The 'core' of computer science as a science

how comprehensive, always has some theoretical bias, as Lakatos (1978*b*) valuably notes:

> History without some theoretical bias is impossible. Some historians look for the discovery of hard facts, inducive generalizations, others for bold theories and crucial negative experiments, yet others for great simplifications, or for progressive and degenerating problemshifts; all of them have some theoretical 'bias'. [...] [N]o set of human judgments is completely rational and thus no rational reconstruction can ever coincide with actual history. (pp. 120, 131, footnotes omitted, emphasis omitted)

The choice of literature sources alone can go a long way in shaping the results and conclusion of a researcher. Also, note that (as in any literature review of the scope we have undertaken for this work) the contention of Sprague and Sprague (1976) holds firmly: "[T]he bulk of articles appearing in the refereed journals are in fact either *toy research* on *real problems* or *real research* on *toy problems*" (p. 57) — some works are about interesting problems but are academically unsound, others theoretically interesting but useless for real world purposes, and still others both unsound and irrelevant. We would claim to have conducted an extremely comprehensive and critical literature review; but, of course, we cannot claim to be free from any preconceived notions, assumptions, or values that would shape our reading and its interpretation. And even if we had been, literature in and of itself only ever goes so far in closing in on 'truth' or even simple 'facts', as Latour (1987) valuably details:

> [A] fact is what is collectively stabilised from the midst of controversies when the activity of later papers does not consist only of criticism or deformation but also of confirmation. The strength of the original statement does not lie in itself, but is derived from any of the papers that incorporate it. (p. 42)

It is thus a difficult and error-prone endeavor to try and ascertain in retrospect the causal forces behind certain historical events in the Internet, the actual incentives behind certain actions, and the principles that usefully apply to a range of observed practices. Notes BBN's Haverty (2009*a*):

> Even if you could somehow prove that someone subscribed to a journal, or actually read a paper, or even understood it, he or she may not have agreed with it — and simply ignored it as noise. I'm equally suspect of anyone who claims to have invented any particular mechanism or approach. It's simply too hard, in my experience at least, to be sure that an idea that pops into your head is original, and not a product of your subconscious working on something you saw, or heard, or read, days or months before.

Also, Haverty argues that the development of the Internet had been very much a hands-on activity with a focus on best practices rather than academic discussions in peer-reviewed journals:

> At the time, there was a lot of pressure to deploy a functional Internet — one which could support successful demonstrations of the kinds of mostly government-oriented applications that would cause the "operational" government gang to keep the

> research funding going and the funds going to ARPA (and then to us and others). That focus, coupled with the fact that BBN was not a university, led to a noticeable bias toward engineering rather than science. Getting it to work, using proven techniques rather than academic ideas, became the primary goal. Writing papers, presenting at conferences, trying new interesting approaches, and other such science-oriented activities got pushed to the back burner. As I remember also, all through that period most of the interesting discussion and argument happened on the various mailing lists, or at the quarterly Internet meetings, rather than in the traditional journals—at least from my personal perspective at the time.

To make up for the many sources of bias from our reliance on literature accounts, we have relied only marginally on secondary accounts—we rarely refer to Hafner and Lyon (1998), and have completely neglected the more cursorily takes such as Abbate (1999) or Naughton (2000). Mostly, we have worked through the primary sources ourselves and backed up all major insights with various means of triangulation: other primary and secondary sources, private communication with knowledgeable authorities (in person or via email), and questions about specific issues to the internet history mailing list (http://www.postel.org/internet-history/) and other mailing lists. Wherever a statement of fact could, despite our best efforts, not be verified to a reasonable extent, we have added a proper indication (see, e.g., note 218). Our take on many questions that this thesis comes to deal with has, in fact, developed appreciably over time. There has no doubt remained scope for subjective bias, but we hope to have applied all prudence and diligence in minimizing it to an acceptably low level.

In all, despite all caveats and qualifications, we feel that history and empirical fact (even if only at approximation) are the best grounds on which to base any higher level philosophy and theory if there is to be any hope of linking those theoretical elaborations back to real world concerns.

12 (2). Arguably, either side have set off entire research programmes that have, at least to a certain extent, successfully developed (along the lines of Lakatos 1978*a*) a hard core of irrefutable statements, a protective belt of auxiliary statements, and a positive heuristic that have provided some useful insights and arguments. Arguably, the articulation and advancement

of those programmes is the very reason for our own efforts at contributing to the competition lined up against those research programmes. To quote yet again from Lakatos:

> The history of science has been and should be a history of competing research programmes (or, if you wish, 'paradigms'), but it has not been and must not become a succession of periods of normal science: the sooner competition starts, the better for progress. (p. 69, emphasis omitted)

13 (3). To quote from Hayek (1973):

> [C]onstructivist rationalism, in its endeavour to make everything subject to rational control, in its preference for the concrete and its refusal to submit to the discipline of abstract rules, comes to join hands with irrationalism. Construction is possible only in the service of particular ends which in the last resort must be nonrational, and on which no rational argument can produce agreement if it is not already present at the outset. (p. 34)

14 (3). See, e. g., Lessig (1999*a*); Lemley and Lessig (2001); Wu (2003); Schewick (2007) arguing for a conceptual link between end-to-end arguments, network neutrality, and a specific notion of innovation. In a recent FCC hearing on network neutrality, Lessig (2008) claims: "It is [. . .] end-to-end, or what we now call net neutrality, [. . .] that gave us transparency, openness, and freedom" (ca. 4:30 min).

15 (3). See the various FCC hearings on the issue of network neutrality in recent years (e. g., at Harvard in February 2008, http://www.fcc.gov/broadband_network_management/hearing-ma022508.html), and also the various public consultations on those matters (for a recent exemplary submission see Clark et al. 2010).

Also see the 2005 FCC policy statement granting Internet users four "Internet freedoms" (Dortch 2005):

> [T]o ensure that broadband networks [i. e., the Internet] are widely deployed, open, affordable, and accessible to all consumers, the Commission adopts the following principles: [. . .] [1] consumers are entitled to access the lawful Internet content

> of their choice. [. . .] [2] consumers are entitled to run applications and use services of their choice, subject to the needs of law enforcement. [. . .] [3] consumers are entitled to connect their choice of legal devices that do not harm the network. [. . .] [4] consumers are entitled to competition among network providers, application and service providers, and content providers. (p. 3, footnotes omitted, emphasis omitted)

As of this writing a fifth principle has been added to the four just quoted. However, a law suit in the aftermath of the 2007 Comcast incident (see our note 323) filed by Comcast questioning the authority of the FCC to regulate ISPs in the first place has been answered in the negative (they do not have the authority); in turn leading to current efforts to restate the legal status of ISPs as 'telecommunications services' rather than 'information services', the former of which warrants broader regulatory scope for intervention. We have not taken the effort to add proper literature resources for those recent events.

16 (3). On the many legislative proposals on net neutrality put forward from 2006 to 2008 in the US Congress (none of which was enacted into law) see Holman (2008, pp. 5–9). See also the recent 2009 effort by Ed Markey und Anna Eshoo (Internet Freedom Preservation Act of 2009, http://markey.house.gov/images/PDFs/netneutralitybill.pdf).

17 (3). Most noteworthy in this respect are the recent works by David D. Clark, e. g., Clark et al. (2004); Clark (2007*a*); Clark and Blumenthal (2007); Clark (2007*b*); Clark (2008*c*).

It bears noting that the group of computer scientists proper are a minority compared to the large and vocal group of legal scholars who claim a stake in the ongoing debate about end-to-end arguments. However, not surprisingly, the positions of the former — especially those featuring daring causalities based on only anecdotal understanding of the technologies involved — have sometimes been criticized by the latter as uninformed and thus irrelevant. E. g., notes Crowcroft (2007) about network neutrality:

> Much of what I have read on the subject of net neutrality by economists is technically naïve and simplistic. (p. 567).

18 (3). For example, compare the articulations put forward by Denning and Martell (2007*c*) and Denning and Martell (2007*b*), both part of a com-

prehensive attempt to list the "great principles" of computing (Denning 2006). From the former:

> In a distributed system, it is more efficient to implement a function in the communicating applications than in the network itself (end-to-end principle).

But, from the latter:

> *End-to-End Principle*—Consider any network in which data are moved from one machine to another. If we check the integrity of the bits at any point on the path, but not the absolute end, there is a possibility that an error can occur in the final segment. Therefore, we must check that the bits at the end are the same as those at the beginning. This is called end-to-end error checking. [. . .]
>
> The only reason to include checks on the path would be to improve performance. For example, routers could cut retransmission times in TCP by caching packets. Such checks do nothing to improve reliability. (pp. 12 f.)

The first formulation is brief, vague, and broad; the second, however, is much longer, but *only* about end-to-end error control, and thus very narrow indeed. Which, then, is the 'real' end-to-end principle and what functions does it pertain to?

19 (3). Broadly speaking, the whole area of technology and regulation has remained an extremely difficult one to tackle in a consistent and sensible manner. As for the Internet, the positions put forward in the literature have been ranging from the complete dismissal of any legitimacy of governmental or legal regulation of 'cyberspace' (Barlow 1996) to the effective denial of any political or legal dimension let alone constitution of the Internet in and of itself (Easterbrook 1996), with various shades of gray in between (e. g., Gillett and Kapor 1997; Lessig 1999*b*). For a recent set of takes on the broader issue of technology and regulation see the collection compiled by Brownsword and Yeung (2008).

As for the end-to-end arguments, we have already noted above that their articulation is non-trivial (see note 18 and accompanying text); but actually arriving at a useful set of implications is even harder still. In fact, the end-to-end notion may be considered a prime example of what Latour (1987) calls a "stable statement" that over time "is slowly eroded, losing its original shape, encapsulated into more and more foreign statements, becoming so familiar and routinised that it becomes part of tacit practice and disappears from view!" (p. 43). Much of the debate about the nature and merit of end-to-end arguments is completely detached from the original paper (Saltzer et al. 1984), and, in fact, detached from any sober technological reality in the first place.

David (2001*a*) points out aptly that any sensible notion of Internet economics (put in more pompous terms: the law and economics of the Internet) will have to entail a proper appreciation of the technology and its history:

> [It is important] to take account of the present dynamism of the Internet's enabling technologies, and also of the limitations imposed by the distinctive architecture that was inherited from its historical precursors. [. . .] [F]or the field of "Internet economics" to mature into an area of disciplinary specialization that has more immediate policy relevance, economists will need to develop a greater appreciation of both of those realities, as well as of the historically contingent processes of technological and institutional co-evolution. (p. 5)

Prior Arguments about End-to-End Arguments

20 (9). It is, indeed, rare to find notions in the history of science that may not be conceived as recombinations of ones. So is it with Darwin's theory of evolution, and so is it with the end-to-end arguments, a principle of sorts first stated explicitly by Saltzer et al. (1981*a*). Much like it is useful and valuable to understand the predecessors to Darwin's theory, it is useful to elaborate the history of the end-to-end arguments.

21 (9). Savigny (1840) made this point succinctly when he argued that interpretation is about "reconstruction of the inherent notion of a coded law". It is not about a narrow purpose, but really about drawing in on the idea that stands behind a given articulation (cf. p. 213). Hence "interpretation" and not "explanation" (cf. p. 216).

22 (10). See on Lakatos (1978*a*) notes 12 and 11 plus accompanying texts.

23 (10). Savigny (1840) famously established four elements that are to be considered when interpreting legal texts: textual, teleological, historical and systematic.

There has been some tendency in secondary literature about the end-to-end arguments to interpret the original paper and some of its more authoritative follow-ups in a rather textual interpretation like fashion. Reed, one of the authors of the 1981 paper and one of its most ardent advocates at that, comments, in a slightly different but altogether fitting context:

> I am afraid that those who treat the RFCs as scripture from high priests mistake dogma for thoughtfulness. [...] The act of granting an RFC a number does not (anymore than acceptance at a peer reviewed journal does not) create a "fact" or a "truth". And now many [...] behave like Talmudic scholars or law professors—somehow thinking that by studying merely the grammar and symbols we can ascertain what is right, what is good, or what is fit to purpose. (Reed 2008*a*)

Our efforts go well beyond such limited approaches, and in later segments of this thesis we shall offer a systematic analysis, too.

24 (10). At times we will in this chapter point to the realities underlying the higher level arguments about the placement of functions in a network, but only to the extent necessary to give context to some of the notions here raised and discussed. E. g., in section 3.3 we briefly mention the realities of host level delegation of functions to a common transport module in order to discuss some of the arguments raised along those lines.

25 (10). The earliest documented general purpose method of encoding and sending arbitrary messages across long distances by optical means rather than human or pigeon messengers goes back to Polybius (1925) (written at around 200 BCE) who describes the following procedure:

> We take the alphabet and divide it into five parts, each consisting of five letters. There is one letter less in the last division, but this makes no practical difference. Each of the two parties who are about signal to each other must now get ready five tablets and write one division of the alphabet on each tablet, and then come to an agreement that the man who is going to signal is

> in the first place to raise two torches and wait until the other replies by doing the same. This is for the purpose of conveying to each other that they are both at attention. These torches having been lowered the dispatcher of the message will now raise the first set of torches on the left side indicating which tablet is to be consulted, i. e. one torch if it is the first, two if it is the second, and so on. Next he will raise the second set on the right on the same principle to indicate what letter of the tablet the receiver should write down. Upon their separating after coming to this understanding each of them must first have on the spot a telescope with two tubes, so that with the one he can observe the space on the right of the man who is going to signal back and with the other that on the left. The tablets must be set straight up in order next the telescope, and there must be a screen before both spaces, as well the right as the left, ten feet in length and of the height of a man so that by this means the torches may be seen distinctly when raised and disappear when lowered. [. . .] This device enables any news to be definitely conveyed. (p. 213 ff.)

The five by five matrix suggested by Polybius is also referred to as Polybius square.

The documentation of explicit point-to-point control procedures such as flow control, forward error correction (by means of redundancy, acknowledgments, and retransmissions), and priority handling can be traced back to theoretical accounts from the 17th Century, namely Hooke (1726); hints can also be found in Wilkins (1641), a comprehensive work on cryptography in long distance optical signaling, which in turn refers back to Polybius (1925). To quote from Hooke (1726):

> There will be also requisite several other Characters, which may, for Expedition, express a whole Sentence, to be continually made use of, whilst the Correspondents are attentive and communicating. The sentences to be express'd by one Character may be such as these in Fig. 2. [Signal 1] I am ready to communicate [synchronization]. [Signal 2] I am ready to observe [idem]. [Signal 3] I shall be ready presently [delay]. [Signal 4]

> I see plainly what you shew [acknowledgment]. Shew the last again [an error code]. Not too fast [rate control]. Shew faster [idem]. Answer me presently. Dixi [I have spoken, i. e., end-of-text]. Make Haste to communicate this to the next Correspondent [priority]. I stay for an Answer; and the like. All which may be expressed by several single Characters, to be exposed on the Top of the Poles [instead of suspended below them, like the characters for message data], by themselves [. . .] so as no Confusion may be created thereby. (pp. 147 f.)

For a comprehensive discussion of the history of control signals in data communication see also Holzmann and Pehrson (1994, ch. 1, particularly pp. 35 ff., and ch. 6, particularly the section on control signals, pp. 211 ff., and the section on protocol rules, pp. 213 ff.). Holzmann and Pehrson also discuss in detail the developments toward telegraphy in France (by Claude Chappe) and Sweden (by Abraham N. Edelcrantz), as well as the first telegraphy 'inter-networking' experiments at around 1800 (pp. 106 ff.).

26 (11). For completeness' sake, here is the whole list of relevant publications (as in public, not confidential or "for official use only") by Baran and his colleagues at RAND: the series of reports (also referred to as the "dozen research memoranda") includes Baran (1964*a*); Boehm and Baran (1964); J. W. Smith (1964); Baran (1964*b*); Baran (1964*e*); Baran (1964*f*); Baran (1964*g*); Baran (1964*h*); Baran (1964*c*); Baran (1964*i*); Baran (1964*j*). This report series is largely based on two earlier papers, also published at RAND: Baran (1960); Baran (1962). And, finally, there was a peer reviewed paper released roughly at the same time the report series was published (Baran 1964*d*), and a 1967 follow-up on the 1964 report series.

27 (11). Such corporate networks were based mostly — very much in the tradition of telegraphy — on punch cards as well as leased telephone lines that would provide for dedicated connections between branches, or to a central entity. Also, they were not of general purpose application nature. At most, they would allow special purpose terminals to communicate to a central computer, transmitting characters or lines of characters as part of a dedicated application serving no more than one specific purpose, e. g., flight reservation or financial reporting (Walden 1990, pp. 341 f.). For a brief account of private networks in the 1950s and 1960s see also Davies and Barber (1973, ch. 4).

28 (11). For a telegraphy system of the late 1950s see Vernam (1958). Roberts (1978) notes:

> Packet switching technology was not really an invention, but a reapplication of the basic dynamic-allocation techniques used for over a century by the mail, telegraph, and torn paper tape switching systems. (p. 1307)

29 (11). Baran (1977) recalls the response of analog communications peoples in the early 1960s:

> The reason that it was necessary to write literally a two-inch thick pile of paper "On Distributed Communications" down to the transistor-by-transistor level was the response by communication experts not familiar with digital processing. They kicked, screamed, grumbled and worse. Their response tended to be emotional, often with anger, and rarely with humor. They were initially certain that proponents did not understand how communications systems work. Part of their response can be appreciated by the realization that the telephone plant even at that time represented an investment in the tens of billions of dollars. When someone comes around and talks about building inexpensive communications networks using unreliable links and nodes, and of networks arranged willy nilly for extremely high survivability, it violates all their basic premises of network design. (p. 460)

30 (11). Digression: Roberts and Wessler (1970) explicitly credit Baran and his RAND reports as a major source of inspiration for the whole Arpanet project:

> The distributed store and forward system [by Baran] was chosen, after careful study, as the ARPA Network communication system. (p. 545)

See also Norberg et al. (1996, p. 166); Hafner and Lyon (1998, p. 77); and Beranek (2000) on the influence of Paul Baran's RAND Reports on ARPA's Lawrence Roberts. Plus, see a reference to minutes of a 1967 ARPA meeting which clearly indicate that the work of Baran had been very much common ground at that time:

> It is anticipated that extremely dynamic traffic routing procedures will be employed, implemented by programs in each IMP. In particular a version of the Baran (of RAND) hot potato method may be employed. The notion of the packet (an entity of 1000 bits maximum) was introduced, where a given message could be composed of many packets. The routing mechanism would deal with the packet, thus packets of the same message may traverse different routes from source to destination. The problem now arises of packets of common message arriving at their common destination out of time sequence. (Engelbart 1967, pp. 1 f.)

In fact, O'Neill (1995, pp. 78 f.) reports that Baran met with ARPA IPTO network project members at least twice, in November 1967 and in March 1968.

BBN's Frank Heart, too, credits Baran with laying the foundations to the later development of Arpanet:

> One of the most important early studies of computer networks was performed by Paul Baran and his colleagues at the RAND Corporation in the early 1960s. Many concepts central to the later development of the Arpanet and other computer networks were first described in the series of reports published by RAND in 1964 [. . .].
>
> Baran anticipated many of the developments in practical networks that came a full decade later. In the Distributed Adaptive Message Block Network [the network put forward by Baran], a "multiplexing station" connects up to 1024 terminals of widely differing characteristics. Automatic user-to-user cryptography is integrated into the network switching technique to ensure efficiency. Both satellite links and low-cost microwave relay systems are suggested as techniques for providing the network with very high data rate circuits. The concept of a "message block" is introduced: a packet of up to 1024 bits of header and data, which is the unit of data transferred in the network. One of the most interesting aspects of this study is that it concluded that a large-scale digital transmission network

> was not only feasible but also highly cost-effective, and proposed that many of the switching functions be implemented in hardware. Baran was considering ways of making extremely reliable networks, and so preferred simple solutions and reliable hardware where possible. (Heart et al. 1978, pp. III-5 f.)

Note, though, that Heart was considering the higher level contribution of Baran, and it was left to the BBN team and the host sites of the Arpanet to work out the myriad of actual implementation issues that would arise in a real network, none of which Baran could come to deal with since his work remained largely a desk based exercise, not a real engineering project. The subtleties of routing; flow control, bandwidth and delay; congestion control and recovery; error control; and the drawing of the line between network and hosts only became relevant issues when work on the Arpanet progressed at around 1970.

Still, Paul Baran was rightly among the first four people to receive the IEEE Internet Award in 2000, the other three being Donald Davies, Leonard Kleinrock, and Lawrence Roberts — "[f]or their early, preeminent contributions in conceiving, analyzing and demonstrating packet-switching networks, the foundation technology of the Internet".

DIGRESSION: Speaking of Donald Davies, and as another lengthy (but instructive) aside, it is apt to briefly summarize the conceptual contributions and actual experiences in computer networking made at the National Physical Laboratory in the UK. Not only did Davies as early as 1965 offer a strikingly accurate prediction of the ultimately dominant uses of public data networking — not resource sharing, but much rather "everyday purposes such as shopping". His group was also well aware of the benefits of packet switching, and by 1967 they had built what to all intents and purposes amounted to a "local network". In fact, the term local network was first introduced in Davies et al. (1967). Davies (1988) recalls from the 1965 to 1969 time frame:

> Our local area network was built around one-megabit lines because we used coaxial cable. [. . .] [The network operated] using a link protocol that is the so called one-bit protocol. In a lot of the theoretical work on protocols, this has been used as an example, because it's so simple and neat. There have even been

> people who have written papers to show it didn't work, but in fact we were using it, and everywhere, on every link, in our local area network, this very simple line protocol was being used. [. . .] [I]t had the possibility of [connecting] 512 terminals [but also minicomputers, PDP-8s, and other small computers], and very soon [. . .] it was working properly. About a year after it first worked, we completely rewrote the software, because we realized we were not going very fast. When it was under full steam, it was carrying about a million packets a day, which was rather more than any single ARPA node, which is not surprising, because we had a lot of people around the laboratory, and as you can imagine, local area communications is always more intense than distant, because you've got more of a community of interest. [. . .]
>
> I'm quite certain we had the world's first local area network of the present era, but it was largely unnoticed because the rest of the local area networks hadn't been trumpeted at all at that time. All the emphasis was on Arpanet, which was fine. Arpanet was a tremendous achievement. Really, we didn't make a great deal of publicity.

Given their budgetary constraints and the typical European PTT politics at the time, Davies' group never had a chance to develop their networking ideas into any form of larger scale or even public service despite their early progress in networking. Davies (1988) concludes:

> The people who ran the Post Office, knew that telephone was their real traffic, and that telephone switching was going to stay circuit switching forever, which possibly it will. I was always being told that the revenue we're going to get from data communication is terribly small. It's never going to approach what we get from our ordinary telephone network, so we concentrate on what matters. People who were making the commercial decisions in the Post Office were very much opposed to it. I think that the guys in industry naturally see that. They wouldn't go out and make a special development of packet switching and hope that the Post Office might come along. There wasn't,

> also, really, much chance of building private networks. Private networks were closely controlled. For a long time, you had to use modems. It was very restrictive. Modems had to be supplied by the Post Office, and if you built a private network, you weren't allowed to let any of it to provide service to anybody else. That was absolutely forbidden.

Pointing to the intricacies of networking that were later to be addressed in the Arpanet efforts R. E. Kahn (1989) thus comments:

> [W]hat he [Donald Davies] did was hook a bunch of terminals up to one mini-computer, just to show you could type on one terminal and it would come out on the other through switching the packets out different lines. So he demonstrated the ability to switch, but he did not have anything that resembled a wide area network with algorithms, much congestion control to worry about, things like that. (p. 12)

Still, a surprising number of original developments stem from the NPL work, anticipating several of the notions that are essentially still with us to this day. First, they made a number of high level observations about generality and flexibility of data networking:

> We have not found it possible to present the design of the network in an entirely logical manner, starting from well-defined users' requirements, because the set of users for which it caters is not determined in advance. There is a wide variety of potential users of digital communication, and we must adapt our design to deal efficiently with the largest range. (Davies et al. 1967, p. 2.2)

And, on end-to-end error control:

> It is thought that all users of the network will provide themselves with some kind of error control and that without difficulty this could be made to show up a missing packet. Because of this, loss of packets, if it is sufficiently rare, can be tolerated. (Davies et al. 1967, p. 2.3)

Second, the whole notion of packet switching may, in fact, plausibly be traced back to Davies (1966)—the first paper to use the term "packet", at that. Davies develops the conceptual separation of user level "messages", and the smaller units of data—"packets"—that those messages would have to be broken up into before being transmitted through the network:

> [I]nformation is carried through the network in relatively small units, which are stored at each node through which they pass. The unit in which information is carried must be distinguished from the message as understood by the user. [. . .] The user is aware of the message as the unit of information he wishes the system to carry, but for its own purposes in allocating channel capacity the network may break up the users' messages into smaller units. Smaller units for transmission must be distinguished and we shall call them "packets". Each packet contains, in addition to the information being carried for the user, certain data, [. . .] which is needed by the communication system ["source, destination, route"]. (p. 9)

Next, Bartlett (1968) is one of the first papers to point to the merit of layered design:

> If interfaces between adjacent levels can be defined, improvements in technology at any one level do not involve redesign or change at any other level. (p. 705)

Last, Davies's group developed a number of key architectural concepts which clearly anticipate some of the later Arpanet design decisions. On the concept of specialized switching equipment serving a host computer:

> We never believed that you should just connect like minicomputers and then program them, and that would be your switching center. It has always seemed to me that since telephone switches were highly specialized mechanisms, so data switches should be. So right from the beginning [. . .] we envisioned special hardware which would do all the input and output and so on, and therefore the packet switching would only be concerned with moving pointers around. A pointer to a packet would be assembled in store and be ready for transmission, then it would be moved. (Davies 1988)

Also, the concept of TIPs had been anticipated in their earlier implementations of terminal processors (Campbell-Kelly 1987, pp. 236 f.).

31 (11). To quote Baran (1964*d*) slightly more extensively:

> Reliability and raw error rates are secondary. The network must be built with the expectation of heavy damage anyway. Powerful error removal methods exist. (p. 5)

And, indeed, while the later end-to-end paper by Saltzer et al. (1984) discusses the example of "careful", meaning reliable, file transfer as the canonical example in which an end-to-end principle applies, the argument that an application requiring reliable data transmission will have to check on this for itself in order to cover potential errors all the way from source to destination is actually so trivial as to be no more than a truism: As for 'correct' file transfer, there is no choice about whether *not* to implement end-to-end checks in the first place — an end-to-end *principle* is thus unnecessary.

Much rather, the crucial point is the logical conclusion that flows from this truism (and that is only imperfectly covered by the metaphor of 'end-to-end'): excessive measures aimed at reliability at lower non-end-to-end levels are futile in a theoretical sense, and, at a pragmatic level, to be weighed against the benefits and costs they entail for the end points to the communication. The end-to-end principle as such adds little insight into how this trade-off is to be resolved. Arguably, it is by historical accident, that the end-to-end arguments proved the powerful frame of reference for arguing about trade-offs in the placement of functions it turned out to remain to this day.

32 (11). Of course, the notion of obtaining arbitrary reliability from the parallel redundancy of unreliable parts owes credits to prior work, too; most notably Neumann (1956). However, the detailed trade-offs in an application to data networking had not been dealt with before Baran.

As an aside, it is all good to be smart and argue that IP's best effort would, strictly speaking, also cover no effort whatsoever. However, the notion of end-to-end arguments was never meant as an excuse for dispensing with *all* efforts in between two end points of a communication. Note Saltzer et al. (1984):

> Clearly, some effort at the lower levels to improve network reliability can have a significant effect on application performance. (p. 281)

33 (11). Even a redundancy level of 1.5, meaning that every node in the network would be connected to three other nodes, would leave virtually all of the nodes perfectly connected should 20 percent of the nodes fail. A redundancy level of four (every node connected to 8 other nodes) would leave the remaining network fully intact should half of the nodes fail. See Baran (1960, pp. 15 ff.), Figure N.2, and Figure N.3. Similar results obtain for the failure of links rather than nodes (Baran 1964*d*, p. 3).

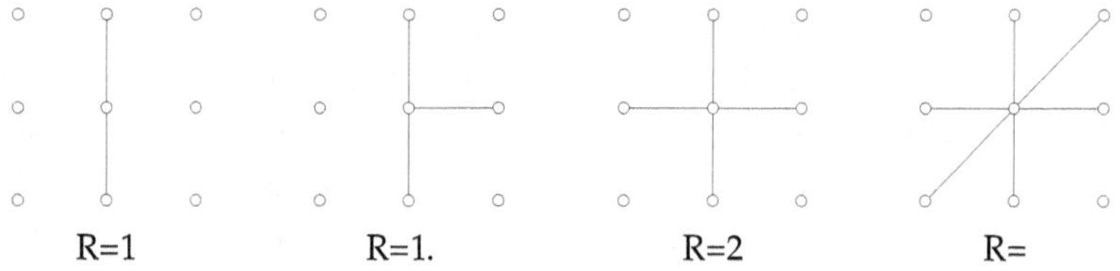

Figure N.2: Paul Baran's redundancy levels; Source: Baran (1964*d*, p. 2)

34 (12). See also Figure 9 at page 15, Figure 15 at page 24, as well as the brief elaboration at page 23 in Baran (1960).

As an aside, the importance of protecting the connectedness of end points has, not surprisingly, been discussed before in other contexts. E. g., Holzmann (1994) quotes a French newspaper article from 1841 discussing the superiority of optical telegraphy links over electrical ones in the face of malicious adversaries:

> [A] single man in a single day could, without interference, cut all the electrical wires terminating in Paris; it is obvious that a single man could sever, in ten places, in the course of a day, the electrical wires of a particular line of communication, without being stopped or even recognized. (p. 8)

35 (12). See note 30.

36 (12). Baran halted the plans for implementing a network in 1966 when the DoD turned responsibility for building the planned network from the Air Force over to the newly formed Defense Communications Agency

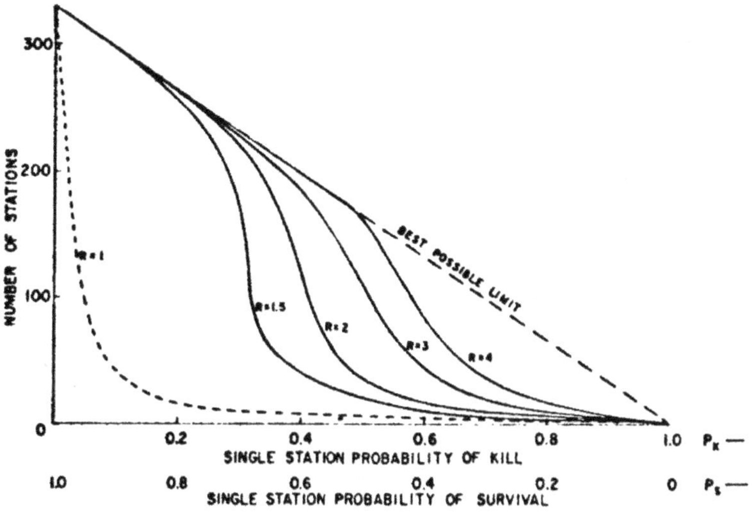

Figure N.3: Sensitivity to node destruction as a function of redundancy of node connectedness; Source: Baran (1960, p. 17, figure 10)

(DCA) (which, as an aside, took over the management of the later Arpanet, but only once it was firmly in place):

> We agreed that DCA had the charter. The legal determination had been made. We also agreed that the then present DCA wasn't up to the task. I felt that they could be almost guaranteed to botch the job since they had no understanding for digital technology, nor for leading edge high technology development. Further, they lacked enthusiasm. Sometimes, if a manager doesn't have the staff but has the drive and smarts to assemble the right team, one could justify taking a chance. But lacking skills, competence, and motivation meant betting on a sure loser.
>
> We found ourselves agreeing that DCA should not be given the funds to proceed, as the chance of their success would be too low to justify the risk. This risk was compounded because we both knew that if the project turned into a botch, it would be extremely difficult to get it going again. Detractors would

> have proof that it couldn't be done. We decided to wait until an organization with the requisite competence could be found that could take on the task within the DoD restrictions. (Baran 1990, p. 34)

See also Hafner and Lyon (1998, pp. 63 f.) for a brief elaboration.

37 (13). To quote from the Arpanet RFQ (Scheblik et al. 1968):

> [T]o guard against burdening connected Hosts with network responsibilities, a communication subnet shall be constructed consisting of store-and-forward computers (called IMPs or interface message processors) located at contractor sites [that is, host sites]. Each IMP shall be connected to several other IMPs by full duplex 50 kbps common carrier communication links creating a strongly-interconnected net. Typically, there will be three or four full duplex lines at each site that can serve to benefit routing and network buffering. (p. 22)

To the hosts the network would appear as a simple I/O system not much different from a printer or a tape drive:

> From the point of view of the ARPA contractors as users of the network, the communication subnet is a self-contained facility whose software and hardware is maintained by the network contractor. In designing Interconnection Software we should only need to use the I/O conventions for moving data into and out of the subnet and not otherwise be involved in the details of subnet operation. Specifically, error checking, fault detection, message switching, fault recovery, line switching, carrier failures and carrier quality assessment, as required to guarantee reliable network performance, are the sole responsibility of the network contractor. (p. 25)

Errors in the IMP subsystem were to be so infrequent as to be negligible:

> It is vitally important that the users have confidence in the overall reliability of the network. Low probability of wrong or lost messages, particularly when undetected, is desired. The mean time between failures due to undetected parity errors is predicted to be less than one message per year; other errors will

> hopefully not increase that rate significantly. Errors that occur after the message is passed to the Host should not be considered. Also, when a Host refuses to accept messages, the loss of those messages, if reported, is not considered as important as other losses. (p. 35)

Heart et al. (1970), still very confident about the prospect of building a virtually error-free subnetwork:

> [T]he mean time between undetected errors in the subnet should be on the order of years. (p. 554)

Of course, it turned out later that the process of ensuring correctness and reliability of the subnetwork involved much more than merely checking for bit errors by means of adding checksums—see our note 163 and accompanying text.

38 (13). For more detailed background on the Arpanet IMPs see various asides throughout, plus especially sections 4.1 through 4.3.

39 (13). To quote slightly more fully from Scheblik et al. (1968):

> Each IMP is required to coordinate its actions with its own Host. These activities include the acceptance of messages from the transmitting Host upon request (at the IMP's convenience), and the delivery of messages to the receiving Host (at the receiving Host's convenience). (pp. 8 f.)

40 (13). Quote:

> The basic notion of a subnet leads directly to a series of questions about the relationship between the Hosts and the subnet: What tasks shall be performed by each? What constraints shall each place on the other? What dependence shall the subnet have on the Hosts? In considering these questions, we were guided by the following principles: (1) The subnet should function as a communications system whose essential task is to transfer bits reliably from a source location to a specified destination. Bit transmission should be sufficiently reliable and error free to obviate the need for special precautions (such as storage for retransmission) on the part of the Hosts; (2) The

> average transit time through the subnet should be under a half second to provide for convenient interactive use of remote computers; (3) *The subnet operation should be completely autonomous. Since the subnet must function as a store and forward system, an IMP must not be dependent upon its local Host. The IMP must continue to operate whether the Host is functioning properly or not and must not depend upon a Host for buffer storage or other logical assistance such as program reloading. The Host computer must not in any way be able to change the logical characteristics of the subnet; this restriction avoids the mischievous or inadvertent modification of the communication system by an individual Host user;* (4) Establishment of Host-to-Host protocol and the enormous problem of planning to communicate between different computers should be an issue separated from the subnet design. (Heart et al. 1970, pp. 552 f., emphasis added)

41 (15). Initially, the IMPs only guarded against line errors; later the checksumming procedures were extended so as to cover the IMPs' own operations, too. See McQuillan (1973) plus the second digression in our note 155 for some elaboration of the use of checksumming in the Arpanet.

42 (15). Rulifson (2009) notes:

> [B]ack then, everything failed a lot, both hardware and software. There were no networks, but the actual hardware and software modules in systems. So, we built in some mechanisms to try to keep the overall system going even when pieces failed. [. . .] I think [Douglas T.] Ross had a [. . .] [large] impact on the way we built the systems for the SDS940 [an early time sharing system used at SRI for the Douglas Engelbart's "oN-Line System" (NLS), an early hypertext system]. Somewhere in the back of my mind, I remember programming to catch exceptions and failures and recover and learning to think about that from Ross. For RFC 1 [S. D. Crocker (1969)], I was taking our experiences from a non-networked machine and anticipating what would happen when we introduced even more components that would fail.

43 (15). Deloche (1969*b*) repeats the concerns with BBN's Host-IMP interface:

> What happens if a message, issued from the Host, reaches the IMP with an error due to the transmission? From the BBN specifications it appears that this error will be transmitted as far [as] the receiving Host. In that case must an Host-Host control procedure be provided? (p. 5)

Deloche (1969*a*) also states that the network program on the host would have to add a checksum to the user program data before sending it, and checking the integrity of the data upon arrival of messages (p. 7, but see also the UCLA Host Message format as in Fig. 1 at page 12 of Deloche 1969*a*), the rationale being:

> This checking procedure allows the verification of the right IMP-to-IMP procedure. It also protects against Host-to-IMP (or IMP-to-Host) bad transmission, and against IMP packet number inversion. (p. 4)

Deloche (1969*c*) in a description of the Network Control Program (NCP) operation (implementing the host-host protocol) mentions "host checksums" (p. 13) and the option for users to request acknowledgments for sent data (p. 11).

And, Deloche (1969*d*) emphasizes that control messages at the host level should have no meaning to the IMPs but are to be treated just like any other user data:

> A control message has a structure identical to that of a regular message; it only differs from it by the text which is for use by Network programs instead of users.
>
> Let us insist that this control procedure is completely unrelated to transmission control procedures implemented in the IMP computers. We are here at the Host level (Network programs), and therefore control messages [. . .] are transmitted over the IMPs like regular messages. (p. 14)

44 (15). See RFCs 39, 40, 46 (Harslem and Heafner 1970*a*; Harslem and Heafner 1970*b*; Meyer 1970*a*).

45 (16). Indeed, the same strategy was used at the IMP level:

> If there is no [checksum] error [in a packet received] by an IMP, an acknowledgment (with its own checksum) is sent back to the transmitting node. If there is an error, no acknowledgment is sent and the packet will be retransmitted (Heart et al. 1978, p. II-16)

Already, BBN (1969*a*), laying out the Initial Design for Interface Message Processors for the ARPA Computer Network, had been very explicit about the usefulness of positive acknowledgments, as well as the uselessness of negative acknowledgments:

> Each time an IMP receives *and accepts* a packet it returns a positive acknowledgment to the transmitting IMP. The transmitting IMP retains its copy of the packet until it receives the positive acknowledgment. The transmitting IMP will retransmit the packet if an acknowledgment is not received within a time-out period. It will continue to try transmissions via a different route if necessary, until such time as a positive acknowledgment is returned. We have explicitly avoided the use of negative acknowledgments which we feel are insufficient and consequently redundant. (pp. 2 f., emphasis in original)

As an aside, already before the Arpanet RFQ was issued, some thought had gone into the problem of error control. R. E. Kahn, by then at BBN, wrote a brief memorandum in 1968 in which he argued for a 24 bit checksum to be added to each packet exchanged in the network (assuming a packet size of around 1000 bits). This checksum requirement became part of the RFQ (p. 49), in turn (as did a maximum packet size of 1024 bits, pp. 46 f.; the same packet size, in fact, that had been proposed by Baran 1964*d*, p. 6).

46 (17). See Metcalfe (1974) as quoted in note 82 for an instructive note on the irrelevance of the source of error for the recovery strategy.

As an aside, note that the problem of disjunct control state in the sender and receiver generally makes necessary a strategy to obtain idempotence of the action in question. Notes Reed (1978):

> The basic problem lies in the knowledge that the requester has of the state of his action after a requesting message has been

> sent. If the requester receives a proper response, then it is sure that the action has been performed. However, if it has received no response, then the requester only knows that the request may not have been processed, not that it has not been wholly or partially processed. Achieving reliable control of remote actions requires some tricky design of the remote actions, so that a request may be repeated if no response has been gotten in an appropriate time, without causing errors due to running the request more than once. (p. 34)

Typically, idempotence is obtained by some identification number scheme. Note that the problem of dealing with duplicate messages is not limited to the lower levels of communication, but extends all the way up to the application level (Reed 1978, p. 36; D. Russell 1989, pp. 301 ff.).

47 (17). We submit that our analysis here is, of course, very much stylized. Simply disregarding errors will not help much in addressing the root causes of the underlying error symptoms. It was for this very reason that (1) IMPs included elaborate error monitoring and reporting facilities, (2) the first node on the Arpanet was with Kleinrock at UCLA who was tasked with running the Arpanet Network Measurement Center, and (3) BBN deployed a Network Control Center (NCC) along with the fifth IMP they installed at BBN, Cambridge, MA.

48 (17). As for acknowledgments in general, this is effectively what any protocol aiming at reliable service effectively does to this day. Sunshine (1975) summarizes:

> A correctly functioning PAR protocol [Positive Acknowledgment/Retransmission protocol] with infinite retry count never loses or duplicates messages. [Corollary:] A correctly functioning PAR protocol with finite retry count never loses or duplicates messages, and the probability of failing to deliver a message can be made arbitrarily small by the sender. (p. 3)

Digression: See also Burton and Sullivan (1972); Pouzin and Zimmermann (1978, p. 1364); Liu et al. (1997, p. 173) for overviews of the various acknowledgment strategies based on positive acknowledgment (ACK) of received data (also referred to as Automatic Repeat Query or ARQ schemes). The most obvious improvement to a simple *send A, wait for*

ACK A, send B, wait for ACK B, etc. scheme (stop-and-wait ARQ) is to decouple data and acknowledgment channels and allow the cumulative acknowledgment of multiple blocks of data (continuous ARQ), thus improving throughput significantly. (Such schemes can easily be traced back to the very early 1960s, see the references in Burton and Sullivan 1972.) For a discussion of the overhead of positive acknowledgments versus negative acknowledgments (NAKs or NACKs), and the trade-off of retransmission timers depending on the expected reliability of the link see also Edge and Hinchley (1978). As an aside, until the early 1970s it was widely believed that Forward Error Correction (FEC) schemes could be designed so as to make redundant the need for any retransmissions:

> The conclusion [that ARQ schemes are superior to FEC schemes] may leave coding theorists somewhat upset, and indeed the authors have been frequently confronted with arguments which have the following general tone: Shannon's capacity theorem [Shannon 1948] states that for any channel there is a quantity called the channel capacity. As long as the information rate through the channel does not exceed this capacity, it is theoretically possible, with the use of forward error-correcting codes alone, to achieve an error probability as low as one desires. Therefore, there should, in principle, be no need for ARQ systems. (Burton and Sullivan 1972, p. 1300)

The belief that FEC schemes could be found that would render all need for ARQ unnecessary has, of course, not come to pass given the subtleties of mixed burst and random errors in real world data transmission systems which are inherently difficult to cover with any reasonable FEC overhead.

Another aside: As for the control over timeouts and number of retransmissions, fixing timers for the termination of a "reliable" connection for lack of acknowledgments has been tried, but turned out not to be a very good idea. Clark (1982*a*) elaborates:

> Clients of TCP can be divided into two classes: those running on immediate behalf of a human, such as Telnet, and those supporting a program, such as a mail sender. Humans require a sophisticated response to errors. Depending on exactly what went wrong, they may want to abandon the connection at once,

> or wait for a long time to see if things get better. Programs do not have this human impatience, but also lack the power to make complex decisions based on details of the exact error condition. For them, a simple timeout is reasonable.
>
> Based on these considerations, at least two modes of operation are needed in TCP. One, for programs, abandons the connection without exception if the TCP timer expires. The other mode, suitable for people, never abandons the connection on its own initiative, but reports to the layer above when the timer expires. Thus, the human user can see error messages coming from all the relevant layers, TCP and ICMP, and can request TCP to abort as appropriate. (pp. 8 f.)

Today's TCP thus allows for timeouts in order to terminate connections after arbitrarily long periods of missing acknowledgment, with the value of the timers being at full discretion of the process using TCP. Braden (1989) put it:

> An application *must* be able to set the value for R2 [a counter for the number of retransmission attempts] for a particular connection. For example, an interactive application might set R2 to "infinity," giving the user control over when to disconnect. (p. 100)

49 (17). In fact, BBN's Frank Heart (who managed the IMP project) chose the computers to be used for the IMPs not least by their ruggedness and thus safeness from "inquisitive graduate students". Hafner and Lyon (1998) recount:

> [T]he reliability issue led Heart to favor the new Honeywell DDP-516, the machine housed in the heavy-duty steel cabinet. [. . .] The 516 [. . .] helped to settle Heart's fear that inquisitive graduate students might bring down the network with their tinkering. He could rest much easier knowing the IMPs would be housed in a box built to withstand war. (p. 97)

50 (17). There were ample grounds for host sites to be cool to the idea of networking. First, until 1967 it was not clear to which extent host sites would have to be involved in running the network, and the amount of

resources they would have to contribute to it. Salus (1995), on the initial plan for the Arpanet (as discussed at the Ann Arbor meeting where it was superseded by Wesley Clark's IMP idea, see note 51):

> The plan [. . .] was to connect all the computers by phone lines and data sets [modems], so that every computer could establish contact with any other by means of circuit switching. (p. 21)

Second, the network to be built was not supposed to be for any "fun" whatsoever; in fact, Roberts (1967*b*) specifically excludes "message services" (such as the later network email) from the motivations behind Arpanet:

> [A] network can be used to handle interpersonal message transmissions. [. . .] However, it is not an important motivations for a network of scientific computers. (p. 3.1)

Rather, the network was intended to be used for sharing data and programs — the benefits of neither were tangible at the time. Roberts put it:

> The advantages which can be obtained when computers are interconnected in a network such that remote running of programs is possible, include advantages due to specialized hardware and software at particular nodes as well as increased scientific communication. (p. 3.1)

The same argument recurs throughout the literature on Arpanet, see, e. g., Roberts and Wessler (1970, p. 543), Schelonka (1974, p. 1045), Heart et al. (1978, pp. II-2 f.), Kleinrock (1978, p. 1321). It is an odd irony that games and personal communication uses of the networks, not "experimentation and resource sharing", arguably turned out to be the decisive drivers of network growth.

51 (18). The core idea to the clean separation of the subnetwork and the hosts goes back to an anecdotally reported episode involving Wesley Clark (then at Washington University, previously working at MIT's Whirlwind and SAGE projects), one of a group of IPTO principal investigators who consulted to Lawrence Roberts and ARPA in the run-up to the Arpanet RFQ. To copiously quote from Roberts (1967*a*), the first ever written record of the Wesley Clark subnetwork design idea:

The concept which Wes [Clark] proposed was to insert a small computer like the PDP-8 between each participant's computer and the transmission line network. The small computer, an Interface Message Processor (IMP), would perform the functions of dial up, error checking, retransmission, routing and verification. Thus the set of IMP's plus the telephone lines and data sets would constitute a Message Switching Network. The protocol which we are intending to establish would define the communication format between the IMP's. The interface between the participant's computer and his IMP would now be a digital interface of a much simpler sort so that no considerations of error checking, retransmission and inter-network routing would have to be considered. Messages could be supplied which merely requested that a message be sent to another node stating the priorities for speed of transmission and, if desired, error probability. That is, if a message consists solely of non-critical data, it could be sent unchecked through the network at a lower cost. [. . .]

The major advantage of this plan is that a unified, straightforward design of the network can be made and implemented without undue consideration of the various contractors' buffer space, interpret speed and other machine requirements. The interface to the contractor's computer would be a much simpler digital connection with an additional flexibility provided by programming the IMP. The network section of the IMP's program would be completely standard and provide guaranteed buffer space and uniform characteristics, thus the entire planning job is substantially simplified. The data sets and transmission lines utilized between the small computers would most likely be standardized upon, but as changes occurred in the communication tariffs or data rates available, it would be much more straightforward to modify just the small computer net rather than twenty different computers. As soon as the need became apparent, additional small computers could be located at strategic connection points within the network to concentrate messages over cross-country lines. Finally, the

> modifications required to currently operating systems would be substantially less if we utilized these small computers since there will be no requirement to find buffer spaces, hold messages for retransmission, verify reception of messages and dial up telephone lines.
>
> The basic advantage of utilizing small computers to run a message switching network is an increased speed for the realization of the network, a decreased load on the main computer and improved flexibility as changes are required. The technique also provides a distinct network entity which is useful in presenting the network publicly. In cases where a participant felt his computer should be used to connect to the telephone system directly, this would, of course, be possible if he followed the approved protocol and conventions; however, the requirements on his computer might be somewhat more demanding as to required buffer space and message rerouting. (Roberts 1967*a*, spelling corrected)

See also Roberts (1967*b*, pp. 3.2 f.) for discussions of the Wesley Clark episode, as well as the recount by Hafner and Lyon (1998, pp. 71 ff., 123), O'Neill (1995, p. 78), and, based on interviews with Lawrence Roberts and Robert W. Taylor (then director of ARPA's IPTO), Norberg et al. (1996, pp. 163 f.).

It is fair to say that the logical and administrative separation between IMP subnetwork and the attached hosts was a very happy coincidence of engineering sensibility and political feasibility. We have already considered in note 49 and accompanying text that BBN was fine with not having to deal with host level issues and rather provide a clean and well defined interface. On operational grounds, this happiness was shared by the military, too, who, after all, funded the whole exercise in the first place. Says Schelonka (1974):

> IMPs/TIP [Terminal IMP] ownership remains with ARPA/RML [Range Measurement Laboratory, Patrick Air Force Base, FL] to insure that network integrity is preserved although custodial responsibilities are delegated to the [host] site. (p. 1046)

On a final side note, Salus (1995) reports that Clark saw his idea of building an IMP subnetwork as very much a logical conclusion to the problem that did not take much ingenuity to arrive at:

> Clark is extremely modest about this [episode]. "Someone else would have thought of it in a few days or weeks," he remarked to me. (p. 21)

And, in fact, as we have seen in note 30, the concept of boxes dedicated to assuming the packet switching functions on behalf of the actual comupters attached to a communication network had been arrived at (probably independently) by Davies's group at NPL when building their local network.

52 (18). Roberts (1986) recalls:

> Robert Kahn of BBN organized the demonstration installing a complete Arpanet node at the conference hotel, with about 40 active terminals permitting access to dozens of computers all over the U. S. This public demonstration was, for many (if not most) of the ICCC attendees, proof that packet switching really worked. At this time, it was difficult for many experienced professionals to accept the fact that a collection of computers, wideband circuits, and minicomputer switching nodes (equipment totaling well over 100 pieces) could all function together reliably. The Arpanet demonstration lasted for three days and clearly displayed its reliable operation in public. The network provided highly reliable service to thousands of attendees during the entire duration of the conference. (p. 53)

53 (18). At the time Pouzin was at Institut de Recherche d'Informatique et d'Automatique (French National Institute for Research in Computer Science and Control, IRIA). The Cyclades project was launched in early 1972 by the French Ministry of Industry. See Pouzin (1973*b*, p. 81), and Zimmermann (1977).

54 (18). Pouzin (1998) credits BBN:

> At the beginning of the Cyclades project, I went to the United States and consulted BBN. (my translation)

Another mention is in Pouzin (1973*b*, p. 85):

> Stimulating discussions with D. Walden (BBN) brought substantial improvement and simplification.

Walden (2009) elaborates that he went over to Paris about once every three months, meeting with and consulting to Louis Pouzin, Hubert Zimmerman and Gerard LeLann. After a while, Alexander McKenzie took over the consulting assignment.

55 (19). Note how this approach is in stark contrast to the 1968 Arpanet RFQ, for it would be "burdening connected Hosts with network responsibilities" and getting them heavily "involved in the details of subnet operation". Recall from note 37 that in the Arpanet "error checking, fault detection, message switching, fault recovery, line switching, carrier failures and carrier quality assessment, as required to guarantee reliable network performance, are the sole responsibility of the network contractor." In Cyclades, most of these functions would sit with the end hosts.

56 (19). Pouzin (1974*b*, section 3.12: Error control):

> In Cigale packets are checked and acknowledged between nodes. However node and line failures coupled with adaptive routing may result in packets being lost or duplicated. Consequently, some control mechanism is necessary to catch this type of error. It can only be done as part of a transmission procedure between a pair of correspondents.

57 (19). To quote from Pouzin (1976*b*):

> [T]he sequencing functions require that all packets be routed through a minimum of two focal points, which insure numbering and sequenced delivery. Alternate routes can only appear in between the focal points. The paths between ports and VC focal points must be unique and sequential. This creates a reliability problem when ports and focal points are not collocated in the same equipment. (p. 486, references omitted)

See also note 174 for an apt observation of this point by McQuillan and Cerf (1978*a*), and see note 64 for Pouzin's observation that carriers offering virtual circuits still use datagram facilities internally.

58 (19). Walden (2009) remembers how he once asked Pouzin about why they departed from the Arpanet approach, and Pouzin replied that they

did so in order for France to have a network that would be different from the U. S. one, and thus help them establish their own international standard.,This take is confirmed by Schafer (2009).

59 (19). It is apt to quote Pouzin more fully on both points. As for the former:

> [Our] design effort bears on a carefully layered architecture, providing for an extensible structure of protocols and network services, tailored to various classes of traffic and applications.
>
> This concern for built-in evolutionism translates itself in putting *as few features as possible at levels buried in the sensitive parts of the network*. With experience gradually building up, and depending on trends in international standards, more stable characteristics will eventually emerge. By putting them at some lower system level, it will be possible to obtain higher efficiency and reduce duplication, at the cost of freezing a few more parameters.
>
> The Cyclades design attempts to be both precise and independent from the implementation at the user level, so that heterogeneous sites can have their way, and still communicate with others in a consistent manner. (p. 80, emphasis added)

And, as for the latter:

> [In inter-network communications] [i]t seems that key-points include simplicity and open-endedness.
>
> The more sophisticated a network, the less likely it is going to interface properly with another. In particular, any function except sending packets is probably just specific enough not to work in conjunction with a neighbor. The result is *an intersection of properties rather than a union*. (p. 84, emphasis added)

60 (20). See Pouzin (1973*a*, pp. 3 ff.) for an earlier version of essentially the same argument. See also note 271 for a lengthy quote from Pouzin (1973*a*).

61 (20). Pouzin (1976*a*) elaborates:

> In such a free wheeling context [as in the U. S.], it does not appear likely that regulations per se will contribute one way

> or the other to the carrier strategy. There are indications that even more competition will be allowed in areas traditionally protected.
>
> The scene is totally different in other parts of the world, such as Europe, where all transmission services are in the hands of state monopolies. Over there [in Europe] regulations are solely designed for the protection of the monopolies. This is not surprising since monopolies are both operators and legislators. [. . .]
>
> In principle, monopolies should offer the best deal, due to economies of scale. Unfortunately, this principle is less and less visible in fact, unless there exists an independent controlling agency. E. g., in Europe the cost per mile of a point to point leased line is 3 to 5 times higher than in the USA. Crossing a national boundary line increases this factor substantially. Thus it seems that state monopolies have gone far beyond the point where they became detrimental to the user interest. [. . .]
>
> In line with those practices, it is predictable that competition will be eliminated in some segments of the data processing market, with a resulting increase in the cost of services. However, the carrier strategy is not yet clear. They may start with variations in attachment costs in order to make their own equipment and services more attractive. This in turn may help the sale of specific data processing applications under the umbrella of protected access through their own terminals. (p. 565)

As for the state of public data networking services:

> The carrier position would be stronger if they had come up with a good set of standards designed in cooperation with users and manufacturers. What everyone would welcome is standards designed for a variety of distributed computer systems, with enough generality and flexibility to meet the requirements of the next generation of systems and terminals. Instead, the carriers do not offer more than handling character terminals for simple time-sharing systems. This is a far

> cry from a useful standard, and *its useless complexity bears little relation with the services it is supposed to bring about.* (p. 566, footnotes omitted, emphasis added)

By the time Pouzin wrote those accounts, the Cyclades network was already well on its way into obscurity, owing to a lack of political commitment that finally lead to the demise of the network project in 1978 (Foucart 2006). Schafer (2009) confirms that by 1979 the Cyclades project was effectively 'dead', given (1) the opposition of the French PTT at the time, (2) the fading support of IRIA and the lack of industry interest to take over sponsorship, and (3) the decreasing strategic importance of high-level political support that had helped start the project in the first place (Maurice Allègre, director of Délégation à l'Informatique was no more there to support the project).

62 (21). The first high-profile paper on TCP (Cerf and Kahn 1974) has grown out of an earlier version that had been discussed in 1973 at a INWG meeting. In May 1973 Cerf sent out a document entitled A Partial Specification of an International Transmission Protocol to a couple of INWG members (Aupperle, Kahn, McKenzie, Metcalfe, Scantlebury, Walden, and Zimmerman) most of whom discussed it at a June meeting in New York. In September 1973, Cerf and Kahn put forward a new version of the document at the INWG meeting in Sussex, UK which integrates the discussions on the earlier version (Towards Protocols for Internetwork Communication). A first manuscript of Cerf and Kahn (1974) was then submitted to the IEEE journal Transactions on Communications in November 1973.

63 (21). As for the general state of the debate about inter-networking by that time, it is only fair to note that the superiority of end-to-end approaches over hop-by-hop approaches was, in fact, very well understood (see also section 2.5 for parts of the debate in the U. S. prior to 1977). E. g., Sunshine (1977*a*, pp. 188 f.) offers a discussion of the benefits to either approach, concluding that the former is more robust, general, and ultimately more universal than the latter.

64 (22). In France, the PTT pursued the plan to build a public VC network from ca. 1971, resulting in the RCP network (operational from 1975, see Després 1974) which was later superseded by the X.25 Transpac network (Bache and Matras 1976; Danet et al. 1976; Bache et al. 1976). Pouzin

(1976*b*) notes that all the networks offering VCs are internally based on the datagram notion:

> Even the carriers have been able to understand the advantages of decoupling the VC protocol from the transport function proper. Datapac (Bell-Canada), EPSS (UK), Telenet (USA) are typical examples of packet networks based on this approach. Thus, it is all the more intriguing that carriers deny users the privilege to adopt the same principles. (p. 487)

Although he does not cite the French RCP and later Transpac network, the argument applies to these, too.

65 (22). See note 61.

66 (24). See for the quote from Heart et al. (1970) in note 40.

67 (24). Large verbatim portions of BBN (1974*d*) can also be found in Crowther et al. (1975) and McQuillan and Walden (1977).

68 (25). Quote from BBN (1974*d*):

> A layering of functions, a hierarchy of control, is essential in a complex network environment:
>
> - For efficiency, IMPs must control subnetwork resources, and Hosts must control Host resources.
> - For reliability, the basic subnetwork environment must be under the effective control of the IMP program — Hosts should not be able to affect the usefulness of the network to other Hosts.
> - For maintainability, the fundamental message processing program should be IMP software, which can be changed under central control and much more simply than all Host programs.
> - For debugging, a hierarchy of procedures is essential, since otherwise the solution of any network difficulty will require investigating all programs (including Host programs) for possible involvement in the trouble.
>
> The nature of the problem of message processing does not change if it is moved out of the network and into the Hosts;

the Hosts would then have this very difficult job even if they do not want it.

Moving this task into the Hosts does not alleviate any network problems such as congestion, Host interference, or suboptimal performance but, in fact, makes them worse since the Hosts cannot control the use of IMP resources such as buffering, CPU bandwidth, and line bandwidth.

It is cheap to do message processing in the IMPs, and it has very few detrimental effects. (pp. 6 f.)

69 (25). BBN (1974*d*) argue:

Whatever is done at the Host level, it is critical for the communications subnetwork to handle its own problems or else it will perform poorly in many dimensions; e. g., message loss, message ordering, etc. *Without such controls, the Hosts will be in conflict with each other, degrading their performance, with no way to resolve these conflicts. (For example, if the subnetwork handles congestion by merely discarding packets whenever congestion occurs, it is as likely to discard packets of "well behaved" Hosts, whose I/O rates are closely coordinated, as to discard packets from streams between Hosts which are not coordinating their rates.)* (pp. 4 f., emphasis added)

70 (25). BBN (1974*d*) argue:

Despite the fact that some Hosts may not care how prone to message loss the subnetwork is, and despite the fact that many Hosts may need to duplicate functions also performed in the subnetwork for those (hopefully rare) instances when the subnetwork does fail, the majority of Hosts will want the subnetwork to do the best job it can so as to minimize Host performance of these functions. Every channel is noisy; and the IMP must do what it can to minimize noise. Furthermore, this is basically inexpensive to do in the IMP, especially when compared to the cost of doing it in all the Hosts and, *generally, what is done at IMP level is in no way detrimental to the Host level, even if it does not help the Host level.* [. . .] In the few areas where the present

> ARPA Network design does present real limitations to some desired types of network use (e. g., transmission of fixed, very low delay traffic such as speech), mechanisms can be added to the ARPA Network in parallel to the existing mechanisms for the purpose of accommodating these desired but presently unobtainable types of traffic service. (p. 5, emphasis added)

As for minimizing the processing of messages destined for inter-networking:

> [I]f it is politically or technically desirable to avoid some of the standard message processing for messages that are destined for internetwork transmission, it is relatively easy to allow parallel mechanisms which are subsets of the full message processing facilities. (We are currently implementing such a parallel mechanism to permit experiments of this type) [the "raw messages" facility, see BBN and Kahn (1976, pp. 3-35 f.)]. (p. 14)

71 (25). As for the problem of coordination:

> [W]ith many independent implementations of this kind, not only will initial implementation cost be high, but coordination and testing of any necessary or desirable changes will be extraordinarily difficult. This is in sharp contrast to the relative ease of making corrections, improvements, and even fundamental design changes in the subnetwork. (p. 6)

In fact, the Arpanet had seen a number of major rollouts of updates to the IMP software, which were coordinated from the BBN NCC in Cambridge, MA without needing any manual assistance at the growing number of host sites that owned an IMP. Changing the IMP software across the whole Arpanet literally required nothing more than pushing one central button, once an IMP had been bootstrapped with a physical copy of the IMP programs. (An aside, the very first few updates to the IMP software were still loaded manually and required physical distribution. But, once BBN became part of the Arpanet themselves, they quickly got the central update facility in place; see BBN 1972*b*, pp. 6 ff. as cited in note 146.)

72 (25). There is not necessarily a conflict between idiosyncratic networks and a lowest common denominator global network. The Arpanet was effectively little more than a large scale 'local' network offering reliable and

transparent data transfer, albeit one that gradually became connected to various other networks by means of special gateways (see note 261 and accompanying text); while the latter took aim at interconnecting different networks by means of a *common* protocol which would span *all* networks and would thus have to be basic enough to potentially comprise as many as possible networks (see section 5.2 for the progression from Arpanet to Internet). Any network to be part of an inter-network can offer as elaborate services to its hosts as it pleases, as long as it also conforms to the global inter-network protocol. No number of protocols and services available at a network exclude the existence of other protocols to be implemented alongside them; and, in principle, no level of Quality of Service (QoS) renders a network unfit for participation in any such 'supernetwork'. In fact, it is not unreasonable to pursue a more-is-more strategy at local scopes, and a less-is-more strategy that aims at a global scope, both at the same time—see for a fine argument about the sensibility of having various protocols at the same 'level' without any loss of generality Cohen and Postel (1983, p. 32).

In all, the sensibility of any set of principles always depends on the context at hand, and both positions make perfect sense—the Arpanet's premise of building a self-contained and reliable network, as well as the Internet's premise of leaving the bulk of network functions to the end hosts so as to allow the common protocol to be implemented by all nodes of the overall network to be as minimal and thus global as possible. It is surprising enough that the latter works (even to those who have thought long and hard about it), but it does; and as long as being part of the Internet does not prejudice the services of a constituent network in its own right, the two notions do little harm to each other.

73 (26). See section 5.1 (particularly note 249 and accompanying text) for a discussion of the requirements of interactive speech applications. Also, Tennenhouse and Wetherall (1996) have put forward a broad and somewhat extreme, though by no means implausible general take:

> There is an untapped reservoir of applications that require sophisticated network-based services to support the distribution and fusion of information. (p. 7)

74 (26). To begin with, the extensible options field in the IP header has proven largely useless:

> IP was supposed to be extensible through the use of IP options, but long ago the introduction of a hardware-assisted fast path through router forwarding engines meant that packets without IP options were forwarded much faster than packets with IP options. Today, using a new IP option would amount to a denial-of-service attack on the routing processor of many fast routers, and so such packets are highly likely to be filtered. Thus IPv4 effectively lost the use of its extension mechanism. (Handley 2006, p. 127)

And, Clark (2009*e*) seconds:

> Over time, the IP option mechanism has fallen into disuse, and it is worth considering why. It might seem that the IP option would fall into the *explicit* class of input, but the processing of the field was still inefficient, because the forwarding device had to parse all of the options to see if one of then represented an input it was to use for its PHB [local "per-hop behavior"]. The router had to process a variable-length field of unpredictable contents, and this was too much computation for a high-performance packet forwarding path; it was almost like deep packet inspection. (p. 9, emphasis in original)

In fact, Clark noted in late 1981 that "[c]urrently, options are most commonly processed by ignoring them" (p. 5). It is fair to argue that very little in this respect has changed ever since.

There have been literally hundreds of fine proposals in the last three decades on how to improve on the basic Internet model and 'instantiation', very few of which have seen widespread inter-ISP deployment. Even the slightest changes to IP have proven virtually impossible to implement, precisely because of the globality of the Internet; see e. g., Sridharan et al. (2007, pp. 6 f.) on the problem of just turning on support for the two Explicit Congestion Notification (ECN) bits (Ramakrishnan et al. 2001) in the IP header. To this very day, ECN support is still turned off by default in all major operating systems, including Linux distributions; even though

Cisco has by now fixed the problem with its home routers that caused the problem pointed to by Sridharan et al. But, since the routers have only been produced and then sold by Cisco, they cannot force users to upgrade the routers' firmware; in fact, many end users may not even be aware that their router runs a firmware that they ought to upgrade in the first place.

But, also, entirely reasonable schemes that may easily be deployed incrementally by ISPs without 'breaking' home routers (e. g., Podlesny and Gorinsky 2008) rarely offer enough benefit to get ISPs interested in deploying them. More adventurous approaches (e. g., Andersen et al. 2008; Braden et al. 2003; Guruprasad 2002) are even less likely to see any deployment, ideas on how to remedy the inflexibility of IP (e. g., Ratnasamy et al. 2005) notwithstanding.

75 (26). Clark (1988) voices a similar concern about the the emerging Internet:

> [A] problem arising from the use of host-resident mechanisms is that poor implementation of the mechanism may hurt the network as well as the host. This problem was tolerated, because the initial experiments involved a limited number of host implementations which could be controlled. However, as the use of Internet has grown, this problem has occasionally surfaced in a serious way. In this respect, *the goal of robustness, which led to the method of fate-sharing, which led to host-resident algorithms, contributes to a loss of robustness if the host misbehaves.* (p. 110, emphasis added)

As an aside, Roberts makes a number of additional points in a discussion of "Datagrams versus VC's [Virtual Circuit]" (p. 1311), but these pertain largely to more mundane cost and overhead considerations, and should probably be considered against the background of Roberts' involvement with Telenet, a company spun off from BBN that was one of the key players in the X.25 specification efforts in the mid 1970s, and specialized in offering virtual circuit interfaces based on X.25 to enterprise customers. In fact, Roberts is to this day an advocate of making the Internet offer virtual circuits rather than best effort facilities to customers (Roberts 2004).

Classic End-to-End Arguments and Beyond

76 (27). Recall that our thesis is based heavily on the records available in the literature and the personal accounts of various people we communicated with—see note 11, particularly pages 172 ff. E.g., J. Saltzer has noted in an email to the author that encryption had been far more important an issue informing the original end-to-end arguments reasoning than it might appear from the literature of the time, thus leaving our thesis slightly imbalanced on this point.

77 (28). At one stage of writing this thesis, there was a whole section, complete with copious endnotes, on the notion of network neutrality as derived from the end-to-end arguments. However, we came to realize that the notion of network neutrality is not so much an advancement of the end-to-end arguments, but rather an instance of their application to political purposes—attempts to establish network neutrality as an end-to-end argument of some sort notwithstanding. Or rather, as Hayek (1973) put it:

> Abstract rules are not likely to be invented by somebody concerned with obtaining particular results. (p. 88)

78 (28). The confusion is well captured in the abstract of the paper which argues that the paper presents a "principle, called the end-to-end argument"; and we thus have "end-to-end arguments" (in the title), "the end-to-end argument" (in the abstract, and referring to a principle to be put forward in the paper), and "end-to-end arguments" yet again (in the conclusion, and considered "part of a set of rational principles for organizing [. . .] layered [communication] systems").

Arguably, all of those notions hold, for the authors have (1) traced arguments of a debate (as in: controversy), (2) made arguments themselves (as in: a course of reasoning), and (3) posited one core argument, the "end-to-end argument" (1984, p. 278).

79 (28). It is fair to argue that the word principle in Saltzer et al. (1984) does not hold the significance that its prominent appearance in the abstract, introduction, and conclusion appears to signal. Clark (2009*c*) acknowledges that the choice of words at the time may not have been the most considerate. And, Reed (2009*c*) goes so far as to argue that "there never was an 'end-to-end principle'" (only arguments).

80 (28). It is worth recalling the remarks by Latour (1987) about the unfortunate downside that inevitably hits the lucky few "stable statements" in the literature of science: they turn into black boxes whose content becomes "slowly eroded, losing its original shape, encapsulated into more and more foreign statements, becoming so familiar and routinised that it becomes part of tacit practice and disappears from view". (See notes 19 and 11.) Saltzer et al.'s 1984 paper (first published in 1981) has thus been one of the most prominent, but also one of the least understood and probably most abused ones in the field of design principles in computer science.

Speaking of misunderstandings (some of which border conspiracy theories, and none of which, arguably, should bear any significance for the actual technical *content* of the paper, but still are often put forward), we note in passing that the Saltzer et al. paper was not intended to add to the debates of TCP/IP versus ITU's notorious X.25/X.75, nor versus ISO/OSI's CLNP/TP4 (which, by the way, emerged only after the paper); rather, it was chiefly about architectural principles and their application (Clark 2009*c*). In fact, Reed (2009*d*) states in writing:

> The end-to-end paper was not written to be a part of any war whatsoever. I say that with knowledge of all of the 3 co-authors' intents and motivations.

81 (29). Note, though, that a good name is an absolutely *essential* part of any principle (see our note 373), as is, for that matter, the possibility of drawing a diagram of it — says Alexander (1979):

> If you think you have a pattern, you must be able to draw a diagram of it. This is a crude, but vital rule. A pattern defines a field of spatial relations, and it must always be possible to draw a diagram for every pattern. In the diagram, each part will appear as a labeled or colored zone, and the layout of the parts expresses the relation which the pattern specifies. If you can't draw it, it isn't a pattern. (p. 267)

The end-to-end arguments certainly have both: a good name and a good diagram to express their main intuition (as for the latter see Figure 3.1).

82 (29). See for an elaboration section 5.2. Note Frank et al. (1975), as for intrinsically lossy networks:

> The value of an End-to-End acknowledgment is sufficiently great that it can be assumed *a priory*. However, the additional use of a Hop-by-Hop acknowledgment is not as clear. (p. 225, emphasis added)

And, note Walden and Rettberg (1975), about the design of a "gateway virtual network":

> [E]ven though gateways provide these functions [pertaining to retransmissions across lossy networks], the TCPs should retain the end-to-end retransmission capability at their level for reliability, since retransmissions performed by the gateway level are for *efficiency* rather than for *complete reliability*. (p. 122, emphasis added)

And, notes Metcalfe (1974) (in the context of the Xerox PARC's PUP Internet) on the redundancy of any control messages from the network nodes to the end hosts:

> There are several reasons why a packet might be discarded and lost at a Gateway: (1) nobody here by that name, (2) Pup too big to fit in transporting packet, (3) congestion too high right now, (4) can't get there from here, or (5) unrecoverable transmission error. The source of a packet can't, no shouldn't, care which of those strikes his packet down in its prime; the recovery procedure is the same, just time-out and retransmit. (p. 9)

By 1981 Lampson et al. conclude:

> Don't go to heroics to make lower levels have ultra reliable design: fault tolerance can be spread throughout the design and you should seriously trade off the cost of losing an occasional (infrequent) datagram. (p. 491)

83 (29). See also note 40.

84 (31). See sections 2.2 and 2.4.

85 (31). See sections 2.1 and 2.4.

86 (31). Sproull and Cohen (1978) note about the voice applications in the Arpanet from the mid-1970s onwards:

> Very few conventional transport services are required by an NVP [Network Voice Protocol]. No retransmission to remedy errors is required because a lost message is not catastrophic; both coding schemes are designed so that a parcel is decoded without knowledge of previous messages. Moreover, retransmission would introduce highly variable delays that cause worse perceptual damage than the loss of the message. (p. 1379)

See also Gray (2005) for a summary of the history of real-time interactive voice applications on the Arpanet, and Gray (2010*a*); Gray (2010*b*) for detailed recounts of the various speech experiments on Arpanet, PRNET, and WBNET (WB Satnet), plus the various specifications (NVP, NVP2) that emerged. Plus, refer to section 5.1 for an elaboration of packet speech in the Arpanet.

87 (32). See the considerations in BBN (1974*d*) as cited in note 70 and accompanying text at page 25.

88 (32). Denning (2003) notes that all great principles are, at their core, little more than "interwoven stories about the structure and behavior of field elements" , or even just the "*title of a story*" (p. 17).

89 (33). Metcalfe and Boggs (1976) put it:

> The design of the transceiver must be an exercise in paranoia. Precautions must be taken to insure that likely failures in the transceiver or station do not result in pollution of the Ether. (p. 398)

Typically, thus, every Ethernet card contains a physically distinct module to detect excessive 'jabber' and cut off the transceiver in case of malfunction. Also, repeaters will typically contain functions to cut off misbehaving network segments.

90 (33). Saltzer et al. have noted themselves that the end-to-end argument must not be interpreted without prudence and care:

> [T[he end-to-end argument is not an absolute *rule*, but rather a *guideline* that helps in application and protocol design analysis. (p. 285, emphasis added)

91 (34). See our elaborations in the preceding section, especially at pages 31 f.

92 (35). To quote more copiously from Clark (1989):

> The stateless gateway was proposed as part of the Internet design in order to insure a robust architecture. If the gateway has no state, then a crash of a gateway cannot endanger an on-going connection. If there is state in a gateway, and that state information is lost because of a crash, then it is possible that a flow would be disrupted.
>
> In moving from a gateway with no state to a gateway which caches information, it is necessary to ensure that the cached information can be lost and reconstructed. The idea of keeping in gateways only that state which can be easily reconstructed I call "soft state." (p. 15)

See also Chiappa (1995) for an elaboration of the problem of defining the notion (and particularly that of 'hard' state) more clearly; and Chiappa (2002) for a related discussion about the difference between the 'end-to-end principle' and the 'fate-sharing principle'.

93 (35). The link between the original end-to-end arguments and the fate-sharing argument is also acknowledged by IAB (1996):

> An end-to-end protocol design should not rely on the maintenance of state (i. e. information about the state of the end-to-end communication) inside the network. Such state should be maintained only in the endpoints, in such a way that the state can only be destroyed when the endpoint itself breaks (known as fate-sharing). (p. 3)

94 (35). Clark (1988) puts it:

> [T]he intermediate packet switching nodes, or gateways, must not have any essential state information about on-going connections. Instead, they are stateless packet switches, a class of network design sometimes called a "datagram" network. (p. 108)

And, IAB (1996):

> [D]atagrams are better than classical virtual circuits. The network's job is to transmit datagrams as efficiently and flexibly

> as possible. Everything else should be done at the fringes. (pp. 3 f.)

95 (35). IAB puts it:

> To perform its services, the network maintains some state information: routes, QoS guarantees that it makes, session information where that is used in header compression, compression histories for data compression, and the like. This state must be self-healing; adaptive procedures or protocols must exist to derive and maintain that state, and change it when the topology or activity of the network changes. The volume of this state must be minimized, and the loss of the state must not result in more than a temporary denial of service given that connectivity exists. Manually configured state must be kept to an absolute minimum. (p. 4)

96 (36). See also Moors (2002) who argues that congestion control and routing are functions that are best dealt with by the network, not the end hosts. However, neither the original end-to-end arguments nor the elaborations put forward subsequently and considered in this section have ever been meant to apply to *all* functions; in fact, functions such as congestion control and routing are rarely analyzed using the end-to-end arguments in the first place.

97 (37). This notion of a "common subroutine which handles all communications" can already be found in Marill and Roberts (1966, p. 429).

98 (37). Both NCP and TCP essentially established virtual circuits on behalf of application processes wishing to communicate with processes at remote host computers, which would in turn also have to communicate through an NCP or TCP on their computer. (The difference, of course, being that NCP would assume a largely reliable subnetwork, whereas TCP would assume the very opposite: an unreliable packet switching 'datagram' network.) To quote from S. D. Crocker (1970*a*):

> Processes within a Host communicate with the network through a NCP. In most Hosts, the NCP will be part of the executive, so that processes will use sysgen calls [probably: system calls] to communicate with it. The primary function of the NCP is

> to establish connections, break connections, and control flow. (p. 4)

To quote from Cerf and Kahn (1974):

> Multiplexing and demultiplexing of segments among processes are fundamental tasks of the TCP. On transmission, a TCP must multiplex together segments from different source processes and produce internetwork packets for delivery to one of its serving packet switches. On reception, a TCP will accept a sequence of packets from its serving packet switch(es). From this sequence of arriving packets (generally from different Hosts), the TCP must be able to reconstruct and deliver messages to the proper destination processes. (p. 640)

99 (37). As an aside: it would probably be possible to devise a distributed scheduling scheme across applications based on global lock variables or a contention scheme much like that in the Ethernet; but such approaches depend on applications well-behaving and honoring the access protocol— particularly, they suffer from defective or malicious applications potentially holding up access to the network. In any setting where applications may not be 'trusted' as much as a tried and tested transport module, such an approach would not only be unreasonable, but be very much untenable.

100 (37). We note here in passing that Moors carries this point beyond the merit it deserves, arguing that TCP is effectively in violation of the end-to-end principle, an assessment that we cannot concur with, especially given that applications are free to bypass TCP and use whichever transport protocol they please. Says Moors:

> It is important that the application be able to disable integrity checking by the transport layer (and this is not possible with the most popular reliable transport protocol, TCP). This is because while most applications can neglect the chance of errors in the local system, some applications will be concerned about errors in the local system (e. g. when writing to disk), and may implement their own, truly end-to-end checks. By the end-to-end argument, such end-to-end checks render lower-layer checks redundant and useful (or detrimental) only in terms of

performance. Also, interactive applications implicitly provide positive acknowledgements (though not error recovery) of receipt of requests by sending the corresponding reply. Again, for such applications, transport layer mechanisms for providing reliable transfer may be redundant and only impede performance. (pp. 1215 f.)

101 (37). As for the descent of the Clark and Blumenthal paper it bears noting that it also loosely relates to the notion of "trust-modulated transparency" (or trust-mediated transparency) as developed in Clark et al. (2004, pp. 39 ff.). The paper considers in great depth the issues raised by the growing lack of trust among virtually all Internet stakeholders owing to its ever increasing scope, and argues that the end points should be offered a choice of whether to assume the responsibilities that come with being a 'raw' end host in the Internet:

> The end-to-end argument [Saltzer et al. 1984] would say that the end node should defend itself from any incoming packet that is not welcome. This is a fine principle. [But] [i]t raises some residual issues:
>
> - First is the problem of flooding the link incoming to a host. If the packets have to come all the way to the host to be discarded, they consume resources, which may raise both performance and cost issues.
> - Second is the problem of protecting an end host with possible security holes from low level security attacks.
>
> Interposing a service of some sort between the end node and the untrusted foreign party can solve both sorts of problems. Firewalls are an example of a device that tries to limit the range of low level attacks. Application-specific servers, such as a mail server that filters incoming mail, are an example of a device that tries to export the first line of constraint for untrusted parties.
>
> Architecturally, a consistent design for trust would require that firewalls and application-specific devices protecting a given

> host be able to tailor their behavior based on a trust specification provided by the end node. The user and its end-node must be able to select and configure any such service they use, and explicit expression of trust must be a part of any such service. (p. 46)

See also Clark et al. (2003) for the notion of "controlled transparency" (pp. 248 f.), developed very much along the same lines as that of "trust-modulated transparency".

102 (37). See Bärwolff (2009*c*), very much building on Clark and Blumenthal (2007), for the notions of vertical and horizontal end-to-end arguments. As for the former:

> [T]he vertical version of the end-to-end arguments addresses the question of which functions to provide at the network layer, the only module in the internet protocol stack that by definition is shared among all its participants. It concludes that those functions should be as few as possible, and even those should not be trusted by the end points that run applications on the internet. (p. 2)

And, as for the latter, somewhat more vaguely:

> The core of the horizontal end-to-end argument is the tradeoff between putting application level functions with the end points or rather with intermediaries in the network that are in the path (physical or logical) between the two ultimate end points. It is not adventurous to premise the futility of insisting on all application level functions (approaching, effectively, the entirety of functions there are) to be under the immediate control of the ultimate end points. Thus the questions arise: where to put them, whom to put in charge, and which remedies to apply? (p. 3)

103 (37). About the original 1984 end-to-end argument they note:

> [T]he argument, as stated [in Saltzer et al. 1984], does not offer advice about how "the rest" should be structured. That paper equates the "rest of the system" with the application, and the application with the end-points. [. . .]

> [However] [a]pplications and services on the Internet today do not just reside at the "end points"; they have become more complex, with intermediate servers and services provided by third parties interposed between the communicating end-points. [...]
>
> The original end-to-end paper, because it uses a simple two-part model of the communications subsystem and "the rest," does not directly speak to the situation where "the rest" has structure. (Clark and Blumenthal 2007, p. 2)

A similar point about the scope of applicability of the original end-to-end arguments is made by Reed et al. (1998):

> End-to-end arguments address design more than implementation and implementation more than execution; that is, they suggest who should provide the code, not on which box it should run. (p. 69)

And, Reed (2002), too, points out that the end-to-end arguments only speak to the vertical division of functions:

> [W]hat about servers that are owned by the network provider, and what about multipoint protocols. Well, the end-to-end principle never talked about ownership. So "economic bundling" has nothing to do with a service being "provided by the network" — the server is not "in the network". The end-to-end argument talked about "endpoints" — some people read the paper as about circuits or sessions — but they would be wrong. One can discuss the ensemble of endpoints [...] as the set of endpoints treated by an end-to-end argument used in the design process.
>
> One of the main conclusions of the end-to-end argument is usually to point out the inflexibility or difficulty of evolution of a design to incorporate requirements not known at the time of system design. Non-end-to-end designs usually fail to meet future needs quickly. That's the point. No one would make an end-to-end design if they had a fully specified problem and

were searching for the absolute optimum performance where all conditions are known.

104 (38). See Clark and Blumenthal (2007, pp. 2 ff.) for a detailed consideration of that issue.

105 (38). In fact, there may be agents assuming application functions on behalf of both end users — the 'application end points' (Clark and Blumenthal 2007, p. 11) would thus collapse into but one point. This is typically the case with regard to applications requiring shared state plus some notion of rule enforcement that is best obtained by an intermediate third party, particularly in cases where there is very limited trust between the actual user end points. Examples are game servers in distributed gaming, and market makers such as eBay. Note that the third party need not continuously be in the physical communication path between the two user end points (pp. 13 ff.).

106 (38). To quote Clark and Blumenthal:

> There is an explicit assumption in the original paper that the communications subsystem is unreliable. This assumption is justified (both then and now) [. . .]. But there is an implicit assumption that the end-node is reliable and trustworthy. The paper assumes that the end-node can compute a checksum reliably, and perform other actions designed to compensate for the unreliability of the communications. It also assumes, implicitly, that the two ends trust each other. One end wants to send the file to the other, and the other wants to receive it. Presumably, the interests of the two ends are aligned in this respect. But let us challenge these assumptions and see what happens. (pp. 4 f.)

107 (38). To quote Clark and Blumenthal again:

> What we see is that function is migrating to the point where it can be done most reliably and efficiently. In some cases, this migration is "naturally" toward the ultimate end-points (because of "natural" limits to the reliability of the communications subsystem), but in other cases function may migrate away from the end-point to a service point somewhere else in the network. (p. 4)

108 (38). This potential superiority of trusting functions to third parties is particularly striking for the today rather typical cases in which "the end-user can no longer trust his own end-node—his own computer" (Clark and Blumenthal 2007, p. 16). The point has been made earlier by Thompson (1984) who notes that total trust (into any system) is very expensive indeed:

> You can't trust code that you did not totally create yourself. [. . .] No amount of source-level verification or scrutiny will protect you from using untrusted code. [. . .] A well installed microcode bug will be almost impossible to detect. (p. 763)

109 (39). Digression: An aside on the link between the Clark and Blumenthal paper and the literature on "active networking" is in order here. Clark and Blumenthal acknowledge the merit of arguments earlier put forward by Bhattacharjee et al. (1997) who argue that placing functions within the network on explicit behalf of the applications terminating at the end hosts does not contradict the end-to-end arguments of Saltzer et al. (1984), but is in fact entirely consistent with them. Bhattacharjee et al. (1997, p. 221) note that "[s]ome services can best be supported or enhanced using information that is only available inside the network." Thus, they argue, "to optimize performance, it is desirable to combine application and network information." While they do not address the larger questions of incentive problems for hosts (and networks), nor the problem of complexity thus introduced to the network, they rightly point out that there is a significant performance gain to be had by moving functions on behalf of the end points into the network. Clark and Blumenthal (2007) make a similar point, but confine the delegation to inside the network firmly to the application layer:

> Putting some mechanism to enhance reliability into the communications subsystem runs the risk of adding mechanism that does not meet the needs of the application. However, when we look at the placement of application-level function inside "the rest," this argument has less relevance. Wherever application-level components are placed, they can be designed so that they are aware of the application-level semantics. (p. 6)

While the grand vision of active networking, the notion of ubiquitous general purpose programmability of network nodes by providing "a uniform platform for network-based computation" for code that may be carried in packets along with the ordinary data payload (Tennenhouse and Wetherall 1996), has by now become something of a historical obscurity in the field of computer networking and superseded by much humbler and more focused notions (e. g., Walfish et al. 2004), the notion that applications spread over multiple physical nodes of a network *at the application layer* and thus beyond the immediate vicinity of the ultimate user has become very much a defining characteristic of today's networking applications. The original end-to-end arguments had been silent on this problem, and the "trust-to-trust" arguments have filled a considerable gap here.

110 (39). Blumenthal and Clark (2001) offer a taxonomy of elements "in" the network, "attached to" the network, and "on" the network, of which the former is vastly more sensitive than the latter two:

> Network designers make a strong distinction between two sorts of elements—those that are "in" the network and those that are "attached to," or "on," the network. A failure of a device that is "in" the network can crash the network, not just certain applications; its impact is more universal. Hence the end-to-end argument at this level states that services that are "in" the network are undesirable because they constrain application behavior and add complexity and risk to the core. Services that are "on" the network, and that are put in place to serve the needs of an application, are not as much of an issue because their impact is narrower. (pp. 80 f.)

For a brief elaboration on this point see also Bärwolff (2009*c*):

> [In the vertical version of the end-to-end arguments one of the most important points about the] potentially large externalities imposed upon other applications by optimising the shared internet layer for specific applications. The horizontal end-to-end argument, on the other hand, does not involve such externalities, since functions in between two end points and at layers above IP do not affect other applications built on IP in the same way that adding functions to the IP protocol itself would. From

> a horizontal viewpoint we are thus free to migrate functions away from the ends. (p. 3)

111 (40). Recall that Clark and Blumenthal (2007) argue that such "construction by analogy may be nonsense" (p. 15). See for the notion of vertical versus horizontal end-to-end arguments Bärwolff (2009*c*) and note 102.

112 (41). Quote:

> I may be willing to trust a router to forward my packets (or, putting this differently, there may be enough constraints that I can count on the router to forward my packets even if I do not fully trust it), but I may not trust it to protect my packets from disclosure. (Clark and Blumenthal 2007, p. 18)

113 (41). Blumenthal and Clark (2001) make the point that technical necessities may speak for distributing an application across intermediaries in between two end points, the prime example here being asynchronous communication, as exemplified by email:

> [A]n end-to-end argument can be employed to decide where application-level services themselves should be attached. Some applications have a very simple end-to-end structure, in which computers at each end send data directly to each other. Other applications may emerge with a more complex structure, with servers that intermediate the flow of data between the end-users. (p. 81)

114 (41). We submit that the trust notion is an important one, not only as one of the factors in a more nuanced decision about offloading functions into the network, but also as an overarching concern in a context where there are very few means of "routing money" between arbitrary parties (payment), and enforcing contractual agreements, often resulting in prohibitive transaction costs to more elaborate economic arrangements, thus leaving us with informal means of economic transacting that depend on trust more than punishment. Ironically, it is the very loss of trust between end users that necessitates the increasing role of intermediaries who in turn will capitalize on building trust with end users (Blumenthal and Clark 2001, pp. 93 f.).

	End based control	Control by third-parties
Off the ends	Email, etc.	The "Zittrain Internet"[a]
At the ends	The "Stallman box"[b]	An MS Windows system

[a]The "Zittrain Internet" is an Internet dominated by "tethered applications", and an audience that has no interest in innovations due to the ubiquity of malicious end users and thus the extreme costs of assuming any control let alone physical hosting of applications and the body of functions they perform.

[b]The "Stallman box" is a computer built from the core by oneself, with the BIOS and *all* software written from the scratch using no external tools (such as compilers) to bootstrap the development process. This computer is then connected to a pure raw medium network with no boxes whatsoever tainting the dominance of the end hosts in performing *all* functions of networking. Thus it provides absolute control over each and every function there can be to an application.

Figure N.4: Functions in a network—physical place and control

115 (41). We may draw a matrix which represents the four basic patterns that can thus emerge (Figure N.4).

116 (42). Hence the horizontal version gives rise to the notion of end point meshes with 'ultimate ends' and 'proxy ends', arranged depending on the application at hand. Compare classic email with modern filesharing applications—the former has a firm notion of ultimate ends and supporting proxies; the latter distributes state among the peers involved in a highly symmetrical fashion.

117 (42). We mean here focal points as in game theory—see Schelling (1957) who has seminally discussed the importance of "focal points", that is, equilibria in games that come about by tacit agreement based on clues such as "analogy, precedent, accidental arrangement, symmetry, aesthetic or geometric configuration, casuistic reasoning, and who the parties are and what they know about each other" (p. 21).

118 (44). Other terms found in the literature are "configurational potentialities" (Sawhney and Lee 2005, pp. 397 ff.) and "virtual freedom" (Nunziato 2009), a list which could certainly be extended a lot further.

Digression: The notion that excessive functionality in the 'common ground' of a system catering to application requirements unspecified in advance may be harmful was, in fact, no news by the time when the end-to-end arguments emerged as notion in networking design. E. g., Ross and Rodriguez (1963) note that minimality at the basis of a system is inextricably related to its flexibility:

> [I]f the system has, built in, a certain way of accomplishing a task, but the individual user does not wish to perform the task in that manner, then unless it is possible for the user to substitute his own way of doing things for the way that is already built in, the system will not satisfy the basic requirement of naturalness and ease of use. Another basic source of the contradiction, and one that may seem to some to carry more weight than the requirement that the system be adaptable to the arbitrary whim of an arbitrary user, is that it is inconceivable to build in beforehand all possible solutions to all possible problems. Thus the very nature of the system must be such that its area of applicability is continually extended by its users to provide new capabilities as the need arises. (p. 306)

The 'Turing tarpit' problem, however, remains: that such system may be one "in which everything is possible but nothing of interest is easy" (Perlis 1982, p. 10).

119 (44). Even routing may be considered a function that had better be performed by the end hosts, not the network. Mere random routing, in which "the choice as to the next node to visit is made according to some probability distribution over the set of of neighboring nodes" (Kleinrock 1964, p. 95), may be a sensible strategy. And, given the prominence of routing overlays on the current Internet one may rightly question the use of routing as a function of the inner network. Kleinrock (1964) on the virtue of random routing:

> Random routing procedures [. . .] are simple, both in conception and in realization in a practical system. Another advantage is that systems operating under a random routing procedure are relatively insensitive to changes in the structure of the network; i. e., if some of the channels disappear, the routing procedure continues to function without considerable degradation in performance. Moreover, since the random routing procedure does not make use of directory information, changes in the network structure need not be made known to all the nodes. (pp. 95 f.)

Of course, Kleinrock is well aware of the inefficiency of random routing when compared to fixed routing and adaptive routing (see pp. 96, 27 f.), but the point is that arriving at an optimum strategy that is global to all conceivable contexts and dynamics is virtually impossible. Random routing may have a dismal performance, but it will work in any setting; and a sufficiently ubiquitous infrastructure of hosts may easily assume the routing of data on a network, leaving full flexibility for host level routing strategies. (As an aside: Arpanet IMPs had the concept of 'fake hosts' which could in principle run arbitrary functions and be addressed much like an ordinary end host to the Arpanet; see also note 188 and accompanying text. Modern routers sometimes come with fully fledged SDKs and are marketed accordingly.)

We may, in theory and given way too much time and money, even dispense with headers altogether and instead just flood the network with arbitrary data at will, with just the end hosts implementing schemes about managing the resulting mess.

120 (44). The Arpanet Completion Report, effectively acknowledging the concerns that had been raised from S. D. Crocker (1969) onwards (see notes 42, 43 and accompanying text at pages 14 f.), admits:

> It was originally thought that the Arpanet would lose a message so seldom that there was no point in hosts ever bothering with message retransmission. Unfortunately, resolving various possible lockups has required the subnetwork to discard a message occasionally, and the topology of the network has evolved into long series of machines and lines that increase the probability of involuntary message loss. However, the host-to-host protocol followed the initial thought and did not provide for message retransmission. Given the realities of the probability of message loss in the network and given the host-to-host protocol which is inordinately sensitive to any abnormality, the host-to-host protocol (and protocols based on it) has proven quite unreliable. (Heart et al. 1978, pp. III-52 f.)

Walden (1990) concludes that all checksumming and reliability overhead inside the subnetwork notwithstanding, obtaining proper end-to-end reliability remains effectively impossible:

> It is hard to checksum all control bits in a way that does not

> take too much calculation and that totally eliminates the possibility of undetected bit errors—that is, somewhere there may be an uncovered seam between calculations or between memory and an I/O channel. [. . .] Thus, achieving a totally bug-free network is very difficult. (p. 361)

In fact, already by 1973 it was clear to BBN that complete reliability could not be achieved by the IMP subnetwork alone, despite heroic subnetwork level source-IMP-to-destination-IMP efforts bordering the paranoid. McQuillan (1973):

> [In light of all the foregoing considerations about network reliability, occasional hardware failures, and the necessary use of checksumming] we are looking into the structure of an optional IMP-Host/Host-IMP checksum to complete Host/Host end-to-end checksum. Under such an arrangement, the IMP and Host could agree to verify the checksums on the messages transferred over the interface between them, and the appropriate signalling mechanisms would be provided to handled errors. With this technique in effect, two Hosts could be certain that their messages were delivered error-free or else they would be notified of an error, and could then retransmit their message if desired. (p. 8)

While BBN have never implemented such a complete chain of end-to-end checksums, the statement is reflective of the growing appreciation of the inevitable role of host computers in end-to-end reliability. See also note 163 and accompanying text for further elaboration on the issue of subnetwork reliability in the Arpanet.

121 (44). Crowcroft (2007) notes about the Internet:

> The core service model supports a very simple definition of performance, which is to say that there is none. (p. 572)

Also, note Kurose and Ross (2005):

> The Internet's network layer provides a single service, known as best effort service. [. . .] [I]t might appear that *best-effort service* is a euphemism for *no service at all*. With best effort

> service, timing between packets is not guaranteed to be preserved, packets are not guaranteed to be received in the order in which they were sent, nor is the eventual delivery of transmitted packets guaranteed. Given this definition, a network which delivered *no* packets to the destination would satisfy the definition best effort delivery service. (p. 305, emphasis in original)

122 (44). R. E. Kahn (2003) recalls the changing premises when moving from Arpanet to Internet:

> We also had to deal with the issue of end-to-end reliability because we knew packets could get lost along the way. The Arpanet was designed to be reliable, so if some packets were lost, it was assumed that something in the net had broken. (This would be as if you were printing to a line printer and the line printer went down, nothing would print.) If packets didn't show up at the destination, then the idea was you just hit the equivalent of a reset button and start over again. Well, that wouldn't work in the Internet environment and so we had to develop an error-detection and retransmission scheme to get around that.

Cerf et al. (1974) (RFC 675, the first 'official' TCP specification) elaborate:

> We specifically assume that fragments are transmitted from Host to Host through means of a Packet Switching Network (PSN). This assumption is probably unnecessary, since a circuit switched network could also be used, but for concreteness, we explicitly assume that the hosts are connected to one or more Packet Switches of a PSN. (p. 2, references omitted)

This early assumption of an effectively arbitrarily unreliable set of intermediate networks has essentially remained in place ever since. Postel (1981*f*) (RFC 793, the ultimate standard specification of TCP) notes:

> Very few assumptions are made as to the reliability of the communication protocols below the TCP layer. TCP assumes it can obtain a simple, potentially unreliable datagram service

> from the lower level protocols. In principle, the TCP should be able to operate above a wide spectrum of communication systems ranging from hard-wired connections to packet-switched or circuit-switched networks. (p. 1)

In fact, one may plausibly argue that the Internet protocol (IP) is hardly a protocol at all, for there are *no* mandatory rules other than a header format with some trivial specifications of the constituent fields (Figure N.5). In particular, there are virtually no control aspects (as op-

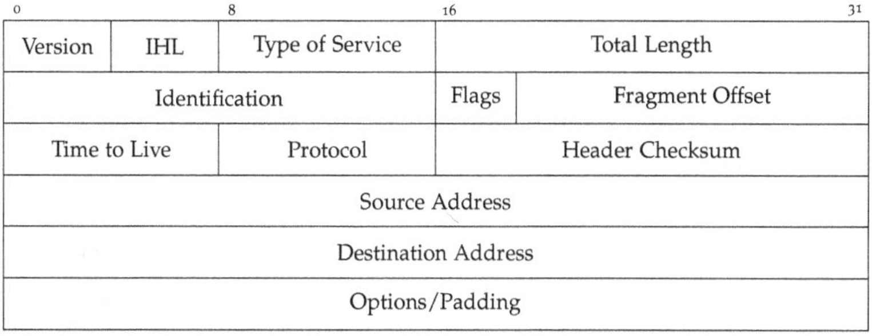

Figure N.5: IP v4 header format

posed to payload data) associated with IP other than the destination address of a packet and flags regarding fragmentation management. While ICMP (Postel 1981*c*) offers some error reporting facilities that may be considered part of the 'Internet', none of the ICMP functions are strictly vital to its logical operation (the strong case for implementing it in both gateways/routers, see Baker et al. 1995, and hosts, see Braden 1989, notwithstanding). Also, the service of the IP layer offers next to no abstraction, as would be required by a clean separation of layers. Tanenbaum (2002) notes:

> The TCP/IP model did not originally clearly distinguish between service, interface, and protocol, although people have tried to retrofit it after the fact to make it more OSI-like. For example, the only real services offered by the internet layer are *Send IP Packet* and *Receive IP Packet*.

And, says Welzl (2010):

> If I had have to pick one major thing that is clearly wrong about the Internet, then it is the *lack of* abstraction. [. . .] [A]n application opening a TCP connection or sending a UDP packet to a specified IP address is not a very abstract concept.

123 (45). See pages 118 ff. on the conceptual issues in defining just what qualifies as Internet service.

124 (45). TCP/IP has been designed with the assumption of a relatively high reliability of the underlying networks (Clark et al. 2004, p. 68; see also the quote at our note 351), and also favors low round trip delays (for various timing reasons). Once this assumption breaks down, performance of TCP drops markedly, and it is more sensible to introduce transport layer aware link layer enhancements that reestablish the assumptions made by TCP, than it is to entirely redesign the transport layer protocols. See Balakrishnan et al. (1995); Balakrishnan et al. (1997); Balakrishnan (1998).

The more general point here is that with TCP/IP firmly in place and in view of QoS considerations, one may actually demand networks to meet the targets specified by a global Internet standard, whereas in the early days of the Internet no such standards were imposed because it needed to be open for any technology to come along (Clark 2010*b*; see also Clark et al. 2004 as quoted in our note 351). Also, it should be noted that the more redundancy in the interconnections in the Internet, the greater the competition between routes—the feasibility of really poor links is thus a function of the relative absence of competing links. Any reasonable routing implementation should avoid such links (see our discussion at pages 129 f.), and it is, in fact, no coincidence that routing overlays have emerged that further optimize the otherwise rather blunt BGP routes (see out discussion at note 363).

125 (46). To quote from Reed et al. (1998):

> While making lower layers more active or programmable is likely to enhance application autonomy, the risk is that programmable lower layers may reduce network transparency. The reason is that a key element of transparency is some ability to predict how the network will behave. [. . .]
>
> To maintain the largest degree of network transparency, then, the end-to-end principle requires that the semantics of any ac-

> tive features be carefully constrained so that interactions among different users of a shared lower level can be predicted by a designer who is using the services and functions of that active layer. Lack of predictability thus becomes a cost for all users, including those that do not use the programmability features. Getting the semantics of active enhancements right is a major challenge, and wrong active enhancements are likely to be worse than none at all, since everyone helps pay the cost of something that is used by only a few but reduces transparency for everyone else. (p. 70)

126 (47). Indeed, Reed et al. call Isenberg's article a "reinvention of the end-to-end arguments". However, the approval by Reed et al. notwithstanding, it should be noted here that while the Isenberg article as well as its successors (Isenberg 1998; Isenberg 2003) may be "entertaining", they do lack the basic rigor that would qualify them as proper statements furthering the end-to-end arguments. We will thus confine a brief discussion of the "stupid network" notion to this footnote only. (See also, however, our notes 433, 434, 436 and accompanying texts.)

Digression: The notion that the Internet would be a 'stupid' network only makes sense in a direct comparison to an 'intelligent' network, and has little actual content beyond highlighting the basic conceptual difference between the Internet and the previously existing telephone network (PSTN). To argue in categorical terms that the Internet is 'stupid', or that the network most desirable from the perspective of the end users would have to be stupid, fails to reflect the host of real-world intricacies of data networking. The telephone network may have stipulated data rates and the whole notion of 'connections', both of which are limiting the flexibility of its uses; but the Internet (or any other large data network for that matter), too, stipulates certain basic notions that cannot be dodged by the applications using it, and thus may also be limiting in certain respects. Plus, any network of appreciable size will have to employ some management and control functions that go beyond the trivial and will invariably interact in one way or another with the concerns of the end hosts.

Largely, the accounts of Isenberg feature idealistic normative notions and gross simplifications coupled with a complete disregard for economics and the complexities of historical fact. While such approach can be useful as a political statement, it does little to advance our understanding of network design principles. To quote from Isenberg (1997):

> The age of plentiful bandwidth is just around the corner [. . .] [and] [a] new network "philosophy and architecture," is replacing the vision of an Intelligent Network. The vision is one in which the public communications network would be engineered for "always-on" use, not intermittence and scarcity. It would be engineered for intelligence at the end-user's device, not in the network. And the network would be engineered simply to "Deliver the Bits, Stupid," not for fancy network routing or "smart" number translation. *Fundamentally, it would be a Stupid Network.* In the Stupid Network, the data would tell the network where it needs to go. (In contrast, in a circuit network, the network tells the data where to go.) In a Stupid Network, the data on it would be the boss. [. . .] End user devices would be free to behave flexibly because, in the Stupid Network the data is boss, bits are essentially free, and there is no assumption that the data is of a single data rate or data type. (emphasis added)

The main thrust of the Isenberg paper goes against the entrenched mindset of telephone companies and the way in which their "network architecture" constrains the uses of the network such that virtually no substantial innovation can occur (a point earlier made by Pouzin 1976*a* and Pouzin 1976*b*). While he has a point (a broad one), he chooses to neglect consideration of issues such as congestion and network abuse which makes the paper somewhat biased and irrelevant for any deeper discussions of principles. The belief that scarcity would simply go away does not add to the credibility of the papers; e. g., Isenberg (2003) argues:

> New entities, such as municipalities, other utilities with rights of way, new kinds of companies (especially wireless ones), and maybe even customers themselves, would gain the freedom to discover successful operating models for end-to-end networks. (p. 38)

More astonishing still is the naiveté with which Isenberg (1997) posits that the network would happily provide any service an end point may desire, all of which would effectively be free of charge and with no issues whatsoever arising from moral hazard and asymmetric informations:

> [I]n the Stupid Network, because the data is the boss, it can tell the network, in real time, what kind of service it needs. And the Stupid Network would have a small repertoire of idiot-savant behaviors to treat different data types appropriately. If the data identified itself as financial data, the Stupid Network would deliver it accurately, no matter how many milliseconds of delay the error checking would take. If the data were two-way voice or video, the Stupid Network would provide low delay, even at the price of an occasional flipped bit. If the data were entertainment audio or video, the Stupid Network would provide wider bandwidth, but would not necessarily give low delay or absolute accuracy. And if there were a need for unique transmission characteristics, the data would tell the Stupid Network in more detail how to treat it, and the Stupid Network would do what it was told. [. . .]
>
> One thing about the Stupid Network is clear — the physical elements that comprise the network would be neither expensive nor scarce.

Two more comments on this quote: First, sweepingly assuming away the scarcity assumption is a gross simplification that is most unlikely ever to come to pass (Clark 2008*a*; Liebowitz 2002). Second, there is an odd reference here to virtual channels, when Isenberg states that "[i]f the data identified itself as financial data, the Stupid Network would deliver it accurately, no matter how many milliseconds of delay the error checking would take." How precisely the notion of a stupid network offering virtual circuits should be compatible with the realities of the Internet as a network of as many as possible networks, and why end-to-end host level error control would thus become dispensable (contra the end-to-end arguments) is not clear from the paper. In fact, the whole notion of support of various data types at the common internet layer is both at odds with the original end-to-end arguments and the actual design decisions of the Internet as recounted by Clark (1988, pp. 108 f.).

Next, Isenberg (2003) advances a false take on the history of the causality between end-to-end arguments and network voice applications. He argues:

> The proponents of the end-to-end principle did not envision Internet telephony; they only knew that a network with less, rather than more, functionality in the middle would be more flexible, and more amenable to as-yet-undreamt-of applications. (p. 38)

This claim is evidently unfounded, for the need to have the network offer an unreliable most basic mode of transport had been understood well before even the 1981 end-to-end arguments were articulated, and precisely because of the very concern for interactive real-time voice applications (Gray 2005; Sproull and Cohen 1978). See section 5.1 for the history of interactive speech research dating back to at least 1974.

Last, we note that Isenberg (2003) goes so far as to sweepingly ascribe the very design of the Internet to the Saltzer et al. paper, a most adventurous claim by all measures—for the conceptual separation of IP and TCP took place well before the end-to-end paper was written (Postel 1977*b*). To quote from Isenberg:

> [I]n the early 1980s, [. . .] [Saltzer et al.] proposed that if functions like error-checking could be implemented at the endpoints of the network, the Internet would be more flexible, and a wider variety of applications—even unknown future applications—could be more easily implemented. The logical conclusion of this argument was the separation into different protocols of functions that had hitherto been bundled together. The first important instance of this new, layered architecture was the separation of the error-checking protocol (the transmission control protocol, or simply TCP) from the Internet protocol (IP). (p. 37)

127 (47). Cerf and Kahn (1973) elaborate on the notion of gateways and their desired simplicity:

> It would be extremely convenient if all the differences between networks could be economically resolved by suitable interfacing at the network boundaries. For many of the differences,

> this objective can be achieved. However, both economic and technical considerations lead us to prefer that the interface be as simple and reliable as possible and deal primarily with passing data between networks that use different packet switching strategies. (p. 4)

(The quote may also be found verbatim in the 1974 successor at page 638.)

128 (48). See section 5.2, particularly pages 88 f., for an elaboration of the eventual 1978 TCP/IP split.

129 (48). Cerf and Kahn (1973) only hinted somewhat indeterminately at the notion that the functions in the network should not mix with host level issues:

> [T]he complexity and dissimilarity of the Host or process level protocols makes it desirable to avoid having to transform between them at the interface [between different networks], even if this transformation were always possible. Rather, compatible Host and process level protocols must be developed to achieve effective internetwork resource sharing. The unacceptable alternative is for every Host or process to implement every protocol (a potentially unbounded number) that may be needed to communicate with other networks. We therefore assume that *a common protocol is to be used between Hosts or processes in different networks* and that *the interface between networks should take as small a role as possible in this protocol.* (p. 4, emphasis added)

(The quote may also be found in the 1974 successor A Protocol for Packet Network Interconnection at page 638.)

130 (48). Hence the early term "catenet"—"an abstract PSN resulting from the juxtaposition of several PSNs" (Pouzin 1973*a*, p. 3)—which, however, did not catch on.

131 (48). See also section 5.2 for substantial elaboration.

Conclusion of Part I

132 (49). To recount from an instructive discussion at the internet history mailing list:

Reed (2009*a*) I would actually like the term "end-to-end argument" to continue to mean what we defined it to mean, rather than what some people have extended it to mean.

D. H. Crocker (2009) Interesting. My sense of things is that the term is not actually defined all that concretely or consistently and that this has made it difficult to use the term constructively.

Reed (2009*b*) I'd suggest reading the paper where it was originally defined. Given that the three authors *and* a crew of peer reviewers touched every word of the definition, it's pretty darned specific.

As an aside, for the original position of Reed it is also instructive to consult his 1978 thesis which anticipates much of the later elaboration of the end-to-end arguments (Reed 1978, pp. 33 ff.).

133 (49). As noted above, we have decided not to include a section on the recent discussion on network neutrality, because the notion—while claiming to derive from and develop upon the end-to-end arguments—adds little to the theory of end-to-end arguments, and it does not obtain any useful design principles that would satisfy the criteria of Denning and Martell (2007*a*).

134 (49). We should like to mention that while our review certainly features some inevitable subjectivity and bias, it is void of the type of preconceived notions and foregone conclusions that has shaped other attempts to write comprehensive histories of the end-to-end arguments; e. g., Schewick (2004) who argues that the end-to-end arguments have been a vital prerequisite for innovation, or Bennett (2009) who argues just the opposite. We have not had a prior hypothesis that narrowed the choice of material for us to consider.

Basic Structures

135 (53). See Dunleavy (2003, pp. 62 ff.) for a fine introduction to the different patterns of explanation, of which descriptive and analytic explanation are two which may usefully be arranged in a matrix pattern (pp. 72 ff.).

136 (54). It bears elaborating briefly why we put such prominent focus on the Arpanet in our history account, when we could also have treated other

networks (Ethernet, Satnet, PRNET, NSFNET, etc.) in greater depth. For one, the Arpanet was the world's first ever large-scale packet switching network which could transmit completely arbitrary application level payload data (no limits on word sizes, no limits on bit combinations) and is in many important respects a direct predecessor of the Internet (which started out as 'ARPA Internet', only later giving way to a completely distributed system of peer networks). Many of the protocols and technical solutions developed for the Arpanet carried over largely unchanged to the Internet — e. g., Telnet and FTP; but also routing approaches and other control issues. For another, the Arpanet was developed not primarily as a commercial venture but by the guidance of a government agency (ARPA). Hence it was documented in minute detail, with most documentation either getting published in the open literature (conference proceedings, journal articles) or at least being reported to ARPA by their various contractors, mostly BBN (technical and management reports). While the development of most other networks of interest (NPL's network, Alohanet, Ethernet, etc.) has been documented to a certain extent, too; none of them matches the level of documentation available for the Arpanet. Finally, we note that our bias toward the early history of the Internet stems largely from the fact that with the growth of the Internet beyond Arpanet and NSFNET it really reduced to the core common protocols; everything else became fair game (see, e. g., MPLS and Diffserv inside ISP networks).

137 (54). We have considered in section 2.1 the role of Baran's prior work for the Arpanet (note 30 and accompanying text), and the lack of conducive general conditions for Baran's packet switching network in the early 1960s (note 36 and accompanying text). Other pertinent work prior to the advent of Arpanet includes the work of Kleinrock on queuing theory and routing (Kleinrock 1962*b*; Kleinrock 1964) as well as a certain body of experiences in local general purpose networking, on the one hand, and wide area special purpose networking, on the other. (See also the credits noted in Walden 1972*b*, p. 2.)

Digression: Earlier experiments had been done connecting two computers across some distance (across the whole of the U. S., in fact; see Marill and Roberts 1966, pp. 430 f., see also Hafner and Lyon 1998, pp. 68 f.), and there had been ample experience with star topology computer to terminal, and even somewhat general purpose computer to computer networks, particularly in the fields of airline reservations (Chretien et al. 1973; Hirsch 1974; Campbell-Kelly and Garcia-Swartz 2005, pp. 16 f.) and banking (Davies and Barber 1973, pp. 116 ff., ch. 4.4; Campbell-Kelly and Garcia-Swartz 2005, p. 17). Also, the notion of data transfer via modems had been in the making since at least 1958, when AT & T — the telecommunications monopoly at the time — introduced commercial modems (initially with a speed of 300 bps). The desire of customers to use third party modems, and that of companies to introduce such modems to the market eventually culminated in the 1967 FCC Carterphone decision which by 1968 was established as a broad rule permitting the attachment of any "foreign equipment" to the AT & T network as long as no publicly detrimental effect ensued (see Pelkey 2009, ch. 1 for a fine summary).

By the time ARPA came to design a national general purpose network, the notion of long distance data transmission across leased telephone lines was thus no novelty. In particular, the designers of the SITA network had already dealt with some of the issues in an open-ended store-and-forward message switching system — error control hop-by-hop and end-to-end (Hirsch 1974, p. 61 f.), the useful modularity of a distributed communication system (p. 61), and the trade-off between routing and performance gains versus simple over-provisioning (p. 63).

But, few of these efforts were well documented or widely discussed at the time. Apart from the seminal work by Davies et al. (see our in-depth discussions at notes 30 and 259) no-one had yet systematically tackled the host of problems entailed by connecting multiple computers in a true general purpose manner using a partially connected wide-area mesh topology — routing had only been dealt with in theory; congestion problems had largely been avoided by over-provision and strict resource reservation schemes; error recovery, remote monitoring and maintenance, etc. had all been addressed by ad-hoc efforts rather than well-reasoned and documented measures.

138 (54). Digression: Computers at the time meant large mainframe computers, with 'dumb' terminals connected to them. The mainframe computers where ridiculously expensive, and the terminals very expensive given their capabilities limited to basic I/O operations. By the early 1970s terminals gradually became 'smarter', but remained still a long way off what we would today consider to be computers proper (Hobbs 1972). S.

D. Crocker (1988) recalls the centralized computing paradigm at the time, which in many ways informed the initial approaches to be pursued in data communication between computers:

> [I]f you looked at the design of an operating system in a computer, the view implicit in the design was that the operating system was the center of the world, and anything that was attached to the computer was a slave device. You could attach tapes and disks and card readers and printers and so forth, but the initiative was in the computer, and it would say when to talk or when to listen to those things. You tried to connect [. . .] two computers together, and they only knew how to talk to each other as if one is the master — well, if one is the master, then the other must be the slave.
>
> We knew that we wanted a much more flexible vision in which the initiative could be at either site, and there would be a coordinated or cooperative model of communications. But the applications that first come to mind — being able to remotely log-in to another thing, or to move a file, or do remote job entry — all are back in the master/slave model. We wanted those to be special cases, rather than being the only thing you could work with. So we knew that if we put those in as our basic model, that more ambitious things would always be fighting against those kind of things [. . .]. So a general-purpose interprocess communication facility was definitely needed, and then you'd build things up on that. [. . .] Those were the days when, instead of viewing the network as an electronic mail system, which was kind of an afterthought in a way, there were all these visions of shared databases and load balancing, or jobs [that] would be shifted from one machine to another.

Despite their aspirations, the first results of the NWG's work on a general host-host protocol were limited to precisely the asymmetric master/slave (or, client/server) schemes they had wanted to overcome (S. D. Crocker 1987, p. 4) — a curiously limited use of the otherwise fully transparent Arpanet IMP subnetwork which allowed completely arbitrary binary data digital messages to be sent between hosts (Walden 1972*b*, p. 13). It took until 1972 to arrive at reasonably useful and stable host-host protocol and implementations, which, at that, were still very much anchored in the paradigm of connection-oriented communication.

Braden (1977*a*, p. 4-2), in his account of the substantial UCLA efforts to implement network host functions, proposes a useful taxonomy of three different models for host level interaction: (1) virtual terminals (the simplest of all, e. g., the early asymmetric "old" Telnet), (2) virtual I/O Devices (a generalization of the virtual terminal model), and (3) distributed processes (communicating across the Arpanet on an equal basis as peers). A number of innovative schemes beyond remote login, file transfer, and remote job entry (the former two of which have remained the defining notions of host level network usage to this day) were proposed in the early days of the Arpanet, but were ultimately not pursued any further. Examples include the decode encode language (del) (Rulifson 1969), a proposal for a network interchange language (Elie 1970), and a follow-up scheme in which "[t]he user treats the network as a single resource and is unconcerned with the location of the services, data files, etc." (Karp et al. 1971, p. 3). By 1972 there would still be elaborate notions about possible applications of the Arpanet — from "multiprocess operation in many machines" to "distributed operating systems" (R. E. Kahn 1972, pp. 1405 f.). However, many of those projections were to remain mere speculation. In fact, the overwhelmingly dominating use of the early Arpanet — its first true 'killer application' — was plain and simple remote terminal access. Roberts (1988) recalls:

> What I had first expected was that traffic would be computer to computer; it would be transfer of software, the remote use of software, the interaction between machines — that people would be on their own machine doing something and they would need another machine for cycles of something. But it turned out that most people just used the network as an individual terminal on the other machine as a remote terminal. The concept of distributed computing was a future concept in a lot of respects, and the short term need was for a much better communication system to get people to their remote computers.

139 (54). Baran had established that much like a fully connected network would be prohibitively expensive, a star topology one would be unreliable given the possibility of the central node failing. Thus a partially connected mesh network would offer the best solution to the trade-off between cost and reliability.

140 (55). At the time, the notion of fully transparent data communication (by means of bit-stuffing so as to allow arbitrary data to be distinguished from control headers and trailers) was not as self-evident as it is today. Notes Walden (1972*b*):

> All too many networks require transmission to be limited to characters from a particular character set. Besides preventing the network's users from sending arbitrary messages, the designers of the network are prevented from such things as loading programs over the network. (p. 13)

141 (55). The very first use of the Arpanet, once in place between the first two host sites UCLA and SRI, was no more than a terminal emulation, thus requiring only minimal changes to the two host computers involved. But even this rather trivial use of the network took considerable effort to get going—BBN had delivered IMP Nr. 2 to SRI on October 6, 1969 (BBN 1970*c*), and the first successful host level remote login from UCLA to SRI only took place at October 29, 1969, with the SRI machine treating the UCLA machine as a "bona fide dumb terminal". Hafner and Lyon (1998) remark:

> There is no small irony in the fact that the first program used over the network was one that made the distant computer masquerade as a terminal. All that work to get two computers talking to each other and they ended up in the very same master-slave situation the network was supposed to eliminate. (p. 154)

More than a year into the Arpanet project, with more than a dozen IMPs in place, there was still no notable operational use of the network. Notes Meyer (1970*b*):

> The feeling at MIT is that to be a success, the network needs desperately to be used operationally. If another year passes

> without significant operational use, it [the Arpanet] might go down the drain. (p. 4)

See also our considerations at note 138.

142 (55). See Hafner and Lyon (1998, pp. 71 ff.) and Norberg et al. (1996, pp. 163 f.).

143 (55). See particularly note 40 and accompanying text.

144 (55). Also, there was an early and basic decision *not* to charge the host sites for volume of usage of the network. Any additional expenses incurred by the host sites were typically offset by increases in their ARPA funding. This was based not only on the consideration of unpredictable and heavy overhead — the traffic patterns typical for remote login sessions would have control data overheads of well above 90 percent — but also to ease the concerns over whether to connect to the network in the first place. Note that at the time the value proposition of the Arpanet was vague at best. Owning a computer was generally considered vastly more desirable than accessing one remotely (see note 142).

145 (55). DIGRESSION: In fact, there had been some debate over access to BBN's IMP software code for interested parties, and only by ca. 1974 was the network software "made available to interested agencies or individuals for the cost of reproduction" (Schelonka 1974, p. 74-1045). However, while the IMP code was now available for others, no-one actually used it — notes Walden (2010*a*):

> I think I eventually sent out copies of the code to 7 or 11 groups. Of course, no one copied our code. They all did something different themselves, costing lots more money, time, and ultimately failing in some instances.

146 (55). See the specification in Scheblik et al. (1968) as quoted in note 37. See also Hafner and Lyon (1998, pp. 122 f.) for a brief recounting of the ARPA/BBN decision to put "maximum logical separation between the IMP and the host". Also, see our extensive discussion of the history of the subnetwork/host separation as initially put forward by Wesley Clark in note 51.

The crucial point of the whole subnetwork idea was that not only would the host computers be spared the hassle of diverting substantial resources to the task of networking (to largely uncertain eventual avail, at that); it would also become much easier to implement and roll out changes to the distributed functions of the network in a coherent and tractable way. Before this notion was introduced by Clark, plans had been to connect the host computers directly, implementing the core networking functions within the very host computers themselves. Later experiences by BBN in managing the networking functions of the Arpanet proved the value of this early intuition. In BBN (1972*b*) they report that coordinating upgrades to the IMP software became ever more cumbersome given the growing heterogeneity of the subnetwork (now including "DDP-516's and H-316's, IMP's and TIP's, TIP's with and without special features") and the human factor at host sites:

> [At one occasion] [w]e planned to reload the Net by telephoning each site and asking that the new copy of IMPLOD be manually loaded and started, at each site in sequence. It proved impossible to reach a person at each site [of the then 29 sites] (in the right order) as promptly as we wished. One site could not even find the tape, although we had previously confirmed that the correct person had received it. (p. 5)

As a result of these experiences BBN devised an automatic rollout procedure capable of loading new IMP software onto IMPs and reverting to previous states at the discretion of BBN's Network Control Center (NCC) at its head quarter in Cambridge, MA (BBN 1972*b*, pp. 6 ff.). Clearly, without proper control over the subnetwork, instituting such a procedure would have been much more difficult if not impossible. (See also Frank et al. 1972, p. 257 noting the same point.)

147 (55). Note though, that once the Arpanet was firmly in place, the balance of functions between hosts and IMPs was subject to some reconsideration. By 1972 Frank et al. made the following observation regarding Arpanet message reassembly:

> Hosts [instead of IMPs] could assume the responsibility for reassembling messages. For an asynchronous IMP-Host channel, this marginally simplifies the IMP's task. However, if every IMP-Host channel were synchronous, and the Host provided the reassembly, the IMP task can be further simplified. In this

> latter case, "IMP-like" software would have to be provided in each Host. [. . .]
>
> A Host that performs reassembly can also [just like an IMP does] assign and process sequence numbers and check for duplicate packets. For many applications, the order of delivery to the destination is immaterial. (pp. 259 f.)

148 (56). The host-IMP interface was initially extremely simple (see note 178 and accompanying text), the assumption being that an IMP and its host computer would be physically so close (typically no more than 30 feet, see BBN and Kahn 1976, p. 2-1) that communication between the two would not be much different from any other typical I/O operation and thus deemed error free. Considering the hosts no more than simple sources and sinks for the data to be transferred was thus no grave omission at first. This changed later on, when hosts moved farther away from the IMPs, thus necessitating a special protocol that would have to add error control including a retransmission facility (McKenzie 1971*b*). In another line of developments the number of hosts per IMP increased markedly. The first increase was from the initial one host per IMP to up to four hosts per IMP and took place in 1969 while BBN was still busy designing the initial IMP software (see note 176 and accompanying text). Later, BBN added to its IMPs the capacity to allow multiple hundreds of terminals to connect to the IMP directly (Ornstein et al. 1971). (See section 4.3 for further elaboration.)

DIGRESSION: The protocol for connecting IMPs and hosts was typically referred to as the 1822 interface, and was specified in the so-called 1822 Report (one version being BBN and Kahn 1976). To digress but briefly, this report covered all versions of the interface that were developed throughout the Arpanet lifetime, from Local Host (LH), to Distant Host (DH), Very Distant Host (VDH), and HDLC Distant Host (HDH). Later, the interface came to be referred to as Arpanet Host-IMP Protocol (AHIP) (see, e. g., Khanna and Malis 1987). Throughout the years the 1822 specification developed considerably from its first version in 1969. Not only did the inner details and lower levels of the interface (link level connection) change considerably, the very core of the interface itself changed as well, and came to encompass various additions such as those of Private Line Interfaces (PLIs) for encrypting or otherwise coding data to be sent between two hosts (circa 1975, see Blumenthal et al. 2010, ch. 17.6). The highest-profile change to the IMP-host interface was the introduction of new message leaders of 96 bit length instead of 32 bit length, the transition from the latter to the former taking place at circa January 1, 1981 (Haughney 1980; Haughney 1981). Also, there was an interesting change from the 1822 protocol to the 1822L protocol starting in 1981, introducing name based routing, or "logical addresses", rather than the previous network interface based routing (Malis 1983). Under the new scheme (which depended on the BBN C/30 IMPs instead of the Pluribus or Honeywell ones, though) hosts would be named with an identifier rather than a permanent physical address; multihoming and mobility where thus supported, as was anycast. (See also Rosen 1981 on an elaboration of 'logical addressing' notion.)

149 (56). R. E. Kahn (1969), addressing concerns raised in Kreznar (1969), states that "We [BBN] do not require a Host to be prepared to repeat transmissions into the network."

150 (56). See notes 42 and 43 and accompanying text.

151 (56). Digression: S. D. Crocker (2008) recalls:

> [A]t the first meeting we had with BBN in February 1969, Frank Heart [head of the IMP project] argued against this [checksums and retransmissions] because *it would add overhead and reduce the efficiency of the overall network.* I asked him how reliable the network would be, and he replied, "as reliable as your accumulator." In those days, the accumulator was the key part of the central processing unit of each computer. If it was not working or if it was even slightly dysfunctional, the entire computer was completely unusable. [...] We acceded and removed the checksums from our design. *The network itself was indeed highly reliable. Strong checksums were included in the transmissions between each IMP, and it was rare for messages to arrive garbled.* (p. 101, emphasis added)

As for the conflict between NWG and BBN, S. D. Crocker (2009) adds:

> [BBN] felt it [end-to-end checksums] was unnecessary overhead, would reduce performance, and would make the net-

> work — and hence them — look bad. They also aspired to have 100 % reliability in the subnet with no discards at all.
>
> There was a significant difference in political power. They were the professionals with the advantage of age, experience and official status. We were an informal, unchartered less experienced group of users. It was a mistake on my part that I caved in on the original plan to have checksums on the messages.

See also Hafner and Lyon (1998, pp. 120 f.) on the BBN versus host sites graduate students 'clash'.

However, note that while initially BBN may have been reluctant to let go of functions that had clearly been specified in the Arpanet RFQ to be the sole province of the IMP subnetwork, at least by 1972 this position relaxed from adamant to openly negotiable. Note Frank et al. (1972):

> A reliable system design insures that each transmitted message is accurately delivered to its intended destination. The occasional time when an IMP fails and destroys a useful in-transit message is likely to occur far less often than a similar failure in the Hosts and has proven to be unimportant in practice, as are errors due to IMP memory failures. A simple end to end retransmission strategy will protect against these situations, if the practical need should arise. (p. 260)

See also note 147 for a quote from Frank et al. (1972) in which they argue that hosts may take over other tasks such as reassembly from the IMPs, too. These relaxations from the original Arpanet specification were hardly surprising given that the Arpanet clearly did not offer a *perfectly* reliable service. Notes Metcalfe (1973):

> [T]here have been enough bits in error in the Arpanet to fill this quota [one undetected transmission bit error per year] for centuries. (p. 7-28)

We will momentarily discuss that while the need for host level error control soon arose, it was not pressing enough to warrant a change of the then entrenched host-host protocol (note 158 and accompanying text).

152 (56). Digression: As for the reliability of the subnetwork, Postel and Crocker (1970*b*) note:

> In the short time the network has been up at UCLA, we have become convinced that the network itself will generate very few errors. We have watched the BBN staff debug and test the IMP program, and it seemed that most of the errors affected timing and throughput rather than validity. *Hence most errors will probably arise from broken Hosts and/or buggy NCP's.* (p. 7, emphasis added)

Bhushan (1973) reports:

> In transferring files we found the Arpanet and the FTP to be quite reliable. On numerous occasions we transferred complete listing of our operating system (about 6 million bits), reassembled it and ran it with no problem. *No data lossage problems have been reported to us as yet.* (p. 6, emphasis added)

Kleinrock and Naylor (1974) conclude from a seven day in-depth measurement series:

> With few exceptions the channels in the network are fairly reliable. Over half of the channels reported packet error rates less than one in 100,000. The average packet error rate was one error in 12,880 packets transmitted. Of the 86 channels in the network 14 reported no errors during the seven days, while six channels had packet error rates worse than one in 1000. The worst case was one in 340 packets for the channel from RADT to LL. While these error rates are large enough to warrant the inclusion of error detection hardware and software, they are small enough so that *traffic flow through the network is not impaired.* (pp. 776 f., emphasis added)

As for IMP uptime, by 1974 Schelonka reports for the period from June 1972 through to November 1973 that the multiple dozens of IMPs in operation were up on average for well above five hours before some hardware or software failure hit, with a mean time to recovery of about 5 minutes (p. 1047). Similar numbers are reported for the September 1971 to June 1972 period by McKenzie et al. (1972). However, the IMPs were not the only sources of failure; preventive maintenance, site environmental problems, retrofits, etc. accounted for roughly the same amount of additional downtime. Still, this would mean that a host site would typically obtain a virtually error free service from the subnetwork for some one or two hours in a row. Occasionally, there would be problems with the IMP-Host interface (Haverty 1980); but, by and large, the network worked as advertised.

It is thus fair to say that, in general, absent serious outages or error conditions, the Arpanet offered a reliable virtual circuit service to its hosts. It should be noted, though, that the absence of error control in the host-host protocol prevented any proper measurements of transmission errors due to subnetwork failures. Metcalfe (1973):

> Because error detection has been missing in Host-Host communication protocols, there are few (if any) real statistics on the magnitude of the error problem. Because the IMP Subnet is advertised as error-free (transmission error-free), protocol designers (e. g., we) have thus far avoided higher level error control and left themselves exposed. (p. 7-29)

However, see our considerations of higher level error control in section 4.4.

153 (56). Schelonka (1974, p. 1046) reports that "[t]he average growth rate of the net is 12 sites per year and the rate is continuing at the present time."

154 (57). See section 5.2.

155 (57). The most important improvements of the Arpanet took place fairly early in its lifetime, ranging from (1) important qualitative changes to operations with respect to subnetwork reliability to (2) somewhat gradual and peripheral performance improvements by adding memory to IMPs and higher level capacities such as the ability of IMPs to serve terminals directly. As for the former, see Walden (1972*b*, pp. 28 ff.) for a concise description of the changes as of ca. 1972.

Digression: An early important concern was that of lockups—"states that the network can enter and from which it cannot recover without being reset" (Kahn et al. 1971, p. 5). The seriousness of the problem was very quickly established by field test conducted by Robert Kahn and David Walden in early 1970. Notes R. E. Kahn (1990):

> It was my contention that we had to worry about congestion and deadlocks. What do you do when the network just fills

> up? Things might come to a grinding halt. [. . .] When Dave Walden and I went out to the west coast at the at the end of 1969 or early 1970 to test the net the very first thing that we did was run deadlock tests. And the network locked up in twelve packets. I had devised these tests to prove that the network could deadlock. There was no way to convince anybody else, particularly the person writing the software, that the network was going to deadlock—except by doing it. And even that wasn't sufficient as it turned out [. . .] [b]ecause everyone thought the experiment must have been contrived. They still didn't think it could happen in actual use. It was about nine months later when some internal work that Bill Crowther of BBN had been doing on simulation led him to the same conclusion and then it all changed. But it was rather contentious for a while. (pp. 20 f.)

Kahn et al. (1971) report on the latter study following the initial field tests, summarizing the problem as follows:

> The ARPA Network has been operational since the fall of 1969. During this time it has evolved from a four-node initial network to a fifteen-node network, as of July 1971, without significant modification to the original system design. A year and one half of experience by BBN and the participating Host organizations both in operating and in using the net has demonstrated that the IMP subnet will handle normal interactive traffic of all message lengths when each Host is prompt in accepting and delivering network traffic. However, under heavy traffic load, as may occur with many continuous file transfers or with unresponsive Hosts, the network performance can become substantially degraded. (p. 1)

At that time, the network could easily have been brought down by a single misbehaving host, thus hosts "were simply asked to not use the network in the way that caused the subnetwork problems, and the hosts did as they were asked" (Heart et al. 1978, p. III-56). As a more solid remedy, however, Kahn et al. (1971) improved on the system algorithms, particularly in the areas of reassembly storage management and routing, with the objective of solving the problems of reassembly lockup (deadlock in the destination IMP), store-and-forward lockup (deadlock in an IMP acting as an intermediary to other IMPs) and poor routes (from oversensitive and counterproductive routing updates in the face of heavy load) (pp. 3 f.).

Kahn et al. (1971, section 3.1, pp. 13 ff.) detail the improved algorithms to deal with lockups. To quote copiously from the subsection dealing with the algorithm applied to multi-packet messages:

> The source IMP will identify a multi-packet message by the absence of an end of message indication at the end of the first packet. Upon receipt of the first packet, the source IMP will stop the Host-to-IMP line and dispatch a small discardable message to the destination IMP asking to reserve 8 buffers in reassembly. When 8 buffers are available, the destination IMP will place them in reserve and then return a message to the source IMP to indicate the reservation. When this message is received by the source IMP, it will then restart the Host-to-IMP line and attempt to transmit the entire multi-packet message.
>
> The first packet of a multi-packet message is held by the source IMP while waiting for space to become available at the destination. The Host-to-IMP line is stopped after the first packet is received (provided space was not previously made available at the destination, as for example during high-bandwidth transfers) and restarted when space is known to be available. This technique typically increases the time to complete the transfer of an occasional 8-packet message or the first of a long sequence of messages from the Host to the IMP by tens of milliseconds in a lightly loaded net.
>
> This additional setup delay is not present for each message after the first of a continuous stream of multi-packet messages. Whenever a multi-packet message is received by a destination IMP, it will not return a RFNM to the source until the first packet has been sent to the Host and an additional 8 buffers have been reserved for that source. The source IMP will keep a record of the new buffer reservation for about 125 msec after completing the transfer of the RFNM to the Host. For each

> such record of a RFNM, the source IMP will allow one multi-packet message to that destination to be transmitted without first sending a discardable message and without halting the Host line.
>
> A Host that wishes to obtain high throughput must complete the transfer (into the source IMP) of the first packet of its next multi-packet message to the given destination within 125 msec after receipt of the RFNM. Any sequence of single-packet or multi-packet messages which fits into the 125 msec interval may precede this next multi-packet message. By continuing to transmit each successive message immediately upon receipt of the RFNM, a Host will be able to avoid the setup delay and thus allow high throughput of data to be achieved. If the source IMP does not receive a multi-packet message for the given destination within the 125 msec time period, it will discard its record of the buffer reservation and dispatch a short message to the destination IMP to free the 8 reserved buffers, and the source Host may then experience the short setup delay when it sends its next multi-packet message. (pp. 15 f.)

A second digression on checksums inside the IMP subnetwork: In the early years of the Arpanet, BBN constantly increased the use of checksums both in hardware and software in order not only to cope with transmission line errors, but also with 'intra-IMP failures'. Eventually, checksums as well as acknowledgment and retransmission schemes were applied to virtually all data that could conceivably become corrupted, be it by line errors, memory errors inside the IMPs, hardware interface errors, etc. Thus not only would packets be checksummed (checking integrity at both ingress and egress), but also control data (particularly routing messages) and the very IMP software itself. BBN (1973*b*) elaborate on those issues (pp. 11 ff.), and reflects on some of the experiences with hardware problems that could only be debugged by software checksums in the first place:

> A partial list of the hardware problems that were uncovered by software checksums, and subsequently fixed, includes:

- One modem interface at the Aberdeen IMP dropped several bits from several successive words in transferring data into memory.
- One modem interface at the Belvoir IMP picked one or two bits in a single word in transferring data into memory.
- One modem interface at the ETAC TIPs dropped the first word in transferring data out of memory.

(pp. 12 f.)

See also McQuillan (1973) for a further elaboration of the ever increasing use of checksumming in the IMP software, largely as a function of the growing difficulties in tracking down errors in the network, and the adverse effects of local errors on the operation of the overall network (see, e. g., the Harvard IMP incident of 1971 which repeatedly brought down the entire Arpanet by advertising false routing updates due to a memory hardware error setting the values for the distances to all other IMPs to zero, p. 2). Plus, see note 120 and accompanying text for further discussion of the points here alluded to.

See also McQuillan et al. (1972) for a concise summary of the IMP software changes regarding lock-up prevention, IMP-IMP acknowledgments, routing, etc.; Kahn and Crowther (1972) for an elaboration of some of the congestion and flow control issues that emerged in the early Arpanet; and Levin (1978) for a brief list of principal Arpanet development milestones.

156 (57). See note 163.

157 (57). We have mentioned in section 2.2, specifically note 45 and accompanying text, that retransmission based on lack of positive acknowledgments is the only complete strategy in dealing with errors end-to-end (Walden 1970*b*). A different algorithm based on explicit inquiries and negative acknowledgments was proposed by Kalin (1970, pp. 6 f.). Along the lines of Walden (1970*b*), an extended take on the theory of error control and the means of achieving reliable communication is then offered by Kalin (1971). Postel takes up the issue of reliability in 1973 yet again, considering three schemes for lost message detection (Postel 1973*b*) and proposing to adopt a retransmission scheme based on Incomplete Message indications rather than one based on host-to-host acknowledgments, noting that "several hosts" already implement the former scheme (p. 2). Then,

Hathaway (1973); Walden (1973*b*); Walden (1973*a*), in discussion of Postel (1973*b*), add further elaboration to a scheme based on Incomplete Message indications and unique message IDs per connection (rather than per host). Finally, Kanodia (1974) puts forward a somewhat complete specification of a lost message detection and recovery protocol which not only addresses the problem of lost data massages but also that of lost control messages. However, the proposal was not pursued any further in the NWG (see Postel 1975*c* who notes that it "is interesting in several features, but some have suggested that is aimed at a non-problem", p. 7).

158 (57). To be sure, it is also true that by 1973 the Arpanet was simply too large to easily change the host-host protocol so as to encompass mandatory retransmission facilities, for this would have involved having to rewrite substantial portions of all of the various NCPs in existence and generally impose much larger resource requirements on the NCPs, most notably retransmission buffers. As Postel (1973*b*) notes:

> Host to host acknowledgements could be required. Such an acknowledgement scheme could be implemented similarly to the IMP to IMP scheme. [However,] [t]his is a serious change to the current protocols so I will not elaborate on it here, feeling that deeper study will be necessary to fully specify a reasonable host to host acknowledgement strategy. (p. 2)

And, Hathaway (1973), advocating a retransmission scheme based on Incomplete Transmission indications of the IMP subnetwork (see note 157), seconds:

> The [. . .] host-to-host acknowledgment scheme is perhaps the best, but as that requires quite major changes to the level 2 protocol, an interim solution such as that proposed here seems of value. (p. 2)

159 (57). Note that even the availability of hosts to begin with was fairly low in the early years of the Arpanet. BBN (1971*a*) reports:

> During the single two-week period in the third quarter for which data was obtained, only five Hosts responded to "login" attempts more than 50 % of the time; further, the usual response of one of these Hosts was to refuse the login. (p. 2)

Similarly, R. E. Kahn (1972) reports:

> [I]n the Arpanet, total uptime of the IMP at any site is currently on the order of 98 or 99 percent, while Host availability is generally no higher than 90 percent. (p. 1402)

Second, even the most basic common intermediary representations such as bytes had to be agreed on (see BBN 1970*a*, p. 9). A still more formidable challenge was that of arriving at standard Telnet and FTP protocols/applications, as evidenced by the host of RFCs documenting the discussion at the time (see ftp://ftp.rfc-editor.org/in-notes/rfc-index.txt).

As late as 1977, UCLA's Braden concluded that getting host computers to adapt to a peer-to-peer rather than master/slave paradigm and thus make proper use of the networking services offered by the Arpanet had been so tricky that "one might well consider it a minor technical miracle that the entire user/server system [at UCLA] seen by an Arpanet user works at all" (p. 4-6). As an instructive example for the intricacies at the host level consider the most impressive number of RFCs issued on the File Transfer Protocol (among the first 1000 RFCs alone)—concerned with little more than the seemingly trivial task of transferring files from one place to another.

160 (57). Notes Sunshine (1975) on the potential fallibility of end-to-end protocols concerned with reliability:

> PAR protocols [positive ACK/retransmission communication protocols] [. . .] successfully mask errors in the transmission medium, but not surprisingly, they cannot guarantee reliable transmission when part of the protocol itself is violated due to failure of one side or the other. The information maintained at both sides of the protocol [IDs used, messages pending] is necessary for correct functioning. (p. 5)

As for NCP, Metcalfe (1973) makes several instructive points:

> It is [. . .] a fact that our complex connection-oriented NCP's drop bits, bytes, and even whole messages on occasion. Unfortunately, the NCP protocol, in all of its efforts to afford user processes a clean bytestream communication system, has failed

to treat error control. We have taken the IMP Subnet's guarantee of (transmission) error-free communication too much to heart (sic) and left ourselves exposed to the dangers of intermittent undetected error. [. . .] The NCP protocol does not explicitly treat situations in which a Host malfunction leads to a specific protocol violation or to a lack of response. Host-Host control messages which arrive in improper context are often discarded and only occasionally logged. Many implementations treat a lack of response after some arbitrary time-out as a protocol violation and take punitive action against all the users on an offending Host. Actions taken (1) usually lose information and/or cause catastrophic Host-wide communication failures, (2) are non-standard, and (3) offer little potential for successful recovery. (pp. 8-14 f., references omitted)

161 (58). Placing the bulk of networking functions under central control increases (1) robustness, manageability, and monitoring; (2) performance as a function of accessing and controlling the distributed processes and resources involved; and (3) maintainability, particularly debugging, recovery, and maintenance updates. (McQuillan and Walden 1977, pp. 281 f.).

The costs to this approach, on the other hand, are primarily a potential loss of generality from the extra level of indirection and, thus, a reduction of flexibility in actual applications of the network. Also, the feasibility of the administrative arrangement here is a directly proportional function of the alignment of interests among the ultimate network users and the entity tasked with running the subnetwork. In the case discussed here it is fair to say that the interests of all stakeholders where largely aligned, but it should be noted that the maintenance of congruent interests without intrinsic conflict resolution mechanisms (such as markets) does not generalize well to larger less tractable network settings (such as the later Internet, see section 8.1 for the notion of tussles).

162 (58). Referring to McKenzie's 1972 Host/Host Protocol for the ARPA Network, Heart et al. (1978, pp. III-63 ff.) recount the early history of the host-host protocol, and conclude that only by January 1972, and following a lengthy process involving not only NWG, but also ARPA and BBN, was there a final version of the host-host protocol that has remained "essentially unchanged since" (p. III-65). The first version of the host-host

protocol had been put forward by S. D. Crocker (1970*a*), but see also S. D. Crocker (1971).

See also Metcalfe (1973, pp. 8-3 ff.) for a fine overview of host-host protocol experiments prior to the 'official' host-host protocol from the NWG.

163 (58). DIGRESSION: With the Arpanet growing, the possible sources of errors in the subnetwork increased, too. Also, with network uses gradually turning from experimental to operational, message losses inside the subnetwork became a somewhat less forgivable. To quote from McQuillan (1973):

> Our idea of the Network has evolved as the Network itself has grown. Initially, it was thought that the only components in the network design that were prone to errors were the communications circuits, and the modem interfaces in the IMPs are equipped with a CRC checksum to detect "almost all" such errors. The rest of the system, including Host interfaces, IMP processors, memories, and interfaces, were all considered to be error-free. We have had to re-evaluate this position in the light of our experience. In operating the network we are faced with the problem of having to perform remote diagnosis on failures which cannot easily be classified or understood. Some examples of such problems include reports from Host personnel of lost RFNMs and lost Host-Host protocol allocate messages, inexplicable behavior in the IMP of a transient nature, and, finally, the problem of crashes — the total failure of an IMP, perhaps affecting adjacent IMPs. These circumstances are infrequent and are therefore difficult to correlate with other failures or with particular attempted remedies. Indeed, it is often impossible to distinguish a software failure from a hardware failure. [. . .]
>
> In the course of the last few years, it has become increasingly clear that such errors were occurring, though it was difficult to speculate as to where, why, and how often. (pp. 1 and 2)

BBN (1974*c*), commenting on the growing reliability problems due to the increasing size of Arpanet, by then including 45 IMPs and TIPs:

The size of the network tends to exaggerate the effects of low-probability failures. For example, a hardware design problem which would result in a failure on a single machine once a month will probably occur somewhere in the network once every 16 hours. Even an event which has a once-a-year probability in a single machine has almost a once-a-week probability in the network. Similarly, if new IMP software has an obscure bug, the probability of this bug showing up in the network in a single day is twice the probability of the bug showing up in the BBN test cell operating in three machines for a week, even ignoring those bugs which are purely related to the size and complexity of the network (dynamic routing, for example, might contain such bugs).

In addition, the number of IMP variations continues to increase: there are 516's and 316's; IMPs and TIPs; Local, Distant, and Very Distant Hosts; circuits running at 7.2, 9.6, 50, and 230 kilobits per second; surface and satellite circuits. Each of these "variables" tends to apply to a machine essentially independently of the values of the other "variables", yet there is some probability that a given combination will interact on the hardware or software in some unexpected way. (For example, a problem first observed at the Ames TIP was due to the interactions of four circuits, one a satellite circuit and two others running at 230 Kbs, with the software in the Ames IMP.)

Finally, site problems (which have always occurred) are magnified in their effect as the average network connectivity has gradually decreased. For example, we are averaging between one and two site power failures per day. There are now several network areas where there are 5 or 6 IMPs strung out in a row; almost any pair of "simultaneous" failures in such a string will isolate some machines between the failing sites. If the failures are in the IMP software it can quickly be re-initialized; if they are in the hardware we can frequently bypass the machine; however, if they are in the site environment (e. g. power) we are not usually able to influence the duration of the isolation. Occasionally the environmental problems are rather

> bizarre; during the month of February one machine was damaged by an internal fire (ISI), power at a second was lost due to computerroom flooding (Rutgers), and a third machine was turned off when the room was filled with dust from building construction (Moffett). (pp. 10 f.)

A less flattering assessment of the growing reliability problems is given by S. D. Crocker (2009):

> As it turned out, he [Frank Heart] was wrong on all counts. Some of the interfaces were not completely reliable, and it would have been very, very helpful to have checksums. Nor would they have added very much in processing time. And it wasn't really up to him to tell us what to do. And, of course, it turned out to be impossible to build a network that never lost a packet. In trying to do so, they suffered various forms of lock up that brought the entire network down from time to time.

164 (58). See Heart et al. (1978).

165 (59). In fact, as we shall see in section 5.1, the Arpanet on the inside not only looked much like today's Internet, it even offered what amounts to a best effort service in addition to its standard virtual circuit service, thus anticipating both the high level architecture, and the low level minimum service aspect of the Internet.

166 (59). From a host level perspective the subtleties of the IMP subnetwork are, of course, entirely immaterial. For example, Crocker et al. (1972) treat the IMP level protocols as but one:

> There are three lower level software protocols which nest in support of the user-level communications interface for the Arpanet. The lowest of these is the IMP-IMP protocol which provides for reliable communication among IMPs. [. . .] At the next higher level is the IMP-Host protocol. [. . .] The Host-Host protocol, finally, is the set of rules whereby Hosts construct and maintain communication between processes (user jobs) running on remote computers. (pp. 271 f.; see also Figure 3 at p. 274)

With hindsight, we can make several observations about this statement. First, while it is a fair simplification to subsume the rules that govern the internal working of the IMP subnetwork under one layer, the differences between the IMP-IMP procedures hop-by-hop versus source-to-destination are so striking as to warrant a firm conceptual separation.

Second, and with a nod to the contributions of the OSI model to the conceptualization of networking structures, to argue that there is one IMP-IMP protocol nested inside the IMP-Host protocol is an oversimplification of the Arpanet architecture that confuses *protocols*, allowing peers at one layer to communicate, and *interfaces*, making available the service of one layer to that logically above it. In truth, the IMP-host protocol affords no peer-to-peer communication across the IMP-IMP protocol. Rather, it extends the IMP-IMP protocol to the hosts by way of concatenation. Thus the more sensible abstraction would hold that the IMP-IMP protocol is at the very *same* level as the IMP-Host protocol (see also Figure 4.1). Clark (1974) elaborates, taking into account both the lower level IMP-IMP protocol and the source-IMP-to-destination-IMP protocol:

> There are several levels of protocol in the network. At the lowest level there are the adjacent IMP-IMP protocol and the Host-IMP protocol, which govern the transfer between adjacent modules. Above this there is the sender to receiver IMP-IMP protocol, between the IMPs which represent the ultimate source and destination of a message; above this there is the Host-Host protocol; and above the Host-Host protocol are special-purpose protocols for such things as transfer of files and allowing a user at one host to log into another host (the Telnet protocol). (pp. 105 f.)

A brief aside on the difference between protocols and interfaces. McQuillan and Cerf (1978*a*) offer a good distinction between the two: Protocols are "rules for communication between *similar* processes", whereas interfaces are "rules for communication between *dissimilar* processes" (p. 2, emphasis added). Also, see Tanenbaum (2002, pp. 44 f., 48 f.) for a general discussion of interfaces versus protocols in the context of TCP/IP.

167 (59). McQuillan and Walden (1977):

> [T]he ARPA Network implementation uses the technique of breaking messages into packets to minimize the delay seen for long transmissions over many hops. The ARPA Network

> implementation also allows several messages to be in transit simultaneously between a given pair of Hosts. However, the several messages and the packets within the messages may arrive at the destination IMP out of order, and in the event of a broken IMP or line, there may be duplicates. The task of the ARPA Network source-to-destination transmission procedure is to reorder packets and messages at their destination, to cull duplicates, and after all the packets of a message have arrived, pass the message on to the destination Host and return an end-to-end acknowledgment called a Ready for Next Message (or RFNM) to the source. (p. 284)

This design plainly reflected the basic principles of datagram networking as expounded by Pouzin (1976*b*) (see our discussion at page 19). It is noteworthy that the basic design decision flowed straight from the Arpanet RFQ:

> A "Normal" message may be broken into several packets according to its size (multiple packet message, MPM), but a packet will contain only one message. The packets in MPM are not bound together until they reach the destination IMP where they are formed back into a normal message. They may even flow through different paths of network and reach the destination IMP out of sequential order. (Scheblik et al. 1968, p. 47 f.)

As for flow control, essentially, in the Arpanet this was handled by returning RFNMs from the destination IMP to the source IMP which would pass it to the source hosts, thus both acknowledging receipt of the message by the destination IMP, plus indicating that a new message may be sent to the destination. Eight messages could be in transit between a pair of hosts at one time, messages falling outside this permissible window would be discarded at destination (McQuillan and Walden 1977; Walden 1974).

Another notable aspect of the source-IMP-to-destination-IMP transmission procedure was that Multi Packet Messages (MPMs) would require a storage allocation prior to sending the message (see note 155). Thus it was made sure that the message could actually be taken by the destination IMP. Plus, the reservation was kept alive for subsequent messages, and would only be torn down once a timer of 125 ms (between RFNM and new host message) elapsed at the source IMP (McQuillan and Walden 1977, p. 285). On the other hand, single-packet messages, that is, *messages* no larger than the maximum permissible *packet* size could be send without any prior reservation, hoping that sufficient storage was available in the destination IMP. In case no storage was available such packets would simply be discarded at the destination IMP, which would then return to the source IMP a reservation acknowledgment message once sufficient storage became available (p. 285). This scheme speeds up small and low frequency messages which are typical for remote login sessions, and takes "advantage of the highly probable case that the destination will be able to find storage for a single packet immediately" (p. 285). To quote from BBN (1978*c*) on the mechanisms that had been in place largely unchanged since 1971:

> No multi-packet message is allowed to enter the network until storage for the message has been allocated at the destination IMP. As soon as the source IMP takes in the first packet of a multi-packet message, it sends a small control message to the destination IMP requesting that reassembly storage be reserved at the destination for this message. It does not take in any further packets from the Host until it receives an allocation message in reply. The destination IMP queues the request and sends the allocation message to the source IMP when enough reassembly storage is free; at this point the source IMP sends the message to the destination.
>
> Effective bandwidth is maximized for sequences of long messages by permitting all but the first message to bypass the request mechanism. When the message itself arrives at the destination, and the destination IMP is about to return the RFNM, the destination IMP waits until it has room for an additional multi-packet message. It then piggybacks a storage allocation on the RFNM. If the source Host is prompt in answering the RFNM with its next message, an allocation is ready and the message can be transmitted at once. If the source Host delays too long, or it the data transfer is complete, the source IMP returns the unused allocation to the destination. With this

> mechanism, the inter-message delay has been minimized and the Hosts can obtain the full bandwidth of the network.
>
> The delay for a short message has been minimized by transmitting it to the destination immediately while keeping a copy in the source IMP. If there is space at the destination, it is accepted and passed on to a Host and a RFNM is returned; the source IMP discards the message when it receives the RFNM. If not, the message is discarded, a request for allocation is queued and, when space becomes available, the source IMP is notified that the message may now be retransmitted. Thus, no setup delay is incurred when storage is available at the destination. (p. 4)

DIGRESSION: Note that the source-IMP-to-destination-IMP procedures in the Arpanet were not fully complete — leaving any end-to-end retransmissions in pursuit of reliability to the end hosts. While McQuillan and Walden (1977) acknowledge in a theoretical elaboration of end-to-end transmission procedures the merit of end-to-end checksums — "[n]ode-to-node checksums do not fulfill the same function as end-to-end checksums because they check only the lines, not the nodes" (p. 278) —, their description of the actual Arpanet source-IMP-to-destination-IMP transmission procedures does not contain such provisions. (See also note 168.) Two more quotes from McQuillan and Walden (1977), one on the theoretical use of a checksum for entire messages end-to-end:

> A checksum is appended to the message at the source and the checksum is checked at the destination; when the checksum does not check at the destination, the incorrect message is discarded, requiring it to be retransmitted from the source. (p. 277)

And, on the actual dealing with incomplete or missing messages end-to-end:

> The source IMP keeps track of whether a response has come in (typically in the form of a Ready For Next Message) for each message sent. The destination IMP keeps track of whether the message is complete (that is, whether all the packets have arrived). The source IMP also times out the message number,

> and if a response has not been received for a message for too long a period (e. g., thirty seconds), the source IMP sends a control message with the timed-out message number questioning the possibility of an incomplete transmission. The destination IMP must always return a Ready for Next Message for such a control message stating whether it saw the original message or not, and the source IMP will send the message number in question every few seconds until it receives a response or one of the other of the IMPs decides that there is a hopeless deadlock and more massive corrective action is required. (p. 284)

BBN and Kahn (1976) elaborate the handling of incomplete message transmissions:

> [W]hen all packets arrive at the destination, they are reassembled to form the original message and passed to the destination Host. The destination IMP returns a positive acknowledgment for receipt of the message to the source IMP, which in turn passes this acknowledgment to the source Host. This acknowledgment is called a Ready for Next Message (RFNM) and identifies the message being acknowledged by name. In some relatively rare cases, however, the message may be lost in the network due to an IMP failure; in such cases an Incomplete Transmission message will be returned to the source Host instead of a RFNM. Again, in this case, the message which was incompletely transmitted is identified by name.
>
> If a response from the destination IMP (either RFNM or Incomplete Transmission) is itself lost in the network, this condition will be detected by the source IMP, which will automatically inquire of the destination IMP whether the original message was correctly transmitted or not, and repeat the inquiry until a response is received from the destination IMP. This inquiry mechanism is timeout-driven, and each timeout period may be as little as 30 or as much as 45 seconds in length. (p. 3-2)

Surely, if the source IMP still had a copy of the incomplete message in question, it would retransmit the message rather than report to its host that transmission of the message was incomplete by issuing a Incomplete

Transmission (type 9, subtype 3) message. After all, in case the destination host was dead, and retransmissions thus futile, the source IMP would return to its host a Destination Host or IMP Dead (type 7) message. The lack of source-IMP-to-destination-IMP retransmission facilities is also confirmed by Cosell (2009):

> IMPs *only* buffered packets at the modem-output queue. There was no source-IMP buffering of data for the destination-IMP. [. . .] It was up to the host to resend the message. (emphasis in original)

It is hard to tell in retrospect the extent to which hosts did engage in end-to-end (as in host-to-host) retransmissions following incomplete message transmission incidents due to subnetwork IMP or circuit failures. While NCP did not include retransmission facilities (the host-host protocol did not have sequence numbers), and any error recovery would thus have to be implemented by higher level protocols or manual human intervention (restarting an application, logging in again, etc.); some special purpose hosts such as BBN's Terminal IMPs, or TIPs, did come to include message retransmission facilities (see section 4.3, particularly pages 66 ff.) Also, higher layer protocols and user application came to encompass some error recovery mechanisms such as checkpoints for data transmissions (see section 4.4).

168 (60). Originally, IMP-to-IMP acknowledgments were sent explicitly for every packet received:

> As a packet moves through the subnet, each IMP stores the packet until a positive acknowledgment is returned from the succeeding IMP. This acknowledgment indicates that the message was received without error and was accepted. Once an IMP has accepted a packet and returned a positive acknowledgment, it holds onto that packet tenaciously until it in turn receives an acknowledgment from the succeeding IMP. Under no circumstances (except for Host or IMP malfunction) will an IMP discard a packet after it has generated a positive acknowledgment. However, an IMP is always free to refuse a packet by simply not returning a positive acknowledgment. It may do this for any of several reasons: the packet may have been

> received in error, the IMP may be busy, the IMP buffer storage may be temporarily full, etc.
>
> At the transmitting IMP, such discard of a packet is readily detected by the absence of a returned acknowledgment within a reasonable time interval (e. g., 100 msec). Such packets are retransmitted, perhaps along a different route. Acknowledgments themselves are not acknowledged, although they are error checked in the usual fashion. Loss of an acknowledgment results in the eventual retransmission of the packet; the destination IMP sorts out the resulting duplication by using a message number and a packet number in the header.
>
> The packets of a message arrive at the destination IMP, possibly out of order, where they are reassembled. (Heart et al. 1970, pp. 554 f.)

Later, the acknowledgment scheme of Bartlett et al. (1969) was adopted, such that acknowledgments would piggyback with data packets as alternating one-bit signals in the reverse direction (using 'null packets' in the absence of other traffic), thus making for a 10–20 % efficiency improvement (Kahn and Crowther 1972, p. 545; McQuillan et al. 1972, pp. 744 f.; BBN 1978*c*, pp. 8 f.).

There was no facility in the Arpanet to retransmit packets or entire messages from source IMP to destination IMP. Once an IMP received an acknowledgment for a packet sent out, it discarded its copy of the packet, thereby freeing buffer space for new packets. It could thus happen that parts of a message got lost inside the IMP subnetwork due to IMP failures, see also note 163. However, subnetwork failures were sufficiently rare to warrant the lack of 'complete and correct' (but also very costly in terms of buffer space) end-to-end reliability mechanisms. Also, it should be noted that the PSN circuits used for linking the IMPs were notoriously prone to all sorts of errors which would corrupt Arpanet packets (the error rate of phone lines being about 0.001 percent; see, e. g., Ornstein et al. 1971, p. 253). Thus dealing with errors hop-by-hop rather than end-to-end made good engineering sense at the time. In fact, Pouzin's Cigale subnetwork of the Cyclades network adopted the Arpanet IMP-IMP procedure, using the very same acknowledgment/retransmission scheme (Pouzin 1982, pp. 99 ff.).

Digression: Note as an aside that some have contested the case for hop-by-hop acknowledgment and retransmissions. Metcalfe (1973, pp. 3-31 ff.) argues that the benefits from hop-by-hop rather the end-to-end error acknowledging are not overwhelming (in fact, he puts the reduction in transfer time at a mere 9 %). On the other hand, the larger the number of hops between two end points and the more error prone the links, the larger the benefit from hop-by-hop error control. However, one may also argue that the total memory required for error control is lower with end-to-end error control.

169 (60). See note 51 and accompanying text.

170 (60). McQuillan and Walden (1977) touch on the various trade-offs that define packet switching, one such trade-off being that of packet loss versus duplicates:

> An attempt to prevent lost and duplicate packets must fail as there is a tradeoff between minimizing duplicate packets and minimizing lost packets. If the nodes avoid duplication of packets whenever possible, more packets are lost. Conversely, it the nodes retransmit whenever packets may be lost, more packets are duplicated. (p. 245)

171 (60). Recall that packets belonging to one and the same message may be routed along different paths across the network. Also, since every IMP-to-IMP packet transmission featured error control by checksumming, acknowledgment, and retransmission, packets encountering line errors may be delayed. McQuillan and Walden (1977):

> [A]n IMP may send the several packets of a message out on different links. Because of retransmission (out of order) of a packet on a link and transmission of packets on alternate links, the packets of a message may arrive at the destination IMP out of order and must be reassembled into the correct order for retransmission into the Host. (p. 245)

Digression: As an aside, one may ask why go to the trouble of splitting up messages into separate and—for the purpose of lower level IMP-IMP operations—unrelated packets in the first place. Walden (1972*b*) remarks:

> There are several reasons for breaking messages into packets: (1) a packet is more convenient to buffer in the IMPs than messages would be; (2) shorter checksums are sufficient for packets than would be required for messages; but, mainly, (3) the earlier packets in a message can begin their journey across the network while the later packets are still coming into the IMP from the Host. (p. 9)

172 (61). Walden (1972*b*):

> Each IMP holds on to a packet until it gets a positive acknowledgment from the next IMP down the line that the packet has been properly received. It is gets the acknowledgment, all is well; the IMP knows that the next IMP now has responsibility for the packet and the transmitting IMP can discard its copy of the packet. (p. 11)

173 (61). Note that, strictly speaking, the design of the Arpanet fell short of perfect completeness and reliability, for missing or incomplete messages (due to intermediary IMPs acknowledging but not sending off a packet) would be dropped without end-to-end retransmission, leaving any retransmissions or other means of error recovery to higher level protocols or human intervention. (See our discussion in notes 167 and 168.) But, then again, achieving *strictly* perfect reliability is impossible even with arbitrarily long checksums, or elaborate end-to-end transmission protocols such as TCP. Remarks Crowcroft (2009) on TCP reliability:

> [T]here's a small, but non zero possibility that transmission errors caused by interference create a packet that is a duplicate of an Ack, from a completely unrelated packet, and happen to create the right link and IP header and TCP checksum to match.

In today's TCP, for that matter, ca. one in 300 million packets is accepted with data corruption; given the 16 bit checksum of TCP and an IP packet corruption rate of 0.02 percent (as measured by Paxson 1999, p. 280).

174 (61). McQuillan and Cerf (1978*a*) note, more generally, about the design choices regarding end-to-end protocols:

> [M]any design issues remain constant whether these functions are performed at the host or subnetwork level. (p. 31)

Particularly, the functional separation between a lower level datagram service and higher level services such as virtual circuits was well established, and used in practically all networks at the time, even if only internally—see note 64 for an apt observation on this matter by Pouzin (1976*b*).

175 (62). As an aside, one may argue that the feasibility of extending the scope of IMP services was a result of the great success with which the IMPs mastered the tasks they were designed for in the first place. The first IMP was delivered by BBN on time, without cost overruns, and working very much as planned if not better (BBN 1969*b*, p. 4)—much to the surprise of UCLA staff (S. D. Crocker 1987, pp. 3 f.). But, not only did the project start well; by and large, it is fair to say that the entire Arpanet project was a huge success that "far exceeded even the most optimistic views at the time of inception" (Heart et al. 1978, p. II-26). However, as with any major IT project, a conceivable result could as well have been that the IMPs worked poorly if at all, in which case increasing their set of tasks would have been much more remote and hence unlikely an option.

176 (63). Hafner and Lyon (1998, pp. 121 f.) recount how representatives from the prospective host sites voiced their request to have more than but one host connected to the IMP, and by February 1969 ARPA's Roberts amended the specification accordingly. BBN (1969*c*, pp. 7 ff.) briefly detail the changes to the initial specification entailed by the increase of hosts per IMP from one to four. (Note as an aside that the number of available I/O ports of the hardware placed an upper bound to the sum of host and modem interfaces.)

177 (63). Initially, the Arpanet had an address space catering for 63 IMPs (6 bits in the 'leader format') and 4 hosts per IMP (another 2 bits) (BBN 1978*c*, p. 94) which was later increased to allow for up to 65,536 IMPs (16 bits in the new-style, extended leader format) and 256 hosts per IMP (another 8 bits) (BBN 1978*c*, p. 95 f.). (See also Walden 1975*c*, p. 1 and Santos 1975, p. 1 on the changes in the IMP/host and host/IMP protocols including the increased address space, plus interesting comments by Postel 1975*a*, p. 1 and Postel 1977*c* on the shortcomings of fixed address schemes. Plus, see Walden 1972*b* as quoted in our note 188 on the 'virtual' fake hosts adding to the 'real' hosts to be placed with an IMP.)

Digression: Note that, unlike the newer BBN Pluribus IMPs and BBN C/30s, the earlier Honeywell type IMPs (H316/516) did not have enough I/O ports to exploit the host address space provided by the new leader format (see Perry et al. 1988, p. 53 for a brief summary of the several generations of IMP hardware). Thus many host sites had to make do with the four hosts restriction, or resort to some combination of gateways and an inter-network addressing scheme logically residing atop of the Arpanet IMP subnetwork protocols up to the IMP-host protocol (as specified in the 1822 Report).

Another less elaborate (but also less elegant) alternative was provided by port expanders (Nelson et al. 1980) — small multiplexers that intervened (more or less) transparently between an IMP and the attached hosts, allowing four instead of one host to be connected to each of the four IMP-host ports (appearing to the IMP as a single host, and to the hosts as an IMP). Thus, using four port expanders, the number of host computers to be attached to one IMP could be raised to a maximum of 16 instead of four. However, in order for the port expanders to multiplex between the attached hosts it was necessary that all but one of the hosts attached to it used the IP protocol in addition to the host-IMP protocol so that the hosts could be distinguished based on the IP address provided in the IP header (Figure N.6). (Decimal values 155–158 in the link field of the Arpanet 1822 leader signified that the payload is an IP packet; see Postel 1973*a*, p. 1 and Postel 1977*a*, p. 2.) Kirstein and Bennett (1979) comment critically on the

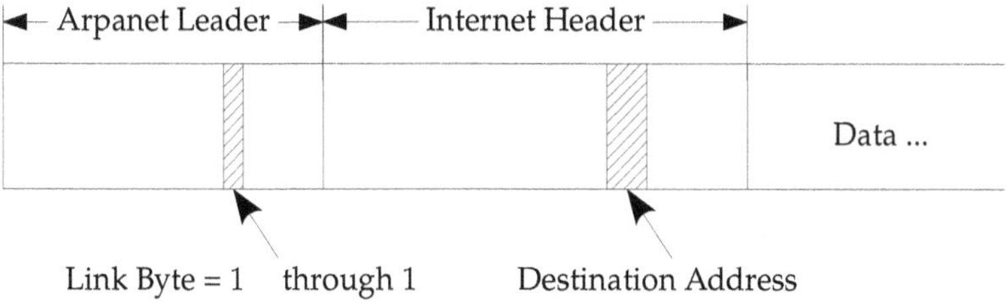

Figure N.6: Arpanet IMP port expander message format; Source: Nelson et al. (1980, p. 5)

port expanders' reliance on an IP header field outside the Arpanet message headers, arguing that any multiplexing should rather be performed based on explicit fields provided by the new extended 96 bit Arpanet IMP-host protocol header (see on the new header format note 148); after all an IP packet is but one of many conceivable payloads to an Arpanet message:

> [Using the expanded 96 bit header] each IMP can theoretically support up to 64 hosts. There is therefore no theoretical reason why port expanders cannot be used to make this function work. [. . .]
>
> Under the scheme proposed here, the hosts on a port expander can be an NCP host, a gateway, or the planet Mars; the only requirement is that it supports the 1822 interface [BBN and Kahn's 1822 Report]. Since port expansion is a local, IMP based function, this is as it should be. (pp. 6 and 7)

As an aside, port expanders were also reported to be coupled with proper gateways in the course of Internet implementation efforts at various Arpanet host sites, thus allowing the connection of arbitrary local networks to the Arpanet (see, e. g., Postel 1979c).

178 (63). As for the standard interface between IMPs and local hosts:

> The standard Host/IMP interface is a full duplex bit-serial unit that is logically divided into a Host-to-IMP section and an IMP-to-Host section. [. . .] In general, words are taken one by one from the sender's memory and transferred bit serially across the interface to the receiver, where they are reassembled into words of the appropriate (i. e., receivers) length and stored into the receiver's memory. The transmission thus consists of a bit train containing no special indications of word boundaries. [. . .] Bit transfer is asynchronous, the transmission of each bit being controlled by a *Ready-For-Next-Bit, There's-Your-Bit* handshaking procedure. Each bit is transferred only when both sender and receiver indicate preparedness. This permits either the sender or the receiver to hold up the transmission between any two bits in order to take as much time as necessary to get a new word from memory, to tuck an assembled word into memory, or to activate an interrupt routine that sets up new input or output buffers. Neither the sender nor the receiver should expect transmission to take place at a pre-determined bit rate

> and each must be able to accept arbitrary delays introduced by the other at any point in the bit train. (BBN and Kahn 1976, p. 4-2, emphasis in original)

An aside note on the "arbitrary delays" just quoted: IMPs did not typically accept infinitely long delays by hosts in sending or receiving messages: hosts have 15 seconds to send a message in its entirety to their IMP (BBN and Kahn 1976, p. 3-4), and 30 seconds to take in a message from their IMP (p. 3-9).

179 (64). This was acknowledged, albeit somewhat reluctantly, by McKenzie (1971*b*):

> The normal method of connecting a Host computer to the ARPA Network is, and will continue to be, placing an IMP at the Host site and making a short-distance hard-wire connection. However, during the past several months we have become increasingly aware of the occasional desire to interface a Host to some IMP via a long-distance connection (where long-distance, in this context, is any cable run longer than 2000 feet but may typically be tens of miles) via either a hard-wire or telephone circuit. (p. 1)

It is apt here to quote once more from Heart et al. (1978) who note that the simple host-IMP interface in the initial Arpanet design, largely flowing from the Arpanet RFQ, may have substantially eased the separation of responsibilities and concerns between subnetwork and hosts; yet it quickly "resulted in a hodge-podge of interface variations, each designed for more distant operation than its predecessors, and none except the first [bit-serial, asynchronous, non-error-controlled] was very elegant" (p. III-57).

180 (64). For an elaboration of the various aspects to the connection of a very distant host to an IMP see BBN and Kahn (1976, Appendix F, pp. F-1 ff.).

181 (64). Walden (2010*c*) informs me that the VDH interface was built by him in full appreciation of the IMP subnetwork internal protocols — "I knew the former, so I did it again for the latter".

182 (65). Transmissions between an IMP and a very distant host would no more be based on a per-bit handshakes but rather be in packets of multiples of 16 bits, up to 1008 bits. BBN (1972*a*) summarize:

> [U]nlike a normal Host, a Very Distant Host must be aware of packets. (p. 12)

183 (65). Acknowledgments were piggybacked on data or 'null' packets just like in IMP-to-IMP acknowledgments BBN (1972*a*, pp. 13 f.).

184 (65). Note that the IMP side modem in Figure 4.5 features just the same error detection (a 24-bit CRC for packets of up to a of maximum 1008 bits) as the host side modem in conjunction with the "Error Detecting Special Host Interface", an information which has been omitted from the figure because the IMP modems have built-in checksum generation and checking, anyway. BBN and Kahn (1976):

> [T]he modem interface in the IMP and the Error Detecting Special Host Interface communicate using the line protocol currently used between IMPs. (p. F-3)

See also BBN and Kahn (1976, section F.3, pp. F-14 ff.) for an elaboration of the line protocol (the conventions for the line format).

The working of the reliable transmission package, again, is based on symmetrical functional equivalence (section F.2, pp. F-5 ff.). The source transmits and retransmits packets until acknowledged; the receiving side issues acknowledgments for packets, discards packets in error, and will "pass on correctly received packets in sequence, waiting for the retransmission of any missing packet" (p. F-7).

185 (65). Note that "local" here means "idiosyncratic", not "limited geographic extent". This take is also common ground in the literature (see, e. g., Cerf 1978*c*, p. 1; Postel et al. 1981, p. 263).

186 (66). As an aside: Over the years the IMP-host interface was further refined, eventually adopting HDLC (the then emerging international standard for link level data transmission protocols) as a link control protocol providing reliable transmission. The resulting interface was called HDLC Distant Host, or HDH (Perry et al. 1988, p. 54). See also Perillo (1981) for a note on the HDH interface introduction in 1981.

The major innovation to the Arpanet design, however, had been the VDH interface introduced in the early 1970s when loosening the ties between IMPs and hosts necessitated no less than a complete redesign of the IMP-host interface based on a proper appreciation of the subtleties here — thus arriving at a structure that in many aspects closely resembled the existing inner structure of the IMP subnetwork: a reliable serial data connection was obtained by augmenting a basic packet service so as to deliver a virtual circuit.

187 (66). We note as an aside that terminals connecting to a host could also involve fairly elaborate 'link level' procedures, and may thus well be considered part of the overall network architecture in their own right. The most trivial case was a terminal connected right to a host computer, both sitting in the same premises. The more elaborate case was to connect hosts via dial-up and modems, thus affording a reliable serial connection between the two.

DIGRESSION: In fact, there could be any type of local network in between a host and its terminals. An interesting case in point has been the Alohanet system, work on which started in 1969, and which connected terminals scattered around the Hawaiian islands via two broadcast radio channels (one uplink, one downlink) to a central host computer (called Menehune) at the University of Hawaii. It was the first network to use a single broadcast channel for various users governed by a completely random access scheme (rather than a conventional time-division multiplexing scheme) — based on the assumption of bursty and largely uncorrelated low volume traffic. Despite its poor channel capacity due to the inevitable collisions and the resulting overload with retransmission traffic entailed by the decentralized random access scheme on the uplink — initial capacity was $1/(2e)$, and ca. 300 users at any one time could be served (Abramson 1970, p. 285); later elaborations increased capacity to ca. 0.35 by adding globally synchronized discrete time interval constraints ("slotted" Aloha, see Roberts 1975); plus, the range of "Aloha channels" was limited to a certain "Sisyphus distance", r_0, which could only be extended by repeaters (Abramson 1975, pp. 4 ff.) — the system performed much better than dial-up connections over Hawaii's telephone lines. Instead of modems it relied on Terminal Control Units (TCUs) which provided a reliable (simplex) link from terminals to central computer by implementing the error control and retransmission schemes required to make up for bit errors (largely due to collisions) (Abramson 1970, p. 283; Abramson 1985, p. 120; Kuo 1990, pp. 107 f.). At its peak, the Alohanet served some forty users on the islands of Oahu and Mauri (Pelkey 2009, ch. 4.10).

In late 1972 the Menehune computer was connected to an Arpanet

IMP, which in turn was connected to the U.S. mainland via a point-to-point satellite channel between Paumalu, Hawaii and Jamesburg, California (using a 56 kb PCM voice channel of the Pacific Ocean Intelsat IV satellite) (Abramson 1985, pp. 120 f.; Kuo 1990, p. 108; see also North 1972 versus Neigus and Feinler 1973; and see Binder et al. 1975, p. 204, Figure 1 for a block diagram illustrating the Alohanet-Arpanet connection). However, note that terminal connections from the Alohanet to the Arpanet only became available in 1974 after NCP and Telnet were sufficiently supported by Menehune, and even then support for terminal connections was still somewhat limited (Abramson 1975, pp. 8 f.). In 1976 Alohanet ceased operation and was discontinued for lack of further funding, see Kuo 1990, p. 109; also, the two managers Norman Abramson and Frank Kuo left Hawaii to work for the DoD, Abramson from 1974 to 1975, and Kuo from 1976 to 1977; however, the Hawaii IMP remained in place, see, e. g., Rosen et al. 1979, pp. 3, 156.

188 (67). For a description of the various programs making up the IMP software see BBN (1978*c*). Quote:

> The programs in the IMP background loop perform a variety of functions: TTY is used to handle the IMP Teletype traffic; DEBUG, to inspect or change IMP core memory; TRACE, to transmit collected information about trace packets; STATISTICS, to take and transmit network and IMP statistics; PARAMETER-CHANGE, to alter the values of selected IMP parameters; PACKET CORE, to transfer portions of core images via the network; and DISCARD to throw away packets. Selected Hosts and IMPs, particularly the Network Control Center, will find it necessary or useful to communicate with one or more of these background loop programs. So that these programs may send and receive messages from the network, they are treated as "fake Hosts." Rather than duplicating portions of the large IMP-to-Host and Host-to-IMP routines, the background loop programs are treated as if they were Hosts, and they can thereby utilize existing programs. [. . .]
>
> Other routines, which send connection protocol messages, send incomplete transmission messages, send allocations, return give-

> backs, send RFNMs, and retransmit single-packet messages also reside in the background program. These routines are called Back Hosts. However, these programs run in a slightly different manner than the fake Hosts in that they do not simulate the Host/IMP channel hardware. They do not go through the Host/IMP code at all, but rather put their messages directly on the task queue. Nonetheless, the principle is the same. (pp. 26, 27)

The conceptual difference between fake hosts and back hosts was thus that the former could properly communicate with other normal hosts or fake hosts, whereas back hosts would be used for subnetwork internal control communication only (Santos 1979*a*, 19:27 min).

Walden (1972*b*) elaborates on the nature of the 'virtual' fake hosts:

> The Host to IMP and IMP to Host routines both think they can handle eight Hosts although there will never be more than four real Hosts on an IMP. The other four Hosts are these background programs which simulate the operation of the Host/IMP data channel hardware so that the Host/IMP routines are unaware they are communicating within anything other than a real Host. This trick saved a large amount of code. (p. 25)

See also BBN and Kahn (1976, ch. 5, pp. 5-1 ff.) and BBN (1973*a*, section 3.2, pp. 59 ff) for a detailed description of the different background programs of an IMP.

189 (67). In fact, the background programs running as fake hosts were quite literally low-profile, in that they were run with the lowest possible priority, only to be executed when no other tasks were present.

190 (67). See BBN (1970*b*); BBN (1970*d*); BBN (1971*a*).

191 (68). Recall that prior to the Arpanet it was thought (if only in the abstract) that computer networking may be achieved by having hosts communicate with one another all by themselves. The only thing that kept normal Arpanet hosts from connecting directly to the telephone lines of the Arpanet and assume all the IMP functions themselves was the prohibitive effort thus incurred, making any such exercise a purely hypothetical one.

DIGRESSION: The first paper published on the design of the Arpanet as implemented in the IMP subnetwork (Heart et al. 1970) considers but one host per IMP (Figure N.7), which is, of course, precisely the topology found by the end of 1969 with the four initial IMPs at UCLA, SRI, UCSB, and University of Utah in place. See also note 146 on the initial idea

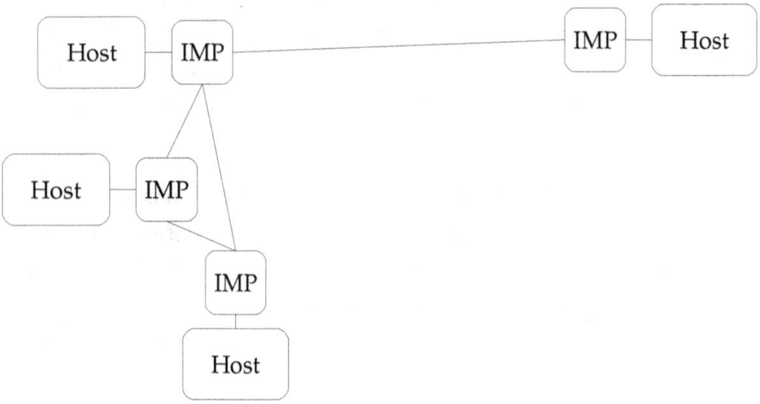

Figure N.7: Hosts and IMPs in the basic Arpanet architecture; Source: Heart et al. (1970, p. 552)

of connecting host computers directly rather than building a subnetwork out of uniform computers that would serve the ultimate host computers. However, see also note 176 about how the number of possible hosts per IMP had increased to four by 1969, already.

192 (68). As for the distribution of computational power in the application now stretching from the ultimate end point (the terminal device with the end user) and its agent (the terminal handler with the Arpanet IMP) Ornstein et al. (1971) reason:

> [W]hat is the proper distribution of computational power among the remote big facility, the terminal processor, and the terminal? Shall the terminal processor be clever, have sizable storage, be user programmable, etc., or shall it be a simpler device whose basic job is multiplexing in a flexible way? [. . .] [W]e decided that the terminal processor should be simple and not programmable from the terminals. The computational load and the storage should be in the Hosts or in the terminals and not in the terminal processor. This simple multiplexing

> approach is amenable to some standardization and is philosophically close to the original IMP notion of a standard nodal device. (p. 246)

It is thus only fair to note that while the TIPs introduced host level functions to the province of BBN's Arpanet IMP subnetwork, they only did so to the minimum degree necessary to support basic Telnet terminal sessions, leaving any additional computational sophistication to the terminal devices. Also, the terminal handler was relatively separate from the IMP part of the overall TIP box (Ornstein et al. 1971, pp. 246 f.; see also note 193).

193 (68). Ornstein et al. (1971, pp. 245 ff.) consider the theoretical reasoning behind the notion of integrating terminal host functionality into an IMP, rather than separating the IMP and host functions into two distinct boxes. While the 'T[erminal]' portion of the T[erminal] I[nterface] [Message] P[rocessor] was, in fact, firmly separated from the classic IMP portion (they shared a processor, but the code for either of them was in different memory banks), there was significant economy from combining the two in but one physical box. Those considerations notwithstanding, the most important point to note is that, from a host level perspective, the combination of the two parts reduced to a host with IMP functions rather than an IMP with host functions:

> Because the terminals connected to a TIP communicate with Hosts at remote sites, the TIP, in addition to performing the IMP function, also acts as intermediary between the terminal and the distant Host. This means that network standards for format and protocol must be implemented in the TIP. One can thus think of the TIP software as containing both a very simpleminded mini-Host and a regular IMP program. (Ornstein et al. 1971, p. 251)

Digression: An aside for completeness' sake: by circa 1982 the TIPs came to be replaced by Terminal Access Controllers (TACs) in BBN's C/30 computers that in turn replaced some of the earlier IMPs/TIPs based on Honeywell DDP-316 machines (Perry et al. 1988, p. 54; Cerf 1982*b*). The TAC physically separated the terminal handling functions from the IMP;

however, remained intimately close to the IMP, thus not very much changing the situation compared to the earlier integrated TIP approach.

194 (68). The Multi-Line Controller, or MLC, allows connection of terminals either locally or via modem connections. It accepts a variety of character sizes (from 5 through to 8 bits) and various data rates, and also allows pairs of the 63 input and output ports to be driven with different character sizes and data rates, so as to support as wide a range of terminals as possible (Ornstein et al. 1971, pp. 248 f.). See Rettberg (1972, Appendix B, pp. 35 ff.) and BBN (1971*a*, pp. 5 f.) for a list of supported terminals as of late 1971, ranging from simple teletypes to various video display terminals of the time. Plus, see BBN (1971*b*) on the hardware specifics of the TIP.

195 (69). For details concerning the precise functioning of the various aspects of the TIPs refer to:

- Ornstein et al. (1971), pp. 247 ff. for a brief description of the hardware, pp 249 ff. for the commands available to users to converse with the TIP, and p. 251 for an rough overview of the TIP software design;
- McKenzie (1971*a*) for a summary of the TIP's implementation of higher level protocols (NCP, ICP, and Telnet);
- as well as BBN (1977) for a comprehensive user guide;
- BBN (1971*b*) for the hardware manual;
- and Rettberg (1972) for a detailed account of the TIP-terminal interface.

Digression: A brief digression on the Network Virtual Terminal (NVT): The problem of character conversion in conversations between different hosts had been a major issue from the very start of the Arpanet project. BBN (1970*a*) note:

> While we have come to believe that the IMP should not do character set conversions, there is still an immediate need for a network-wide teletype character set into and out of which each Host translates his messages. The choice is arbitrary, and the need for a decision has become urgent (already we see Hosts converting to the language of the destination). We recommend the adoption of 8-bit ASCII with the 8th bit (checksum bit) set

> to 1, which is the IMP's internal character set. This choice has the small additional advantage that Hosts may send messages to local or remote IMP teletypes without an additional conversion. As network use develops, other standards (such as a display language) will be needed. (p. 9)

By mid-1970 some early ideas on a network-wide standard character set emerged, S. D. Crocker (1970*b*) notes:

> We next agreed [in a meeting with BBN and MIT representatives] on an initial network standard console: 7-bit ASCII in 8 bit fields with the eight bit on, transmitted in contiguous streams. The specific codes are listed in appendix H of the IMP Operations manual, BBN report #1877 [BBN 1973*a*]. This seems to work only some hardship on PDP-10's and be fine for all others. (p. 3)

By 1971 a firm consensus on the issue was taking shape in the 'Telnet Committee' featuring participants from various host sites plus BBN (for a list of participants see O'Sullivan 1971*b*, p. 2). The Telnet protocol (O'Sullivan 1971*b*) thus contains an "official network virtual terminal code" (figure 3, pp. 9 f.) based on ASCII, and more specifically the ASCII Format For Network Interchange (Cerf 1969). Quote from O'Sullivan (1971*b*):

> The Telnet protocol provides for a Network Virtual Terminal (NVT) through which users may transmit and receive data over connections between the using site and the serving site. The code of the NVT will be full ASCII. The seven-bit code will be transmitted in eight-bit bytes, the high order bit set to zero. It will be the responsibility of the using site to provide its users with a means of producing all 128 ASCII codes, as well as a selected set of special Telnet control signals (see Figure 3). (p. 4)

In RFC 139 (O'Sullivan 1971*a*) the group provide an interesting discussion of the reasoning behind their choice of an ASCII based code as a network-wide intermediate representation of terminal code, and the various advantages and disadvantages to their ultimate decision to settle for a fairly simple and limited rather than complex and powerful protocol (pp. 2 ff.). Particularly, in order to increase the character set beyond 128 (7 bits) an escape character was to be used to provide for more complex mappings between the NVT code and local systems. Braden (2010) notes that the design of NVT as a "least-common-denominator terminal" has been substantially influenced by the characteristics of the IBM 2741 terminal (Winett 1971*b*; Winett 1971*a*; O'Sullivan 1971*b*). Also, Braden attributes the adoption of CR LF as an EOL (end-of-line) convention to Jonathan B. Postel (see also Braden and RFC editors 2004). Finally, see Padlipsky (1982*a*, pp. 9 ff.) for a general discussion of the benefits of "common intermediate representations" such as NVT.

Leaving our digression, and returning to our topic here, we close by noting that the TIPs assumed the burden of converting the local terminal's character set to the NVT code, much like a normal host offering Telnet services for its users:

> Because of the large number of different terminal types used in the network, the concept of the Network Virtual Terminal was developed. This is an imaginary but well-defined type of terminal. The TIP translates typed data to virtual terminal code before shipping it into the network, and conversely translates the remote system's response back into the local terminal's code. Thus, each Host system must deal only with this single terminal type. (Ornstein et al. 1971, p. 249)

(See on the TIP use of NVT also BBN 1977, p. 6.)

196 (69). Vertical layering was a concept that only took shape when data communications based on the packet switching paradigm took hold. In the world of telephony with next to no applications atop of voice communication and audio baseband signals modulated virtually straight onto the carrier, a vertical layering model was of very little use indeed.

197 (70). It is only fair to note that, in a sense, TIPs have not fundamentally changed the architecture of the Arpanet — host level functions were horizontally inside the network, but remained vertically at the host level. In this respect, the terminal handling portion of the TIPs was no different than a host proper being connected to an IMP by conventional means. However, it bears repeating that the crucial difference between the two cases is that of who controls those host level functions. Again, in the early 1970s there was little conflict of interest between ARPA, BBN, and the host

sites that could not be addressed by straightforward contractual remedies and funding distribution. But, the decentralized and massive scale Internet (well beyond that which in 1983 was considered to be tractable for centralized monitoring and control, Hinden et al. 1983) later introduced far greater scope for destructive tussles.

DIGRESSION: It would be an interesting exercise to recount the crucial steps in the gradual loss of central (or at least potentially central) control, moving from the early Arpanet to today's Internet which is almost completely decentralized, requiring virtually no central coordination other than the assignment of unique IP addresses. However, we leave this for another day.

198 (71). E. g., Ford et al. (2009, p. 3) argue for a "fuzzy ends" principle which allows some delegation of 'soft' state into the network, but firmly argues against the delegation of 'hard' state.

199 (71). Most germane here are the principles of complexity avoidance and cascadability, both of which we discuss in section 7.2.

200 (72). Arguably, given the wide array of stakeholders, the overall pace of developments toward tangible results at the host layer was somewhat slower than that displayed by BBN in developing the IMP subnetwork of the Arpanet. The history of the Network Working Group (NWG) and the Request for Comments (RFC) series closely associated with it is one of the classic stories in broader-brush accounts of the Internet, see, e. g., Hafner and Lyon (1998, pp. 143 ff.) or S. D. Crocker (1987).

On another note, it has been argued that the somewhat random development of higher level protocols and applications has been detrimental to the overall advancement of the Arpanet as well as the later Internet. Abbate (1999) deplores in her chapter 3, pp. 95 f. that Lawrence Roberts of ARPA refused to support the efforts of a group called the Arpanet User Interest Working Group (USING) in "user-oriented network development" (Iseli et al. 1973) (see also Crocker et al. 1973), thus harming the advance of the network at large. However, it turns out that her account is based exclusively on an interview with John Day (who makes a similar point in his 2008 book, too; and argued in 1982 that "[p]rotocol research in the Arpanet terminated in 1973, so that many of the improvements that were intended were never made" and "[s]ince that time almost all protocol research has been done in Europe", Day 1982, p. 444). A plausible refutation of such claims may simply be that Roberts first and foremost wanted the network and its core functions in place, and there were no bad intentions whatsoever against the work of that group. Note also that Roberts and the ARPA IPTO in general did very much take part and offered some guidance to NWG's efforts in application level development efforts. In fact, it was Roberts himself who is said to have written the first ever email client (called RD).

D. H. Crocker confirms this innocent take:

> The USING effort had some meetings and did a tiny amount of useful work, but I never felt that it gained serious traction. We simply were not that focused and enthusiastic. [. . .] If we had had real community traction, IPTO would have supported it, in my opinion. (D. H. Crocker 2010)

201 (72). To repeat from S. D. Crocker (1988) (see also note 138):

> Those were the days when, instead of viewing the network as an electronic mail system, which was kind of an afterthought in a way, there were all these visions of shared databases and load balancing, or jobs would be shifted from one machine to another.

202 (72). Deloche (1969*d*):

> The basic idea is that several users, at a given Host, should simultaneously be able to utilize the network by time-sharing its physical facilities.
>
> This implies that within each Host operating system, there must exist a special program that multiplexes outgoing messages from the users into the network and distributes incoming messages to the appropriate users. We will call this special program the Network program [later referred to as the Network Control Program, or NCP]. (p. 2)

Padlipsky (1982*a*) recounts:

> As best we can reconstruct things, the NWG was much taken with the Computer Science buzzword of the times, "modularity". "Everybody knew" modularity was a Good Thing. In

> addition, we were given a head start because the IMP's weren't under our direct control anyway, but could possibly change at some future date, and we didn't want to be "locked in" to the then-current IMP-Host protocol. So it was enunciated that protocols which were to be members of the ARM suite [Arpanet reference model suite] [. . .] were to be layered. It was widely agreed that this meant a given protocol's control information [. . .] should be treated strictly as data by a protocol "below" it, so that you could invoke a protocol interpreter (PI) through a known interface, but if either protocol changed there would not be any dependencies in the other on the former details of the one, and as long as the interface didn't change you wouldn't have to change the PI of the protocol which hadn't changed. (p. 7)

See also Padlipsky (1984, pp. 77 ff.) for a related discussion of the virtues of layering.

203 (72). By 1971 at the latest, there were three clearly distinguishable Arpanet protocol levels:

level 1 the host-IMP interface (BBN and Kahn 1976, 1822 Report);

level 2 the host-host protocol as implemented by NCP (Bressler et al. 1971; McKenzie 1972); and

level 3 "the place to which and from which the NCP communicates internally in its own host"; that is, any user process or intermediary process on behalf of a user process.

While the precise origin of the three layer model of the Arpanet (see, e. g., the articulation in O'Sullivan 1971*b*) is somewhat foggy; conceptually it emerged the very moment the necessity and reasonableness of a network-wide host-host protocol was generally agreed upon. Deloche (1969*c*) refers to a distinct network program that multiplexes connections, and S. D. Crocker (1970*a*) explicitly refers to the "first level protocol or Host-IMP protocol" (p. 1) and a "second level or Host-Host protocol" (p. 2), as well as a "fundamental requirement of the Host-Host protocol to provide for process-to-process communication over the network" (p. 4), at least implicitly alluding to the notion of a "third level". S. D. Crocker (1971) offers some initial elaboration to the structure above the "second level", pointing to ICP, Telnet, DTP, and FTP (pp. 2 f.). (For ICP see also note 204, and for DTP see Bhushan et al. 1971*a*.)

As an aside, and as we have already observed in note 166, the host-IMP (IMP-host) interface is, of course, neither a layer nor a protocol. Much rather, it is an *interface* making available the *services* of the IMP subnetwork *layer*, specifically its source-IMP-to-destination-IMP *protocol*. (See also Tanenbaum 2002, pp. 44 f., 48 f. and Day 2008, pp. 7 ff. for discussions of the terminologies of layer, protocol, service, and interface.)

204 (73). ICP refers to Initial Connection Protocol, a "third level" protocol at the Arpanet's early host layer to be used in order to connect processes between two hosts. See Postel's 1971 RFC 165 and the various RFCs leading up to it. At first, it was thought that such a general mechanism was needed to establish connections between peer processes; however, it quickly turned out that this was actually unnecessary (Walden 1972*a*; Bressler et al. 1972*a*), and was later (with the introduction of TCP) abandoned in favor of the notion of (well known) ports at which receiving processes would 'listen' (or not), rather than having a separate process setting up explicit connections on behalf of the eventual application processes.

Digression: Arguably, the whole notion of connections inherent to the host-host protocol approach was a serious limitation to the generality of the host layer, and owed much of their apparent attractiveness to the previous telephone communication paradigms, on the one hand, and the master-slave paradigms dominating computer 'communication' with peripherals at the time, on the other. A more general notion proposed by Walden (1970*a*) and taken up by Pouzin (1973*b*) and Cerf et al. (1976) was based on the notion of exchanging discrete host layer messages rather than streams of data on dedicated 'connections'—why bother with setting up a connection every time you want to send a message to someone, or elicit no more than a casual response? Walden (1978) puts it succinctly:

> At present one cannot call a library square root subroutine across the network without going through all that [the ICP procedures] and considerably more to get the library routine actually running. How much more convenient it would be if the square root routine was just "hanging around" on a well-known socket to which a user could send a number directly

along with a socket to which to return the answer. (p. 190)

A final aside on the perpetuation of the 'connection paradigm' even today when much of the data traffic on the Internet effectively boils down to dissemination of pre-existing pieces of discrete data (Jacobson 2006)—the most prominent example being the different pieces making up a website. HTTP, in its first widely used version (1.0), opened a TCP connection for each and every piece of different data to be obtained from a web server (Berners-Lee et al. 1996), thus making for a poor performance given TCP's connection setup and slow start overhead which prejudice short-lived connections (Padmanabhan and Mogul 1994). In HTTP/1.1 this inefficiency was addressed by using one TCP "persistent" connection for the transfer of multiple files (Fielding et al. 1999, pp. 44 f.). (See also CSTB 2001, pp. 56 f. for a brief discussion.) However, arguably, implementing such a scheme on top of TCP adds another source of complexity (and overhead by having to maintain connections which may be torn down, eventually, anyway), compared to some discrete message based scheme right on top of UDP.

205 (73). See note 195 on the Network Virtual Terminal or NVT.

206 (73). Davidson et al. (1977) summarize (with no claim to originality):

> [The Host/Host layer] specifies methods of establishing communications paths between Hosts, managing buffer space at each end of a communications path, etc. Next, the Initial Connection Protocol or ICP specifies a standard way for a remote user (or process) to attract the attention of a network Host, preparatory to using the Host. [. . .] In the next layer is the Telecommunications Network or Telnet protocol which was designed to support terminal access to remote Hosts. [. . .] The next logical protocol layer consists of function oriented protocols [. . .] [two of which are File Transfer Protocol (FTP) and Remote Job Entry protocol (RJE)]. Finally, at any point in the layering process, it is possible to superimpose ad hoc protocols. (p. 4-10, references omitted, footnotes omitted)

Note that virtually *all* of the host level protocols effectively emerged from earlier ad hoc protocol experiments. (See for an overview of some of the ad hoc protocols Walden 1978, pp. 178 ff.)

207 (73). This is an important aside: strict modularity following unambiguous layer boundaries may be a fine and laudable endeavor in principle; yet there are also be sizable benefits from choosing which layers to build on at the discretion of the actual application developers. Notes McKenzie (1973):

> There are many advantages to a layered approach; for example, it certainly makes thinking about the protocols easier than a monolithic approach would. In addition, implementations divide cleanly, and there can be a well defined interface between programs implementing various portions of the protocol. Nevertheless, there is at least one important difficulty with the layered protocol approach. The difficulty is in the number of interfaces between processes which a message must cross between the time that the data is generated and the time that it is sent into the network. If there are many such interfaces, there is likely to be a lot of wheel spinning involved in massaging the data to translate it into the form suitable for the next layer of protocol. (quoted in Walden 1978, p. 196)

Walden (1975*b*) discusses the problem of excessive layering when elaborating the examples of RJE and FTP both of which build on Telnet, ICP, and the host-host protocol, and thus fail to make sensible use of the message boundaries afforded by the host-IMP interface (which are suppressed by the host-host protocol). As for the generality thus obtained, Walden (1978) notes:

> [FTP] provides five different modes of representing files to be transferred, four different modes for actually transferring the files, and the necessary error recovery and restart mechanisms for all of these modes. It specifies dozens of commands and replies. To my mind, FTP gets its generality in a primitive way, by throwing in a little something for everybody.
>
> My view, perhaps an extreme view, is that there should be a single, general, simple, albeit inefficient protocol that could be used by all casual users of RJE, file transfer, and similar functions. This would perhaps be embedded in Telnet. All

> communication between pairs (or other natural groups) of serious users should be done using special-purpose protocols. (pp. 197 f.)

Turning to the later TCP/IP protocols, it is instructive to quote from Clark (1982*c*) on the importance of not unnecessarily hiding lower level layers:

> It must be remembered that things other than TCP are expected to run on top of IP. The IP interface must be made accessible, even if TCP sits on top of it inside the kernel. (p. 12)

Also, it is apt here to point in passing to the ISO/OSI versus Arpanet/Internet debate of the 1970s. For early critical comments on the strict layering approach of the ISO/OSI Reference Model (Zimmermann 1980; ISO 1983) see Cohen and Postel (1983) and Padlipsky (1982*b*). Note Cohen and Postel (1983):

> We suggest that any a priori assignment of levels to issues is superficial and not necessarily consistent. For example, as a part of connection management it might be important to establish reconnection procedures for recovery from failures of subsystems. However, there is no unique level for this task. In some situations, it could be the job of all the levels, in others of some levels only, and in still others of none (i. e., it could be left to the user). [. . .]
>
> As early as 1970, the ARPA community thought that there were three levels, soon after it became four, then three again, then four, then five. It took several years to notice the constant need for the $N + 1st$ level and to realize that the number of levels is not fixed. (p. 30)

See also Padlipsky (1982*a*, pp. 9 f.) for an exemplary discussion of FTP and its optional use of Telnet facilities.

208 (73). Note that even though the host-host protocol became the prime spanning layer for Arpanet hosts, there was nothing that kept hosts from implementing other protocols on a bilateral or more widespread basis and based directly on the host-IMP interface rather than a higher level abstraction — see again Figure 4.9. In fact, the introduction of TCP (see section 5.2) proceeded very much in parallel to the initial host-host protocol

based on NCP. Also, the fake hosts and back hosts within the IMPs implemented their own specialized communication protocol.

DIGRESSION: As for the notion of spanning layers, see Clark (1997c) for a comprehensive discussion, albeit largely in the context of the Internet rather than Arpanet. Note that while there is some economy to the notion of having but one spanning layer, there need not necessarily be a singular spanning layer in a network — there may well be a choice of spanning layers at various 'levels'. In fact, there may even be multiple potential spanning layers at one level. See the instructive example of Internet email (Clark 1997c, pp. 136 f.). (See Clark et al. 2004, pp. 19 ff. for a slightly updated version of the spanning layer discussion.) Also, see IAB (1996, pp. 2 f.) for a brief discussion of the "inter-networking layer" of the Internet, Clark (1988, p. 112) for a discussion of the architectural role of IP datagrams as an all-encompassing spanning layer, and Postel et al. (1981, pp. 262 f.) for a brief discussion of the IP protocol as the "point of convergence" in the Internet.

As for the Arpanet: In addition to the host level spanning layer (the host-host protocol), there were, in fact, multiple spanning layers in the IMP subnetwork, each with its own distinct scope (see section 4.2). First, there was the IMP-IMP protocol governing the procedures between two neighboring IMPs. And, second, there was a de facto source to destination IMP protocol governing the data communication between IMPs on behalf of the hosts attached to them. Both of these protocols had by definition to be implemented by each and every IMP in the Arpanet.

209 (73). While some consensus on network-wide notions such as that of ICP, Telnet, and FTP emerged relatively quickly; there was a lot of experimentation in application level inter-process communication ranging from thought experiments (such as those referred to in note 138), to sloppy bilateral terminal emulation protocols (such as the early idiosyncratic terminal access protocols), to more widespread standards (Telnet, FTP, and RJE all remained very active research topics in the first years of the Arpanet). See also Heart et al. (1978, pp. III-66 ff.) on the evolution of Telnet and other host protocols, plus see Crocker et al. (1972, p. 277) on the early file transfer mechanisms based on Telnet.

210 (73). See, particularly, note 152 and accompanying text.

211 (74). See note 157 in section 4.1 for the largely unsuccessful efforts aimed

at introducing error control and retransmission to the host-host protocol.

212 (74). E. g., in remote terminal sessions one could ask the remote host to echo all characters sent, then keep comparing the echo with the data actually sent, and in case of error delete and resend the last characters. More generally, data received could be checked for signs of corruption ("This doesn't look right"), or be explicitly checked for integrity (by high-level checksums). And, users could also engage in interactive 'user-level' end-to-end acknowledgments and retransmissions (such as "I just got a message with the number 123 containing the letters ABC from you, if that's not what you intended to send, send it to me again.").

213 (74). See Pyke (1971).

214 (75). Negative acknowledgments never do for complete reliability, see our discussion in section 2.2, particularly note 48 and accompanying text.

215 (75). Note that applying policies at the NCP level based largely on error indications available from the IMP-host interface did in principle neither require changes to the host-host protocol, nor did it require the peer NCP at the destination host to be even aware of such retransmission strategies. As RFC 55 (A Prototypical Implementation of the NCP, Newkirk et al. 1970) put it:

> There is, of course, absolutely no requirement to implement anything which is contained in this document. The only rigid rules which an NCP *must* conform to are stated in NWG/RFC #54 [Official Protocol Proffering]. (p. 1)

The more general underlying notion here is that a given set of *mechanisms* typically give rise to a variety of feasible *policies* with potentially very different outcomes.

However, in case more than one message was to be sent between two hosts at a time (given the possibility of unordered arrival and message losses), some mutually agreed upon sequence number scheme is, of course, required. Conceptually, a retransmission scheme based on such sequence numbers may be conceived as a reliability enhancement below the host-host protocol layer. See for a discussion of such schemes the references listed in note 157, e. g., Walden (1973*b*).

Digression: As an aside, limited experiments outside the virtual circuit provided by normal host-host protocol had been tried as early as

1971. Cerf (1974) reports of an assay which logically moved significant functions of error control, retransmissions, and reassembly of packets to the host level, effectively virtualizing a host level connection by rapidly cycling through a large number of IMP-host interface logical links (dozens of which were available between any two hosts), thus significantly improving throughput compared to the 'standard' use of host level connections afforded by the NCP and ICP:

> An experiment between Tinker and McClellan Air Force Bases in 1971 achieved burst rates as high as 40 kb/sec, but this was achieved by the use of a non-standard Host/Host protocol which transmitted data over multiple logical connections, and which used Host level re-assembly and acknowledgement to achieve reliable, ordered transmission. (p. 3, footnotes omitted)

Note that the Tinker/McClellan experiment did not necessitate any changes in the IMP level procedures (RFNMs and flow control worked as usual, raw uncontrolled messages — which we discuss in section 5.1 — did not yet exist at the time). Rather, it used a "Gatling gun" approach over multiple links (with the given one message per link allowance) augmented by host level reliability measures; thus neither did hold-ups due to outstanding RFNMs greatly affect overall throughput, nor did packet losses go unremedied (Cerf 2010).

A final aside on the scarce documentation of NCP implementations in general: There had been an effort at UCSB to gather information about the NCPs and higher level applications at different Arpanet host sites (Bryan 1972); however, Pickens (1972, p. 5) had to conclude: "Information about each node's NCP, which was requested in February, 1972 [Bryan 1972], is still unavailable." Later efforts (Kline 1973) where not to be much more successful (Kantrowitz 1973*b*; Kantrowitz 1973*a*).

216 (75). At first, there could only be up to four messages in transit between two hosts at a time, in 1974 the permissible number was increased to eight (Walden 1974).

217 (75). Note that the overwhelming majority of Arpanet traffic was single-packet messages, often consisting of little more than a few characters — an obvious artifact of the dominance of remote terminal applications:

> Most of the messages on the Arpanet contain very little user data, usually one or several characters. (Cohn 1983, p. 9)

Cohn (1983) concludes from a measurement in May 1982 that 97.9 percent of traffic were single-packet messages (p. 11).

218 (75). Unfortunately, primary sources about the design of NCP implementations at the various host sites of the Arpanet are rare, and so are secondary sources. It has thus been hard for us to properly verify some of the concepts inferred from our readings and inquiries. However, some facts could be established with reasonable certainty: Postel (1973*b*) states that message retransmissions based on Incomplete Transmission indications had been implemented by "several hosts" (p. 2), albeit without going into any details. It is worthy of note here that initially the error messages from the IMP to the host were rather vague, and only by 1972 did a more precise and much less ambiguous set of such messages become available; in particular, a more specific indication of the causes to an Incomplete Transmission (message type 9) was now provided, with subtype 3 indicating a message loss inside the subnetwork rather than due to errors induced by the source or destination host. E. g., retransmission would clearly be futile if a message is too large to begin with (more than 8095 bits), or the destination host repeatedly fails to take in a message from its IMP (see McQuillan and Walden 1972, p. 3). Arguably, the finer-grained error messages were provided not only for debugging, but also for the very retransmission scheme we are on about here.

Another well documented development was the augmentation of the TIPs so as to retransmit messages in case an Incomplete Transmission message was returned from the IMP level. Cosell and Walden (1972) submit:

> Occasionally, an IMP crashes somewhere in the network and takes a packet of a message along with it. Eventually, the source of the message gets an incomplete transmission message from the network. When the TIP gets this message, it closes the connection and calls the destination dead. This is what most other Hosts do also, we understand. A more reasonable thing to do might be to retransmit the message or to tell the user and then let him continue; we would like to do one of these. (p. 3)

By 1973 the TIPs were changed accordingly, McQuillan (1973) explains:

> Since a TIP acts as a Host for its users, its resilience when these types of failures [Incomplete Transmission errors due to subnetwork failures] occur has a major effect on user satisfaction. Prior to this time the TIP program "aborted" the user's connection if it received an Incomplete Transmission indication from the IMP program. In March [1973] the TIP program (and the programs of several other Hosts) was changed to retransmit messages for which the Incomplete Transmission indication was returned; some Hosts (e. g. MULTICs) have done this from the start. This modification has turned out to be relatively simple, and we urge other Hosts to consider implementing some sort of error recovery software. (p. 7)

Parenthetically, we have not been able to obtain closer details about the precise nature of the Multics retransmission features alluded to in the above quote. But, it seems to confirm the general statement made in Postel (1973*b*).

219 (75). Again, we are left to guess about how precisely those features manifested and worked out in detail (a research exercise for another day). However, there is an evident progression from early FTP without any checkpoint and restart features to one which includes said features. In spite of suggestions such as Sunberg (1971) neither the Data Transfer Protocol (Bhushan et al. 1971*a*) nor the File Transfer Protocol (Bhushan et al. 1971*b*) initially included any data error control and recovery mechanisms (see the discussion in Bhushan 1972*a*, pp. 6 f.). Checkpoints became part of the FTP protocol by 1972, however:

> There is no provision [in FTP] for detecting bits lost or scrambled in data transfer. This issue is perhaps handled best at the NCP level where it benefits most users. However, a restart procedure [based on checkpoints] is provided to protect users from gross system failures (including failures of a Host, an FTP-process, or the IMP subnet). (Bhushan 1972*b*, p. 12)

Also, by 1973 the TIPs came to include higher layer error recovery mechanisms for magnetic tape file transfers (based on Telnet), very much along the lines of the restart facilities provided by File Transfer Protocol (Bhushan 1972*b*). McQuillan (1973) explains:

> A different situation [from interactive terminal sessions] pertains to tape transfers involving TIPs with the magnetic tape option. In these cases, the user would like to start the process and then ignore it until the transfer is finished. Network partitions, even if infrequent, may occur when tape transfers many hours in length are in progress. Therefore, we made a significant modification to the TIP magnetic tape option to include a sequencing mechanism in the tape transfer protocol which permits automatic recovery and transmission continuation after most kinds of network transients. With this mechanism in effect, and assuming a tape is mounted at the "other end", the complete transfer of a tape is possible with a single command given at either end. If the connection goes dead in mid-transfer, the TIP magnetic tape software will attempt to reopen the connection until successful and then continue the transfer from where it was left off. (p. 7)

(Note as an aside that McQuillan 1973 copies the above quote verbatim from BBN 1973*b*, p. 17.)

220 (75). See also D. Russell (1989, pp. 271 ff.) for a discussion of checkpoint recovery in FTP as a mechanism that almost necessarily has to be placed at application level — the highest possible level just below the 'user level' — given that "networks have the habit of failing in ever more inventive ways in order to thwart the intent of the designers [of lower level error recovery mechanisms]."

221 (75). Curiously, it was the host-host protocol that saw the fewest changes, whereas the only 'external given', from the perspective of the host level, to be imposed on the the continuum of approaches to using the Arpanet — the source-IMP-to-destination-IMP procedures as exposed be the IMP-host interface specified in the 1822 Report — was in constant flux, as was everything else other than the host-host protocol.

Digression: An aside on applications other than Telnet and FTP, which we have not covered here: Arguably, Telnet and FTP have been the two most prominent applications at the time. And, of the two, Telnet has been the more important one, with early ad hoc file transfer applications having been based on Telnet (Crocker et al. 1972, p. 277). But, there have also been other protocols and applications, most notably Remote Job Entry (RJE). We have only given scant attention to RJE, for this application was largely built on both Telnet and FTP (the former to issue the commands, the latter to retrieve the output), and was also driven largely by ad hoc rather than concerted standards efforts (Crocker et al. 1972, pp. 277 ff.). However, see Heart et al. (1978, pp. 68 f.) for a brief summary of the developments concerning RJE on the Arpanet, most notably UCLA's Remote Job Service (RJS) implementation. As for error control, RJE protocols typically assumed a virtual circuit service (see, e. g., Day and Grossman 1977, p. 4), discarding jobs in case of failures in data transmission or host operation (see, e. g., Braden 1977*b*), and leaving it to users or the RJE user program to retransmit jobs or try again to retrieve outputs of completed jobs (see, e. g., Bressler et al. 1972*b*, p. 13).

A fourth important application/protocol was network voice, which did not gain big prominence on the Arpanet for various reasons, but turned out to be a crucial impact on the later design of the Internet, particularly the split between IP and TCP. We will discuss the history of packet speech in proper detail in section 5.1.

222 (76). It is, of course, true that the only complete means to achieve end-to-end reliability is by end-to-end acknowledgments and retransmission; however, this does not entail that lower level hints about transmission errors are useless on a practical level, especially when the marginal costs to host computers for implementing end-to-end retransmission schemes is so large as to render them uneconomical.

223 (77). See note 315 on the priority orders in treating different kinds of data packets in the Arpanet; and, see note 317 on the implicit precedence scheme (differentiating between interactive terminal traffic and bulk data transfers); plus note 167 for copious quotes regarding the latter.

Letting Go

224 (79). By the end of the 1980s much of the Internet's core architecture became ossified to the extent that it has remained largely unchanged to this day. This is, of course, not to say that there have been no innovations

above and below the IP layer, the one common spanning layer, only that it has proven virtually impossible to add even the slightest changes to the parts of the Internet that provide the common ground between different stakeholders across trust boundaries.

225 (79). Examples of more recent developments to address the problems of the Internet can be found at any IETF meeting agenda. There is little indication that the amount of problems to solve is going to decrease any time soon, given the ever expanding size and use of the Internet which has gone way beyond what was anticipated in the early 1980s.

226 (80). More precisely speaking, the IMP subnetwork tried to optimize for both delay and throughput given a strict reliability requirement. See our discussion of multi-packet versus single-packet message handling in note 155, particularly the quote from Kahn et al. (1971, section 3.1, pp. 13 ff.).

227 (80). BBN (1974*a*):

> [A] problem for some Host applications, related to the Host being stopped, is the 30-second incomplete transmission timeout on message numbers. Some Hosts need to have accurate accounting of all messages, while others would prefer to go ahead, giving up on a lost message or reply in much less than 30 seconds. That is, they are willing to trade off a higher rate of lost messages, declaring messages older than a few seconds as lost, for the ability to always send a message every few seconds. Here again, we are considering allowing the Hosts to specify their preference in this regard, once message number sequences are kept separately for each Host pair. (p. 54)

228 (80). Interactive voice traffic is the most prominent example of a class of applications that also includes sensor data traffic, and generally every application which places very low value on strict reliability versus low latency and jitter. To quote from BBN (1974*a*):

> An example of a Host application with special performance requirements is the transmission of real-time, synchronous data such as vocoded speech, the output of physical sensing devices, and so on. These users represent a new demand for network performance — low delay and high throughput at the

> same time. The current ARPA Network is optimized to deliver short messages with low delay, and long messages with high throughput. Speech transmission, for instance, requires a guaranteed minimum throughput level (depending on the vocoding technique), and a "guaranteed" maximum delay (depending on the tolerance of the people speaking). Users are probably willing to trade a slightly higher message loss rate for the "guarantees". This is a good example of an environment in which reliability, in terms of accurate reporting of message loss, is less important than steady high performance. (pp. 54 f.)

And, Sproull and Cohen (1978) add:

> Very few conventional transport services are required by an NVP. No retransmission to remedy errors is required because a lost message is not catastrophic; both coding schemes are designed so that a parcel is decoded without knowledge of previous messages. Moreover, retransmission would introduce highly variable delays that cause worse perceptual damage than the loss of the message. (p. 1379)

Thus not only was the service delivered by the subnetwork excessive (or rather: unbalanced), the host-host protocol was equally unsuitable if not detrimental for real time voice applications:

> The NVP requires real-time transport of parcels. Unfortunately, none of the standard transport facilities designed for HLP [high-level protocol] use in the ARPA network could provide such service; the NVP designed its own real-time protocol using only the facilities of the IMP-based communication subnet [and not those of the host-host protocol]. (p. 1379, references omitted)

229 (80). Again, to quote from BBN (1974*a*):

> Another area of interest is network interconnection. It can be argued that (1) message processing facilities offered by the several interconnected networks vary greatly and there may be no need for elaborate processing in one network if it is not provided in another; and (2) some functions, such as sequencing,

> might lead to degraded overall performance if performed in each network (total delay is increased if each net in the path performs sequencing in turn instead of passing unordered data to the ultimate destination for sequencing). (pp. 55 f.)

230 (80). BBN (1974*a*), on voice applications:

> It has been argued that the requirements of such applications as speech are so stringent that the network should do no message processing at all, to avoid introducing artificial performance limits, and leave these functions to the Hosts. We feel this argument is specious [. . .]. Furthermore, we believe that we can modify the algorithms in the subnetwork to provide appropriate service to such Hosts, without prejudicing the network services provided to other Hosts (as would happen if the subnetwork abandoned all message processing). (p. 55)

And, on network interconnection:

> Some networks may not function well if services are removed which do not exist in other networks. For instance, flow control might be important to keep in one network even though some other network does not perform flow control. [However,] [i]n the Arpanet case, if it is politically or technically desirable to avoid some of the standard message processing for messages that are destined for internetwork transmission, it is relatively easy to allow parallel mechanisms which are subsets of the full message processing facilities. (We are currently implementing such a parallel mechanism to permit experiments of this type). (p. 56)

231 (80). To quote copiously from Walden (1974):

> For certain limited experiments which are being carried on using the network, it is thought to be desirable for specified Hosts to be able to communicate outside the normal ordered, error controlled message sequences. Thus, the following expansion to the IMP/Host protocol is being provided.

i. A single packet message coming from the source Host to the source IMP with a (new) special message type, 3 [later changed from type 3 to type 0, subtype 3; see Walden 1975*c*, p. 2 and BBN 1978*c*, p. 101], will be put directly into the IMP store-and-forward logic with a mark saying the packet is this special kind of message. A multi-packet message of type 3 will be discarded. [That is, there are no multi-packet messages.]
ii. Such messages (packets) are routed normally to the destination IMP, possibly arriving out of order.
iii. At the destination IMP, messages of the special type will be put directly on the destination Host output queue skipping the reassembly logic and marked with a special (new) IMP to Host message type, also 3 [again, later changed to type 0, subtype 3].
iv. There is no source-to-destination retransmission logic, no reassembly, no RFNMs, no incomplete transmissions, etc.
v. If at any time there are insufficient resources in the network to handle one of these special messages (e. g., the destination Host won't take it), the message will be discarded.

(Walden 1974, p. 2)

See also BBN (1978*c*, pp. 8, 52, and 101), as well as BBN and Kahn (1976, pp. 3-35 f.).

It is interesting to note that raw messages where given no below standard treatment by intermediary IMPs. Especially, one would think it fairly reasonable for an IMP, in the face of imminent congestion, to issue an acknowledgment for a raw message received, and throw it away nevertheless (as was done in Cyclades, see Pouzin 1982, p. 44). However, neither the Arpanet Completion Report, nor Technical Information Report 89, nor any other of the reports issued to ARPA at the time offer an indication of this having been done. Walden (2010*b*) summarizes:

> If the document [The Interface Message Processor Program] does not mention special handling of raw packets in the Task-Store-and-Forward routine, then my guess is that the normal

> ACK-and-retransmit mechanism was used. It wouldn't cause much delay to get them reliably through IMP-to-IMP and perhaps we thought the chances or an inter-IMP line error were high enough to justify a slight increase in the average delay, and the odds of no packet buffering in the receiving IMP of an IMP-IMP transmission were not so high. It probably was a statistical issue. Maybe we considered it better to get the packets to the destination IMP rather than lose lots of packets along the way across the network, e. g., from flakey inter-IMP lines.

232 (81). BBN's Alexander McKenzie confirms this general point in an email conversation with David Walden in early 2010, on file with the author. It is also not unlikely that at least at some point in late 1974 the then introduced logical subnetwork mechanism (BBN 1974*b*, pp. 9, 13 f.; BBN 1974*a*, pp. 4, 32) was used to manage access to the RMI — using a specific reserved private subnet to restrict raw packet sending. However, given that BBN (1974*a*) mention packet speech experiments (p. 4), too, other means may have been employed prior to the availability of the logical subnetwork feature.

233 (81). There are no definitive statistics on the spread of RMI access by hosts; however, there are some scattered data points, plus reasonable (if vague) inferring. E. g., even by as late as 1986 use of uncontrolled messages was largely negligible:

> Up to now, the EE's [end-to-end protocol's] flow control has been (in the absence of subnet congestion control) the only governor of the amount of traffic a host can submit to the network. When you take that away by using uncontrolled messages, you are really introducing the possibility of debilitating congestion on the network.
>
> As a result, the use of uncontrolled messages has been, shall we say, controlled (administratively). There are, I believe, no hosts on the MILNET that have permission to send them, and only a small number on the Arpanet (mostly associated with packet speech). I know of no TOPS-20s that are currently allowed to submit uncontrolled messages. As an example, neither of the hosts at SUMEX are enabled, and at the ISI complex, the only

enabled host is ISI-SPEECH11 (I just checked these). (Malis 1986)

234 (81). Braden (2009*a*) reports informally on an episode in which BBN may have denied permission for an experiment using uncontrolled messages for TCP traffic. However, this account could not be confirmed by other sources; we mention it here merely for completeness' sake, not to make any argument or accusation about the role of BBN as a 'gatekeeper' for the uncontrolled message facility.

235 (81). See also BBN (1975, p. 47).

236 (81). The estimate is drawn from Crispin (1979) which lists all Arpanet hosts at the time, indicating whether they were being used for dedicated speech experiments, or used to serve as gateways to networks outside Arpanet.

As for the packet voice experiments, D. Cohen (1977*b*) names ISI, LL, Culler-Harrison (CHI), and SRI as the main participating sites. Gold (1977, pp. 1652 f.) adds that a total of eight ARPA contractors were eventually involved in the experiments: SRI, ISI, CHI, LL, BBN, as well as the speech communication research laboratory (SCRL) at CHI, plus MIT and Utah.

However, note that raw messages were also used by the IMPs themselves for sending statistics (status and throughput reports) to the NCC (Santos 1979*b*, 50:16 min)—an early (albeit undocumented) application of having low priority messages sent with an unreliable "datagram type facility" (19:38 min) message service.

237 (81). As for inter-networking experiments, RMI was implemented in some Unix systems so as to allow simultaneous use of normal NCP, on the one hand; and TCP, NVP, and other protocols requiring raw message support, on the other (BBN 1978*a*, pp. 40 f.; BBN 1978*b*, pp. 42 ff.). In fact, by 1978 some machines were reported not to contain an NCP, but only an RMI (plus TCP).

However, TCP could also be run using normal messages, and there were apparently few significant efforts using raw messages rather than normal messages for TCP. Arguably, neither the IMP level error control and retransmission, nor the reordering of multi-packet messages incurred performance discounts large enough to render the raw message service substantially superior to that of normal controlled messages. While one would think that the RMI would have been particularly useful to experiment with TCP, it turns out that most TCPs used the normal controlled message service of the IMP subnetwork. Some TCP hosts did not even bother with implementing the RMI facility in the first place (see, e. g., Chiappa 2009) — not only because uncontrolled messages were restricted to a size of ca. 120 bytes (thus incurring rather severe if not prohibitive fragmentation/defragmentation penalties, see Kent and Mogul 1987 for a general discussion of the case against network level fragmentation), but also because there was simply no explicit need to dispense with the reliability offered by the Arpanet. As Cerf (2009) put it:

> [P]acket radio, packet satellite and ethernets as well as Bill Plummer's Flakeway gateway ["flakey gateway", a test gateway implementation set to deliberately and randomly reorder, delay, and/or drop packets with some set specified frequency distributions] provided us with plenty of opportunity to deal with packet loss.

238 (81). Gray (2005, p. 88) reports that the packet voice research was initiated by Robert E. Kahn in 1972 (then at ARPA) and involved a number of participants from various host sites plus BBN who formed the Network Secure Communications (NSC) group (also referred to as the Network Speech Compression program, see Makhoul 2006, p. 34). In fact, it is fair to say that the raw message facility was introduced first and foremost in order to allow packet voice experiments outside the normal VC service of the IMP subnetwork in the first place. Weinstein and Forgie (1983):

> The Arpanet characteristics lead to upper bounds on speech throughput due to the 50 kbit/s links and the transmission overhead, and lower bounds on delay due to the multiple hops generally required between source and destination. In addition, the original protocols developed for the Arpanet included reliability and flow control features which were designed appropriately for data communication, but which caused undesirable and unnecessary limitations on the throughput and delay for real-time speech. These limitations were present both in the packet delivery service provided by the IMP subnet between source and destination host, and in the original host/host or network control protocol (NCP) used in the Arpanet.

> Because of these limitations a new host/host protocol (NVP) was developed for speech and a new type of "uncontrolled" packet delivery service (suggested by Dr. R. E. Kahn) was introduced into the Arpanet. (p. 970)

(As an aside, Dave Walden informs me that the continual reference to his involvement—see e. g., Gray 2005; Gray 2010*b*—is in mistake, he "really was not involved" in any other way than possibly having his name on some BBN contract; see Walden 2010*c*.)

239 (81). Control messages would be sent using normal (controlled) messages, whereas data could be sent with either uncontrolled or normal messages (D. Cohen 1977*b*, p. 1).

240 (81). Arguably, the most important development was that of Linear Predictive Coding (LPC), and variable compression schemes so as to reduce the data rate from ca. 64 kb/s down to as little as 2.4 kb/s (Gray 2005; Makhoul 2006, pp. 34 f.). D. Cohen (1981, p. 20) even puts the lowest data rate required to support LPC vocoded speech at a mere 1 kb/s.

241 (81). A 1971 experiment at MIT (locally, using a fake host at the IMP, see Pfeifer and McAfee 1973, pp. 1 f.; Weinstein and Forgie 1983, p. 972) had established the general feasibility of packet voice:

> It was concluded that packet speech in a system with characteristics similar to a lightly-loaded Arpanet could be quite satisfactory from a human factors point of view. (Weinstein and Forgie 1983, p. 972)

Pfeifer and McAfee (1973) discuss a 1973 real-time voice experiment at UCLA and UCSB, and Weinstein and Forgie (1983, p. 972) mention a mid-1974 experiment between ISI and Lincoln Labs, both using the normal message service. While the reliability measures inside the IMP subnetwork resulted in sometimes large transmission delays, the service obtained was often sufficient for interactive voice applications:

> Fortunately, the rarity of packet errors in Arpanet did allow some successful speech communication despite this [the IMP subnetwork's] error control and sequencing. (Weinstein and Forgie 1983, p. 971)

In fact, Pfeifer and McAfee (1973) conclude that significant delays are typically "attributable to the host computers and not the network" (p. 9).

242 (81). Note that the values used in Figure 5.1 are only approximations without any claim to scientific correctness. Note also that the choice of the three parameters delay, throughput, and reliability is not to say that there are not more parameters that could enter into the trade-off analysis. In fact, D. Cohen (1977*a*), in a thoughtful analysis on flexibility and generality of network transport services in view of real-time speech communication requirements, adds cost and security as possible parameters for such considerations (p. 2), and also puts forward an orthogonal taxonomy of the more general 'issues' involved: sorting, acknowledgment, retransmission, size, reliability, priority, error-control, security, and routing (p. 3). (As an aside, refer to Table 6.1 for a recent take on the different throughput requirements of various application types.)

243 (82). The Arpanet was specified in the Arpanet RFQ to have maximum delays of no more than 0.5 seconds. The implementation of Arpanet turned out to easily meet this target figure as of 1972, if only at light to moderate loads—once a certain threshold load was hit, the delay increased rapidly (Frank et al. 1972, p. 258, 265 f., Figure 3 at p. 266).

244 (82). See also Weinstein and Forgie (1983, p. 971, Figue 6).

245 (82). Thus a fixed delay of half a second at the receiver, plus a speech processing algorithm making up for at most 1 percent packet loss, will obtain a perfectly uniform speech rate at the receiver; allowing for a 5 percent packet loss would accordingly reduce the delay necessary for a uniform rate to 0.35 seconds.

246 (82). Further measurements and elaboration can be found in Casner et al. (1978). Plus, Forgie (1979) details the general requirements for packet speech communication, noting that a delay above 0.25 seconds typically reduces the interactivity of a communication markedly (p. 3). Also, he puts the acceptable packet loss rate (that is, packets either lost, or arriving after the fixed delay at the receiver)—provided that the "amount of speech" per packet is sufficiently low,—at the order of "1 % or less to be considered acceptable for everyday (non-crisis) use" (pp. 3 f.).

247 (82). Packet voice experiments were also successfully conducted with satellite connections, most notably the Atlantic packet satellite network (Satnet) and the wide-band packet satellite network (WB Satnet) (Weinstein and Forgie 1983, pp. 972 ff.). (The latter even saw real-time video communication experiments, see D. Cohen 1984. For general references

on ARPA efforts in packet satellite networking see also Cerf 1982*a*.) However, despite promising results (and the fact that packet switching is a far superior model for integrating data and voice networks than traditional circuit switching, see Gitman and Frank 1978), packet voice was to remain a niche application with largely experimental character until very recent times and the advent of broadband Internet along with popular mass market VoIP applications such as Skype (commercial and proprietary) and RTP/SIP telephony (Rosenberg et al. 2002; Schulzrinne et al. 2003; Rosenberg 2009). As Weinstein and Forgie (1983) put it:

> The vast investment in circuit-switched systems currently in existence makes it unlikely that packet techniques will soon become the dominant method for speech communication. (p. 978)

248 (82). See section 5.2, particularly pages 88 f.

249 (82). By an odd irony, thus, the application of interactive voice communication, which in virtually every aspect other than that of perfect reliability has, in fact, *more* stringent quality of service requirements than either file transfer or remote terminal sessions (see Figure 5.1), paved the way for a relaxation of the hitherto almost sacrosanct network reliability criterion — the crucial paradigm shift in networking theory that would ultimately allow for the interconnection of idiosyncratic networks on a global scale, using a protocol that does little more than establish an inter-network address space, and offers neither reliability, nor rate, nor delay guarantees. E. g., Postel et al. (1981) explicitly credits "applications in which it is desirable to receive data even though there are a few bits in error" for the limitation of IP's checksumming to the header, not the content of a packet, for "[i]f the IP enforced a data checksum and discarded datagrams with data checksum failures such applications would be restricted unnecessarily" (p. 267).

Digression: The most prominent (though ultimately futile) result of the efforts in shaping packet switched networks so as to support robust real-time voice conversations was theInternet Stream Protocol (ST), first specified in Forgie (1979), and later amended by Topolcic et al. (1990) and Delgrossi et al. (1995). As an aside, ST (or rather: the ST datagram mode, see Forgie 1979, p. 7) was assigned IP Version number 5 in Postel (1980*a*), so it may be considered to be "IPv5".

Packet Speech Requirements	ST Approach
Guaranteed data rate	Know requirements in advance Request reserved network resources when available (e. g., PODA streams) Assign loads to links statistically in routing virtual circuits
Controlled delay (predictable dispersion)	Prevent congestion by controlling access on a call basis
Small quantity of speech per packet	Set up virtual circuit routes so that abbreviated headers can be used Aggregate small packets for efficiency
Efficiency equal to or better than circuit switching without TASI	Abbreviated headers for packet efficiency Goal of high link utilization with effective traffic control
Efficient use of broadcast media	Control multiaddress setup for conferencing and replicate only packets when necessary

Table N.1: Packet speech requirements and ST protocol approach; Source Weinstein and Forgie (1983, p. 976)

The idea behind ST was to establish an inter-network layer protocol beside IP that would allow virtual circuits with rate and delay guarantees as well as multicast groups by direct manipulation (or 'conditioning') of the constituent networks (mostly: resource reservation and access control) rather than by having to go through an intrinsically unreliable ('best effort' only) Internet layer protocol — see Table N.1 for the approach taken by ST. (See also Weinstein and Forgie 1983, p. 966, Figure 3 and Topolcic et al. 1990, p. 6, Figure 1 for an overview of the protocol hierarchy for ST.)

ST became necessary (or rather, was felt to be necessary) once end-to-end voice paths were to be extended beyond the rather well-behaved Arpanet where in light loads NVP (right above the IMP-host interface) would provide satisfactory service. The inevitable limitations to the universal deployability of the protocol were acknowledged in Forgie (1979), and have kept it from wider-scale adoption ever since:

> [ST] is not likely to find useful application in the current ARPA

> internet environment where the networks and gateways lack the capacity to handle significant speech communication. Instead, ST is aimed at application in wideband networks, in particular those intended to carry a large fraction of packet voice in their traffic mixes. (p. 2)

Much of the experimentation with voice and video communications thus took place on the wide-band packet satellite network (WB Satnet) (Weinstein and Forgie 1983, pp. 973 ff.) rather than on the Arpanet or the then emerging Internet.

The initial failure of interactive voice communication as a popular application of packet switched networks was due not only to limited bandwidths, but also due to the efficiency disadvantages of packet switching versus circuit switching — the problem was largely that of "[o]vercoming the inability of datagram nets to maintain data rates and delay characteristics as offered load increases" (Forgie 1979, p. 5). Despite its failure to become a standard inter-network protocol, many of the concepts of ST have made it into MPLS (Davie and Farrel 2008), which has become an extremely popular technology inside ISPs.

250 (83). By the mid-1970s it was well understood that the error characteristics in radio networks often called for a trade-off with respect to perfection of link level data transmission, thus necessitating fairly high level error control and retransmission strategies. E. g., the early Alohanet retransmission strategy in the face of collisions on the shared random access channel was to have the TCUs retransmit packets three times at most, and then leave it to the terminal user to initiate retransmission. "This in effect introduces a long interval between every three retransmissions, allowing time for retransmissions from other users to succeed" (Binder et al. 1975, p. 206). While the channel traffic load was typically so low that manual retransmissions were only seldom necessary (Binder 2010), and some flexibility was later added when the TCUs were replaced by Programmable Control Units (PCUs) that would allow to implement retransmission strategies in software rather than relying on users to manually re-initiate retransmissions, the rationale behind the original scheme nicely reflects the trade-off found in nondeterministic systems: leave decisions about low level strategies to higher level applications or even users themselves, rather than retransmitting packets in vain.

Another instructive example of the trade-offs in subnetwork reliability can be found in the design of Alohanet's broadcast channel (that is, the channel used for transmitting data from the central computer Menehune to the dispersed nodes). Given the poor economy of acknowledging every data packet received from the Menehune on the random access channel—for every acknowledgment lost on the random access channel the system would have to spuriously retransmit packets on the broadcast channel, too—Binder et al. (1975) explain the Alohanet trade-off taken here:

> This problem was "resolved" for the initial implementation by simply not sending ACK's from user nodes. Because of the high received signal strengths at the nodes, a very low error rate was anticipated; considering also that user nodes consisted only of human terminal users, it was decided that a simple error detection/user notification scheme would be sufficient. (p. 209)

This scheme was later augmented by optional acknowledgments for file transfer and other uses that typically need greater reliability than remote terminal sessions. But, again, the solution here neatly points to the subtle trade-offs in dealing with inherently unreliable subnetworks.

251 (83). See the Alohanet case considered in section 4.3, note 187 and accompanying text.

252 (84). The frictions between BBN and the NWG about the shape of the host-host protocol, alluded to in previous sections (see notes 151 and 163 and accompanying text) thus turned out to be something of a red herring. While at the (inter)network level there might be a good case for a least common denominator service, once we move to the host level the necessity of and need for such notion markedly decreases. One set of applications might require perfect reliability and will want to implement the necessary functions themselves, or trust them to a more general transport protocol such as TCP (or NCP, with the assumption of perfect subnetwork service). Others may instead have tight delay constraints and will want to keep the number of hops in the requisite real-time data communications as low as possible, choose uncongested links, and may even want to integrate with the communication service in some way. And, still other applications may require large bandwidths and will thus want to make

sure to multihome adequately or otherwise see to it to obtain the due data rates. Plus, considering parameters of cost and security (to name but two), and the various combinations between any of them, the list could be extended almost arbitrarily. The crucial point is: there is no one-size-fits-all transport service at the host layer.

253 (84). See Partridge (2008) for a comprehensive history of email (or: "Internet mail"), arguably *the* killer application of both Arpanet and the early Internet.

254 (84). See note 195 for a digression on common intermediate representations, or "standard representations" (Crocker et al. 1972, p. 279).

255 (85). On an instructive aside note, interconnecting networks at the packet level, and striving for simplicity at the common low level ground in inter-networking (the notion of datagrams) is not merely to reduce complexity in the gateways; it may, in fact, be impossible to map two protocols at all, e. g., when the one requires acknowledgments of individual records sent in sequence, and the other one requires the full set of records sent at once — as is the case with the sequential FTP protocol versus MIT's experimental Blast file transfer protocol (see D. Russell 1989, pp. 429 for a discussion of this example). In a datagram network, such complexity to impede cascadability will rarely be found; note, however, that the seeming clarity of approach at the inter-network level is obvious only by hindsight — at the time, not only was the concatenation of X.25 virtual circuit networks a serious effort pursued by various parties, the high-level "protocol translation" approach was considered by some to be a potential contender to the lower-level "media conversion" one, for it would spare end hosts the trouble of implementing a common inter-network protocol in the first place. See Postel 1982*a*, pp. 513 ff.; Sunshine 1977*a*, pp. 188 f. for elaboration and critique.

256 (85). See note 187 for a summary on the Alohanet connection to the Arpanet.

257 (85). Norway was the first country outside the U. S. to become part of the Arpanet, having had been connected to the U. S. to transmit seismic data from the NORSAR seismic array, thus complementing a set of three seismic arrays (the other two being in Alaska and Montana). In June 1973 a TIP at Kjeller, near Oslo (Norway), was linked to the U. S. mainland via the existing satellite link from Tanum, Sweden over to the NASA's So-

lar Data Analysis Center (SDAC) in Greenbelt, MD, and the University of Southern California Information Sciences Institute (USC-ISI) branch facility in Arlington, VA. Note that there was no local network proper at Kjeller, only host computers connected to the IMP.

258 (85). A TIP at University College London (UCL) was connected to the Arpanet at July 25, 1973, initially via a cable link to the NORSAR array in Kjeller, later directly by a satellite link from Goonhilly Downs, UK. This TIP was used to connect the NPL network to the Arpanet. See Kirstein (2009); Kirstein (1999); Stokes (1973).

259 (85). Those local networks ranged from the arguably obvious simple star topology networks (hosts or terminals connecting to an IMP, TIP, or port expander); to various other, more elaborate local networks, the most prominent ones of which were to become bus networks (mostly Xerox PARC's Ethernet), and, to a lesser extent, ring networks (e. g., UC Irvine's Distributed Computing System, the Cambridge Net, or the later IBM Token Ring). For a comprehensive and (still) very much authoritative overview of the theoretical and practical aspects of local area networks (also vis à vis long-haul packet networks) see Clark et al. (1978).

Digression: The development of local area networks, or LANs, has been a most decisive factor in driving the growth of the Arpanet from very early on. In fact, local networking between different hosts on one site has been one of the chief uses of the first Arpanet IMPs. Recall that up to four hosts could connect to one IMP. Thus, and particular as long as no common host-host protocol had yet been arrived at, many sites used their IMPs to connect terminals at different hosts, effectively using the IMP as a switch to exchange local traffic (Naylor and Opderbeck 1974, p. 5; Kleinrock and Naylor 1974, pp. 771, 773; Walden 1975*a*, p. 4 in preprint PDF version; Pelkey 2009, ch. 4.8). Local networking was getting another important impetus in 1971 when the TIPs arrived on the scene, allowing terminals to network without having to go through an Arpanet host proper, simply using a dial-up connection to a TIP. Further broadening of the scope for local networking along 'IMP centric' lines was obtained by 1980 with SRI's port expanders that may well be considered proper, if fairly simple, gateways between two distinct networks (see note 177).

While local networking based on IMP switching was an early surprise, the rise of 'real' local networks, most notably the contention access broadcast Ethernet (Metcalfe 1973; Metcalfe and Boggs 1976) (derived from the earlier Alohanet and its 'pure' Aloha broadcast access scheme, see note 187) was to become one of the most crucial development lines in the early Internet, allowing hundreds of computers to connect to one another with relatively trivial and robust means, and in a completely distributed fashion. Ring networks also saw some deployments and elaboration (Farmer and Newhall 1969; Farber and Larson 1972*b*; Farber and Larson 1972*a*; Pierce 1972; Farber et al. 1973), and were favored by some over Ethernet for their seemingly deterministic behavior. However, due to their complexity and proneness to even the slightest misconfiguration (or simply the finite probability of having tokens destroyed due to physical level transmission errors, see Saltzer et al. 1981*b*, p. 215) they turned out to be far less robust and thus, in fact, much *less* deterministic and flexible than the Ethernet (Boggs et al. 1988), and have not nearly seen as high a deployment rate as Ethernets have. (For a discussion of the reliability characteristics of both network types see also Clark et al. 1978, p. 1502 f.)

Speaking of LANs, it is indispensable to mention the early advances in local area networking by Donald Davies' group at the National Physical Laboratory in the UK. By 1968 their local network was advanced enough be presented in a series of papers at the IFIP Congress in Edinburgh (Davies et al. 1968; Wilkinson and Scantlebury 1968; Bartlett 1968; Davies 1968; Scantlebury et al. 1968). Their network was connected to the Arpanet in 1973 (see also note 258). See also note 30 for a lengthy aside on their network, and their various contributions to networking at large.

Finally, there were some noteworthy and well documented experiments with mobile nodes creating ad hoc packet radio networks in the Packet Radio Network (PRNET) in the San Francisco area—another line of research that stemmed from the original Alohanet network scheme (R. E. Kahn 1975; Frank et al. 1975). Given its unmistakable delay and reliability issues, PRNET featured prominently in the a number of 1976/1977 inter-network TCP experiments and demonstrations (Nielson 2002, pp. 4 f.; see also Cerf and Kirstein 1978, p. 1404 for a brief summary) (Figure N.8). In fact, Clark (1988) goes so far as to attribute the whole rationale behind the TCP work to the desire to link PRNET to the Arpanet (pp. 106 f.). While this may be a bit of a stretch, Robert Kahn and Vinton Cerf certainly personified a solid logical connection between the Stanford University work on TCP, the funding and guidance of ARPA, and the PRNET experiments which made plain beyond reasonable doubt the potential differences in local networks that any inter-networking scheme would be required to bridge if it was to be successful.

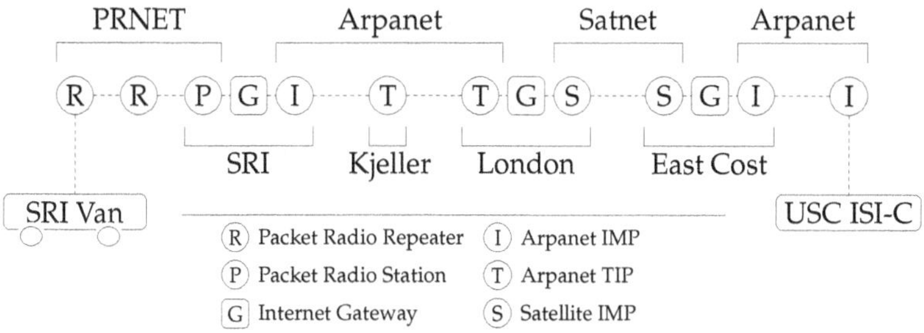

Figure N.8: First ARPA multinetwork TCP demonstration in November 1977; Source: Adapted from Kunzelman et al. (1978) as quoted in Nielson (2002, p. 5) (see also http://www.sri.com/about/timeline/images/1977map_000.jpg for a good quality diagram of the demonstration)

260 (85). Some local networks even relegated the Arpanet to a mere transit network bridging a set of remote networks of the same type—see e. g., the PUP network using the Arpanet to connect different Ethernets (Shoch 2010).

261 (85). Any such gateway will have to deal with flow control on either side of its connections, plus manage protocol conversion, addressing, and, possibly, even routing. It may also have to ensure utmost reliability and thus support the error control mechanisms of both networks, plus feature elaborate error control mechanisms itself. Most such gateways provided application level protocol conversion or concatenation—largely for Telnet and email (see, e. g., Shoch 2010), but also printer access, etc (see, e. g., C. M. Rogers 2010). However, even if a site gets one of its hosts to be simultaneously on the local network and the Arpanet at a lower conceptual level, the generality of the approach is strictly limited by the ability of the gateway to sensibly convert protocols between the one and the other. Such concatenation will rarely scale well to more than two different networks. (See also our considerations at note 255 and accompanying text.)

Digression: Shoch (2010) recalls that making do with such limited approaches was no longer considered a feasible option, once their local networks at Xerox PARC started blossoming:

> As soon as the lab started to envision hundreds of Altos, on dozens of Ethernets, it was clear that the Arpanet protocol design was not appropriate. Thus, we designed our own internet architecture, PUP; created at about the same time as TCP, but actually implemented and refined well in advance of TCP (and its successor, the more layered TCP/IP) [see Boggs et al. 1980]. This internet architecture allowed Alto users on our multiple networks (all around the world) to access our own set of PUP file servers, print servers (first laser printers), mail servers, etc. [. . .] I think you could Telnet from an Alto to Maxc [which was connected as a host to an Arpanet IMP] (via a PUP-based internet telnet protocol), and from there Telnet out to a legacy Arpanet site; but there was little need or desire to do this. We also had a gateway link from the PUP architecture using the Arpanet as a transit network. So, for example, after we gave some Alto computers to MIT, CMU, and others we could communicate with them using our internet architecture, and the Arpanet as a transit network.

While the PUP Internet ultimately lost out to TCP/IP, the connection of largely identical networks (mostly Ethernets) by means of long-distance bridges using an effectively arbitrary intermediary network between them (see Clark et al. 1978, p. 1514 f.) was arguably an important conceptual step toward conceiving a truly global inter-networking design, for it raises many of the issues that apply to any general purpose Internet system.

Two more asides here, one on Alohanet, one on the NPL link. We have in note 187 alluded to the experiences with the gateway between Alohanet and Arpanet. It took a long time to implement the gateway such that Alohanet terminals could access Arpanet resources in a meaningful way, and once the necessary protocol implementations and conversions were in place, the Alohanet terminal support was still incomplete (Abramson 1975, p. 8). As for the UK connection, Kirstein (1999, p. 4) details the emulation efforts necessary to connect their existing computers to the TIP: facing the Arpanet side they implemented the whole stack of common Arpanet host protocols (Host-IMP, Host-Host, Telnet, and FTP); and facing their internal hosts part of the NPL network they emulated an IBM terminal because they were for various reasons not in a position to change the hosts to be connected. See on this episode also Kirstein (2009, p. 22). Such an emulation approach is very similar to the one taken by the Arpanet TIPs, which also, for the most part, appear to the terminals connected to them as a terminal handler, not an IMP, thus providing a transparent gateway between the Arpanet on the one hand, and the TIP-terminals 'networks' on the other (see our considerations at pages 66 ff.). At that, it features the same limitations — connecting two networks by using an idiosyncratic RJE interface (as was done in the NPL case) may be a reasonable 'hack' for some time, but is hardly a sensible basis to a robust general purpose inter-network. See also Clark et al. (1978) for a discussion of the limitations of using "front-end processors" to mediate between a host and a network by "mimicking a standard method of attachment to the [host] system, such as a group of remote interactive terminal lines, or a remote job entry (RJE) port" (p. 1505).

262 (85). D. Cohen (1978*b*) puts it:

> All the networks involved in the interconnection of [. . .] networks are of equal level, unless we decide otherwise for administrative reasons. The internet communication environment does not have up-and-down relations, except in the eyes of some users, which may be very subjective. (p. 9)

263 (85). See also section 5.1 for a discussion of voice applications on the Arpanet, and the difficulties of even serving all sensible application needs in but one, centrally controlled and managed network. As for interconnection, not only did the hotch-potch of ad-hoc solutions for converting protocols between the attached networks and the Arpanet soon become unbearable, even the centrally managed amendments of the Arpanet subnetwork itself in view of the growing diversity of hosts and terminals to be served directly became ever less feasible.

264 (86). See note 52 and accompanying text.

265 (86). INWG largely drew participants from the Arpanet NWG (Vinton Cerf, Alexander McKenzie, Robert Kahn, etc.), but also from European

networking efforts (e. g., Louis Pouzin, Donald Davies), and commercial companies (e. g., Xerox PARC's Robert Metcalfe).

DIGRESSION: A brief aside on the origin of the INWG: Even though the Cerf and Kahn TCP line eventually was to become the core of the now dominant Internet protocol suite, the initial effort resulting in a forum for discussing inter-networking goes back to Louis Pouzin. To quote copiously from Pelkey (2009, ch. 6.3):

> After returning to Paris [from a 1971 trip to the U. S. which exposed him to the Arpanet], Pouzin began designing the computer communications network [Cyclades] and organizing a conference of Europeans interested in networking. Most participants attending the June 1972 meeting were French. Notable exceptions were Steve Crocker of DARPA, Donald Davies of the NPL and Peter Kirstein of University College, London. Two decisions came easy. First, they agreed they needed to meet again and function much like the Network Working Group, NWG, of Arpanet. So they assumed the name of the International Network Working Group or INWG. Second, they agreed [that] the institutional conditions of Europe were very different from those in the United States. How to work with the all-powerful Public Telephone and Telegraph companies (PTTs) and their omnipotent standards-making body, the International Telegraph and Telephone Consultative Committee (CCITT), was bound to be complicated and time consuming. Most attendees believed they needed the credibility and authority of an existing organization to level the playing field. Pouzin, a member of the newly created International Federation of Information Processing (IFIP) Technical Committee 6 (TC 6) on Data Communications, suggested INWG look into affiliating with IFIP, a body of computer scientists interested in international harmony and information sharing organized under the auspices of the United Nations. The INWG members authorized Pouzin to talk with Alex Curan, chairman of IFIP TC-6. They also scheduled the next meeting for November at the University of Kent, England, after the upcoming ICCC demonstration in Washington D. C. [which first introduced the Arpanet to a

> broader audience beyond the researchers and contractors immediately involved]. [. . .]
>
> In November 1972, just weeks after the heady experience of ICCC, the workshop at the University of Kent convened. With the Arpanet success serving as both an inspiration to those with computer communication ideas and a proof of principal to be improved upon, workshop organizers hoped to foster new collaborations. Participants from the United States, Canada, Japan and several European countries heard presentations on Arpanet, the NPL of Davies, and the network Pouzin was planning called Cyclades. [. . .]
>
> The confusion over how to best design a computer communications network also embroiled the debates within the group now named IFIP Working Group 6.1. In 1973, when Pouzin approached Alex Curran, chairman of IFIP TC-6, regarding the recently formed INWG becoming associated with IFIP TC-6, he readily agreed and they renamed INWG: IFIP Working Group 6.1 (WG 6.1) on Network Interconnection. Steve Crocker, chairman of the original Arpanet NWG, recommended Vint Cerf became Chairman, a suggestion readily approved. Quickly the WG 6.1 meetings became a must for anyone wanting to influence computer communications. For what was recognized by but a handful of people in mid-1973 became, in the short span of twenty-four months, received knowledge by nearly all those involved in computer communications: the world was going to be populated by many computer networks, networks that inevitably would need to be interconnected.

Note that the recount by Pelkey is based on a set of interviews with an impressive number of key people from the time, among them Vinton Cerf, Robert Kahn, Lawrence Roberts, Jon Postel, Stephen Crocker, David Clark, Frank Heart, Robert Metcalfe, Louis Pouzin, Hubert Zimmerman, and Donald Davies, see http://historyofcomputercommunications.info/CC_Individuals/IndividualsInterviewed.html?pab=3_1 — lending fairly solid credibility to his account. See also Cerf (1994) and Curran and Cerf (1975, p. 20), but also Cerf (1972*a*) and Cerf (1972*b*) for some triangulation. Finally, note as an aside that INWG initially consisted of two subgroups, one on "communication system requirements" (Cerf 1972*a*) and one on "host-host protocol requirements" (Cerf 1972*b*), with Pouzin and Cerf taking part in the latter.

266 (87). To quote again from Cerf (1973):

> The interconnection of two networks can be achieved through an interface or gateway which is connected to the nodes of two or more distinct networks. [. . .] The gateway must accept messages from one network and pass them to another, reformatting the message as necessary for transmission in the new network. (p. 4)

267 (87). Recall that the checksum in the IP header only checks the header, not the payload of an IP packet — see the Postel et al. (1981) quote at our note 249.

268 (87). The most crucial characteristic of the TCP design was its explicit assumption of less than reliable service delivered to the end hosts — thus the conspicuous emphasis on end host TCP reliability measures.

DIGRESSION: The existing networks at the time had made it clear that a network in itself may only offer a certain level of reliability without incurring unreasonable costs, and the only way to improve upon this state of affairs is for the end hosts to implement reliability measures themselves, typically via some acknowledgment, timeout, and retransmission strategy. To give an extreme illustration, PRNET lost so many packets ("5–10 % in severe cases", McQuillan and Cerf 1978*b*, p. 255) that end-to-end retransmission was the only way to obtain any reasonable service in the first place. Not surprisingly, thus, Frank et al. (1975) argue that "[t]he value of an End-to-End acknowledgment is sufficiently great that it can be assumed a priory" (p. 225).

This is true, in principle, for any network, even those with the luxury of abundant overhead. As we have seen in previous sections, while the Arpanet was initially specified and designed to offer fully reliable message transmission service in all but the most exceptional circumstances, it fell markedly short of perfect reliability in reality. Thus the designers of the Ethernet system made it very clear that even though their network was extremely robust and dependable, packets may get lost without the

Ethernet correcting for those losses, a situation which aggravates when building larger networks out of multiple individual Ethernets:

> Protocols used to communicate through an Ethernet must assume that packets will be received correctly at intended destinations *only with high probability*.
>
> An Ethernet gives its *best efforts* to transmit packets successfully, but it is the responsibility of processes in the source and destination stations to take the precautions necessary to assure reliable communication of the quality they themselves desire. Recognizing the costliness and dangers of promising "error-free" communication, we refrain from guaranteeing reliable delivery of any single packet to get both economy of transmission and high reliability averaged over many packets. Removing the responsibility for reliable communication from the packet transport mechanism allows us to tailor reliability to the application and to place error recovery where it will do the most good. This policy becomes more important as Ethernets are interconnected in a hierarchy of networks through which packets must travel farther and suffer greater risks. (p. 398, emphasis in original, references omitted)

Note that the lack of perfect reliability in the Ethernet is not due to poor engineering (in fact, by virtue of its distributed CSMA/CD control scheme it goes to considerable lengths to prevent collisions and make up for the ones that do occur), but is simply reflective of a basic philosophical assumption that is neatly captured in Boggs et al. (1980):

> Packet management strategies that attempt to guarantee perfect reliability must be designed to operate correctly under *worst case* conditions, whereas strategies that have the option of discarding packets when necessary need operate correctly only under *most* conditions. The idea is to sacrifice the guarantee of reliable delivery of individual packets and to capitalize on the resulting simplicity to produce higher reliability and performance overall. (p. 615, emphasis in original)

It is instructive here to venture an excursus on the very origin of the best effort notion — the philosophical basis to the lack of perfect reliability guarantee in the Ethernet (and, indeed, properly, any other network; see, e. g., Clark et al. 1978, p. 1499). Metcalfe (1973, ch. 6) develops the rationale for "best effort" in minute detail; in fact, we cannot recommend highly enough reading chapter 6 of his thesis. The crucial insight of Metcalfe was to appreciate the very nature and implications of *distributed* computing:

> We begin to have distributed computing environments when the distance in space or time between components becomes a factor in basic organization. [. . .] [T]he essence of distributed interprocess communication is dealing with a high degree of isolation and uncertainty. (p. 6-13)

To elaborate:

> A most important contrast to be drawn between centralized and distributed computing is that of reliability. When a disk controller sends a buffer to a user Job, it is assumed that the transfer will complete successfully. When the transfer fails, the operating system typically initiates some drastic procedure (e. g., halt) until the difficulty is found and fixed. The malfunction of even a single bit in a single word of a computer system's central memory may lead to a total collapse. *In a distributed computing system, errors are the rule. Because distributed systems are constructed by many different people at many different times, the potential for malfunction is considerably higher than that of centralized systems; the potential for error recovery in distributed systems is, fortunately, also very high. Because remote processes have only their communications in common (and not their memory and processor) the malfunction of one does not necessarily lead to the death of some other.* (p. 6-16, emphasis added)

From this basic insight, Metcalfe develops the notion of what he calls "'best effort' philosophy of interprocess communication":

> A system which depends jointly on a large number of its components to sustain operation will have poor reliability for the

> simple reason that the unreliability of the components will accumulate multiplicatively in the unreliability of the system. [. . .]
>
> Imagine that we are a component process in the midst of some large system. There are two extreme attitudes we might have toward the system and toward the several component processes upon which we depend. We might believe the processes around us to be so reliable, irreplaceable, and interdependent that, if one should fail, there would be little point in trying to carry on. Or, we might believe the processes around us to be so unreliable, expendable, and independent that, if some should fail, there would be considerable potential in our being able to patch things up to struggle on, weakened, but doing our job. This second attitude is characteristic of what we call *the "best-efforts" philosophy of interprocess communication; it is based on our desire to give the system our best efforts and, to do so, on our expecting only as much from the processes upon which we depend.* (pp. 6-25 f., emphasis added)

The principle put forward by Metcalfe is only seemingly obvious, however:

> But why make an issue out of something as simple as this "best-efforts" idea? Why call it a philosophy? Why give it a name at all? For the simple reason that, without a conscious effort to do otherwise, computer people (especially) find it easy to neglect the potential offered by thin-wire isolation — they've worked in centralized environments for so long. (p. 6-27)

And, sure enough, history offers more than one example of networks built with precisely the premise of offering no less than perfectly reliable virtual circuits to hosts, even if those networks were planned to scale well beyond anything that might be considered 'local'. Clark (2009*d*) recalls an episode about IBM's SNA network which demonstrates the absurdity of effectively outruling any node failure so as to 'guarantee' that no packets are being lost. The SNA specification held that no incoming packets must ever be discarded. Of course, in a packet switched network subject to statistical aggregation there is always a possibility — however minuscule — that a buffer overflows, leading to the inevitable discarding of additional incoming packets. Yet the implementers could not allow such a situation to occur, because that would run counter to the specification. However, what they could do—and did do—was to make the whole machine simply crash and reboot whenever it would otherwise have had to discard a packet—insane, but at least not in violation of the specification.

269 (87). The datagram notion has only been coined in the mid-1970s (Davies 1976; Pouzin 1976*b*). It goes back, in turn, to the much older notion of packet switching—"not really an invention, but a reapplication of the basic dynamic-allocation techniques used for over a century by the mail, telegraph, and torn paper tape switching systems" (Roberts 1978, p. 1307). In the mid-1960s the packet switching notion was elaborated chiefly by Baran and Davies, the former showing its feasibility in copious theory, and the latter implementing an actual (if locally confined) network based on the principle of packet switching. And, of course, packet switching was the defining paradigm for the Arpanet as we have discussed in previous sections.

Digression: The difference between the notion of packets and that of datagrams is largely one of elaboration of and adamancy about vertical layering between a most simple packet switching subnetwork, and a host level transport layer which from the packet switching service derives the more specific services a user might require. The latter philosophical elaboration is largely absent from the initial packet switching notion. Baran (1964*d*) introduces the general concept of "standard message blocks"—reasoning that their principal advantages are the better use of transmission lines by avoiding the utilization inefficiency and setup overhead of connections, and thus allow more users to share the transmission plant, catering for widely different bandwidth and service type requirements (p. 6).

Davies et al. (1967) offer more detail and anticipate some of the conceptual premises of datagrams, explicitly introducing the notion of of a "high level network" based on lower level "store-and-forward" links, with the high-level network carrying "packets" on behalf of users of the network. While the packet switching network is to be largely transparent to the user ("[t]o the user, the store-and-forward nature of the network might in some instances be hidden", p. 2), Davies et al. already appreciate the role that users (or, more generally, hosts) might have to play in error control:

> A computer failure in a node would probably destroy the few packets that are stored there. The question then arises whether duplication of the computer at each node is needed to guard against this possibility. It is thought that all users of the network will provide themselves with some kind of error control and that without difficulty this could be made to show up a missing packet. Because of this, loss of packets, if it is sufficiently rare, can be tolerated. (pp. 2 f.)

The datagram notion proper goes back to Pouzin and his Cyclades network, which by mid-1973 was coming to be developed with a firm notion of separating between a most simple packet switching subnetwork and higher level protocols assuming the responsibility of deriving reliable message or VC services for the users at their discretion. Notes Pouzin (1973*b*):

> Cyclades uses a packet-switching sub-network, which is a transparent message carrier, completely independent of host-host conventions. While in many ways similar to Arpanet, it presents some distinctive differences in address and message handling, intended to facilitate interconnection with other networks. In particular, addresses can have variable formats, and messages are not delivered in sequence, so that they can flow out of the network through several gates toward an outside target. (p. 80)

And, on layering:

> [W]e have been very strict in insulating logically, and even physically, functions related to computer network on one hand, and those germane to packet switching on another hand. (p. 84)

A similar notion can be found in the INWG proposals by Pouzin (1973*a*):

> The minimum service to be expected is the capability to send messages to a receiver, given some sort of global address, which can be understood by the traversed networks. The message should not be altered in any way between reception from its source and delivery to its destination. (p. 3)

Though not using the term datagram yet, the notion itself can clearly be seen from those early drafts. (For another apt quote from Pouzin 1973*a* see note 271.)

By 1976 the 'datagram paradigm' as distinct from the more general 'packet switching paradigm' was beginning to shape up properly against that of virtual circuit efforts (such as those pursued by CCITT, resulting in the X.25 standard). Notes Pouzin (1976*b*):

> The *DG protocol* consists only in formatting packets to be sent and dispatching received packets to specified ports. It may also include some conventions for flow control, when there exists a possibility of flooding some limited resource along the way. Thus, DGs appear as a *very simple transport facility*, without mechanisms normally associated with an orderly and reliable transfer of information. [. . .] *DGs are not intended to be used as a self-contained transport facility*. On the contrary, they should normally be accessed through *an embedding higher level protocol*. This higher level protocol may be a VC protocol, or *any other protocol* well suited to a specific class of applications. (p. 486. emphasis in original)

See also Pouzin (1982, pp. 35 ff.) for a retrospective on the advantages of a pure datagram subnetwork.

270 (87). Digression: Just like any 'normal' host level protocol is virtual in that it abstracts from and builds on lower level services down to the actual physical transmission of data, so is the inter-network produced from the protocols connecting hosts and gateways. In fact, it is precisely because it virtualizes from the local networks by means of a host level inter-network protocol (with the gateways operating at the lowest logical host level), that an inter-network can encompass a wide variety of different networks, so long as their services can reasonably be mapped to and from the common intern-network protocol. Note Gien et al. (1975):

> [I]t is not actually essential that the internal formats of a constituent network conform to some standard, since the important feature of Catenet [the early term for Internet, see Pouzin 1973*a*; Cerf 1978*c*] is the commonality of external service provided to subscribers and to other communication networks.

> [. . .] If amongst their customer services two communication networks offer a common service, and if the means for interworking between the two networks exists such that this service can be mutually exchanged, then there exists the basis for the interworking of their subscribers using that service. (p. 245)

Adding to the benefit of allowing the integration of widely different local networks into a "supernetwork" (Pouzin 1973*a*, p. 5) with gateways as "supernodes" (Sunshine 1977*a*, p. 175), interconnecting different networks at the host layer rather than some lower network specific level allows "to maintain the sovereignty of the networks involved" (Walden and Rettberg 1975, p. 115). More precisely:

> If the point of connection [between networks] is the host level [. . .], each network can protect itself against activities of the gateway to the same extent as it may protect itself against the activities of any other host. (Walden and Rettberg 1975, p. 115)

The notion of a 'virtual gateway network' also proved to help in separating intra-network from inter-network routing. Note Michel and Tasman (1984):

> Over the years, as more and more gateways were deployed, it became evident that the original model of a gateway was inadequate. Often it was desired to send a message to a computer on a network several gateways away. Thus, it became necessary for gateways to be able to do routing, in a manner similar to an IMP on the Arpanet. In fact, the evolving interconnected set of networks (the Internet) can itself be viewed at a higher level of abstraction as a network. The nodes of this network are the gateways, and the "hosts" are the component networks. Thus, the gateways of today have extensive routing capabilities, and these capabilities are becoming still more sophisticated as time goes on. (pp. 5 f.)

271 (87). It is apt to quote here from Pouzin (1973*a*) on the principal reasoning behind simplicity in inter-networking protocols:

A cursory examination may suggest that this is the way to get around network peculiarities, by burying them within gateways. But a closer look reveals that this is not so.

For example we might have network-1, with virtual circuits, end to end acknowledgments, and sequencing, while network-2 has none of these features. If we want network-1 properties be extended across network-2, then gateways all over must implement virtual circuits, end to end acknowledgment, and sequencing on the same way as network-1 does. As a consequence, all gateways would have to implement all network properties, which is clearly unrealistic.

On the opposite, we may want network-1 properties to be entirely masked out, so that network-1 appears no different from network-2. Only gateways to network-1 would be dependent on network-1 properties, which is undoubtedly more satisfactorily. But this is only possible to the extent that network-1 users disregard all network-1 properties that are not matched by network-2. I. e. virtual circuits, end to end acknowledgments, and sequencing. If network-1 interface does not allow such simplification, then a local gateway must be interposed between network-1 and its users that want to access network-2. [...]

We gradually come to the conclusion that users and gateways cannot assume anything about other networks but the simplest possible properties, the reason is that gateways cannot give to networks properties that they do not have. They can only screen out undesirable or unusable ones.

One might also think of gateways as nodes of a super-network, in which transmission lines happen to be local networks. Then, one could implement within gateways whatever properties should be deemed fit for inter-network communications, using more of less of the local features to carry messages between gateways.

Actually, this last approach boils down to the construction of yet another network, and ultimate at that. The very feasibility

> of such an objective can be seriously in doubt. Should network interconnection depend on a universal network, schisms would indefinitely raise the problem one level up.
>
> This is not to say that a general inter-network agreement will never happen, but that it will happen gradually, starting with a few recommendations on fundamental issues, rather than a whole network. (p. 5)

Gien and Zimmermann (1979) thus conclude:

> In many cases, there do not exist equivalent and cascadable services in networks to be interconnected. In order to match these constraints, it is necessary either to select a common cascadable subset of both services (i. e., to realize only a partial interconnection) or to add a new layer to one or both networks to reach equivalent cascadable services. This new layer appears only in the user equipment and in the gateway, thus wrapping (end-to-end) the original network without requiring any modification to intermediate nodes in the network. (p. 112)

In short, an inter-network protocol will necessarily have to abstract away from potentially useful but idiosyncratic local network mechanisms (such as broadcast). While mechanisms may be placed in a destination network's gateway that make such services accessible, they come at the cost of markedly increased gateway complexity and statefulness (Walden and Rettberg 1975, pp. 125 f.). Also, there are protocols which cannot be mapped onto each other (let alone be put in cascades of three or more mapped protocols) without violating their respective protocol semantics (see note 255).

272 (87). Digression: Our account here is, of course, and despite its apparent comprehensiveness, still a gross simplification itself. The design philosophy of TCP and the later TCP/IP was for years subject to various competitive efforts aiming at producing networks that would offer reliable service to hosts without requiring any extensive cooperation or efforts on their part — much along the lines of Arpanet. We will not here venture a detailed discussion of the X.25 protocol and deployment efforts (however, see Hovey 1976 for an overview; Sirbu and Zwimpfer 1985 for a detailed case study of the standards process; and Cerf and Kirstein 1978, pp. 1401 ff. for a critical discussion of the disadvantages of X.25/X.75). Suffice it here

to say that, at the time, the superiority of the datagram network paradigm was by no means universally acknowledged. In fact, even in circles close to the TCP and larger INWG discussions, it was not considered unreasonable to pursue efforts aimed at increasing the range of inter-network services beyond an unreliable datagram facility. E. g., argue Lloyd and Kirstein (1975):

> We consider that a user could build up whatever kind of communication he might require, given this set of three basic facilities:
>
> - A simple, single message, with comprehensive control header, which can be delivered reliably without further action or intervention by the user. (Datagram)
> - An ordered sequence of messages in each direction which, thanks to an end-to-end set-up procedure, requires fewer control fields per packet. (Virtual Circuit)
> - A longer sequence of messages in one direction, which has a minimal overhead of control information per packet. This requires a special end-to-end set-up scheme. (Bulk Data Transfer)
>
> (p. 506)

See also note 249 on the efforts toward a 'Stream Protocol' at the inter-network layer which were pursued until the mid-1990s, but ultimately proved futile.

Also, note that there were a number of competing inter-networking schemes built on essentially the same notions than TCP/IP. Most notably, Xerox PARC's "PUP Internet" (Boggs et al. 1980) (later turned into XNS) was not only similar to TCP/IP, but also had a considerable influence on its design. In fact, XNS came to have a lot of traction with entrepreneurs ad venture capitalists in the Silicon Valley area at the time—it was somewhat less general, and thus less complex and easier to implement than TCP/IP. However, it instantly fell out of general favor once Xerox put forward its specification of the InterPress printing protocol in 1982 which was encumbered with intellectual property reservations that made clear to all stakeholders involved the danger of trusting stewardship of inter-networking standards to a private commercial enterprise (Clark 2010*a*). Xerox later freed the InterPress specification from its proprietary licensing terms, but the damage was done. Also, adding insult to injury, Adobe's PostScript had by then become the de facto standard for a universal and general purpose intermediary representation for graphical printing output. Had Xerox chosen a different licensing model and product policy for its XNS protocol suite in general, it might well have become the dominant inter-network solution (Pelkey 2009, ch. 9.8).

The success of TCP/IP may at least in part be the result of historical chance—the concerted management efforts of ARPA, and the conducive, non-proprietariness driven governance context notwithstanding. One notable event was the implementation of TCP/IP into BSD Unix (the dominant operating system used at universities at the time, see Quarterman 1990, pp. 282 f.) under most liberal licensing terms—the design of which proved to be seminal, but which took place largely outside the ARPA funded TCP/IP implementation efforts. By 1982 TCP/IP became part of BSD Unix 4.2 due largely to UC Berkeley's William Joy's coding efforts (Joy and Fabry 1981) based on the prior BBN TCP/IP implementation for VAX Unix (Gurwitz 1981) ("the Berkeley team would sometimes justify bugs in their TCP by pointing out that the original BBN code had the same bug", Partridge and Blumenthal 2006, p. 59). Together with Ethernet (as the lower layers of Xerox' XNS) available for VAX machines, anyway, "market forces swept TCP/IP forward in a way no one could have planned" (Pelkey 2009, ch. 9.8). In fact, the BSD TCP/IP networking stack and its "socket abstraction" (Leffler et al. 1993, p. 18-6) have remained most popular to this day, and have by virtue of their utterly liberal licensing terms been incorporated into most if not all Unix systems since, and also formed the basis for today's Microsoft Windows' as well as Apple's Mac OS X TCP/IP stack. By 1986—the year the first TCP/IP Implementers Workshop, the later Interoperability Conference, or Interop, was held in Monterey, CA—TCP/IP was becoming the technology of choice for an ever increasing number of vendors, given that the much-touted ISO/OSI protocol suite was yet to be finalized, and there had been ample experience with TCP/IP in U. S. federal and military networks at the time (Shaw 1988).

273 (88). Cerf and Kahn (1973), on addressing in an inter-network:

> Since the Gateway must understand the address of the source and destination Hosts, this information must be available in a standard format in every packet which arrives at the Gateway. This information is contained in an *internetwork header* prefixed to the packet. (p. 5, emphasis in original)

And, further:

> If the [destination] TCP is to determine for which process an arriving packet is intended, every packet must contain a *process header* (distinct from the internetwork header) which completely identifies the destination process [and we select this method as a part of the *internetwork transmission protocol*]. (p. 10, emphasis in original)

See for the two header formats and the fields they contain Cerf and Kahn (1973, Figure 3 at p. 6, and Figure 7 at p. 13). The same quotes and illustrations can be found in Cerf and Kahn (1974, p. 638, Figure 3 at p. 639, p. 640, Figure 6 at p. 642).

Further elaboration of the two headers is provided in Cerf and Postel (1977, pp. 68 ff., ch. 4.3). In fact, Cerf and Postel (1977) already speak of a "basic internet header" and a "TCP header [that] follows the internet header", thus allowing for "the existence of internet protocols other than TCP, and for experimentation with TCP variants" (p. 68), with the internet header's format field specifying a first set of different protocol types beside TCP (p. 70).

See also Cerf (1977) for a brief discussion of end-to-end flow control versus gateway-to-gateway 'flow control' (congestion control).

274 (88). Pouzin (1973*a*) noted that gateways are effectively two hosts:

> Gateways would look like a host for each network, i. e. receive receive and forward messages, exchange adequate signaling information, perform some error and flow control, accounting, etc. In other words, a gateway could be viewed as two hosts face to face. (p. 4)

Also, to quote from Cerf (1977):

> A gateway has always been regarded as a host, at least to the extent that it obeys host/subnet protocols. (p. 2)

And, note Walden and Rettberg (1975) on the gateway sitting logically between two hosts facing two different networks—all of which could well reside in but one physical machine:

> [T]he gateway connecting two networks could [. . .] take the form of a program running in a host which is connected to both networks. (p. 120)

Finally, Boggs et al. (1980) remark (albeit in the context of the PUP internetwork):

> [T]he hosts *are* the internet. [. . .] Gateways are simply hosts in the internet that are willing to forward packets among constituent networks. Thus, most of the properties of the internet are primarily artifacts of host software. (p. 613, emphasis in original)

The interesting question which had been in limbo prior to the 1978 TCP/IP split is, of course, to which degree the inter-network functions in the gateways and hosts overlap, thus introducing structural dependencies between the two which may inhibit later amendments.

275 (88). Note that even though hosts would generally be considered to implement the gateway level protocol themselves, they could as well connect to a gateway of their choice by any mutually agreed procedure. Equally, a gateway could implement TCP, and offer some idiosyncratic interface to less potent host computers or terminals (very much along the lines of the Arpanet TIP); however, in this case it would become a de facto host, itself. The crucial point is that TCP was no more a protocol to be implemented in a cascaded fashion, it had now become a true end-to-end protocol. The concatenation of the constituent networks was to be the sole responsibility of the IP part of TCP/IP.

276 (89). As an aside note on UDP, Reed (2008*b*) recalls the very conception of UDP as a "placeholder " for non-VC protocols:

> UDP was actually "designed" in 30 minutes on a blackboard when we decided pull the original TCP protocol apart into TCP and IP, and created UDP on top of IP as an alternative for multiplexing and demultiplexing IP datagrams inside a host among the various host processes or tasks. But it was a placeholder

> that enabled all the non-virtual-circuit protocols since then to be invented, including encapsulation, RTP, DNS, [. . .], without having to negotiate for permission either to define a new protocol or to extend TCP by adding "features".

See also Reed (2004) for a more extensive recount on the TCP/IP split as driven largely by John Shoch (given his PUP background), Daniel Cohen (given his packet speech background), and David Reed (given his consideration of messages versus streams as basic building blocks for higher level applications outside the telephony inspired connection paradigm).

277 (89). UDP adds to the IP header nothing but the source and destination port, plus checksum and message length, and has remained effectively unchanged to this day (see Postel 1980*c*). Applications requiring still less protocol logic could, of course, use the IP protocol right away (provided their host systems catered for such access, see also Clark 1982*c*, p. 12, and provided they needed no additional protocol or port multiplexing logic).

278 (89). The most obvious application for UDP (other than packet voice experiments and such) has been for message exchanges in simple request/ response communication patterns—see the square root example cited in note 204. The first widespread application along those lines (which even predates the first specification of UDP) was the Internet Name Server (first specified in Postel 1978*b*, with the successor version, Postel 1979*d*, using UDP), the predecessor to today's DNS system (beginning with Mockapetris 1983). Another example for the use of UDP is TFTP (Sollins 1980), which was designed so as to allow 'trivial' file transfers with as little as possible protocol overhead, just using IP and a simple data transfer protocol without any of the bells and whistles typically afforded by FTP. Today, UDP is frequently used for streaming media applications, but also applications demanding extremely high throughput.

See also Clark et al. (1978, pp. 1511 f.) for a discussion of the relative advantages of virtual circuits versus message exchanges, including an instructive comment on the problem of acknowledgment strategies in message exchange communications.

279 (89). The inter-network packet format specified in TCP Version 2 (Cerf and Postel 1977) contained a format field that could take the value 0 for "raw internet packets" (p. 78). However, the record on any such uses of TCP is scarce to non-existent.

280 (90). Cerf and Kahn (1973) is a substantial elaboration on the fairly summary initial draft offered in Cerf (1973).

281 (90). To quote slightly more copiously on the fragmentation issue:

> Unless all transmitted packets are legislatively restricted to be small enough to be accepted by every individual network, the Gateway may be forced to split a packet into two or more smaller packets. This must be done in such a way that the destination is able to piece together the fragmented packet. We believe it to be undesirable to restrict the size of the internetwork packets to the smallest maximum size available and therefore conclude that the Gateways must be prepared to break up packets into smaller pieces when necessary. It is conceivable that one might desire the Gateway to perform the reassembly to simplify the task of the destination Host (or process) and/or to take advantage of a larger packet size. We take the position that Gateways should not perform this function since Gateway reassembly can lead to serious buffering problems, potential deadlocks, the necessity for all fragments of a packet to pass through the same Gateway, and increased delay in transmission. Furthermore, it is not sufficient for the Gateways to provide this function since the final Gateway may also have to fragment a packet for transmission. Thus, the destination Host must be prepared to do this task. (Cerf and Kahn 1973, pp. 7 f.)

The above quote made it almost verbatim into their famous 1974 paper (Cerf and Kahn 1974, p. 639).

Note as an aside that the term denoting the PDUs in question gradually moved from *message* to *packet* (as in today's IP packets, too); however, the meaning remains essentially the same and does not change the pertinent analyses.

282 (91). In principle, a local network could relay TCP messages by any means — the specifics of any individual networks are completely transparent to the end hosts. It is thus irrelevant to the inter-networking operations of an end host whether its packets are subjected to avian carriers or elaborate X.25 Virtual Circuits, as long as the intermediate networks move some of the packets at all.

283 (91). Cerf and Kahn (1974) is heavily based on the Cerf and Kahn (1973) draft.

284 (91). To quote slightly more copiously from Pouzin (1975*b*):

> [The Cerf and Kahn (1974) proposal] includes additional machinery allowing further fragmentation of messages within gateways between PSNs. Final reassembly is performed at station level [that is, at the end host] [. . .]. The goal is to preserve the possibility of using longer messages with some PSNs. The other side of the coin is that E-E protocols are definitely tied up with the design of gateways. As a consequence, evolutions in E-E protocols could become completely dependent on PTTs. (Pouzin 1975*b*, p. 2-10)

285 (92). As an aside, Xerox' PUP inter-network (which shared many of its principal design choices with TCP, and was used at least inside Xerox since the mid-1970s) did not implement an inter-network fragmentation scheme, "requiring that every agent in the [PUP] internet handle Pups [the equivalent to IP packets] up to a standard maximum size, using network-specific fragmentation where necessary" (Boggs et al. 1980, p. 616). See Metcalfe (1988) for a comprehensive insider take on the history of Ethernet, PUP, XNS, and Xerox's mixed successes in bringing these technologies to the market.

286 (92). Digression: Sunshine (1977*a*, p. 190) notes:

> Although adoption of such a scheme [Cerf and Kahn 1973; Cerf and Kahn 1974] allows arbitrary local net packet sizes, it complicates selection of optimal packet sizes for internet communication. Presumably small packets (from interactive traffic) will traverse all nets on a one-to-one basis with no complications. High throughput applications, on the other hand, tend to use large packet sizes to reduce overhead. In this case, passing through even a single "small packet" net may cause degradation, since once packets are fragmented in the small packet net, they are not reassembled. All the fragments must be carried through subsequent nets which might have accepted the original packets more efficiently, or at lower cost. In such cases a user may wish to forgo the added robustness of independent

> fragmentation propagation in favor of local net fragmentation/ reassembly.

Note that even in the worst case — a network not capable of forwarding a packet due to its size drops it without any indication to the source — a sending TCP has several options other than reducing its packet sizes: it may avoid the network by manually setting up a chain of Telnet or FTP connections; or it may resort to source routing (which was then still considered a viable solution to the inter-network routing problem, Sunshine 1977*b*; and was, in fact, made available as an option in the IP protocol (see our digression in note 381).

And, for gateways to do fragmentation they "cannot merely use a network-specific technique, and may need to know some intimate details about the internals of an inter-network packet" (Shoch 1978*a*, p. 2) which may arguably 'inhibit the long range growth and development of inter-network communication' more than legislating a maximum packet size to be handled by every network connecting to to the TCP Internet. The full quote reads:

> [With inter-network fragmentation] [t]he gateway must be able to suitably divide up the original inter-network packet into pieces that the destination — any destination — can properly reassemble; it cannot merely use a network-specific technique, and may need to know some intimate details about the internals of an inter-network packet. (Shoch 1978*a*, p. 2)

For an extended version of Shoch (1978*a*) see also Shoch (1979).

Note also that just about any network may be connected to an inter-network using intra-network not inter-network fragmentation. Failing to meet a minimum datagram size target may complicate the tasks of the gateways involved, and take away some routing flexibility (e. g., to obtain Arpanet subnetwork like load balancing), but it does not make interconnection impossible, and need not even make it markedly more expensive (in terms of complexity, fallibility, etc.).

287 (92). All of the versions prior to the 1977 discussions on TCP Version 4 (Postel 1977*e*) maintained the original fragmentation scheme — TCP Version 1 introduced the notion of allowing gateway level fragmentation requiring host level reassembly (Cerf et al. 1974, p. 3), TCP Version 2 offered

some elaboration (Cerf and Postel 1977, pp. 82 f.), which carried over almost verbatim into TCP Version 3 (Cerf and Postel 1978, pp. 69 f.). However, by that time serious reservations had surfaced that would finally help separating the gateway level issues from the host level issues by a firm structural separation of two protocols. IEN 2 (Postel 1977*b*) had laid out the the case for a separation between the hop-by-hop gateway level 'Internet part' and the end host level 'TCP part', and Postel (1977*e*) came to conclude:

> The idea of a separate internet protocol that routes TCP segments through the internet system [see also Postel 1977*b* for the initial IEN memo on this matter] is gaining favor, and if such an internet protocol is to exist perhaps it should be the site of fragmentation and reassembly. [. . .] [T]he current TCP fragmentation description will be in TCP-3, but it may be removed in TCP-4. (p. 6)

TCP Version 3 (Cerf and Postel 1978) was left to acknowledge:

> It is possible that fragmentation of segments may be removed from responsibility of TCP and placed at the gateway level only. (p. 68)

Thus it happened, the TCP version 4 draft specification (Postel 1978*e*) was consequently void of any fragmentation considerations, for they were moved to the IP version 4 draft specification (Postel 1978*c*). (See also Postel 1978*a* for the IP version 2 specification, a slightly earlier but largely similar IP version.)

288 (92). Moving fragmentation and reassembly from the connection oriented TCP protocol to the datagram IP protocol required some changes, since one could no longer use the TCP sequence numbers which had made inter-network fragmentation virtually indistinguishable from the initial packaging of TCP messages at the source host. IP fragmentation had to introduce complexity for both fragmentation (Postel 1978*c*, pp. 17 f.; Postel 1981*d*, pp. 8 f.) and reassembly (Clark 1982*b*) at the IP level, largely adding to the TCP message processing machinery previously in place.

289 (92). Ironically, now the source of contention — that had lead to a major rift between the 'TCP community' and the more Cyclades inspired broader

INWG debate—was resolved very much in the spirit of Pouzin's 1975 objections.

Digression: A brief aside on the fate of the competitive effort inside INWG based on many of the notions introduced by Pouzin's Cyclades project. In parallel to the initial TCP specifications the INWG produced a set of specification documents for an alternative scheme that would leave fragmentation to the host layer alone—largely inspired by Pouzin's notion of letters at Transport Station (TS) level based on unreliable datagram networks. In fact, Cerf et al. (1974)—TCP Version 1—was an attempt to incorporate some of the notions put forward by Pouzin (1973*a*). However, Cerf et al. would allow gateway level fragmentation, and Pouzin was decidedly unhappy with the mingling of "matters that belong to the transport level, and matters that belong to the end-to-end protocol" (Pouzin 1988). Yet unlike Pouzin's TS, the TCP specification quickly turned from specification to several implementations, backed by substantial ARPA guidance and funding:

> In early 1975, DARPA gave three contracts to test whether the TCP specifications were detailed and explicit enough to enable different implementations to function seamlessly. The three teams were headed by Cerf at Stanford, Ray Tomlinson and Bill Plummer at BBN, and by Peter Kirstein at University College in London, England. (Pelkey 2009, ch. 6.4)

On a related note, TCP was much less complex than the competing INWG line of specification: while TCP was initially conceived as (and has largely remained to this day) a one-size-fits-all host level transport program comparable to Arpanet's NCP, it provided a fairly limited level of abstraction. Pouzin's TS concept, on the other hand, was far more elaborate to begin with. Whereas TCP simply set up connections and then implemented a reliable virtual circuit largely using a set of techniques relatively well understood at the time (safe some refinements such as three-way handshakes to avoid confusion in message reassembly, see Tomlinson 1975; or improving flow control so as to avoid Silly Window Syndrome performance degradation, see Clark 1982*e* and Braden 1989), the TS concept involved elaborate subscriber management (Pouzin 1973*b*, p. 82), subscriber name based addressing (p. 82), and four different service classes (pp. 82 f.). Also, the system put forward by Pouzin was to be so general as to allow virtually arbitrary multiplexing at all levels below the end-to-end protocol at the port level—gateways, DTEs, and Transport Stations:

> [I]f a station is likely to be associated with a physical host computer, nothing prevents from having several stations within the same computer, or to have distributed stations not associated with any identifiable computer. [. . .] Each station may exchange traffic through several DTEs, and conversely, any DTE may multiplex traffic with several stations. (Pouzin 1975*b*, p. 2-9)

While there were some inter-networking experiments based on the Cyclades inspired TS line of end-to-end protocols (Gien et al. 1975, pp. 247 ff.), they remained fairly limited, given that neither Cyclades, nor the NPL network, nor EIN ever approached near the size of the Arpanet, let alone an inter-network built around Arpanet. (Cyclades never had more than 20 hosts, see Pouzin 1982, p. 3 and Schafer 2009; the NPL network was always confined to the NPL site, see Campbell-Kelly 1987; and as for EIN, "because of its delay, and because it never had any appreciable usage, its impact was minimal", see Kirstein 2009, p. 22.)

Still, many of the TS notions found their way into a Cerf et al. (1976) proposal (first released in mid-1975) that was largely due to an effort of BBN's Alexander McKenzie to "bridge the differences between the TCP and European communities" (Pelkey 2009, ch. 6.4). The document, also dubbed INWG 96 End-to-End Protocol, featured a number of noteworthy departures from TCP—subscriber name based addressing, sharing of ports between several "associations" in parallel, fragmentation at the host level only, two different association modes ("Liaison" and "Lettergram"), and optional error control. However, the proposal was met with little enthusiasm in the larger TCP community, which had already embarked on several implementation efforts for TCP. Notes Cerf (1988):

> [We could not] persuade the TCP community to adopt the compromise given the state of implementation experience of TCP at the time and the untested nature of the IFIP document [Cerf et al. 1976].

Not only was the Cerf et al. (1976) proposal left largely neglected by the larger TCP community—adding insult to injury, CCITT, largely owing to its firm telephony background, in 1976 decided to go with the virtual circuit protocol X.25 that had been in the making from ca. 1975 (Campbell-Kelly and Garcia-Swartz 2005, pp. 22 f.; ITU 2009; see also Hovey (1976) and Sirbu and Zwimpfer (1985); and, for a critical discussion, Cerf and Kirstein 1978, pp. 1401 ff.). The only forum thus left for the INWG datagram networks proponents in competition to TCP was ISO, which they had approached in late 1975, already. However, the ISO's "leisurely, democratic processes" (Campbell-Kelly and Garcia-Swartz 2005, p. 28) proved poor competition to the fast paced networking industry, and ISO/OSI has (its conceptual contributions to the theory of networking notwithstanding) largely been written out of the relevant Internet history (with textbooks gradually dropping the ISO/OSI model as frame of reference, see e. g., Pahlavan and Krishnamurthy 2009). With ARPA deciding to continue going with TCP, rather than turning to X.25 (Partridge and Blumenthal 2006, p. 59) or waiting for ISO to produce useful results, the larger INWG efforts (outside CCITT and ISO) effectively stopped, and INWG ceased to be a relevant forum for work on inter-networking protocols and standards. The interesting action thus firmly moved to the TCP community, and outside the INWG (Walden 1990, pp. 361 f.).

290 (93). The major problem with fragmentation of IP packets is that it introduces sizable overhead penalties, and suffers from poor performance when fragments get lost—loss of a single fragment of an IP packet requires retransmission of the entire packet by way of higher layer timeouts, for IP does not include timeout and retransmission mechanisms itself.

291 (93). It is worthy of note that a sizable percentage of routers or other middleboxes in a given path block the ICMP packets involved in classic path MTU discovery (Medina et al. 2005, pp. 41 f.). End hosts thus either turn to detecting the path MTU based on observed loss rates ("black hole detection") (Mathis and Heffner 2007), or simply pick a reasonably safe MTU (e. g., 1024 bytes, cf. Mathis and Heffner 2007, p. 16) and dispense with MTU discovery altogether.

292 (93). Indeed, today "it is near impossible for an application to force TCP to send segments large enough to require fragmentation" (Stevens 2002, p. 149).

293 (93). Digression: A brief aside elaboration on fragmentation: As a practical matter, there have always been some size limitations to the packets a network could handle without resorting to fragmentation or discarding — Arpanet single-packet messages (eligible for raw message expedited handling): some 100 bytes; Arpanet messages subject to intra-network fragmentation: up to some 1000 bytes; Experimental Ethernet 'messages': 500 bytes (Metcalfe and Boggs 1976); Ethernet specification 1.0 'messages': 1500 bytes (Shoch et al. 1982). The INWG 96 End-to-End Protocol (as well as its predecessors, Pouzin 1974*a*; Zimmermann and Elie 1974) was based on host level fragmentation of messages of up to 128 times 216 bytes which would then be fragmented into fixed length 216 bytes fragments for delivery to the datagram network interface. The assumption here is, of course, that every network to be potentially encountered be able to deal with 216 bytes packets. Some argued that this minimum maximum size was sufficient for all virtually every network (Gien et al. 1975, p. 246), others found it rather large (Shoch 1979, p. 7).

As we have discussed, TCP allowed gateway level fragmentation, essentially on par with host fragmentation of messages into inter-network packets (Cerf et al. 1974, p. 3). In fact, gateways are allowed to this day to fragment IP packets at their discretion provided the "don't fragment" flag is off. However, IPv6 provides no gateway level fragmentation anymore, instead requiring a maximum MTU of at least 1280 bytes (Deering and Hinden 1998, p. 24).

Given the disadvantages of gateway level inter-network fragmentation (Kent and Mogul 1987), a default maximum transmission unit (MTU) has quickly been standardized on, which may only be exceeded if both end hosts agree upon it. While this default maximum IP packet size has little to do with fragmentation, it still proved to be a focal point that characterized much of the IP traffic at the time, and allowed IP packets to traverse most networks without any need for fragmentation. Postel (1979*b*) first points to the emerging default MTU:

> An internet datagram of 576 octets may be sent by any internet host with expectation that all internet hosts will be able to accept internet datagrams that large. It may be that such datagrams will be fragmented to transit certain networks and that destination hosts will have to reassemble the fragments. Every

> internet host should be prepared to assemble a set of fragments totaling 576 octets.
>
> [. . .] [E]very internet module should be prepared to pass a 68 octet datagram with out fragmentation. The maximum internet header is 60 octets, and the minimum data fragment is 8 octets. (p. 12)

Postel (1979*a*) (IP Version 4) thus says:

> All hosts must be prepared to accept datagrams of up to 576 octets (whether they arrive whole [or] in fragments). It is recommended that hosts only send datagrams larger than 576 octets if they have assurance that the destination is prepared to accept the larger datagrams. (p. 10)

This early consensus allowed for a minimum common ground that would allow any two hosts to exchange IP traffic without prior negotiations, and would also be small enough a size to be handled without fragmentation by most typical networks (safe packet radio networks like PRNET). (For a list of common ARQs see Mogul and Deering 1990, Table 7-1 at p. 17.) The 576 byte MTU recommendation has remained in place to this day (Braden 1989, pp. 58 ff.).

Note well, though, that even though the 576 byte figure might have provided a focal point for networks and their gateways (Stine 1988, pp. 22 f.), and has to this day been used as a fallback in case of path MTU discovery problems (Medina et al. 2005, pp. 41 f.), it has logically been a completely irrelevant figure for the operation of the gateways:

> Gateways must be prepared to accept the largest datagrams that are allowed on each of the directly attached networks, even if it is larger than 576 octets. Gateways must be prepared to fragment datagrams to fit into the packets of the next network, even if it smaller than 576 octets. (Postel 1983, p. 7)

Thus, in order to to be absolutely certain that no packets are fragmented along the way, a host must determine the MTU of a given path between source and destination of its IP traffic — either using ad hoc measures (Mathis and Heffner 2007), or using dedicated gateway ICMP feedback (Mogul and Deering 1990).

Nowadays, very few routes have MTUs lower than 1492 bytes, and fragmentation has generally become a rare phenomenon, largely confined to streaming media, misconfigured tunneling and some UDP message applications with very tight delay requirements (Shannon et al. 2002). Thus IP packets with 1492 bytes are now almost guaranteed not to encounter any fragmentation.

294 (94). Digression: Even though the transition from NCP to TCP is often depicted in retrospect as a flag day transition; in actual fact, it has been a gradual transition, starting in late 1982 and largely finished by ca. mid-1983, preceded by a five year run-up period.

By 1978, with the draft specifications of TCP and IP in place (Postel 1978*e*; Postel 1978*c*), ARPA had decided to adopt "a set of DoD standard host-to-host protocols based on the Transmission Control and Internet Protocol" with exceptions "only for networks that can be shown to have no future requirements for interoperability" (Dinneen 1978). By 1980, TCP/IP implementation efforts funded by ARPA were well underway (see also Postel et al. 1979), and the two protocols (TCP and IP) were ratified as DoD standards (Dinneen 1980).

However, many sites were largely happy with NCP and the application level email gateways in place between different networks. It thus took considerable persuasion to get some of the host sites to go along with the transition (Cerf 2001, p. 28; R. E. Kahn 1990, pp. 32 ff.). In order to smoothen the transition the NCP/TCP Transition Plan contained a number of provisions for application layer gateways (or "relays") that would allow NCP hosts and TCP hosts to communicate at the level of Telnet, FTP, and Email, respectively (Postel 1981*e*; Cerf and Postel 1980).

By late 1981 TCP/IP was implemented in dozens of gateways, already (Postel 1981*e*, pp. 16 ff.); by 1982 the Arpanet was able to connect to Satnet, PRNET, and LAN type networks via the DARPA Internet Gateway (Hinden and Sheltzer 1982, pp. 27 f.); and by 1983 "TCP/IP had been successfully ported to all the leading computers of the day" (Pelkey 2009, ch. 9.11). Yet, despite the initial plan to cut over to TCP/IP on January 1, 1983, sharp ("the pressure is uncomfortable, but we will probably be able to make it", Muuss 1982), a substantial number of hosts took well into 1983 to finish their TCP/IP implementations. R. E. Kahn (1990) recalls:

> [T]he biggest problem was just getting people to believe that

> it was real. It is like any major change; it is not real until it happens. We sent messages to everybody, alerting them to the timing and yet one week before we were still getting messages, "Is this really going to happen next week?" or "Let us know if you decide to really go ahead with this." The day after we did the transition, people were saying "Hey, how come I didn't know about this?" or "It was impossible for me to convert; I need another six months." We would say, "You had two years' lead notice; why is it that suddenly you need six more months?" [. . .] Even the places that thought they were going to convert properly suddenly found that while theirs worked with the three or four places that they thought it would, or had tried it out with, it didn't work with some others. So there was quite a bit of time required to smooth out the rough edges. (pp. 32 f.)

Thus, while on January 1, 1983, the transition "took place as scheduled", a significant number of exceptions were granted to continue using NCP (Heiden 1983). Absent such official exception a host would be cut off from the Arpanet, by having the IMPs filter and block their NCP traffic. (Already, Postel 1981*a* had noted in a response to Crispin 1981 that "a quite simple modification to the IMP program would enable the IMPs to filter out and discard all NCP traffic".) Still, by late February 1983 only little more than 50 percent of all hosts surveyed in a series of connectivity tests provided Telnet, FTP, and SMTP services over TCP in full accordance with the NCP/TCP Transition Plan (Westine et al. 1983). It was only by ca. June 1983, that the transition may reasonably be considered to have been successfully finished (Abbate 1999, p. 142).

295 (94). For a current overview of "Open Research Issues in Internet Congestion Control" see Papadimitriou et al. (2009). Also, see Bauer et al. (2009) for another current discussion of Internet congestion issues.

296 (94). The basic problem with congestion is not primarily in buffer queues building up, round-trip times (RTT) increasing, and even packets having to be dropped for lack of additional buffer space—the real problem sets in when hosts are too slow in updating their maximum retransmission intervals to a sudden RTT increase, and start introducing ever more retransmissions of the same datagrams already sent out, leading to a congestion

collapse that seriously degrades the overall network performance and is hard to recover from. Nagle (1984*a*) puts it succinctly:

> [A] sudden load on the net can cause the round-trip time to rise faster than the sending hosts['] measurements of round-trip time can be updated. Such a load occurs when a new bulk transfer, such a file transfer, begins and starts filling a large window. Should the round-trip time exceed the maximum retransmission interval for any host, that host will begin to introduce more and more copies of the same datagrams into the net. The network is now in serious trouble. Eventually all available buffers in the switching nodes will be full and packets must be dropped. The round-trip time for packets that are delivered is now at its maximum. Hosts are sending each packet several times, and eventually some copy of each packet arrives at its destination. This is congestion collapse.
>
> This condition is stable. Once the saturation point has been reached, if the algorithm for selecting packets to be dropped is fair, the network will continue to operate in a degraded condition. In this condition every packet is being transmitted several times and throughput is reduced to a small fraction of normal. (p. 2)

It is important to note that increasing buffer sizes will not remedy the problem; in fact, it may make things *worse*, for it potentially increases delays and does nothing to address the problem of excess retransmissions filling the network up duplicate packets (Nagle 1985). Gross excess capacity, possibly maintained by tight access control and 'traffic policing', will render the issue of congestion irrelevant (recall the administrative and technical restrictions for access to the Arpanet raw message interface considered at pages 80 f.), but it comes with considerable overhead which may be reasonable in wire-based LAN scenarios with inexpensive bandwidth, but much less so in wide-area networks with comparatively expensive bandwidth and large delays (Clark et al. 1978, p. 1510).

In order to avoid any onset of congestion in a router in the first place, queues should on average be held at a low enough level to allow for the accommodation of brief intermittent bursts of traffic without having to drop packets. This can be achieved by Active Queue Management (AQM) schemes (Braden et al. 1998) such as Random Early Detection (RED) (Floyd and Jacobson 1993).

297 (95). See Davies and Barber (1973, pp 404 ff.) and Price (1973) on an isarithmic congestion control scheme based on controlling admission using a "permit pool" of tokens. Also Davies and Barber introduce the distinction between "local", "end-to-end", and "global" congestion control methods, concluding:

> A distributed method of [congestion] control is preferred [to a centralized one]. There seems to be a need for both end-to-end control (which in any case is part of the mechanism of end-to-end protocol) and global control. (p. 405)

298 (95). This reasoning holds for the Ethernet, too. Even though components that are logically part of the network sit physically with the host computers (making the design of those components an "exercise in paranoia", Metcalfe and Boggs 1976, p. 398), the locality of the Ethernet setting aids administrative control and individual accountability. Any network problems in an Ethernet are thus far more likely to stem from misconfiguration (too many hosts, too large a shared bus segment, etc.) than misbehaving hosts (e. g., tweaking their jabber timers).

Later networks built and operated by BBN also had a global congestion control scheme based on closed-loop feedback systems and dedicated throttlers policing the traffic every host could inject to the network (Robinson et al. 1990).

299 (96). Arguably, the best effort packet transmission function has become cemented once the Internet grew beyond the tractable confines of a small research community. No amendments have since been made to the IP protocol and the gateway functions immediately concerned with IP. Notes Haverty (2009*b*):

> Once TCP/IP got out of the realm where all of the implementors could sit together in a room or on a mailing list and argue, it became harder to change things. Research goals never seem to include "must be easily upgradeable without disruption to current operations."

Browsing through accounts from the time, one often finds statements such as "Yes, we should really think about accounting and security some time"; however, those items have rarely featured prominently on the lists of priorities in 'designing' the Internet (Clark 1988).

It is important to recall that the possibility of adding any complexity to the Internet gateways beyond best effort packet transmission has always been limited sharply by the requirement of arbitrary cascadability of inter-network functions. Even if a consensus could be reached about additional functions (other than dropping packets) in the gateways (an adventurous assumption in itself, see Pouzin 1973*a*, pp. 4 f.) — there seems to be a fundamental limit to the functions amenable to cascading across multiple networks without either driving up gateway and inter-network protocol complexity and fallibility, or exclude less potent networks not capable of implementing the function in question. In fact, protocols may differ in subtle ways, such that they cannot be cascaded at all without violating their semantics. (See notes 271 and 255.)

Also, recall that it is a lot easier to build a potentially global network with the assumption of zero trustworthiness on any of the components outside one's immediate control, than build a network which relies on complex inter-network functions to be carried out in concert with gateways and hosts well beyond any central accountability or control. To repeat the due quote from Metcalfe (1973) (see note 268.):

> [W]e might believe the processes around us to be so unreliable, expendable, and independent that, if some should fail, there would be considerable potential in our being able to patch things up to struggle on, weakened, but doing our job. This [...] attitude is characteristic of what we call the "best-efforts" philosophy of interprocess communication; it is based on our desire to give the system our best efforts and, to do so, on our expecting only as much from the processes upon which we depend. (pp. 6-25 f.)

300 (96). To quote from Strazisar (1979):

> The gateway may discard internet packets if it does not have the buffer space needed to queue the packets for output to the next network on the route to the destination network. If the

> gateway discards a packet, it sends a source quench message to the internet source host of the packet. The source quench message is a request to the host to cut back the rate at which it is sending traffic to the internet destination. The gateway sends a source quench message for every message that it discards. On receipt of a source quench message, hosts should cut back the rate at which they are sending traffic to the specified destination until they no longer receive source quench messages from the gateway. The hosts can then gradually increase the rate at which they are sending traffic to the destination until they again receive source quench messages from the gateway. (pp. 9 f.)

The source quench message became part of Internet Protocol (Postel 1980*b*, pp. 19 f.), using the option field in the IP header which had previously only been used to hold a "General Error Report" reporting "errors in internet packet processing" (Postel 1978*c*, p. 14). With Postel (1981*b*) the error reporting from gateways to hosts was moved to a separate protocol specification, based on IP null packets and using the IP header options (Internet Control Message Protocol). Postel (1981*b*, pp. 7 f.) and Postel (1981*c*, pp. 10 f.) thus refer to the source quench mechanism in greater depth again, using much of the initial wording from Strazisar (1979).

As for the deeper history of the source quench notion, an early discussion of congestion control goes back to Davies (1976). Speaking of "congestion due to excess traffic at the destination" Davies notes:

> At a higher queue level it will be necessary to discard packets that arrive on the queue and in this case the source of the packets should receive a diagnostic message. [. . .]
>
> After warning of network output queue level, [a terminal should] reduce the level of activity or give more priority to accepting packets. (pp. 8, 10)

While pertaining to congestion of end hosts rather than intermediary network nodes, the basic reasoning very much anticipates the later source quench notion.

301 (96). Like normal IP packets, ICMP packets were not acknowledged. Also, any failures in ICMP packet communication was supposed *not* to trigger subsequent ICMP packets to be sent. Notes Postel (1981*b*):

> The ICMP messages typically report errors in the processing of datagrams, to avoid the infinite regress of messages about messages etc., no ICMP messages are sent about ICMP messages. (p. 1)

302 (96). An Internet router in the initial network that a host resides at may control or reset to a proper value the IP source address field. However, there is no immediate benefit for the router from incurring the effort of doing so, other than acting for the 'common good' (and possibly irritating customers with faulty but innocent host configuration). As of 2009, the MIT ANA Spoofer project (http://spoofer.csail.mit.edu) find in a fairly large sample of probes that "31 % of clients are able to spoof an arbitrary, routable source address" and "77 % of clients otherwise unable to spoof can forge an address within their same /24 subnetwork" (Beverly et al. 2009, p. 357).

303 (96). Notes Pouzin (1973*a*) on the questionable benefit of error messages in an inter-network:

> Customarily PSNs send some error messages back to the source whenever they recognize conditions precluding the correct forwarding of a regular message.
>
> Even in the case of a single PSN, it is not clear whether this is actually useful. This is even more debatable in Catenet, as it could raise a tariff question about whom should be charged for diagnostics traffic. Furthermore, some precautions are necessary so that successive failures do not wind up in priming a message explosion. Finally, some standardization would be mandatory if they are to be any useful for end recipients. (p. 18)

304 (97). A statement along similar lines of reasoning can be found in Lampson (1983):

> Use hints to speed up normal execution. A hint, like a cache entry, is the saved result of some computation. It is different in

> two ways: it may be wrong, and it is not necessarily reached by an associative lookup. Because a hint may be wrong, there must be a way to check its correctness before taking any unrecoverable action. It is checked against the *truth*, information which must be correct, but which can be optimized for this purpose and need not be adequate for efficient execution. Like a cache entry, the purpose of a hint is to make the system run faster. Usually this means that it must be correct nearly all the time. (p. 43, emphasis in original)

305 (97). Notes Nagle (1984*a*):

> Implementations of Source Quench entirely within the IP layer are usually unsuccessful because IP lacks enough information to throttle a connection properly. Holding back acknowledges tends to produce retransmissions and thus unnecessary traffic. Holding back retransmissions may cause loss of a connection by a retransmission timeout. (p. 8)

306 (97). Note that following Jacobson's 1988 work on congestion avoidance and control (Jacobson 1988*b*; Jacobson 1988*a*) TCP gained such capabilities. But the problem, of course, remains the same to this day: A TCP that does *not* reduce its rate in spite of "being asked to" can be punished only if (access) routers police traffic, thus incurring the overhead of holding state information about ongoing traffic flows.

307 (97). The core problem with UDP throttling is that a typical process generating UDP data may long have terminated when the source quench signal is received. UDP is thus not only unreliable, but it also offers very little chance of managing rate control the way the connection-oriented and relatively long-lived TCP does (Stevens 2002, pp. 160 ff.). See also Robinson et al. (1990, pp. 78 ff.) for a general discussion of the problems of open-loop congestion control systems.

308 (98). Digression: Says Braden (1989):

> If a Source Quench message is received, the IP layer *must* report it to the transport layer (or ICMP processing). In general, the transport or application layer *should* implement a mechanism to respond to Source Quench for any protocol that can send a

> sequence of datagrams to the same destination and which can reasonably be expected to maintain enough state information to make this feasible. (p. 41, emphasis in original)

Plus:

> UDP *must* pass to the application layer all ICMP error messages that it receives from the IP layer. (p. 78, emphasis in original)

And:

> TCP *must* react to a Source Quench by slowing transmission on the connection. The *recommended* procedure is for a Source Quench to trigger a "slow start," as if a retransmission timeout had occurred. (p. 103, emphasis in original)

By 1995 the source quench mechanism was firmly seen to be more of a liability than an asset. Already, Braden and Postel (1987) were undecided on the value of sending such messages (p. 17). Baker et al. (1995) elaborated the case against source quench:

> When a router receives a packet beyond its storage capacity it must (by definition, not by decree) discard it or some other packet or packets. Which packet to discard is the subject of much study but, unfortunately, little agreement so far. The best wisdom to date suggests discarding a packet from the data stream most heavily using the link. However, a number of additional factors may be relevant, including the precedence of the traffic, active bandwidth reservation, and the complexity associated with selecting that packet. [. . .] ICMP Source Quench is a very weak mechanism, so it is not necessary for a router to send it, and host software should not use it exclusively as an indicator of congestion. (pp. 95 ff.)

Not only is there ambiguity about whether or not a router should send source quench messages in the first place; for security reasons alone most TCP/IP implementation disregard any such messages (Gont 2010, p. 17), as do most firewalls. While this is in violation of RFC 1122 (Braden 1989, "Requirements for Internet Hosts—Communication Layers"), it is arguably the most reasonable thing to do:

> Given today's security environment, it is inadvisable for hosts to act on indications provided by routers without careful consideration. (Aboba and IAB 2007, p. 30)

See also Gont (2010) for an in-depth discussion of security concerns regarding ICMP messages.

309 (98). In particular, the Arpanet became ever more of a bottleneck (Gardner 1986), and a somewhat erratically-behaved one at that (Jacobson 1987*b*, p. 11).

310 (98). The accounts here cited also comport with the Jacobson (1988*a*) statement about an October 1986 "series of 'congestion collapses'" (p. 314). But, see, of course, also the seminal description of congestion collapse by Nagle (1984*a*) as quoted in note 296.

311 (99). Digression: On the rationale for relying on packet losses rather than explicit signals:

> If packet loss is (almost) always due to congestion and if a timeout is (almost) always due to a lost packet, we have a good candidate for the "network is congested" signal. Particularly since this signal is delivered automatically by all existing networks, without special modification. (Jacobson 1988*a*, p. 319)

The mechanism devised by Jacobson has first been publicly discussed in 1987 at the 6th IETF meeting (Jacobson 1987*b*). It was further developed in Jacobson (1987*a*) and Jacobson (1988*c*), the latter of which explicitly draws upon earlier work of Jain et al. (1987) who had devised a congestion avoidance algorithm, already. The Jain et al. scheme relied on explicitly congestion marked packets rather than packet losses as a proxy for congestion. Floyd and Jacobson (1993) proposed using such a marking scheme for IP, too; and ECN for IP was later standardized (Ramakrishnan and Floyd 1999; Ramakrishnan et al. 2001). However, whilst ECN is still not widely used (Medina et al. 2005, pp. 40 f), largely due to its requiring intermediary routers to support the scheme (Sridharan et al. 2007; Thaler 2008), Jacobson's scheme based on packet dropping alone saw very rapid adoption and has been in use ever since, because (1) it was deceptively simple to implement, (2) did not require any changes to intermediary gateways, and (3) payed off right away for a host using it, without requiring other hosts to adopt the scheme simultaneously. As for the latter point, Jacobson (1987*a*) notes:

> These improvements [slow start and congestion avoidance] to TCP increased the throughput on a heavily loaded SATNET link from 70 bps to 1 kbps. (p. 15)

And, Partridge (2004) recalls:

> Actually the great thing about Van's patch was that the existing TCPs were so bad, that being the only one running Van's patch meant you got *better* performance. Only later did people figure out how to create unresponsive TCP's that were well-behaved enough they'd win in this fight. (emphasis in original)

DIGRESSION: Today, the economics of TCP well-behaved versus 'TCP unfriendly' protocols (or "non-responsive flows") have changed, given that "in environments of high statistical multiplexing, the delay and loss rate experienced by a flow are largely independent of its own sending rate" (Floyd 2000, p. 5). A dominant strategy for the individual flow vis à vis other flows (which is becoming increasingly popular with P2P and streaming applications) is thus not to cooperate with other flows by being TCP compatible:

> A growing proportion of Internet traffic comes from applications designed not to use congestion control at all, or worse, applications that add more forward error correction the more losses they experience. (Papadimitriou et al. 2009, p. 28)

Moreover, even perfectly well-behaved and benign TCP senders may be turned into sources of excess traffic by certain TCP receiver attacks (Savage et al. 1999*b*; Allman et al. 2009, p. 13).

All those qualifications notwithstanding, TCP slow start and congestion avoidance have to this day remained the central mechanisms to deal with congestion at the host layer.

312 (99). From ca. 1980 onwards gateways began to be referred to as "routers" See Haverty (2006) for a brief overview of the principal reasons behind the introduction of the term router in lieu of gateway.

313 (99). Note that a host is effectively a peer to the Internet routers; it may thus inject traffic at any rate permissible by the local networks it is attached to. While enforcing rate limits per host in the initial local network is trivial for an Internet router, there is very little it can do about congestion in downstream networks. Also, there are very few incentives in place today for Internet access providers to enforce a 'global fairness regime' by policing traffic into the access networks beyond what is necessary to manage their own network and stay within their immediate contractual obligations with other networks. Thus the only place that can ultimately control the traffic a router is subjected to is that very router itself.

314 (99). Framing the problem as one of "unwanted traffic" (versus 'wanted traffic') (Andersson et al. 2007)—a notion that can be traced to early laments about unsolicited and unwanted inbound traffic, both benign (Bressler 1972) and malicious (Postel 1975*b*)—may, in fact, not be the most meaningful exercise to begin with. For in a network with perfect accountability, payment mechanisms, and low transaction costs to these, malice and high utility (and thus cost for the immediate stakeholders to a high volume traffic causing congestion in a router or an end point) would simply collapse into one. Note Arkko et al. (2009):

> DDoS attacks can be considered as a disconnect between the ability to send traffic and being accountable for the congestion it causes. (p. 44)

And, Briscoe (2006) elaborates:

> A DDoS attack is just another innovative use of the Internet. In stopping DDoS, should we also stop VoIP? Fortunately, there is a huge difference in degree between the two. But, streaming video—hundreds of times more bandwidth than VoIP—and still not responding to congestion can be seriously anti-social and selfish, though probably inadvertently so. Where do we draw the line? Should we block streaming video? Should we block holographic cinema?
>
> Our answer is that we, the designers, should not draw the line. Instead the line should be drawn by the invisible hand of the market. If we had a properly functioning market, the network

> (supply-side) would attract enough capacity investment to adequately support video streaming if there was sufficient demand. But if any link became excessively congested, the internal price seen by the network would go stupidly high, automatically drawing the line at the right level. (p. 6, footnotes omitted, references omitted, emphasis omitted)

The crucial question is, of course, how to obtain accountability and marketability when the Internet was conceived without these items as intrinsic properties — as of 2010, IETF work is underway to resolve those issues (Conex WG). See also note 328 and accompanying text.

315 (99). When the IP protocol was originally defined it was thought to be useful to allow the end hosts to signal their "type of service" requirements to the networks (Postel et al. 1981, pp. 266 f.); but, due to the inherent credibility problem absent economic incentives to signal such requirements truthfully, few routers ever took note of those flags — hence the demise of the ToS field in the IP header. While the ToS field is still used inside ISPs for traffic differentiation purposes (Zhang et al. 2009, pp. 110 f.), it has never been a mechanism for signalling service requirements from end hosts to Internet gateways across administrative domains or trust boundaries more generally (Ramakrishnan et al. 2001, pp. 58 ff.).

A feasible way to solve this dilemma without having to introduce accounting and payment mechanisms in the Internet would be to frame the choice of service alternatives in terms of one between equivalent likes of which one could then choose some mixture — e. g., between low delay and high throughput. See Podlesny and Gorinsky (2008) for a recent proposal along those lines. However, as with any such proposals, there is always the question of whether deployment is beneficial enough for an individual ISPs to venture, or whether the combined benefits are large enough to warrant some concerted effort by a sufficient multitude of ISPs.

Digression: Note, as an instructive aside, that such a scheme had already featured in the Arpanet as part of a general priority scheme in the IMPs; allowing hosts to choose between a priority (low delay) and normal (high throughput) service (McQuillan et al. 1972, pp. 743 f.). IMPs amongst one another would also treat packets according to a priority scheme giving precedence to (1) management traffic over (2) priority packets over (3) normal packets over (4) retransmissions (McQuillan et al. 1972, pp. 744 f.). To quote from BBN (1978*c*):

> In view of the large number of channels, and the delay that is encountered on long lines, some packets may have to wait an inordinately long time for transmission. A one-character packet should not have to wait for several thousand-bit packets to be transmitted, multiplying by 10 or more the effective delay seen by the source. Therefore, the following transmission ordering scheme has been instituted: priority packets which have never been transmitted are sent first; next sent are any regular packets which have never been transmitted; finally, if there are no new packets to send, previously transmitted packets are periodically retransmitted even when there is a continuous stream of new traffic. (p. 9)

The complete priority order can be found in the "IMP to Modem Task" (summarized in BBN 1978*c*, p. 37) — internal control and management packets go first, then retransmissions, and only then the packet types listed in the above quote. Also, see p. 39 for the priority order in the "IMP to Host Task", which largely mirrors the IMP-IMP routines (control messages first, then priority messages, then normal messages, then retransmissions). Last, see pp. 99, 101 for the priority flag in the host message headers, and pp. 100, 102 for the priority flag in control message headers (always set). For a fine narrative description of the source-IMP-to-destination-IMP and IMP-IMP priority schemes see also McQuillan et al. (1972, pp. 743 ff.).

316 (100). As for fair queuing (Nagle 1985; Nagle 1986), Jacobson (1988*c*) argues that a simple random packet discard scheme (proper random, not just tail drop) might be more useful than any attempt at achieving elaborate per-flow fairness:

> I worry that fair-queuing requires the gateway to know something about the transport protocols (something I think we should avoid since there are several new transport protocols on the horizon and it will be a lot of work to keep gateway implementations current with the protocol mix) and fair queuing requires a lot of state in the gateways (something we should avoid to make the next generation packet switch — the state

> maintenance adds a lot to the packet processing time and the space used for end-to-end state could probably be better used as packet buffers or routing cache). (p. 14)

Stine (1988) also recommends random dropping over both tail drop (p. 22), and fair queuing (p. 23).

On a related note, even if a router had infinite processing capacity and speed, allowing it to distinguish between flows at an arbitrarily fine-grained level of granularity, it would be hard if not impossible to obtain a defendable notion of the 'fairness weights' to apply in the first place (Briscoe 2007*c*), which at least reduces its terminological appropriateness (Floyd and Allman 2008, p. 6).

317 (100). Recall from BBN (1978*c*, p. 4):

> The delay for a short message has been minimized by transmitting it to the destination immediately while keeping a copy in the source IMP. If there is space at the destination, it is accepted and passed on to a Host and a RFNM is returned; the source IMP discards the message when it receives the RFNM. If not, the message is discarded, a request for allocation is queued and, when space becomes available, the source IMP is notified that the message may now be retransmitted. Thus, no setup delay is incurred when storage is available at the destination. (p. 4)

The general reasoning behind this policy was that interactive terminal traffic is rarely larger than one packet (ca. 1000 bits), which makes the 'no larger than one packet' criterion a good test for determining whether the payload data requires low delays, as opposed to high throughput — regardless of any priority flag indications.

See also note 167 for the Arpanet resource reservation and flow control schemes; and note 315 on the priority orders in treating different kinds of data packets in the Arpanet.

318 (100). Digression: To quote from Mills (1988) on the precedence scheme in the NSFNET's Fuzzball routers:

> As the NSFNET Backbone has reached its capacity, various means have been incorporated to improve interactive service

> at the possible expense of deferable (file-transfer and mail) service. An experimental priority-queueing discipline has been established based on the precedence specification. Queues are serviced in order of priority, with FIFO service within each priority level. However, many implementations lack the ability to provide meaningful values and insert them in this field. Accordingly, the Fuzzball cheats gloriously by impuning a precedence value of one in case the field is zero and the datagram belongs to a TCP session involving the virtual-terminal Telnet protocol. [. . .] Customers of the NSFNET Backbone were thrilled when Telnet response dramatically improved after the new scheme was installed. (p. 119)

Regarding the 'secrecy' of the scheme Bohn et al. (1994) add:

> Because the backbone administrators did not have any way to provide an incentive to not use the highest priority, they did not publicize the priority-based treatment of traffic, and end users did thus not know it was possible to give high precedence to other applications [than certain interactive applications, specifically Telnet] (p. 2 in technical report version)

Mills (2004) offers another retrospect comment on the details of the scheme and the need to keep it secret:

> Steve Wolff of NSF and I had a nasty little secret we did not tell the NSFnet maintenance crew who could never keep a secret. I built in priority queueing and preemption in the fuzzball routers. The former wiretapped the telnet port and made it just below NTP on the priority scale. We put mail on the bottom just below ftp. A lot of telnet users stopped complaining because they thought we "fixed" the network.

The need for the prioritization scheme only disappeared when the NSFNET upgraded to T1 capacity leading to an "overabundance of bandwidth", and thus "the designers did not reintroduce the priority queuing for end-user traffic" (Bohn et al. 1994, p. 2).

However, dealing with basic fairness issues has remained an important issue, and a concern very much separate from congestion management at large. Mills (1988) reports that the Fuzzball routers implemented a basic version of AQM, aiming at "shooting the elephants" (to use a metaphor from Mills et al. 2004) so as to offer reasonable service to the 'mice':

> Every customer has equal claim to critical system resources, most importantly buffer space. In case of insufficient resources, the quench and preemption mechanisms operate to reduce the allocations of those customers claiming the most resources, so that the available resources will tend to be equally allocated among all customers. (p. 120)

Mills and Braun (1988) elaborate on the preemption scheme:

> When preemption is necessary, each output queue is scanned separately to find the customer with the largest number of 512-octet blocks. Then the queue with the largest number of such blocks is determined and the last buffer for the associated customer is preempted, even if the buffer preempted was the one just filled. In case of ties, the queue with the most packets transmitted since the last preemption is chosen. The entire process is repeated until sufficient buffer space is available for the input buffer request. (p. 194)

And, again, a recount from Mills (2004):

> The other thing was to shoot the elephants. When a new packet arrived and no buffer space was available, the output queues were scanned looking for the biggest elephant (total byte count on all queues from the same IP address) and killed its biggest packet. Gunshots continued until either the arriving packet got shot or there was enough room to save it. It all worked gangbusters and the poor ftpers never found out.

319 (100). In fact, many routers do not even implement packet drop algorithms beyond tail drop; likely because the overhead is simply not warranted by the added benefits of doing so.

To be sure, there is always the possibility of "flash crowds", sudden collective rushs of traffic due to certain external events that trigger surges of highly correlated application activity on the Internet resulting in well above average combined load. However, most of those events are predictable and effectively reduce to broadcast patterns which may easily be mitigated for in some controlled fashion, dissipating traffic by targeted CDN deployments.

Also, it should be noted that some evidence of traffic differentiation based on application type has been found for backbone ISPs. Without any claim to generality, the general picture emerging from one study seems to be that BGP and VoIP traffic tend to be favored over SMTP and P2P file sharing traffic, typically dependent on the total offered load, and considering HTTP to be served with some 'baseline service' (Zhang et al. 2009). This assessment is not surprising, especially given that typical router equipment today offers fairly trivial configuration options to filter the most common P2P applications and protocols by port number and apply some basic differentiation policies (e. g., setting a ToS value in the IP header) (Zhang et al. 2009, pp. 112 f.).

320 (101). Beverly et al. (2007) report on 'benign' blocking:

> For instance, the MIT network drops traffic destined for TCP ports 135 and 137-139, ports associated with Microsoft file sharing. With the same intent, but slightly different effect, Comcast residential broadband blocks the entire 135-139 port range. Interestingly, Comcast's policy results in the collateral blocking of port 136, assigned to the innocuous Profile naming service. The fact that MIT and other non-profit organizations block the Windows file sharing ports potentially provides justifiable evidence that Comcast's intentions in blocking the same ports are not abuses of market power. Indeed, here *the motivation for blocking is based upon operators' concerns for end-user security and privacy*. (footnotes omitted, emphasis added)

321 (101). Wireless networks typically exhibit much more pronounced loss rates and capacity constraints that may require substantial overprovisioning, depending on the scale of aggregation and relatedness of individual traffic spikes. In such cases congestion may be more prevalent, and packets may be lost much more frequently than in larger, wire-based networks.

322 (101). Just as it was reasonable to prioritize interactive terminal sessions over less delay-sensitive file transfers in the early NSFNET, it is reasonable today to prioritize interactive computer game traffic and voice traffic. This is especially useful given the high latencies often found in residential

broadband networks due to either contention or (more frequently) TDMA schemes in cable access networks (Dischinger et al. 2007, p. 54) Also, it has proven popular with some ISPs to 'boost' HTTP traffic and other short lived traffic by increasing the maximum allowable bandwidth per user for a brief period of, say, 1 second (Dischinger et al. 2007, p. 50).

323 (101). It is useful here to briefly discuss the most prominent 'network neutrality violation' to date, the 2007 high-profile Comcast incident in which they closed TCP connections by injecting forged RST packets, applying this scheme to BitTorrent uploads (without, however, affecting any of the ongoing downloads in a BitTorrent client) (Dischinger et al. 2008). Following the public outcry once the blocking became public in October 2007 (Soghoian 2007; Svensson 2007), Comcast was subject to intense scrutiny and suffered from extremely bad publicity on the whole issue. In response to the FCC memorandum opinion and order (FCC 2008) they disclosed details of the scheme (Zachem 2008*a*) and replaced it with a protocol agnostic scheme (Zachem 2008*b*; Peterson and Cooper 2009, pp. 6 f.) that has been in place ever since. See also http://networkmanagement.comcast.net.

It is fair to say that following the Comcast BitTorrent blocking incident such blunt measures cannot be found anymore. As of 2010 there is still some evidence of rate limiting BitTorrent applications; however, only a fraction of users is affected by such traffic shaping, and often only at certain peak traffic periods (Dischinger et al. 2010, pp. 415 f.).

324 (101). Indeed, just measuring traffic and discrimination patterns is a highly active area of current research; see (in addition to the sources already mentioned) Tariq et al. (2009) for a large scale passive measurement approach, and the MIT Internet Traffic Analysis Study (MITAS) project (http://mitas.csail.mit.edu) which aims at gathering traffic and congestion data in collaboration with major ISPs.

325 (101). Note that some loss of IP packets is always to be expected in the Internet, even though maximum rates are often throttled at either the server side or at the access network used by a client. Using loss rates of inter-PoP segments from the iPlane project at University of Washington (Madhyastha et al. 2006) from April 15, 2010, (http://iplane.cs.washington.edu/data/per_segment_loss_rate.txt), and calculating the arithmetic mean of the entire sample of 570,671 values with a small c++ program, we arrive at an average loss rate of 1.16 percent. Reducing the set to all values below

10 percent leaves a sample size of 552,871 and an average loss rate of 0.31 percent. Datasets from other days in that month give similar results. However, note that the iPlane samples cover the whole world; and RTTs and losses are generally much better in the U. S., Europe, Australia, and South America, than they are in other parts of the world (see, e. g., data and reports from the PingER project at University of Stanford, SLAC National Accelerator Laboratory, http://www-iepm.slac.stanford.edu/pinger).

326 (101). Technically speaking, "packet dropping and source back-off are two open-loop control systems" (Robinson et al. 1990, p. 80).

327 (101). Note that the cooperation here is not between end hosts and 'the network'. Rather, it is cooperation amongst end hosts at the transport layer, as it is manifested in the Jacobson congestion avoidance and control scheme, that is the critical ingredient here. For abiding by the "packet conversation principle" (Jacobson 1988*a*, p. 314) is not primarily in the interest of the Internet router; it is in the ultimate interest of the end hosts, lest they will see their performance become severely degraded by having to retransmit data over and over again.

328 (101). Briscoe (2007*c*) elaborates this notion and has put forward a detailed scheme to allow the pricing and accounting for "congestion volume" (Briscoe 2009) while keeping with the customary flat pricing for residential Internet access (Anania and Solomon 1997; Odlyzko 2001), only requiring special traffic policing boxes to be placed at the Internet fringes to monitor subscribers' traffic and prejudice packets beyond the allowed congestion volume. His work goes back to notes such as MacKie-Mason and Varian (1995), considering a market approach to the problem of congestion in theory; Clark (1995); Clark (1997*b*); Clark (1997*a*); Clark and Fang (1998), adding some technical elaboration and discussion; and, more intimately, to the work of Kelly (1997) and Kelly (2000), working out the mathematics for the incentives and pricing to obtain value maximization in a congestable Internet. (See also the references cited in Lehr and Weiss 1996*a*, p. 220, footnotes 2, 3.)

329 (102). See Briscoe (2006, pp. 11 ff.) for an in-depth discussion of the deployment incentives, noting that the potential to solve the problem of DDoS attacks may incentivize some providers and operating system vendors to move to the new scheme. However, thus far no deployment has taken place, and no Internet Standard has yet been finalized. Also, note

that it may not be enough to deploy a Re-ECN scheme in IP routers only; given the popularity of MPLS inside ISPs it may prove important (though not strictly necessary) to design a solution that takes MPLS into some account, too. Plus, operating system vendors would have to implement the scheme. And, most importantly, application level protocols would have to be designed so as to make meaningful use of the congestion feedback provided by the system.

330 (103). Note Clark et al. (2005*a*):

> The Internet was designed in simpler times, when the user community was smaller. It was reasonable to trust most of the users, and it was possible to track down and deal with misbehavior. It is clear today that the Internet, like the real world, includes a population of malicious users. Policing is difficult since the Internet crossed jurisdictional boundaries. War in cyberspace is a possibility, and terrorist manipulation of the Internet is likely. Greed is leading to a range of anti-social behavior, including spam, spyware and adware, and phishing. (p. 93)

331 (103). The typical argument against end-to-end solutions to the congestion problem is captured by Moors (2002):

> [C]ongestion control is not amenable to end-to-end implementation for the following reasons: First, like routing, congestion is a phenomenon of the network, and since multiple endpoints share the network, it is the network that is responsible for isolating endpoints that offer excessive traffic so that they do not interfere with the ability of the network to provide its service to other endpoints. Second, it is naive in today's commercial Internet to expect endpoints to act altruistically, sacrificing the performance that they receive from the network in order to help the network limit congestion. (pp. 1218 f.)

However, this take fails to appreciate that hosts, not the network. are the proper parties to deal with congestion in a way compatible to economic utility considerations or even basic fairness concerns.

DIGRESSION: An aside on the 'tragedy of the commons' notion: While the term has been coined by Hardin (1968)—"[f]reedom in a commons brings ruin to all" (p. 1244)—, the notion itself may be traced back much longer. Particularly, it had been developed in proper economics terms by Demsetz (1967) who offers a sound analysis of the problem in transaction costs and incentive terms (pp. 354 ff.) concluding:

> Communal property results in great externalities. The full costs of the activities of an owner of a communal property right are not borne directly by him, nor can they be called to his attention easily by the willingness of others to pay him an appropriate sum. Communal property rules out a "pay-to-use-the-property" system and high negotiation and policing costs make ineffective a "pay-him-not-to-use-the-property" system. (p. 355)

Krier (1992) valuably observes that many of the remedies proposed ever since, particularly those advocating property and private control in the resources at hand (Demsetz 1967; Hardin 1968; Hardin 1974), suffer from precisely the problem that gave rise to the dilemma in the first place: the infeasibility of coordinating of a large community. Despite all headway toward understanding and managing commons problems so as to escape the trap of rational actors in prisoners' dilemma type situations (Ostrom 1990; Ostrom 2005) and the marked shift in economics toward psychology and biology (Bowles 2004), there is no simple overall theory about how to approach such issues consistently that goes much beyond the general design principles put forward by Ostrom (1990, p. 90). The current consensus in large parts of the debate is that sustainable solutions can be achieved with community governance and punishment of defectors (Bowles 2004).

Conclusion of Part II

332 (105). We should like to mention that we have gone to great lengths to base all of the statements made in the course of this part on solid historical evidence from primary literature resources and personal communication with persons involved with the matters at the time. Hence the many endnote asides in eloborate support and copious development of points made in the main text. See also note 11 and accompanying textfor a detailed discussion of our methodology.

Revisiting the Classic End-to-End Arguments

333 (111). RFCs 791 and 793 (Internet Protocol and TCP) have been in place since 1981; RFC 1122 (Requirements for Internet Hosts—Communication Layers) since 1989; and RFC 1812 (Requirements for IP Version 4 Routers) since 1995.

334 (113). The wealth of research on transport layer issues subsequent to the introduction of TCP offers impressive testament to its (potential) limitations.

335 (113). There may be other parameters that can be modified by end-to-end measures alone. But, reliability is the only one of the trinity of reliability, throughput, and delay that can be arbitrarily improved, no matter how dismal the performance of the underlying networks. See section 5.1 for some elaboration of this point.

336 (113). See section 5.1 for the history of packet speech starting in the early 1970s.

337 (114). Recall the history of the Internet Stream Protocol (ST) that aimed at offering a more complete common service at the inter-network level, but failed to gain sufficient traction—see note 249 and accompanying text.

338 (114). Note that this is so even though all the functions could be implemented in the end systems.

339 (114). Neither TCP nor NCP offer through their service interface any departure from the virtual circuit service between two fixed end points. As for UDP, it offers only the unreliable plain message service, again with no variation in the service to be obtained.

340 (115). We are basing this conclusion on both the wording found in Saltzer et al. (1984) and the prominence of what may be named the 'TCP/IP, UDP/IP version' of the end-to-end arguments.

341 (115). Saltzer et al. (1984) acknowledge that TCP performance will drop markedly once a certain packet loss threshold is exceeded.

On a related note, see the considerations in BBN (1974*d*) as cited in our note 70 and accompanying text at section 2.5, page 25 about the general intuition that a multitude of service levels in a network need not necessarily prejudice applications with very limited requirements, a reasoning that may as well be applied to the 'supernetwork' that is today's Internet.

342 (115). It is only fair to note that such argument may be leveled at most

any principle safe the most adamant ones; yet it is also true that end-to-end arguments have necessarily been very explicit about their limitations, particularly the performance trade-off that virtually always apply.

343 (115). Consider, on a related note, the fitting point about government provided infrastructures made by Hayek (1973):

> Where government is concerned with providing particular services, most of them of the kind which have recently come to be described as the "infrastructure" of the economic system, the fact that such services will often aim at particular effects raises difficult problems. [. . .] The crucial point has been well expressed by the statement that there can be no "equality before a measure" as there is equality before the law. What is meant by this is that most measures of this sort will be 'aimed', in the sense that, although their effects cannot be confined to those who are prepared to pay for the services provided by them, they will yet benefit only some more or less clearly discernible group and not all citizens equally. Probably most of the services rendered by government, other than the enforcement of just conduct, are of this sort. (p. 139, footnotes omitted)

344 (116). Also, recall the notion of Turing tarpits — "in which everything is possible but nothing of interest is easy." (Perlis 1982, p. 10).

345 (116). Note Postel et al. (1981):

> There are several issues related to more flexible addressing that the current IP does not deal with. One case is a host with two (or more) internet addresses, either on one network or even on different networks. Sometimes this serves to distinguish between logically separate hosts, but in other cases it is desirable to consider both addresses the "same place" as far as higher level protocols are concerned. It is not clear how a gateway could know when or how to route messages sent to one address to another address (e. g. if the first address was unreachable). A particularly difficult example of this problem is a mobile packet radio which moves from one network to another while trying to maintain unbroken communication. (p. 270)

Cerf and Cain (1983), too, acknowledge the problem of mobility and multihoming with TCP as one of the "loose ends" of the existing Internet architecture left for future evolution:

> The addressing structure of the Internet Protocol assigns host addresses on a hierarchical (i. e., relative) basis, as a function of the network to which the host is attached. The TCP protocol depends upon the IP network and host addresses for part of its connection identifiers; the full identifiers include port numbers assigned by the TCP level and carried in its header. If a host were to move from one net to another (e. g., via an airborne packet radio), its network (and host) addresses would change and this would affect the connection identifiers used by the TCP to maintain state information. In effect, roving hosts require some means of dynamically re-defining TCP connection identifiers. This is rather like a problem called "dynamic reconnection" which has plagued network designers since the inception of the Arpanet project in 1968. The crux of the problem lies in the use of the IP network and host addresses by the TCP level of protocol. The DoD Internet Model accommodates the re-binding of host names to internetwork addresses through the use of the distributed name server protocol, however use of this mechanism requires that the TCP connections be broken and re-established. (pp. 314 ff.)

346 (117). Again, TCP offers a good illustration of this point, with its semantics tied to the physical network interface IDs (the IP addresses).

347 (117). To briefly elaborate, a design whose set of common core functions are too minimal will foreclose certain applications, and so will a design that is too elaborate. A second relevant continuum of concerns is that of performance versus cost — while it is largely true that "[g]etting bandwidth out all the way to the user is something we can do without loss of generality [. . .] [and] anything else you do on the network may later come back to bite you because of profound uncertainty about what is happening" (M. Shaw, in Clark et al. 1998, p. 35), it is also true that a higher performance Internet affects the balance of applications, may trigger unexpected side effects by violating previous tacit assumptions in parts of

the system, and, last not least, is inevitably more expensive than a lower performance network, thus prejudicing applications with very low service requirements.

348 (118). The prospect of 'pervasive computing' with very simple 'end' devices adds to these considerations, for their limitations in virtually all engineering aspects (most notably computing power and battery life) drastically increase their attack tolerance, thus very much necessitating the interposition of proxies that assume substantial functionalities on behalf of such devices; see Briscoe (2004).

349 (118). Note that the 'non-zero percentage' criterion is, strictly speaking, worthless; for IP has no notion of time-outs or acknowledgments, and higher level time-outs below infinity may — given long enough round-trip times — cause imprudent data losses. Thus even a system with zero transmission rates theoretically qualifies as part of the Internet.

350 (119). Without any performance criterion there would be no line between the Internet, on the one hand; and postal mail (e. g., mail art, cf. Gangadharan 2009) and pigeons (Waitzman 1990), on the other. Quarterman and Carl-Mitchel (1996) put it:

> [I]f *being part of a community of discussion* was enough, we would have to also include anyone with a fax machine or a telephone. [. . .] With edges so vague, what would be the point in calling anything the Internet? We choose to stick with a definition of the Internet as requiring the *interactive services*. (p. 6, emphasis added)

Note that the line defining the limits of the Internet is likely to shift along with the dynamics of the ecosystem of products and stakeholders in the Internet. See also Kiousis (2002) and Rafaeli (1988) for detailed elaborations of the notion of interactivity as an attribute of communication processes.

351 (119). Digression: Note Clark et al. (2004) about the link layer requirements in the existing Internet:

> [T]he phrase "minimum assumptions" does not mean no assumptions. At the minimum, a subnet technology used in the Internet must support the delivery of packets, i. e., it must carry

> a byte stream and support synchronization of bytes and packets. In fact, the current Internet architecture makes additional demands on the subnet, for example:
>
> - TCP performs badly if the subnet packet loss exceeds a few percent; the solution has been to enhance the underlying subnet reliability when needed.
> - The requirement for QoS in the Internet [RFC 1633] implies QoS mechanisms within subnets.
> - Subnet technology is allowed to be sufficiently packet-aware to "mess" with packets, e. g., to lose data on packet boundaries, or to reorder packets.
> - The subnet must provide some mechanism to map IP addresses into link-layer addresses, e. g., the Address Resolution Protocol (ARP).
>
> (p. 68)

In fact, they note that the set of requirements could safely be extended given the commanding dominance of the Internet:

> [W]e are [now] in a position to ask that new subnet technologies be tailored to the Internet's needs [rather than the other way around]. This would mean allowing a future Internet to operate over highly diverse technologies while taking advantage of enhanced link-layer functionality where it exists. This would require a careful definition of desirable link layer enhancements; for example, these might include: congestion indication, QoS, self-characterization of performance parameters, or context setup. (p. 73)

352 (119). The full quote from Clark et al. (1991):

> As the Internet has grown and the technology on which it is based has gained widespread commercial acceptance, the sense of what it means for a system to be "on the Internet" has changed, to include:
>
> - Any system that has partial IP connectivity, restricted by policy filters.

- Any system that runs the TCP/IP protocol suite, whether or not it is actually accessible from other parts of the Internet.
- Any system that can exchange RFC-822 mail, without the intervention of mail gateways or the transformation of mail objects.
- Any system with e-mail connectivity to the Internet, whether or not a mail gateway or mail object transformation is required.

These definitions of "the Internet", are still based on the original concept of connectivity, just "moving up the stack". (p. 10)

353 (119). It has become very much customary to speak of a "core Internet" and a "consumer Internet" (Quarterman and Carl-Mitchel 1996), the main distinction between the two notions being that in the core Internet there are "supplier-capable computers (not firewalled)", and in the consumer Internet there are only "consumer-capable computers (firewalled)" (pp. 3 f.). Along those lines, the current mission statement for the IETF (Alvestrand 2004) defines the Internet as:

> A large, heterogeneous collection of interconnected systems that can be used for communication of many different types between any interested parties connected to it. The term includes both the "core Internet" (ISP networks) and "edge Internet" (corporate and private networks, often connected via firewalls, NAT boxes, application layer gateways and similar devices). (p. 2)

See also Klensin (2005) for another recent elaboration of the various 'grades' of Internet connectivity found in today's access networks.

	Core internet	Consumer internet
"Up the stack"	Servers, app gateways	Web browsers, email clients
IP only	Interconnected IP routers	Firewalled/NAT IP systems

Figure N.9: Conceptual dimensions to the Internet

354 (120). Aside from the practical work toward the Domain Name System (DNS) (Mockapetris 1983; Mockapetris 1987*a*; Mockapetris 1987*b*), there has been some theoretical work about the proper understanding of bindings between names, addresses, network attachment points, and routes (nost notably Saltzer 1993*b*, but see also Shoch 1978*b*; D. Cohen 1978*a*; D. Cohen 1978*b*; Clark 1982*d*). We refrain here from elaborating the subject of DNS in further detail, but see Stallings (2007, pp. 774 ff.); Peterson and Davie (2007, pp. 657 ff.) for recent descriptions.

355 (120). See Quarterman and Hoskins (1986, pp. 939) and Quarterman (1990, pp. 217 ff.) for a brief introduction to the subtleties of sending email across email gateways in the 1980s.

356 (120). See our pages 129 f. for a brief elaboration of the routing functions found in the Internet.

357 (120). See note 361 for a brief consideration of caching in the context of the WWW application.

358 (121). As an aside, to quote from Perlis (1982), "[o]ne man's constant is another man's variable" (p. 7).

359 (121). Digression: Note, as an aside, that we have not included in our list the manipulation of payload data along the way between two end points on one or both of their behalf or consent. While there has been some work on specifying an architecture that would allow for such application level intermediary functions (Open Pluggable Edge Services, or OPES—Barbir et al. 2004; see also http://tools.ietf.org/wg/opes/ for an overview), the whole notion of introducing or explicitly catering for entities that take over potentially unbounded content and application specific functions from the end nodes proper has been met with considerable and not always rational suspicion by many observers (see IAB 2002, plus a comment by Clark and Blumenthal 2007, p. 19) and has turned into something of a dead end with neither any significant practical adoption nor sufficient interest in the industry to pursue the OPES work any further (Hofmann and Beaumont 2007, p. 73).

360 (121). The asynchronous nature of email makes intermediate persistent storage a trivial requirement. Email servers thus featured prominently in the overall application design as it emerged from the 1970s to the 1980s (see SMTP, Postel 1982*b*). Generally speaking, an email user may choose which server(s) to rely on for email messages destined to themselves; in

fact, they may run a server at their own computer. Also, users typically advertise their mail servers via DNS MX records. Nowadays, the overwhelming majority of email users subscribes to web based email services by specialized email providers who manage all the intricacies of email management, often including the filtering of spam, on behalf of the user. Delegation of control may thus range from none at all to virtually complete. See also Clark and Blumenthal (2007, pp. 5 f.) for a brief discussion.

361 (121). The World Wide Web started out as an end based application concerned with the dissemination of content in a way that was more intuitive and accessible than the previous Telnet, FTP, and Gopher applications (Berners-Lee 1989; Berners-Lee and Fischetti 1999). In particular, while instituting a strict star topology communication approach for every web server hosting some web content, it allowed for easy logical 'hyperlinking' to other such servers, so that a web client would in effect be forwarded to other servers in a seamlessly integrated fashion. The whole system does not maintain any intrinsic state about the hyperlinked structure other than forward links between two pieces of web content, and is thus highly robust to errors or disruptions. In a sense, the WWW may be considered the application layer equivalent to best effort IP packet switching (Dam 2009), especially given that very little of the conceivable elaboration in the design of an optimal distributed system of hyperlinked data (see Saltzer 1993*a* for an overview) have even remotely come to pass (Nelson 2008).

Largely due to the scalability problems with the initial star topology client/server communication model, HTTP caches (as well as caching proxies and surrogates) have been featuring prominently in the WWW (see, e. g., Blumenthal and Clark 2001, p. 87). While reducing "semantic transparency", they have markedly improved "performance, availability, and disconnected operation" (Fielding et al. 1999, p. 74). As in the case of email, while end users may generally choose not to make use of any caches they consider untrustworthy or feel otherwise uncomfortable with, they may as well choose to trade off semantic end-to-end transparency with concerns about performance and cost in general. (See also the discussion in Cooper et al. 2001.) On a related note, consider the various general application level services beyond caches that have emerged to further augment applications such as WWW and email—e. g., anonymizing message forwarders and content filters (see, e. g., Blumenthal and Clark

2001, p. 86).

362 (121). Google has over the last 10 years come to assume an increasingly pivotal position not only in Web search but also in a host of other respects, with countless services ranging from basic ones such as DNS and email to more elaborate ones such as advertising and Web based productivity applications. To many Internet users today Google *is* the Internet — an interpretation not actually too inaccurate, for Google has come not only to dominate much of the application level sphere of the Internet, it has also steadily increased its global footprint by collocating its servers with major ISPs, running a number of large data centers themselves, and even acquiring physical communication lines so as to sidestep data carriers. As of 2003 it stored "dozens of copies of the Web across its clusters", already (Barroso et al. 2003, p. 24), a figure that has likely increased since then, given the growth of YouTube (a division of Google) alone.

363 (121). Akamai is probably the example par excellence for higher level general purpose intermediary structures in between application end points. Not only do they offer routing services — improving significantly on the substantial inefficiencies in 'normal' routing (Savage et al. 1999*a*, pp. 51 f.) —, they also provide caching, content distribution, and application hosting services, all of which combine to a value added service that has come to take over a comfortable double digit percentage of the world's 'Web' traffic. Clark and Blumenthal (2007) comment:

> Today, much Web content is not delivered to the ultimate recipient directly from the Web server belonging to the original creator, but via a content delivery network (CDN) — a collection of servers that cache the content and deliver it on demand. This, like email, has no end-to-end confirmation of correct delivery. Is this design being careful? Is it trustworthy? Commercial CDNs such as Akamai depend on their reputation as a reliable and trustworthy provider. There are no features built into the Web standards that assure that they are reliable, but only the discipline of the competitive marketplace. If they were not reliable and trustworthy, they would go out of business. So they build highly reliable systems, the content creators trust them, and the result is a more efficient overall system. (p. 6)

See also our notes 387 and 388 for further Akamai related considerations.

On a related note, it is apt here to mention the recent efforts in "content networking" (Jacobson et al. 2009; Jacobson 2006) which depart from the received notion of connections between sources and destinations, replacing it with the notion of "networking named content". Unlike the Akamai system, a widespread adoption of such a scheme would be potentially more encompassing and inclusive, bringing about a more competitive CDN landscape. However, no dedicated IETF work has yet been instituted that would allow a broader constituency of stakeholders to take on a more active role in the development of the technology.

364 (121). Both standard RTP/SIP telephony (Rosenberg et al. 2002; Schulzrinne et al. 2003; Rosenberg 2009) and the proprietary Skype application typically go along with a distributed application structure involving more or less transparent intermediary servers for various application specific purposes ranging from NAT traversing to higher value intermediary services such as interconnecting to POTS and billing.

365 (121). We have discussed above the intrinsic need of intermediate storage for email given that destinations may not be constantly available for delivery. It is for much the same reason that email clients typically 'pull' their emails off a remote POP or IMAP server, rather than have servers signal the availability of new emails to the user — the server may simply not know the current address of a user in the first place. While polling a mail server once every few minutes with a significant risk of not finding any new messages is usually a fairly low overhead operation, it may become a sizable cost factor in mobile contexts. RIM's BlackBerry was the first 'push' email system that delivered emails to mobile clients without requiring them to constantly poll an email server or keep an open connection to any server. To this end the system extends the classic email application by an ALG (the BlackBerry Internet Service, or, as a more elaborate version, the BlackBerry Enterprise Server) that connects the Internet (as in IP) with the wireless mobile phone network that a registered BlackBerry device is attached to. The crucial point here is that the 'wireless half' of the gateway knows the current address of a BlackBerry device and may thus deliver any new email straight away (or inform the device about new emails, depending on the specific configuration of the account), rather than have the device poll the server (potentially in vain). While the push function-

ality of RIM's BlackBerry email system has been somewhat original, it is similar to earlier email gateways in so far as it extends the scope of the email system at large across the narrower borders of the Internet proper by using email level gateways. (See http://docs.blackberry.com/en/ for current documentation of BlackBerry email.)

366 (122). To quote more copiously:

> [T]here remains the question of when a global agreement is really an agreement, and when it is the illusion of agreement. An example from the Internet might be the initial assumption that the Internet was based on the global agreement that there was a single global address space. It was thought that this agreement was important, and one of the basic tenets of the stable IP platform, but then Network Address Translation devices were introduced, and the Internet survived. Some would say that because NAT devices impair certain classes of applications (in particular, passive servers located behind NAT devices), we should view NATs (and the loss of global addresses) as a significant violation of the stable architecture. However, if the Internet was equipped with a protocol that allowed state to be installed dynamically in NAT devices (perhaps an example of the theory of the building block), the Internet could support essentially all the applications it did in the era of global addresses. [...] Clever reconceptualization may allow what was seen as a global agreement to be set aside with no loss of power. (Clark 2009*a*, p. 10)

And, on a very much related note, Clark (2009*e*) argues:

> NAT boxes are a wonderful example of how one can disrupt two of the most fundamental assumptions of the original Internet and still have enough functions mostly work that we accept the compromise. The assumptions of the original Internet were that there was a single, global address space, and there was no per-flow state in forwarding elements. NAT boxes, of course, have per-flow state [maintained by various "tricks"]. However, it is easy to imagine that if there were some scheme to allow end-nodes to set up state along the path to them, it would be

> straight-forward to manage the full range of forwarding tasks done by NAT boxes. (p. 8)

And:

> [M]ostly, the Internet continues to work, even with NAT boxes, VPNs, and private address spaces, because the consequences of messing with addresses are restricted to regions within which there is agreement to assign a common meaning to those addresses. Those self-consistent regions need not be global. (pp. 1 f.)

Arguably, NATs are, in fact, an entirely reasonable way of decentralizing and thus flexibilizing the otherwise highly centralized and strict IP address management scheme—they distribute a potentially arbitrary number of 'peer' inter-network scopes, leaving uniqueness of addressing scope to a conceptually higher layer global name space, or to the ad-hoc formation of unique 'super paths' across such NATs. Notes Hain (2000):

> Breaking the semantic overload of the IP address will force applications to find a more appropriate mechanism for endpoint identification and discourage carrying the locator in the data stream. (p. 10)

367 (122). See note 355.

368 (122). Consider the instructive case of DNS—see notes 354 and 393.

369 (122). We are not arguing that each and every application necessarily develops toward such structure of elaborate distributiveness and arbitrary cascadability, thus reducing the conceptual role of application level end points in the first place. But it bears noting that, particularly in the realm of content distribution (which is undoubtedly one of the core uses of the Internet), the application level structure is often highly malleable so as to flexibly bridge arbitrary 'user level' end points. See also in this respect the rise of CDNs which very much anticipate many of the notions lately raised by Jacobson about content centric networking (see, e. g., Jacobson et al. 2009); plus see filesharing applications which are typically designed in a symmetric fashion such that any 'end' is also a potential intermediary node for third parties. On a related note, see also the brief comment about "application design patterns" in Clark (2009*f*, p. 42).

370 (122). Schewick (2004) put forward an elaborate attempt to articulate and defend a "broad version" of the end-to-end arguments that would imply a very strict prohibition of functions 'in' the network as opposed to in the end points. Of course, the origination end-to-end arguments articulation by (Saltzer et al. 1984) does not support such interpretation, and neither do more recent statements by any of the three authors. We have already quoted Clark and Blumenthal (2007) at our page 39 who argue that such "construction by analogy may be nonsense". Also, Reed (2009*a*) notes that "[in] the original paper, there is no claim whatever that says either: (1) that all functions should be done at the edges, [. . .][or] (2) that one should never include optimizations of functions that must (to be correct) be done at the edges, in the network". And, as for Saltzer, his most recent tome (Saltzer and Kaashoek 2009) offers no indication for the merit of a dogmatic interpretation of the end-to-end arguments as a principle of sorts, either:

> The end-to-end argument can be applied to a variety of system design issues in addition to network design. It does not provide an absolute decision technique, but rather a useful argument that should be weighed against other arguments in deciding where to place function. (p. 7-31)

Toward a Systematic Analysis

371 (125). See Hayek (1973).

372 (125). See Alexander (1979).

373 (125). Denning (2003) considers "the title of a story" that seeks "to make simple the complex history of a complex area" to be the defining moment for many good computer science engineering principles (p. 17). Similarly, in a variation of the classic Wittgenstein theme, Alexander (1979) notes about architectural principles:

> The search for a name is a fundamental part of the process of inventing or discovering a pattern. So long as a pattern has a weak name, it means that it is not a clear concept, and you cannot tell me to make "one". (p. 267)

374 (127). Clark et al. (2004, pp. 31) argue that lack of end user control over routing may be unfortunate in so far as there is next to no incentive for intermediate ISPs to offer QoS and other service enhancements since customers would have no convenient means to monitor, let alone control, the routes their traffic takes. Neither do today's routers implement any of IPv4's optional source routing facilities, nor is there a control plane that gives end points the relevant information about available paths and their properties. The only choice that they have is the residential ISP they connect to. Beyond that, it is largely infeasible to affect the route one's packets take through the network towards their eventual destination. Notes Yang (2003):

> If the consumer could pick the routes his packets took, this might entice some providers to enter the market with a QoS offering, and a set of ISPs might in time team up to make this widely available. But there is no motivation to offer such a service today, since the consumer has no way to get it. So one can speculate that lack of competition in the form of user-selected routes is one cause of stagnation in Internet services today. (p. 302)

Overlay alternatives by third parties (such as Akamai) have their own inefficiencies; again, Yang (2003) notes:

> The limitation of the overlay networks is that they are not ubiquitous. Only nodes on the overlay network can control their paths by tunneling traffic through other nodes on the overlay network. It is unlikely that that overlay networks can scale up to include every user on the Internet. Besides its limited scope, an overlay architecture is less efficient than source routing. An overlay path may traverse duplicate physical links. (p. 304)

375 (127). See, e.g., Yang (2003); Feamster et al. (2004); Lakshminarayana et al. (2006).

376 (127). See section 6.1, pages 114 f.

377 (128). We have argued in section 6.2 that any function beyond the most trivial datagram forwarding is inevitably related in non-orthogonal ways to the ultimate end points of the network.

378 (129). It is apt here to repeat from our pages 93 f. the Postel (1978*c*) quote:

> [T]he gateways must have the least possible knowledge of end-to-end protocols. (p. 5)

379 (129). Note that routing, much like fragmentation and congestion control, went through an evolution from 'original design' to a markedly different 'eventual practice'. In 1977 source routing was still considered a reasonably viable solution to the inter-network routing problem (Sunshine 1977*b*); and is, in fact, still part of the IPv4 set of options (Postel 1981*d*). However, it has since faded to obliteration — see our note 381.

380 (129). While random routing is a possible approach, it is rarely an efficient one — see note 119 for some pertinent considerations by Kleinrock (1964).

381 (130). It is conceivable to choose paths based on static information and prior computation — possibly even information imposed on the network at runtime. However, it is generally not prudent in today's Internet to assume a static connectivity graph, making such an approach a poor choice for any stable routing strategy. (This is notwithstanding the fact that today's routers typically select but a single path to any given destination; see, e. g., Savage et al. 1999*a*, p. 52.)

Digression: See also Sunshine (1977*b*) and Sunshine (1977*a*, pp. 181 f.) for an early discussion of the trade-offs in source routing. Sunshine (1977*a*) remarks on benefits from source routing:

> Source routing eliminates the need for global agreement on network names, since the name of each destination becomes equivalent to a path specification for reaching the destination node. This simplifies addition of new networks, or replacement of a single Host by a network, because the new nodes may be addressed by adding one more address element to existing path specifications. [. . .]
>
> Source routing is most appropriate where greater source participation in route selection and non-optimal routing are acceptable in order to simplify routing at intermediate nodes or to allow more general addressing. (p. 182)

As Sunshine acknowledges (p. 182), the problem to such primacy of routes are legion — ranging from the sheer cost of administration to the lack of robustness from effectively allowing addresses to collapse into routes (thus reducing the very role of topological addresses distinct from the actual routing). Source routing has thus remained a limitedly viable option, and one that has never seen any noticable deployment across Internet providers, despite its potential usefulness as a means of decentralizing interconnection and enabling ad-hoc arrangements without having to involve the Internet at large (Postel et al. 1981, pp. 269 f.).

A brief elaboration on the early history of source routing in the Internet: It was first mentioned as one of several open "technical points" in Postel (1978*c*):

> [I]n some cases the sender may wish or need to specify the route to be traversed through the internetwork system rather than the address of the destination. Current plans call for an option to be developed to carry such information. (p. 8)

The same statement carried over verbatim to Postel (1978*d*, p. 8), but was left undealt with for the time being (Postel 1977*d*, p. 10) getting people in the ARPA sponsored Internet Meetings increasingly concerned about whether there would be any progress on the issue at all (Postel 1979*b*, p. 15). Eventually, the IP Version 4 specification (Postel 1979*a*) came to include a "source routing option" along with the following description:

> The source routing option provides a means for the source of an internet datagram to supply routing information to be used by the gateways in forwarding the datagram to the destination. A source route is composed of a series of internet addresses. The pointer is initially zero, which indicates the first octet of the source route. The segment is routed to address in the source route indicated by the pointer. As that internet module the pointer is advanced to the next address in the source route. This routing and pointer advancing is repeated until the source address is exhausted. At that point the destination may have been reached, if not, the protocol module must attempt to route the packet to the destination in the destination address field by the ordinary routing procedure. (pp. 14 f.)

However, even though Vinton Cerf "expected all gateways to process the source routing options" (Postel 1979*b*, p. 15) and the source routing option has remained part of the Internet Protocol standard ever since, it is plausible to speculate that source routing *never* saw any appreciable coherent implementation in the Internet gateways at the time, much less in today's Internet routers. Cohen and Postel (1979) discuss some of the pertinent issues in the proper design of a robust (and incrementally deployable) source routing scheme—pointing to the intricacies of dealing with legacy gateways and the recording of return routes. While Cohen and Postel come up with an elaborate scheme (that is essentially still part of today's Internet Protocol) based on gateways continuously replacing the destination address field proper with the next hop from the source routing string provided as an option field, thus allowing source routed messages to "pass through intermediate gateways and nodes which are not capable of handling source routing" (p. 1), the cost of even the moderate complexity implied by the scheme appear not to have been offset by its vague benefits.

382 (130). As an aside, the nodes could also flood the entire Internet with their connectivity data; but that would, of course, be truly silly if not downright stupid.

383 (130). See note 74, and Clark (2009*e*) for further elaboration.

384 (131). It is no coincidence that ICMP, the protocol designed for passing control information from Internet routers to end hosts, is nowadays almost as useless as are the IP options (designed to pass control information from the end hosts to the routers). ICMP packets not already filtered by a typical firewall are often disregarded by the end hosts due to security concerns alone. We have already pointed to some of the reliability issues inherent in the whole notion of ICMP type feedbacks (pages 96 f.); and it is instructive to note that virtually the only ICMP message that has remained useful to this day is the "destination unreachable" one—the very one which signals that there is no end host peer to communicate in the first place. In all other cases the net benefits from 'router-to-end' communication are no larger than some according end-to-end mechanisms; or, where there is no such pendant, the router signal may be so unreliable or untrustworthy that there is no average benefit to begin with.

385 (131). As an aside, the notion of focal points (as in game theory, see Schelling 1957) comes to mind here and adds useful explanation to the observation of the perversion and demise of explicit interfaces. The crucial point is that such implicit focal points may also feature prominently

when there are mechanisms for explicit bargaining:

> [S]ince even much so-called "explicit" bargaining includes maneuver, indirect communication, jockeying for position, or speaking to be overheard, or is confused by a multitude of participants and divergent interests, the need for convergent expectations and the role of signals that have the power to co-ordinate expectations may be powerful. (Schelling 1957, p. 32)

For a discussion of the notion of focal points see also Dixit and Nalebuff (1991, pp. 250 ff).

386 (131). The success of any such effort critically hinges on the ubiquity of the routing agents (see also Yang 2003, p. 304), which is inherently limited to the gateway level virtual network (outside of the local intra-ISP routing). Lakshminarayana et al. (2006, p. 5) suggest that (as of 2006) the number of relevant 'virtual links' that would have to be managed in order to reasonably deal with the entire Internet topology and available routes might be as low as 18,000.

387 (131). The obvious example that comes to mind as of the year 2010 is that of Akamai, but similar efforts have been in the making by large players in the content industry — most notably Amazon and Google. See Clark et al. (2005*b*) for a comprehensive discussion of overlay networks in general. There has also been some work on arriving at some standard notion of interdomain routing so as to help create a competitive 'routing service industry' on behalf of end users (Feamster et al. 2004; Lakshminarayana et al. 2006). Most of that work has, however, remained largely on the theoretical side, not least because "the providers and their suppliers had the economic incentive to drive the engineering and standardization of BGP, and there was no corresponding economic drive to tilt the playing field toward users control of policies [e. g., the Clark 1989 scheme]" (Clark et al. 2005*c*).

388 (132). It is instructive to note that Akamai (or any other CDN for that matter) typically contracts not with the end users at the receive side of Internet content, but with the sending side — those content providers large enough to improve their offerings by delegating the task of 'getting the content to the consumers as efficiently as possible' to a specialized third party. This is an example of a two-sided market structure (Tirole and Rochet 2003)

(see also Hagiu 2007; Hagiu and Lee 2007; Hagiu and Jullien 2007), in which the intermediary party interfaces with content providers on the one hand, and content consumers on the other hand, facing a trade-off about whom to charge for the services it renders to both. Clearly, contracting with providers who are typically the larger entities is far more efficient than contracting with the end users in the terminating eyeball networks. (See also note 363 for a related account of the Akamai case.)

There are instructive cases other than CDNs — see, e. g., DNS providers such as OpenDNS, or consider the case of public WLAN access points with authentication and registration via HTTP/HTML (also referred to as universal access method, or UAM). In both cases, control is very much an out-of-band 'user layer' matter.

389 (132). See note 317 and accompanying text.

390 (132). To offer some aside elaboration we may generalize from our considerations the following taxonomy for the functions of networking:

- application related functions that can only be implemented 'completely and correctly' based on the knowledge of the specific application requirements and by mechanisms implemented in the ultimate application ends (reliability, data integrity, encryption, etc., cf. Saltzer et al. 1984);
- application related functions that can only be implemented at all based on the knowledge of the specific application requirements and by mechanisms in the network nodes rather than the ultimate end hosts (obtain a given maximum delay, minimum throughput, etc.);
- functions of networking orthogonal to any application requirements which are best implemented by mechanisms in the ultimate end hosts (proper choice of maximum packet size, congestion avoidance) *or* by mechanisms horizontally inside the network at the host level (routing, network management, etc.).

And, typically, the following broad rules seem to apply to the question of whether a function comes to reside with the end hosts or with the network:

- As for any application specific function, if it is possible to implement it sufficiently well in the end hosts, then the end hosts are the logical place for it to be performed; if not, then it might be possible to implement it with help from the network, but only if the elaboration of control communication between end hosts and network can be reduced to an absolute minimum.

- As for any function that is orthogonal to application specific requirements, it might be implemented either in the end hosts *or* in the network, depending on the general cost and performance trade-offs. Barring the feasibility of such exclusive or, any control communication between end hosts and network must be kept to an absolute minimum.

This taxonomy largely covers the examples considered thus far, and implies a strong prejudice for end-to-end solutions which only relaxes for functions that are either (1) fully orthogonal to the application needs in the end hosts, or (2) involved with the network in such ways that render end-based solutions prohibitively expensive or downright impossible. Any function that is remotely related to the applications in the end hosts is best performed by the end hosts, lest the communication and interface costs outweigh the benefits from the function in the first place. If the management costs to distributing certain functions at the host level toward inside the Internet can be kept to a minimum, then such functions may be delegated from the ultimate application ends to third parties inside the Internet. Hence the popularity of implicit control communication over explicit communication protocols for the 'management' of functions distributed between end hosts and network — even at the cost of considerable vagueness.

391 (132). See Table N.2.

392 (133). Often, it is feasible to move functions that end up with the network up to a higher level where they offer more scope for variation and the participation of third parties in rendering the services in question to the application end hosts. However, we have found that no matter at which level a function is implemented away from the end host, there is precious little scope for explicit cooperation between end hosts and network, due to the intricacies of the necessary control interface.

393 (133). Thus far we used the term architecture in a very loose sense (as in 'there is an Internet architecture', Cerf and Cain 1983; 'there is no Internet architecture', Crowcroft et al. 2007; but also in combinations with

Function	Distribution and organization
WWW	Clients and servers in end hosts plus ALGs and servers in the network; delegation mostly implicit (contingent or topological)
Email	Clients in end hosts plus servers in the network; delegation both explicit (intentional or contingent), and implicit (contingent or topological)
Reliable transport	'Completely and correctly' only in the application ends; however, cost and performance trade-offs dictate substantial effort in the network (implicit; contingent or topological)
QoS guarantees	'Completely and correctly' only by efforts in the network, thus no part of the Internet at large; sometimes implicit invocation (contingent or topological); explicit invocation only inside trust boundaries
Congestion control	Source back-off in the sender, based on packet drop rates (implicit invocation), or, less often, explicit feedback from routers to end hosts
Fragmentation	Probing for maximum packet size by the sender, based on packet drop rates (implicit) or tacit focal point (Ethernet MTU 1500 bytes), or, increasingly less often, explicit router feedback
Routing	Mostly confined to the router-to-router level of the Internet, no input from end hosts; source hosts only get to choose the first hop, destination host gets no choice at all; in the case of CDNs, more control for the source host, but again no control for the destination host
Packet forwarding	Intrinsic province of the network nodes; hosts take no part whatsoever

Table N.2: Horizontal distribution of various functions across the network protocol stack (using the function invocation taxonomy by Clark 2009*e*, pp. 4, 5 ff.)

'layered', 'end-to-end', 'versatile, robust, and scalable', 'Arpanet', 'Pup Internet', and 'TCP/IP Internet') and we have in this chapter dealt with the question of what principles inform those 'architectures'.

Clark (2005) usefully elaborates about the applicability of the architecture notion to the design of the Internet:

> [A]rchitecture (like most human endeavors) benefits from what has already been tried and learned. It is a discipline to be studied and learned. Architects study existing buildings, and CS students study existing systems. [. . .] In (building) architecture school, students are taught about design patterns. [. . .] Similarly, different aspects of CS have their own design patterns: [. . .] network protocol designers are taught about layering and abstraction, and more specific patterns such as the end to end arguments. (p. 2)

And, on the scope of the Internet architecture notion:

> If the Internet is defined narrowly by the IP layer, it is conceptualized broadly by a set of features, capabilities and services that are defined in common across the net, and are generally useful, even if not mandatory. The DNS is not part of the specification of IP, but most would consider it to be a part of the Internet. TCP is not mandatory (one can choose to use alternatives), but it is clearly part of the architecture. Individual applications have an application-specific architecture in their own right, as do technologies such as Ethernet. (pp. 2 f.)

394 (134). Alexander (1979) put it succinctly:

> [O]f course, it is not possible to make something beautiful, merely by combining fixed components. [. . .] Each pattern is a field — not fixed, but a bundle of relationships, capable of being different each time that it occurs, yet deep enough to bestow life wherever it occurs. A collection of these deep patterns, each one a fluid field, capable of being combined, and overlapping in entirely unpredictable ways, and capable of generating an entirely unpredictable system of new and unforeseen relationships. (p. 223)

See also Alexander (1979, pp. 268 ff.) for the notion of tentativeness of principles subject to articulation, promulgation, and debate.

395 (134). See note 30 for a pertinent aside on the pioneering work of Baran and Davies.

396 (134). Note that, internally, the prior Arpanet was a datagram network very much comparable to the Internet — see section 4.2.

397 (134). See, e. g., Postel et al. (1981, pp. 269 f.); Clark (1988); Gien and Zimmermann (1979); Leiner et al. (2003).

398 (134). See section 6.1.

399 (134). It is instructive to consider in due detail what qualifies a statement about observed regularities to be denoted principle in the first place. On the one hand, it needs to be precise enough to carry any meaning; on the other hand, principles necessarily contain a certain amount of vagueness — otherwise they would be inviolable laws of natures (see, e. g., Alexander 1979, pp. 261). Denning and Martell (2007*a*) suggest three criteria that have to be met for a principle to come about: it needs to be (1) universal, (2) recurrent, and (3) broadly influential:

> A principle is a statement that guides or constrains action. We used three criteria to select computing principles:
>
> 1. Universal: The principle arises from taking care of a pervasive concern. Everyone is affected. It is unavoidable. The concern is durable if not permanent.
> 2. Recurrent: The principle has been encountered repeatedly in many contexts. Different groups have independently discovered it. It is reproducible. It is useful for prediction and design.
> 3. Broadly Influential: The principle informs and constrains all the technologies and applications of computing. It shapes standard practice; its impact is wide and deep in science, industry, and society.
>
> Although related, these criteria are not the same. The universality criterion says that people everywhere find it relevant to their success. The recurrence criterion says that people in different fields, places, and times are likely to independently rec-

> ognize the principle. The breadth criterion says that everybody is practicing it, whether they are aware of it or not.
>
> It is tempting but misleading to say that principles are invariant. Over time, the interpretation of a principle can change — for example, the US Constitution is constantly reinterpreted by the courts. Moreover, the set of active principles can change as new principles are discovered and older principles go out of use. A principle may become obsolete, outmoded, or irrelevant.

At the same time, for it to be of any non-trivial interest, it needs to be specific enough so as to be non-obvious. We submit that such test is non-trivial in itself, to quote from Edelcrantz (1796) (as translated in Holzmann 1994, p. 278):

> It often happens, with regard to new inventions, that one part of the general public finds them useless and another part considers them to be impossible. When it becomes clear that the possibility and the usefulness can no longer be denied, most agree that the whole thing was fairly easy to discover and that they knew about it all along.

Yet we should we should generally be careful to avoid principles or sets of principles that amount to tautologies or trivial restatements of existing principles.

400 (135). A more thorough exercise along the lines sketched in this section will be left for another day, and would probably result in a series of books rather than a single thesis.

401 (135). We submit that there can be no conclusive proof that the principles here chosen are the most useful and relevant ones; our choice is arbitrary in that it mostly follows intuition and reflection of the host of literature consumed in the course of this work. Caveats very much comparable to those stated by Lampson (1983, p. 33) thus apply: our principles and their elaboration are neither novel, nor foolproof, absolute, precise, consistent, always appropriate, universally approved, or guaranteed to work.

However, some of the principles here referred to are so universally acknowledged that it is hard to exclude them from any such exercise — layering, best effort, and running code are probably prime examples. Others spring from the subjective appreciation of the thesis author alone (symmetry) or have been suggested in private communication with other researchers (least privilege). See also note 399 for the relevant criteria for stating principles in the first place.

402 (135). As we have noted in section 4.2 (pages 61 f.), much of the end-to-end arguments stems from the very success and profoundness of packet switching, and datagrams in particular.

403 (136). Notably, like the original end-to-end arguments, which developed as a descriptive notion from the experiences in the 1970s (see note 82 and accompanying text), the layering *principle* developed in the early 1970s from the de facto layering *practice* that quickly came to dominate the broader protocol stack architecture in the Arpanet. See pages 72 f. for a discussion of the Arpanet layered architecture. The notion of layering was later developed in excessive elaboration in the ISO work the OSI reference model (Zimmermann 1980; ISO 1983) — see the critical comments by Cohen and Postel (1983) quoted in our note 207.

DIGRESSION: We have in section 4.4, specifically at pages 72 f., elaborated the notion of layering in the context of the early Arpanet. It is fair to argue that the NWG, in fact, invented the concept:

> The NWG [. . .] pioneered and probably invented the notion of doing intercomputer networking/resource sharing via hierarchical, layered protocols for interprocess communication over logical connections of common intermediate representations/virtualizations. (Padlipsky 1982*a*, p. 4)

Although the term 'layering' can be traced back at least to 1972 (Crocker et al. 1972), it bears noting that at that time the notion of a hierarchy of functions separated by distinct interfaces was generally referred to in terms of 'levels' rather than 'layers'. E. g., Clark (1974) on the 'levels' covered by NCP:

> [T]he network control program in a host must deal with three levels of protocol. First, it must deal at the hardware level with the handshake-procedure necessary to transfer each bit to the adjacent IMP. Second, it must deal with the Host-IMP messages, which do such things as report errors. Third, it must

> deal with the Host-Host messages which are concerned with multiplexing and flow control. (p. 108)

The precise origin of the term layering is somewhat obscure. Accordingly, Pouzin (1982) argues that layering has been a concept rooted in practices that predate networking:

> The concept of a layered structure is by no means an innovation. It has always more or less inspired designers of complex systems, or large application programs. Difficulties in the design of layered systems are not at all in reinventing the principles of embedded layers, but in the identification of appropriate intra- and inter-layer relationships. It is quite easy to draw boxes that look like independent layers on a piece of paper. It is much less easy to maintain independence at the implementation stage. (pp. 24 f.)

Cohen and Postel (1983) offer a good definition of the notion of layering:

> Layering permits protocols to be designed so as to deal with specific tasks independently. Low level protocols deal with more primitive communication details than do high level protocols; the higher the protocol level, the more abstract and idealized the communication procedures (with respect to the physical hardware).
>
> Layering is a consequence of modularity in protocol architecture, just as subroutines and procedures result from modularity in software. Lower level protocols are like lower level, or more primitive subroutines: They encapsulate idiosyncratic knowledge about lower level details and hide them from higher layers. Thus, the higher level entities can defer binding to these details until run time. These details can change significantly between design time and run time. The higher level protocols, which are, again, very like higher level subroutines, augment the capabilities of the lower-level hardware to provide more powerful virtual capabilities. (p. 29)

Padlipsky (1984) puts forward a more concise definition:

> The principle of layering is perhaps best stated as an insistence that control information at a given level of protocol must be treated as data by the next "lower" level of protocol. (pp. 77 f.)

404 (136). The principle of modularity is a high level argument about hiding difficult and dynamic design decisions from other parts of a system. Parnas (1972):

> [I]t is almost always incorrect to begin the decomposition of a system into modules on the basis of a flowchart. [. . .] [O]ne [should] begin with a list of difficult design decisions or design decisions which are likely to change. Each module is then designed to hide such a decision from the others. Since, in most cases, design decisions transcend time of execution, modules will not correspond to steps in the processing. (p. 1058)

Stevens et al. (1974) add:

> The fewer and simpler the connections between modules, the easier it is to understand each module without reference to other modules Minimizing connections between modules also minimizes the paths along which changes and errors can propagate into other parts of the system, thus eliminating disastrous "ripple" effects, where changes in one part cause errors in another, necessitating additional changes elsewhere, giving rise to new errors, etc. [. . .]
>
> Each element in the common environment adds to the complexity of the total system to be comprehended by an amount representing all positive pairs of modules sharing that environment. Changes to, and new uses of, the common area potentially impact all modules in unpredictable ways. Data references may become unplanned, uncontrolled, and even unknown. (pp. 117, 118)

The layering principle, on the other hand, has proven a specific instantiation of this general design rule, one that shapes a highly versatile, robust, and scalable vertical hierarchy of functions — the famous hourglass architecture of the Internet — and thus goes well beyond the principle of modularity as such.

★ Digression: We note in passing that Baldwin and Clark (2000) have written about the concept of modularity and its various attendant value trade-offs. While their book features a number of notable omissions — e. g., in elaborating the notion of option value they refer to Black and Scholes (1973) on pages 235 and 104 f. without mentioning the 1998 collapse of the investment fond managed by Black and Scholes on the very basis of their very option valuation methods; at page 98 they offer a curious take on the nature of money as a "numeraire good" which is markedly at odds with the received notion that money has no value of its own, but rather serves as a means of recording credits and debts (Innes 1914); and throughout the book they attribute the notion of evolution firmly to Darwin (1859), which is at least debatable (Hayek 1973, p. 22) — they make a number of useful observations about modularity as (1) a means to limit complexity, allow independent progression, and accommodate uncertainty (p. 90), plus (2) a conducive structure for intersystem competition, because "[m]odules created via augmentation [. . .] embody new concepts, [and] such modules change the 'value landscape' not only in their original system but in all systems" (pp. 306 f.). See also Bresnahan (1998, pp. 13 ff.) for an earlier seminal development of the latter notion.

405 (136). Note that a vertical protocol stack implementation need not be modularized along layer boundaries; especially on performance grounds such congruence is typically ill-advised (see, e. g., McKenzie 1973; Jensen 1981; Clark 1982*c*; Cohen and Postel 1983; Clark et al. 1989; Clark and Tennenhouse 1990), see also note 207, and also Bush and Meyer (2002, pp. 7 ff.) for a broader discussion of the notion of layering versus complexity. Fry (1992) summarizes:

> A fundamental cause of implementation inefficiency is that the layer *abstraction* is often also used as a prescription for *modularization*. [. . .] The general principle [toward greater efficiency] is that modularization should reflect the objects being processed (messages), rather than the protocol layers. (p. 5)

And, Parnas (1972), to whom the seminal elaboration of the notion of modularity is due, notes:

> [H]ierarchical structure and "clean" decomposition are two desirable but independent properties of a system structure. (p. 1058)

While modules in one physical place (host computers, network nodes) may be combined in a monolithic fashion, no such combination is feasible in the 'thin wire' contexts that are intrinsic to communication networks spanning non-trivial distances. The horizontal modularization is thus very much an exogenous given, whereas vertical modularization along layer boundaries is a much more elastic function of the performance benefits to monolithic implementation. Layering as a vertical decomposition of functions has thus been augmented by the orthogonal notion of 'planes', which is less restricted than that of layers, but is also more vague and less powerful an abstraction.

406 (136). Note Clark and Tennenhouse (1990):

> Layered engineering designs should not be thought of as fundamental, but only as one approach, which must be evaluated on the basis of overhead and simplicity against other designs. (p. 205)

Also, some have argued that layering is useless not only as a guide to modularization and implementation, but that it also offers little use as an abstraction, for it hides too much of the actual system complexity and is thus inferior to proper subsystem dependency graphs (Braden et al. 2003; Crowcroft et al. 2003; Crowcroft et al. 2007; Crowcroft 2008).

407 (136). The Internet protocol stack is typically regarded to have four layers (Braden 1989, pp. 8 ff.):

- network (ISO layers 1 and 2),
- internet (ISO layer 3),
- transport (ISO layer 4),
- application layer (ISO layers 5 through 7).

However, even though the transport layer has been almost exclusively defined by common standards (UDP and TCP), end hosts are entirely free to place arbitrary protocols on top of IP. To repeat a quote from Clark (1982*c*) (see note 207):

> It must be remembered that things other than TCP are expected to run on top of IP. The IP interface must be made accessible, even if TCP sits on top of it inside the kernel. (p. 12)

408 (136). See note 208 for a brief elaboration of the spanning layer notion. As an aside, the notion of minimality in the spanning layer — the one layer that by definition encompasses all entities partaking in the Internet — may be considered a variant of the "least common mechanism" principle put forward by Saltzer and Schroeder (1975):

> [A]ny mechanism serving all users must be certified to the satisfaction of every user, a job presumably harder than satisfying only one or a few users. For example, given the choice of implementing a new function as a supervisor procedure shared by all users or as a library procedure that can be handled as though it were the user's own, choose the latter course. Then, if one or a few users are not satisfied with the level of certification of the function, they can provide a substitute or not use it at all. Either way, they can avoid being harmed by a mistake in it. (p. 1283)

409 (136). We have in our note 74 considered how the IP options fell into almost complete disuse in the Internet at large. While the lack of interface for hosts to specify QoS requirements and the general lack of a QoS in the Internet at large is regrettable, the irreducible minimality of the Internet Protocol has helped achieve its almost universal dominance in the first place. Plus, there is nothing (apart from the cost and effort involved) that keeps higher layers from instituting sufficiently wide-spread host layer structures integrated with Internet routers to an extent that allows the 'conditioning' of lower layers so as to obtain arbitrarily reliable QoS guarantees (see note 387).

As for the lack of control data to be passed via IP (and, in fact, ICMP, too — see note 384), it is apt to quote once more from Stevens et al. (1974):

> Modules must at least pass data or they cannot functionally be a part of a single system. Thus connections that pass data are a necessary minimum. (Not so the communication of control. In principle, the presence or absence of requisite input data is sufficient to define the circumstances under which a module should be activated, that is, receive control. Thus the explicit passing of control by one module to another constitutes an additional, theoretically inessential form of coupling.) (p. 120)

410 (137). To quote from CSTB (1994):

> One way of visualizing the layer modularity is to see the layer stack as an hourglass, with the bearer service at the narrow waist of the hourglass. Above the waist, the glass broadens out to include a range of options for transport, middleware, and applications. Below the waist, the glass broadens out to include the range of network technology substrate options. Imposing this narrow point in the protocol stack isolates the application builder from the range of underlying network facilities, and the technology builder from the range of applications. In the Internet protocols, the IP protocol itself sits at this waist in the hourglass. Above IP are options for transport (TCP, UDP, or other specialized protocols); below are all the technologies over which IP can run.
>
> The benefit of this architecture is that it forces a distinction between the low-level bearer service and the higher-level services and applications. The network provider that implements the basic bearer service is thus not concerned with the standards in use at the higher levels. This separation of the basic bearer service from the higher-level conventions is one of the tools that ensures an open network; it precludes, for example, a network provider from insisting that only a controlled set of higher-level standards be used on the network, a requirement that would inhibit the development and use of new services and might be used as a tool to limit competition. (p. 51)

It has been noted that the once narrow waist of the hourglass has by now broadened substantially (Deering 2001; Aguiar 2008); yet despite all the control protocols that have come to accrue at the level of IP, the IP protocol is to this day the sole strictly mandatory protocol in the Internet.

411 (137). CSTB (1994) had still argued that QoS would be an important addition to IP:

> We must resist the temptation to define the bearer service using simplistic measures such as raw bandwidth alone. We must instead look for measures that directly relate to the ability of the facilities to support the higher-level services, measures that

> specify QoS parameters such as bandwidth, delay, and loss characteristics. (p. 52)

Yet, to this day, no IP level solution for service discrimination has been adopted in the Internet at large.

A side effect to this lack of control communication has been the ossification of certain implicit assumptions and communication schemes that have tended to perpetuate along with the level of adoption they command, and thus become de facto part of the overall institutional setting of the Internet (Thaler 2009). See also our pages 100 f. for some of the implicit precedence schemes used in the history of the Internet and Arpanet—largely due to the lack of meaningful explicit communication channels between end hosts and intermediary network nodes.

DIGRESSION: Similarly, Cerf and Cain (1983) argue that some implicitness about the nature of functions at certain levels of the protocol hierarchy may be both inevitable and useful:

> [T]here is often an implicit assumption that one can easily substitute one protocol for another in a particular layer without affecting the functionality of the protocols which depend on it. This assumption (or goal) is sometimes unwarranted, although it seemingly makes life easier for the protocol architecture designer. The problem lies in the nature of the functionality of the protocols in a particular layer and the nature of the services they can easily offer.
>
> For example, broadcast service or multiaddress service is more easily achieved by networks whose natural medium is broadcast in nature, such as the Ethernet or broadcast packet satellite. Substitution of the Arpanet or a public data network which provides an X.25 interface, may fail to provide the service needed by higher level protocols which *assumed* the existence of a broadcast or multicast feature in a lower layer.
>
> This observation leads to the view that a particular model and especially the protocols fitting that model, may form a self-consistent protocol suite [. . .], but arbitrary substitution of a new protocol within the hierarchy may violate these implicit

> assumptions. This observation is not to say that no substitutions can work, but only that it is probably too much to assume that any layer N protocol (to use the ISO terminology) may replace any other layer N protocol without impact on layer N+1 and above. Furthermore, it is the view of the authors that the goal of total interchangeability of layer N protocols is unnecessary. It is reasonable to expect that distinct types of service may be offered at a given layer in the hierarchy (e.g. transaction/connectionless and virtual circuit). (pp. 308 f., references omitted)

412 (137). See also note 268 for some elaboration.

413 (138). Metcalfe (1973) notes:

> Arpanet IMPs [. . .] treat telephone circuits as unreliable, expendable, independent components of the packet-switching system. Telephone circuits are individually asked to give their best efforts to the transmission of digital data. Realizing that a telephone circuit's best is not perfect, the IMPs take steps to monitor circuit performance and, detecting a malfunction, to retry, and, failing some number of retrys, to take alternative action, namely to use alternate paths to get packets closer to their destination. Beyond this, the IMPs are suspicious of one another and can recover in various ways to provide partial service in the face of IMP failures. (p. 6-26)

In fact, as Walden (1972*b*) notes, IMPs were suspicious enough of themselves so as to allow them to check for their own sanity before blaming others for any malfunctions:

> [A]ll the interfaces on the IMP, both to the Hosts and to the [telephone] lines, can be be automatically cross patched, output back into input, under program control. We are able to experiment and to decide whether a fault is in our IMP or the telephone lines or the Host. If we tell the telephone company it is their phone line, then it always is their phone line; we are never wrong about that. [. . .]
>
> [Also, there] is a system called the watchdog timer. Every few hundred milliseconds if it is operating correctly, the program

> resets the watchdog timer. It the watchdog timer is not reset for too long, it decides that program is not operating properly and [. . .] [triggers a reload of] a new copy of the whole IMP program from one of the neighboring IMPs. (pp. 15, 16)

414 (138). To quote from Saltzer (1974):

> The principles of least privilege [holds that] [e]very program and every privileged user of the system should operate using the least amount of privilege necessary to complete the job. The purpose of this principle is to reduce the number of potential interactions among privileged programs to the minimum necessary to operate correctly, so that one may develop confidence that unintentional, unwanted, or improper uses of privilege do not occur. If this principle is followed, the effect of accidents is reduced. Put another way, if one has a mechanism available which can provide "firewalls," the principle of least privilege provides a rationale for where to install the firewalls. (p. 389)

See also Saltzer and Schroeder (1975, pp. 1282 f.) for an almost verbatim predecessor of the above quote, and Needham (1972, p. 571) for an earlier formulation to largely the same effect.

Note that the principle of least privilege has originally been about security rather network design. However, we feel that it applies equally well to the design of the Internet.

415 (138). Put in more colloquial terms, while 'best effort' means that we don't expect much from others and don't guarantee much to others, ourselves; 'least privilege' here means that we don't give others the authority (as in security jargon) to mess with our state, and don't expect others to give us much authority to mess with theirs, in turn.

Our notion of least privilege also relates to the above discussion of minimal coupling afforded by the IP layer, see pages 136 f.

Digression: There has been some discussion lately about the merit of least privilege as a useful principle in computer security. Lampson (2005) has argued:

> The principle of least privilege has done an enormous amount of damage to security, because what it encourages you to do

> is to make everything fine-grained, and work out all the dependencies very carefully. It's too complicated, you can't keep track of it, you're bound to mess it up. Even if you get it right today it will be wrong in three months from now. [. . .] So I say absolutely not least privilege, absolutely not fine-grained protection. Everything should be as coarse-grained as possible, because otherwise you won't be able to administer it. (ca. 14:34 min; slide 10)

However, while such qualifications may usefully apply to operating system design and efforts such as NSA's Security-Enhanced Linux ("What is the #1 SELinux FAQ? 'How do I turn it off?'"), they are probably much less germane to our context in which least privilege goes along with irreducibly minimal coupling at the very natural layer boundary exemplified by IP, plus the very minimality of both the the IP protocol and the typical IP module (which is really only concerned about forwarding IP packets as fast and efficient as possible). Put differently, in our context the means to obtain least privilege are very much as coarse-grained as Lampson argues they should be. Also, as with any other design principle, there is little point in taking the principle of least privilege in any absolute sense without considering other principles and more general cost/benefit analyses.

416 (138). See the discussion of IP options and ICMP messages at note 384 and accompanying text, as well as a brief aside on active networking at note 109. Also, note how the IP architecture — the commandingly dominant inter-networking system of our times — contrasts with more elaborate hop-by-hop inter-networking approaches, as had been discussed in the 1970s. See Sunshine (1977*a*, pp. 188 f.) (but also Sunshine 1990, pp. 4 ff.) for a discussion of the excessive and evidently prohibitive user involvement required to achieve reasonably useful inter-network connections with a hop-by-hop translation approach.

As an aside, it is only fair to note that the principle of least privilege evades perfect implementation in a distributed system based on the notion of passing data via contingent (rather than explicitly 'called') intermediary modules. Unlike in an operating system, it is the task of each individual module to protect itself from privilege escalation by other modules. Much like a router should be suspicious of any packet addressed to himself, an application end point should be mindful of the possibility of routers unraveling the IP packet payload it is supposed to be treating as transparent data only. Arguable, a proper 'codification' of the least privilege principle in data networking would have to involve both the low level authentication of headers and the end-to-end encryption of application level payload data as an integral part of the overall system design (Kent 1976; Kent 1977; Voydock and Kent 1983; Kent and Seo 2005), not merely as an option to informed end users. For various reasons, mostly technical (Kent 1989, p. 11), but also political (Reed 2008*b*), such security architecture has not become a part of the Internet at large. It is instructive, nevertheless, to observe how higher level security measures such as SSL/TLS have come to be built into critical Internet applications such as online banking, given sufficient economic incentive to move the relevant stakeholders in concert. A current instructive example along those lines is the gradual deployment of DNSSEC. Also, the TOR system (Dingledine et al. 2004) can be seen as a rather complete effort to reduce the amount of interesting data available for possible leakage by untrusted parties to a minimum (not a complete minimum, though, given the open nature of the Internet; see, e. g., Edman and Syverson 2009).

417 (138). As for cascadability, Cohen and Postel (1983, pp. 32 f.) emphasize the importance of a "catenation principle" based on a proper separation of control (addressing and type of service) from payload data aiding the "catenation of [different] communication systems"; but they also note that such principle (which is comparable, at least in name, to ours) hitherto had been absent from the literature on inter-networking.

418 (138). See also note 271, as well as note 60 and accompanying text for some elaboration. Generally, see Gien and Zimmermann (1979, p. 112) for a fine discussion of the problem of choosing the proper "common cascadable" set of services to be implemented in gateways connecting different networks so as to form a supernetwork.

419 (138). See note 255 for an example, albeit at the application level.

420 (138). Conceptually, this lack of control goes back to Arpanet's raw messages, but it also shares commonalities with the Ethernet approach to communication. See section 5.1, particularly pages 80 ff. on raw messages. As an aside, classic Ethernet and other such networks have no need for network based routing, making them even simpler than IP packet forwarding.

DIGRESSION: Note that the principle of cascadability of protocols first and foremost applies to the packet level spanning layer as exemplified by the Internet Protocol — allowing almost arbitrary expansion, and generally allowing any end point to turn into an intermediary node simply by establishing another 'hop' further outwards (or back into the network so as to increase its connectivity redundancy). The only problem with the Internet Protocol's cascadability as a practical matter has been the limitation of its address space while conceptually relying on a model of global connectivity based on IP addresses as unique identifiers. While an earlier draft of the IP protocol specified a "variable length quantity" IP address field, allowing arbitrary multiplexing of networks, hosts, and processes (Cerf and Postel 1978, pp. 56 f.), the eventual Internet Protocol specification provided for the 32 bits address field in place to this day — a trade-off between pragmatic engineering and future flexibility. Postel et al. (1981):

> Perhaps the most difficult design decision was the choice of address size and structure. The size of the address field is a compromise that allows enough addresses for the anticipated growth of the Catenet yet is not an excessive overhead burden. (p. 269)

Braden (2009*b*) offers some more perspective:

> I recall rather vividly the variable vs fixed length address discussion. Jon Postel and Danny Cohen strongly favored variable length addresses, for architectural reasons. I assume that Jon slipped them into IEN 21. In your DARPA role, you [Vinton Cerf] then decreed (and it was perfectly clear to the rest of us that this was non-negotiable) that addresses would be 32 bits and fixed length. Your argument was that it would significantly simplify implementations of the protocols, and that would strengthen the acceptability of TCP/IP in the struggle with OSI. I have often wondered who was right. In the short run, you were probably right about the threat of OSI. In the long run, would variable length addresses have avoided the IPv4/IPv6 mess? I can only speculate.

In all, the fixed size address field of IP limits the cascadability of the very Internet Protocol, if only to a magnitude that few would have predicted ever to be achieved. Note also that few at the time thought that the 1981 Internet Protocol would ever become so entrenched that it would be almost impossible to dislodge it and have it replaced by an updated protocol version. See also note 299 for further elaboration of this point.

Another aside on the notion of cascadability: as a principle it applies much less strictly to protocols at layers above IP, for the trade-off between local optimality of specific problem solution versus open-endedness is typically much less pronounced here. Still, cascadability in places other than the IP layer is often beneficial as an additional means of flexibility — not least in extending application level structures to beyond the core Internet (as in "roughly transitive closure of IP-speaking systems", see pages 118 ff.) — see the case of BlackBerry email considered in note 365, but also the world of email level interconnection prior to the dominance of the TCP/IP Internet, see, e. g., Quarterman and Hoskins (1986, pp. 936 f.) for a compilation of networks most of which were connected at the 'email level' only). A related use of higher level cascadable protocols is in managing transitions in the common spanning layer at the packet level. In fact, employing ALGs is the only meaningful way of gradually migrating from one protocol to another without requiring a flag day type transition. ALGs, particularly for email, featured prominently in the transition from NCP to TCP in 1983 (see pages 344 f.), and they have also been acknowledged as potentially crucial for the introduction of IPv6 (Blanchet 2006, ch. 18). The prominence of email gateways is no coincidence, though, for email is a classic store and forward application with no elaborate control features that impede concatenation of mail relays at the application protocol level rather than the IP packet level. Finally, email gateways have been used as filtering and blocking devices between Arpanet and Milnet following their split in 1983 (Michel and Tasman 1984), somewhat anticipating the modern notion of firewalls.

421 (139). E. g., note Walden and McKenzie (1979):

> While there are some exceptions, workers have found it useful to have symmetric protocols, that is, protocols with a participant at each end, with neither participant a master nor slave. (p. 35)

And, Perlis (1982), in a related context:

> Symmetry is a complexity reducing concept (co-routines include sub-routines); seek it everywhere. (p. 7)

422 (139). The IMP level forwarding of packets was a simple operation between peers, designed not to raise any asymmetric issues (see note 168 and accompanying text). Also, note that the IMP-host hardware interface was symmetric in that it was full-duplex, and either side could start and stop transmissions at any time (Walden 1972*b*, p. 7). The host-host protocol, too, was symmetric by design, Requests for Connection (RFCs) could be issued by either side without running into any race conditions; and once the connection was established, either side could send data. Another oft-quoted example still higher 'up the stack' is the Telnet symmetric option negotiation introduced by Cosell and Walden (1973) that greatly increased the usefulness of Telnet for applications other than asymmetric remote terminal sessions. For a recount see Cosell and Walden (2003); but also, for a broader discussion, Davidson et al. (1977).

423 (139). In particular, special purpose protocols for specific applications that are intrinsically about some master-slave situation often have very little need for symmetry. See, e. g., DHCP, ARP, but also TLS, HTTP, IMAP, etc.

424 (139). The notion of "rough consensus and running code" was coined by Clark (1992*a*), the full quote reading:

> As the Internet and its community grows, how do we manage the process of change and growth?
>
> - Open process — let all voices be heard.
> - Closed process — make progress.
> - Quick process — keep up with reality.
> - Slow process — leave time to think.
> - Market driven process — the future is commercial.
> - Scaling driven process — the future is the Internet.
>
> We reject: kings, presidents and voting. We believe in: rough consensus and running code. (slide 19)

IAB (1996) re-emphasize these notions:

> [Internet] evolution depends on rough consensus about technical proposals, and on running code. Engineering feed-back from real implementations is more important than any architectural principles. [. . .]
>
> [In fact,] [n]othing gets standardised until there are multiple instances of running code. (pp. 4, 5)

It is important to note that the principle of rough consensus is by no means an arbitrary choice, but a logical conclusion from the very nature of both the Internet and the IETF. Just like the Internet may be expanded largely at will, in a decentralized fashion with little central control; so does the IETF lack any formal notion of membership. IETF Secretariat and Malkin (1994) put it:

> There is no membership in the IETF. Anyone may register for and attend any meeting. The closest thing there is to being an IETF member is being on the IETF or working group mailing lists. (p. 3)

Without clear borders between the inside and the outside there is, of course, little point in insisting on majority votes, or any votes at all, for that matter.

See also A. L. Russell (2006) for a comprehensive discussion of the two notions and their contextual history, plus the broader history of the IETF and its predecessors, the ICCB and IAB. As for the latter, see also Cerf (1990, pp. 1 f.) and Cerf (2001).

425 (139). See Alvestrand (2004) for a concise statement on the scope and legitimacy of the IETF. Also, there are other technical forums outside the IETF which occupy important roles in certain aspects of work on the Internet at large—most notably IEEE and W3C whose work overlaps only in part with that of the IETF (and who have structures and processes very different from the IETF). Plus, the IETF is a body explicitly concerned with technical problems, not political, moral, or legal ones. IAB and IESG (2000) put it succinctly:

> Since the IETF deals with protocol standardization, not protocol deployment, it is not in a position to dictate that its product is only used in moral or legal ways. (p. 5)

426 (139). It is often surprisingly difficult for observers (especially legal scholars, but also some IETF critics insisting on a more scientific approach to networking) to appreciate the centrality of rough consensus and running code as a legitimate means of shaping the structure of the Internet — along with the corollary that no-one is necessarily bound to follow any of the rules thus arrived at, or need to abide by any of the principles which may be postulated to apply to the Internet (including, of course, those we elaborate in this thesis). No matter how grand a design principle, or how standard an RFC, pragmatism, running code, and rough consensus have been very much primary to any abstraction or normative codification. As for the end-to-end arguments, notes D. H. Crocker (2000):

> Unfortunately, the production Internet (i. e., since 1983) has never been fully end-to-end at the IP layer. Never. Arguably it has never been end-to-end at the application layer, either, nor even application-layer data. Gateways have always been a part of the Internet. We have simply chosen to ignore them, except for the case of email (smtp/x.400). It's fine to create a clean architecture, but not very helpful to ignore or complain about market-driven extensions (or work-arounds) to it. Folks — people would not be making those extensions unless they experienced benefit in them. We claim to believe that the market is the ultimate venue for resolving choice among standards. We need to acknowledge that that applies to missing standards, as well as competing standards.

Also, it is apt to quote here from Tanenbaum and Renesse (1985) who had already noted about LANs:

> One of the great difficulties in implementing efficient communication is that it is more of a black art than a science. [. . .] Abstract formulations and simulations are not enough. (pp. 431 f.)

427 (139). Complexity, as Saltzer and Kaashoek (2009) aptly put it, is the "lack of simple, methodical description [. . .] that remains despite the use of abstraction" (p. 12).

428 (139). E. g., note Saltzer and Schroeder (1975) (albeit in the context of security rather than networking):

> Economy of mechanism [means to] [k]eep the design *as simple and small as possible.* This well-known principle applies to any aspect of a system, but it deserves emphasis for protection mechanisms for this reason: design and implementation errors that result in unwanted access paths will not be noticed during normal use (since normal use usually does not include attempts to exercise improper access paths). As a result, techniques such as line-by-be inspection of software and physical examination of hardware that implements protection mechanisms are necessary. For such techniques to be successful, a small and simple design is essential. (p. 1282, emphasis added)

The simplicity of the core Internet architecture can be firmly traced to the very early accounts anticipating the Internet, see note 127 and accompanying text.

A tangible example of "simple and small" design further up the stack has undoubtedly been the Jacobson slow start and congestion avoidance scheme for TCP, the addition of which took no more than "one new state variable and three lines of code in the sender" (Jacobson 1988*a*, p. 315).

429 (139). Put in game theoretic terms, all actors are trapped in a stable but suboptimal equilibrium—commonly referred to as "prisoner's dilemma" (see, e. g., Kuhn 2009)—which is aggravated by the costs of rearranging the allocation of assets and the relationships between the actors. In the Internet, rarely can one component or facet be changed without entailing all sorts of side effects that render it unfeasible. The lucky introduction of Jacobson's TCP slow start and congestion avoidance scheme has been one of the very few prominent exceptions to this unfortunate rule—see the Partridge (2004) quote in our note 311.

430 (141). In fact, the ultimate end points are not the applications, but the users invoking them or being otherwise subject to them. Notes Clark (1992*b*):

> It is not proper to think of networks as connecting computers. Rather, they connect people using computers to mediate. (p. 15)

The Elusive Normativity of End-to-End Arguments

431 (143). While being a bit of a stretch, it is germane to mention in passing the seminal Radbruch dictum about the impossibility of unjust legal rules — no law which is evidently unjust must be upheld by courts of law:

> Where justice is no part of the objective, where equality, the very core of justice, is consciously repudiated in the articulation of positive law — there the law is not only "unjust law", but is is, in fact, no law at all. (Radbruch 1946, p. 107, my translation)

432 (144). See the US DoJ (2007) comment quoted in the second digression of our note 436.

433 (145). DIGRESSION: Wu (2004) acknowledges the centrality of innovation as a purpose for those trying to argue for "network neutrality":

> Whatever its meaning elsewhere, in [. . .] [for us] e2e [the end-to-end principle] stands for a theory of innovation. It rejects centralized, planned innovation, and holds that the greatest rate of technological development is driven by delegating decisional authority to the decentralized "ends" of any network. The reason is fairly simple: the "ends" of the network are numerous, or nearly unlimited, and delegating authority to the ends opens the door to more approaches to a given technological challenge. The e2e principle assumes that innovation is an evolutionary process, driven by contests between competing approaches to a problem. For Openists, the e2e principle puts as many players in the contest as possible to ensure the true champion emerges. (pp. 73 f.)

Schewick (2004) briefly develops the innovation purpose, and arrives at a broad (or, in fact, narrow) definition that explicitly emphasizes the process of invention (as in content creation and application development) over the process of dissemination and adoption of such (p. 62). She argues that an invention that does not get adopted by others is still an innovation since "the time and money the innovator invested to develop the innovation were incurred" (footnote 162). Later in her thesis, when considering the "ability to innovate in end-to-end networks" she claims that intermediaries concerned with turning an invention into an innovation by disseminating it and furthering its adoption are completely irrelevant to her argument: "[c]ontent distribution [on the WWW] is almost costless" (p. 228). And, even if it were not (of course, content distribution is costly, cf. Clark 2008*a*), to Schewick the creation of content or applications have nothing to do whatsoever with their distribution and thus need not be considered at all:

> [A]part from making the new applications available for download, an application developer [the "innovator"] in an end-to-end network does not need to engage in additional activities to enable the adoption and deployment of the innovation by someone else. (p. 231)

While this statement may technically be true, it completely neglects the dynamics of innovations in real world situations — even on the Internet. In fact, despite her claiming otherwise (footnote 162 and accompanying text), her conception of innovation is in stark contrast to the "standard definition of innovation used in the literature" that considers the successful dissemination and adoption of an invention the *defining* moment of an innovation (E. M. Rogers 2003).

Zittrain (2008), in his account of "tethered" and "locked-down" devices and Web 2.0 services that he fears customers will resort to in the face of increasing security concerns in an open network, thus departs from the notion of innovation and puts forward that of "generativity". However, other than various musings about the responsibility of the computer science community to protect and further "recursive generativity, repeated up through the layers of the hourglass" (p. 94), and the suggestion to replace the end-to-end principle with a "new generativity principle" — "a rule that asks that any modifications to the Internet's design or to the behavior of ISPs be made where they will do the least harm to generative possibilities." (p. 165) — his account adds very little to a reasoned debate about either end-to-end arguments or innovation.

434 (145). Gillett et al. (2001*a*); Gillett et al. (2001*b*) persuasively argue with reference to various empirical (if anecdotal) cases that Internet innovation is largely exogenous to local idiosyncrasies; thus innovation at large can hardly be restricted as long as at least *some* actors are willing to experiment, and as long as a reasonably predictable general purpose Internet

service is available in a sufficiently large part of the Internet. Also, most appliances are relatively inexpensive and any lock-in is thus bound to be weak. If a vendor restricts too much what users can do with their devices, then others will step in and provide better ones:

> Consumers, it seems, are willing to replace fixed function appliances reasonably quickly if there is a compelling reason to do so — and if the devices are relatively inexpensive. (Gillett et al. 2001*b*, pp. 42 f.)

Thus the likely result of market forces is going to be a happy medium in which "lightly walled garden with the well marked exit" (p. 44) are going to be most successful, one example of which is Japanese mobile operator NTT's DoCoMo system. While Zittrain (2008, ch. 5) has gone to some lengths to establish a theory of "power of fear" (p. 102, explicitly contra Gillett et al. 2001*a*) that will drive *all* users to "tethered, locked-down devices" and Web 2.0 services, the argument of Gillett et al. (2001*a*) much more plausibly explains the dynamics of application level innovation in the Internet:

> The truly fixed function appliances [. . .] are unlikely to place a serious drag on innovation, because they are only likely to succeed in the marketplace if they are inexpensive, frequently replaced devices. Rather than [. . .] [such] appliances threatening to retard Internet innovation, the already existing fact of rapid Internet innovation threatens to preclude the emergence of expensive [. . .] [such] devices in the first place. (p. 50)

Digression: In passing we note that — the common-place reference to the notion of 'unanticipated application level innovation' notwithstanding — for the most part the evolution of Internet applications has arguably proceeded much along the lines of long-standing and well-understood taxonomies. The most obvious taxonomy has been between delay-sensitive applications and delay-tolerant applications, a distinction used for various discrimination policies ever since the Arpanet (see note 317 and accompanying text). Pouzin (1973*b*) puts forward a general taxonomy of lower host level usage patterns — (1) "regular letters [. . .] for conversational traffic", (2) "liaisons [. . .] for bulk traffic", (3) "connections [. . .] for I/O streams", and (4) "events [. . .] for [higher priority] control information". Along similar lines, Shenker et al. (1994) suggest a taxonomy of elastic applications — (1) asynchronous bulk (e. g., email), (2) interactive bulk (e. g., file transfer), (3) interactive burst (e. g., remote terminal sessions) — on the one hand; and real-time applications — (4) delay/jitter tolerant (speech), (5) delay intolerant (applications requiring a "firm worst-case bound on delay") — on the other hand (pp. 146 f.). See also our taxonomy in Figure 5.1 and accompanying text.

As for actual applications, it is fair to say that neither 'peer-to-peer filesharing', nor VoIP, nor even WWW have been as unanticipated as is sometimes claimed. Peer-to-peer systems have been anticipated in the early thinkings about distributed databases in the Arpanet (see the considerations of R. E. Kahn 1972 as quoted in note 138), VoIP is an obvious successor to the speech experiments in the early Arpanet (see section 5.1), and the WWW goes back directly to systems such as Engelbart's NLS built in the mid-1960s (Engelbart and English 1968; but see also DeRose and Dam 1999; Nielsen 1988, pp. 29 f.; Oinas-Kukkonen 2007 for historical accounts; Simpson et al. 1996 for an instructive discussion between various hypertext pioneers; and Nelson 2008 for an opinionated take on the history of hypertext systems), and may be traced still further back to intellectual predecessors such as the seminal notes of Bush (1945) and even the still earlier efforts by Otlet (1934). (It is somewhat ironic that the earlier hypertext systems were putting far greater emphasis on a symmetrical balance between reading *and* writing as an intrinsic part of the system, rather than having the write part tied to either intimate expertise of the users or the use of third party Web services such as today's Facebook, Twitter, and Blogger.) Not even email was an entirely novel application when it took off as the Arpanet 'killer application' in the early 1970s, for it is a direct successor to earlier message systems in time-sharing computers of the 1960s (Partridge 2008, pp. 3 f.).

Note that none of the above is to say that there is no scope on the Internet for genuinely new applications, usage patterns, and content; it is merely to argue that it is possible to reason about application level Internet uses without resorting to vague rhetorics about 'unanticipated innovations', 'recursive generativity' (Zittrain 2008, p. 94), etc. Developing a complete history of Internet applications, the interplay between applications and content, and the patterns thus emerging is beyond our scope here, but it would certainly be a worthwhile effort for future research.

435 (145). See Gaynor and Bradner (2004); Frischmann (2005); Frischmann and Schewick (2007).

436 (145). DIGRESSION: A note on the desirability of an Internet with complete end point discretion over the use of the system. A popular analogy about normative high-level end-to-end arguments is that they bring about the equivalent of a 'free market', void of transaction costs and inefficiencies. Faulhaber (2000) summarizes:

> End-to-end advocates are essentially arguing [. . .] that end-to-end in engineering is the equivalent of the perfect competitive market that economists know and love. It is the thing that makes it all transparent and open, anybody can do anything.

However, he then comments:

> But, in fact, that is not the way the real world world works. It is neither the economist nirvana of perfect competition, nor is it the engineering nirvana of end-to-end. It does not work that way.

Adding to the economic futility of the perfectly competitive market, there are strong legal arguments against complete freedom of contract in an economic system. Notes Kimel (2003) on the limits of freedom of contract both as a descriptive and normative notion:

> The law takes measures to protect various types of relatively weak or vulnerable contract parties — consumers, employees, tenants — sometimes in general, sometimes in specific categories of contract or commercial activity. Intervention is introduced in some cases in the name of protecting contracting individuals, in others in the name of public (economic or other) interests. The law sometimes dictates contractual terms, introduces special requirements for the formation of certain contracts, or prohibits or imposes sanctions for a refusal to contract with certain parties or in certain circumstances; it sometimes renders agreed terms illegal, void, voidable, or unenforceable, and sometimes limits the obtainable remedy for breach. And apart

> from various forms of statutory intervention, courts have routinely applied broad interpretations of various contract law doctrines — fraud, duress, implied terms, consideration, unconscionability — to impose further conditions for the validity or enforceability of contracts, and to protect parties from the consequences of unfortunate, yet genuine, exercises of their very freedom to make contracts. [. . .]
>
> [Not only is] the rigid conception of freedom of contract [. . .] highly unrealistic [on the descriptive level], [on the normative level] many, probably most, of the instances of intervention in freedom of contract that are to be found in modern legal systems appear to be justified. They often fit neatly into desirable social, economic, and legal policies, and reflect perfectly valid (and sometimes overlapping) concerns—for vulnerable individuals, for social justice, for individual and public well-being. (pp. 118 f., 13 footnotes pointing to various English common law references omitted)

In fact, personal liberty and autonomy are not a strictly increasing function of the available choices:

> To lead valuable, autonomous lives, people need a sufficient range of valuable options to choose from, but they do not need worthless options, let alone *all* the worthless options; and while promoting personal autonomy requires, among other things, making available a sufficient range of valuable options, it does not entail a favourable attitude to the availability of bad ones. On the contrary: when the availability of certain bad options would significantly decrease people's chances of leading valuable autonomous lives, or exercising their autonomy in a valuable way in particular circumstances, or, more generally, of leading valuable lives, concern for autonomy could only require their elimination. (p. 132, emphasis in original)

See for similar points also Rosa (2003).

On a very much related note, it is instructive to observe how little the arguments of network neutrality research programme have developed over the years, and how they have remained theoretical, and almost completely void of more empirically grounded research—e. g., compare Gaynor and Bradner (2001) to Gaynor and Bradner (2008), or Schewick (2004) to Schewick (2010*a*). In particular, they have found no good empirical cases to support their theoretical notions—e. g., Schewick (2007), elaborating on the work of MacKie-Mason (2000), makes extensive references to the year 2000 merger of AOL and Time Warner as evidence for the harm caused by monopoly network operators, even though most of the fears voiced back then have now virtally evaporated. Not surprisingly, US DoJ (2007) conclude:

> On the empirical side, despite the [Federal Communication] Commission's request for evidence of harmful discrimination or behavior [. . .] *commenters failed to present evidence suggesting that a problem exists*. To the contrary, it appears that the Internet is flourishing without the proposed sectoral regulation. (p. 5, emphasis added)

(For a related discussion of the poor empirical backing behind network neutrality see Bärwolff 2008, e. g., footnote 8 at pp. 3 f.)

Thus Schewick's bold conclusions of (1) banning intermediaries from application level innovation and vertical integration, and (2) requiring end hosts irrespective of their requirements to partake in arbitrary application level innovation, have gradually given way to various qualifying statements—e. g., Frischmann and Schewick (2007), in seeking to rebut Yoo (2002); Yoo (2005); Yoo (2006), submit:

> We do not claim that we stand on stronger empirical ground than [opponents of network neutrality]. (p. 16, footnote 42)

As of 2010, most network neutrality advocates have largely retreated to very loose arguments about free speech, rather than further pursuing previous arguments about grander purposes such as innovation and economic welfare—see for example Wu (2010). Arguably, the scope for novel research results has thus become rather limited, given that Sola Pool (1983) has already produced a very complete analysis of the problem of free speech and electronic communication media—see the copious quote at our note 438.

Last, a critique on the Gaynor and Bradner (2004) approach mentioned above, for theirs is probably coming closest to a reasonable theoretical treatment in support of network neutrality. The most curious feature of their theory is the use of standard deviation as an independent variable, thus turning the conventional conception of standard deviation on its head. Say Gaynor and Bradner (2004):

> The probability of the best experiment greatly exceeding the mean increases as the number of experiments grows or the standard deviation increases. (p. 33)

The causality implied here is that standard deviation is the lever that when increased makes extraordinarily successful experiments accordingly more likely. However, the trouble with this argument is that standard deviation is not typically a variable that determines the shape of a series of 'experimentation results'. It could be a normal distribution, but it could as well be a myriad of other distributions — standard deviation is simply a function of a given series and says nothing whatsoever about specific values in that series. Moreover, even if we accept that the results from experimentation are distributed in some bell shaped fashion, it does not follow that the maximum value achieved in the series of experiments determines the overall value of the whole series. It seems as though the authors have not only disregarded the costs of every single experiment, but also succumbed to assuming that the value generated by the most successful experiment would eventually spread through the entire economy, that is to all experimenters.

While the (slim) empirical evidence presented by Gaynor and Bradner can be construed so as to fit their model, we doubt that their model has much explanatory value. This is for two reasons: *First*, uncertainty in a market and experimentation in the face of that uncertainty usually results in a substantial premium adding to costs. Uncertainty is not as manageable as is risk; rather, it creates a fundamental incentive problem, for no one even knows even the expected value of one's efforts. That is, the mean of whatever distribution of "experimentation values" turns out to arise is unknown in advance. In fact, it is not even known if there is a market at all. It is strange then that Gaynor and Bradner (2004) argue:

> [W]hen the standard deviation is high and your experiment is the most successful at meeting the market, then it is likely you will win big by capturing most of the market because your

> product better meets users wants in a market where products are differentiated by features. This chance to win big will induce many vendors to experiment, which increases the probability of a superior match and big win for the lucky (or smart) vendor or service provider. (p. 33)

What they say is, in effect, that rational investors will prefer uncertain investments irrespective of the costs incurred simply because there might be a "superior match and big win". This, we believe, is highly unlikely if not outright false.

Second, even if there were "big wins" in the face of uncertainty, we do not see how that would raise the mean of those uncertain experiments—which to all intents and purposes is a more realistic measure of the overall value—above the mean of less exciting but more certain and less risky experiments that are better targeted at known market demands. It is certainly reasonable to assume that the mean of the latter will be higher than that of the former.

A final comment about their conclusion which reads:

> [F]irewalls and NATs make network experimentation harder, and thus, according to our real options framework, reduce the overall value of the network since users will have fewer choices. (pp. 36 f.)

An obvious objection to this (popular) assessment is that there is value from firewalls and NATs in that they raise the mean value of the "experiments" by providing for increased security, and an increase in available addresses for end hosts. The Gaynor and Bradner model does not convincingly show how dispensing with firewalls and NATs would increase overall value vis à vis the very tangible value provided by both.

437 (145). Any value (such as innovation, generativity, improved democratic discourse, etc.) imposed upon the stakeholders of a complex system in pursuit of higher level ends may easily destroy the abstract order and the rules (those that were there as regularities to be observed, not mandated by an authority) that created the complexity in the first place. Customers might prefer a "sheltered environment or at least preferential offering of selected services and content" (CSTB 2001, p. 145), and it is thus hard to uphold rules in opposition to such outcomes (Clark 2009*b*, pp. 4 f.). Put

differently, there is very little scope for overarching values in a sufficiently complex system consisting of non-uniform legitimate stakeholders, for it is the purposes of those stakeholders that ought to be served, not those of a central authority who can never know and process all the local preferences and circumstances, let alone make informed decisions based on these and act accordingly. Hayek (1973) put it:

> [T]he rules governing a spontaneous order must be independent of purpose [. . .]. They will have to be applied by the individuals in the light of their respective knowledge and purposes; and their application will be independent of any common purpose, which the individual need not even know. (p. 50)

And, slightly more elaborate:

> The reason why [. . .] isolated commands requiring specific actions by members of the spontaneous order can never improve but must disrupt that order is that they will refer to a part of a system of interdependent actions determined by information and guided by purposes known only to the several acting persons but not to the directing authority. The spontaneous order arises from each element balancing all the various factors operating on it and by adjusting all its various actions to each other, a balance which will be destroyed if some of the actions are determined by another agency on the basis of different knowledge and in the service of different ends. (p. 51)

Rawls (1972), in his elaboration of the notion of justice, famously makes a similar point about the primacy of individual liberty and purposes:

> Each person possesses an inviolability founded on justice that even the welfare of society as a whole cannot override. For this reason justice denies that the loss of freedom for some is made right by a greater good shared by others. It does not allow that the sacrifices imposed on a few are outweighed by the larger sum of advantages enjoyed by many. (pp. 3 f.)

Finally, to return to the realm of computer science, it is apt to quote from Friedman and Nissenbaum (1996) who argue that computer systems should be designed so as to be as unbiased as possible and allow for maximum user autonomy, thus adding to our notion of limiting the values of the Internet to serving the local purposes of individual stakeholders on the one hand, and the overall 'good order' on the other:

> [B]iases in computer systems can be difficult to identify let alone remedy because of the way the technology engages and extenuates them. Computer systems, for instance, are comparatively inexpensive to disseminate, and thus, once developed, a biased system has the potential for widespread impact. If the system becomes a standard in the field, the bias becomes pervasive. If the system is complex, and most are, biases can remain hidden in the code, difficult to pinpoint or explicate, and not necessarily disclosed to users or their clients. Furthermore, unlike in our dealings with biased individuals with whom a potential victim can negotiate, biased systems offer no equivalent means for appeal. (p. 331)

438 (146). DIGRESSION: As we have observed in our note 436, many network neutrality proponents have lately come to restate their arguments in terms of free speech rather than innovation. However, it is instructive to note that many of the notions that are now considered in the research and activism programme of network neutrality have been dealt with in considerable detail by Sola Pool (1983). With respect to the purpose of free speech, Sola Pool's analysis provides a much better basis for a comprehensive set of principles guiding the regulation of the Internet than conjectures building on a dogmatic interpretation of the end-to-end arguments. It is apt to quote copiously from Sola Pool (1983):*

> [W]hen there is severe scarcity, there is an unavoidable need to regulate access. Caught in the tension between the tradition of freedom and the need for some controls, the communications system then tends to become a mix of uncontrolled and common carrier elements — of anarchy, of property, and of enfranchised services. A set of principles must be understood

*Reprinted with permission of the publisher from TECHNOLOGIES OF FREEDOM: ON FREE SPEECH IN AN ELECTRONIC AGE by Ithiel de Sola Pool, pp. 245–250, Cambridge, Mass.: The Belknap Press of Harvard University Press, Copyright © 1982 by the President and Fellows of Harvard College.

if communications in the electronic era are to hold as fully as possible to the terms of the First Amendment. The technology does not make this hard. Confusion about principles may.

The *first* principle is that the First Amendment applies fully to all media. It applies to the function of communication, not just to the media that existed in the eighteenth century. It applies to the electronic media as much as to the print ones.

Second, anyone may publish at will. The core of the First Amendment is that government may not prohibit anyone from publishing. There may be no licensing, no scrutiny of who may produce or sell publications or information in any form.

Third, enforcement of the law must be after the fact, not by prior restraint. In the history of communications law this principle has been fundamental. Libel, obscenity, and eavesdropping are punishable, but prior review is anathema. In the electronic media this has not been so, but it should be. Traffic controls may be needed in cases where only one communicator can function at a particular place at a particular time, such as street meetings or use of radio frequencies, but this limited authority over time and place is not the same as power to choose or refuse to issue a license.

Fourth, regulation is a last recourse. In a free society, the burden of proof is for the least possible regulation of communication. If possible, treat a communications situation as free for all rather than as subject to property claims and a market. If resource constraints make this impossible, treat the situation as a free market rather than as a common carrier. But if resources for communication are truly monopolistic, use common carrier regulation rather than direct regulation or public ownership. Common carriage is a default solution when all must share a resource in order to speak or publish.

Under common law in the nineteenth century, vendors could not be made common carriers against their will. If they offered a service to the general public, it had to be without discrimination, but if they chose to serve a limited clientele, that was their right. This philosophy applies well to publishing. One would not require the Roman Catholic *Pilot* to carry ads for birth control or a trade union magazine to carry ads against the closed shop. But these cases assume that diverse magazines exist. A dilemma arises when there is a monopoly medium, as when a monopoly newspaper in a town refuses ads to one party and carries them for another.

In the world of electronic communications some but not all of the basic physical carriers, and only those, seem likely to continue to have significant monopoly power. It is hard to imagine a value-added network having the dominance in a community that a local newspaper has today. Even now the communications monopolies that exist without privileged enforcement by the state are rare. Even basic physical conduits become monopolies precisely because they cannot exist without public favors. They need permissions that only the state can grant. These favors, be they franchises to dig up the city streets or spectrum to transmit through the air, may properly be given to those who choose to serve as common carriers. This is not a new idea. In 1866 telegraph companies were given the right to string wires at will along post roads and across public lands, but only if they became common carriers. Where monopoly exists by public favor, public access is a reasonable condition.

Fifth, interconnection among common carriers may be required. The basic principle of common carriage, namely that all must be served without discrimination, implies that carriers accept interconnection from each other. This principle, established in the days of the telegraph, is incorporated in the 1982 AT&T consent decree. All long-distance carriers have a right to connect to all local phone companies. That is the 1980s outgrowth of the 1968 Carterphone decision which required AT&T to interconnect with an independent radio-telephone service. Universal interconnection implies both adherence to technical standards, without which interconnection can be difficult, and a firm recognition of the right to interconnect.

Carriers may sometimes raise valid objections to interconnection. Some will wish to use novel technologies that are incompatible with generally accepted standards, claiming that they are thereby advancing the state of the art. Also, when they handle highly sensitive traffic, such as funds transfers or intracompany data, they may not wish to be common carriers and bear the risks of having outsiders on their system. Such arguments are often valid, though they may also be used to lock a group of customers out of using the carrier.

An argument in favor of general interconnectivity is that it facilitates market entry by new or small carriers. It also makes universal service easier. It may even be useful for national security, since a highly redundant system is less likely to be brought down. In short, there are conflicting considerations that must be balanced. As a policy, the requirement of interconnection is a reasonable part of a common carriage system.

Sixth, recipients of privilege may be subject to disclosure. The enforcement of nondiscrimination depends critically on information. Without control of accounting methods, regulatory commissions are lost in swamp. I once asked the head of the Common Carrier Bureau of the FCC what he would ask for if he could rob Aladdin's lamp. "Revelatory books" was his reply.

Yet American lawmakers, who have imposed far more oppressive and dubious kinds of regulation, such as exit, entry, and tariff controls, have never pushed the mild requirement for visibility. Apart from requiring accounts, legislators have been highly considerate of proprietary information. A firm that enjoys the monopoly privileges which lead to being a common carrier should perhaps forgo, like government, some privileges of privacy. Unbundled rates for cable leasing, for example, help reveal who is being charged for what. Disclosure is not a new idea. Patents and copyrights are privileges won only by making their object public. The same principle might well apply to action under franchises too.

Seventh, privileges may have time limits. Patents and copyrights are for finite periods. and then the right expires. Radio and television licenses and cable franchises, though also for fixed periods, are typically renewable. Some monopoly privileges that broadcasters and cablecasters have in their licenses could expire after a fixed period. This is a way to favor infant industries but limit their privileges when they become giants.

Eighth, the government and common carriers should be blind to circuit use. What the facility is used for is not their concern. There may be some broad categories of use. Emergency communications often have priority. Special press rates for telegraph have been permitted, though their legality in the United States has been questioned. But in general, control of the conduit may not become a means for controlling content. What customers transmit on the carrier is no affair of the carrier.

Ninth, bottlenecks should not be used to extend control. Rules on undeliverable mail have been used to control obscene content. Cablecasting, in which there is no spectrum shortage, has been regulated by the FCC as ancillary to broadcasting. Telegraph companies have sought to control news services, and cable franchisees have sought to control the programs on the cable. Under the First Amendment, no government imposition on a carrier should pass muster if it is motivated by concerns beyond common carriage, any more than the carrier should be allowed to use its service to control its customers.

Tenth, and finally, for electronic publishing, copyright enforcement must be adapted to the technology. This exceptional control on communication is specifically allowed by the Constitution as a means of aiding dissemination, not restricting it. Copyright is temporary and requires publication. It was designed for the specific technology of the printing press. It is in its present form ill adapted to the new technologies. The objective of copyright is beyond dispute. Intellectual effort needs compensation. Without it, effort will wither. But to apply a print scheme of compensation to the fluid dialogue of interactive electronic publishing will not succeed. Given modern technologies, there is no conceivable way that individual copies can be effectively protected from reproduction when they are already either on a sheet of paper or in a computer's memory. The task is to design new forms of market organisation that will provide compensation and at the same time reflect the character of the new technology.

The question boils down to what users at a computer terminal will pay for. For one thing, they will pay for a continuing relationship, as they will continue to need maintenance. It may be easy to pirate a single program or some facts from a data base by copying from a friend of a friend of a friend who once bought it. But to get help in adapting it or to get add-on versions or current data, one might pay a fee as a tender for future relations. The magazine subscription model is closer to the kind of charging system that will work for electronic publishing than is the one-time book purchase with a royalty included.

A workable copyright system is never enacted by law alone. Rather it evolves as a social system, which may be bolstered by law. The book and music royalty systems that now exist are very different from each other, reflecting the different structures of the industries. What the law does is to put sanctions behind what the parties already consider right. So too with electronic publishing on computer networks, a normative system must grow out of actual patterns of work. The law may then lend support to those norms.

If language were as fluid as the facts it represents, one would talk in the electronic era of serviceright, not copyright. But as language is used, old words are kept regardless of their derivation, and their meanings are changed. In the seventeenth century reproducing a text by printing was a complex operation that could be monitored. Once the text was printed on paper, however, it required no further servicing, and no one could keep track of it as it passed from reader to reader. In the electronic era copying may become trivially easy at the work stations people use. But both the hardware and the software in which the text is embodied require updating and maintenance. In ways that cannot yet be precisely identified, the bot-

> tleneck for effective monitoring and charging is migrating from reproduction to the continuing service function. (pp. 245–250, emphasis in original, emphasis of numbers added)

439 (146). As for the former, see Koreng (2009):

> With respect to the Internet one cannot speak of any lack of plurality; much to the contrary, there is currently no other medium as pluralistic as the Internet. (p. 759, my translation)

As for the latter, see the elaborations of Sola Pool (1983) as cited in our note 438.

440 (146). Internet design principles—much like any *norms* as in *normative* rules—ought to be shaped by all of their stakeholders, not just by those considering themselves authorities 'who understand the science' (see for a seminal statement along those lines Häberle 1975). Such a premise will also provide a better framing to incorporate actions of end users that are seemingly in violation of end-to-end principles (NATs, firewalls, etc.), and those of ISPs that are subject to plausible economic constraints (DPI, etc.). Both sides have a stake in the Internet and its principles, and the way forward should not be to develop principles into categorical rules, but rather to have them evolve in a fair and open way. (See also our discussion at note 426.)

Contrary to popular belief, if our primary objective is to uphold a just and orderly overall system (in the sense of Hayek 1973), then it is *not* useful merely to appeal to the 'technologically sophisticated' to resolve our problems with the Internet (see, e. g., Zittrain 2006, pp. 2035 f.), for both legislation and interpretation of norms in the Internet (including those of 'constitutional' rank) are better left to an "open society" that acknowledges all stakeholders, not just a self-proclaimed élite group (Jessen 2010; Häberle 1975).

441 (146). We note in passing that a popular notion often raised in this context is that of the Internet designed as a general purpose technology (Schewick 2007, pp. 385 f.) or platform (Baldwin and Woodard 2008, p. 10). While the notion of general purpose technologies (Bresnahan and Trajtenberg 1995) may or may not have merit beyond the abstract, the main problem with such accounts is typically that they resort to tautological arguments about the appropriateness of the set of stable components found in the Internet

that are creating the general purpose technology or platform, and say little about contradictory notions such as active networking, network based services more generally, or any of the principles we have considered in section 7.2. It is apt in this context to recall that "[w]e must not take the present form of the Internet as a given" (Clark 2008*b*).

442 (146). The 2002 conference paper by Clark et al. was eventually published in a slightly edited version as Clark et al. (2005*c*).

443 (146). To quote more fully from Clark et al. (2005*c*):

> [I]t is our opinion that design for choice — design that accommodates tussle rather than attempt to preclude it — has been a beneficial option in the past. It has preserved the option for evolution, it has preserved the option for innovation and the creation of new value, and it has allowed the Internet to keep pace with the computer industry as that industry evolves. (p. 466)

444 (146). Notes Briscoe (2007*a*):

> [Instead of] blaming operators for acting in their own self-interest [. . .] [we should probably rather] blame the designers of the [Internet] architecture for not expecting operators to act in their own interests.

445 (147). Notes Briscoe (2007*b*):

> [W]e're actually a long way off an analytical understanding. Unlike the e2e principle, the original tussle paper [Clark et al. 2002] doesn't really even have a good concrete example (there are some high level arm-wavy examples, but not anything as concrete as the TCP reliability example in the e2e principle paper [Saltzer et al. 1981*a*]).

446 (147). Remarkably, the research programme of network neutrality (Wu 2003; Schewick 2004) has remained ignorant of the tussles notion to this day, by choosing to pursue and advocate efforts that run very much counter to those implied by Clark et al. Clark (2009*b*) notes that network neutrality is very much about "drawing a line through the middle of a grey area"

and thus "[c]omplete precision in rule-making will not be possible in advance" (p. 1). (See also Clark et al. 2010 for an edited and extended version.) While we are left to speculate about the precise reasons for this fundamental ignorance, it bears noting that the network neutrality advocates' disregard for the tussles notion is consistent with the dynamics of competing research programmes as elaborated by Lakatos (1978*a*).

447 (147). An apt comment by Hardie (2009) about the broader merit of the 'neutrality' notion for the IETF in the first place:

> We made a choice a while back about what our values were. And it wasn't for network neutrality, it was for liberty. We chose to try and design a network that enabled the maximum number of end-to-end flows, that enabled people to connect, for communities to form, and to allow all of us not to be mere consumers but actual providers of content onto the network.

(Of course, this statement must not be taken as representative of the position of IETF, IAB, and ISOC. Statements leaning more towards neutrality than choice can easily be found, too; see, e. g., ISOC's statement about their values and public policy principles, ISOC 2010.)

448 (147). Not only does the network neutrality notion arrive at a different position here; it may also be in plain violation of the tussle separation principle in that it does not have any scope for allowing 'non-neutral' design decisions that may ensue from tussle isolation concerns. By carrying the end-to-end arguments to the extreme, it is concerned with but one logical separation line: that between end users and network operators—foreclosing precisely the very tussle that Clark et al. (2005*c*) aim to *accommodate*, not *preclude*. As Sandvig (2006) noted about the network neutrality notion:

> The best outcome that normative claims premised on the end-to-end argument can offer us is to produce the right result for the wrong reasons. (p. 2)

In comparison, the tussle separation principle seems to be a far better candidate for a useful normative principle to uphold the "goodness" of the Internet—not by forcing a result based on the theoretical development of an originally technical design principle, but by allowing conflicting choices to play out in the ultimately most conducive manner.

449 (147). Notes Feldmann (2007):

> [T]here is a need for an economic model as well as a technical one that makes sense for the evolution of the network and its services, and the continued viability of both. (p. 61)

Plus, Clark (2003) notes:

> As consumers, our instinct is to build systems that appropriate all excess utility, but we might need to build mechanisms that deliberately give up some of that utility to the providers. Letting the industry sectors with sunk costs recover more of the value associated with consumer utility could be the best compromise to ensure industry stability. (p. 95)

Note also that the existence of mechanisms that give ISPs a greater share of power in the tussles has not led to the 'network neutrality violations' predicted by network neutrality proponents. See the US DoJ (2007) comment quoted in the second digression in note 436. Examples of prejudicial discrimination such as those listed in Windhausen (2006) are exceptions rather than rules, and none which would make a solid case for preemptive ex ante rules. See in this respect also our considerations in note 462.

450 (147). Notes Liebowitz (2002):

> [The] scarcity assumption, although a bit of a downer, is not going to be overturned. Beware of anyone who says otherwise. (p. 208)

And, Braden et al. (1994):

> The incredibly large carrying capacity of an optical fiber leads some to conclude that in the future bandwidth will be so abundant, ubiquitous, and cheap that there will be no communication delays other than the speed of light, and therefore there will be no need to reserve resources. However, we believe that this will be impossible in the short term and unlikely in the medium term. While raw bandwidth may seem inexpensive, bandwidth provided as a network service is not likely to become so cheap that wasting it will be the most cost-effective design principle. Even if low-cost bandwidth does eventually

> become commonly available, we do not accept that it will be available everywhere in the Internet. Unless we provide for the possibility of dealing with congested links, then real-time services will simply be precluded in those cases. We find that restriction unacceptable. (p. 3)

451 (148). If normative statements are primarily defined by the actual disobedience with which they are met, then the history of normative end-to-end arguments may be extended back to the early articulations such as Pouzin (1976*b*)—see our section 2.3, particularly pages 20 f. Those type of arguments reappeared in the late 1990s along with the rousing growth of commercial activities surrounding the Internet—see our discussion of Isenberg (1997) at note 126.

A related strand of arguments came from the authors of the original end-to-end arguments. Saltzer, lead author of the classic paper on end-to-end arguments (Saltzer et al. 1981*a*; Saltzer et al. 1984), put forward a brief note of his concerns about the future development of the Internet (Saltzer 1999). He argues that ISPs are increasingly employing various restrictions to the service offered to end users, some clandestine, others backed up by "technical excuses", all operating to prejudice the end users—namely (1) limits on streaming video, (2) restrictions on setting up servers, (3) choosing large delay paths when better ones would be available, so as to prevent Internet telephony, (4) filtering applied to file sharing applications and objectionable content in general, (5) restricting the number of end devices per home, handing out but one IP number to end users. These actions, Saltzer argues, are in conflict with the end-to-end argument which he quotes as saying "don't force any service, feature, or restriction on the customer; his application knows best what features it needs, and whether or not to provide those features itself." Also, Saltzer (1999) considers the end-to-end argument to be "the principle that has enabled the thousands of innovative applications we see today and it will continue to enable that kind of innovation only so long as it is not interfered with." Very similar points can be found in Reed (2000) as well as Blumenthal and Clark (2001, p. 74).

Yet by 2001 it was also well established that the most sensible remedies to such problems would likely be to increase transparency about service restrictions and market choice of providers for end users. Note CSTB:

> [F]ull disclosure of filtering practices provides consumers with the means to make informed choices when selecting an ISP. (CSTB 2001, p. 150)

And, despite their concerns about some of the ISP actions at the time and a certain bias in favor of end user empowerment and control, and despite their very different personal opinions on normative matters beyond the scope of the original end-to-end arguments, all three authors of the Saltzer et al. (1981*a*) paper agree that the end-to-end arguments must not be extended arbitrarily from their original scope and meaning. Blumenthal and Clark concluded by 2001:

> The end-to-end arguments are no more "validated" by the belief in end-user empowerment than they are "'invalidated" by a call for a more complex mix of high-level functional objectives. (p. 80)

The Blumenthal and Clark statement is accompanied by a footnote pointing to a personal communication with J. Saltzer at November 11, 1998. And, Reed (2009*a*) notes that the goal of having all functions at the edges may be a "'Reed research guideline' not an architecture argument." See also our note 370.

Concurrently, however, the notions put forward by Saltzer (1999) were taken up by legal scholars (see, e. g., Lessig 2001 who refers to Saltzer at pp. 156 ff.) and economists (e. g., David 2001*a*, see particularly pp. 19 f.). Ever since then, 'network neutrality' advocates (starting with Wu 2003) have prominently featured the link between the original end-to-end arguments and their decisively normative positions — Schewick (2004) tries to give credence to the Lessig take, and as of 2008 Lessig still claims: "It is [. . .] end-to-end, or what we now call net neutrality, [. . .] that gave us transparency, openness, and freedom" (Lessig 2008, ca. 4:30 min). Suffice it here to point to Sandvig (2006) who has offered a fine rebuttal of such claims, casting serious doubt on the alleged causality between (1) the Internet as an artifact, (2) the end-to-end arguments, and (3) the network neutrality calls for regulation of network providers.

452 (148). Notes Clark (2003):

> Leaving a feature out of an interface does not make it go away. It can drive it under the covers, outside the architecture, but not

> out of existence. Creative market entrants are already finding clever ways to bypass the basic interface's architectural limitations and impose price discrimination. ISPs are seeking ways to introduce value stratification, and they will do it whether the building blocks are in the architecture or not. (p. 95)

453 (148). In fact, it is hard to state the network neutrality principle so that it can be sensibly applied by regulators at all. Note Mueller et al. (2007):

> Properly defined, the principle of network neutrality combines and integrates concepts of universal access to the resources connected to the Internet, freedom of expression, economic innovation, and free trade in digital products and services. (p. 2)

Going into greater detail and establishing guidelines that are genuine part of a distinct network neutrality notion has proven vastly more complicated, however. E. g., Schewick (2010*b*) proposes that:

- "[n]etwork neutrality rules should not prevent the evolution of the network's core more than absolutely necessary to protect the values that network neutrality rules are designed to protect", leaving open the question of what values and what tests for her rule to apply;
- "[i]f a network provider decides to offer QoS, the choice of whether and when to use QoS must be left to the user", leaving unaddressed the problem of the due application level changes, negotiations between users and network providers, and the overhead thus entailed;
- "[t]he rules should prohibit network providers from charging application or content providers for enhanced or prioritized transport [. . .] [but allow them] to charge their own Internet service customers for the type of QoS described above", implying a firm separation between providers on the one hand, and consumers on the other—precisely the type of distinction network neutrality proponents are fond of doing away with.

In all, articulating sensible and defendable network neutrality positions beyond the 'technically naïve and simplistic' is not at all trivial.

454 (148). See the elaboration by Saltzer (1999) as recounted in our note 451.

455 (148). Unlike many of the 'technically naïve and simplistic' arguments of network neutrality proponents, Mueller et al. (2007) acknowledge:

> The claim [. . .] that the Internet protocol itself somehow embodies an agreement to treat all packets equally [. . .] is not accurate. The TCP/IP protocols define an address space and a way to chop information into packets, assign addresses to them, and reassemble them at the destination. The protocols don't care whether someone reads what is inside the packet or makes a routing priority decision based on the header information or the payload along the way; TCP/IP continues to work as designed whether or not that happens. [. . .]
>
> [C]oncerns [about Deep Packet Inspection, DPI] are real and important. But they are relevant only insofar as bandwidth management techniques are part of a strategy of vertical integration by network operators into content and applications, or when they are used to censor or block access to Internet resources. In other words, the issue is not bandwidth differentiation per se, but blocking or gatekeeping, or anti-competitive discrimination. (pp. 4 f.)

Sandvig (2006), too, argues against "conflating the technical and the normative" — technical 'proxy' arguments on the one hand, and public policy about transparency, participation, and flexibility on the other:

> Indeed, it is not end-to-end design per se that is normatively positive, but the transparency, openness, and participatory design consultation that have come to be associated with this model of network intelligence through history and tradition. Loading the end-to-end argument with these social goals (rather than addressing normative goals directly) is a dangerous and misguided strategy because it shifts policy discourse away from normative ends in favor of traditional means that may no longer lead where we expect.

456 (149). To repeat the due Baran (1960) quote (from our page 12):

> [In case of random node or link failures] most of the non-connected stations are found on the periphery of the matrix. This result is caused by the number of probable connections being lower for those stations on the outside fringe. [. . .] [A] higher

degree of redundancy is desirable at the outside edge of distributed networks than needed in the interior. (p. 23)

457 (149). Recall from our note 443 and accompanying text that there is little point in precluding tussles in the Internet, for such restrictions run the risk of adversely affecting the overall order and structure of the Internet (Clark et al. 2005c). In a sense, the Internet may be conceived as an economic system that gives incentives to its various stakeholders — and very little has changed since A. Smith observed in 1776 that, above all, people react to incentives, and most if not all of the 'goodness' in a system stems from this very fact ("people respond to incentives", Landsburg 1995). Our argument thus implies that it is fair enough to have ISPs peek into IP packets (Clark et al. 2005c, p. 472). As long as the end users have a reasonable choice of providers (and may even distribute a logical communication across several of them), there is hardly a problem that would spell the need for ex ante limitations of ISP behavior.

458 (149). The typical U. S. household has at least three principal options for Internet access: (1) cable or DSL, (2) POTS modem dial-up, and (3) satellite Internet access. As always, there are trade-offs:

cable/DSL offers high bandwidth and low delay, but there are usually not too many providers to choose from;

dial-up offers almost unlimited choice of providers, but very low bandwidth;

satellite reaches everywhere with line of sight to the sky, generally offers good bandwidth, but comes with substantial delays (depending on whether satellites are geostationary or low orbit).

The costs of either option are within the same order of magnitude — option 1 usually comes with a flat rate pricing (in the U. S. from some $ 30 per month, in Germany from ca. € 30 per month); option 2 with a per minute charge of a few cents; and option 3 comes flat starting at some $ 40 per month (e. g., with WildBlue and a download speed of 512 kbps, a upload speed of 128 kbps as of July 2010). Increasingly, mobile phone infrastructures such as GSM, EDGE, and UMTS are becoming viable and popular options for stationary Internet access, too.

'Innovators' of the type that Schewick and Lessig are concerned about, are, of course, even less constrained than the average end user, for they may generally host their application or content wherever they please.

459 (149). TCP has no way of using several network attachment points, or IP addresses, in distributing the load of a connection's traffic. Work on "multipath TCP" is underway — see the IETF's Multipath TCP working group as well as Han et al. (2006). Also, applications based on the notion of "named content" rather than dedicated end-to-end connections offer great potential for using a multitude of access links in a seamless fashion (Jacobson et al. 2009).

460 (150). The fate of policy routing offers another example for the difficulty of organizing end users in pursuit of aims that have few beneficiaries other than themselves (Clark et al. 2005*c*, p. 469).

461 (150). See Bärwolff (2009*b*) for a brief elaboration:

> On what grounds is access granted to one's Internet connection for unknown third parties? What about monitoring, accounting of credits and debts, and, possibly, payments in money terms? Who shall be accountable for any wrongs committed by third parties via one's Internet connection, and how should identity of those third parties be managed?
>
> Many of those questions have been touched on in the literature, case law, and legislation on liability and identity management for wireless hotspots and arbitrary third parties gaining Internet access through them. The legal situation with respect to wireless hotspots dispensing with any identity management is somewhat sketchy and inconclusive, and the state of the art of managing such hotspots has thus become one where (1) access to unknown and untrustworthy third parties is prevented by encryption and other security measures, and (2) wherever public access is granted it is based on proper identification of the ones using the hotspot.
>
> While browser-based access (universal access method, or UAM) is a feasible solution for acquiring casual access to one hotspot, it is too difficult a solution for seamless roaming and multihoming; however, some sort of automatic authentication may

> be achieved in a similar manner. Plus, managing credits and debts from using others' services or providing services to others calls for some kind of global arrangement on how to account for and manage the due figures as a distributed and highly available service. It would be desirable to have a scheme that allows for individual users to accrue credits and debts within a certain range, so as to do away with the need to transfer any credits within the system or manage actual payments. The possibility for such transfers, however, may later be added as an out-of-band or add-on service to the system. (pp. 10 f., footnotes omitted)

462 (150). It is not at all clear whether ISP interests are, in fact, diametrically opposed to those of consumers as MacKie-Mason et al. (1996*a*) valuably observe in terms of the trade-offs in the different conceivable network architectures. True, all other things being equal, providers prefer an "aware" architecture over a "blind" one, for the former allows them to pursue conventional price discrimination; while consumers prefer the latter, for it leaves them with the bulk of social surplus. However, in reality there are sizeable costs to either architecture: the aware architecture suffers from *liability*, *reputation*, and *gateway effects* (pp. 10 ff.), and the blind architecture suffers from *clutter* and *attention effects* (pp. 13 ff.). Thus providers may shy away from a perfectly aware architecture, and consumers may not be too happy with a perfectly blind architecture either. Curiously, despite the attendant costs, the overall balance may well be favor of the blind architecture:

> [T]he blind architecture may encourage more vigorous creation of content than the aware architecture for two reasons. First, the blind architecture leaves more profits for early entrants to markets, thereby encouraging the rapid filling of unmet consumer needs. Second, in the presence of significant uncertainty about the profitability of various goods, networks with a blind architecture benefit from the diversity of beliefs among content creators; taken as a collective whole, the community of content creators experiments widely with new goods in the blind architecture. The increased content creation in the blind archi-

> tecture not only increases consumer surplus, but can also lead to a higher level of revenue for the network provider because of the increased total demand for goods. (p. 22)

The empirical indications to date—particularly the developments from 'walled gardens' to virtually ubiquitous plain IP level access provision (MacKie-Mason et al. 1996*c*, p. 216)—very much support this conjecture.

463 (150). We have noted in section 8.1 (note 449 and accompanying text) that it is vital to allow ISPs to recover their fixed costs so as to incentivize investments in physical infrastructure build-outs; and it is obvious that ISPs are in a far more competitive situation than higher-level service providers such as Akamai, Google, Amazon, Yahoo, etc. Yet our scheme would not necessarily have an adverse effect on the overall ISP business case. In fact, it is perfectly compatible with their natural profit orientation, for it entails no normative preference for neutrality on the part of network providers, thus allowing them to differentiate their offers and avert commodification of their services. Such improved scope for differentiation would also go very well with traditional industry practices which prefer flat rate pricing (Odlyzko 2001). While there has been some competition on price, most of the competition takes place under the premise of an industry wide reference price tag, and with the specific product attributes varying. Already, Chamberlin (1950) noted in his treatise about monopolistic competition:

> [P]rices may not be free to move at all. They may be set by custom or tradition. A particular price may have come generally to be associated with a product so that it cannot be changed without disaster. (p. 108)

464 (150). This point had been acknowledged as early as 1972 in the context of the Arpanet—notes Mathison and Walker (1972):

> While the question of regulating the ARPA network is somewhat academic today, since the network is a government-sponsored experimental project exclusively serving ARPA contractors, the next logical step after completion of the research stage is to consider commercial operation of the network and expansion of the user base. At that time, what effect will regulation, or the threat of regulation, have upon industry's interest in pro-

> viding such services on a commercial basis? Given the uncertain commercial prospects for a communications service based upon the ARPA technology, will firms be willing to undertake such a service offering with the added uncertainties of limited profit margins, delays due to lengthy regulatory proceedings, and reduced control of one's business activities? Is it more desirable, from a public interest point of view, to authorize a single common-carrier ARPA-like network or to permit several competitive networks to go into operation? The answers to these questions are not clear. *However, the possibilities for variety and innovation in services of this type suggest that they would flourish best in a competitive rather than a regulated common-carrier environment.* (p. 1259, emphasis added)

Moreover, to quote from the seminal discussion of the economics of regulation, A. E. Kahn (1971) notes about the problem of specifying the level of mandatory service and permissible restrictions:

> Service standards [. . .] [w]here they can be specified, they are often essentially uncontroversial. Where they cannot — and this is particularly the case when it comes to innovations, to the dynamic improvement of service — in a system in which the private companies do the managing and the government the supervision, there is no choice but to leave the initiative with the company itself. The only role the regulation commission can typically play is a negative one — formulating minimum standards and using periodic inspections to see that they are met; investigating customer complaints and issuing orders when service has been obviously poor, when management or subordinates have been blatantly inefficient or unfair, or when it wishes to insist that the companies take on or retain unremunerative business. (p. 22)

We are not saying that there is no merit whatsoever in articulating and enforcing restrictive rules on service providers (and neither has A. E. Kahn, for that matter); but, given the choice between (1) upholding overall order and individual liberty by monitoring and punishing ISPs, and (2) rewarding diversification at the edges on the other hand, the latter option seems far more attractive — after all, people respond much better to rewards than to punishments.

465 (151). As an aside, there are two potential implication of such principle: (1) the need for liability exemptions for end points serving as intermediaries for other end points, and (2) some appreciation of identifiers beyond IP addresses along the line of login credentials or OpenIDs.

466 (151). See the qualifications stated by Blumenthal and Clark (2001), quoted at our page 114.

467 (151). See note 335 and accompanying text, but also note 249 and accompanying text. Functions other than throughput and delay may be cost and security — see also note 242 for a useful list by D. Cohen (1977*a*) of 'issues' of potential concern for end points. The crucial thing about all these functions is that they typically involve a certain level of cooperation across trust boundaries, plus a useful interface to capture all the necessary control information to be exchanged. Hence, we have argued in section 7.1, such functions are generally implemented either in the network or in the end hosts, rarely in both — even at the cost of incompleteness and sizable inefficiencies.

Conclusion of Part III

468 (153). IAB (1996) conclude:

> The principle of constant change is perhaps the only principle of the Internet that should survive indefinitely. (p. 1)

The resulting challenge is thus to find and articulate regularities and structures beyond the trivial, that help shape the normative reasoning about practices, principles and values.

469 (153). The importance of this point can hardly be overemphasized: in classic architecture one may say that "5 percent of all the buildings in the world" are built by architects, with the rest coming "from the work of thousands of different people" (Alexander 1979, pp. 199 f.); but in the Internet, we have not had a 'chief protocol architect' for the last twenty years — the constituency has diffused to the point that it is hard for anyone to claim to have *any* control over parts of the Internet not under his immediate control.

470 (153). Recall from Clark (1992*b*) that "networks connect people using computers to mediate" (p. 15).

Conclusion

471 (157). Kleinrock (1978) once argued:

> [I]f one leaves design decisions in the hands of the users (or even network designers) then those individuals must be informed as to the effect of their decisions regarding these parameter settings; they cannot be expected to understand the consequence of their actions without being so informed. (p. 1329)

The interesting question then is, who has a legitimate claim to the articulation of Internet design principles. If we follow Häberle (1975), then the power to interpret and develop principles — even and especially when they have a quasi constitutional character — properly belongs to every person who comes into contact with them. There cannot thus be a definitive authority on the end-to-end arguments, not even the original authors have a claim to such authority.

472 (159). While our thesis may contribute to and inform the ongoing high-profile debate about network neutrality, we feel that considering it merely as a statement within that debate does little justice to its conceptual breadth.

473 (159). Note that the main predecessor to this notion — Clark and Blumenthal (2007) — has only been published as a conference paper; and so has our 2009 paper on the issue (Bärwolff 2009*c*).

474 (159). There have been limited efforts before ours to put the end-to-end arguments in a meaningful context of other principles; however, to our knowledge these have not gone beyond the consideration of layering and modularity as a theoretical exercise based on presumptions or secondary accounts (see, e. g., Gaynor and Bradner 2004; Schewick 2004).

475 (159). While we have here given explicit consideration to the notions of rough consensus and running code as core principles of the Internet evolution, we have done so only in a high-level abstract way of reasoning. An empirical study of cases to inform the descriptive content of this principle would likely add much to our broader understanding of the dynamics of normative principles in the Internet evolution at large.

476 (160). See, e.g., the IETF Multipath TCP working group (see also note 459).

477 (160). Notes Dunleavy (2003):

> [T]he act of writing may often be constitutive of your thinking. Left to ourselves we can all of us keep conflicting ideas in play almost indefinitely, selectively paying attention to what fits our needs of the moment and ignoring the tensions with what we said or thought yesterday, or the day before that. (p. 26)

Interesting Asides

Acronyms

ACM Association for Computing Machinery

AFIPS American Federation of Information Processing Societies

AHIP Arpanet Host-IMP Protocol

ALG Application Level Gateway

AQM Active Queue Management

ARP Address Resolution Protocol

ARPA Advanced Research Projects Agency

ARQ Automatic Repeat Query

ASCII American Standard Code for Information Interchange

BBN Bolt, Beranek, and Newman, Inc.

BGP Border Gateway Protocol

BSD Berkeley Software Distribution

CCITT Comité Consultatif Internationale de Télégraphie et Téléphonie

CDN Content Delivery Network

CHI Culler-Harrison

CLNP Connectionless Network Protocol

CRC Cyclic Redundancy Check

CS Computer Science

CSMA/CD Carrier Sense Multiple Access with Collision Detection

CVC Carrier Virtual Circuit

CVSD Continuously Variable Slope Delta Modulation

DARPA Defense Advanced Research Projects Agency

DCA Defense Communications Agency

DDoS Distributed Denial-of-Service

DG Datagram

DH Distant Host

DHCP Dynamic Host Configuration Protocol

DNS Domain Name System

DNSSEC Domain Name System Security Extensions

DoD U. S. Department of Defense

DPI Deep Packet Inspection

DSL Digital Subscriber Line

DTE Data Terminal Equipment

DTP Data Transfer Protocol

E-E User Protocol End-End User Protocol

ECN Explicit Congestion Notification

EDGE Enhanced Data rates for GSM Evolution

EIN European Informatics Network

FCC Federal Communications Commission

FEC Forward Error Correction

FTP File Transfer Protocol

GSM Global System for Mobile Communications

HDH HDLC Distant Host

HTML Hypertext Markup Language

HTTP Hypertext Transfer Protocol

I/O Device Input/Output Device

IAB Internet Architecture Board

ICCB Internet Configuration Control Board

ICCC International Conference on Computer Communication

ICMP Internet Control Message Protocol

ICP Initial Connection Protocol

IEEE Institution of Electrical and Electronics Engineers

IETF Internet Engineering Task Force

IFIP International Federation of Information Processing

IHL Internet Header Length

IMAP Internet Message Access Protocol

IMP Interface Message Processor

INWG International Packet Network Working Group

IP Internet Protocol

IPTO Information Processing Techniques Office

IRIA Institut de Recherche d'Informatique et d'Automatique

ISI University of Southern California Information Sciences Institute

ISO International Organization for Standardization

ISOC Internet Society

ISORM ISO/OSI Reference Model

ISP Internet Service Provider

ITP International Transport Protocol

ITU International Telecommunication Union

LAN Local Area Network

LH Local Host

LL Lincoln Labs

LNI Local Network Interface

LPC Linear Predictive Coding

MIT Massachusetts Institute of Technology

MLC Multi-Line Controller

Modem Modulator-Demodulator

MPLS Multiprotocol Label Switching

MPM Multi Packet Message

MTBF Mean Time Between Failure

MTTR Mean Time To Recovery

MTU Maximum Transmission Unit

MX Mail Exchange

NAT Network Address Translation

NCC Network Control Center

NCP Network Control Program

NPL National Physical Laboratory

NSC Network Secure Communications

NTP Network Time Protocol

NVP Network Voice Protocol

NVT Network Virtual Terminal

NWG Network Working Group

OPES Open Pluggable Edge Services

OSI Open Systems Interconnection

P2P Peer-to-Peer

PAR Positive Acknowledgment/ Retransmission

PCM Pulse-Code Modulation

PCU Programmable Control Unit

PDF Portable Document Format

PDU Protocol Data Unit

PLI Private Line Interface

PMTU Discovery Path MTU Discovery

PODA Priority-Oriented Demand Assignment

POP Post Office Protocol

POTS Plain Old Telephone Service

PRNET Packet Radio Network

PS Packet Switch

PSN Packet Switching Network

PSTN Public Switched Telephone Network

PTT Postal Telephone and Telegraph

PUP PARC Universal Packet

QoS Quality of Service

RED Random Early Detection

RFC Request for Connection

RFC Request for Comments

RFNM Ready for Next Message

RFQ Request for Quotations

RIM Research In Motion, Ltd.

RJE Remote Job Entry

RJS Remote Job Service

RMI Raw Message Interface

RML Range Measurement Laboratory, Patrick Air Force Base, FL

RST TCP Reset

RTP Real-time Transport Protocol

RTP Reliable Transmission Package

RTT Round-Trip Time

SAGE Semi-Automatic Ground Environment

SELinux Security-Enhanced Linux

SIP Session Initiation Protocol

SITA Société Internationale de Télécommunications Aéronautiques

SMTP Simple Mail Transfer Protocol

SNA IBM System Network Architecture

SRI Stanford Research Institute

SSL Secure Socket Layer

ST Internet Stream Protocol

TAC Terminal Access Controller

TCP Transmission Control Protocol

TCP Transmission Control Program

TCU Terminal Control Unit

TDMA Time Division Multiple Access

Telnet Telecommunications Network

TFTP Trivial File Transfer Protocol

TIP Terminal Interface Message Processor

TLS Transport Layer Security

TOR The Onion Router

ToS Type of Service

TP4 Transport Protocol Class 4

TS Transport Station

UAM Universal Access Method

UCLA University of California, Los Angeles

UCSB University of California, Santa Barbara

UDP User Datagram Protocol

UMTS Universal Mobile Telecommunications System

VC Virtual Circuit

VDH Very Distant Host

VoIP Voice over IP

VPN Virtual Private Network

W3C World Wide Web Consortium

WLAN Wireless Local Area Network

WWW World Wide Web

Xerox PARC Xerox Palo Alto Research Center

XNS Xerox Network Services

Figures

Tables

Literature

Abbate, J. (1999). *Inventing the Internet*. MIT Press. See pp. 175, 285, 345.

Aboba, B., ed. (1994). *The Online User's Encyclopedia: Bulletin Boards and Beyond*. Addison-Wesley.

Aboba, B. and Internet Architecture Board (2007). *Architectural Implications of Link Indications*. RFC 4907. Informational. IETF. URL: http://www.rfc-editor.org/rfc/rfc4907.txt. See p. 353.

Abramson, N. (1970). "The Aloha System — Another Alternative for Computer Communications". In: *AFIPS '70: Proceedings of the AFIPS 1970 Fall Joint Computer Conference*. Houston, TX. November 17–19, 1970. Vol. 36, pp. 295–298. URL: http://ethernethistory.typepad.com/papers/Alohanet.pdf (1970 Technical Report version). See p. 277.

—— (1975). *The Aloha System*. Tech. rep. B75-1. Final Technical Report for Contract Number NAS2-6700. Honolulu, HI: University of Hawaii. URL: http://www.bitsavers.org/pdf/univOfHawaii/B75-1_NAS2-6700_FinalReport_Jan75.pdf. See pp. 277, 278, 316.

NOTE: This section features the entirety of bibliography records referred to in the body of this thesis, plus a few records that are intimately related to them. Virtually all items are on file with the author, either as electronic versions (PDF, HTML, or plain text files) or printed copies. Some items have been loaned from libraries; we have taken copies of the most important parts of harder to come by ones such as Pouzin (1982).

MINOR TECHNICAL NOTES: Geographical references default to the U.S., with the state indicated by the common two-letter abbreviations (see, e.g., http://www.usps.com/ncsc/lookups/abbr_state.txt) unless indicated otherwise. Addresses are sometimes omitted for major publishing houses such as Springer or MIT Press. Abbreviations have been used wherever appropriate (e.g., NWG for Network Working Group, and RFC for Request for Comments). Overlong URLs where abbreviated using bit.ly. Lists of authors longer than 10 names have been abbreviated to "[first author] et al.". Abbreviated names used for the references in the text (such as IAB and BBN) are always spelled out in full in the bibliography (e.g., BBN will thus point to Bolt, Beranek, and Newman, Inc.).

Abramson, N. (1985). "Development of the ALOHANET". In: *IEEE Transactions on Information Theory* 31.2, pp. 119–123. ISSN: 0018-9448. See pp. 277, 278.

Aggarwal, V., A. Feldmann, and C. Scheideler (2007). "Can ISPs and P2P Users Cooperate for Improved Performance?" In: *ACM SIGCOMM Computer Communication Review* 37.3, pp. 29–40. ISSN: 0146-4833. DOI: 10.1145/1273445.1273449. See p. 121.

Aguiar, R. L. (2008). "Some Comments on Hourglasses". In: *ACM SIGCOMM Computer Communication Review* 38.5, pp. 69–72. ISSN: 0146-4833. DOI: 10.1145/1452335.1452346. See p. 396.

Alexander, C. (1979). *The Timeless Way of Building*. Vol. 1. 3 vols. New York, NY: Oxford University Press. ISBN: 0-19-502248-3. See pp. 109, 134, 164, 167, 215, 378, 387, 388, 437.

Allman, M., V. Paxson, and E. Blanton (2009). *TCP Congestion Control*. RFC 5681. Draft Standard. IETF. URL: http://www.rfc-editor.org/rfc/rfc5681.txt. See p. 354.

Alvestrand, H. T. (2004). *A Mission Statement for the IETF*. RFC 3935. Best Current Practice. IETF. URL: http://www.rfc-editor.org/rfc/rfc3935.txt. See pp. 371, 405.

Anania, L. and R. J. Solomon (1997). "Flat—The Minimalist Price". In: *Internet Economics*. Ed. by L. W. McKnight and J. P. Bailey. Cambridge, MA: MIT Press, pp. 91–118. See p. 363.

Andersen, D. G., H. Balakrishnan, N. Feamster, T. Koponen, D. Moon, and S. Shenker (2008). "Accountable Internet Protocol (aip)". In: *ACM SIGCOMM Computer Communication Review* 38.4, pp. 339–350. ISSN: 0146-4833. DOI: 10.1145/1402946.1402997. URL: http://www.cs.cmu.edu/~dga/papers/aip-sigcomm2008.pdf. See p. 213.

Andersson, L., E. Davies, and L. Zhang (2007). *Report from the IAB workshop on Unwanted Traffic March 9–10, 2006*. RFC 4948. Informational. IETF. URL: http://www.rfc-editor.org/rfc/rfc4948.txt. See p. 355.

Arkko, J., R. Briscoe, L. Eggert, A. Feldmann, and M. Handley (2009). "Dagstuhl Perspectives Workshop on End-to-end Protocols for the Future Internet". In: *ACM SIGCOMM Computer Communication Review* 39.2. Summary of a June 2008 workshop at Schloss Dagstuhl, Wadern, Germany, pp. 42–47. ISSN: 0146-4833. DOI: 10.1145/1517480.1517489.

URL: https://fit.nokia.com/lars/papers/2009-ccr-dagstuhl-fi.pdf. See p. 355.

Bache, A. and Y. Matras (1976). "Fundamental Choices in the Development of RCP, the Experimental Packet-Switching Data Transmission Service of the French PTT". In: *ICCC '76: Proceedings of the Third International Conference on Computer Communication*. Toronto, Canada. August 3–6, 1976. Ed. by P. K. Verma, pp. 311–316. URL: http://www.rogerdmoore.ca/PS/RCPBAC/RB.html. See p. 207.

Bache, A., L. Guillou, H. Layec, B. Lorig, and Y. Matras (1976). "RCP, the Experimental Packet-Switched Data Transmission Service of the French PTT: History, Connections, Control". In: *ICCC '76: Proceedings of the Third International Conference on Computer Communication*. Toronto, Canada. August 3–6, 1976. Ed. by P. K. Verma, pp. 37–43. See p. 207.

Baker, F., P. Almquist, and F. Kastenholz (1995). *Requirements for IP Version 4 Routers*. RFC 1812. Proposed Standard. Updated by RFC 2644. IETF. URL: http://www.rfc-editor.org/rfc/rfc1812.txt. See pp. 98, 233, 352, 366.

Balakrishnan, H. (1998). "Challenges to Reliable Data Transport over Heterogeneous Wireless Networks". PhD thesis. University of California at Berkeley, Department of Electrical Engineering and Computer Sciences. URL: http://nms.lcs.mit.edu/papers/hari-phd/ (requires ghostview or GNU gv). See p. 234.

Balakrishnan, H., S. Seshan, and R. H. Katz (1995). "Improving Reliable Transport and Handoff Performance in Cellular Wireless Networks". In: *Wireless Networks* 1.4, pp. 469–481. ISSN: 1022-0038. DOI: 10.1007/BF01985757. URL: http://www.cs.cmu.edu/~srini/Papers/1995.Balakrishnan.winet.pdf (pre-publication version). See p. 234.

Balakrishnan, H., V. N. Padmanabhan, S. Seshan, and R. H. Katz (1997). "A Comparison of Mechanisms for Improving TCP Performance Over Wireless Links". In: *IEEE/ACM Transactions on Networking (TON)* 5.6, pp. 756–769. ISSN: 1063-6692. DOI: 10.1109/90.650137. URL: http://pdos.csail.mit.edu/decouto/papers/balakrishnan97.pdf. See p. 234.

Baldwin, C. Y. and K. B. Clark (2000). *The Power of Modularity*. Vol. 1. Design Rules. MIT Press. See p. 393.

Baldwin, C. Y. and C. J. Woodard (2008). *The Architecture of Platforms: A Unified View*. Working Paper 09-034. Harvard Business School. URL: http://hbswk.hbs.edu/item/6025.html. See p. 424.

Baran, P. (1960). *Reliable Digital Communications Systems Using Unreliable Network Repeater Nodes*. The RAND Corporation Paper P-1995. RAND Corporation. URL: http://rand.org/pubs/papers/2008/P1995.pdf. See pp. 12, 182, 189–191, 431.

—— (1962). *On Distributed Communications Networks*. The RAND Corporation Paper P-2626. RAND Corporation. URL: http://www.rand.org/pubs/papers/2005/P2626.pdf. See pp. 182, 183.

—— (1964*a*). *On Distributed Communications: I. Introduction to Distributed Communications Networks*. Research Memorandum RM-3420-PR. RAND Corporation. URL: http://rand.org/pubs/research_memoranda/2006/RM3420.pdf. See p. 182.

—— (1964*b*). *On Distributed Communications: IV. Priority, Precedence, and Overload*. Research Memorandum RM-3638-PR. RAND Corporation. URL: http://www.rand.org/pubs/research_memoranda/2006/RM3638.pdf. See p. 182.

—— (1964*c*). *On Distributed Communications: IX. Security, Secrecy, and Tamper-Free Considerations*. Research Memorandum RM-3765-PR. RAND Corporation. URL: http://www.rand.org/pubs/research_memoranda/2006/RM3765.pdf. See p. 182.

—— (1964*d*). "On Distributed Communications Networks". In: *IEEE Transactions on Communications* 12.1, pp. 1–9. ISSN: 0096-2244. See pp. 11, 12, 107, 182, 189, 190, 196, 324, 388.

—— (1964*e*). *On Distributed Communications: V. History, Alternative Approaches, and Comparisons*. Research Memorandum RM-3097-PR. RAND Corporation. URL: http://www.rand.org/pubs/research_memoranda/2008/RM3097.pdf. See p. 182.

—— (1964*f*). *On Distributed Communications: VI. Mini-Cost Microwave*. Research Memorandum RM-3762-PR. RAND Corporation. URL: http://www.rand.org/pubs/research_memoranda/2006/RM3762.pdf. See p. 182.

—— (1964*g*). *On Distributed Communications: VII. Tentative Engineering Specifications and Preliminary Design for a High-Data-Rate Distributed Network Switching Node*. Research Memorandum RM-3763-PR. RAND Corporation. URL: http://www.rand.org/pubs/research_memoranda/2006/RM3763.pdf. See p. 182.

—— (1964*h*). *On Distributed Communications: VIII. The Multiplexing Station*. Research Memorandum RM-3764-PR. RAND Corporation. URL: http://www.rand.org/pubs/research_memoranda/2006/RM3764.pdf. See p. 182.

—— (1964*i*). *On Distributed Communications: X. Cost Estimates*. Research Memorandum RM-3766-PR. RAND Corporation. URL: http://www.rand.org/pubs/research_memoranda/2006/RM3766.pdf. See p. 182.

—— (1964*j*). *On Distributed Communications: XI. Summary Overview*. Research Memorandum RM-3767-PR. RAND Corporation. URL: http://rand.org/pubs/research_memoranda/2006/RM3767.pdf. See p. 182.

—— (1967). *Some Remarks on Digital Distributed Communications Networks*. The RAND Corporation Paper P-3536. RAND Corporation. URL: http://www.rand.org/pubs/papers/2008/P3536.pdf. See p. 182.

—— (1977). "Some Perspectives on Networks — Past, Present and Future". In: *Information Processing '77: Proceedings of the IFIP Congress 1977*. Toronto, Canada. August 8–12, 1977. Ed. by B. Gilchrist. Amsterdam, Netherlands: North-Holland, pp. 459–464. ISBN: 0-7204-0755-9. See p. 183.

—— (1990). *An Interview with Paul Baran (by Judy O'Neill)*. Oral History Interview (see http://www.cbi.umn.edu/oh/oralhistories.html). Minneapolis, MN: Charles Babbage Institute for the History of Information Technology, University of Minnesota. URL: http://special.lib.umn.edu/cbi/oh/pdf.phtml?id=295. See p. 192.

Barbir, A., R. Penno, Y.-F. R. Chen, M. Hofmann, and H. Orman (2004). *An Architecture for Open Pluggable Edge Services (OPES)*. RFC 3835. Informational. IETF. URL: http://www.rfc-editor.org/rfc/rfc3835.txt. See p. 372.

Barlow, J. P. (1996). *A Declaration of the Independence of Cyberspace*. Online. URL: http://homes.eff.org/~barlow/Declaration-Final.html. See p. 178.

Barroso, L. A., J. Dean, and U. Hölzle (2003). "Web Search for a Planet: The Google Cluster Architecture". In: *IEEE Micro* 23.2, pp. 22–28. URL: http://labs.google.com/papers/googlecluster-ieee.pdf. See p. 374.

Bartlett, K. A. (1968). "Transmission Control in a Local Data Network". In: *Information Processing '68: Proceedings of IFIP Congress 1968*. Edinburgh, UK. August 5–10, 1968. Ed. by A. J. H. Morrell. Vol. 2.3. Amsterdam, Netherlands: North-Holland, pp. 704–708. See pp. 188, 314.

Bartlett, K. A., R. A. Scantlebury, and P. T. Wilkinson (1969). "A Note on Reliable Full-Duplex Transmission Over Half-Duplex Links". In: *Communications of the ACM* 12.5, pp. 260–261. ISSN: 0001-0782. DOI: 10.1145/362946.362970. See p. 269.

Bauer, S., D. D. Clark, and W. H. Lehr (2009). "The Evolution of Internet Congestion". In: *TPRC 2009: 37th Research Conference on Communication, Information and Internet Policy*. Arlington, VA. September 25–27, 2009. Papers online. URL: http://www.tprcweb.com/images/stories/papers/Bauer_Clark_Lehr_2009.pdf (also at http://mitas.csail.mit.edu/papers/Bauer_Clark_Lehr_2009.pdf). See p. 345.

Bennett, R. (2009). *Designed for Change: End-to-End Arguments, Internet Innovation, and the Net Neutrality Debate*. Report. Information Technology and Innovation Foundation (ITIF). URL: http://www.itif.org/files/2009-designed-for-change.pdf. See p. 240.

Beranek, L. (2000). "Roots of the Internet: A Personal History". In: *The Massachusetts Historical Review* 2. URL: http://www.historycooperative.org/journals/mhr/2/beranek.html. See p. 183.

Berners-Lee, T., W. Hall, J. A. Hendler, K. O'Hara, N. Shadbolt, and D. J. Weitzner (2006). "A Framework for Web Science". In: *Foundations and Trends in Web Science* 1.1, pp. 1–130. DOI: 10.1561/1800000001. URL: http://www.nowpublishers.com/getpdf.aspx?doi=1800000001&product=WEB. See p. 171.

Berners-Lee, T. (1989). *Information Management: A Proposal*. Internal Proposal. Switzerland and France: CERN. URL: http://www.w3.org/History/1989/proposal.html (also at http://info.cern.ch/Proposal.html). See p. 373.

Berners-Lee, T. and M. Fischetti (1999). *Weaving the Web: The Original Design and Ultimate Destiny of the World Wide Web*. London: Orion Business Books. See p. 373.

Berners-Lee, T., R. T. Fielding, and H. Frystyk Nielsen (1996). *Hypertext Transfer Protocol—HTTP/1.0*. RFC 1945. Informational. IETF. URL: http://www.rfc-editor.org/rfc/rfc1945.txt. See p. 289.

Beverly, R., S. Bauer, and A. Berger (2007). "The Internet's Not a Big Truck: Toward Quantifying Network Neutrality". In: *PAM 2007: Proceedings of the 8th Passive and Active Measurement Conference*. Louvain-la-neuve, Belgium. April 5–6, 2007. URL: http://www.mit.edu/~rbeverly/papers/truck-pam07.pdf. See p. 361.

Beverly, R., A. Berger, Y. Hyun, and K. C. Claffy (2009). "Understanding the Efficacy of Deployed Internet Source Address Validation Filtering". In: *IMC '09: Proceedings of the 9th ACM SIGCOMM Conference on Internet Measurement*. Chicago, IL. New York, NY: ACM, pp. 356–369. ISBN: 978-1-60558-771-4. DOI: 10.1145/1644893.1644936. URL: http://rbeverly.net/research/papers/spoofer-imc09.pdf. See p. 350.

Bhattacharjee, S., K. L. Calvert, and E. W. Zegura (1997). "Active Networking and the End-to-End Argument". In: *ICNP '97: Proceedings of the 1997 International Conference on Network Protocols*. Atlanta, GA. October 28–31, 1997. Washington, DC: IEEE Computer Society, pp. 220–228. ISBN: 0-8186-8061-X. URL: http://www.ieee-icnp.org/1997/papers/1997-23.pdf. See p. 225.

Bhushan, A. K. (1972*a*). *Another Look at Data and File Transfer Protocols*. RFC 310. Historic. NWG. URL: http://www.rfc-editor.org/rfc/rfc310.txt. See p. 296.

——— (1972*b*). *File Transfer Protocol*. RFC 354. Historic. Obsoleted by RFC 542, updated by RFCs 385, 454, 683. NWG. URL: http://www.rfc-editor.org/rfc/rfc354.txt. See pp. 296, 297.

——— (1973). *Data and File Transfer: Some Measurement Results*. RFC 573. Historic. NWG. URL: http://www.rfc-editor.org/rfc/rfc573.txt. See p. 251.

Bhushan, A. K., R. B. Braden, W. R. Crowther, E. Harslem, J. Heafner, A. A. McKenize, J. Melvin, B. Sundberg, D. Watson, and J. White (1971*a*). *The Data Transfer Protocol*. RFC 264. Historic. Obsoleted by RFC 354, updated by RFC 310. NWG. URL: http://www.rfc-editor.org/rfc/rfc264.txt. See pp. 288, 296.

——— (1971*b*). *The File Transfer Protocol*. RFC 265. Historic. Obsoleted by RFC 354, updated by RFCs 281, 294, 310. NWG. URL: http://www.rfc-editor.org/rfc/rfc265.txt. See p. 296.

Binder, R. (2010). *Re: [ih] Fate of Alohanet*. internet history mailing list. Mar. 13, 2010. URL: http://mailman.postel.org/pipermail/internet-history / 2010 - April / 001305.html (forwarded copy, original email to the author). See p. 310.

Binder, R., N. Abramson, F. F. Kuo, A. Okinaka, and D. Wax (1975). "ALOHA Packet Broadcasting: A Retrospect". In: *AFIPS '75: Proceedings of the AFIPS 1975 National Computer Conference and Exposition*. Anaheim, CA. May 19–22, 1975. New York, NY: ACM, pp. 203–215. DOI: 10.1145/1499949.1499985. See pp. 278, 310, 311.

Black, F. and M. Scholes (1973). "The Pricing of Options and Corporate Liabilities". In: *Journal of Political Economy* 81.3, pp. 637–654. See p. 393.

Blanchet, M. (2006). *Migrating to IPv6: A Practical Guide to Implementing IPv6 in Mobile and Fixed Networks*. Wiley. See p. 403.

Blumenthal, M. S. (2002). "End-to-End and Subsequent Paradigms". In: *The Law Review of Michigan State University—Detroit College of Law* 3, pp. 709–717. See p. 144.

Blumenthal, M. S. and D. D. Clark (2001). "Rethinking the Design of the Internet: The End-to-End Arguments vs. the Brave New World". In: *ACM Transactions on Internet Technology* 1.1, pp. 70–109. URL: http://mia.ece.uic.edu/~papers/Networking/pdf00002.pdf (pre-publication version). See pp. 41, 114, 127, 226, 227, 373, 428, 429, 437.

Blumenthal, S. H., A. A. McKenzie, C. Partridge, and D. C. Walden (2010). "Data Networking @ BBN". In: *A Culture of Innovation: Insider Accounts of Computing and Life at BBN*. Ed. by D. C. Walden and R. S. Nickerson. East Sandwich, MA: Waterside Publishing. Chap. 17. See p. 249.

Boehm, S. P. and P. Baran (1964). *On Distributed Communications: II. Digital Simulation of Hot-Potato Routing in a Broadband Distributed Communications Network*. Research Memorandum RM-3103-PR. RAND Corporation. URL: http://www.rand.org/pubs/research_memoranda/2006/RM3103.pdf. See p. 182.

Boggs, D. R., J. F. Shoch, E. Taft, and R. M. Metcalfe (1980). "Pup: An Internetwork Architecture". In: *IEEE Transactions on Communications* 28.4, pp. 612–624. ISSN: 0090-6778. URL: http://ia360911.us.archive.org/2/items/PupAnInterworkArchitecture/PupAnInterworkArchitecture.djvu. See pp. 316, 321, 330, 333, 336.

Boggs, D. R., J. C. Mogul, and C. A. Kent (1988). "Measured Capacity of an Ethernet: Myths and Reality". In: *SIGCOMM '88: Symposium on Communications Architectures and Protocols*. Stanford, CA. August 16–18,

1988. New York, NY: ACM, pp. 222–234. ISBN: 0-89791-279-9. DOI: 10.1145/52324.52347. See p. 314.

Bohn, R., H.-W. Braun, K. C. Claffy, and S. Wolff (1994). "Mitigating the Coming Internet Crunch: Multiple Service Levels Via Precedence". In: *Journal of High Speed Networks* 3.4, pp. 335–349. URL: http://www.caida.org/publications/papers/1994/mcic/ (also at http://moat.nlanr.net/Papers/precedence.asc, both CAIDA working paper version). See p. 359.

Bolt, Beranek and Newman Inc. (1969*a*). *Initial Design for Interface Message Processors for the ARPA Computer Network*. BBN Report 1763. Bolt, Beranek and Newman Inc. (BBN). URL: http://www.bitsavers.org/pdf/bbn/imp/BBN1763_IMP_InitialDesign_Jan69.pdf. Also published in the 2008 Salus book. See p. 196.

——— (1969*b*). *Interface Message Processors for the Arpa Computer Network*. BBN Report 1890. Quarterly Technical Report No. 3, 1 July 1969 to 30 September 1969. Bolt, Beranek and Newman Inc. (BBN). See p. 272.

——— (1969*c*). *Interface Message Processors for the Arpa Computer Network*. BBN Report 1783. Quarterly Technical Report No. 1, 1 January 1969 to 31 March 1969. Bolt, Beranek and Newman Inc. (BBN). URL: http://ia311503.us.archive.org/2/items/QuarterlyTechnicalReport1/QuarterlyTechnicalReport1.djvu (http://www.archive.org/details/QuarterlyTechnicalReport1). See pp. 272, 280.

——— (1970*a*). *Interface Message Processors for the Arpa Computer Network*. BBN Report 1928. Quarterly Technical Report No. 4, 1 October 1969 to 31 December 1969. Bolt, Beranek and Newman Inc. (BBN). See pp. 64, 258, 282.

——— (1970*b*). *Interface Message Processors for the Arpa Computer Network*. BBN Report 2055. Quarterly Management Report, 1 July 1970 to 30 September 1970. Bolt, Beranek and Newman Inc. (BBN). See pp. 67, 279.

——— (1970*c*). *Interface Message Processors for the Arpa Computer Network*. BBN Report 1928. Quarterly Management Report, 1 October 1969 to 31 December 1969. Bolt, Beranek and Newman Inc. (BBN). See p. 245.

——— (1970*d*). *Interface Message Processors for the Arpa Computer Network*. BBN Report 2059. Quarterly Technical Report No. 7, 1 July 1970 to 30 September 1970. Bolt, Beranek and Newman Inc. (BBN). See p. 279.

Bolt, Beranek and Newman Inc. (1971*a*). *Interface Message Processors for the Arpa Computer Network*. BBN Report 2270. Quarterly Technical Report No. 11, 1 July 1971 to 30 September 1971. Bolt, Beranek and Newman Inc. (BBN). See pp. 67, 257, 279, 282.

—— (1971*b*). *The BBN TIP: Hardware Manual*. BBN Report 2184. Bolt, Beranek and Newman Inc. (BBN). See p. 282.

—— (1972*a*). *Interface Message Processors for the Arpa Computer Network*. BBN Report 2198. Quarterly Technical Report No. 4, 1 October 1971 to 31 December 1971. Bolt, Beranek and Newman Inc. (BBN). See pp. 64, 65, 275, 276.

—— (1972*b*). *Interface Message Processors for the Arpa Computer Network*. BBN Report 2396. Quarterly Technical Report No. 14, 1 April 1972 to 30 June 1972. Bolt, Beranek and Newman Inc. (BBN). See pp. 210, 247.

—— (1973*a*). *Interface Message Processor Operating Manual*. Operating Manual for Interface Message Processors: 516 IMP, 316 IMP, TIP. BBN Report 1877. Revised edition. Bolt, Beranek and Newman Inc. (BBN). See pp. 279, 283.

—— (1973*b*). *Interface Message Processors for the Arpa Computer Network*. BBN Report 2541. Quarterly Technical Report No. 1, 1 January 1973 to 30 March 1973. Bolt, Beranek and Newman Inc. (BBN). Republished partly in RFC 528. See pp. 255, 297.

—— (1974*a*). *Interface Message Processors for the Arpa Computer Network*. BBN Report 2913. Quarterly Technical Report No. 7, 1 July 1974 to 30 September 1974. Bolt, Beranek and Newman Inc. (BBN). See pp. 80, 299–301, 303.

—— (1974*b*). *Interface Message Processors for the Arpa Computer Network*. BBN Report 2852. Quarterly Technical Report No. 6, 1 April 1974 to 30 June 1974. Bolt, Beranek and Newman Inc. (BBN). See pp. 63, 303.

—— (1974*c*). *Interface Message Processors for the Arpa Computer Network*. BBN Report 2816. Quarterly Technical Report No. 5, 1 January 1974 to 31 March 1974. Bolt, Beranek and Newman Inc. (BBN). See p. 260.

—— (1974*d*). *Network Design Issues*. BBN Report 2918. Bolt, Beranek and Newman Inc. (BBN). URL: http://www.cs.utexas.edu/users/chris/DIGITAL_ARCHIVE/ARPANET/bbn2918.pdf. Based on BBN Report 2913. See pp. 24–26, 208, 209, 217, 366.

—— (1975). *Interface Message Processors for the Arpa Computer Network*. BBN Report 3106. Quarterly Technical Report No. 2, 1 April 1975 to 3 June 1975. Bolt, Beranek and Newman Inc. (BBN). See p. 304.

—— (1977). *Terminal Interface Message Processor: User's Guide*. BBN Report 2183. Revised version. Bolt, Beranek and Newman Inc. (BBN). First published in 1971. See pp. 282, 284.

—— (1978*a*). *Packet Broadcast by Satellite, Pluribus Satellite IMP Development, Unix System Development*. BBN Report 3911. Combined Quarterly Technical Report No. 10, Volume I. Bolt, Beranek and Newman Inc. (BBN). See p. 304.

—— (1978*b*). *Packet Broadcast by Satellite, Pluribus Satellite IMP Development, Unix System Development, Remote Site Maintenance*. BBN Report 3984. Combined Quarterly Technical Report No. 11, Volume I. Bolt, Beranek and Newman Inc. (BBN). See p. 304.

—— (1978*c*). *The Interface Message Processor Program*. BBN Technical Information Report 89. Updated for IMP version 3244. Bolt, Beranek and Newman Inc. (BBN). First published in 1973. See pp. 265, 269, 272, 278, 302, 357, 358.

Bolt, Beranek and Newman Inc. and R. E. Kahn (1976). *Interface Message Processor—Specifications for the Interconnection of a Host and an IMP*. BBN Report 1822. Bolt, Beranek and Newman Inc. (BBN). URL: http://www.bitsavers.org/pdf/bbn/imp/BBN1822_Jan1976.pdf (January 1976 revision). See pp. 63–65, 210, 248, 267, 273–276, 279, 287, 297, 302.

Boulez, P. (1989). *Jalons (Pour Une Décennie): Dix Ans d'Enseignement au Collège de France (1978-1988)*. Paris, France: Christian Bourgois. ISBN: 2-267-00631-6. See p. 164.

Bowles, S. (2004). *Microeconomics: Behavior, Institutions, and Evolution*. Princeton University Press. See p. 365.

Braden, R. T. (1977*a*). "A Server Host System on the Arpanet". In: *Proceedings of the Fifth Data Communications Symposium*. Snowbird, UT. September 27–29, 1977. Ed. by J. F. Marchese and F. E. Heart. ACM and IEEE. New York, NY: IEEE, pp. 4-1–4-9. See pp. 244, 258.

—— (1977*b*). *NETRJS Protocol*. RFC 740. Historic. NWG. URL: http://www.rfc-editor.org/rfc/rfc740.txt. See p. 298.

—— (1989). *Requirements for Internet Hosts—Communication Layers*. RFC 1122. Standard. Updated by RFCs 1349, 4379. IETF. URL: http://www.

rfc-editor.org/rfc/rfc1122.txt. See pp. 98, 199, 233, 339, 343, 351, 352, 366, 394.

Braden, R. T. (2009*a*). *[ih] ARPAnet Type 3 packets (datagrams)*. internet history mailing list. Nov. 25, 2009. URL: http://mailman.postel.org/pipermail/internet-history/2009-November/001057.html. See p. 304.

—— (2009*b*). *Re: [ih] internet-history Digest, Vol 37, Issue 6*. internet history mailing list. Nov. 8, 2009. URL: http://mailman.postel.org/pipermail/internet-history/2009-November/000983.html. See p. 402.

—— (2010). *[ih] The origin of the NVT*. internet history mailing list. Jan. 22, 2010. URL: http://mailman.postel.org/pipermail/internet-history/2010-January/001214.html. See p. 284.

Braden, R. T. and J. B. Postel (1987). *Requirements for Internet Gateways*. RFC 1009. Historic. Obsoleted by RFC 1812. IETF. URL: http://www.rfc-editor.org/rfc/rfc1009.txt. See p. 352.

Braden, R. T. and RFC editors (2004). *The End-of-Line Story*. Online. URL: http://www.rfc-editor.org/EOLstory.txt. See p. 284.

Braden, R. T., D. D. Clark, and S. Shenker (1994). *Integrated Services in the Internet Architecture: An Overview*. RFC 1633. Informational. IETF. URL: http://www.rfc-editor.org/rfc/rfc1633.txt. See pp. 370, 427.

Braden, R. T. et al. (1998). *Recommendations on Queue Management and Congestion Avoidance in the Internet*. RFC 2309. Informational. IETF. URL: http://www.rfc-editor.org/rfc/rfc2309.txt. See p. 347.

Braden, R. T., T. Faber, and M. Handley (2003). "From Protocol Stack to Protocol Heap: Role-Based Architecture". In: *ACM SIGCOMM Computer Communication Review* 33.1, pp. 17–22. ISSN: 0146-4833. DOI: 10.1145/774763.774765. URL: http://conferences.sigcomm.org/hotnets/2002/papers/braden.pdf and http://www.isi.edu/newarch/DOCUMENTS/hotrba.paper.pdf (version presented at the First Workshop on Hot Topics in Networks (HotNets-I). Princeton, NJ. October 28–29, 2002). See pp. 213, 394.

Braithwaite, R. B. (1953). *Scientific Explanation: A Study of Theory, Probability and Law in Science*. Cambridge University Press. See p. 170.

Bresnahan, T. F. and M. Trajtenberg (1995). "General Purpose Technologies: 'Engines of Growth'?" In: *Journal of Econometrics* 65.1, pp. 83–108. URL: http://www.tau.ac.il/~manuel/pdfs/general_purpose.pdf. See p. 424.

Bresnahan, T. F. (1998). "New Modes of Competition and the Future Structure of the Computer Industry". In: *Progress and Freedom Foundation Conference*. Competition, Convergence, and the Microsoft Monopoly. Washington, DC. February 5, 1998. URL: http://www.stanford.edu/~tbres/research/pff.pdf. See p. 393.

Bressler, R. D. (1972). *"But my NCP costs $500 a day . . . "* RFC 425. Historic. NWG. URL: http://www.rfc-editor.org/rfc/rfc425.txt. See p. 355.

Bressler, R. D., S. D. Crocker, W. R. Crowther, G. R. Grossman, R. S. Tomlinson, and J. E. White (1971). *Output of the Host-Host Protocol Glitch Cleaning Committee*. RFC 107. Historic. Updated by RFCs 111, 124, 132, 154, 179. NWG. URL: http://www.rfc-editor.org/rfc/rfc107.txt. See p. 287.

Bressler, R. D., D. Murphy, and D. C. Walden (1972*a*). *Proposed Experiment with a Message Switching Protocol*. RFC 333. Historic. NWG. URL: http://www.rfc-editor.org/rfc/rfc333.txt. See p. 288.

Bressler, R. D., R. Guida, and A. A. McKenzie (1972*b*). *Remote Job Entry Protocol*. RFC 407. Historic. NWG. URL: http://www.rfc-editor.org/rfc/rfc407.txt. See p. 298.

Briscoe, R. (2004). "The Implications of Pervasive Computing on Network Design". In: *BT Technology Journal* 22.3, pp. 170–190. ISSN: 1358-3948. DOI: 10.1023/B:BTTJ.0000047131.43151.f3. See p. 369.

—— (2006). "Using Self-Interest to Prevent Malice: Fixing the Denial of Service Flaw of the Internet". In: *Workshop on the Economics of Securing the Information Infrastructure*. Washington, DC. October 23–24, 2006. URL: http://www.bobbriscoe.net/presents/0610wesii_dos_refb/0610briscoe_wesii.pdf (presentation slides), http://www.bobbriscoe.net/projects/2020comms/refb/refb_dplinc_wesii06.pdf (paper). See pp. 355, 363.

—— (2007*a*). *[e2e] Time for a new Internet Protocol*. end2end-interest mailing list. May 21, 2007. URL: http://www.postel.org/pipermail/end2end-interest/2007-May/006857.html. See p. 425.

—— (2007*b*). *[e2e] Time for a new Internet Protocol*. end2end-interest mailing list. May 22, 2007. URL: http://www.postel.org/pipermail/end2end-interest/2007-May/006870.html. See p. 425.

—— (2007*c*). "Flow Rate Fairness: Dismantling a Religion". In: *ACM SIGCOMM Computer Communication Review* 37.2, pp. 63–74. ISSN:

0146-4833. DOI: 10.1145/1232919.1232926. URL: http://www.sigcomm.org/ccr/drupal/files/fair_ccr0.pdf (pre-publication version). See pp. 358, 363.

Briscoe, R. (2008). "A Fairer, Faster Internet Protocol". In: *IEEE Spectrum* 45.12, pp. 42–47. URL: http://www.spectrum.ieee.org/dec08/7027. See p. 26.

—— (2009). "Re-Feedback: Freedom with Accountability for Causing Congestion in a Connectionless Internetwork". PhD thesis. University College London (UCL). URL: http://www.cs.ucl.ac.uk/staff/B.Briscoe/pubs.html\#refb-dis. See pp. 26, 363.

Briscoe, R., A. Jacquet, C. Di Cairano-Gilfedder, A. Salvatori, A. Soppera, and M. Koyabe (2005). "Policing Congestion Response in an Internetwork Using Re-Feedback". In: *ACM SIGCOMM Computer Communication Review* 35.4, pp. 277–288. ISSN: 0146-4833. DOI: 10.1145/1090191.1080124. See p. 101.

Brownsword, R. and K. Yeung, eds. (2008). *Regulating Technologies: Legal Futures, Regulatory Frames and Technological Fixes*. Hart Publishing. See p. 178.

Bryan, R. F. (1972). *Exercising The Arpanet*. RFC 302. Historic. NWG. URL: http://www.rfc-editor.org/rfc/rfc302.txt. See p. 294.

Burton, H. and D. Sullivan (1972). "Errors and Error Control". In: *Proceedings of the IEEE* 60.11, pp. 1293–1301. See pp. 197, 198.

Bush, R. and D. Meyer (2002). *Some Internet Architectural Guidelines and Philosophy*. RFC 3439. Informational. IETF. URL: http://www.rfc-editor.org/rfc/rfc3439.txt. See pp. 35, 393.

Bush, V. (1945). "As We May Think". In: *The Atlantic Monthly* 176.1, pp. 101–108. URL: http://www.theatlantic.com/doc/print/194507/bush. See p. 411.

Bärwolff, M. (2008). *The (In)essentiality of Monopoly Power in Network Neutrality Violations*. Online. URL: http://works.bepress.com/mbaer/1/. See p. 414.

—— (2009*a*). "Discrimination, Liberty, and Innovation: Some Thoughts on the Invariable Trade-Offs of Normative Purposes and Technical Means in the Internet". In: *ReArch '09: Proceedings of the 2009 Workshop on Re-Architecting the Internet*. Rome, Italy. December 1–4, 2009. New York,

NY: ACM, pp. 25–30. ISBN: 978-1-60558-749-3. DOI: 10.1145/1658978.1658985.

—— (2009*b*). *Towards Extending the Equilibrium of Discrimination in the Internet to its Fringes*. Online. Complete rewrite of the 2009 ReArch paper. URL: http://works.bepress.com/mbaer/4/. See p. 433.

—— (2009*c*). "Vertical and Horizontal End-to-End Arguments in the Internet". In: *ICC 2009: Proceedings of the IEEE International Conference on Communications Workshops*. Dresden, Germany. June 14–18, 2009. IEEE. DOI: 10.1109/ICCW.2009.5207972. See pp. 5, 41, 222, 226, 227, 438.

Campbell, D. T. and D. W. Fiske (1959). "Convergent and Discriminant Validation by the Multitrait-Multimethod Matrix". In: *Psychological Bulletin* 56.2, pp. 81–105. See p. 170.

Campbell-Kelly, M. (1987). "Data Communications at the National Physical Laboratory (1965-1975)". In: *IEEE Annals of the History of Computing* 9.3/4, pp. 221–247. ISSN: 1058-6180. DOI: 10.1109/MAHC.1987.10023. URL: http://www.archive.org/details/DataCommunicationsAtTheNationalPhysicalLaboratory. See pp. 189, 340.

Campbell-Kelly, M. and D. D. Garcia-Swartz (2005). *The History of the Internet: The Missing Narratives*. Working Paper. URL: http://ssrn.com/abstract=867087. See pp. 242, 341.

Carpenter, B. E. (2000). *Internet Transparency*. RFC 2775. Informational. IETF. URL: http://www.rfc-editor.org/rfc/rfc2775.txt. See p. 134.

Carr, C. S., S. D. Crocker, and V. G. Cerf (1970). "Host-Host Communication Protocol in the ARPA Network". In: *AFIPS '70: Proceedings of the AFIPS 1970 Spring Joint Computer Conference*. Atlantic City, NJ. May 5–7, 1970. New York, NY: ACM, pp. 589–597. DOI: 10.1145/1476936.1477024. Also published as RFC 33 with Stephen Crocker as the lead author.

Casner, S. L., E. R. Mader, and E. R. Cole (1978). "Some Initial Measurements of Arpanet Packet Voice Transmission". In: *NTC '78; National Telecommunications Conference Record*. Birmingham, AL. December 3–6, 1978. Vol. 1. IEEE. Piscataway, NJ, pp. 12.2.1–12.2.15. See p. 307.

Cerf, V. G. (1969). *ASCII Format For Network Interchange*. RFC 20. Historic. NWG. URL: http://www.rfc-editor.org/rfc/rfc20.txt. See p. 283.

—— (1972*a*). *Report of Subgroup 1 on Communication System Requirements*. INWG Note 1. IFIP WG 6.1 (INWG). URL: http://baerwolff.de/

public/Cerf-1972-Report-of-Subgroup-1-on-Communication-System-Requirements--INWG-Note-1.pdf. See pp. 47, 319, 320.

Cerf, V. G. (1972*b*). *Report of Subgroup 2 on Host-Host Protocol Requirements*. INWG Note 2. IFIP WG 6.1 (INWG). URL: http://baerwolff.de/public/Cerf-1972-Report-of-Subgroup-2-on-HOST-HOST-Protocol-Requirements--INWG-Note-2.pdf. See pp. 319, 320.

—— (1973). *A Partial Specification of an International Transmission Protocol*. INWG General Note 28. Sent in May 1973 to the INWG mailing list with the subject line "First pass draft of International Transmission Protocol". IFIP WG 6.1 (INWG). URL: http://www.cs.utexas.edu/users/chris/DIGITAL_ARCHIVE/TCPIP/Cerf.pdf (different pagination). See pp. 86, 90, 207, 320, 335.

—— (1974). *An Assessment of Arpanet Protocols*. RFC 635. Historic. NWG. URL: http://www.rfc-editor.org/rfc/rfc635.txt. See pp. 24, 25, 294.

—— (1977). *Gateways and Network Interfaces*. Internet Experiment Note (IEN) 6. Internet Notebook Section 2.3.3.3. URL: ftp://ftp.rfc-editor.org/in-notes/ien/scanned/ien6.pdf. See p. 332.

—— (1978*a*). *A Proposal for TCP Version 3.1 Header Format*. Internet Experiment Note (IEN) 27. Internet Notebook Section 2.4.2.1. URL: ftp://ftp.rfc-editor.org/in-notes/ien/scanned/ien27.pdf. See p. 92.

—— (1978*b*). *A Proposed New Internet Header Format*. Internet Experiment Note (IEN) 26. Internet Notebook Section 2.3.2.1. URL: ftp://ftp.rfc-editor.org/in-notes/ien/scanned/ien26.pdf. See p. 92.

—— (1978*c*). *The Catenet Model for Internetworking*. Internet Experiment Note (IEN) 48. Internet Notebook Section 2.1.1.1. URL: ftp://ftp.rfc-editor.org/in-notes/ien/ien48.txt. See pp. 276, 326.

—— (1980). *DoD Protocol Standardization*. Internet Experiment Note (IEN) 152. URL: ftp://ftp.rfc-editor.org/in-notes/ien/ien152.txt.

—— (1982*a*). *Packet Satellite Technology Reference Sources*. RFC 829. Historic. NWG. URL: http://www.rfc-editor.org/rfc/rfc829.txt. See p. 308.

—— (1982*b*). *The C/30 Upgrade on the Arpanet*. DoD Network Newsletter (ANEWS) 10. Network Info Center for Defense Communications Agency (DCA) Defense Data Network (DDN) Program Management Office (SRI NIC). URL: ftp://ftp.rfc-editor.org/in-notes/museum/ARPANET_News.mail (copies also at http://ring.nict.go.jp/pub/doc/RFC/museum/ddn-news/ddn-news.n10.1). See p. 281.

—— (1988). *Interview with Vinton Cerf by James Pelkey*. Excerpts in the James Pelkey online book. URL: http://historyofcomputercommunications.info/index.html. See p. 340.

—— (1990). *Internet Activities Board*. RFC 1160. Informational. IETF. URL: http://www.rfc-editor.org/rfc/rfc1160.txt. See p. 405.

—— (1994). "How the Internet Came to Be". In: *The Online User's Encyclopedia: Bulletin Boards and Beyond*. Ed. by B. Aboba. Addison-Wesley, pp. 527–534. URL: http://virtualschool.edu/mon/Internet/CerfHowInternetCame2B.html (1993 pre-publication version). See p. 319.

—— (2001). *An Interview with Vinton G. Cerf*. http://www.cwhonors.org/archives/histories/cerf.pdf. Interview conducted by Daniel S. Morrow on November 1, 2001; Computerworld Honors Program International Archives. See pp. 344, 405.

—— (2009). *Re: [ih] Arpanet raw messages, voice, and TCP*. internet history mailing list. Nov. 26, 2009. URL: http://mailman.postel.org/pipermail/internet-history/2009-November/001070.html. See p. 305.

—— (2010). *Re: Experiments outside IMP subnetwork VCs by 1971, as reported in your RFC 635*. Email to the author. Feb. 15, 2010. See p. 294.

Cerf, V. G. and E. Cain (1983). "The DoD Internet Architecture Model". In: *Computer Networks* 7.5, pp. 307–318. See pp. 368, 385, 397.

Cerf, V. G. and R. E. Kahn (1973). *Towards Protocols for Internetwork Communication*. INWG General Note 39. Presented at the September 1973 INWG meeting in Sussex, UK. IFIP WG 6.1 (INWG). URL: http://ia300241.us.archive.org/1/items/HostAndProcessLevelProtocolsForInternetworkCommunication/. Sent to INWG mailing list with the subject line "Host and Process Level Protocols for Internetwork Communication"; also published as NIC 18764. See pp. 90, 207, 238, 239, 331, 332, 335, 336.

—— (1974). "A Protocol for Packet Network Interconnection". In: *IEEE Transactions on Communications* 22.5. Based on an earlier version prepared as a working paper for a September 1973 INWG meeting), pp. 637–648. URL: http://www.cs.princeton.edu/courses/archive/fall06/cos561/papers/cerf74.pdf. See pp. 24, 25, 91, 207, 220, 239, 318, 332, 335, 336.

Cerf, V. G. and P. T. Kirstein (1978). "Issues in Packet-Network Interconnection". In: *Proceedings of the IEEE* 66.11, pp. 1386–1408. ISSN: 0018-9219. See pp. 314, 329, 341.

Cerf, V. G. and J. B. Postel (1977). *Specification of Internet Transmission Control Program TCP (Version 2)*. Internet Experiment Note (IEN) 5. Internet Notebook Section 2.4.2. URL: ftp://ftp.rfc-editor.org/in-notes/ien/ien5.pdf (also at http://www.postel.org/ien/pdf/ien005.pdf; and at http://www.cs.utexas.edu/users/chris/DIGITAL_ARCHIVE/TCPIP/IEN5.pdf, OCR version, different pagination). See pp. 332, 334, 337, 338.

——— (1978). *Specification of Internetwork Transmission Control Program TCP Version 3*. Internet Experiment Note (IEN) 21. Internet Notebook Section 2.4.2.1. URL: ftp://ftp.rfc-editor.org/in-notes/ien/ien21.pdf (also at http://www.cs.utexas.edu/users/chris/DIGITAL_ARCHIVE/TCPIP/IEN21.pdf, OCR version, different pagination). See pp. 82, 88, 239, 333, 338, 402.

——— (1980). *Mail Transition Plan*. RFC 771. Historic. NWG. URL: http://www.rfc-editor.org/rfc/rfc771.txt. See p. 344.

Cerf, V. G., Y. Dalal, and C. A. Sunshine (1974). *Specification of Internet Transmission Control Program*. RFC 675. Historic. INWG General Note 72. Network Working Group, IFIP Working Group 6.1. URL: http://www.rfc-editor.org/rfc/rfc675.txt. See pp. 232, 337, 339, 342.

Cerf, V. G., A. A. McKenzie, R. A. Scantlebury, and H. Zimmermann (1976). "Proposal for an International End to End Protocol". In: *ACM SIGCOMM Computer Communication Review* 6.1 (Jan. 1976), pp. 63–89. ISSN: 0146-4833. DOI: 10.1145/1015828.1015832. Also published as INWG Note 96, July 1975. See pp. 288, 340–342.

Chamberlin, E. H. (1950). *The Theory of Monopolistic Competition: A Re-Orientation of the Theory of Value*. 6th ed. Harvard University Press. First published in 1933. See p. 435.

Chiappa, J. N. (1995). *"Soft" and "Hard" State*. Online. URL: http://ana.lcs.mit.edu/~jnc/tech/hard_soft.html. Slight revision of an email message sent to the mailing list flows@research.ftp.com (an open list for general discussion of 'flows' in the Internet architecture) on November 2, 1995 (also sent to big-internet mailing list at munnari.oz.au, see http://www.sobco.com/ipng/archive/big-i/1995-11-Nov). See p. 218.

—— (2002). *Will The Real "End-End Principle" Please Stand Up?* Online. URL: http://ana.lcs.mit.edu/~jnc/tech/end_end.html (see also http://www.postel.org/pipermail/end2end-interest/2002-April/001980.html for a contextual note). See p. 218.

—— (2009). *Re: [ih] Arpanet raw messages, voice, and TCP.* internet history mailing list. Nov. 25, 2009. URL: http://mailman.postel.org/pipermail/internet-history/2009-November/001063.html. See p. 305.

Chretien, G. J., W. M. Konig, and J. H. Rech (1973). "The SITA Network". In: *Proceedings of the NATO Advanced Study Institute on Computer Communication Networks.* Sussex, UK. September 9–15, 1973. Noordhoff International Publishing, pp. 373–396. URL: http://rogerdmoore.ca/PS/SITAB.html (different pagination). See p. 242.

Clark, D. D. (1974). "An Input/Output Architecture for Virtual Memory Computer Systems". PhD thesis. Cambridge, MA: Massachusetts Institute of Technology. URL: http://publications.csail.mit.edu/lcs/pubs/pdf/MIT-LCS-TR-117.pdf. Submitted in 1973. Published as MIT Laboratory for Computer Science Technical Report 117. See pp. 263, 390.

—— (1981). *Internet Short Term Service Goals.* Internet Experiment Note (IEN) 201. URL: ftp://ftp.rfc-editor.org/in-notes/ien/ien201.txt. See pp. 98, 212.

—— (1982*a*). *Fault Isolation and Recovery.* RFC 816. Historic. NWG. URL: http://www.rfc-editor.org/rfc/rfc816.txt. See pp. 97, 198.

—— (1982*b*). *IP Datagram Reassembly Algorithms.* RFC 815. Historic. NWG. URL: http://www.rfc-editor.org/rfc/rfc815.txt. See p. 338.

—— (1982*c*). *Modularity and Efficiency in Protocol Implementation.* RFC 817. Historic. NWG. URL: http://www.rfc-editor.org/rfc/rfc817.txt. See pp. 291, 334, 393, 394.

—— (1982*d*). *Name, Addresses, Ports, and Routes.* RFC 814. Historic. NWG. URL: http://www.rfc-editor.org/rfc/rfc814.txt. See p. 372.

—— (1982*e*). *Window and Acknowledgement Strategy in TCP.* RFC 813. http://tools.ietf.org/html/rfc813. See p. 339.

—— (1988). "The Design Philosophy of the DARPA Internet Protocols". In: *ACM SIGCOMM Computer Communication Review* 18.4, pp. 106–114. ISSN: 0146-4833. DOI: 10.1145/52325.52336. URL: http://nms.csail.mit.edu/6829-papers/darpa-internet.pdf (also at http://ccr.sigcomm.org/

archive/1995/jan95/ccr-9501-clark.pdf, 1995 SIGCOMM reprint). See pp. 34, 35, 45, 165, 213, 218, 237, 292, 314, 348, 388.

Clark, D. D. (1989). *Policy Routing in Internet Protocols*. RFC 1102. Historic. IETF. URL: http://www.rfc-editor.org/rfc/rfc1102.txt. See pp. 35, 218, 383.

—— (1992*a*). "A Cloudy Crystal Ball—Visions of the Future". In: *IETF 24: Proceedings of the Twenty-Fourth Internet Engineering Task Force Meeting*. Massachusetts Institute of Technology (MIT), Cambridge, MA. July 13–17, 1992. Ed. by M. Davies, C. Clark, and D. Legare. IETF. Corporation for National Research Initiatives, pp. 539–543. URL: http://www.ietf.org/old/2009/proceedings/prior29/IETF24.pdf (presentation slides at http://xys.ccert.edu.cn/reference/future_ietf_92.pdf). See pp. 73, 139, 404.

—— (1992*b*). *Untitled subsection of: "Who's Who in the Internet—Biographies of IAB, IESG and IRSG Members"*. RFC 1336. Informational. IETF, p. 15. URL: http://www.rfc-editor.org/rfc/rfc1336.txt. See pp. 407, 438.

—— (1995). "Adding Service Discrimination to the Internet". In: *TPRC 1995: Proceedings of the 23rd Annual Telecommunications Policy Research Conference*. Solomons, MD. September 30 to October 2, 1995. URL: http://www.cnaf.infn.it/~ferrari/papers/ispn/TPRC2-0.ps.gz (also at ftp://ftp.ccs.neu.edu/pub/people/matta/Ex-Internet/InetClark.ps). Also published in Telecommunications Policy, Vol. 20, No. 3, April 1996. See p. 363.

—— (1997*a*). "Combining Sender and Receiver Payments in the Internet". In: *Interconnection and the Internet: Selected Papers from the 1996 TPRC*. Ed. by G. Rosston and D. Waterman. Lawrence Earlbaum Associates. URL: http://www.gta.ufrj.br/diffserv/csrp-ddc.ps.gz. See p. 363.

—— (1997*b*). "Internet Cost Allocation and Pricing". In: *Internet Economics*. Ed. by L. W. McKnight and J. P. Bailey. Cambridge, MA: MIT Press, pp. 215–252. Largely based on a 1995 version titled "Adding Service Discrimination to the Internet". See p. 363.

—— (1997*c*). "Interoperation, Open Interfaces, and Protocol Architecture". In: *The Unpredictable Certainty: White Papers*. Complement to the CSTB report "The Unpredictable Certainty: Information Infrastructure Through 2000". Washington, DC: National Academy Press. Chap. 16, pp. 133–144. URL: http://www.nap.edu/openbook.php?record_id=6062&page=133. See p. 292.

—— (2003). "Economics and the Design of Open Systems". In: *IEEE Internet Computing* 7.2, pp. 96, 94–95. ISSN: 1089-7801. DOI: 10.1109/MIC.2003.1189196. See pp. 427, 429.

—— (2005). *What is "Architecture"?* Future Internet Network Design (FIND) Meeting 2005. Background paper. URL: http://find.isi.edu/presentation_files/Dave_Clark-What_is_architecture_4.pdf. See p. 387.

—— (2007*a*). *Application Design and the End-to-End Arguments.* MIT Communications Futures Program Bi-Annual Meeting. Philadelphia, PA. May 30–31, 2007. Presentation slides. URL: http://cfp.mit.edu/events/may07/presentations/CLARK%20Application%20Design.ppt. See pp. 61, 177.

—— (2007*b*). "Net Neutrality: Words of Power and 800-Pound Gorillas". In: *International Journal of Communication* 1, pp. 701–708. URL: http://ijoc.org/ojs/index.php/ijoc/article/view/158/83. See p. 177.

—— (2008*a*). "A Simple Cost Model for Broadband Access: What Will Video Cost?" In: *TPRC 2008: 36th Telecommunications and Communications Policy Research Conference.* Arlington, VA. September 26–28, 2008. Papers online. URL: http://tprcweb.com/files/Cost%20analysis%20TPRC.pdf. See pp. 237, 409.

—— (2008*b*). *What Would a More Secure Future Look Like?* Online. URL: http://publius.cc/2008/06/10/david-clark-what-would-a-more-secure-future-look-like/. See p. 425.

—— (2008*c*). *Written Statement.* FCC public hearing on network management, Harvard Law School, Cambridge, MA, February 25, 2008. URL: http://www.fcc.gov/broadband_network_management/022508/clark.pdf. See p. 177.

—— (2009*a*). *A Multi-Theory Analysis of Long-Lived Networks.* Version 2.1. URL: http://groups.csail.mit.edu/ana/People/DDC/Longevity%202-1.pdf. See pp. 122, 376.

—— (2009*b*). *Getting a Clear Signal: Decoding Network Neutrality.* Working Paper. Version 2.0 of October 10, 2009; on file with the author. Cambridge, MA: MIT, CSAIL. See pp. 119, 416, 425.

—— (2009*c*). *Private Communication with Matthias Bärwolff.* Notes on file with the author. Phone call. Oct. 23, 2009. See pp. 214, 215.

Clark, D. D. (2009*d*). *Private communication with Matthias Bärwolff. SNA: Reliability versus statistical aggregation.* Notes on file with the author. Interview in Cambridge, MA. Feb. 26, 2009. See p. 323.

—— (2009*e*). *The Expressive Power of the Internet Design.* Version 5.0. URL: http://groups.csail.mit.edu/ana/People/DDC/Expressive%20power%205.pdf. See pp. 212, 376, 382, 386.

—— (2009*f*). *Toward the Design of a Future Internet.* Online. Version 7. URL: http://groups.csail.mit.edu/ana/People/DDC/Future%20Internet%207-0.pdf. See pp. 121, 377.

—— (2010*a*). *Private Communication with Matthias Bärwolff.* Notes on file with the author. Phone call. Apr. 6, 2010. See pp. 91, 331.

—— (2010*b*). *Re: Chapter 2 – End-to-End Arguments in the Literature.* Email to the author. Jan. 1, 2010. See p. 234.

Clark, D. D. and M. S. Blumenthal (2007). "The End-to-End Argument and Application Design: The Role of Trust". In: *TPRC 2007: 35th Telecommunications and Communications Policy Research Conference.* Arlington, VA. September 28–30, 2007. Papers online. URL: http://web.si.umich.edu/tprc/papers/2007/748/End%202%20end%20and%20trust%2010%20final%20TPRC.pdf. See pp. 37–41, 50, 118, 148, 177, 221–225, 227, 372–374, 378, 438.

Clark, D. D. and W. Fang (1998). "Explicit Allocation of Best-Effort Packet Delivery Service". In: *IEEE/ACM Transactions on Networking (TON)* 6.4, pp. 362–373. ISSN: 1063-6692. DOI: 10.1109/90.720870. See p. 363.

Clark, D. D. and D. L. Tennenhouse (1990). "Architectural Considerations for a New Generation of Protocols". In: *ACM SIGCOMM Computer Communication Review* 20.4, pp. 200–208. ISSN: 0146-4833. DOI: 10.1145/99517.99553. See pp. 393, 394.

Clark, D. D., K. T. Pogran, and D. P. Reed (1978). "An Introduction to Local Area Networks". In: *Proceedings of the IEEE* 66.11, pp. 1497–1517. ISSN: 0018-9219. See pp. 313, 314, 316, 317, 322, 334, 346.

Clark, D. D., V. Jacobson, J. Romkey, and H. Salwen (1989). "An Analysis of TCP Processing Overhead". In: *IEEE Communications Magazine* 27.6, pp. 23–29. DOI: 10.1109/35.29545. See p. 393.

Clark, D. D., L. Chapin, V. G. Cerf, R. T. Braden, and R. Hobby (1991). *Towards the Future Internet Architecture.* RFC 1287. Informational. IETF. URL: http://www.rfc-editor.org/rfc/rfc1287.txt. See pp. 118, 119, 370.

Clark, D. D., E. A. Feigenbaum, J. Hartmanis, R. W. Lucky, R. M. Metcalfe, R. Reddy, and M. Shaw (1998). "Innovation and Obstacles: the Future of Computing". In: *Computer* 31.1 (Jan. 1998). Excerpts from a panel discussion moderated by David Clark, pp. 29–38. ISSN: 0018-9162. DOI: 10.1109/2.641975. See p. 368.

Clark, D. D., J. Wroclawski, K. R. Sollins, and R. T. Braden (2002). "Tussle in Cyberspace: Defining Tomorrow's Internet". In: *SIGCOMM '02: Proceedings of the 2002 Conference on Applications, Technologies, Architectures, and Protocols for Computer Communication*. Pittsburgh, PA. August 19–23, 2002. New York, NY: ACM, pp. 347–356. ISBN: 1-58113-570-X. DOI: 10.1145/633025.633059. URL: http://www.sigcomm.org/sigcomm2002/papers/tussle.pdf (also at http://groups.csail.mit.edu/ana/Publications/PubPDFs/Tussle2002.pdf). See pp. 146, 425.

Clark, D. D., K. R. Sollins, J. Wroclawski, and T. Faber (2003). "Addressing Reality: An Architectural Response to Real-World Demands on the Evolving Internet". In: *FDNA '03: Proceedings of the ACM SIGCOMM Workshop on Future Directions in Network Architecture*. Karlsruhe, Germany. New York, NY: ACM, pp. 247–257. URL: http://poet.mit.edu/events/020107/addressing.pdf. See p. 222.

Clark, D. D. et al. (2004). *New Arch: Future Generation Internet Architecture*. Final Technical Report AFRL-IF-RS-TR-2004-235. URL: http://www.isi.edu/newarch/iDOCS/final.finalreport.pdf (another, presumably more 'official', version with different pagination is at http://www.dtic.mil/cgi-bin/GetTRDoc?AD=ADA426770&Location=U2&doc=GetTRDoc.pdf). See pp. 111, 177, 221, 234, 292, 369, 379.

Clark, D. D. et al. (2005*a*). "Making the World (of Communications) a Different Place". In: *ACM SIGCOMM Computer Communication Review* 35.3, pp. 91–96. ISSN: 0146-4833. DOI: 10.1145/1070873.1070887. URL: http://www.ir.bbn.com/~craig/e2e-vision.pdf. See p. 364.

Clark, D. D., W. H. Lehr, P. Faratin, S. Bauer, and J. Wroclawski (2005*b*). "The Growth of Internet Overlay Networks: Implications for Architecture, Industry Structure and Policy". In: *TPRC 2005: 33th Telecommunications and Communications Policy Research Conference*. Arlington, VA. September 23–25, 2005. Papers online. URL: http://web.si.umich.edu/tprc/papers/2005/466/TPRC_Overlays_9_8_05.pdf. See p. 383.

Clark, D. D., J. Wroclawski, K. R. Sollins, and R. T. Braden (2005*c*). "Tussle in Cyberspace: Defining Tomorrow's Internet". In: *IEEE/ACM Transactions on Networking (TON)* 13.3, pp. 462–475. ISSN: 1063-6692. DOI: 10.1109/TNET.2005.850224. See pp. 146, 147, 150, 383, 425, 426, 432, 433.

Clark, D. D., W. H. Lehr, and S. Bauer (2010). *In the Matter of Preserving the Open Internet Broadband Industry Practices.* Filing to the FCC WC Docket No. 07-52; GN Docket No. 09-191. Massachusetts Institute of Technology. URL: http://fjallfoss.fcc.gov/ecfs/comment/view?id=6015522681. See pp. 176, 426.

Cohen, D. (1977*a*). *Internetting or Beyond NCP.* Internet Experiment Note (IEN) 11. Internet Notebook Section 2.3.3.4. URL: http://www.postel.org/ien/pdf/ien011.pdf. Featuring comments by Carl A. Sunshine, Vinton G. Cerf, Robert E. Kahn, and Jonathan B. Postel. See pp. 307, 437.

—— (1977*b*). *Specifications for the Network Voice Protocol (NVP).* RFC 741. Historic. NWG. URL: http://www.rfc-editor.org/rfc/rfc741.txt. Also published as Network Secure Communications (NSC) group Note Nr. 68, a revision of NSC Notes 26, 40, and 43. See pp. 81, 304, 306.

—— (1978*a*). *On Names, Addresses and Routings.* Internet Experiment Note (IEN) 23. Internet Notebook Section 2.3.3.7. URL: ftp://ftp.rfc-editor.org/in-notes/ien/ien23.txt. See p. 372.

—— (1978*b*). *On Names, Addresses and Routings (II).* Internet Experiment Note (IEN) 31. Internet Notebook Section 2.3.3.11. URL: ftp://ftp.rfc-editor.org/in-notes/ien/ien31.txt. See pp. 317, 372.

—— (1981). "A Voice Message System". In: *Computer Message Systems.* Proceedings of the IFIP TC-6 International Symposium on Computer Message Systems. Ottawa, Canada. April 6–8, 1981. Ed. by R. P. Uhlig. Amsterdam, Netherlands: North-Holland, pp. 17–27. ISBN: 0-444-85253-6. See p. 306.

—— (1984). "Satellite Communication of Real-Time Packet Video Images". In: *ICCC '84: Proceedings of the Seventh International Conference on Computer Communication.* Sidney, Australia. October 30 to November 2, 1984. Ed. by J. M. Bennett and T. Pearcy. Amsterdam, Netherlands: North-Holland. URL: http://www.dtic.mil/cgi-bin/GetTRDoc?Location=U2&doc=GetTRDoc.pdf&AD=ADA143613 (ISI Reprint Series version, ISI/RS-83-6; Information Sciences Institute at University of Southern California). See p. 307.

Cohen, D. and J. B. Postel (1979). *Source Routing*. Internet Experiment Note (IEN) 95. URL: ftp://ftp.rfc-editor.org/in-notes/ien/ien95.txt (also at ftp://ftp.rfc-editor.org/in-notes/ien/scanned/ien76.pdf). See p. 382.

—— (1983). "The ISO Reference Model and Other Protocol Architectures". In: *IFIP '83: Proceedings of the Ninth World Congress of the International Federation for Information Processing*. Paris, France. September 19–23, 1983. Ed. by R. E. A. Mason. Amsterdam, Netherlands: North-Holland, pp. 29–34. ISBN: 0-444-86729-5. Also published as ISI/RS-83-6 (Information Sciences Institute at University of Southern California, ISI Reprint Series), November 1983. See pp. 211, 291, 390, 391, 393, 401.

Cohen, M. R. (1931). *Reason and Nature: An Essay on the Meaning of Scientific Method*. New York, NY: Harcourt, Brace. See p. 9.

Cohn, S. N. (1983). *Measurement and Analysis of ARPANET Traffic: May 1982 and March 1983*. BBN Report 5349. Bolt, Beranek and Newman Inc. (BBN). See p. 295.

Computer Science and Telecommunications Board (1994). *Realizing the Information Future: The Internet and Beyond*. Authored by the NRENAISSANCE Committee; Computer Science and Telecommunications Board; Commission on Physical Sciences, Mathematics, and Applications; National Research Council. Washington, DC: National Academy Press. ISBN: 0-309-05044-8. URL: http://www.nap.edu/openbook.php?record_id=4755. See p. 396.

—— (2001). *The Internet's Coming of Age*. Authored by Committee on the Internet in the Evolving Information Infrastructure; Computer Science and Telecommunications Board; Commission on Physical Sciences, Mathematics, and Applications; National Research Council. Washington, DC: National Academy Press. URL: http://www.nap.edu/openbook.php?record_id=9823. See pp. 289, 416, 428, 429.

Cooper, I., I. Melve, and G. Tomlinson (2001). *Internet Web Replication and Caching Taxonomy*. RFC 3040. Informational. IETF. URL: http://www.rfc-editor.org/rfc/rfc3040.txt. See p. 373.

Cooper, M. N., ed. (2004). *Open Architecture as Communications Policy: Preserving Internet Freedom in the Broadband Era*. Center for Internet and

Society, Stanford Law School. URL: http://cyberlaw.stanford.edu/attachments/openarchitecture.pdf.

Cosell, B. P. (2009). *Re: [ih] ARPAnet Type 3 packets (datagrams).* internet history mailing list. Nov. 26, 2009. URL: http://mailman.postel.org/pipermail/internet-history/2009-November/001074.html. See p. 268.

Cosell, B. P. and D. C. Walden (1972). *Letter to TIP Users—2.* RFC 386. Historic. NWG. URL: http://www.rfc-editor.org/rfc/rfc386.txt. See p. 295.

—— (1973). *Telnet Issues.* RFC 435. Historic. NWG. URL: http://www.rfc-editor.org/rfc/rfc435.txt. See p. 404.

—— (2003). "Developing Telnet's Negotiated Options". In: *IEEE Annals of the History of Computing* 25.2, pp. 80–82. ISSN: 1058-6180. DOI: 10.1109/MAHC.2003.1203060. See p. 404.

Crispin, M. R. (1979). *Universal Host Table.* RFC 752. Historic. NWG. URL: http://www.rfc-editor.org/rfc/rfc752.txt. See p. 304.

—— (1981). *TOPS-20 TCP Implementation.* tcp-ip mailing list. TCP/IP Digest, Monday, 19 October 1981, Volume 1, Issue 3. URL: http://securitydigest.org/tcp-ip/archive/1981/10 (also at http://ftp.arl.army.mil/ftp/tcp-ip-digest/tcp-ip-digest.v1n3.1). See p. 345.

Crocker, D. H. (1982). *Standard For the Format of ARPA Internet Text Messages.* RFC 822. Standard. Obsoleted by RFC 2822, updated by RFCs 1123, 2156, 1327, 1138, 1148. NWG. URL: http://www.rfc-editor.org/rfc/rfc822.txt. See p. 371.

—— (2000). *levels of end-to-end; lack thereof.* IETF Discussion mailing list. Dec. 19, 2000. URL: http://www.ietf.org/mail-archive/web/ietf/current/msg15623.html. See p. 406.

—— (2009). *Re: [e2e] Protocols breaking the end-to-end argument.* end2end-interest mailing list. Oct. 23, 2009. URL: http://www.postel.org/pipermail/end2end-interest/2009-October/007832.html. See p. 240.

—— (2010). *Re: The fate of Arpanet Users Interest Working Group (USING).* Email to the author. Feb. 3, 2010. See p. 286.

Crocker, D. H., N. Neigus, E. J. Feinler, and J. Iseli (1973). *ARPANET Users Interest Working Group Meeting.* RFC 585. Historic. NWG. URL: http://www.rfc-editor.org/rfc/rfc585.txt. See p. 285.

Crocker, S. D. (1969). *Host Software*. RFC 1. Historic. NWG. URL: http://www.rfc-editor.org/rfc/rfc1.txt. See pp. 14, 15, 194, 230.

——— (1970*a*). *Host-Host Protocol Document No. 1*. NIC 5143. ARPA/NWG. URL: http://www.baerwolff.de/public/Crocker-1970-Host-Host-Protocol-Document-No-1-NIC5143.pdf. See pp. 16, 37, 219, 260, 287.

——— (1970*b*). *NIC — Third Level Ideas and Other Noise*. RFC 66. Historic. Obsoleted by RFC 123, updated by RFCs 80, 93. NWG. URL: http://www.rfc-editor.org/rfc/rfc66.txt. See p. 283.

——— (1971). *Host/Host Protocol for the ARPA Network*. NIC 7147. ARPA/NWG. URL: http://ia300210.us.archive.org/1/items/HostHostProtocolForTheArpaNetwork/. See pp. 260, 287.

——— (1987). *The Origins of RFCs*. RFC 1000. Historic. Part of: "Request For Comments Reference Guide". IETF, pp. 1–5. URL: http://www.rfc-editor.org/rfc/rfc1000.txt. See pp. 243, 272, 285.

——— (1988). *Interview with Stephen D. Crocker by James Pelkey*. Excerpts in the James Pelkey online book. Interview conducted at April 26, 1988. URL: http://historyofcomputercommunications.info/index.html. See pp. 242, 286.

——— (2008). "Retrospective of the Arpanet Protocols and RFCs". In: *The Arpanet Sourcebook: The Unpublished Foundations of the Internet*. Ed. by P. H. Salus. Charlottesville, VA: Peer-to-Peer Communications LLC, pp. 97–102. See p. 249.

——— (2009). *Re: The migration of errror detection and correction towards the ends (both spatially and "up the stack") in the years from 1969 onwards*. Email to the author. May 12, 2009. See pp. 249, 262.

Crocker, S. D., C. S. Carr, and V. G. Cerf (1970*a*). *New Host-Host Protocol*. RFC 33. Historic. Updated by RFCs 36, 47. NWG. URL: http://www.rfc-editor.org/rfc/rfc33.txt. See p. 15.

Crocker, S. D., J. B. Postel, J. Newkirk, and M. Kraley (1970*b*). *Official Protocol Proffering*. RFC 54. Historic. Updated by RFC 57. NWG. URL: http://www.rfc-editor.org/rfc/rfc54.txt. See pp. 15, 16, 293.

Crocker, S. D., J. F. Heafner, R. M. Metcalfe, and J. B. Postel (1972). "Function-Oriented Protocols for the ARPA Computer Network". In: *AFIPS '72: Proceedings of the AFIPS 1972 Spring Joint Computer Conference*. Atlantic City, NJ. May 16–18, 1972. New York, NY: ACM, pp. 271–279. DOI: 10.1145/1478873.1478908. See pp. 262, 292, 298, 312, 390.

Crowcroft, J. (1997). *Comment on Christopher D. Clack's note on "PhD Thesis Structure and Content"*. Online. URL: http://www.cs.ucl.ac.uk/staff/C.Clack/phd.html. See p. 172.

——— (2007). "Net Neutrality: The Technical Side of the Debate—A White Paper". In: *International Journal of Communication* 1, pp. 567–579. URL: http://ijoc.org/ojs/index.php/ijoc/article/view/159/84. See pp. 177, 231.

——— (2008). "Toward a Network Architecture that Does Everything". In: *Communications of the ACM* 51.1, pp. 74–77. ISSN: 0001-0782. DOI: 10.1145/1327452.1327486. See p. 394.

——— (2009). *Re: [e2e] Some questions about TCP*. end2end-interest mailing list. Nov. 27, 2009. URL: http://www.postel.org/pipermail/end2end-interest/2009-November/007978.html. See p. 271.

——— (2010). *[e2e] Fie on future internet*. end2end-interest mailing list. Feb. 28, 2010. URL: http://www.postel.org/pipermail/end2end-interest/2010-February/007994.html.

Crowcroft, J., S. Hand, R. Mortier, T. Roscoe, and A. Warfield (2003). "Plutarch: An Argument for Network Pluralism". In: *ACM SIGCOMM Computer Communication Review* 33.4, pp. 258–266. ISSN: 0146-4833. DOI: 10.1145/972426.944763. See p. 394.

Crowcroft, J., J. Scott, P. Hui, C. Diot, and M. Roscoe (2007). *Network Architecture Research Considerations Or The Internet Conspiracy*. Editorial contribution to the ACM SIGCOMM Computer Communication Review (CCRonline), based on an earlier talk at 2006 ACM CoNEXT conference. Presentation slides. URL: http://ccr.sigcomm.org/online/files/conext-hag-arch-crowcroft.pdf. See pp. 385, 394.

Crowther, W. R., F. E. Heart, A. A. McKenzie, J. M. McQuillan, and D. C. Walden (1975). "Issues in Packet Switching Network Design". In: *AFIPS '75: Proceedings of the AFIPS 1975 National Computer Conference and Exposition*. Anaheim, CA. May 19–22, 1975. New York, NY: ACM, pp. 161–175. DOI: 10.1145/1499949.1499981. URL: http://www.archive.org/details/IssuesInPacketSwitchingNetworkDesign. Based on BBN Report 2918. See p. 208.

Curran, A. and V. G. Cerf (1975). "The Work of IFIP Working Group 6.1". In: *ACM SIGCOMM Computer Communication Review* 5.2, pp. 18–27. ISSN: 0146-4833. DOI: 10.1145/1024916.1024919. See p. 319.

Dam, A. van (2009). *Private communication with Matthias Bärwolff. On FRESS and Other Early Hypertext Systems*. Notes on file with the author. Interview in Providence, RI. Apr. 8, 2009. See p. 373.

Danet, A., R. Després, A. Le Best, G. Pichon, and S. Ritzenthaler (1976). "The French Public Packet Switching Service: The Transpac Network". In: *ICCC '76: Proceedings of the Third International Conference on Computer Communication*. Toronto, Canada. August 3–6, 1976. Ed. by P. K. Verma, pp. 251–260. See p. 207.

Darwin, C. R. (1859). *On the Origin of Species by Means of Natural Selection, or the Preservation of Favoured Races in the Struggle for Life*. London, England: John Murray. URL: http://www.gutenberg.org/etext/1228. See pp. 179, 393.

David, P. A. (2001*a*). *The Beginnings and Prospective Ending of "End-to-End": An Evolutionary Perspective on the Internet's Architecture*. URL: http://www-econ.stanford.edu/faculty/workp/swp01012.pdf. Revised version of the Oxford Review of Economic Policy version. See pp. 179, 429.

—— (2001*b*). "The Evolving Accidental Information Super-Highway". Ed. by A. Glyn and A. Graham. In: *Oxford Review of Economic Policy (Special Issue: "The Economics of the Internet")* 17.2, pp. 159–187. ISSN: 0266-903X; 1460-2121 (online).

Davidson, J., W. Hathaway, J. B. Postel, N. Mimno, R. Thomas, and D. C. Walden (1977). "The Arpanet Telnet Protocol: Its Purpose, Principles, Implementation, and Impact on Host Operating System Design". In: *Proceedings of the Fifth Data Communications Symposium*. Snowbird, UT. September 27–29, 1977. Ed. by J. F. Marchese and F. E. Heart. ACM and IEEE. New York, NY: IEEE, pp. 4–10–4–18. See pp. 289, 404.

Davie, B. S. and A. Farrel (2008). *MPLS: Next Steps*. The Morgan Kaufmann Series in Networking. Morgan Kaufmann (Elsevier). ISBN: 9780123744005. LCCN: 2008004669. See p. 310.

Davies, D. W. (1965). *Remote On-line Data Processing and its Communication Needs*. Aide-mémoire. UK: National Physical Laboratory (NPL). URL: http://www.cs.utexas.edu/users/chris/DIGITAL_ARCHIVE/NPL/Davies02.pdf. See p. 185.

—— (1966). *Proposal for a Digital Communication Network*. Lecture. March 1966. UK: National Physical Laboratory (NPL). URL: http:

//bit.ly/bnrU2x (http://www.archive.org/details/NationalPhysicalLaboratoryProposalForADigitalCommunicationNetwork; also at http://www.cs.utexas.edu/users/chris/DIGITAL_ARCHIVE/NPL/Davies05.pdf, different pagination). See pp. 107, 188, 324, 388.

Davies, D. W. (1968). "The Principles of a Data Communication Network for Computers and Remote Peripherals". In: *Information Processing '68: Proceedings of IFIP Congress 1968*. Edinburgh, UK. August 5–10, 1968. Ed. by A. J. H. Morrell. Vol. 2.3. Amsterdam, Netherlands: North-Holland, pp. 709–715. See p. 314.

—— (1976). *Some Possible Features of a Datagram Service*. INWG Note 112. IFIP WG 6.1 (INWG). See pp. 324, 349.

—— (1988). *Interview with Donald W. Davies by James Pelkey*. Supplement to the James Pelkey online book. Interview conducted at May 27, 1988, in London, UK. URL: http://historyofcomputercommunications.info/CC_Individuals/DaviesDonald/InterviewDonaldDavis.html. See pp. 185, 186, 188, 203.

Davies, D. W. and D. L. A. Barber (1973). *Communication Networks for Computers*. Ed. by C. A. Lang. Wiley Series in Computing. John Wiley & Sons. See pp. 182, 242, 347.

Davies, D. W., K. A. Bartlett, R. A. Scantlebury, and P. T. Wilkinson (1967). "A Digital Communication Network for Computers Giving Rapid Response at Remote Terminals". In: *SOSP '67: Proceedings of the First ACM Symposium on Operating System Principles*. Gatlinburg, TN. October 1–4, 1967. New York, NY: ACM, pp. 2.1–2.17. DOI: 10.1145/800001.811669. URL: http://www.cs.utexas.edu/users/chris/DIGITAL_ARCHIVE/NPL/Davies06.pdf (different pagination). See pp. 185, 187, 324.

—— (1968). "Communication Networks to Serve Rapid-Response Computers". In: *Information Processing '68: Proceedings of IFIP Congress 1968*. Edinburgh, UK. August 5–10, 1968. Ed. by A. J. H. Morrell. Vol. 2.3. Amsterdam, Netherlands: North-Holland, pp. 650–658. See pp. 242, 314.

Day, J. D. (1982). "Terminal Support Protocols". In: *Computer Network Architectures and Protocols*. Ed. by P. E. Green Jr. Applications of Communications Theory. New York, NY: Plenum Press. Chap. 15, pp. 437–457. ISBN: 0-306-40788-4. See p. 285.

—— (2008). *Patterns in Network Architecture: A Return to Fundamentals*. Prentice Hall. See pp. 164, 285, 288.

Day, J. D. and G. R. Grossman (1977). *RJE Protocol for a Resource Sharing Network*. RFC 725. Historic. NWG. URL: http://www.rfc-editor.org/rfc/rfc725.txt. See p. 298.

Day, J. D., I. Matta, and K. Mattar (2008). ""Networking is IPC": A Guiding Principle to a Better Internet". In: *Re-Arch 2008: First Workshop on Re-Architecting the Internet; part of the 4rd International Conference on Emerging Networking Experiments and Technologies (ACM CoNEXT)*. Madrid, Spain. December 9–12, 2008. ACM, pp. 1–6. ISBN: 978-1-60558-210-8. DOI: 10.1145/1544012.1544079. URL: http://www.cs.bu.edu/fac/matta/Papers/IPC-arch-rearch08.pdf. See p. 164.

Deering, S. E. (2001). *Watching the Waist of the Protocol Hourglass*. 51th IETF Meeting. London, UK. August 5–10, 2001: Plenary. August 30, 2001. Presentation slides. URL: http://www.iab.org/documents/docs/hourglass-london-ietf.pdf (also at http://www.ietf.org/proceedings/51/slides/plenary-1/). See p. 396.

Deering, S. E. and R. M. Hinden (1998). *Internet Protocol, Version 6 (IPv6) Specification*. RFC 2460. Draft Standard. IETF. URL: http://www.rfc-editor.org/rfc/rfc2460.txt. See p. 342.

Delgrossi, L., L. Berger, D. Duong, S. Jackowski, S. Schaller, C. Topolcic, S. L. Casner, C. Lynn Jr., P. Park, and K. Schroder (1995). *Internet Stream Protocol Version 2 (ST2) Protocol Specification — Version ST2+*. RFC 1819. Experimental. IETF. URL: http://www.rfc-editor.org/rfc/rfc1819.txt. See p. 308.

Deloche, G. (1969*a*). *Functional Specifications for the ARPA Network*. RFC 8. Historic. NWG. URL: http://www.rfc-editor.org/rfc/rfc8.pdf. See p. 195.

—— (1969*b*). *Host-IMP Interface*. RFC 7. Historic. NWG. URL: http://www.rfc-editor.org/rfc/rfc7.txt. See p. 195.

—— (1969*c*). *Host Software*. RFC 9. Historic. NWG. URL: http://www.rfc-editor.org/rfc/rfc9.pdf. See pp. 195, 287.

—— (1969*d*). *Implementation of the Host-Host software procedures in GORDO*. RFC 9. Historic. Obsoleted by RFC 33. NWG. URL: http://www.rfc-editor.org/rfc/rfc11.pdf (also at http://www.rfc-editor.org/rfc/rfc11.txt). See pp. 195, 286.

Demsetz, H. (1967). "Toward a Theory of Property Rights". In: *The American Economic Review* 57.2, pp. 347–359. See p. 365.

Denning, P. J. (2003). "Great Principles of Computing". In: *Communications of the ACM* 46.11, pp. 15–20. ISSN: 0001-0782. DOI: 10.1145/948383.948400. See pp. 165, 217, 378.

—— (2006). "A New Interview with Peter Denning on The Great Principles Of Computing". In: *Ubiquity* 7.44. URL: http://www.acm.org/ubiquity/interviews/v8i22_denning.html. See p. 178.

Denning, P. J. and C. Martell (2007*a*). "Criteria for Principle Statements". In: *Great Principles of Computing*. Ed. by P. J. Denning. "Library" of great computing principles. Online. URL: http://cs.gmu.edu/cne/pjd/GP/gp_criteria.html. See pp. 240, 388.

—— (2007*b*). "Design". In: *Great Principles of Computing*. Ed. by P. J. Denning. "Library" of great computing principles. Online. URL: http://cs.gmu.edu/cne/pjd/GP/gp_narratives.html. See p. 177.

—— (2007*c*). "Top Level Summary of Great Principles". In: *Great Principles of Computing*. Ed. by P. J. Denning. "Library" of great computing principles. Online. URL: http://cs.gmu.edu/cne/pjd/GP/gp_summary_toplevel.html. See p. 177.

DeRose, S. and A. van Dam (1999). "Document Structure and Markup in the FRESS Hypertext System". In: *Markup Languages: Theory and Practice* 1.1, pp. 7–32. This article is often refered to as "The Lost Books of Hypertext", I have no idea why; let me know if you do. See p. 411.

Dertouzos, M. L. (1980). "Another Reply to Weizenbaum". In: *Computer Age: A Twenty-Year View*. Ed. by M. L. Dertouzos and J. Moses. Vol. 6. MIT Bicentennial Studies. Cambridge, MA: MIT Press. Chap. 20, pp. 463–464. See p. 168.

Després, R. (1974). "RCP, The Experimental Packet-Switched Data Transmission Service of the French PTT". In: *ICCC '74: Proceedings of the Second International Conference on Computer Communication*. Stockholm, Sweden. August 12–14, 1974, pp. 171–185. URL: http://www.rogerdmoore.ca/PS/RCPDEP/RD.html. See p. 207.

Dingledine, R., N. Mathewson, and P. Syverson (2004). "Tor: The Second-Generation Onion Router". In: *SSYM'04: Proceedings of the 13th Conference on USENIX Security Symposium*. San Diego, CA. August 9–13, 2004. Berkeley, CA: USENIX Association, pp. 303–320. URL: http://www.

usenix.org / events / sec04 / tech / full_papers / dingledine / dingledine. pdf. See p. 401.

Dinneen, G. P. (1978). *Host-to-Host Protocols for Data Communications Networks*. Distributed to various DoD agencies; and published as an attachment to the 1980 Internet Experiment Note (IEN) 152 by V. Cerf. Including the "Management Plan for Executive Agent for Standardization of Host-to-Host Data Communications Protocols in the DoD". Dec. 1978. URL: ftp://ftp.rfc-editor.org/in-notes/ien/ien152.txt. See p. 344.

—— (1980). *Host-to-Host Data Communications Protocols*. Distributed to various DoD agencies; and published as an attachment to the 1980 Internet Experiment Note (IEN) 152 by V. Cerf. Apr. 1980. URL: ftp://ftp.rfc-editor.org/in-notes/ien/ien152.txt. See p. 344.

Dischinger, M., A. Haeberlen, K. P. Gummadi, and S. Saroiu (2007). "Characterizing Residential Broadband Networks". In: *IMC '07: Proceedings of the 7th ACM SIGCOMM Conference on Internet Measurement*. San Diego, CA. October 24–26, 2007, pp. 43–56. URL: http://www.imconf.net/imc-2007/papers/imc137.pdf. See p. 362.

Dischinger, M., A. Mislove, A. Haeberlen, and K. P. Gummadi (2008). "Detecting BitTorrent Blocking". In: *IMC '08: Proceedings of the 8th ACM SIGCOMM Conference on Internet Measurement*. Vouliagmeni, Greece. October 20–22, 2008. New York, NY: ACM, pp. 3–8. ISBN: 978-1-60558-334-1. DOI: 10.1145/1452520.1452523. URL: http://broadband.mpi-sws.org/transparency/results/08_imc_blocking.pdf. See p. 362.

Dischinger, M., M. Marcon, S. Guha, K. P. Gummadi, R. Mahajan, and S. Saroiu (2010). "Glasnost: Enabling End Users to Detect Traffic Differentiation". In: *NSDI '10: Proceedings of the 7th USENIX Symposium on Networked Systems Design and Implementation*. San Jose, CA. April 28–30, 2010. USENIX Association, pp. 405–418. URL: http://www.usenix.org/events/nsdi10/tech/full_papers/dischinger.pdf. See p. 362.

Dixit, A. K. and B. J. Nalebuff (1991). *Thinking Strategically: The Competitive Edge in Business, Politics, and Everyday Life*. 1st ed. New York, London: W. W. Norton. See p. 383.

Dortch, M. H. (2005). *Policy Statement Regarding the Four Internet Freedoms for Internet Users*. Policy Statement FCC 05-151. Federal Communications Commission of the US (FCC). URL: http://hraunfoss.fcc.gov/edocs_public/attachmatch/FCC-05-151A1.pdf. See p. 176.

Dunleavy, P. (2003). *Authoring a PhD: How to Plan, Draft, Write and Finish a Doctoral Thesis or Dissertation.* Palgrave Study Guides. Palgrave Macmillan. See pp. 240, 439.

Easterbrook, F. H. (1996). "Cyberspace and the Law of the Horse". In: *University of Chicago Legal Forum* 1996, pp. 207–216. URL: http://www.law.upenn.edu/fac/pwagner/law619/f2001/week15/easterbrook.pdf. See p. 178.

Edelcrantz, A. N. (1796). *Afhandling om Telegrapher och Försök Til en ny Inrättning däraf.* Stockholm, Sweden: J. P. Lindh. Translated version in Holzmann and Pehrson 1994 book. See p. 389.

Edge, S. W. and A. J. Hinchley (1978). "A Survey of End-to-End Retransmission Techniques". In: *ACM SIGCOMM Computer Communication Review* 8.4, pp. 1–18. ISSN: 0146-4833. DOI: 10.1145/1015856.1015857. See p. 198.

Edman, M. and P. Syverson (2009). "AS-Awareness in Tor Path Selection". In: *CCS '09: Proceedings of the 16th ACM Conference on Computer and Communications Security.* Chicago, IL. November 9–13, 2009. New York, NY: ACM, pp. 380–389. ISBN: 978-1-60558-894-0. DOI: 10.1145/1653662.1653708. See p. 401.

Elie, M. (1970). *Proposal for a Network Interchange Language.* RFC 51. Historic. NWG. URL: http://www.rfc-editor.org/rfc/rfc51.pdf. See p. 244.

Engelbart, D. C. (1962). *Augmenting Human Intellect: A Conceptual Framework.* Summary Report AFOSR-3233. Menlo Park, CA: Stanford Research Institute (SRI). URL: http://www.dougengelbart.org/pubs/augment-3906.html (see also http://www.liquidinformation.org/ohs/62_paper_full.pdf). See p. 411.

——— (1967). *Minutes of the ARPA Contractors Meeting, October 9–10, 1967.* Meeting of ARPA contractors organized by Lawrence G. Roberts of ARPA. Pentagon, Washington, DC. October 9–10, 1967. URL: http://sloan.stanford.edu/MouseSite/EngelbartPapers/B1_F20_CompuMtg.html. See pp. 183, 184.

Engelbart, D. C. and W. K. English (1968). "A Research Center for Augmenting Human Intellect". In: *AFIPS '68: Proceedings of the AFIPS 1968 Fall Joint Computer Conference.* San Francisco, CA. December 9–11, 1968.

New York, NY: ACM, pp. 395–410. DOI: 10.1145/1476589.1476645. URL: http://sloan.stanford.edu/MouseSite/Archive/ResearchCenter1968/ResearchCenter1968.html. For the video of the December 9, 1968 FJCC demonstration, also refered to as the "mother of all demos", see http://video.google.com/videoplay?docid=-8734787622017763097. See p. 411.

Epstein, R. A. (2003). *Scepticism and Freedom: A Modern Case for Classical Liberalism*. University of Chicago Press. See p. 166.

Fano, R. M. (1972). "On the Social Role of Computer Communications". In: *Proceedings of the IEEE* 60.11, pp. 1249–1253. See p. 167.

Farber, D. J. (2009). "Point/Counterpoint: Network Neutrality Nuances". In: *Communications of the ACM* 52.2, pp. 34–36, 37. ISSN: 0001-0782. DOI: 10.1145/1461928.1461942. URL: http://lauren.vortex.com/ACM209.pdf (also at http://idisk.mac.com/dfarber-Public). See p. 3.

Farber, D. J. and K. C. Larson (1972*a*). "The Structure of a Distributed Computing System — Software". In: *Symposium on Computer Communications Networks and Teletraffic*. New York, NY. April 4–6, 1972. Brooklyn Polytechnic Press, pp. 539–545. See p. 314.

—— (1972*b*). "The System Architecture of the Distributed Computer System — The Communication System". In: *Symposium on Computer Communications Networks and Teletraffic*. New York, NY. April 4–6, 1972. Brooklyn Polytechnic Press, pp. 21–27. See p. 314.

Farber, D. J., J. Feldman, F. R. Heinrich, M. D. Hopwood, and C. Larson (1973). "The Distributed Computing System". In: *Digest of Papers from the 7th Annual IEEE Computer Society International Conference*. San Francisco, CA. February 27 to March 1. New York, NY: IEEE, pp. 31–34. See p. 314.

Farmer, W. D. and E. E. Newhall (1969). "An Experimental Distributed Switching System to Handle Bursty Computer Traffic". In: *Proceedings of the First ACM Symposium on Problems in the Optimization of Data Communications Systems*. Pine Mountain, GA. October 13–16, 1969. New York, NY: ACM, pp. 1–33. DOI: 10.1145/800165.805236. The http://portal.acm.org version features only the abstract of the paper. See p. 314.

Fastner, C. (2007). "Genialisch Bizarr". In: *Die ZEIT* 2007.40 (Sept. 27, 2007), p. 72. URL: http://www.zeit.de/2007/40/Diabelli-Variationen. See p. 164.

Faulhaber, G. (2000). "Comments made at Panel 5 (G. Faulhaber and M. Nuway)". In: *The Policy Implications of End-to-End*. Stanford Law School. December 1, 2000. URL: http://cyberlaw.stanford.edu/e2e/papers/e2e.panel5.pdf. See p. 412.

Feamster, N., H. Balakrishnan, J. Rexford, A. Shaikh, and J. van der Merwe (2004). "The Case for Separating Routing from Routers". In: *FDNA '04: Proceedings of the ACM SIGCOMM Workshop on Future Directions in Network Architecture*. Portland, OR. August 30, 2004. New York, NY: ACM, pp. 5–12. ISBN: 1-58113-942-9. DOI: 10.1145/1016707.1016709. See pp. 379, 383.

Federal Communications Commission (2008). *Memorandum Opinion and Order. In the Matters of Formal Complaint of Free Press and Public Knowledge Against Comcast Corporation for Secretly Degrading Peer-to-Peer Applications, Broadband Industry Practices Petition of Free Press et al. for Declaratory Ruling that Degrading an Internet Application Violates the FCC's Internet Policy Statement and Does Not Meet an Exception for "Reasonable Network Management"*. FCC 08-183. Aug. 20, 2008. URL: http://hraunfoss.fcc.gov/edocs_public/attachmatch/FCC-08-183A1.pdf. See p. 362.

Feldmann, A. (2007). "Internet Clean-Slate Design: What and Why?" In: *ACM SIGCOMM Computer Communication Review* 37.3, pp. 59–64. ISSN: 0146-4833. DOI: 10.1145/1273445.1273453. See p. 427.

Fielding, R. T., J. Gettys, J. C. Mogul, H. F. Nielsen, L. Masinter, P. J. Leach, and T. Berners-Lee (1999). *Hypertext Transfer Protocol — HTTP/1.1*. RFC 2616. Draft Standard. Updated by RFC 2817. IETF. URL: http://www.rfc-editor.org/rfc/rfc2616.txt. See pp. 289, 373.

Floyd, S. (2000). *Congestion Control Principles*. RFC 2914. Best Current Practice. IETF. URL: http://www.rfc-editor.org/rfc/rfc2914.txt. See p. 354.

Floyd, S. and M. Allman (2008). *Comments on the Usefulness of Simple Best-Effort Traffic*. RFC 5290. Informational. IETF. URL: http://www.rfc-editor.org/rfc/rfc5290.txt. See p. 358.

Floyd, S. and V. Jacobson (1993). "Random Early Detection Gateways for Congestion Avoidance". In: *IEEE/ACM Transactions on Networking* 1.4, pp. 397–413. ISSN: 1063-6692. DOI: 10.1109/90.251892. URL: http://www.icir.org/floyd/papers/early.twocolumn.pdf (pre-publication version). See pp. 347, 353.

Ford, A., P. Eardley, and B. van Schewick (2009). "New Design Principles for the Internet". In: *ICC 2009: Proceedings of the IEEE International Conference on Communications Workshops*. Dresden, Germany. June 14–18, 2009. IEEE. DOI: 10.1109/ICCW.2009.5207995. See p. 285.

Forgie, J. W. (1979). *ST — A Proposed Internet Stream Protocol*. Internet Experiment Note (IEN) 119. URL: ftp://ftp.rfc-editor.org/in-notes/ien/ien119.txt. See pp. 307–310.

Foucart, S. (2006). "Louis Pouzin: l'homme qui n'a pas inventé Internet". In: *Le Monde* August 5, 2006. URL: http://lists.parinux.org/pipermail/linux/2006-August/001962.html. See p. 207.

Frank, H., R. E. Kahn, and L. Kleinrock (1972). "Computer Communication Network Design: Experience with Theory and Practice". In: *AFIPS '72: Proceedings of the AFIPS 1972 Spring Joint Computer Conference*. Atlantic City, NJ. May 16–18, 1972. New York, NY: ACM, pp. 255–270. DOI: 10.1145/1478873.1478907. URL: http://bit.ly/cqPREt (http://ia300209.us.archive.org/2/items/ComputerCommunicationNetworkDesignExperienceWithTheoryAndPractice/). See pp. 247, 250, 307.

Frank, H., I. Gitman, and R. van Slyke (1975). "Packet Radio System: Network Considerations". In: *AFIPS '75: Proceedings of the AFIPS 1975 National Computer Conference and Exposition*. Anaheim, CA. May 19–22, 1975. New York, NY: ACM, pp. 217–231. DOI: 10.1145/1499949.1499987. See pp. 215, 314, 320.

Friedman, B. and H. Nissenbaum (1996). "Bias in Computer Systems". In: *ACM Transactions on Information Systems (TOIS)* 14.3, pp. 330–347. ISSN: 1046-8188. DOI: 10.1145/230538.230561. URL: http://depts.washington.edu/vsdesign/publications/pdf/64_friedman.pdf. See p. 417.

Friedman, M. (1953). "The Methodology of Positive Economics". In: *Essays in Positive Economics*. University of Chicago Press. Chap. 1, pp. 3–43. See p. 171.

Frischmann, B. M. (2005). "An Economic Theory of Infrastructure and Commons Management". In: *Minnesota Law Review* 89.4, pp. 917–1030. URL: http://ssrn.com/abstract=588424. See p. 412.

Frischmann, B. M. and B. van Schewick (2007). "Network Neutrality and the Economics of an Information Superhighway: A Reply to Professor Yoo". In: *Jurimetrics: The Journal of Law, Science and Technology* 47.4, pp. 383–428. URL: http://ssrn.com/abstract=1014691 (2007 working paper version). See pp. 412, 414.

Fry, M. (1992). "Practical Trade-Offs for Open Interconnection". In: *CSC '92: Proceedings of the 1992 ACM Annual Conference on Communications*. Kansas City, MO, pp. 1–8. ISBN: 0-89791-472-4. DOI: 10.1145/131214.131215. See p. 393.

Gangadharan, S. P. (2009). "Mail Art: Networking Without Technology". In: *New Media Society* 11.1-2, pp. 279–298. DOI: 10.1177/1461444808099581. See p. 369.

Gardner, M. (1986). "Arpanet Congestion". In: *Proceedings of the 4th Joint Meeting of the Internet Engineering and Internet Architecture Task Forces*. Menlo Park, CA. October 15–17, 1986. Ed. by P. Gross. Internet Engineering Task Force and Internet Architecture Task Force, pp. 48–58. URL: http://www.ietf.org/proceedings/04.pdf. See pp. 98, 353.

Gaynor, M. S. and S. O. Bradner (2001). "Using Real Options to Value Modularity in Standards". In: *Knowledge, Technology, and Policy* 14.2, pp. 41–66. URL: http://www.sobco.com/papers/kt&p.pdf. See p. 414.

——— (2004). "A Real Options Metric to Value Network, Protocol, and Service Architecture". In: *ACM SIGCOMM Computer Communication Review* 34.5, pp. 31–38. URL: http://people.bu.edu/mgaynor/papers/ccr-small-final.pdf (edited version with slightly different title). See pp. 412, 414–416, 438.

——— (2008). "Statistical Framework to Value Network Neutrality". In: *Media Law and Policy* 17.1, pp. 24–38. URL: http://www.nyls.edu/user_files/1/3/4/30/84/88/Vol%2017,%20No%201%20Gaynor%20Article.pdf. See p. 414.

Gien, M. and H. Zimmermann (1979). "Design Principles for Network Interconnection". In: *SIGCOMM '79: Proceedings of the Sixth Symposium on Data Communications*. Pacific Grove, CA. New York, NY: ACM, pp. 109–119. DOI: 10.1145/800092.802988. See pp. 329, 388, 401.

Gien, M., J. Laws, and R. A. Scantlebury (1975). "Interconnection of Packet Switching Networks: Theory and Practice". In: *Eurocomp 1975: Proceedings of the European Computing Conference on Communications Networks*. London, UK. September 23–25, 1975. Ed. by D. L. A. Barber. Online Conferences, pp. 241–260. ISBN: 0903796058. See pp. 91, 92, 326, 340, 342.

Gilles, S. G. (2003). "United States v. Carroll Towing Co., The Hand Formula's Home Port". In: *Torts Stories*. Ed. by R. Rabin and S. Sugarman, pp. 11–39. See p. 166.

Gillett, S. E., W. H. Lehr, J. T. Wroclawski, and D. D. Clark (2001*a*). "Do Appliances Threaten Internet Innovation?" In: *IEEE Communications Magazine* 39.10, pp. 46–51. ISSN: 0163-6804. DOI: 10.1109/35.956112. See pp. 145, 409, 410.

—— (2001*b*). "The Disruptive User — Internet Appliances and the Management of Complexity". In: *BT Technology Journal* 19.4, pp. 40–45. ISSN: 1358-3948. DOI: 10.1023/A:1013774312186. See pp. 145, 409, 410.

Gillett, S. E. and M. Kapor (1997). "The Self-Governing Internet: Coordination by Design". In: *Coordinating the Internet*. Ed. by B. Kahin and J. H. Keller. Cambridge, MA: MIT Press, pp. 3–38. URL: http://ccs.mit.edu/papers/CCSWP197/CCSWP197.html (1996 workshop version). See p. 178.

Gitman, I. and H. Frank (1978). "Economic Analysis of Integrated Voice and Data Networks: A Case Study". In: *Proceedings of the IEEE* 66.11, pp. 1549–1570. ISSN: 0018-9219. See p. 308.

Glaser, B. G. and A. L. Strauss (1967). *The Discovery of Grounded Theory: Strategies for Qualitative Research*. Aldine. See p. 170.

Gold, B. (1977). "Digital Speech Networks". In: *Proceedings of the IEEE* 65.12, pp. 1636–1658. See pp. 82, 304.

Gont, F. (2010). *ICMP Attacks Against TCP*. Internet Draft. Informational (intended status). Version 12. IETF. URL: http://tools.ietf.org/html/draft-ietf-tcpm-icmp-attacks-12. See pp. 352, 353.

Gray, R. M. (2005). "The 1974 Origins of VoIP". In: *IEEE Signal Processing Magazine* 22.4, pp. 87–90. See pp. 217, 238, 305, 306.

—— (2010*a*). "Linear Predictive Coding and the Internet Protocol". A Survey of Linear Predictive Coding. In: *Foundations and Trends in Signal Processing* 3.3, pp. 153–202. ISSN: 1932-8346; 1932-8354 (online). DOI: 10.1561/2000000029. See p. 217.

—— (2010*b*). "Linear Predictive Coding and the Internet Protocol". A History of Realtime Digital Speech on Packet Networks. In: *Foundations and Trends in Signal Processing* 3.4, pp. 203–303. ISSN: 1932-8346; 1932-8354 (online). DOI: 10.561/2000000036. See pp. 217, 306.

Griffiths, C., J. Livingood, L. Popkin, and R. Woundy (2009). *Comcast's ISP Experiences in a Proactive Network Provider Participation for P2P (P4P) Technical Trial.* RFC 5632. Informational. IETF. URL: http://www.rfc-editor.org/rfc/rfc5632.txt. See p. 121.

Guba, E. G. and Y. S. Lincoln (1994). "Competing Paradigms in Qualitative Research". In: *Handbook of Qualitative Research.* Ed. by N. K. Denzin and Y. S. Lincoln. Thousand Oaks, CA: Sage Publications. Chap. 6, pp. 105–117. See p. 170.

Guruprasad, V. (2002). "A Self-Managing Addressing, Naming and Routing Service". In: *Proceedings of the 4th IEEE International Workshop on Networked Appliances.* Gaithersburg, MD. January 15–16, 2002. Ed. by A. Mink, pp. 186–195. DOI: 10.1109/IWNA.2001.980848. See p. 213.

Gurwitz, R. F. (1981). *VAX-UNIX Networking Support Project Implementation Description.* Internet Experiment Note (IEN) 168. URL: ftp://ftp.rfc-editor.org/in-notes/ien/ien168.txt. See p. 331.

Hafner, K. and M. Lyon (1998). *Where Wizards Stay up Late: The Origins of the Internet.* New York, NY: Touchstone. See pp. xi, 175, 183, 192, 199, 202, 241, 245, 246, 250, 272, 285.

Hagiu, A. (2007). *Proprietary vs. Open Two-Sided Platforms and Social Efficiency.* Harvard Business School Working Paper 07-095. Harvard Business School. URL: http://www.hbs.edu/research/pdf/07-095.pdf. See p. 384.

Hagiu, A. and B. Jullien (2007). *Designing a Two-Sided Platform: When to Increase Search Costs?* Harvard Business School Working Paper 08-010. Harvard Business School. URL: http://www.hbs.edu/research/pdf/08-010.pdf. See p. 384.

Hagiu, A. and R. S. Lee (2007). *Exclusivity and Control.* Harvard Business School Working Paper 08-009. Harvard Business School. URL: http://www.hbs.edu/research/pdf/08-009.pdf. See p. 384.

Hain, T. (2000). *Architectural Implications of NAT.* RFC 2993. Informational. IETF. URL: http://www.rfc-editor.org/rfc/rfc2993.txt. See p. 377.

Han, H., S. Shakkottai, C. V. Hollot, R. Srikant, and D. Towsley (2006). "Multi-Path TCP: A Joint Congestion Control and Routing Scheme to Exploit Path Diversity in the Internet". In: *IEEE/ACM Transactions on Networking (TON)* 14.6, pp. 1260–1271. ISSN: 1063-6692. DOI: 10.1109/TNET.2006.886738. See p. 433.

Handley, M. (2006). "Why the Internet only just Works". In: *BT Technology Journal* 24.3, pp. 119–129. See pp. 26, 212.

Hardie, T. (2009). *Comment*. Voiced at Technical Plenary, July 30, 2009; 75th IETF Meeting. Stockholm, Sweden. July 26–31, 2009. URL: ftp://videolab.uoregon.edu/pub/videolab/media/ietf75/ietf75-thur-tech-plenary.mp3 (audio recording, starting at 125.19 minutes). See p. 426.

Hardin, G. (1968). "The Tragedy of the Commons". In: *Science* 162.3859, pp. 1243–1248. URL: http://www.garretthardinsociety.org/articles/art_tragedy_of_the_commons.html. See pp. 364, 365.

—— (1974). "Living on a Lifeboat". In: *BioScience* 24.10, pp. 561–568. URL: http://www.garretthardinsociety.org/articles/art_living_on_a_lifeboat.html. See p. 365.

Harslem, E. and J. F. Heafner (1970*a*). *Comments on Protocol Re: NWG/RFC #36*. RFC 39. Historic. NWG. URL: http://www.rfc-editor.org/rfc/rfc39.txt. See p. 195.

—— (1970*b*). *More Comments on the Forthcoming Protocol*. RFC 40. Historic. NWG. URL: http://www.rfc-editor.org/rfc/rfc40.txt. See p. 195.

Hathaway, W. (1973). *More on Lost Message Detection*. RFC 512. Historic. NWG. URL: http://www.rfc-editor.org/rfc/rfc512.txt. See p. 257.

Haughney, J. (1980). *Arpanet Newsletter*. Arpanet Newsletter (ANEWS) 3. Network Info Center for Defense Communications Agency (DCA) Defense Data Network (DDN) Program Management Office (SRI NIC). URL: ftp://ftp.rfc-editor.org/in-notes/museum/ARPANET_News.mail. See p. 249.

—— (1981). *Arpanet Newsletter*. Arpanet Newsletter (ANEWS) 6. Network Info Center for Defense Communications Agency (DCA) Defense Data Network (DDN) Program Management Office (SRI NIC). URL: ftp://ftp.rfc-editor.org/in-notes/museum/ARPANET_News.mail. See p. 249.

Haverty, J. (1980). *HOSTs as IMPs*. Internet Experiment Note (IEN) 139. URL: ftp://ftp.rfc-editor.org/in-notes/ien/ien139.txt. See p. 252.

—— (2006). *Re: [ih] origins of the term "router"*. internet history mailing list. May 17, 2006. URL: http://mailman.postel.org/pipermail/internet-history/2006-May/000617.html. See p. 354.

Haverty, J. (2009*a*). *Re: [ih] Baran and Davies and respetive roles in Apra design*. internet history mailing list. Mar. 20, 2009. URL: http://mailman.postel.org/pipermail/internet-history/2010-February/001219.html (resent in February 2010, for the original mail did not make it to the list). See p. 174.

—— (2009*b*). *Re: [ih] [ipv6] IP versions explained*. internet history mailing list. Nov. 7, 2009. URL: http://mailman.postel.org/pipermail/internet-history/2009-November/000978.html. See p. 347.

Hayek, F. A. von (1973). "Rules and Order". In: *Law, Legislation and Liberty: A New Statement of the Liberal Principles of Justice and Political Economy*. Vol. 1. 3 vols. University of Chicago Press. See pp. v, 3, 51, 125, 143, 145, 147, 157, 159, 166, 176, 214, 367, 378, 393, 417, 424.

Heart, F. E., R. E. Kahn, S. M. Ornstein, W. R. Crowther, and D. C. Walden (1970). "The Interface Message Processor for the ARPA Computer Network". In: *AFIPS '70: Proceedings of the AFIPS 1970 Spring Joint Computer Conference*. Atlantic City, NJ. May 5–7, 1970. New York, NY: ACM, pp. 551–567. DOI: 10.1145/1476936.1477021. URL: http://www.archive.org/details/TheInterfaceMessageProcessorForArpaComputerNetwork. See pp. 13, 14, 29, 193, 194, 208, 269, 279, 280.

Heart, F. E., A. A. McKenzie, J. M. McQuillan, and D. C. Walden (1978). *Arpanet Completion Report*. BBN Report. Bolt, Beranek and Newman Inc. (BBN). Also published in an edited version as BBN Report 4799. See pp. 58, 63, 67, 185, 196, 200, 230, 253, 259, 262, 272, 275, 292, 298, 302.

—— (1981). *A History of the Arpanet—The First Decade*. BBN Report 4799. Bolt, Beranek and Newman Inc. (BBN). URL: http://www.dtic.mil/cgi-bin/GetTRDoc?AD=ADA115440&Location=U2&doc=GetTRDoc.pdf (also at http://www.darpa.mil/Docs/A%20History%20of%20the%20ARPANet.pdf and http://www.cs.utexas.edu/users/chris/DIGITAL_ARCHIVE/ARPANET/DARPA4799.pdf). Reprint (with different pagination) of the Arpanet Completion Report submitted to ARPA in 1978.

Heiden, H. B. (1983). *TCP/IP Conversion Effective 1 Jan 83*. DoD Network Newsletter (ANEWS) 20. Network Info Center for Defense Communications Agency (DCA) Defense Data Network (DDN) Program Management Office (SRI NIC). URL: ftp://ftp.rfc-editor.org/in-notes/museum/ARPANET_News.mail. See p. 345.

Hinden, R. M. and A. Sheltzer (1982). *The DARPA Internet Gateway*. RFC 823. Historic. NWG. URL: http://www.rfc-editor.org/rfc/rfc823.txt. See p. 344.

Hinden, R. M., J. Haverty, and A. Sheltzer (1983). "The DARPA Internet: Interconnecting Heterogeneous Computer Networks with Gateways". In: *Computer* 16.9, pp. 38–48. DOI: 10.1109/MC.1983.1654494. See p. 285.

Hirsch, P. (1974). "SITA: Rating a Packet-Switched Network". In: *Datamation* 20.3, pp. 60–63. See p. 242.

Hobbs, L. C. (1972). "Terminals". In: *Proceedings of the IEEE* 60.11 (Nov. 1972), pp. 1273–1284. ISSN: 0018-9219. See p. 242.

Hofmann, M. and L. R. Beaumont (2007). "Open Pluggable Edge Services: An Architecture for Networked Content Services". In: *IEEE Internet Computing* 11.1, pp. 67–73. ISSN: 1089-7801. DOI: 10.1109/MIC.2007.19. See p. 372.

Holman, J. (2008). "The Way They See Us: Net Neutrality and the Public Image of Telecommunications Policymaking". In: *TPRC 2008: 36th Telecommunications and Communications Policy Research Conference*. Arlington, VA. September 26–28, 2008. Papers online. URL: http://tprcweb.com/files/The%20Way%20They%20See%20Us.pdf. See p. 177.

Holzmann, G. J. (1994). "Data Communications: The First 2500 Years". In: *IFIP '94: Proceedings of the IFIP 13th World Computer Congress*. Hamburg, Germany. August 28 to September 2, 1994. Ed. by B. Pehrson and I. Simon. Amsterdam, Netherlands: North-Holland, pp. 271–278. URL: http://spinroot.com/gerard/pdf/hamburg94b.pdf (pre-publication version). See pp. 190, 389.

Holzmann, G. J. and B. Pehrson (1994). *The Early History of Data Networks*. IEEE Computer Society Press. URL: http://people.seas.harvard.edu/~jones/cscie129/papers/Early_History_of_Data_Networks/The_Early_History_of_Data_Networks.html (excerpts). See pp. 10, 182.

Hooke, R. (1726). "Dr. Hook's Discourse to the Royal Society, May 21. 1684. shewing a Way how to communicate one's Mind at great Distances". In: *Philosophical experiments and observations of the late Eminent Dr. Robert Hooke, S. R. S. and Geom. Prof. Gresh. and Other Eminent Vir-*

tuoso's in his Time. Ed. by W. Derham. London, At the West End of St. Paul's: W. and J. Innys, Printers to the Royal Society, pp. 142–150. URL: http://libcoll.mpiwg-berlin.mpg.de/libview?url=/mpiwg/online/permanent/library/RT3R12V8/pageimg&pn=1&mode=imagepath. See p. 181.

Hovey, R. B. (1976). "Packet-Switched Networks Agree on Standard Interface". In: *Data Communications* 5.3, pp. 25–39. Republished in the 1978 McQuillan and Cerf IEEE Tutorial. See pp. 329, 341.

Häberle, P. (1975). "Die offene Gesellschaft der Verfassungsinterpreten". In: *Juristenzeitung (JZ)* 30.10, pp. 297–305. See pp. 424, 438.

IETF Secretariat and G. S. Malkin (1994). *The Tao of IETF — A Guide for New Attendees of the Internet Engineering Task Force*. RFC 1718. Informational. Obsoleted by RFC 3160. IETF. URL: http://www.rfc-editor.org/rfc/rfc1718.txt. See p. 405.

Innes, A. M. (1914). "The Credit Theory of Money". In: *Banking Law Journal* 31, pp. 151–168. See p. 393.

International Organization for Standardization (1983). *Information Technology — Open Systems Interconnection — Basic Reference Model: The Basic Model*. ISO/IEC International Standard 7498-1. International Organization for Standardization (ISO). URL: http://www.ecma-international.org/activities/Communications/TG11/s020269e.pdf (1994 second edition). See pp. 291, 390.

International Telecommunication Union (2009). *Short History of Study Group 17*. Online. URL: http://www.itu.int/ITU-T/studygroups/com17/history.html (as of March 2010). See p. 341.

Internet Architecture Board (1996). *Architectural Principles of the Internet*. RFC 1958. Informational. Updated by RFC 3439. IETF. URL: http://www.rfc-editor.org/rfc/rfc1958.txt. See pp. 35, 218, 219, 292, 404, 437.

—— (2002). *IAB Architectural and Policy Considerations for Open Pluggable Edge Services*. RFC 3238. Informational. IETF. URL: http://www.rfc-editor.org/rfc/rfc3238.txt. See p. 372.

—— (2004). *The Rise of the Middle and the Future of End-to-End: Reflections on the Evolution of the Internet Architecture*. RFC 3724. Informational. IETF. URL: http://www.rfc-editor.org/rfc/rfc3724.txt. See pp. 134, 145, 165.

—— (2009). *RFC Editor Model (Version 1)*. RFC 5620. Informational. IETF. URL: http://www.rfc-editor.org/rfc/rfc5620.txt.

Internet Architecture Board and Internet Engineering Steering Group (2000). *IETF Policy on Wiretapping*. RFC 2804. Informational. IETF. URL: http://www.rfc-editor.org/rfc/rfc2804.txt. See p. 405.

Internet Society (2010). *Principles*. Online. URL: http://www.isoc.org/pubpolpillar/principles.shtml. See p. 426.

Iseli, J., D. H. Crocker, and N. Neigus (1973). *Charter for ARPANET Users Interest Working Group*. RFC 584. Historic. NWG. URL: http://www.rfc-editor.org/rfc/rfc584.txt. Also published as USING Note 6. See p. 285.

Isenberg, D. S. (1997). "Rise of the Stupid Network". In: *Computer Telephony* 5.8, pp. 16–26. URL: http://www.hyperorg.com/misc/stupidnet.html. See pp. 47, 235–237, 428.

——— (1998). "The Dawn of the "Stupid Network"". In: *ACM netWorker* 2.1, pp. 24–31. URL: http://www.isen.com/papers/Dawnstupid.html. See p. 235.

——— (2003). "The End of the Middle". In: *IEEE Spectrum* 40.1, pp. 37–38. See pp. 235, 236, 238.

Jacobson, V. (1987*a*). "Round Trip Delay Estimation". In: *Proceedings of the 7th IETF Meeting*. McLean, VA. July 27–29, 1987. Ed. by A. Mankin and P. Gross. IETF, pp. 14–16. URL: http://www.ietf.org/proceedings/07.pdf. See pp. 353, 354.

——— (1987*b*). "TCP Enhancements". In: *Proceedings of the 6th IETF Meeting*. Draft. Cambridge, MA. April 22–24, 1987. Ed. by P. Gross. IETF, pp. 9–11. URL: http://www.ietf.org/proceedings/06.pdf. See p. 353.

——— (1988*a*). "Congestion Avoidance and Control". In: *SIGCOMM '88: Symposium Proceedings on Communications Architectures and Protocols*. Stanford, CA. August 16–18, 1988. New York, NY: ACM, pp. 314–329. ISBN: 0-89791-279-9. DOI: 10.1145/52324.52356. URL: http://ee.lbl.gov/papers/congavoid.pdf (revised version). See pp. 94, 98, 99, 103, 351, 353, 363, 407.

——— (1988*b*). *Dynamic Congestion Avoidance / Control (long message)*. tcp-ip mailing list. Feb. 11, 1988. URL: http://ee.lbl.gov/tcp.html (also at http://securitydigest.org/tcp-ip/archive/1988/02). See p. 351.

——— (1988*c*). "Recent Congestion Control Efforts for 4 BSD". In: *Proceedings of the 8th IETF Meeting*. Boulder, CO. November 2–4, 1987. Ed. by A. Mankin and P. Gross. IETF, pp. 13–14. URL: http://www.ietf.org/proceedings/08.pdf. See pp. 353, 357.

Jacobson, V. (1990). *Modified TCP Congestion Avoidance Algorithm*. end2end-interest mailing list. Apr. 20, 1990. URL: ftp://ftp.ee.lbl.gov/email/vanj.90apr30.txt/. See p. 353.

—— (2006). *A New Way to Look at Networking*. Presentation at Google Tech Talk. URL: http://video.google.com/videoplay?docid=-6972678839686672840. See pp. 289, 375.

—— (2009). "A Conversation with Van Jacobson". In: *ACM Queue* 7.1. Interview conducted by Craig Partridge, pp. 8–16. ISSN: 1542-7730. DOI: 10.1145/1508211.1508215. URL: http://m-cdn.dashdigital.com/queue/200901/data/queue200901-dl.pdf. See p. 377.

Jacobson, V., D. K. Smetters, J. D. Thornton, M. F. Plass, N. H. Briggs, and R. L. Braynard (2009). "Networking Named Content". In: *CoNEXT '09: Proceedings of the 5th International Conference On Emerging Networking Experiments And Technologies*. Rome, Italy. December 1–4, 2009. New York, NY: ACM, pp. 1–12. ISBN: 978-1-60558-636-6. DOI: 10.1145/1658939.1658941. See pp. 375, 377, 433.

Jain, R., K. K. Ramakrishnan, and D. Chiu (1987). *Congestion Avoidance in Computer Networks with a Connectionless Network Layer*. Tech. rep. DEC-TR-506. DEC. URL: http://www.cs.wustl.edu/~jain/papers/ftp/cr5.pdf. Reprinted in C. Partridge, Ed., "Innovations in Internetworking", pp. 140–156, Artech House, 1988. See p. 353.

Jensen, E. D. (1981). "Hardware/Software Relationships in Distributed Systems". In: *Distributed Systems—Architecture and Implementation*. An Advanced Course. Ed. by B. W. Lampson, M. Paul, and H. J. Siegert. Lecture Notes in Computer Science 105. Springer. Chap. 17, pp. 413–420. ISBN: 3-540-10571-9, 0-387-10571-9. See p. 393.

Jessen, J. (2010). "Das Netz gehört uns". In: *Die ZEIT* 2010.17 (Apr. 22, 2010), p. 45. See p. 424.

Jick, T. D. (1979). "Mixing Qualitative and Quantitative Methods: Triangulation in Action". In: *Administrative Science Quarterly* 24.4, pp. 602–611. See p. 170.

Joy, W. N. and R. S. Fabry (1981). *Berkeley Enhanced TCP/IP for 4BSD UNIX*. tcp-ip digest contribution. tcp-ip mailing list. TCP/IP Digest, Wednesday, 11 Nov 1981, Volume 1, Issue 6. Nov. 11, 1981. URL: http://securitydigest.org/tcp-ip/archive/1981/11 (also at http://ftp.arl.army.mil/ftp/tcp-ip-digest/tcp-ip-digest.v1n6.1). See p. 331.

Kaczynski, T. (1995). *Industrial Society and Its Future*. Also referred to as "Unabomber Manifesto". Jolly Roger Press. URL: http://en.wikisource.org/wiki/Industrial_Society_and_Its_Future. See for contextual information http://en.wikipedia.org/wiki/Theodore_Kaczynski. See p. 168.

Kahn, A. E. (1971). "Economic Principles". In: *The Economics of Regulation: Principles and Institutions*. Vol. 1. 2 vols. John Wiley & Sons, Inc. See p. 436.

Kahn, R. E. (1968). *Error Control in the Arpa Network*. Memorandum to ARPA Network Committee. Dated January 25, 1968. Bolt, Beranek and Newman Inc. URL: http://www.cs.utexas.edu/users/dragon/sigcomm/t1/kahn68memo.ppt (plain text version at http://www.baerwolff.de/public/kahn-1968-memorandum.txt). See p. 196.

—— (1969). *Re: Some Questions Re: HOST-IMP Protocol*. RFC 17a. Historic. NWG. URL: http://www.rfc-editor.org/rfc/rfc17a.txt. See p. 249.

—— (1972). "Resource-Sharing Computer Communications Networks". In: *Proceedings of the IEEE* 60.11, pp. 1397–1407. URL: http://people.scs.carleton.ca/~soma/distos/2008-01-14/kahn1972-resource.pdf. See pp. 244, 258, 411.

—— (1975). "The Organization of Computer Resources into a Packet Radio Network". In: *AFIPS '75: Proceedings of the AFIPS 1975 National Computer Conference and Exposition*. Anaheim, CA. May 19–22, 1975. New York, NY: ACM, pp. 177–186. DOI: 10.1145/1499949.1499983. See p. 314.

—— (1989). *An interview with Robert E. Kahn (by William Aspray)*. Oral History Interview (see http://www.cbi.umn.edu/oh/oralhistories.html). Minneapolis, MN: Charles Babbage Institute for the History of Information Technology, University of Minnesota. URL: http://www.archive.org/details/AnInterviewWithRobertKahnOh158 (also at http://www.cbi.umn.edu/oh/display.phtml?id=119). See p. 187.

—— (1990). *An Interview with Robert E. Kahn (by Judy O'Neill)*. Oral History Interview (see http://www.cbi.umn.edu/oh/oralhistories.html). Minneapolis, MN: Charles Babbage Institute for the History of Information Technology, University of Minnesota. URL: http://special.lib.umn.edu/cbi/oh/pdf.phtml?id=167 (also at http://ia331308.us.archive.org/0/items/Inet95/). See pp. 252, 344.

Kahn, R. E. (2003). "Putting it all together with Robert Kahn (Interview)". In: *Ubiquity* 4.3. DOI: 10.1145/764024.764025. URL: http://www.acm.org/ubiquity/interviews/pf/r_kahn_1.html. See p. 232.

Kahn, R. E. and W. R. Crowther (1972). "Flow Control in a Resource-Sharing Computer Network". In: *IEEE Transactions on Communications* 20.3, pp. 539–546. ISSN: 0096-2244. See pp. 256, 269.

Kahn, R. E., W. R. Crowther, and Bolt, Beranek and Newman Inc. (1971). *A Study of the Arpa Network Design and Performance.* BBN Report 2161. Bolt, Beranek and Newman Inc. (BBN). See pp. 252–254, 299.

Kalin, R. B. (1970). *Simplified NCP Protocol.* RFC 60. Experimental. NWG. URL: http://www.rfc-editor.org/rfc/rfc60.txt. See p. 256.

——— (1971). *Achieving Reliable Communication.* RFC 203. Historic. NWG. URL: http://www.rfc-editor.org/rfc/rfc203.txt. See p. 256.

Kanodia, R. K. (1974). *Lost Message Detection and Recovery Protocol.* RFC 663. Historic. NWG. URL: http://www.rfc-editor.org/rfc/rfc663.txt. See p. 257.

Kantrowitz, W. (1973*a*). *Network Make-Work.* RFC 514. Historic. NWG. URL: http://www.rfc-editor.org/rfc/rfc514.txt. See p. 294.

——— (1973*b*). *Network Questionnaires.* RFC 459. Historic. NWG. URL: http://www.rfc-editor.org/rfc/rfc459.txt. See p. 294.

Karp, P. M., D. B. McKay, and D. C. M. Wood (1971). *Views on Issues Relevant to Data Sharing on Computer Networks.* RFC 146. Historic. NWG. URL: http://www.rfc-editor.org/rfc/rfc146.txt. See p. 244.

Kay, A. C. (1977). "Microelectronics and the Personal Computer". In: *Scientific American* 237.3, pp. 230–244. URL: http://www.guidebookgallery.org/articles/microelectronicsandthepersonalcomputer (also at http://www.digibarn.com/collections/books/xerox-parc-1970-80/alto-article/). See p. 171.

Kelly, F. P. (1997). "Charging and Rate Control for Elastic Traffic". In: *European Transactions on Telecommunications* 8, pp. 33–37. URL: http://www.statslab.cam.ac.uk/~frank/elastic.html (edited version). See p. 363.

——— (2000). "Models for a Self-Managed Internet". In: *Philosophical Transactions: Mathematical, Physical and Engineering Sciences* 358.1773, pp. 2335–2348. ISSN: 1364503X. See p. 363.

Kent, C. A. and J. C. Mogul (1987). "Fragmentation Considered Harmful". In: *ACM SIGCOMM Computer Communication Review* 17.5, pp. 390–401.

ISSN: 0146-4833. DOI: 10.1145/55483.55524. URL: http://www.hpl.hp.com/techreports/Compaq-DEC/WRL-87-3.pdf (revised version). See pp. 93, 305, 342.

—— (1988). "Fragmentation Considered Harmful". In: *SIGCOMM '87: Proceedings of the ACM Workshop on Frontiers in Computer Communications Technology*. Stowe, VT. August 11–13, 1987. New York, NY: ACM, pp. 390–401. ISBN: 0-89791-245-4. URL: http://www.hpl.hp.com/techreports/Compaq-DEC/WRL-87-3.pdf (revised version).

Kent, S. T. (1976). "Encryption-Based Protection Protocols for Interactive User-Computer Communication". PhD thesis. Cambridge, MA: Massachusetts Institute of Technology. URL: http://publications.csail.mit.edu/lcs/pubs/pdf/MIT-LCS-TR-162.pdf. Published as MIT Laboratory for Computer Science Technical Report 162. See p. 401.

—— (1977). "Encryption-Based Protection for Interactive User/Computer Communication". In: *SIGCOMM '77: Proceedings of the Fifth Symposium on Data Communications*. Snowbird, UT. September 27–29, 1977. New York, NY: ACM, pp. 5.7–5.13. DOI: 10.1145/800103.803345. See p. 401.

—— (1989). "Comments on "Security Problems in the TCP/IP Protocol Suite"". In: *ACM SIGCOMM Computer Communication Review* 19.3, pp. 10–19. ISSN: 0146-4833. DOI: 10.1145/74674.74675. See p. 401.

Kent, S. T. and K. Seo (2005). *Security Architecture for the Internet Protocol*. RFC 4301. Proposed Standard. IETF. URL: http://www.rfc-editor.org/rfc/rfc4301.txt. See p. 401.

Khanna, A. and A. G. Malis (1987). *ARPANET AHIP-E Host Access Protocol (Enhanced AHIP)*. RFC 1005. Historic. IETF. URL: http://www.rfc-editor.org/rfc/rfc1005.txt. See p. 248.

Kimel, D. (2001). "Neutrality, Autonomy, and Freedom of Contract". In: *Oxford Journal of Legal Studies* 21.3, pp. 473–494.

—— (2003). *From Promise to Contract: Towards a Liberal Theory of Contract*. Oxford: Hart Publishing. See p. 412.

Kincheloe, J. L. and P. McLaren (2005). "Rethinking Critical Theory and Qualitative Research". In: *The Sage Handbook of Qualitative Research*. Ed. by N. K. Denzin and Y. S. Lincoln. 3rd ed. Sage Publications. Chap. 12, pp. 303–342. See p. 170.

Kiousis, S. (2002). "Interactivity: A Concept Explication". In: *New Media & Society* 4.3, pp. 355–383. DOI: 10.1177/146144480200400303. See p. 369.

Kirstein, P. T. (1999). "Early Experiences with the Arpanet and Internet in the United Kingdom". In: *IEEE Annals of the History of Computing* 21.1, pp. 38–44. ISSN: 1058-6180. DOI: 10.1109/85.759368. URL: http://nrg.cs.ucl.ac.uk/mjh/kirstein-arpanet.pdf (pre-publication version), http://nrg.cs.ucl.ac.uk/internet-history.html (ditto). See pp. 313, 316.

—— (2009). "The Early History of Packet Switching in the UK". In: *IEEE Communications Magazine* 47.2, pp. 18–26. DOI: 10.1109/MCOM.2009.4785372. See pp. 313, 317, 340.

Kirstein, P. T. and C. J. Bennett (1979). *Addressing Through Port Expanders.* Internet Experiment Note (IEN) 83. URL: ftp://ftp.rfc-editor.org/in-notes/ien/ien83.txt. Also published as INDRA Note 743. See p. 273.

Kleinrock, L. (1962*a*). "Information Flow in Large Communication Nets". In: *RLE Quarterly Progress Report* 65. URL: http://www.lk.cs.ucla.edu/REPORT/report-4-62-01.html through to http://www.lk.cs.ucla.edu/REPORT/report-4-62-05.html.

—— (1962*b*). "Message Delay in Communication Nets with Storage". PhD Thesis. Cambridge, MA: Massachusetts Institute of Technology. URL: http://dspace.mit.edu/bitstream/handle/1721.1/11562/33840535.pdf (also at http://www.lk.cs.ucla.edu/REPORT/PhD/). See p. 241.

—— (1964). *Communication Nets: Stochastic Message Flow and Delay.* McGraw-Hill. See pp. 44, 229, 241, 380.

—— (1978). "Principles and Lessons in Packet Communications". In: *Proceedings of the IEEE* 66.11, pp. 1320–1329. ISSN: 0018-9219. See pp. 200, 438.

Kleinrock, L. and W. E. Naylor (1974). "On Measured Behavior of the ARPA Network". In: *AFIPS '74: Proceedings of the AFIPS 1974 National Computer Conference and Exposition.* Chicago, IL. May 6–10, 1974. New York, NY: ACM, pp. 767–780. DOI: 10.1145/1500175.1500320. See pp. 251, 313.

Klensin, J. C. (2005). *Terminology for Describing Internet Connectivity.* RFC 4084. Best Current Practice. IETF. URL: http://www.rfc-editor.org/rfc/rfc4084.txt. See p. 371.

Kline, C. S. (1973). *NCP Survey.* RFC 460. Historic. NWG. URL: http://www.rfc-editor.org/rfc/rfc460.txt. See p. 294.

Koreng, A. (2009). "Meinungsmarkt und Netzneutralität. Kommunikationsgrundrechtliche Aspekte des diskriminierungsfreien Netzzugangs". In: *Computer und Recht* 11, pp. 758–760. See p. 424.

Kreznar, J. E. (1969). *Some Questions Re: Host-IMP Protocol*. RFC 17. Historic. NWG. URL: http://www.rfc-editor.org/rfc/rfc17.txt. See p. 249.

Krier, J. E. (1992). "The Tragedy of the Commons, Part Two". In: *Harvard Journal of Law and Public Policy* 15, pp. 325–47. See p. 365.

Kuhn, S. (2009). "Prisoner's Dilemma". In: *The Stanford Encyclopedia of Philosophy*. Ed. by E. N. Zalta. Spring 2009 Edition. URL: http://plato.stanford.edu/entries/prisoner-dilemma/ (http://plato.stanford.edu/archives/spr2009/entries/prisoner-dilemma). See p. 407.

Kunzelman, R. C., V. D. Cone, N. S. Klemba, J. E. Mathis, J. L. McClurg, and D. L. Nielson (1978). *Progress Report an Packet Radio Experimental Network*. Progress Report. SRI. See p. 315.

Kuo, F. F. (1990). "ALOHA Packet Broadcasting System". In: *Encyclopedia of Communications*. Ed. by F. E. Froehlich and A. Kent. Vol. 1. New York, NY: Marcel Dekker, pp. 105–110. See pp. 277, 278.

Kurose, J. F. and K. W. Ross (2005). *Computer Networking: A Top-Down Approach Featuring the Internet*. 3rd ed. Addison-Wesley. See pp. xi, 231.

Lakatos, I. (1970). "Falsification and the Methodology of Scientific Research Programmes". In: *Criticism and the Growth of Knowledge*. Ed. by I. Lakatos and A. Musgrave. Vol. 4. Proceedings of the International Colloquium in the Philosophy of Science, London, 1965. Cambridge University Press, pp. 91–195.

——— (1978*a*). "Falsification and the Methodology of Scientific Research Programmes". In: *The Methodology of Scientific Research Programmes*. Ed. by J. Worrall and G. Currie. Vol. 1. Philosophical Papers. Cambridge University Press. Chap. 1, pp. 8–101. First published in 1970; see Lakatos (1970). See pp. 10, 170, 171, 175, 176, 180, 426.

——— (1978*b*). "History of Science and its Rational Reconstructions". In: *The Methodology of Scientific Research Programmes*. Ed. by J. Worrall and G. Currie. Vol. 1. Philosophical Papers. Cambridge University Press. Chap. 2, pp. 102–138. See p. 173.

Lakshminarayana, K., I. Stoica, S. Shenker, and J. Rexford (2006). *Routing as a Service*. Tech. rep. UCB/EECS-2006. UC Berkeley. URL: http://www.cs.princeton.edu/~jrex/papers/ras.pdf. See pp. 379, 383.

Lampson, B. W. (1983). "Hints for Computer System Design". In: *ACM SIGOPS Operating Systems Review* 17.5, pp. 33–48. ISSN: 0163-5980. DOI: 10.1145/773379.806614. URL: http://research.microsoft.com/en-us/um/people/blampson/33-Hints/Acrobat.pdf (pre-publication version). See pp. 350, 389.

—— (2005). "Computer Security in the Real World". In: *Security '05: 14th Usenix Security Symposium.* Baltimore, MD. July 31 to August 5, 2005. Keynote at Technical Session, August 3, 2005. USENIX Association. URL: http://www.usenix.org/events/sec05/tech/lampson.pdf (presentation slides); http://www.usenix.org/events/sec05/tech/mp3/sec05_keynote_small.mp3 (audio). See pp. 399, 400.

Lampson, B. W., M. Paul, and H. J. Siegert, eds. (1981). *Distributed Systems—Architecture and Implementation.* An Advance Course. Lecture Notes in Computer Science 105. Springer. ISBN: 3-540-10571-9, 0-387-10571-9. See p. 216.

Landsburg, S. E. (1995). *The Armchair Economist: Economics and Everyday Life.* New York, NY: Free Press. See p. 432.

Latour, B. (1987). *Science in Action: How to Follow Scientists and Engineers Through Society.* Harvard University Press. See pp. 27, 163, 174, 179, 215.

Leffler, S. J., W. N. Joy, R. S. Fabry, and M. J. Karels (1993). *Networking Implementation Notes (4.4 BSD Edition).* Part of the UNIX System Manager's Manual (SMM) (4.4 Berkeley Software Distribution). 1993 revision, unchanged from the 1991 edition. URL: http://people.debian.org/~adamm/doc/smm/18.net/paper.pdf (also at http://people.debian.org/~adamm/doc/smm/18.net/paper.html). Also published in the 1994 O'Reilly book. See p. 331.

—— (1994). *4.4 BSD System Manager's Manual.* Originally released in 1993 as UNIX System Manager's Manual (SMM) (4.4 Berkeley Software Distribution) by Computer Systems Research Group, Computer Science Division, Department of Electrical Engineering and Computer Science, University of California Berkeley; first version published in 1979. O'Reilly. ISBN: 978-1565920804. URL: http://people.debian.org/~adamm/doc/index.html#smm (PS, PDF, and ASCII versions of most chapters of the 1993 UCB version).

Lehr, W. H. and M. B. H. Weiss (1996*b*). "The Political Economy of Congestion Charges and Settlements in Packet Networks". In: *The Internet and Telecommunications Policy*. Selected Papers from the 1995 Telecommunications Policy Research Conference. Ed. by G. W. Brock and G. L. Rosston. Mahwah, NJ: Lawrence Erlbaum. Chap. 6, pp. 79–96.

—— (1996*a*). "The Political Economy of Congestion Charges and Settlements in Packet Networks". In: *Telecommunications Policy* 20.3, pp. 219–231. ISSN: 0308-5961. DOI: 10.1016/0308-5961(96)00004-3. See p. 363.

Leiner, B. M., V. G. Cerf, D. D. Clark, R. E. Kahn, L. Kleinrock, D. C. Lynch, J. B. Postel, L. G. Roberts, and S. Wolff (2003). *A Brief History of the Internet*. Online. Version 3.32. URL: http://www.isoc.org/internet/history/brief.shtml. See p. 388.

Lemley, M. A. and L. Lessig (2001). "The End of End-to-End: Preserving the Architecture of the Internet in the Broadband Era". In: *UCLA Law Review* 48.4, pp. 925–972. URL: http://repositories.cdlib.org/cgi/viewcontent.cgi?article=1052&context=blewp. Also published in the 2004 Cooper book. See p. 176.

Lessig, L. (1999*a*). *Code and Other Laws of Cyberspace*. New York: Basic Books. URL: http://www.code-is-law.org/toc.html. See p. 176.

—— (1999*b*). "The Law of the Horse: What Cyberlaw Might Teach". In: *Harvard Law Review* 113.501, pp. 501–549. See p. 178.

—— (2001). *The Future of Ideas*. The Fate of the Commons in a Connected World. New York: Random House. See pp. 429, 433.

—— (2008). *Official Testimony*. Federal Communications Commission's Second Public En Banc Hearing on Broadband Network Management Practices at Stanford University, Stanford, CA, April 17, 2008. Presentation. URL: http://www.lessig.org/blog/2008/04/testifying_fcc_stanford.html. See pp. 165, 176, 429.

Levin, J. (1978). *Arpanet/IMP Software History — Principal Milestones*. BBN Report. Bolt, Beranek and Newman Inc. (BBN). URL: http://www.cs.utexas.edu/users/chris/DIGITAL_ARCHIVE/ARPANET/milestones.pdf (also at http://www.cs.utexas.edu/users/chris/DIGITAL_ARCHIVE/ARPANET/milestones.txt). See p. 256.

Licklider, J. C. R. and A. Vezza (1978). "Applications of information networks". In: *Proceedings of the IEEE* 66.11, pp. 1330–1346. See p. 115.

Liebowitz, S. J. (2002). *Re-Thinking the Network Economy: The True Forces That Drive the Digital Marketplace*. New York, NY: Amacom. See pp. 237, 427.

Liu, H., H. Ma, M. El Zarki, and S. Gupta (1997). "Error Control Schemes for Networks: An Overview". In: *Mobile Networks and Applications* 2.2, pp. 167–182. ISSN: 1383-469X. DOI: 10.1023/A:1013676531988. URL: http://vip.ics.uci.edu/publications/1997/monet97.pdf. See p. 197.

Lloyd, D. and P. T. Kirstein (1975). "Alternative Approaches to the Interconnection of Computer Networks". In: *Eurocomp 1975: Proceedings of the European Computing Conference on Communications Networks*. London, UK. September 23–25, 1975. Ed. by D. L. A. Barber. Online Conferences, pp. 499–515. ISBN: 0903796058. See p. 330.

Lovink, G. (2008). *Zittrain's Foundational Myth of the Open Internet*. Online. URL: http://networkcultures.org/wpmu/geert/2008/10/12/zittrains-foundational-myth-of-the-open-internet/. See p. 165.

MacKie-Mason, J. K. and H. R. Varian (1995). "Pricing Congestible Network Resources". In: *IEEE Journal on Selected Areas in Communications* 13.7, pp. 1141–1149. ISSN: 0733-8716. DOI: 10.1109/49.414634. See p. 363.

MacKie-Mason, J. K. (2000). *An AOL/Time Warner Merger Will Harm Competition in Internet Online Services*. Report submitted to the U.S. Federal Trade Commission. University of Michigan. URL: http://www-personal.umich.edu/~jmm/papers/aol-twoo-public.pdf. See p. 414.

MacKie-Mason, J. K., S. Shenker, and H. R. Varian (1996*a*). *Network Architecture and Content Provision: An Economic Analysis*. Online. Extended version of earlier conference papers (titled "Service Architecture and Content Provision: The Network Provider as Editor"). URL: http://people.ischool.berkeley.edu/~hal/Papers/UM/tprc.pdf. See p. 434.

—— (1996*b*). "Service Architecture and Content Provision: The Network Provider as Editor". In: *The Internet and Telecommunications Policy*. Selected Papers from the 1995 Telecommunications Policy Research Conference. Ed. by G. W. Brock and G. L. Rosston. Mahwah, NJ: Lawrence Erlbaum. Chap. 11, pp. 191–212. URL: http://people.ischool.berkeley.edu/~hal/Papers/UM/tprc.pdf (edited version titled "Network Architecture and Content Provision: An Economic Analysis").

—— (1996c). "Service Architecture and Content Provision: The Network Provider as Editor". In: *Telecommunications Policy* 20.3, pp. 203–217. ISSN: 0308-5961. DOI: 10.1016/0308-5961(96)00003-1. See p. 435.

Madhyastha, H. V., T. Isdal, M. Piatek, C. Dixon, T. Anderson, A. Krishnamurthy, and A. Venkataramani (2006). "iPlane: An Information Plane for Distributed Services". In: *OSDI '06: Proceedings of the 7th USENIX Symposium on Operating Systems Design and Implementation*. Seattle, WA. November 6–8, 2006. Berkeley, CA: USENIX Association, pp. 367–380. URL: http://www.usenix.org/events/osdi06/tech/madhyastha.html. See p. 362.

Makhoul, J. (2006). "Speech Processing at BBN". In: *IEEE Annals of the History of Computing* 28.1, pp. 32–45. ISSN: 1058-6180. DOI: 10.1109/MAHC.2006.19. See pp. 305, 306.

Malis, A. G. (1981). *ARPANET 1822L Host Access Protocol*. RFC 802. Historic. Obsoleted by RFC 851. NWG. URL: http://www.rfc-editor.org/rfc/rfc802.txt. See p. 249.

—— (1983). *ARPANET 1822L Host Access Protocol*. RFC 878. Historic. NWG. URL: http://www.rfc-editor.org/rfc/rfc878.txt. See p. 249.

—— (1986). *Re: major change to 1822 (IMP) software*. tcp-ip mailing list. Mar. 16, 1986. URL: http://securitydigest.org/tcp-ip/archive/1986/03. See pp. 303, 304.

Marill, T. and L. G. Roberts (1966). "Toward a Cooperative Network of Time-Shared Computers". In: *AFIPS '66: Proceedings of the AFIPS 1966 Fall Joint Computer Conference*. San Francisco, CA. November 7–10, 1966. New York, NY: ACM, pp. 425–431. DOI: 10.1145/1464291.1464336. URL: http://www.packet.cc/files/toward-coop-net.html. See pp. 219, 241.

Mathis, M. and J. Heffner (2007). *Packetization Layer Path MTU Discovery*. RFC 4821. Proposed Standard. IETF. URL: http://www.rfc-editor.org/rfc/rfc4821.txt. See pp. 93, 341, 343.

Mathison, S. L. and P. M. Walker (1972). "Regulatory and Economic Issues in Computer Communications". In: *Proceedings of the IEEE* 60.11, pp. 1254–1272. ISSN: 0018-9219. See p. 435.

Mathison, S. (1988). "Why Triangulate?" In: *Educational Researcher* 17.2, pp. 13–17. See p. 170.

McKenzie, A. A. (1971*a*). *NCP, ICP, and Telnet: The Terminal IMP Implementation.* RFC 215. Historic. NWG. URL: http://www.rfc-editor.org/rfc/rfc215.txt. See p. 282.

——— (1971*b*). *"Very Distant" Host interface.* RFC 263. Historic. NWG. URL: http://www.rfc-editor.org/rfc/rfc263.txt. See pp. 64, 248, 275.

——— (1972). *Host/Host Protocol for the ARPA Network.* NIC 8246. ARPA/NWG. URL: http://www.cs.utexas.edu/users/chris/DIGITAL_ARCHIVE/ARPANET/nic8246.pdf. See pp. 57, 244, 259, 287.

——— (1973). *Host/Host Protocol Design Considerations.* INWG General Note 16. IFIP WG 6.1 (INWG). See pp. 290, 393.

McKenzie, A. A., B. P. Cosell, J. M. McQuillan, and M. J. Thrope (1972). "The Network Control Center for the ARPA Network". In: *ICCC '72: Proceedings of the First International Conference on Computer Communication.* Washington, DC. October 24–26, 1972. URL: http://www.archive.org/details/TheNetworkControlCenterForTheArpaNetwork. See p. 251.

McQuillan, J. M. (1973). *Software Checksumming in the IMP and Network Reliability.* RFC 528. Historic. NWG. URL: http://www.rfc-editor.org/rfc/rfc528.txt. See pp. 57, 194, 231, 256, 260, 296, 297.

McQuillan, J. M. and V. G. Cerf (1978*a*). "Choices in the Design of Computer Communications Systems". In: *Tutorial: A Practical View of Computer Communications Protocols.* Ed. by J. M. McQuillan and V. G. Cerf. New York, NY: IEEE, pp. 3–36. ISBN: 0818602015. LCCN: 78061492. See pp. 204, 263, 271.

——— (1978*b*). "Network Sampler". In: *Tutorial: A Practical View of Computer Communications Protocols.* Ed. by J. M. McQuillan and V. G. Cerf. New York, NY: IEEE, pp. 254–258. ISBN: 0818602015. LCCN: 78061492. See p. 320.

McQuillan, J. M. and D. C. Walden (1972). *Three Aids to Improved Network Operation.* RFC 381. Historic. Updated by RFC 394. NWG. URL: http://www.rfc-editor.org/rfc/rfc381.txt. See p. 295.

——— (1977). "The ARPA Network Design Decisions". In: *Computer Networks* 1.5, pp. 243–289. URL: http://www.walden-family.com/public/whole-paper.pdf (OCR version at http://citeseerx.ist.psu.edu/viewdoc/download?doi=10.1.1.83.9752&rep=rep1&type=pdf). Based on Crowther et al. (1975), which is based on BBN Report 2918, which in turn is an extract from BBN Report 2913, both from 1974. See pp. 208, 259, 263–266, 270.

McQuillan, J. M., W. R. Crowther, B. P. Cosell, D. C. Walden, and F. E. Heart (1972). "Improvements in the Design and Performance of the ARPA Network". In: *AFIPS '72: Proceedings of the AFIPS 1972 Fall Joint Computer Conference*. Anaheim, CA. December 5–7, 1972. New York, NY: ACM, pp. 741–754. DOI: 10.1145/1480083.1480096. See pp. 256, 269, 356, 357.

Medina, A., M. Allman, and S. Floyd (2004). "Measuring Interactions Between Transport Protocols and Middleboxes". In: *IMC '04: Proceedings of the 4th ACM SIGCOMM conference on Internet measurement*. Taormina, Sicily, Italy. New York, NY: ACM, pp. 336–341. ISBN: 1-58113-821-0. DOI: 10.1145/1028788.1028835.

—— (2005). "Measuring the Evolution of Transport Protocols in the Internet". In: *ACM SIGCOMM Computer Communication Review* 35.2, pp. 37–52. ISSN: 0146-4833. DOI: 10.1145/1064413.1064418. Extended version of the 2004 IMC version. See pp. 341, 343, 353.

Merton, R. K. (1936). "The Unintended Consequences of Purposive Social Action". In: *American Sociological Review* 1, pp. 894–904. See p. 143.

Mestmäcker, E.-J. (2007). *A Legal Theory Without Law: Posner v. Hayek on Economic Analysis of Law*. Vol. 174. Beiträge zur Ordnungstheorie und Ordungspolitik. Tübingen: Mohr Siebeck. See pp. 7, 166.

Metcalfe, R. M. (1973). "Packet Communication". PhD thesis. Cambridge, MA: Harvard University. URL: http://publications.csail.mit.edu/lcs/pubs/pdf/MIT-LCS-TR-114.pdf (revised edition, published as MIT Laboratory for Computer Science Technical Report 114). Mostly written at MIT Project MAC and Xerox PARC. See pp. 87, 137, 250, 252, 258, 260, 270, 314, 322, 323, 348, 398.

—— (1974). *A Proposed Pup—Parc Universal Packet*. Internal Memorandum. Dated March 19, 1974. Xerox PARC. Posted to internet history mailing list at May 24, 2010 with the subject line "RE: [ih] Early interconnection between Ethernets and Arpanet", copy on file with the author. See pp. 196, 216.

—— (1988). *Interview with Robert M. Metcalfe by James Pelkey*. Supplement to the James Pelkey online book. Interview conducted at February 16, 1988, in Portola Valley, CA. URL: http://historyofcomputercommunications.info/CC_Individuals/MetcalfBob/InterviewMetcalfBob.html. See p. 336.

Metcalfe, R. M. and D. R. Boggs (1976). "Ethernet: Distributed Packet Switching for Local Computer Networks". In: *Communications of the ACM* 19.7, pp. 395–404. ISSN: 0001-0782. DOI: 10.1145/360248.360253. URL: http://ethernethistory.typepad.com/papers/EthernetPaper.pdf (1980 reprint). See pp. 217, 314, 342, 347.

Meyer Jr., E. W. (1970*a*). *ARPA Network Protocol Notes*. RFC 46. Historic. NWG. URL: http://www.rfc-editor.org/rfc/rfc46.txt. See p. 195.

——— (1970*b*). *Network Meeting Notes*. RFC 82. Historic. Minutes from three network meetings held in Houston during the 1970 Fall Joint Computer Conference. NWG. URL: http://www.rfc-editor.org/rfc/rfc82.txt. See p. 245.

Michel, A. and M. Tasman (1984). *Mail Bridge Final Design Report*. BBN Report 5612. Bolt, Beranek and Newman Inc. (BBN). See pp. 327, 403.

Mills, D. L. (1988). "The Fuzzball". In: *SIGCOMM '88: Symposium Proceedings on Communications Architectures and Protocols*. Stanford, CA. August 16–18, 1988. New York, NY: ACM, pp. 115–122. ISBN: 0-89791-279-9. DOI: 10.1145/52324.52337. URL: http://citeseerx.ist.psu.edu/viewdoc/summary?doi=10.1.1.29.8650 (different pagination). See pp. 100, 358, 359.

——— (2004). *Re: [ih] Global congestion collapse*. internet history mailing list. Dec. 13, 2004. URL: http://mailman.postel.org/pipermail/internet-history/2004-December/000439.html. See pp. 359, 360.

Mills, D. L. and H. Braun (1988). "The NSFNET Backbone Network". In: *SIGCOMM '87: Proceedings of the ACM Workshop on Frontiers in Computer Communications Technology*. Stowe, VT. August 11–13, 1987. New York, NY: ACM, pp. 191–196. ISBN: 0-89791-245-4. DOI: 10.1145/55482.55502. URL: http://www.cs.utexas.edu/users/chris/sigcomm/t1/mills.nsfnet.materials.pdf also at http://www.cis.udel.edu/~mills/database/papers/bone.pdf. See p. 360.

Mills, D. L., J. Levine, R. Schmidt, and D. Plonka (2004). "Coping with Overload on the Network Time Protocol Public Servers". In: *Proceedings of Precision Time and Time Interval (PTTI) Applications and Planning Meeting*. Washington, DC. December 7–9, 2004, pp. 5–16. URL: http:

//www.eecis.udel.edu/~mills/database/papers/ptti/ptti04a.pdf. See p. 360.

Mockapetris, P. V. (1983). *Domain Names: Concepts and Facilities.* RFC 882. Historic. Obsoleted by RFCs 1034, 1035, updated by RFC 973. NWG. URL: http://www.rfc-editor.org/rfc/rfc882.txt. See pp. 334, 372.

—— (1987*a*). *Domain Names — Concepts and Facilities.* RFC 1034. Standard. Updated by RFCs 1101, 1183, 1348, 1876, 1982, 2065, 2181, 2308, 2535, 4033, 4034, 4035, 4343, 4035, 4592. IETF. URL: http://www.rfc-editor.org/rfc/rfc1034.txt. See p. 372.

—— (1987*b*). *Domain Names — Implementation and Specification.* RFC 1035. Standard. Updated by RFCs 1101, 1183, 1348, 1876, 1982, 1995, 1996, 2065, 2136, 2181, 2137, 2308, 2535, 2845, 3425, 3658, 4033, 4034, 4035, 4343. IETF. URL: http://www.rfc-editor.org/rfc/rfc1035.txt. See p. 372.

Mockapetris, P. V. and K. Dunlap (1986). "Implementation of the Domain Name System". In: *Proceedings of the 4th Joint Meeting of the Internet Engineering and Internet Architecture Task Forces.* Menlo Park, CA. October 15–17, 1986. Ed. by P. Gross. Internet Engineering Task Force and Internet Architecture Task Force, pp. 132–142. URL: http://www.ietf.org/proceedings/04.pdf. See p. 98.

Mogul, J. C. and S. E. Deering (1990). *Path MTU Discovery.* RFC 1190. Draft Standard. IETF. URL: http://www.rfc-editor.org/rfc/rfc1191.txt. See pp. 93, 343.

Moors, T. (2002). "A Critical Review of "End-to-End Arguments in System Design"". In: *ICC 2002: Proceedings of IEEE International Conference on Communications.* Vol. 2. IEEE, pp. 1214–1219. DOI: 10.1109/ICC.2002.997043. URL: http://www.seas.upenn.edu/~farooq/tcom512/a-critical-review-of_e2e.pdf (2000 working paper version). See pp. 37, 219, 220, 364.

Mueller, M., D. Cogburn, J. Mathiason, and J. Hofmann (2007). *Net Neutrality as Global Principle for Internet Governance.* Research Paper. School of Information Studies, Syracuse University, Syracuse, NY: Internet Governance Project. URL: http://www.internetgovernance.org/pdf/NetNeutralityGlobalPrinciple.pdf. See p. 430.

Muuss, M. (1982). *To TCP or not to TCP?* tcp-ip mailing list. TCP/IP Digest, Thursday, 14 Jan 1982, Volume 1, Issue 12. Jan. 14, 1982. URL: http:

//securitydigest.org/tcp-ip/archive/1982/01 (also at http://ftp.arl.army.mil/ftp/tcp-ip-digest/tcp-ip-digest.v1n12.1). See p. 344.

Nagle, J. (1984*a*). *Congestion Control in IP/TCP Internetworks*. RFC 896. Historic. NWG. URL: http://www.rfc-editor.org/rfc/rfc896.txt. Also published as ACM SIGCOMM CCR paper. See pp. 346, 351, 353.

—— (1984*b*). "Congestion Control in IP/TCP Internetworks". In: *ACM SIGCOMM Computer Communication Review* 14.4, pp. 11–17. ISSN: 0146-4833. DOI: 10.1145/1024908.1024910.

—— (1985). *On Packet Switches with Infinite Storage*. RFC 970. Historic. NWG. URL: http://www.rfc-editor.org/rfc/rfc970.txt. See pp. 100, 101, 346, 357.

—— (1986). "Congestion in the Internet: Doing Something About It". In: *Proceedings of the Fourth DARPA Gateway Algorithms and Data Structures Task Force Meeting*. San Diego, CA. January 16–17, 1986. Ed. by P. Gross. Presentation slides. Internet Engineering Task Force and Internet Architecture Task Force, pp. 88–103. URL: http://www.ietf.org/proceedings/01.pdf. See pp. 98, 357.

Naughton, J. J. (2000). *A Brief History of the Future: From Radio Days to Internet Years in a Lifetime*. Woodstock, NY: The Overlook Press. See p. 175.

Naylor, W. E. and H. Opderbeck (1974). *Mean Round-Trip Times in the ARPANET*. RFC 619. Historic. NWG. URL: http://www.rfc-editor.org/rfc/rfc619.txt. See p. 313.

Needham, R. M. (1972). "Protection Systems and Protection Implementations". In: *AFIPS '72: Proceedings of the AFIPS 1972 Fall Joint Computer Conference*. Anaheim, CA. December 5–7, 1972. New York, NY: ACM, pp. 571–578. DOI: 10.1145/1479992.1480073. See p. 399.

Neigus, N. and E. J. Feinler (1973). *Host Status*. RFC 597. Historic. Updated by RFC 603. NWG. URL: http://www.rfc-editor.org/rfc/rfc597.txt. See p. 278.

Nelson, H. A., J. E. Mathis, and J. M. Lieb (1980). *The Arpanet IMP Port Expander*. Technical Report 1080-140-1. Menlo Park, CA: SRI International. URL: http://www.dtic.mil/cgi-bin/GetTRDoc?AD=ADA155753&Location=U2&doc=GetTRDoc.pdf. See pp. 273, 313.

Nelson, T. H. (2008). *Geeks Bearing Gifts*. How the Computer World Got this Way. Lulu.com. See pp. 373, 411.

Neumann, J. von (1956). "Probabilistic Logics and Synthesis of Reliable Organisms from Unreliable Components". In: *Automata Studies*. Ed. by C. E. Shannon and J. McCarthy. Annals of Mathematics Studies. Princeton University Press. Chap. 2, pp. 43–98. See p. 189.

Newkirk, J., M. Kraley, J. B. Postel, and S. D. Crocker (1970). *A Prototypical Implementation of the NCP*. RFC 55. Historic. NWG. URL: http://www.rfc-editor.org/rfc/rfc55.txt. See pp. 15, 16, 293.

Nielsen, J. (1988). "Trip Report: Hypertext'87, Chapel Hill, North Carolina, 13–15 November 1987". In: *ACM SIGCHI Bulletin* 19.4, pp. 27–35. ISSN: 0736-6906. DOI: 10.1145/43950.43953. URL: http://www.useit.com/papers/tripreports/ht87.html. See p. 411.

Nielson, D. L. (2002). "The SRI Van and Computer Internetworking". In: *Core* 3.1, pp. 2–7. URL: http://www.computerhistory.org/core/backissues/pdf/core_3_1.pdf (see also http://ed-thelen.org/comp-hist/CORE-3-1-SRI-TCP-IP.html). Heavily based on the 2004 book. See pp. 314, 315.

——— (2004). *A Heritage of Innovation: SRI's First Half Century*. SRI International.

Norberg, A. L., J. E. O'Neill, and K. J. Freedman (1996). *Transforming Computer Technology: Information Processing for the Pentagon, 1962–1986*. Ed. by M. R. Smith. John Hopkins Studies in the History of Technology 18. Baltimore, MD and London, UK: The John Hopkins University Press. See pp. xi, 183, 202, 246.

North, J. B. (1972). *Official Site Idents for Organizations in the ARPA Network*. RFC 384. Historic. NWG. URL: http://www.rfc-editor.org/rfc/rfc384.txt. See p. 278.

Nunziato, D. C. (2009). *Virtual Freedom: Net Neutrality and Free Speech in the Internet Age*. Stanford University Press. See p. 228.

Odlyzko, A. M. (2001). "Internet Pricing and the History of Communications". In: *Computer Networks* 36.5/6, pp. 493–517. URL: http://www.dtc.umn.edu/~odlyzko/doc/history.communications1b.pdf (pre-publication version). See pp. 363, 435.

Oinas-Kukkonen, H. (2007). "From Bush to Engelbart: 'Slowly, Some Little Bells Were Ringing'". In: *IEEE Annals of the History of Computing* 29.2, pp. 31–39. ISSN: 1058-6180. DOI: http://doi.ieeecomputersociety.org/10.1109/MAHC.2007.22. See p. 411.

O'Neill, J. E. (1995). "The Role of ARPA in the Development of the ARPA-NET, 1961–1972". In: *IEEE Annals of the History of Computing* 17.4, pp. 76–81. See pp. 184, 202.

Ornstein, S. M., F. E. Heart, W. R. Crowther, H. K. Rising, S. B. Russell, and A. Michel (1971). "The Terminal IMP for the ARPA Computer Network". In: *AFIPS '71: Proceedings of the AFIPS 1971 Fall Joint Computer Conference*. Las Vegas, NV. November 16–18, 1971. New York, NY: ACM, pp. 243–254. DOI: 10.1145/1478873.1478906. See pp. 68, 248, 269, 280–282, 284.

Ostrom, E. (1990). *Governing the Commons: The Evolution of Institutions for Collective Action*. Cambridge University Press. See p. 365.

—— (2005). *Understanding Institutional Diversity*. Princeton University Press. See p. 365.

O'Sullivan, T. C. (1971*a*). *Discussion of Telnet Protocol*. RFC 139. Historic. Updated by RFC 158. NWG. URL: http://www.rfc-editor.org/rfc/rfc139.txt. See p. 283.

—— (1971*b*). *Telnet Protocol*. RFC 137. Historic. Updated by RFC 139. NWG. URL: http://www.rfc-editor.org/rfc/rfc137.txt. See pp. 283, 284, 287.

Otlet, P. (1934). *Traité de documentation. Le livre sur le livre. Théorie et pratique*. Editiones Mundaneum. Brussels, Belgium: D. van Keerberghen & Fils. URL: http://hdl.handle.net/1854/5612 (also at https://archive.ugent.be/retrieve/4607/Traite_de_documentation_ocr.pdf). See p. 411.

Padlipsky, M. A. (1982*a*). *A Perspective on the Arpanet Reference Model*. RFC 871. Historic. NWG. URL: http://www.rfc-editor.org/rfc/rfc871.txt. See pp. 284, 286, 291, 390.

—— (1982*b*). *Critique of X.25*. RFC 874. Historic. NWG. URL: http://www.rfc-editor.org/rfc/rfc874.txt. See p. 291.

—— (1984). *The Elements of Networking Style And Other Essays and Animadversions on the Art of Intercomputer Networking*. Prentice Hall. See pp. 287, 391.

Padmanabhan, V. N. and J. C. Mogul (1994). "Improving HTTP Latency". In: *Proceedings of the Second International World Wide Web Conference*. Chicago, IL. October 17–21, 1994, pp. 995–1005. See p. 289.

——— (1995). "Improving HTTP Latency". In: *Computer Networks and ISDN Systems* 28.1-2, pp. 25–35. ISSN: 0169-7552. DOI: 10.1016/0169-7552(95)00106-1. Revised version of the 1994 paper.

Pahlavan, K. and P. Krishnamurthy (2009). *Networking Fundamentals: Wide, Local, and Personal Area Communications*. Wiley. See p. 341.

Papadimitriou, D., M. Welzl, M. Scharf, and R. Briscoe (2009). *Open Research Issues in Internet Congestion Control*. Internet Draft. Expired. Version 5. IETF. URL: http://tools.ietf.org/html/draft-irtf-iccrg-welzl-congestion-control-open-research-05. See pp. 102, 345, 354.

Parnas, D. L. (1972). "On the Criteria to be Used in Decomposing Systems into Modules". In: *Communications of the ACM* 15.12, pp. 1053–1058. ISSN: 0001-0782. DOI: 10.1145/361598.361623. URL: http://www.cs.umd.edu/class/spring2003/cmsc838p/Design/criteria.pdf. See pp. 136, 146, 392, 393.

Partridge, C. (2004). *[ih] Re: Global congestion collapse*. internet history mailing list. Dec. 26, 2004. URL: http://mailman.postel.org/pipermail/internet-history/2004-December/000451.html. See pp. 354, 407.

——— (2008). "The Technical Development of Internet Email". In: *IEEE Annals of the History of Computing* 30.2, pp. 3–29. ISSN: 1058-6180. DOI: 10.1109/MAHC.2008.32. URL: http://www.net-tech.bbn.com/~craig/email.pdf (pre-publication version). See pp. 312, 411.

Partridge, C. and S. H. Blumenthal (2006). "Data Networking at BBN". In: *Annals of the History of Computing, IEEE* 28.1, pp. 56–71. ISSN: 1058-6180. DOI: 10.1109/MAHC.2006.7. See pp. 331, 341.

Paxson, V. (1999). "End-to-End Internet Packet Dynamics". In: *IEEE/ACM Transactions on Networking (TON)* 7.3, pp. 277–292. ISSN: 1063-6692. DOI: 10.1109/90.779192. See p. 271.

Pelkey, J. (2009). *Entrepreneurial Capitalism: A History of Computer Communications 1968–1988*. Online. URL: http://www.historyofcomputercommunications.info/CC_Book/BookIndex.html. See pp. 242, 277, 313, 318, 319, 331, 339, 340, 344.

Perillo, F. (1981). *The Arpanet HDH Host Interface*. DoD Network Newsletter (ANEWS) 9. Network Info Center for Defense Communications Agency (DCA) Defense Data Network (DDN) Program Management Office (SRI NIC). URL: ftp://ftp.rfc-editor.org/in-notes/museum/ARPANET_News.mail. See p. 276.

Perlis, A. J. (1982). "Epigrams on Programming". In: *SIGPLAN Notices* 17.9, pp. 7–13. ISSN: 0362-1340. DOI: 10.1145/947955.1083808. See pp. 163, 229, 367, 372, 403.

Perry, D. G., S. H. Blumenthal, and R. M. Hinden (1988). "The ARPANET and the DARPA Internet". In: *Library Hi Tech* 6.2, pp. 51–62. DOI: 10.1108/eb047726. See pp. 273, 276, 281.

Peterson, J. and A. Cooper (2009). *Report from the IETF Workshop on Peer-to-Peer (P2P) Infrastructure, May 28, 2008.* RFC 5594. Informational. IETF. URL: http://www.rfc-editor.org/rfc/rfc5594.txt. See p. 362.

Peterson, L. L. and B. S. Davie (2007). *Computer Networks: A Systems Approach.* 4th ed. The Morgan Kaufmann Series in Networking. Morgan Kaufmann (Elsevier). See pp. xi, 372.

Pfeifer, L. and J. McAfee (1973). *Real-Time Data Transmission on the Arpanet.* RFC 508. Historic. NWG. URL: http://www.rfc-editor.org/rfc/rfc508.txt. See p. 306.

Pickens, J. R. (1972). *Evaluation of Arpanet services January–March, 1972.* RFC 369. Historic. NWG. URL: http://www.rfc-editor.org/rfc/rfc369.txt. See p. 294.

Pierce, J. R. (1972). "How Far Can Data Loops Go?" In: *IEEE Transactions on Communications* 20.3, pp. 527–530. See p. 314.

Piscitello, D. M. and A. L. Chapin (1993). *Open Systems Networking: TCP/IP and OSI.* Addison Wesley. ISBN: 0201563347. URL: http://www.interisle-group.com/OSN/OSN.html. See p. 120.

Podlesny, M. and S. Gorinsky (2008). "RD Network Services: Differentiation through Performance Incentives". In: *ACM SIGCOMM Computer Communication Review* 38.4, pp. 255–266. ISSN: 0146-4833. DOI: 10.1145/1402946.1402988. URL: http://www.arl.wustl.edu/~gorinsky/pdf/RD_Services_SIGCOMM_2008.pdf. See pp. 213, 356.

Polybius (1925). "Fragments of Book X". In: *The Histories.* Ed. by T. E. Page, E. Caps, W. H. D. Rouse, L. A. Post, and E. H. Warmington. Vol. IV. 6 vols. The Loeb Classical Library. With an English Translation by W. R. Paton. Harvard University Press, pp. 101–225. URL: http://penelope.uchicago.edu/Thayer/E/Roman/Texts/Polybius/10*.html. See pp. 180, 181.

Popper, K. R. (1935). *Logik der Forschung.* Vienna: Julius Springer. Published in English as "The Logic of Scientific Discovery". See p. 170.

Posner, R. A. (2003). *Law, Pragmatism, and Democracy*. Harvard University Press. See p. 166.

Postel, J. B. (1971). *A Proferred Official Initial Connection Protocol*. RFC 165. Historic. NWG. URL: http://www.rfc-editor.org/rfc/rfc165.pdf (also at http://www.rfc-editor.org/rfc/rfc165.txt, albeit with a misspelled title). See p. 288.

——— (1973*a*). *Assigned Link Numbers*. RFC 604. Historic. Obsoleted by RFC 739. NWG. URL: http://www.rfc-editor.org/rfc/rfc604.txt. See p. 273.

——— (1973*b*). *Lost Message Detection*. RFC 516. Historic. NWG. URL: http://www.rfc-editor.org/rfc/rfc516.txt. See pp. 256, 257, 295, 296.

——— (1975*a*). *Comments on the Proposed Host/IMP Protocol Changes*. RFC 690. Historic. Updated by RFC 692. NWG. URL: http://www.rfc-editor.org/rfc/rfc690.txt. See p. 272.

——— (1975*b*). *On the Junk Mail Problem*. RFC 706. Historic. NWG. URL: http://www.rfc-editor.org/rfc/rfc706.txt. See p. 355.

——— (1975*c*). *Protocol Information*. RFC 694. Historic. NWG. URL: http://www.rfc-editor.org/rfc/rfc694.txt. See p. 257.

——— (1977*a*). *Assigned Numbers*. RFC 739. Historic. Obsoleted by RFC 750. NWG. URL: http://www.rfc-editor.org/rfc/rfc739.txt. See p. 273.

——— (1977*b*). *Comments on Internet Protocol and TCP*. Internet Experiment Note (IEN) 2. Internet Notebook Section 2.3.3.2. URL: ftp://ftp.rfc-editor.org/in-notes/ien/ien2.txt. See pp. 21, 207, 238, 338.

——— (1977*c*). *Extensible Field Addressing*. RFC 730. Historic. NWG. URL: http://www.rfc-editor.org/rfc/rfc730.txt. See p. 272.

——— (1977*d*). *Internet Meeting Notes — 30 & 31 October 1978*. Internet Experiment Note (IEN) 63. URL: ftp://ftp.rfc-editor.org/in-notes/ien/scanned/ien63.pdf. See p. 381.

——— (1977*e*). *TCP Meeting Notes — 13 & 14 October 1977*. Internet Experiment Note (IEN) 66. URL: ftp://ftp.rfc-editor.org/in-notes/ien/scanned/ien66.pdf. See pp. 92, 337, 338.

——— (1978*a*). *Draft Internetwork Protocol Specification*. Version 2. Internet Experiment Note (IEN) 28. Internet Notebook Section 2.3.4.1. URL: ftp://ftp.rfc-editor.org/in-notes/ien/scanned/ien28.pdf. See pp. 92, 338.

——— (1978*b*). *Internet Name Server*. Internet Experiment Note (IEN) 61. Internet Notebook Section 2.5.6.1. URL: ftp://ftp.rfc-editor.org/in-notes/ien/ien61.txt. See p. 334.

Postel, J. B. (1978*c*). *Internetwork Protocol Specification Version 4*. Draft. Internet Experiment Note (IEN) 41. Internet Notebook Section 2.3.2.1. URL: ftp://ftp.rfc-editor.org/in-notes/ien/scanned/ien41.pdf. See pp. 88, 92, 93, 338, 344, 349, 379, 381.

——— (1978*d*). *Internetwork Protocol Specification Version 4*. Draft. Internet Experiment Note (IEN) 54. Internet Notebook Section 2.3.2.1. URL: ftp://ftp.rfc-editor.org/in-notes/ien/scanned/ien54.pdf. See p. 381.

——— (1978*e*). *Transmission Control Protocol Version 4*. Draft. Internet Experiment Note (IEN) 40. Internet Notebook Section 2.4.2.1. URL: ftp://ftp.rfc-editor.org/in-notes/ien/scanned/ien40.pdf. See pp. 88, 338, 344.

——— (1979*a*). *Internet Datagram Protocol Specification Version 4*. Internet Experiment Note (IEN) 80. URL: ftp://ftp.rfc-editor.org/in-notes/ien/scanned/ien80.pdf. See pp. 343, 381.

——— (1979*b*). *Internet Meeting Notes—25 & 26 January 1979*. Internet Experiment Note (IEN) 76. URL: ftp://ftp.rfc-editor.org/in-notes/ien/scanned/ien76.pdf. See pp. 342, 381.

——— (1979*c*). *Internet Meeting Notes—10, 11, 12 & 13 September 1979*. Internet Experiment Note (IEN) 121. URL: ftp://ftp.rfc-editor.org/in-notes/ien/ien121.txt. See p. 274.

——— (1979*d*). *Internet Name Server*. Internet Experiment Note (IEN) 89. URL: ftp://ftp.rfc-editor.org/in-notes/ien/ien89.txt. See p. 334.

——— (1980*a*). *Assigned Numbers*. RFC 762. Historic. Obsoleted by RFC 770. NWG. URL: http://www.rfc-editor.org/rfc/rfc762.txt. See p. 308.

——— (1980*b*). *DoD Standard Internet Protocol*. RFC 760. Historic. IEN 128, Obsoleted by RFC 791, updated by RFC 777. NWG. URL: http://www.rfc-editor.org/rfc/rfc760.txt. See p. 349.

——— (1980*c*). *User Datagram Protocol*. RFC 768. Standard. NWG. URL: http://www.rfc-editor.org/rfc/rfc768.txt. See pp. 334, 394.

——— (1981*a*). *Disabling NCPs*. tcp-ip mailing list. TCP/IP Digest, Wednesday, 11 Nov 1981, Volume 1, Issue 6. Nov. 11, 1981. URL: http://securitydigest.org/tcp-ip/archive/1981/11 (also at http://ftp.arl.army.mil/ftp/tcp-ip-digest/tcp-ip-digest.v1n6.1). See p. 345.

——— (1981*b*). *Internet Control Message Protocol*. RFC 777. Historic. Obsoleted by RFC 792. NWG. URL: http://www.rfc-editor.org/rfc/rfc777.txt. Issues at April 1, but no April Fools' Day RFC. See pp. 349, 350.

——— (1981c). *Internet Control Message Protocol — DARPA Internet Program Protocol Specification*. RFC 792. Standard. NWG. URL: http://www.rfc-editor.org/rfc/rfc792.txt. See pp. 233, 349.

——— (1981d). *Internet Protocol — DARPA Internet Program Protocol Specification*. RFC 791. Standard. NWG. URL: http://www.rfc-editor.org/rfc/rfc791.txt. See pp. 79, 93, 95, 121, 136, 138, 163, 338, 366, 380–382, 395, 402, 403.

——— (1981e). *NCP/TCP Transition Plan*. RFC 801. Historic. NWG. URL: http://www.rfc-editor.org/rfc/rfc801.txt. See pp. 344, 345.

——— (1981f). *Transmission Control Protocol — DARPA Internet Program Protocol Specification*. RFC 793. Standard. NWG. URL: http://www.rfc-editor.org/rfc/rfc793.txt. See pp. 37, 232, 366, 394.

——— (1982a). "Internetwork Protocol Approaches". In: *Computer Network Architectures and Protocols*. Ed. by P. E. Green Jr. Applications of Communications Theory. New York, NY: Plenum Press. Chap. 18, pp. 511–526. ISBN: 0-306-40788-4. See p. 312.

——— (1982b). *Simple Mail Transfer Protocol*. RFC 821. Standard. Obsoleted by RFC 2821. NWG. URL: http://www.rfc-editor.org/rfc/rfc821.txt. See p. 372.

——— (1983). *The TCP Maximum Segment Size and Related Topics*. RFC 879. Historic. NWG. URL: http://www.rfc-editor.org/rfc/rfc879.txt. See p. 343.

Postel, J. B. and S. D. Crocker (1970a). *BBN's Comments on NWG/RFC #33*. RFC 47. Historic. NWG. URL: http://www.rfc-editor.org/rfc/rfc47.txt. See p. 14.

——— (1970b). *Possible Protocol Plateau*. RFC 48. Historic. NWG. URL: http://www.rfc-editor.org/rfc/rfc48.txt. See pp. 15, 250.

Postel, J. B., M. Wingfield, N. Abramovitz, R. T. Braden, G. Grossman, B. Plummer, J. Mathis, A. Stensby, and D. D. Clark (1979). *TCP Implementation Status*. Internet Experiment Note (IEN) 98. URL: ftp://ftp.rfc-editor.org/in-notes/ien/ien98.txt. See p. 344.

Postel, J. B., C. A. Sunshine, and D. Cohen (1981). "The Arpa Internet Protocol". In: *Computer Networks* 5, pp. 261–271. See pp. 93, 134, 276, 292, 308, 320, 356, 367, 381, 388, 402.

Pouzin, L. (1973a). *Interconnection of Packet Switching Networks*. INWG Note 42. IFIP WG 6.1 (INWG). URL: http://baerwolff.de/public/Pouzin-

1973-Interconnection-of-Packet-Switching-Networks--INWG-Note-42.pdf. See pp. 205, 239, 325–327, 332, 339, 348, 350.

Pouzin, L. (1973*b*). "Presentation and Major Design Aspects of the Cyclades Computer Network". In: *DATACOMM '73: Proceedings of the Third ACM Symposium on Data Communications and Data Networks.* Saint Petersburg, FL. November 13–15, 1973. New York, NY: ACM, pp. 80–87. DOI: 10.1145/800280.811034. URL: http://rogerdmoore.ca/PS/CYCLB.html. Also published as INWG Protocol Note 36. See pp. 19, 22–25, 43, 48, 50, 203, 205, 288, 325, 339, 410.

—— (1974*a*). *A Proposal for Interconnecting Packet Switching Networks.* INWG Note 60. An extended version of INWG Note 42. IFIP WG 6.1 (INWG). Also published in Proceedings of EUROCOMP 1974, Brunel University, Uxbridge, UK, May 1974, pp. 1023-1036; and reprinted in "The Auerbach Annual 1975 Best Computer Papers", Isaac L. Auerbach (Ed.), pp. 105–117. See pp. 20, 138, 339, 342.

—— (1974*b*). "Cigale, the Packet Switching Machine of the Cyclades Computer Network". In: *Information Processing '74: Proceedings of IFIP Congress 1974.* Stockholm, Sweden. August 5–10, 1974. Ed. by J. L. Rosenfeld. Amsterdam, Netherlands: North-Holland, pp. 155–159. ISBN: 0-7204-2803-3. URL: http://rogerdmoore.ca/PS/CIGALE/CIGALE.html. See pp. 19, 204.

—— (1975*a*). "An Integrated Approach to Network Protocols". In: *AFIPS '75: Proceedings of the AFIPS 1975 National Computer Conference and Exposition.* Anaheim, CA. May 19–22, 1975. New York, NY: ACM, pp. 701–707. DOI: 10.1145/1499949.1500100. See p. 164.

—— (1975*b*). "Standards in Data Communications and Computer Networks". In: *Network Structures in an Evolving Operational Environment.* Fourth Data Communications Symposium. Quebec City, Canada. October 7–9, 1975. Ed. by F. E. Glave and W. W. Chu. ACM and IEEE. New York, NY: IEEE, pp. 2-8–2-12. See pp. 91, 336, 339, 340.

—— (1976*a*). "The Network Business—Monopolies and Entrepreneurs". In: *ICCC '76: Proceedings of the Third International Conference on Computer Communication.* Toronto, Canada. August 3–6, 1976. Ed. by P. K. Verma, pp. 563–567. Also published as INWG Legal/Political Note 6. See pp. 205, 236.

——— (1976*b*). "Virtual Circuits vs. Datagrams: Technical and Political Problems". In: *AFIPS '76: Proceedings of the AFIPS 1976 National Computer Conference and Exposition*. New York, NY. June 7–10, 1976. New York, NY: ACM, pp. 483–494. DOI: 10.1145/1499799.1499870. See pp. 19–21, 106, 204, 207, 236, 264, 272, 324, 326, 428.

——— ed. (1982). *The Cyclades Computer Network: Towards Layered Network Architectures*. Vol. 2. Monograph Series of the International Council for Computer Communications. Chapters not explicitly matched with authors. Authors include Edouard André, Jean Claude Chupin, Michel Gien, Jean-Louis Grangé, Jean Le Bihan, Gérard Le Lann, Najah Naffan, Louis Pouzin, Vincent Quint, Guy Sergeant, and Hubert Zimmermann. Amsterdam, Netherlands: North-Holland. See pp. 269, 302, 326, 340, 391, 453.

——— (1988). *Interview with Louis Pouzin by James Pelkey*. Excerpts in the James Pelkey online book. Interview conducted at November 28, 1988. URL: http://historyofcomputercommunications.info/index.html. See p. 339.

——— (1998). *Le "père" du réseau Cyclades*. Interview by Alain Simeray. URL: http://www.hsc.fr/presse/www.isocfrance.org/archives/AUTRANS98/lpouzin.htm (English translation of an excerpt at http://www.baerwolff.de/public/index.html#pouzin). See p. 203.

Pouzin, L. and H. Zimmermann (1978). "A Tutorial on Protocols". In: *Proceedings of the IEEE* 66.11, pp. 1346–1370. See pp. 29, 197.

Price, W. L. (1973). "Simulation of Packet-Switching Networks Controlled on Isarithmic Principles". In: *DATACOMM '73: Proceedings of the Third ACM Symposium on Data Communications and Data Networks*. Saint Petersburg, FL. November 13–15, 1973. New York, NY: ACM, pp. 44–49. DOI: 10.1145/800280.811029. See p. 347.

Pyke Jr., T. N. (1971). *Toward Reliable Operation of Minicomputer-Based Terminals on a TIP*. RFC 230. Historic. NWG. URL: http://www.rfc-editor.org/rfc/rfc230.txt. See p. 293.

Quarterman, J. S. (1990). *The Matrix: Computer Networks and Conferencing Systems Worldwide*. Digital Press. ISBN: 1-55558-033-5. See pp. 331, 372.

Quarterman, J. S. and S. Carl-Mitchel (1996). *What is the Internet, Anyway?* RFC 1935. Informational. IETF. URL: http://www.rfc-editor.org/rfc/rfc1935.txt. See pp. 118, 369, 371.

Quarterman, J. S. and J. C. Hoskins (1986). "Notable Computer Networks". In: *Communications of the ACM* 29.10, pp. 932–971. ISSN: 0001-0782. DOI: 10.1145/6617.6618. URL: http://phlogiston.usc.edu/dshell/tmp/p932-quarterman.pdf. Also republished in Denning's 1990 book "Computers under Attack". See pp. 372, 403.

Radbruch, G. (1946). "Gesetzliches Unrecht und übergesetzliches Recht". In: *Süddeutsche Juristische Zeitung (SJZ)*, pp. 105–108. See p. 408.

Rafaeli, S. (1988). "Interactivity. From New Media to Communication". In: *Advancing Communication Science: Merging Mass and Interpersonal Processes*. Ed. by R. P. Hawkins, J. M. Wiemann, and S. Pingree. Newbury Park, CA: Sage Publications, pp. 110–134. See p. 369.

Ramakrishnan, K. K. and S. Floyd (1999). *A Proposal to Add Explicit Congestion Notification (ECN) to IP*. RFC 2481. Experimental. Obsoleted by RFC 3168. IETF. URL: http://www.rfc-editor.org/rfc/rfc2481.txt. See p. 353.

Ramakrishnan, K. K., S. Floyd, and D. L. Black (2001). *The Addition of Explicit Congestion Notification (ECN) to IP*. RFC 3168. Proposed Standard. IETF. URL: http://www.rfc-editor.org/rfc/rfc3168.txt. See pp. 212, 353, 356.

Ramberg, B. and K. Gjesdal (2005). "Hermeneutics". In: *The Stanford Encyclopedia of Philosophy*. Ed. by E. N. Zalta. URL: http://plato.stanford.edu/entries/hermeneutics/. See p. 170.

Ratnasamy, S., S. Shenker, and S. McCanne (2005). "Towards an Evolvable Internet Architecture". In: *SIGCOMM '05: Proceedings of the 2005 Conference on Applications, Technologies, Architectures, and Protocols for Computer Communications*. Philadelphia, PA. August 22–26, 2005. New York, NY: ACM, pp. 313–324. ISBN: 1-59593-009-4. DOI: 10.1145/1080091.1080128. URL: http://berkeley.intel-research.net/sylvia/f300-ratnasamy.pdf. See p. 213.

Rawls, J. (1972). *A Theory of Justice*. Oxford: Clarendon Press. See pp. 143, 417.

Reed, D. P. (1978). "Naming and Synchronization in a Decentralized Computer System". PhD thesis. Cambridge, MA: Massachusetts Institute of Technology. URL: http://publications.csail.mit.edu/lcs/pubs/pdf/MIT-LCS-TR-205.pdf. Published as MIT Laboratory for Computer Science Technical Report 205. See pp. 196, 197, 240.

—— (2000). *The End of the End-to-End Argument.* Online. URL: http://www.reed.com/dpr/locus/Papers/endofendtoend.html. See p. 428.

—— (2002). *Re: [e2e] Clarifying the End-to-End Principle.* end2end-interest mailing list. Mar. 5, 2002. URL: http://www.postel.org/pipermail/end2end-interest/2002-March/001853.html. See p. 223.

—— (2004). *On the Separation of TCP and IP.* internet history mailing list. Posted by Ian Peter with the subject line "[ih] (LONG) - Separating TCP and IP". Sept. 30, 2004. URL: http://mailman.postel.org/pipermail/internet-history/2004-September/000431.html (also at http://www.nethistory.info/Archives/tcpiptalk.html). See p. 334.

—— (2008*a*). *Re: [e2e] end of interest — BP metadata / binary vs text.* end2end-interest mailing list. May 11, 2008. URL: http://www.postel.org/pipermail/end2end-interest/2008-May/007239.html. See p. 180.

—— (2008*b*). *UDP and Me.* Online. URL: http://www.reed.com/blog-dpr/?page_id=6. See pp. 333, 401.

—— (2009*a*). *Re: [e2e] Protocols breaking the end-to-end argument.* end2end-interest mailing list. Oct. 23, 2009. URL: http://www.postel.org/pipermail/end2end-interest/2009-October/007831.html. See pp. 240, 378, 429.

—— (2009*b*). *Re: [e2e] Protocols breaking the end-to-end argument.* end2end-interest mailing list. Oct. 23, 2009. URL: http://www.postel.org/pipermail/end2end-interest/2009-October/007834.html. See p. 240.

—— (2009*c*). *Re: [e2e] Protocols breaking the end-to-end argument.* end2end-interest mailing list. Oct. 23, 2009. URL: http://www.postel.org/pipermail/end2end-interest/2009-October/007838.html. See p. 214.

—— (2009*d*). *Re: [e2e] Protocols breaking the end-to-end argument.* end2end-interest mailing list. Oct. 25, 2009. URL: http://www.postel.org/pipermail/end2end-interest/2009-October/007866.html. See p. 215.

Reed, D. P. and J. B. Postel (1979). *User Datagram Protocol.* Internet Experiment Note (IEN) 71. URL: ftp://ftp.rfc-editor.org/in-notes/ien/scanned/ien71.pdf. See pp. 89, 334.

Reed, D. P., J. H. Saltzer, and D. D. Clark (1998). "Commentary on "Active networking and end-to-end arguments"". In: *IEEE Network* 12.3, pp. 69–71. DOI: 10.1109/65.690972. Part of a collection of three "Commentaries" edited by Thomas M. Chen and Alden W. Jackson. See pp. 46, 112, 223, 234, 235.

Rettberg, R. D. (1972). *Specifications for the Interconnection of Terminals and the Terminal IMP*. BBN Report 2277. Bolt, Beranek and Newman Inc. (BBN). URL: http://www.archive.org/details/TerminalInterfaceMassageProcessorReport2277SpecificationsForTheInterconnectionOfTerminalsAndTheTerminalImp. Also published as NIC 11625. See pp. 68, 282.

Reynolds, J. K. and J. B. Postel (1987). *Request For Comments Reference Guide*. RFC 1000. Historic. IETF. URL: http://www.rfc-editor.org/rfc/rfc1000.txt.

Rheingold, H. (1985). *Tools for Thought: The History and Future of Mind-Expanding Technology*. New York: Simon & Schuster. URL: http://www.rheingold.com/texts/tft/. See p. 172.

Roberts, L. G. (1967*a*). *Message Switching Network Proposal*. Meeting notes of the ARPA IPTO Principal Investigators Meeting, Ann Arbor, MI, April 1967. Dated April 24, 1967. ARPA/IPTO. URL: http://www.dod.mil/pubs/foi/reading_room/977.pdf (pages 10 and 12 of PDF file). Also available from National Archives Branch Depository, Suitland, MD, RG-330-78-0085 Box 2, Folder: Networking 1968–1972. See pp. 199, 200, 202.

——— (1967*b*). "Multiple Computer Networks and Intercomputer Communication". In: *SOSP '67: Proceedings of the First ACM Symposium on Operating System Principles*. Gatlinburg, TN. October 1–4, 1967. New York, NY: ACM, pp. 3.1–3.6. DOI: 10.1145/800001.811680. URL: http://www.packet.cc/files/multi-net-inter-comm.html. See pp. 200, 202.

——— (1975). "ALOHA Packet System With and Without Slots and Capture". In: *ACM SIGCOMM Computer Communication Review* 5.2, pp. 28–42. ISSN: 0146-4833. DOI: 10.1145/1024916.1024920. Originally distributed informally as ARPA Satellite System Note 8 on June 26, 1972. See p. 277.

——— (1978). "The Evolution of Packet Switching". In: *Proceedings of the IEEE* 66.11, pp. 1307–1313. ISSN: 0018-9219. See pp. 26, 183, 213, 324.

——— (1986). "The Arpanet and Computer Networks". In: *Proceedings of the ACM Conference on The History of Personal Workstations*. Palo Alto, CA.

New York, NY: ACM, pp. 51–58. ISBN: 0-89791-176-8. DOI: 10.1145/12178.12182. See p. 203.

—— (1988). *Interview with Lawrence G. Roberts by James Pelkey*. Excerpts in the James Pelkey online book. Interview conducted at June 17, 1988. URL: http://historyofcomputercommunications.info/index.html. See p. 244.

—— (2004). *Is Best Effort IP Really Economic?* Online. URL: http://www.packet.cc/larry-news/Is%20Best%20Effort%20IP%20Really%20Economic2.htm. See p. 213.

Roberts, L. G. and B. D. Wessler (1970). "Computer Network Development to Achieve Resource Sharing". In: *AFIPS '70: Proceedings of the AFIPS 1970 Spring Joint Computer Conference*. Atlantic City, NJ. May 5–7, 1970. New York, NY: ACM, pp. 543–549. DOI: 10.1145/1476936.1477020. See pp. 183, 200.

Robinson, J., D. Friedman, and M. Steenstrup (1990). "Congestion Control in BBN Packet-Switched Networks". In: *ACM SIGCOMM Computer Communication Review* 20.1, pp. 76–90. ISSN: 0146-4833. DOI: 10.1145/86587.86592. See pp. 347, 351, 363.

Rogers, C. M. (2010). *Re: [ih] Early interconnection between Ethernets and Arpanet*. internet history mailing list. Mar. 11, 2010. URL: http://mailman.postel.org/pipermail/internet-history/2010-March/001260.html. See p. 315.

Rogers, E. M. (2003). *Diffusion of Innovation*. 5th ed. Simon & Schuster International. See p. 409.

Romer, P. (2001). "Post-Scarcity Prophet". Economist Paul Romer on Growth, Technological Change, and an Unlimited Human Future. In: *reason* 12.01 (Dec. 2001). Interview with Paul Romer by Ronald Bailey, pp. 52, 56. URL: http://reason.com/archives/2001/12/01/post-scarcity-prophet. See p. 79.

Rosa, H. (2003). "Social Acceleration: Ethical and Political Consequences of a Desynchronized High-Speed Society". In: *Constellations* 10.1, pp. 3–31. DOI: 10.1111/1467-8675.00309. See p. 413.

Rosen, E. C. (1981). *Logical Addressing*. Internet Experiment Note (IEN) 183. Edited version of BBN Report 4473, "Arpanet Routing Algorithm Improvement, Volume 1". URL: ftp://ftp.rfc-editor.org/in-notes/ien/ien183.txt. See p. 249.

Rosen, E. C., J. M. McQuillan, J. G. Herman, and I. Richer (1979). *Arpanet Routing Algorithm Improvements*. BBN Report 4088. Third Semiannual Technical Report, 1 October 1978 to 1 April 1979. Bolt, Beranek and Newman Inc. (BBN). URL: http://www.dtic.mil/cgi-bin/GetTRDoc?AD=ADA086340&Location=U2&doc=GetTRDoc.pdf. See p. 278.

Rosenberg, J. (2009). *A Hitchhiker's Guide to the Session Initiation Protocol (SIP)*. RFC 5411. Informational. IETF. URL: http://www.rfc-editor.org/rfc/rfc5411.txt. See pp. 308, 375.

Rosenberg, J., H. Schulzrinne, G. Camarillo, A. Johnston, J. Peterson, R. Sparks, M. Handley, and E. Schooler (2002). *SIP: Session Initiation Protocol*. RFC 3261. Standards Track. Updated by RFCs 3265, 3853, 4320, 4916. IETF. URL: http://www.rfc-editor.org/rfc/rfc3261.txt. See pp. 308, 375.

Ross, D. T. and J. E. Rodriguez (1963). "Theoretical Foundations for the Computer-Aided Design System". In: *AFIPS '63: Proceedings of the AFIPS 1963 Spring Joint Computer Conference*. Detroit, MI. May 21–23, 1963. New York, NY: ACM, pp. 305–322. DOI: 10.1145/1461551.1461589. See p. 228.

Rulifson, J. (1969). *Decode Encode Language (DEL)*. RFC 5. Historic. NWG. URL: http://www.rfc-editor.org/rfc/rfc5.txt. See p. 244.

—— (2009). *RE: Pre-ARPANET Networking at SRI*. Email to the author. Apr. 13, 2009. See pp. 15, 194.

Russell, A. L. (2006). "'Rough Consensus and Running Code' and the Internet-OSI Standards War". In: *IEEE Annals of the History of Computing* 28.3, pp. 48–61. ISSN: 1058-6180. DOI: 10.1109/MAHC.2006.42. See p. 405.

Russell, D. (1989). *The Principles of Computer Networking*. Ed. by J. S. Rohl, H. Whitfield, and D. J. Cooke. Cambridge Computer Science Texts 25. Cambridge, UK: Cambridge University Press. ISBN: 0-521-33992-8 (paperback). See pp. 197, 297, 312.

Saltzer, J. H. (1974). "Protection and the Control of Information Sharing in Multics". In: *Communications of the ACM* 17.7, pp. 388–402. ISSN: 0001-0782. DOI: 10.1145/361011.361067. See pp. 138, 399.

—— (1993*a*). "Needed: A Systematic Structuring Paradigm for Distributed Data". In: *ACM SIGOPS Operating Systems Review* 27.2, pp. 77–81. ISSN: 0163-5980. DOI: 10.1145/155848.155862. URL: http://web.mit.edu/

Saltzer / www / publications / linking / linking.html (different layout). See p. 373.

—— (1993*b*). *On the Naming and Binding of Network Destinations.* RFC 1498. Informational. IETF. URL: http://www.rfc-editor.org/rfc/rfc1498.txt. See p. 372.

—— (1999). *"Open Access" is Just the Tip of the Iceberg.* Online. URL: http://web.mit.edu/Saltzer/www/publications/openaccess.html. See pp. 428–430.

Saltzer, J. H. and M. F. Kaashoek (2009). *Principles of Computer System Design.* An Introduction. Morgan Kaufman (Elsevier). ISBN: 978-0123749574. URL: http://ocw.mit.edu/Saltzer-Kaashoek (chapters 7 through 11, Version 5.0; online only, not part of the printed book). See pp. 378, 406.

Saltzer, J. H. and M. D. Schroeder (1975). "The Protection of Information in Computer Systems". In: *Proceedings of the IEEE* 63.9, pp. 1278–1308. ISSN: 0018-9219. URL: http://web.mit.edu/Saltzer/www/publications/protection/ (edited version). See pp. 395, 399, 406.

Saltzer, J. H., D. P. Reed, and D. D. Clark (1981*a*). "End-to-End Arguments in System Design". In: *Proceedings of the Second International Conference on Distributed Computing Systems.* Paris, France. April 8–10, 1981. IEEE Computer Society, pp. 509–512. See pp. vii, ix, xi, 3–5, 9–11, 17, 23, 26–30, 32–35, 43, 49, 53, 71, 118, 135, 179, 180, 215, 217, 238, 425, 428, 429.

Saltzer, J. H., D. D. Clark, and K. T. Pogran (1981*b*). "Why a Ring?" In: *SIGCOMM '81: Proceedings of the Seventh Symposium on Data Communications.* Mexico City, Mexico. October 27–29, 1981. New York, NY: ACM, pp. 211–217. DOI: 10.1145/800081.802676. See p. 314.

Saltzer, J. H., D. P. Reed, and D. D. Clark (1984). "End-to-End Arguments in System Design". In: *ACM Transactions in Computer Systems* 2.4, pp. 277–288. URL: http://web.mit.edu/Saltzer/www/publications/endtoend/endtoend.pdf (different pagination). First published in 1981. See pp. 9, 29, 30, 36, 46, 49, 107, 114, 179, 189, 214, 215, 221, 222, 225, 366, 378, 384, 428.

Salus, P. H. (1995). *Casting the Net: From ARPANET to Internet and Beyond.* Addison-Wesley. ISBN: 0201876744. See pp. 200, 203.

Salus, P. H. (2002). "Book Review: The Elements of Networking Style". In: *The Internet Protocol Journal* 5.2, pp. 32–34. URL: http://www.cisco.com/web/about/ac123/ac147/archived_issues/ipj_5-2/book_review.html.

——— ed. (2008). *The ARPANET Sourcebook: The Unpublished Foundations of the Internet*. Computer Classics Revisited. Charlottesville, VA: Peer-to-Peer Communications LLC. ISBN: 978-1-57398-000-5.

Sandvig, C. (2006). "Shaping Infrastructure and Innovation on the Internet: The End-to-End Network that Isn't". In: *Shaping Science and Technology Policy: The Next Generation of Research*. Ed. by D. H. Guston and D. Sarewitz. Madison, WI: University of Wisconsin Press. URL: http://www.spcomm.uiuc.edu/users/csandvig/research/Communication_Infrastructure_and_Innovation.pdf (pre-publication version). See pp. 426, 429, 431.

——— (2007). "Network Neutrality is the New Common Carriage". In: *Info: The Journal of Policy, Regulation and Strategy for Telecommunications, Information and Media* 9.2/3, pp. 136–147. URL: http://www.spcomm.uiuc.edu/csandvig/research/Network_Neutrality_is_the_New_Common_Carriage.pdf (different pagination). See p. 165.

Santos Jr., P. J. (1975). *IMP/Host and Host/IMP Protocol Change*. RFC 704. Historic. NWG. URL: http://www.rfc-editor.org/rfc/rfc704.txt. See p. 272.

——— (1979*a*). *Arpanet End to End; Host to IMP; IMP to Host; Backhosts*. Presentation at BBN, Cambridge, MA. DVD, Number 0009; held internally at BBN, Cambridge, MA. See p. 279.

——— (1979*b*). *Arpanet End to End; IMP to Host; Host to IMP*. Presentation at BBN, Cambridge, MA. DVD, Number 0008; held internally at BBN, Cambridge, MA. See p. 304.

Savage, S. et al. (1999*a*). "Detour: Informed Internet Routing and Transport". In: *IEEE Micro* 19.1, pp. 50–59. ISSN: 0272-1732. DOI: 10.1109/40.748796. See pp. 374, 380.

Savage, S., N. Cardwell, D. Wetherall, and T. Anderson (1999*b*). "TCP Congestion Control with a Misbehaving Receiver". In: *ACM SIGCOMM Computer Communication Review* 29.5, pp. 71–78. ISSN: 0146-4833. DOI: 10.1145/505696.505704. URL: http://www.cs.washington.edu/homes/tom/pubs/CCR99.pdf. See p. 354.

Savigny, F. C. von (1840). "Buch I. Quellen des heutigen Römischen Rechts". In: *System des heutigen Römischen Rechts*. Vol. 1. 7 vols. Berlin: Veit und Camp, pp. 1–330. URL: http://www.archive.org/details/systemdesheutige01saviuoft (transcription of pages 212 to 216, book 1, chapter 4, Auslegung der Gesetze, § 33, A. Auslegung einzelner Gesetze, Grundregeln der Auslegung at http://www.baerwolff.de/public/index.html#savigny). See pp. 179, 180.

Sawhney, H. and S. Lee (2005). "Arenas of Innovation: Understanding New Configurational Potentialities of Communication Technologies". In: *Media Culture Society* 27.3, pp. 391–414. DOI: 10.1177/0163443705051750. URL: http://mcs.sagepub.com/cgi/content/abstract/27/3/391. See p. 228.

Scantlebury, R. A., P. T. Wilkinson, and K. A. Bartlett (1968). "The Design of a Message Switching Centre for a Digital Communication Network". In: *Information Processing '68: Proceedings of IFIP Congress 1968*. Edinburgh, UK. August 5–10, 1968. Ed. by A. J. H. Morrell. Vol. 2.3. Amsterdam, Netherlands: North-Holland, pp. 723–727. See p. 314.

Schafer, V. (2009). *Cyclades*. Email to the author. Dec. 30, 2009. See pp. 205, 207, 340.

Scheblik, T. J., D. B. Dawkins, and Advanced Research Projects Agency (1968). *RFQ for ARPA Computer Network*. Request for Quotations. Advanced Research Projects Agency (ARPA), Department of Defense (DoD). URL: http://www.cs.utexas.edu/users/chris/DIGITAL_ARCHIVE/ARPANET/RFQ-ARPA-IMP.pdf. See pp. 13, 61, 72, 74, 192, 193, 196, 200, 204, 246, 250, 264, 275, 307.

Schelling, T. C. (1957). "Bargaining, Communication, and Limited War". In: *Conflict Resolution* 1.1, pp. 19–36. ISSN: 07314086. See pp. 228, 382, 383.

Schelonka, E. P. (1974). "Resource Sharing with Arpanet". In: *NTC '74: Proceedings of the National Telecommunications Conference*, pp. 1045–1048. Also published in 1976. See pp. 200, 202, 246, 251, 252.

——— (1976). "Resource Sharing with Arpanet". In: *Computer Networks: Text and References for a Tutorial*. Ed. by M. Abrams, R. P. Blanc, and I. W. Cotton. IEEE Computer Society Publications Office.

Schewick, B. van (2004). "Architecture and Innovation: The Role of the End-to-End Argument in the Original Internet". PhD thesis. Berlin,

Germany: Technische Universität Berlin. Available from the university library of Technische Universität Berlin, signature 4TA3016 (http://www.ub.tu-berlin.de). See pp. 164, 165, 240, 378, 408, 409, 414, 425, 429, 433, 438.

Schewick, B. van (2007). "Towards an Economic Framework for Network Neutrality Regulation". In: *Journal on Telecommunications and High Technology Law* 5.2, pp. 329–392. URL: http://jthtl.org/content/articles/V5I2/JTHTLv5i2_vanSchewick.PDF. See pp. 44, 176, 414, 424.

—— (2009). "Point/Counterpoint: Network Neutrality Nuances". In: *Communications of the ACM* 52.2, pp. 31–34, 36–37. ISSN: 0001-0782. DOI: 10.1145/1461928.1461942. URL: http://lauren.vortex.com/ACM209.pdf (also at http://idisk.mac.com/dfarber-Public). See pp. 3, 145.

—— (2010*a*). *Factors that Foster Application Innovation*. FCC Open Internet Workshop: Innovation, Investment, and the Open Internet. MIT, Cambridge, MA. January 13, 2010. Presentation slides. URL: http://www.openinternet.gov/workshops/docs/ws-innovation-investment-and-the-open-internet/schewick.pdf. See p. 414.

—— (2010*b*). *Outline of Proposal for Open Internet Rules*. Filing to the FCC WC Docket No. 07-52; GN Docket No. 09-191. Stanford Law School, Center for Internet and Society. URL: http://fjallfoss.fcc.gov/ecfs/document/view?id=7020493601. See p. 430.

Schinzel, B. (2006). "Informatik – Wissenschaft im Spannungsfeld zwischen (technologischer) Determination und (kultureller) Vision". In: *Mikrokosmos Wissenschaft: Transformationen und Perspektiven*. Ed. by B. Liebig, M. Dupuis, I. Kriesi, and M. Peitz. Vol. 39. Zürcher Hochschulforum. Zürich: vdf Hochschulverlag, pp. 169–186. URL: http://mod.iig.uni-freiburg.de/cms/fileadmin/publikationen/online-vortraege/Zuerich1.doc (original lecture). See pp. 167, 171.

Schulzrinne, H. (2010). *Collection of RTP Resources*. Online. URL: http://www.cs.columbia.edu/~hgs/rtp/.

Schulzrinne, H., S. L. Casner, R. Frederick, and V. Jacobson (2003). *RTP: A Transport Protocol for Real-Time Applications*. RFC 3550. Standards Track. IETF. URL: http://www.rfc-editor.org/rfc/rfc3550.txt. See pp. 308, 375.

Shadbolt, N. and T. Berners-Lee (2008). "Web Science Emerges". In: *Scientific American* 299.4, pp. 31–37. See p. 171.

Shakkottai, S. and R. Srikant (2007). "Network Optimization and Control". In: *Foundations and Trends in Networking* 2.3, pp. 271–379. DOI: 10.1561/1300000007. URL: http://www.ifp.illinois.edu/~srikant/Papers/shasri07.pdf. See p. 101.

Shannon, C. E. (1948). "A Mathematical Theory of Communication". In: *Bell System Tech Journal* 27, pp. 379–423, 623–656. URL: http://cm.bell-labs.com/cm/ms/what/shannonday/paper.html. See pp. 117, 198.

Shannon, C., D. Moore, and K. C. Claffy (2002). "Beyond Folklore: Observations on Fragmented Traffic". In: *IEEE/ACM Transactions on Networking (TON)* 10.6, pp. 709–720. ISSN: 1063-6692. DOI: 10.1109/TNET.2002.805028. See p. 344.

Shaw, S. J. (1988). "TCP/IP Still Rules Federal Nets. Losing the Crown Not the Power". In: *Network World* 5.11 (Mar. 14, 1988), pp. 1, 44, 46. See p. 331.

Shenker, S., D. D. Clark, and L. Zhang (1994). "Services or Infrastructure: Why We Need a Network Service Model". In: *Proceedings of the 1st International Workshop on Community Networking Integrated Multimedia Services to the Home*. San Francisco, CA. July 13–14, 1994, pp. 145–149. DOI: 10.1109/CN.1994.337354. URL: http://groups.csail.mit.edu/ana/Publications/PubPDFs/Services%20or%20Infrastructure.pdf. See p. 411.

Shoch, J. F. (1978a). *A Note on Inter-Network Fragmentation and the TCP*. Internet Experiment Note (IEN) 20. Internet Notebook Section 2.3.3.6. URL: ftp://ftp.rfc-editor.org/in-notes/ien/scanned/ien20.pdf. Also published in an extended version in Computer Networks 3 (1979). See p. 337.

——— (1978b). *A Note on Inter-Network Naming, Addressing, and Routing*. Internet Experiment Note (IEN) 19. Internet Notebook Section 2.3.3.5. URL: ftp://ftp.rfc-editor.org/in-notes/ien/ien19.txt. Also published in IEEE Comp-Con 1978 Proceedings. See p. 372.

——— (1978c). "Inter-Network Naming, Addressing, and Routing". In: *COMPCON Fall '78: Proceedings of the 17th IEEE Computer Society International Conference*. Washington, DC. September 5–8, 1978. IEEE. New York, NY, pp. 72–79. Extended version of IEN 19.

——— (1979). "Packet Fragmentation in Inter-Network Protocols". In: *Computer Networks* 3.1, pp. 3–8. See pp. 337, 342.

Shoch, J. F. (2010). *Re: [ih] Early interconnection between Ethernets and Arpanet*. internet history mailing list. Mar. 12, 2010. URL: http://mailman.postel.org/pipermail/internet-history/2010-March/001262.html (forwarded copy, original email to the author). See p. 315.

Shoch, J. F., Y. K. Dalal, D. D. Redell, and R. C. Crane (1982). "Evolution of the Ethernet Local Computer Network". In: *Computer* 15.8, pp. 10–27. ISSN: 0018-9162. URL: http://ethernethistory.typepad.com/papers/EthernetEvolution.pdf. See p. 342.

Simon, H. A. (1971). "Designing Organizations for an Information-Rich World". A discussion with Karl W. Deutsch and Martin Shubik, moderated by Emilio Q. Daddario. In: *Computers, Communications, and the Public Interest*. Ed. by M. Greenberger. Baltimore, MD: The Johns Hopkins Press. Chap. 2, pp. 37–72. ISBN: 0-8018-1135-X. See p. 169.

Simpson, R., A. Renear, E. Mylonas, and A. van Dam (1996). "50 years after "As We May Think": the Brown/MIT Vannevar Bush Symposium". In: *interactions* 3.2, pp. 47–67. ISSN: 1072-5520. DOI: 10.1145/227181.227187. See p. 411.

Sirbu, M. A. and L. E. Zwimpfer (1985). "Standards Setting for Computer Communication: The Case of X.25". In: *IEEE Communications Magazine* 23.3, pp. 35–45. ISSN: 0163-6804. URL: http://www.archive.org/details/standardssettingoosirb. See pp. 329, 341.

Smallberg, D. (1982*a*). *Who talks TCP?* RFC 832. Historic. NWG. URL: http://www.rfc-editor.org/rfc/rfc832.txt.

——— (1982*b*). *Who talks TCP?* RFC 833. Historic. NWG. URL: http://www.rfc-editor.org/rfc/rfc833.txt.

——— (1982*c*). *Who talks TCP?* RFC 834. Historic. NWG. URL: http://www.rfc-editor.org/rfc/rfc834.txt.

——— (1982*d*). *Who talks TCP?* RFC 835. Historic. NWG. URL: http://www.rfc-editor.org/rfc/rfc835.txt.

——— (1983*a*). *Who talks TCP?* RFC 836. Historic. NWG. URL: http://www.rfc-editor.org/rfc/rfc836.txt.

——— (1983*b*). *Who talks TCP?* RFC 837. Historic. NWG. URL: http://www.rfc-editor.org/rfc/rfc837.txt.

——— (1983*c*). *Who talks TCP?* RFC 838. Historic. NWG. URL: http://www.rfc-editor.org/rfc/rfc838.txt.

—— (1983*d*). *Who talks TCP?* RFC 839. Historic. NWG. URL: http://www.rfc-editor.org/rfc/rfc839.txt.

—— (1983*e*). *Who talks TCP?—Survey of 1 February 1983*. RFC 842. Historic. NWG. URL: http://www.rfc-editor.org/rfc/rfc842.txt.

—— (1983*f*). *Who talks TCP?—Survey of 8 February 1983*. RFC 843. Historic. NWG. URL: http://www.rfc-editor.org/rfc/rfc843.txt.

—— (1983*g*). *Who talks TCP?—Survey of 15 February 1983*. RFC 845. Historic. NWG. URL: http://www.rfc-editor.org/rfc/rfc845.txt.

—— (1983*h*). *Who talks TCP?—Survey of 22 February 1983*. RFC 846. Historic. NWG. URL: http://www.rfc-editor.org/rfc/rfc846.txt.

Smith, A. (1910). *An Inquiry into the Nature and Causes of the Wealth of Nations*. Vol. 1. London: J. M. Dent & Sons Ltd. First published 1776. See p. 432.

Smith, J. W. (1964). *On Distributed Communications: III. Determination of Path-Lengths in a Distributed Network*. Research Memorandum RM-3578-PR. RAND Corporation. URL: http://www.rand.org/pubs/research_memoranda/2006/RM3578.pdf. See p. 182.

Soghoian, C. (2007). *Is Comcast's BitTorrent Filtering Violating the Law?* Online. Sept. 4, 2007. URL: http://www.cnet.com/8301-13739_1-9769645-46.html. See p. 362.

Sola Pool, I. de (1983). *Technologies of Freedom*. Cambridge, MA: Belknap Press. See pp. 414, 418, 424.

Sollins, K. R. (1980). *The TFTP Protocol*. Internet Experiment Note (IEN) 133. URL: ftp://ftp.rfc-editor.org/in-notes/ien/ien133.txt. See p. 334.

Sprague, L. G. and C. R. Sprague (1976). "Management *Science*?" In: *Interfaces* 7.1 (Part 1 of Two), pp. 57–62. ISSN: 00922102. See p. 173.

Sproull, R. F. and D. Cohen (1978). "High-Level Protocols". In: *Proceedings of the IEEE* 66.11, pp. 1371–1386. ISSN: 0018-9219. See pp. 216, 238, 300.

Sridharan, M., D. Bansal, and D. Thaler (2007). *Implementation Report on Experiences with Various TCP RFCs*. 68th IETF Meeting. Prague, Czech Republic. March 18–23, 2007. Presentation slides. URL: http://www.ietf.org/proceedings/07mar/slides/tsvarea-3/sld1.htm. Proceedings compiled and edited by R. Bunch. See pp. 212, 213, 353.

Stallings, W. (2007). *Data and Computer Communication*. 8th ed. Pearson Prentice Hall. See pp. xi, 119, 372.

Stevens, W. P., G. J. Myers, and L. L. Constantine (1974). "Structured Design". In: *IBM Systems Journal* 13.2, pp. 115–139. URL: http://www.research.ibm.com/journal/sj/132/ibmsj1302C.pdf. See pp. 136, 392, 395.

Stevens, W. R. (2002). "The Protocols". In: *TCP/IP Illustrated*. English Reprint Edition. Vol. 1. 2 vols. Reprint of the 1994 Addison-Wesley book. China Machine Press and Pearson Education. See pp. 341, 351.

Stine, R. (1988). "Summary of the 2 Nov 87 Meeting of the Congestion Control Working Group". In: *Proceedings of the 8th IETF Meeting*. Boulder, CO. November 2–4, 1987. Ed. by A. Mankin and P. Gross. IETF, pp. 20–25. URL: http://www.ietf.org/proceedings/08.pdf. See pp. 343, 358.

Stokes, A. V. (1973). *London Node is Now Up*. RFC 588. Historic. NWG. URL: http://www.rfc-editor.org/rfc/rfc588.txt. See pp. 313, 314.

Strazisar, V. (1979). *How to Build a Gateway*. Internet Experiment Note (IEN) 109. URL: ftp://ftp.rfc-editor.org/in-notes/ien/ien109.txt. See pp. 96, 348, 349.

Sunberg, R. L. (1971). *File Transfer and Error Recovery*. RFC 133. Historic. NWG. URL: http://www.rfc-editor.org/rfc/rfc133.txt. See p. 296.

Sunshine, C. A. (1975). *Issues in Communication Protocol Design—Formal Correctness*. Draft. INWG Protocol Note 5. IFIP WG 6.1 (INWG). See pp. 197, 258.

— (1977*a*). "Interconnection of Computer Networks". In: *Computer Networks* 1, pp. 175–195. See pp. 92, 207, 312, 327, 336, 380, 400.

— (1977*b*). "Source Routing in Computer Networks". In: *ACM SIGCOMM Computer Communication Review* 7.1, pp. 29–33. ISSN: 0146-4833. DOI: 10.1145/1024853.1024855. See pp. 337, 380.

— (1990). "Network Interconnection and Gateways". In: *IEEE Journal on Selected Areas in Communications* 8.1, pp. 4–11. ISSN: 0733-8716. See p. 400.

Svensson, P. (2007). *Comcast blocks some Internet traffic*. Tests confirm data discrimination by number 2 U.S. service provider. The Associated Press. Oct. 19, 2007. URL: http://www.msnbc.msn.com/id/21376597/. See p. 362.

Tanenbaum, A. S. and R. van Renesse (1985). "Distributed Operating Systems". In: *ACM Computing Surveys (CSUR)* 17.4, pp. 419–470. URL: http:

//cactus.eas.asu.edu/Partha/Teaching/531-common-files/p419-tanenbaum.pdf. See p. 406.

Tanenbaum, A. S. (2002). *Computer Networks*. 4th ed. Prentice Hall. URL: http://authors.phptr.com/tanenbaumcn4/ (excerpts). See pp. 233, 263, 288.

Tariq, M. B., M. Motiwala, N. Feamster, and M. Ammar (2009). "Detecting Network Neutrality Violations with Causal Inference". In: *CoNEXT '09: Proceedings of the 5th International Conference on Emerging Networking Experiments and Technologies*. Rome, Italy. December 1–4, 2009. New York, NY: ACM, pp. 289–300. ISBN: 978-1-60558-636-6. DOI: 10.1145/1658939.1658972. URL: http://www.gtnoise.net/papers/2009/tariq:nano:conext09.pdf. See p. 362.

Tennenhouse, D. L. and D. J. Wetherall (1996). "Towards an Active Network Architecture". In: *ACM SIGCOMM Computer Communication Review* 26.2, pp. 5–17. ISSN: 0146-4833. DOI: 10.1145/231699.231701. URL: http://ccr.sigcomm.org/online/files/p81-tennenhouse.pdf (2007 SIGCOMM reprint). See pp. 211, 226.

Thaler, D. (2008). *Evolution of the IP Model*. Dagstuhl Perspectives Workshop: End-to-End Protocols for the Future Internet. Schloss Dagstuhl, Wadern, Germany. June 2008. Presentation slides. URL: http://kathrin.dagstuhl.de/files/Materials/08/08242/08242.ThalerDave.Slides.pdf. See p. 353.

——— (2009). "Evolution of the IP Model". In: *IETF Journal* 4.3, pp. 1, 7–11. URL: http://www.isoc.org/tools/blogs/ietfjournal/wp-content/uploads/2009/02/IETFJournal0403.pdf. See p. 397.

Thompson, K. (1984). "Reflections on Trusting Trust". In: *Communications of the ACM* 27.8, pp. 761–763. URL: http://www.acm.org/classics/sep95/. See p. 225.

Tirole, J. and J.-C. Rochet (2003). "Platform Competition in Two-Sided Markets". In: *Journal of the European Economic Association* 1.4. http://www.dauphine.fr/cgemp/Publications/Articles/TirolePlatform.pdf (2001 working paper version), pp. 990–1029. DOI: 10.1162/154247603322493212. See p. 383.

Tomlinson, R. S. (1975). "Selecting Sequence Numbers". In: *ACM SIGOPS Operating Systems Review* 9.3, pp. 11–23. ISSN: 0163-5980. DOI: 10.1145/563905.810894. See p. 339.

Topolcic, C., S. L. Casner, C. Lynn Jr., P. Park, and K. Schroder (1990). *Experimental Internet Stream Protocol: Version 2 (ST-II)*. RFC 1190. Experimental. Obsoleted by RFC 1819. IETF. URL: http://www.rfc-editor.org/rfc/rfc1190.txt. See pp. 308, 309.

Tsiavos, P. and I. Hosein (2003). "Beyond Good and Evil: Why Open Source Development for Peer-to-Peer Networks Does not Necessarily Equal to an Open Society, is as Imbalanced as Copyright Law, and Definitely is not Going to Make You a Better Person." In: *ECIS 2003: Proceedings of the 11th European Conference on Information Systems*. Naples, Italy. June 16–21, 2003. URL: http://csrc.lse.ac.uk/asp/aspecis/20030062.pdf. See p. 172.

United States Department of Justice (2007). *In the Matter of Broadband Industry Practices*. Ex Parte Filing to the FCC WC Docket No. 07-52. United States Department of Justice. URL: http://www.justice.gov/atr/public/comments/225767.htm. See pp. 408, 414, 427.

Vernam, G. S. (1958). "Automatic Telegraph Switching System Plan 55-A". In: *Western Union Technical Review* 12.2, pp. 37–50. See p. 183.

Voydock, V. L. and S. T. Kent (1983). "Security Mechanisms in High-Level Network Protocols". In: *ACM Computing Surveys (CSUR)* 15.2, pp. 135–171. ISSN: 0360-0300. DOI: 10.1145/356909.356913. See p. 401.

Waitzman, D. (1990). *A Standard for the Transmission of IP Datagrams on Avian Carriers*. RFC 1149. Experimental. Updated by RFC 2549. IETF. URL: http://www.rfc-editor.org/rfc/rfc1149.txt. See p. 369.

Walden, D. C. (1970*a*). *A System for Interprocess Communication in a Resource Sharing Computer Network*. RFC 62. Historic. NWG. URL: http://www.rfc-editor.org/rfc/rfc62.txt. See p. 288.

—— (1970*b*). *Comments on Host/Host Protocol Document #1 (S. Crocker—8/3/70)*. RFC 65. Historic. NWG. URL: http://www.rfc-editor.org/rfc/rfc65.txt. Note that the document referred to in the title is *not* RFC 1. See pp. 16, 256.

—— (1972*a*). "A System for Interprocess Communication in a Resource Sharing Computer Network". In: *Communications of the ACM* 15.4, pp. 221–230. ISSN: 0001-0782. DOI: 10.1145/361284.361288. Also published as RFC 62. See p. 288.

—— (1972*b*). "The Interface Message Processor, Its Algorithms, and Their Implementation". In: *AFCET Journées d'Études: Réseaux de Calculateurs*

(AFCET Workshop on Computer Networks). Paris, France. May 25–26, 1972. Association Française pour la Cybernétique Économique et Technique (AFCET). URL: http://www.walden-family.com/public/1972-afcet-paris.pdf. See pp. 241, 243, 245, 252, 270–272, 279, 398, 404.

—— (1973*a*). *Lost Message Detection*. RFC 534. Historic. NWG. URL: http://www.rfc-editor.org/rfc/rfc534.txt. See p. 257.

—— (1973*b*). *Message-ID Numbers*. RFC 533. Historic. NWG. URL: http://www.rfc-editor.org/rfc/rfc533.txt. See pp. 257, 293.

—— (1974). *Some Changes to the IMP and the IMP/Host Interface*. RFC 660. Historic. NWG. URL: http://www.rfc-editor.org/rfc/rfc660.txt. See pp. 5, 75, 80, 81, 238, 264, 294, 301, 302.

—— (1975*a*). "Experience In Building, Operating, and Using the Arpa Network". In: *Proceedings of the Second USA-Japan Computer Conference*. Tokyo, Japan. August 26–28, 1975, pp. 21–31. URL: http://ia310810.us.archive.org/3/items/ExperienceInBuildingOperatingAndUsingTheArpaNetwork/ (pre-publication version). See p. 313.

—— (1975*b*). "Host-to-Host Protocols". In: *Network Systems and Software*. Ed. by D. Bates. 24. Maidenhead, UK: Infotech Information, pp. 287–316. See pp. 73, 290.

—— (1975*c*). *IMP/Host and Host/IMP Protocol Changes*. RFC 687. Historic. Obsoleted by RFC 704, updated by RFC 690. NWG. URL: http://www.rfc-editor.org/rfc/rfc687.txt. See pp. 81, 272, 302.

—— (1978). "Host-to-Host Protocols". In: *Tutorial: A Practical View of Computer Communications Protocols*. Ed. by J. M. McQuillan and V. G. Cerf. New York, NY: IEEE, pp. 172–204. ISBN: 0818602015. LCCN: 78061492. Verbatim reprint of the 1975 paper. See pp. 73, 288–290.

—— (1990). "Arpanet, the Defense Data Network, and Internet". In: *Encyclopedia of Communications*. Ed. by F. E. Froehlich and A. Kent. Vol. 1. New York, NY: Marcel Dekker, pp. 341–361. See pp. 182, 230, 341.

—— (2009). *Private Communication with Matthias Bärwolff*. Notes on file with the author. Interview in Boston, MA. May 6, 2009. See p. 204.

—— (2010*a*). *Re: story of IMP code availability*. Email to the author. June 9, 2010. See p. 246.

—— (2010*b*). *Re: your earlier query about source IMP to destination IMP error control*. Email to the author. Mar. 1, 2010. See p. 302.

Walden, D. C. (2010c). *Various notes in feedback to an early thesis chapter 3 draft*. Notes on file with the author. June 1, 2010. See pp. 275, 306.

Walden, D. C. and A. A. McKenzie (1979). "The Evolution of Host-to-Host Protocol Technology". In: *Computer* 12.9, pp. 29–38. ISSN: 0018-9162. DOI: 10.1109/MC.1979.1658891. See p. 403.

Walden, D. C. and R. D. Rettberg (1975). "Gateway Design for Computer Network Interconnection". In: *Eurocomp 1975: Proceedings of the European Computing Conference on Communications Networks*. London, UK. September 23–25, 1975. Ed. by D. L. A. Barber. Online Conferences, pp. 113–128. ISBN: 0903796058. URL: http://www.walden-family.com/public/gateway-paper.pdf. See pp. 87, 216, 327, 329, 333.

Walfish, M., J. Stribling, M. Krohn, H. Balakrishnan, R. Morris, and S. Shenker (2004). "Middleboxes No Longer Considered Harmful". In: *OSDI '04: Proceedings of the 6th Usenix Symposium on Operating System Design and Implementation*. San Francisco, CA. December 6–8, 2004. Berkeley, CA: USENIX Association, pp. 215–230. See pp. 122, 226.

Weinstein, C. J. and J. W. Forgie (1983). "Experience with Speech Communication in Packet Networks". In: *IEEE Journal on Selected Areas in Communications* 1.6, pp. 963–980. See pp. 82, 305–310.

Weizenbaum, J. (1980). "Once More: The Computer Revolution". In: *Computer Age: A Twenty-Year View*. Ed. by M. L. Dertouzos and J. Moses. Vol. 6. MIT Bicentennial Studies. Cambridge, MA: MIT Press. Chap. 20, pp. 439–458. See p. 168.

Welzl, M. (2010). *Re: [e2e] Fie on future internet*. end2end-interest mailing list. Mar. 3, 2010. URL: http://www.postel.org/pipermail/end2end-interest/2010-March/008002.html. Reply to Crowcroft note sent to end2end-interest mailing list. See p. 233.

Westine, A., D. Smallberg, and J. B. Postel (1983). *Summary of Smallberg Surveys*. RFC 847. Historic. NWG. URL: http://www.rfc-editor.org/rfc/rfc847.txt. See p. 345.

Wilkins, I. (1641). *Mercury, or the Secret and Swift Messenger: Shewing How a Man may with Privacy and Speed communicate his Thoughts to a Friend at any distance*. Published anonymously using the initials I.W. only. London: Printed by I. Norton, for Iohn Maynard and Timothy Wilkins. URL: http://www.light-of-truth.com/Secret_Messenger/secret.html. See p. 181.

Wilkinson, P. T. and R. A. Scantlebury (1968). "The Control Functions in a Local Data Network". In: *Information Processing '68: Proceedings of IFIP Congress 1968*. Edinburgh, UK. August 5–10, 1968. Ed. by A. J. H. Morrell. Vol. 2.3. Amsterdam, Netherlands: North-Holland, pp. 734–738. See p. 314.

Windhausen Jr., J. (2006). *Good Fences Make Bad Broadband: Preserving an Open Internet through Net Neutrality*. Public Knowledge White Paper. Washington, DC: Public Knowledge. URL: http://www.publicknowledge.org/pdf/pk-net-neutrality-whitep-20060206.pdf. See p. 427.

Winett, J. M. (1971*a*). *Conventions for Using an IBM 2741 Terminal as a User Console for Access to Network Server Hosts*. RFC 110. Historic. Updated by RFC 135. NWG. URL: http://www.rfc-editor.org/rfc/rfc110.txt. See p. 284.

——— (1971*b*). *Level III Server Protocol for the Lincoln Laboratory NIC 360/67 Host*. RFC 109. Historic. NWG. URL: http://www.rfc-editor.org/rfc/rfc109.txt. See p. 284.

Wittgenstein, L. (2001). *Tractatus logico-philosophicus*. 2nd ed. Routledge Classics. Routledge. URL: http://www.gutenberg.org/etext/5740 (1921 first edition in German). See p. 378.

Wright, R. W. (2003). "Hand, Posner, and the Myth of the "Hand Formula"". In: *Theoretical Inquiries in Law* 4.1. URL: http://www.bepress.com/til/default/vol4/iss1/art4. See p. 166.

Wu, T. (2003). "Network Neutrality, Broadband Discrimination". In: *Journal of Telecommunications and High Technology Law* 2.1, pp. 141–179. URL: http://ssrn.com/abstract=388863. See pp. 176, 425, 429.

——— (2004). "The Broadband Debate: A User's Guide". In: *Journal of Telecommunications and High Technology Law* 3.1, pp. 69–95. URL: http://ssrn.com/abstract=557330. See p. 408.

——— (2010). "Net Neutrality and Creative Freedom". In: *re:publica 2010*. Berlin, Germany. April 14–16, 2010. Keynote at Session: Net Neutrality and Free Speech, April 15, 2010. URL: http://re-publica.de/10/event-list/net-neutrality-and-free-speech/ (video). See p. 414.

Yang, X. (2003). "NIRA: A New Internet Routing Architecture". In: *FDNA '03: Proceedings of the ACM SIGCOMM Workshop on Future Directions in Network Architecture*. Karlsruhe, Germany. August 27, 2003. New York,

NY: ACM, pp. 301–312. ISBN: 1-58113-748-0. DOI: 10.1145/944759.944768. URL: http://www.isi.edu/newarch/DOCUMENTS/yang.nira.pdf. See pp. 379, 383.

Yoo, C. S. (2002). "Vertical Integration and Media Regulation in the New Economy". In: *Yale Journal on Regulation* 19.1, pp. 171–300. DOI: 10.2139/ssrn.319122. URL: http://ssrn.com/abstract=319122. See p. 414.

—— (2005). "Beyond Network Neutrality". In: *Harvard Journal of Law and Technology* 19.1, pp. 1–77. URL: http://jolt.law.harvard.edu/articles/pdf/v19/19HarvJLTech001.pdf. See p. 414.

—— (2006). "Network Neutrality and the Economics of Congestion". In: *Georgetown Law Journal* 94.6, pp. 1847–1908. URL: http://lgst.wharton.upenn.edu/cmcl/papers/2005/Yoo.pdf. See p. 414.

Zachem, K. A. (2008*a*). *Description of Current Network Management Practices.* Attachment A of letter to FCC "Re: In the Matter of Formal Complaint of Free Press and Public Knowledge Against Comcast Corporation for Secretly Degrading Peer-to-Peer Applications, File No. EB-08-IH-1518; In the Matter of Broadband Industry Practices; Petition of Free Press et al. for Declaratory Ruling that Degrading an Internet Application Violates the FCC's Internet Policy Statement and Does Not Meet an Exception for "Reasonable Network Management," WC Docket No. 07-52". Comcast Corp. Sept. 19, 2008. URL: http://downloads.comcast.net/docs/Attachment_A_Current_Practices.pdf. See p. 362.

—— (2008*b*). *Description of Planned Network Management Practices to be Deployed Following the Termination of Current Practices.* Attachment B of letter to FCC "Re: In the Matter of Formal Complaint of Free Press and Public Knowledge Against Comcast Corporation for Secretly Degrading Peer-to-Peer Applications, File No. EB-08-IH-1518; In the Matter of Broadband Industry Practices; Petition of Free Press et al. for Declaratory Ruling that Degrading an Internet Application Violates the FCC's Internet Policy Statement and Does Not Meet an Exception for "Reasonable Network Management," WC Docket No. 07-52". Comcast Corp. Sept. 19, 2008. URL: http://downloads.comcast.net/docs/Attachment_B_Future_Practices.pdf. See p. 362.

Zhang, Y., Z. M. Mao, and M. Zhang (2009). "Detecting Traffic Differentiation in Backbone ISPs with NetPolice". In: *IMC '09: Proceedings of the 9th ACM SIGCOMM Conference on Internet Measurement*. Chicago,

IL. New York, NY: ACM, pp. 103–115. ISBN: 978-1-60558-771-4. DOI: 10.1145/1644893.1644905. See pp. 356, 361.

Zimmermann, H. (1977). "The Cyclades Experience—Results and Impacts". In: *Information Processing '77: Proceedings of the IFIP Congress 1977*. Toronto, Canada. August 8–12, 1977. Ed. by B. Gilchrist. Amsterdam, Netherlands: North-Holland, pp. 465–469. ISBN: 0-7204-0755-9. See p. 203.

—— (1980). "OSI Reference Model—The ISO Model of Architecture for Open Systems Interconnection". In: *IEEE Transactions on Communications* 28.4, pp. 425–432. See pp. 291, 390.

Zimmermann, H. and M. Elie (1974). *Transport Protocol: Standard Host-Host Protocol for Heterogeneous Computer Networks*. INWG Note 61. IFIP WG 6.1 (INWG). See p. 342.

Zittrain, J. L. (2006). "The Generative Internet". In: *Harvard Law Review* 119.7, pp. 1974–2040. URL: http://www.harvardlawreview.org/issues/119/may06/zittrain.pdf. See p. 424.

—— (2008). *The Future of the Internet—And How to Stop It*. Yale University Press. ISBN: 0300124872. URL: http://ssrn.com/abstract=1125949. See pp. 43, 409–411.

Matthias Bärwolff has worked for two solid years on this tome, completing all the research and wrapping it up in writing. He has a broad academic background, has written extensively about open source economics as well as Internet design principles, and lives in Berlin, Germany.

www.ingramcontent.com/pod-product-compliance
Lightning Source LLC
Chambersburg PA
CBHW070930050326
40689CB00014B/3152
* 9 7 8 1 4 5 6 3 3 1 3 5 1 *